CHRISTABEL PA

CW00816329

Together with her mother, Emmeline, Christabel Pankhurst co-led the single-sex Women's Social and Political Union (WSPU), founded in 1903 and soon regarded as the most notorious of the groupings campaigning for the parliamentary vote for women. A First Class Honours Graduate in Law, the determined and charismatic Christabel, a captivating orator, revitalised the women's suffrage campaign by rousing thousands of women to become suffragettes, as WSPU members were called, and to demand rather than ask politely for their democratic citizenship rights. A supreme tactician, her advocacy of 'militant', unladylike tactics shocked many people, and the political establishment.

When an end to militancy was called on the outbreak of war in 1914, she encouraged women to engage in war work as a way to win their enfranchisement. Four years later, when enfranchisement was granted to certain categories of women aged thirty and over, she stood unsuccessfully for election to parliament, as a member of the Women's Party.

In 1940 she moved to the USA with her adopted daughter, and had a successful career there as a Second Adventist preacher and writer. However, she is mainly remembered for being the driving force behind the militant wing of the women's suffrage movement.

This full-length biography, the first for forty years, draws upon feminist approaches to biography writing to place her within a network of supportive female friendships. It is based upon an unrivalled range of previously untapped primary sources.

June Purvis is Emeritus Professor of Women's and Gender History, University of Portsmouth, UK. She has published extensively on the suffragette movement in Edwardian Britain, her *Emmeline Pankhurst: A Biography* (Routledge, 2002) receiving critical acclaim. She is the Founding and Managing Editor of *Women's History Review*, the Editor for a Women's and Gender Book Series with Routledge, the Chair of Women's History Network and the Secretary and Treasurer of the International Federation for Research in Women's History.

WOMEN'S AND GENDER HISTORY
Edited by June Purvis

CHRISTABEL PANKHURST

A Biography

June Purvis

Routledge
Taylor & Francis Group

LONDON AND NEW YORK

First published 2018
by Routledge
2 Park Square, Milton Park, Abingdon, Oxon OX14 4RN

and by Routledge
711 Third Avenue, New York, NY 10017

Routledge is an imprint of the Taylor & Francis Group, an informa business

© 2018 June Purvis

British Library Cataloguing in Publication Data
A catalogue record for this book is available from the British Library

Library of Congress Cataloging in Publication Data
Names: Purvis, June, author.
Title: Christabel Pankhurst : a biography / June Purvis.
Description: Abingdon, Oxon ; New York, NY : Routledge, 2018.
Identifiers: LCCN 2017036685| ISBN 9780415279475 (hardback : alk. paper) |
ISBN 9780815371496 (pbk.) | ISBN 9781351246668 (ebook)
Subjects: LCSH: Pankhurst, Christabel, Dame, 1880-1958. | Suffragists—Great
Britain—Biography. | Feminists—Great Britain—Biography. |
Women—Political activity—Great Britain—History—20th century.
Classification: LCC HQ1595.P33 P87 2018 | DDC 305.42092 [B] —dc23
LC record available at https://lccn.loc.gov/2017036685

ISBN: 978-0-415-27947-5 (hbk)
ISBN: 978-0-8153-7149-6 (pbk)
ISBN: 978-1-351-24666-8 (ebk)

Typeset in Goudy
by Swales & Willis Ltd, Exeter, Devon, UK
Printed and bound by CPI Group (UK) Ltd, Croydon, CR0 4YY

FOR ALL FEMINISTS, PAST,
PRESENT AND FUTURE, AND THEIR
STRUGGLE FOR EQUALITY FOR WOMEN

CONTENTS

CONTENTS

ILLUSTRATIONS

ACKNOWLEDGEMENTS

I would like to thank those numerous people who have helped me in various ways with the writing of this book. Special thanks must be given to those with whom I have had discussions over the years, including Beverley Cook, Krista Cowman, Irene Cockcroft, Elizabeth Crawford, Nancy Everett, Ken Florey, Sarah Gavron, the late Myrna and Philip Goode, June Hannam, Sandra Stanley Holton, Angela John, the late Warwick Kenney-Taylor, the late Eveline Bennett, Timothy Larsen, Joseph Lennon, Jill Liddington, Chase Livingston, Linda Martz, Hilary McCollum, Jackie More, Sue Morgan, Helen Pankhurst, Antonia Raeburn, Catherine Shaw, Mari Takayanagi and Melanie Unwin. I owe a special debt to Elizabeth Crawford and Elizabeth Hodgson who located some additional infor-mation about Christabel's adopted daughter when I had come to a dead end. The late Jill Craigie was exceptionally kind in allowing me access to her suffrage collection and her husband, the late Michael Foot, after Jill's death, generously granted me exclusive access to these papers before I persuaded him to deposit them in the Women's Library, the London School of Economics. The late Richard Pankhurst, nephew of Christabel Pankhurst, was always most helpful and readily responded to queries. I keep in regular touch with Helen Pankhurst, Richard's daughter, and thank her for her insights and comments. My husband Michael and our daughter, Catherine, have given emotional and culinary sup-port over many years while friends and colleagues on the conference circuit have offered advice and critical comments. I am indebted for financial support to the British Academy's Small Grants Scheme and to the Centre for European and International Studies at the University of Portsmouth. Mark Jones, at the University of Portsmouth, has kindly helped with computer issues.

I am also grateful for the assistance given me by people at the following whose papers I have consulted – Aberdeen Art Gallery and Museum; the British Library; the Bodleian Library; Special Collections at the University of East Anglia; the Fales Library at the Elmer Holmes Bobst Library of New York University; the Fryer Library at the University of Queensland; the House of Lords Record Office; Girton Library Cambridge; the Institute of Social History in Amsterdam; the Walter Clinton Jackson Library at the University of North Carolina; the Sydney Jones Library at Liverpool University; Special Collections at the University of

Leeds; Library of Congress at Washington DC; Lilly Library at Indiana University; Manchester High School Archives; Manchester Public City Libraries Archives; the Mitchell Library at the State Library of New South Wales; the Museum of London; the National Archives; the National Library of Australia in Canberra; the National Library of Scotland; the National Library of Ireland in Dublin; the National Trust (Dryham Park); Special Collections at Northwestern University Illinois; Nottinghamshire Record Office; Princeton University Library; the Public Record Office; the Harry Ransom Humanities Research Center at the University of Texas at Austin; John Rylands Library at the University of Manchester; Schlesinger Library at Radcliffe College Massachusetts; Smith College at Northampton Massachusetts; Trinity College Cambridge; Wallace-Dunlop Family Archive; and the Women's Library at the London School of Economics.

Grateful thanks must also be expressed to the Mary Evans Picture Library, the Heritage Image Partnership Ltd/Alamy, the Institute of Social History in Amsterdam and Nancy Everett to reproduce some photographs. Every attempt has been made to contact copyright holders. The author and publisher would like to apologise in advance for any inadvertent use of copyright material.

Last, but not least, I would like to thank all the staff at Routledge involved in the production of this book, including Eve Setch and especially Michael Bourne who has been extremely supportive and helpful in sorting out queries.

ABBREVIATIONS

APW	Adela Pankhurst Walsh
APWP	Adela Pankhurst Walsh Papers
BH	Beatrice Harraden
BL	British Library
CP	Christabel Pankhurst
DMC	David Mitchell Collection
ELFS	East London Federation of the Suffragettes
EP	Emmeline Pankhurst
EPL	Emmeline Pethick-Lawrence
ESP	E. Sylvia Pankhurst
ESPA	E. Sylvia Pankhurst Archive
EWE	Elizabeth Wolstenholme Elmy
EWEP	Elizabeth Wolstenholme Elmy Papers
FPL	Frederick Pethick-Lawrence
FW	*Freewoman*
HLRO	House of Lords Record Office
HRHRC	Harry Ransom Humanities Research Center
ILP	Independent Labour Party
LG	Lloyd George Papers
LL	*Labour Leader*
MASC	Maud Arncliffe Sennett Collection
NAWSA	National American Woman Suffrage Association
NUWSS	National Union of Women's Suffrage Societies
P-L	Pethick-Lawrence
SFC	Suffragette Fellowship Collection
SSC	Sophia Smith Collection
TNA	The National Archives
TS	*The Suffragette*

TWL	The Women's Library
VfW	*Votes for Women*
WDFA	Wallace-Dunlop Family Archive, Private Collection
WFLMB	Women's Freedom League Minute Book
WSPU	Women's Social and Political Union

INTRODUCTION

When Christabel Pankhurst died in 1958, aged seventy-seven, many tributes were paid to her younger days when she had been the Chief Organiser of the Women's Social and Political Union (WSPU or Union), the most notorious of the various groupings campaigning for the parliamentary vote for women in Edwardian Britain. She had shared the leadership of the WSPU with her widowed mother, Emmeline, and as a key leader of the 'militant suffragettes', as members of the WSPU became known, she became a household name.[1] The attractive, graceful Christabel was what we would now call a 'celebrity'. Her image was reproduced in newspapers and on postcards, badges and posters; she was represented in a wide range of cultural forms such as songs, drama, poetry, fiction, paintings and cartoons. No other young feminist has probably been so admired as she was, in her heyday, by men and women alike.[2]

For Christabel Pankhurst, the subordinate status that women experienced in Edwardian society was due to the power of men and so she saw the separatist WSPU, which only admitted women as members, as an important vehicle for women to foster a sense of sisterhood that would enable them to stand on their own two feet and articulate their demands. As Olive Banks, Elizabeth Sarah and myself have pointed out, she pioneered a number of concerns that were later central to 'radical feminists' in the 'Second Wave' of the women's movement in Western Europe and the USA from the late 1960s and 1970s – the power of men over women in a male-defined world, the importance of a women-only movement as a means for raising women's consciousness, the commonalities that all women share despite their differences and the primacy of putting women first rather than considerations of social class, political affiliation or socialism.[3]

Yet, despite the importance of Christabel Pankhurst to feminism, she has not been popular with feminist writers or with male historians. Two of the most influential early feminist accounts of the women's suffrage campaign were written by former participants, namely Ray [Rachel] Strachey's *'The cause': a short history of the women's movement in Great Britain* and Sylvia Pankhurst's *The suffragette movement*, published in 1928 and 1931, respectively. Both books were subsequently reprinted in cheap paperback editions in the 1970s and 1980s and have consequently been widely read and widely cited.[4] Although written from differing perspectives which we may classify as 'liberal feminist' and 'socialist feminist', both books helped to establish a dominant narrative about Christabel Pankhurst that, at best, ignored her women-centred approach to politics and, at worst, misrepresented her views.[5]

Strachey had been a keen supporter of the main suffrage grouping, the National Union of Women's Suffrage Societies (NUWSS), which, under the leadership of the liberal feminist leader Millicent Garrett Fawcett, engaged in constitutional, law-abiding tactics such as petitions to parliament and polite discussion with sympathetic male supporters. Thus the key players in *'The cause'* are not the WSPU leaders who tried to force change by endorsing 'sensational public protest' and illegal violent methods such as damaging property, that put them in the position of 'outlaws dogged by the police', but Fawcett who worked patiently for women's suffrage to arrive as a natural progression.[6] As Kathryn Dodd persuasively argues, Strachey uses the political vocabulary of liberalism to position the NUWSS and Millicent Garrett Fawcett as the 'rational' wing of the women's movement that was responsible for the partial enfranchisement of women in 1918 and their full enfranchisement, on equal terms with men, in 1928. Christabel, Emmeline and their followers are cast 'out of the making of women's history' because of their reckless activity and passion for change.[7]

Such a representation of Christabel Pankhurst exercised a considerable sway on subsequent accounts of the women's suffrage campaign, but it was especially Sylvia Pankhurst's portrayal of Christabel, her elder sister, in *The suffragette movement* which appeared in 1931, three years after Strachey's book, that has been influential. As a socialist feminist in the women's suffrage campaign, Sylvia had often been at odds with the women-centred views of Christabel and their mother. She had been unhappy when Christabel and Emmeline resigned their membership of the Independent Labour Party (ILP) since she wanted to keep the WSPU closely allied to the socialist movement. Nor did she like the undemocratic structure of the WSPU at the central level or the policies and tactics that were formulated. From 1913, Sylvia began re-building WSPU branches among the poor in the East End of London, forming her own grouping, the East London Federation. The East London Federation, although formally affiliated to the WSPU, differed from it in a number of important respects which led Christabel and Emmeline to expel Sylvia and her organisation from the WSPU early in 1914. The bitterness that Sylvia felt at the way she had been treated by her relatives was intensified during the First World War when Christabel and Emmeline supported the war effort while Sylvia, a pacifist, saw such action as a betrayal of the ideals of her father, Dr Richard Pankhurst, a radical lawyer, pacifist and socialist. It is hardly surprising, therefore, that in *The suffragette movement* she has little to say that is positive about Christabel and their mother.

As I have argued elsewhere, in *The suffragette movement* Sylvia offers a seething portrayal of the hated Christabel, their mother's favourite child. Christabel is presented as an evil force upon the easily swayed Emmeline. Christabel, who resigns her membership of the ILP, does not affiliate the WSPU to socialism and recruits middle-class women of all political persuasions, is demonised as the betrayer of socialist feminism.[8] As Jane Marcus has perceptively observed, in *The suffragette movement* Sylvia inscribes herself as her father's daughter, the only member of the family to uphold his socialist principles of maintaining an alliance with Keir Hardie, a key figure in the founding of the Labour Party. Christabel and Emmeline are presented as the 'separatist feminists' and 'isolated man-haters' who caused split after split in the suffragette movement. Sylvia presents herself as the 'heroine' of the campaign, not Christabel and their mother. It is her success in getting the Liberal Prime Minister Herbert Asquith, an ardent anti-suffragist, to receive her East London delegation of working-class women in June 1914 that is the key to winning the vote. Thus suffrage victory is claimed in the name of socialist feminism, a victory less over the Government than over Sylvia's 'real enemies', her mother and her sister.[9]

What historians have rarely commented upon when reiterating all too frequently this scenario is the way in which this portrayal of Christabel differs from other accounts Sylvia wrote much earlier, in the WSPU newspaper *Votes for Women* and especially in her 1911 book *The suffragette*.[10] In *The suffragette*, Sylvia praises Christabel for her inspired leadership. Also, in this early book she speaks of working women being present in the WSPU but in her later influential 1931 text, *The suffragette movement*, gives the impression that it is almost exclusively middle class, except for her own work in the East End. In Jill Craigie's telling phrase, Sylvia 'misrepresents by omission', presenting the WSPU as elitist and unattractive to working-class and socialist women, which it was not.[11] Yet, despite the inconsistences in Sylvia's various writings, *The suffragette movement* has become the accepted authoritative account of the Pankhurst family, especially after George Dangerfield adopted and adapted Sylvia's script in his influential *The strange death of Liberal England*, first published in 1935.[12]

Dangerfield, writing from a 'masculinist' perspective that assumes that the category 'man' is a universal category that typifies all that is human, views the suffragette movement as a deviant, marginal, even dangerous diversion from the established male political norm.[13] He ridicules and mocks the suffragette movement, drawing upon Freudian theory to explain this 'melodramatic' and 'hysterical' curiosity, suggesting that the cause of militancy is to be found in an 'irrational and conscious element' of the human soul that comes to the fore when women enter political life.[14] The militant suffragettes, wanting to throw off traditional notions of femininity and depart from the company of men, he suggests, were linked to the 'homosexual movement', as a form of 'pre-war lesbianism'.[15] The WSPU, Dangerfield asserts, is a 'puppet show' where the strings are carefully manipulated by Christabel and Emmeline Pankhurst, the 'infernal queens' of the WSPU who 'dictated every move, and swayed every heart, of a growing army of intoxicated women'.[16] In particular, Christabel is portrayed as opportunistic, unprincipled, egocentric and snobbish, setting herself up 'not merely as man's enemy but as man's superior'.[17] However, Sylvia Pankhurst escapes Dangerfield's condemnatory eye. He presents Sylvia as she represented herself in *The suffragette movement*, as the great 'realist' leader who, languishing pale and helpless on a stretcher on the steps of the House of Commons, wins the parliamentary vote for women.[18]

The Sylvia Pankhurst/George Dangerfield narrative about the women's suffrage movement has held a particular sway from which few commentators have been able to break free. Even the popular 1974 BBC television series about the militant suffragettes, *Shoulder to Shoulder*, was framed by Sylvia's *The suffragette movement*, the story told, yet again, through her eyes.[19] Unsurprisingly, it is Sylvia Pankhurst who has attracted the attention of historians, especially socialist feminist historians, rather than her more famous sister, Christabel, who, from the early 1920s, became a Second Adventist, preaching and writing about the imminent Second Coming of Christ. Consequently, Sylvia has been the subject of numerable scholarly assessments, including at least six biographies – and undoubtedly more to come.[20] To date there is only one full-length biography of Christabel, *Queen Christabel*, written by David Mitchell and published in 1977.

The very title of Mitchell's biography indicates something of his approach to his subject whom he clearly does not like. Like Dangerfield before him, Mitchell mocks and insults this important political figure, describing her as 'the great feminist manipulator making her puppets dance to the tune she called'.[21] Christabel is presented as a ruthless, cold, ambitious, autocratic, self-seeking, single-minded, calculating and selfish lesbian – as well as charismatic and quick of tongue and mind. But her life as a feminist is filtered through all the former adjectives.

Among Mitchell's papers, deposited in the Museum of London, can be found distasteful comments about how puzzling he found Christabel's sexuality, let alone her advocacy of militancy and later conversion to Second Adventism. 'C never had boy friends, any really satisfactory [sic] human relationship, now she makes herself [as a Second Adventist] the Bride of Christ, untouched by male hands, lusts, dirt.'[22] That Christabel, apparently, might not have experienced sexual intercourse with a man is difficult for Mitchell to comprehend. Indeed, sexual innuendo is rife throughout *Queen Christabel*, from the opening page where the enthusiastic suffragette response to Christabel's inspirational leadership is described as 'a warm quasi-orgasmic

4

gush of gratitude and heroine worship'. Mitchell even analyses the close relationship between Christabel and her mother as unhealthy, rooted in 'incestuous feelings'.[23] While Sylvia saw her mother as being swayed by Christabel, Mitchell sees it the other way round – that Christabel was driven by her mother 'who was tremendously ambitious for herself and for her children'. In one interview, he asserted that Christabel's psychic development as a human being was so 'stunted' by her partnership with her mother that she was 'almost certifiable, clinically psychotic'.[24]

Thus the image of Christabel as a mad, 'abnormal' lesbian has reached its apogee. Indeed, the final chapter of *Queen Christabel*, where she is compared with radical feminists of the 1970s, is notoriously titled 'Bitch power'. Fearful of these 'Second Wave' feminist harpies who dared to challenge male power, Mitchell goes so far as to suggest that some of Christabel's editorials 'came very near' to the threats of Valerie Solanas, of the Society for Cutting up Men.[25] As Ann Morley and Liz Stanley comment sarcastically, they can picture Mitchell, 'poor man, writing while frequently glancing nervously over his shoulder with one protective hand cupped over his crotch'.[26]

Recent debates within women's history expose the sexism and sheer nastiness of Mitchell's assessment of Christabel Pankhurst. Although some feminists have offered sympathetic appraisals of this much-maligned feminist, many of the old prejudices linger on.[27] The Sylvia Pankhurst/George Dangerfield narrative has become firmly established and repeated in Martin Pugh's 2001 group biography, *The Pankhursts*. Pugh idolises Sylvia, presenting her as a socialist who remained true to her cause while Christabel is an evil Svengali who leads their mother away from socialism. Lacking any sympathy with Christabel's feminism, Pugh condemns her for leaving the ILP and for seeking an end to gender discrimination in the electoral system rather than the elimination of class bias whereby some working-class men did not have the vote.[28] The problem for Pugh is not the opposition of men in government and in the labour movement to women's suffrage, but the WSPU demand for a limited franchise measure that would grant votes to women on the same terms as men, namely on a property qualification as a head of household, a criterion that could effectively include single women and widows but exclude married women. By using such an analysis, Pugh lets men off the hook, blaming the prolonged nature of the suffrage struggle upon the leadership strategy of Christabel and Emmeline.

Like Mitchell before him, Christabel's sexuality is also a matter for Pugh's prurient male gaze, especially in a newspaper article where he claims that she, like the other suffragette leaders, was involved in promiscuous 'lesbian love trysts'.[29] And like Mitchell, Pugh mocks Christabel's turn to Second Adventism, depicting her life as a preacher for the imminent Second Coming of Christ as 'a job creation scheme'.[30] A full-length biography of Christabel Pankhurst that assesses her life, in all its complexity, is long overdue.

This biography of Christabel Pankhurst will offer a different interpretation to the dominant narratives about her that we have considered so far. As Liz Stanley has emphasised, biographers need to acknowledge the subject position from which they stand as a 'socially-located person'.[31] I write as a white, middle-class, heterosexual feminist historian who, as a student embroiled in the feminist debates of the 1970s, understands Christabel Pankhurst's feminist standpoint. I have already published a biography of her mother and my approach to writing this biography will be similar to that adopted previously, namely following a chronological structure while also placing my subject within a network of women's friendships.[32]

Trying to find out what Christabel Pankhurst was 'really like' is not an easy task. Biography writing involves not just historical enquiry but also 'an act of imaginative faith', interpreting the sources, ignoring the silences, making a seamless web of what is often much more messy.[33] We need to discuss not only the views of Christabel's contemporaries, but also her own voice, her own articulation of her subjective experience.[34] Fortunately, many of the public documents that Christabel wrote as a key strategist during the suffrage campaign have survived, as well as her later writings as a successful Second Adventist author. However, finding out about her private life, especially her sexuality, is much more problematic since she kept no diary that might reveal her innermost feelings, although a number of personal letters to and from friends are extant.

The very term 'lesbian' is itself subject to definitional uncertainty, and especially the significance or not of sexual activity.[35] All the extant sources reveal that there is no evidence that Christabel Pankhurst was involved in any lesbian sexual relationship or experienced erotic sexual desire for women; nor did she self-identify as a 'lesbian'. She upheld traditional Christian morality, that sex should be confined to heterosexual married couples, and spoke on more than one occasion about the joys of her single, celibate life.[36] Judith Bennett suggests that rather than being obsessed with finding sexually active lesbians in the past, we use instead the term 'lesbian-like' to include those many women – such as sexual rebels, gender rebels, marriage resisters, cross-dressers and single women – whose life circumstances were such that their rejection of patriarchal norms opened up lesbian possibilities. Might sexual practice be less determinate of lesbianism in the past, asks Bennett, than '*desire* for women, *primary love* for women . . . or even *political* commitment to women?'[37] Such a broad, open-ended, fluid approach is in itself problematic; whether it should be applied to Christabel Pankhurst is debatable, although some recent commentators have done so.[38] Single all her life, outside patriarchal, heterosexual marriage, Christabel had a deep political commitment to women. During the suffrage campaign in particular, she was embedded in networks of warm, supportive female friendships, whether they may be labelled 'lesbian-like' or not.[39]

Although Christabel wrote her autobiography in the 1930s, she did not wish it to be published until after her death. In 1959, one year after she had passed away, that volume appeared edited by someone else and titled *Unshackled: the story of how we won the vote*.[40]

With its rather sparse prose, *Unshackled* was no match for Sylvia's richly textured *The suffragette movement* which continues to be the dominant narrative of the Pankhurst family and the most frequently cited of the Pankhurst memoirs.[41] Pugh in *The Pankhursts*, for example, cites Sylvia's book fifty-eight times but Christabel's only thirteen. For Pugh, the accounts written by other WSPU militants, including Christabel and her mother, 'are largely fantasy'.[42] The only autobiographies that Pugh considers 'useful' for the suffrage historian are Sylvia's *The suffragette movement* and that written by another socialist feminist, Hannah Mitchell.[43] Such a biased assessment, which places Christabel's own interpretation of events out of history, must be challenged.

All biographical interpretations are selective, and this biography of Christabel Pankhurst is no exception. In the following pages, I hope to capture something of the charm, charisma and vitality of Christabel during her suffrage days, her brilliance as the WSPU key strategist and her witty repartee as a speaker – as well as present a fair portrait of her second career, as a successful preacher and writer of Second Adventism.

Notes

1 I am using the term 'militant' to refer to a broad range of confrontational and assertive tactics used to force women's issues into the political arena; for example, protesting at Liberal Party political meetings, as well as illegal more violent tactics that were adopted especially from 1912, such as setting fire to pillar boxes. On this topic see L. E. Nym Mayhall, Defining militancy: radical protest, the constitutional idiom, and women's suffrage in Britain, 1908–1909, *Journal of British Studies*, 39, 1994, pp. 340–71; C. R. Jorgensen-Earp, '*The transfiguring sword': the just war of the Women's Social and Political Union* (Tuscaloosa, AL, University of Alabama Press, 1997); L. E. Nym Mayhall, *The militant suffrage movement: citizenship and resistance in Britain, 1860–1930* (Oxford, Oxford University Press, 2003); J. Purvis, Christabel Pankhurst and the struggle for suffrage reform in Edwardian Britain, and K. Cowman, What was suffragette militancy? An exploration of the British example, both in *Suffrage, gender and citizenship: international perspectives on parliamentary reforms*, eds I. Sulkunen, S-L. Nevala-Nurmi and P. Markkola (Newcastle upon Tyne, Cambridge Scholars Publishing, 2009), pp. 278–98 and 299–322, respectively.
2 I am defining as a 'feminist' a woman who believes that her sex are discriminated against and subordinated by men. Throughout this book I shall adopt the convention of the day and refer to Christabel and her sisters Sylvia and Adela by their Christian names.
3 O. Banks, *The biographical dictionary of British feminists, Vol. 1 1800–1930* (Brighton, Harvester Press, 1985), pp. 146–52; E. Sarah, Christabel Pankhurst: reclaiming her power, in *Feminist theorists: three centuries of women's intellectual traditions*, ed D. Spender (London, Women's Press, 1983), pp. 256–84; J. Purvis, A 'pair of . . . infernal queens'? A reassessment of the dominant representations of Emmeline and Christabel Pankhurst, First Wave feminists in Edwardian Britain, *Women's History Review*, 5, 2, 1996, pp. 259–80; J. Purvis, Christabel Pankhurst and the Women's Social and Political Union, in *The women's suffrage movement: new feminist perspectives*, eds M. Joannou and J. Purvis (Manchester, Manchester University Press, 1998), pp. 157–72; and J. Purvis,

Christabel Pankhurst – a Conservative suffragette? in *Women, gender and the Conservative Party, 1880s to the present*, eds C. Berthezene and J. Gottlieb (Manchester, Manchester University Press, 2017), pp. 29–45. Three categories of feminist thought are usually identified in the 'Second Wave' of the women's movement – liberal, socialist and radical. Liberal feminists emphasise gradual, piecemeal reform as a way to gain equal rights for women and stress the importance of women and men working together to attain this end. Socialist feminists emphasise the nature of capitalism and the control that men exercise over women as being central to women's subordination. Thus inequalities of social class and gender are integral to their analyses. They also stress the importance of men and women working together, as comrades, in the building of an egalitarian, socialist society. Radical feminists, in contrast, emphasise that it is male control over women that has primacy over all other subordinations. This idea of a shared subordination leads to an emphasis upon the sisterhood of women and a focus upon their similarities, while not denying their differences. Radical feminism encourages a degree of separation from men, usually involving the formation of women-only organisations and women-only communities. The celebration of the power of womanhood is welcomed while the liberal approach of fitting women into a male-centred world is rejected in favour of a transformation of society.

4 R. Strachey, '*The cause': a short history of the women's movement in Great Britain* (London, G. Bell and Sons, Ltd., 1928, reprinted in 1978, London, Virago); E. S. Pankhurst, *The suffragette movement: an intimate account of persons and ideals* (London, Longmans, 1931, reprinted 1977, London, Virago, hereafter ESP, TSM). All page numbers refer to the original editions.

5 See note 3 for definitions of 'liberal' and 'socialist' feminism.

6 Strachey, '*The cause*', p. 310.

7 K. Dodd, Cultural politics and women's historical writing: the case of Ray Strachey's *The Cause*, *Women's Studies International Forum*, 13, 1/2, 1990, p. 134, and K. Dodd, Introduction: the politics of form in Sylvia Pankhurst's writing, in her edited *A Sylvia Pankhurst reader* (Manchester, Manchester University Press, 1993), p. 21.

8 ESP, TSM, pp. 247–8.

9 J. Marcus, Introduction, re-reading the Pankhursts and women's suffrage, in her edited *Suffrage and the Pankhursts* (London and New York, Routledge and Kegan Paul, 1987), pp. 5–6.

10 ESP, *The suffragette: the history of the women's militant suffrage movement 1905–1910* (New York, Sturgis & Walton Co., 1911), p. 96.

11 J. Craigie, Sylvia, the revolutionary who ended in a feudal palace, *Times*, 1 May 1982.

12 G. Dangerfield, *The strange death of Liberal England* (London, MacGibbon and Kee, 1966, first pub. 1935).

13 S. Stanley Holton, Challenging masculinism: personal history and microhistory in feminist studies of the women's suffrage movement, *Women's History Review*, 5, 2011, pp. 829–41; J. Purvis, Gendering the historiography of the suffragette movement in Edwardian Britain: some reflections, *Women's History Review*, 4, 2013, pp. 576–90.

14 Dangerfield, *The strange death*, pp. 122 and 128.

15 Dangerfield, *The strange death*, p. 128.

16 Dangerfield, *The strange death*, pp. 155–6.

17 Dangerfield, *The strange death*, pp. 165–6.

18 Dangerfield, *The strange death*, pp. 311 and 293.

19 J. Purvis, The march of the women: a BBC drama from 1974 highlights the tensions in writing feminist history, *History Today*, November 2014, p. 5.

20 See R. Pankhurst, *Sylvia Pankhurst: artist and crusader, an intimate portrait* (New York and London, Paddington Press Ltd., 1979); P. W. Romero, *E. Sylvia Pankhurst: portrait of a radical* (New Haven, CT and London, Yale University Press, 1987); B. Harrison, Two utopians:

Sylvia Pankhurst and Henry Harben, in his *Prudent revolutionaries: portraits of British feminists between the wars* (Oxford, Oxford University Press, 1987); I. Bullock and R. Pankhurst eds, *Sylvia Pankhurst: from artist to anti-fascist* (Houndmills, Macmillan, 1992); R. Taylor, *In letters of gold: the story of Sylvia Pankhurst and the East London Federation of the Suffragettes in Bow* (London, Stepney Books, 1993); K. Dodd, ed, *A Sylvia Pankhurst reader*; B. Winslow, *Sylvia Pankhurst: sexual politics and political activism* (London, UCL Press, 1996); M. Davis, *Sylvia Pankhurst: a life in radical politics* (London, Pluto Press, 1999); S. Harrison, *Sylvia Pankhurst: a crusading life 1882–1960* (London, Aurum Press, 2003, reprinted as *Sylvia Pankhurst: the rebellious suffragette*, Newhaven, East Sussex, 2012); K. Connelly, *Sylvia Pankhurst: suffragette, socialist and scourge of empire* (London, Pluto Press, 2013). A joint biography, B. Castle, *Sylvia and Christabel Pankhurst* (Harmondsworth, Penguin, 1987), merely reiterates Sylvia's story.

21 D. Mitchell, *Queen Christabel: a biography of Christabel Pankhurst* (London, MacDonald and Jane's, 1971), p. 189.

22 D. Mitchell comments on C. Pankhurst (hereafter CP), *Pressing problems of the closing age* (1924), 73.83/31, David Mitchell Collection (hereafter DMC).

23 Mitchell, *Queen Christabel*, pp. 1 and 207.

24 M. Stott, The missing years, *The Guardian*, 6 October 1977.

25 Mitchell, *Queen Christabel*, pp. 319–20.

26 A. Morley with L. Stanley, *The life and death of Emily Wilding Davison* (London, The Women's Press, 1988), p. 79.

27 D. Spender, *Women of ideas and what men have done to them: from Aphra Behn to Adrienne Rich* (London, Routledge and Kegan Paul, 1982), pp. 394–403; Sarah, Christabel Pankhurst; Purvis, Christabel Pankhurst and the Women's Social and Political Union; Purvis, Christabel Pankhurst and the struggle for suffrage reform; and Purvis, Christabel Pankhurst – a Conservative suffragette?

28 M. Pugh, *The Pankhursts* (London, Allen Lane, Penguin Press, 2001), p. 111.

29 V. Thorpe and A. Marsh, Diary reveals lesbian love trysts of suffragette leaders, *The Observer*, 11 June 2000.

30 Pugh, *The Pankhursts*, p. 382.

31 L. Stanley, *The auto/biographical I: the theory and practice of feminist auto/biography* (Manchester, Manchester University Press, 1992), p. 7.

32 J. Purvis, *Emmeline Pankhurst: a biography* (London, Routledge, 2002). M. Bostridge calls this biography 'revisionist' in his review, The Conservative suffragette, *Times Literary Supplement*, 16 August 2002.

33 R. Holmes, *This long pursuit: reflections of a romantic biographer* (London, William Collins, 2016), p. 17.

34 See B. Caine, Feminist biography and feminist history, *Women's History Review* 3, 1994, p. 251.

35 For a useful overview on this issue see S. Morgan, Theorising feminist history: a thirty-year retrospective, *Women's History Review*, 18, 2009, pp. 388–407, especially pp. 388–92.

36 See, for example, CP, Why I never married, *Weekly Dispatch*, 3 April 1921 and CP, The sexless life, *Daily Express*, 20 July 1925.

37 J. M. Bennett, 'Lesbian-like' and the social history of lesbianisms, *Journal of the History of Sexuality*, 9, 2000, p. 10.

38 See H. McCollum, Sapphic suffragettes, a talk delivered at The National Archives, 11 February 2017.

39 L. Stanley, Romantic friendship? Some issues in researching lesbian history and biography, *Women's History Review*, 1, 1992, in her survey about whether some suffragettes were 'lesbian' or not comes to the conclusion on p. 202 that such 'interpretive issues . . . are actually irresolvable given the nature of the historical record that exists'.

40 CP, *Unshackled: the story of how we won the vote*, edited by Lord Pethick-Lawrence (London, Hutchinson, 1959).
41 Emmeline Pankhurst's autobiography *My own story* (London, Eveleigh Nash, 1914) was compiled by American journalist Rheta Childe Dorr from interviews with her and from suffragette literature.
42 M. Pugh, *Women's suffrage in Britain 1867–1928* (London, Historical Association, 1980), p. 40.
43 G. Mitchell, ed, *The hard way up: the autobiography of Hannah Mitchell, suffragette and rebel* (London, Faber and Faber, 1968).

1

'EVERY STRUGGLING CAUSE
SHALL BE OURS . . .'

1880–8

Christabel Harriette Pankhurst was born on 22 September 1880 at 1 Drayton Terrace, Old Trafford, Manchester, England, the home of her radical parents, Dr Richard Pankhurst, a barrister, and his much younger wife Emmeline. Emmeline was twenty-two years old and Richard forty-five when this first of five children arrived. Since Richard thought that pretty names were indispensable for girls, he chose 'Christabel' as suggested by Coleridge's poem, 'the lovely lady Christabel whom her father loves so well'.[1] Both parents were actively involved in the progressive causes of their day, especially women's suffrage and socialism. Over the next nine years, sisters and brothers for Christabel arrived with regularity – Estelle Sylvia (known as Sylvia) in 1882, Henry Francis Robert ('Frank') in 1884, Adela Constantia Mary in 1885 and Henry Francis ('Harry') in 1889. Sources of information about Christabel's family background and childhood are mainly her autobiography, *Unshackled*, but especially her sister Sylvia's *The suffragette movement*. The youngest Pankhurst daughter, Adela, also wrote some reminiscences but these are unpublished papers which have not been extensively mined. Although, unsurprisingly, all three Pankhurst daughters wrote differing accounts of events, as will be evident throughout this book, it is Sylvia's *The suffragette movement* that has become the dominant narrative not only about the suffragette movement but also about Pankhurst family life.[2] One thing on which all three sisters agreed, however, was that as children their lives were not kept separate from the social reform interests of their parents. In Rebecca West's memorable words, they 'bobbed like corks on the tide of adult life', attending political meetings and handing out political leaflets.[3]

Richard, the dutiful son of a Baptist auctioneer and his wife, Margaret, had moved from Stoke-on-Trent to Manchester in 1847. Educated at Manchester Grammar School and then Owen's College (later Manchester University), he had been barred from attending Oxford University because of his Nonconformity. Undeterred, the gifted Richard then became a student at London University from which he graduated in 1859 with a Bachelor of Law and then a Doctorate and Gold Medal, in 1863. After being called to the Bar in 1867, he joined the Northern Circuit, based in Manchester.[4]

Of below medium height for a man of his time, with a high-pitched shrill voice, gold-red beard, a broad, lofty forehead crowned by a mane of ruddy hair and small, blue-grey, twinkling eyes, Richard Pankhurst was not considered particularly handsome. Yet he was regarded as not only a learned man but also an eloquent speaker, both in the law courts and on great civic occasions. A convinced republican and anti-imperialist, he was a member of the Liberal Party but regarded as a political extremist. Fired by a mission to end injustices in society, he supported unpopular causes such as free state education for working-class children, the abolition of the House of Lords, nationalisation of the land, the abolition of slavery, women's suffrage and international peace. The local newspapers affectionately referred to him as 'our learned Doctor' or the 'Red Doctor'.[5]

Richard was an admirer of John Stuart Mill who, as an MP, had unsuccessfully suggested a women's suffrage amendment to the 1867 Reform Bill which extended the parliamentary franchise only to all male householders and men paying more than ten pounds in annual rent in the boroughs.[6] Much to Richard's annoyance, Mills' statement had been greeted with laughter and cheers. A member of the Executive Committee of the Manchester Committee for the Enfranchisement of Women, Richard's support for women's suffrage included, among other activities, acting as counsel in the 1869 case for the right of women to be placed on the parliamentary voting register (known as Chorlton v. Lings), and drafting the first bill aimed at giving women the vote, introduced unsuccessfully in the House of Commons in 1870 by Jacob Bright, another radical Liberal MP.[7]

The earnest Dr Richard Pankhurst had resolved to remain single all his life for the sake of his public work. His good intentions, however, were turned upside down when, in 1879, he met the beautiful and spirited Emmeline Goulden. Despite the fact that the twenty-one-year-old Emmeline was young enough to be his daughter, Richard fell in love with her and was soon to make her his bride. 'They were made for one another', Christabel remembered affectionately in later years. 'Father . . . found in her the woman who shared all his own thought and feeling about life, a helpmate as idealistic and self-regardless as he was.'[8]

Emmeline's parents had always taken a keen interest in politics. Her father, Robert Goulden, a self-made businessman who had risen from a mere errand boy to a partnership in Seedley Printworks, a calico printing and bleaching business in Pendleton, Lancashire, had as a young man followed his own parents in protesting against the Corn Laws which, by imposing duties on imported foodstuffs to protect British producers, had made the cost of living soar for the working classes. After he married, Robert was the Liberal representative for some five or six years for the Seedley Ward of Salford Town Council, becoming a 'favourite with the working classes' for the part he took in several agitations for the benefit of Salford ratepayers.[9] With his wife Sophia Jane, born on the Isle of Man, he was also an ardent campaigner during the American Civil War for the abolition of slavery. Robert and Sophia Jane supported other advanced causes, including franchise reform. After all, the Isle of Man was independent from Britain and in

1881 had given women the parliamentary vote. Emmeline Goulden, the eldest and most precocious girl in a family of ten surviving children, not only listened to family political discussions from an early age but sometimes participated in political events. When just five years old she had collected pennies in a 'lucky bag' to help relieve the poverty of emancipated American slaves. The *Women's Suffrage Journal* was delivered to the Goulden household every week and at the age of fourteen, she begged her mother to take her to a women's suffrage meeting. 'I left the meeting a conscious and confirmed suffragist', recollected the passionate Emmeline.[10]

Emmeline was sent to Paris, to one of the better 'finishing' schools for middle-class girls that also offered some advanced instruction, the École Normale in the Avenue de Neuilly. She quickly became proficient in French as she explored Paris with her room-mate, Noemie Rochefort, only daughter of Henri Rochefort, the well-known republican, communist, journalist and swordsman. Henri, who had renounced his title of Marquis de Rochefort-Lucay, had narrowly escaped execution for his part in the commune uprising in Paris the previous year and Emmeline listened in awe to the stories about how the dashing Henri, whose whereabouts were still unknown, had dared all for his democratic, republican beliefs. It was the year after the Franco-Prussian war, and she saw all around her the battle scars of the conflict as well as the hatred of the defeated French towards the occupying power. From now on, Emmeline developed a deep love for France and a lifelong prejudice against all things German.[11]

After four years in Paris, Emmeline returned home an elegant young woman, having acquired a Parisian taste in dress and fluency in the French language.[12] She found life at Seedley Cottage exceedingly dull and was delighted when she was allowed to accompany her younger sister, Mary, to the French capital where Mary, in her turn, would attend the École Normale. Noemie, now married to a Swiss artist and mother of a baby girl, was anxious that her dear friend Emmeline should marry too and settle near her. A willing suitor was found, provided the charming Emmeline would bring a dowry with her. However, when the prospective bride approached her father about the matter, Robert Goulden was furious. Declaring he would not 'sell' his daughter to any man, especially a foreigner, the enraged father summoned his daughter to come home immediately.[13]

In high dudgeon, the eighteen-year-old Emmeline returned to Manchester in the summer of 1879, accompanied by the discontented Mary whose wish to train as an actress had been sternly refused by their angry father. Matters did not improve when their mother insisted that they should make the home a welcoming place for her tall, handsome sons, who she feared might marry imprudently. The unhappy Emmeline later told Christabel that at this time in her life she wanted to do 'some great thing' but was aware of the limited possibilities for middle-class daughters such as herself.[14] She knew about Dr Richard Pankhurst's work for social reform and so decided to accompany her parents to a meeting where he was speaking. When she saw him step out of his cab, greeted by cheers from the crowd, her heart leapt. Here was her hero, a fighter for just causes, so unlike the immature male friends of her brothers. Richard immediately noticed the strikingly beautiful young woman among the throng and was smitten. Bowled over by his attentions, and flattered that an older man who was a public figure should have any interest in her, Emmeline headily returned his affection.[15]

During their short engagement, Richard wrote to his beloved on 23 September 1879, speaking not only of their joyous love but also of their shared, wider desire for social reform. 'In all my happiness with you, I feel most deeply the responsibilities gathering round us . . . Every struggling cause shall be ours.'[16] They were married on 18 December 1879. Passionately in love, it is highly likely that Christabel was conceived on their wedding night since she was born just over nine months later.

Emmeline doted on her firstborn and unlike her four subsequent children, breastfed and nursed this baby. This early bonding between mother and offspring helped to establish a particularly warm relationship between the two; Christabel, the contented baby, who 'slept much and cried little', was always to be her mother's favourite, something that her siblings soon learnt.[17] Before she was two years old, Christabel had a sister, born on 5 May 1882, who from an early age would only respond to the name 'Sylvia' despite the fact that her first name was 'Estelle'. A nurse, Susannah, was employed to look after the children and help around the house since Emmeline had no desire to be a full-time mother at home, nor did Richard want his wife to be anything other than a partner in his public work for struggling causes.[18] Indeed, when she was pregnant with Christabel, Emmeline had joined Richard on the Executive Committee of the Manchester National Society for Women's Suffrage and had also been co-opted onto the Executive Committee of the Manchester Married Women's Property Committee. After the Married Women's Property Act of 1882 was passed, which allowed married women the same property rights as unmarried women and upheld that wives and husbands should have separate interests in their property, Emmeline threw herself 'with renewed energy' into women's suffrage work.[19]

From an early age, therefore, Christabel had a politically active mother as a role model, not a woman content to be a full-time housewife and mother. Yet the radical politics which both parents supported did not attract the well-off clients who could afford to pay for Richard's legal services. Sophia Jane and Robert Goulden, concerned about the financial plight of their eldest daughter and their grandchildren, invited them to come and live with them, at Seedley Cottage, a kind gesture that was gratefully accepted. But Emmeline and Richard were still devoted to their struggling causes, the adoring Emmeline cherishing the hope that one day Richard would become an MP and do 'great things for the people', delivering them from poverty and exploitation.[20] A chance came in July 1893, when Christabel was nearly three years old. The idealistic Richard decided to contest a by-election in Manchester, not as a Liberal Party candidate but as an Independent Liberal. Lacking the support of party machinery and spending just £541 on his campaign in comparison with the £5,559 of his Conservative opponent, he lost the election – gaining just 6,216 votes to the 18,188 of his rival.[21] The Seedley Cottage household were upset by this news which conveyed an important lesson: fighting for just but unpopular causes was not easy.

Such serious matters were lightened for Christabel and Sylvia by hours of play with their resident aunts and uncles. One memorable Christmas-time, a household pantomime was organised with the four-year-old Christabel resplendent as Prince Charming while the flaxen-haired toddler Sylvia was Cinderella, attired in a dress of pink tulle, with a stiff little ballet skirt that came out of a giant cracker. The girls were taken to the ball on the backs of two uncles who had transformed themselves into an elephant. Christabel's visits to the large kitchen with her grandmother, a bustling housewife, were fun too since granny liked to help the maids make butter, jam, bread and pickles. On one such occasion, she proudly brought back to the nursery a grey piece of dough, dirtied by her grimy small hands, and promptly stuck an orange pip in it, declaring it was an apple tart that should be cooked on the hob. Both Christabel and Sylvia were occasionally allowed the special treat of being taken to see the doll's house prized by their young aunt Ada, just twelve years old, and to hold, for a brief moment, the fragile dolls whose calico bodies were stuffed with sawdust, the heads and lower sections of the arms and legs being made of white pot, daubed very roughly with paint. Then there were the chasing games that the girls would play around the big mahogany table in the breakfast room with its massive claw feet. When a dizzy Sylvia was running away from Christabel one day, she fell accidentally onto the fireplace, hitting her head on a large lump of coal, one arm and hand thrown onto the glowing fire. As a shocked Christabel sat in silence, not knowing what to do, Aunt Effie crept into the room, trying to avoid her father's eye since she was very late for breakfast. On seeing the stunned Sylvia in such a perilous state, the horrified Effie picked up her dazed niece, shouting out for help. After Sylvia's burns were dressed and her arm put in a sling, she was bought a black rabbit for her bravery in not crying. But the rabbit died soon afterwards and the broken-hearted girls often tended to its tiny gravestone in the garden.[22]

A happier time for Christabel and Sylvia was when they were taken to see their new brother, Henry Francis Robert, born on 27 February 1884. They admired his dark hair, black eyelashes and especially his tiny fingernails. For the middle-aged Richard, a son, who soon became known as 'Frank', was a particular joy. Since Emmeline favoured the bright Christabel who, like her mother, had learnt to read at an incredibly early age, it was a difficult situation for the middle child Sylvia who, with her weak eyes, had not been encouraged to read and was considered slower than her big sister.[23]

The welcoming of baby Frank into the large extended household was soon overshadowed by increasing tensions. Richard, who had to pay his own election costs, found that he was boycotted by prospective wealthier clients. His championship of the working classes and of women's suffrage, a cause that was frequently ridiculed, did not attract the support of rich businessmen. Worse, having forsaken Christianity and become an agnostic, Richard was now also articulating strong socialist opinions. Robert Goulden, whose support for his son-in-law had lost him business contracts from which he was never to recover, found himself disagreeing passionately with the 'Red Doctor'. Family quarrels flared up as Mary and Emmeline, pregnant with her fourth child, took Richard's part while Sophia Jane sided with her husband. Richard and Emmeline decided that they had to leave Seedley Cottage and Mary, who ardently supported their socialist views, asked if she could make her home with them.[24]

Christabel and Sylvia, in child-like fashion, were excited about the move from the country back into grimy Manchester. 'Old Trafford!' cried Christabel, as they drove through that part of the city where they were born, 'did you see it?'[25] It was at their new home, 66 Carter Street, Chorlton-upon-Medlock, that Adela Constantia Mary was born, on 19 June 1885. Christabel, Sylvia, Frank and baby Adela slept in the nursery with its two windows, one large and the other narrow and high. It was to the high window that Christabel and Sylvia ran each morning, standing on tiptoes, to wave goodbye to father, waiting till he turned round to wave back. Every evening he brought home a book for the excited children, read aloud to them and told them stories. They admired his slender hands, especially his long nails which he let grow over the finger tips. 'How splendid', the girls murmured, 'to have nails like father; they would never need brushing!'[26] When he stood resplendent in his evening dress, while Emmeline lovingly put in his father's diamond studs, ready to attend some function where he had to speak, they gazed in admiration. They would hear him every morning when the ever-busy Richard, using every moment of the day, read aloud or recited poetry during his ablutions in the bathroom. Richard, with his wide-ranging knowledge, spoke to the children about history, literature and social questions. 'I never met anyone one tithe part so clever', Christabel commented to Sylvia some fifteen years or so later.[27]

But the middle-aged Richard, set in his ways and yet active in the advanced movements of the day, also believed that above all else his children should be taught about the importance of their responsibilities to society. '[K]eep down private interests; work for great public ends' was his philosophy, recollected Christabel.[28] Sylvia remembered how their father would say, 'If you do not grow up to help other people you will not have been worth the upbringing!' 'Drudge and drill! drudge and drill!' was another favourite exhortation as well as 'To do, to be, and to suffer!' and 'Life is nothing without enthusiasms!'[29] Thus was bred in Christabel, Sylvia and Adela the expectation that their duty in life was not to follow the traditional route for Victorian middle-class girls of full-time wifehood and motherhood but to engage in the noble endeavour of serving the people.

Richard practised what he preached. Despite his earlier election defeat, he still wanted to become an MP and Emmeline, keen that her husband should take part in national affairs, thought he would stand a better chance of being elected to parliament in the more anonymous city of London. The opportunity came sooner than expected when the Rotherhithe Liberal and Radical Association invited Richard to be their parliamentary candidate in the November 1885 general election. Although not completely recovered from the birth of Adela, Emmeline travelled to London to support Richard in his campaign while the children stayed in Manchester, with Susannah.

Richard found a formidable foe in his Conservative opponent, Colonel Hamilton, who was determined to present his rival as a man of dubious character. Dr Pankhurst, who spoke to the poor constituents on street corners, was called a 'slum politician' and, on a hastily printed handbill, accused of atheism, a belief system that was considered shocking in Victorian Britain. Although Richard denied the libel, it was well known that he was no longer a practising Christian but an agnostic. But worse than this scandal was the fact that Charles Stewart Parnell, the leader of the Irish nationalists, advocated that his own followers should vote against all Liberal candidates, whether they supported Irish Home Rule (as Richard did) or not; such action, Parnell believed, would substantially reduce the hostile majority that the Liberals enjoyed under William Gladstone and force through a Home Rule Bill. Unsurprisingly, on polling day, the Colonel was returned with 3,327 votes against 2,800 for Richard. An indignant Emmeline protested bitterly about the result but Richard insisted that Parnell's policy was right. Since the Irish nationalists were such a small party, Parnell could never hope to win Home Rule from a hostile majority that opposed the Irish cause, but by constant obstruction he could in time 'wear out' the Government, and 'force it' to surrender to their demands. 'That was a valuable political lesson', Emmeline commented, 'one that years later I was destined to put into practice.'[30] The Rotherhithe election was a critical incident in the political education of Emmeline; she never forgot that the hard line taken by the Irish nationalists yielded results and frequently reiterated the point in the Pankhurst household. Emmeline and Christabel were later, as leaders of the suffragette movement, to utilise Parnell's tactics as a key way to campaign for votes for women.

The immediate aftermath of the Rotherhithe election was more mundane. Richard decided to bring a libel case for slander not only against Colonel Hamilton but also against other involved parties – and lost. Faced with heavy financial burdens, Emmeline and Richard decided to move to London where Richard's professional and political work was increasingly taking him. Listening to Richard's musings about the continual conflict he faced between purse and politics, Emmeline determined on a plan. She would open a fancy goods shop that would make so much money that her gifted husband could give up his legal work and devote himself full-time to progressive causes in parliament.

Emmeline hunted for suitable premises and eventually found a shop and house to rent at 165 Hampstead Road in St Pancras. While the new home was being prepared, Susannah brought Christabel, Sylvia, Frank and Adela to London where they lived in dismal lodgings. All the children fell ill, even the normally robust Christabel. The enthusiastic Emmeline used the family's limited finances to buy an array of fancy goods, including milking stools and photo frames which she enamelled in pastel colours. Mary, who had moved to London with the family, decorated the goods with paintings of flowers. However, despite all the high expectations and effort, 'Emerson and Co.', as the shop was called, was soon to fail. Emmeline understood little about running a business. Although the estate agent had assured the eager Mrs Pankhurst that Hampstead Road was in a 'rising neighbourhood', run-down market stalls selling meat, vegetables and other perishables were directly outside her shop door. The poor women searching for cheap produce to feed their large families had no money to spare for the goods she wanted to sell.[31]

When a worried Emmeline wrote to Richard, away from home on legal business, about her lack of customers, he merely reassured her that all would be well. However, despite her financial worries, Emmeline employed a Miss Pearson and then her sister, 'Miss Annie', as a daily governess to tutor Christabel and Sylvia. Miss Annie thought that the best way to teach the girls was to read aloud to them the novels of Charles Dickens, William Makepeace Thackeray, Walter Scott and George Eliot. Such unsystematic formal schooling, not uncommon for girls in less affluent middle-class homes, was supplemented by Aunt Mary helping the girls to dramatise well-known passages from the classic books of these authors or from fairy-tales by the Brothers Grimm, Hans Christian Andersen or Heinrich Hoffman. Hoffman's *Harriet and the matches*, which the girls knew by heart, was a particular favourite. Sylvia, with her hair in plaits, played the foolish Harriet who disobeyed her mother and nurse and played with matches when her parents were out. Christabel and Adela were the mewing cats who warned her not to do so and watched in sorrow as she burnt to death, leaving just her little scarlet shoes.[32]

Such a haphazard schooling and curriculum did not include the teaching of those subjects that might make the Pankhurst daughters 'good wives and mothers', such as decorative needlework so commonly learnt by middle-class girls in Victorian England. Nor did Christabel engage in another common pursuit of her class and gender: playing with dolls and doll's houses. Although the Pankhurst daughters did have dolls, given to them by visitors rather than their parents who invariably bought them books, the dolls were rarely played with. They were usually brought out twice a year, when Emmeline, Susannah and a seamstress were busy making the spring and summer clothes for the children so that the girls could try their hand at dressing the dolls out of the left-over scraps of material. But once the dressmaking had been completed, the dolls were put away again and soon forgotten. It was not dolls that interested Christabel and her sisters, or the occasional game of chase, played when their parents were away, when the children and servants ran up and down the stairs in the house, hiding in the large, unused communicating cupboards which could hold several people.[33] As Christabel noted, 'Politics interested us and we children were playing election games at an early age.'[34]

Financial stringency in the Pankhurst household meant that the idealistic parents could not afford to buy presents for the seven-year-old Christabel and her siblings that Christmas of 1887, but gave them instead unsold stock from the shop. Christabel, a contented and serious child, made do with an empty red plush square handkerchief box, complete with a large clasp, but the emotional five-year-old Sylvia, who was given an oblong glove case, in the same material, could not hide her disappointment and burst into tears. At least there were other unsold goods that the children could enjoy, including the cardboard cut-outs of Tower Bridge, perforated with holes, ready for cross-stitching. Christabel and Sylvia also worked in blue silk a set of pale-yellow cloth dressing-table mats punched with holes as a wedding present for Alice Brisbane, Aunt Mary's American friend from her schooldays. In preparation for the wedding, Miss Annie had bought some new buttons for their high black boots but found they were too large and so took them back to the shop. Christabel, however, who had definite likes and dislikes, preferred the big shiny buttons and suggested to Sylvia that they cut off the small ones since then the governess might accidentally be given the bigger ones and not bother to exchange them. The deed committed, the girls were punished for their naughtiness by not being allowed to accompany their mother when she visited the bride-to-be with the presents. Many years later Emmeline confessed that she would have relented but felt she could not afford to replace their shabby clothes with the new ones thought necessary for such a visit. On the day of the wedding, however, the girls were allowed to go to the church, accompanied by Susannah. They sat in wonder, in a dimly lit side pew, as they watched the ceremony.[35]

Richard Pankhurst, the busy father, was often away from Hampstead Road on legal business in Manchester, and whenever it was possible Emmeline would accompany him, leaving Mary in charge of the children. While away on one such trip, in early September 1888, shortly before Christabel's eighth birthday, little Frank fell ill with a cold, flushed cheeks and persistent hoarse cough. A worried Aunt Mary sent for Emmeline who came hurrying back. The family doctor was away and so two unknown doctors were called. As four-year-old Frank's condition worsened, terror gripped the household. Croup was diagnosed and the sick boy was sat in a hot bath, with a towel over his head, to breathe in the steam. Sylvia and Adela were in bed by the time the family doctor arrived. Christabel remembered vividly, many years after the event, that she stood alone anxiously on the stairs outside Frank's room, waiting for news, hoping their own doctor had a cure. But it was not to be. It was discovered too late that Frank had been given the wrong treatment since he did not have croup but diphtheria. When Frank passed away, some hours later on 11 September 1888, Christabel and Sylvia heard their mother's wailing of despair.

The fifty-three-year-old Richard was shattered by the news. Christabel commented:

> Fatherhood that begins in ripe years is doubly serious . . . and Frank was his heart's core. The grief remained with him always and seemed to give him new tenderness for the children that remained. Frank's death was the first and the one real sorrow that came to Father and Mother in their years of marriage.[36]

The household was now hushed in silence as the children grieved and crept away from their sorrowful parents, not knowing what to do, or approached them, from a sense of duty.[37] Christabel's birthday was not a happy occasion, despite the fact that Sylvia had bought her a little present out of carefully saved pocket money.[38] Much had been expected of Frank, the only boy in the family.

When defective drains at the rear of 165 Hampstead Road were found as the cause of Frank's diphtheria, the children were hurried away to Richmond until new accommodation could be found. The shop was hastily closed. However, Richard had taken out a long lease on the property and was frequently unable to sub-let it, adding to the financial burdens. Emmeline was still convinced that she could help her husband socially and financially in his quest to become an MP and, what was more, badly needed some venture to occupy her time and ease her aching heart. She thus rented for her growing family a big house at 8 Russell Square, in a respectable district close to the British Museum. What particularly appealed to her was that the first floor of the building consisted only of two large communicating drawing rooms that would form a space suitable for political gatherings and conferences. Emmeline also reopened Emerson's, first in Bernard Street, off fashionable Oxford Street, and then, when the premises were demolished, in Regent Street itself, with its high overhead charges.

Notes

1 CP, *Unshackled*, p. 24.
2 Christabel devoted only forty pages in *Unshackled* to these topics; Sylvia, in *The suffragette movement*, nearly one hundred and fifty. Adela's unpublished writings question many of Sylvia's claims and are to be found in the Adela Pankhurst Walsh Papers (hereafter APWP), National Library of Australia, Canberra.
3 R. West, Mrs. Pankhurst, in *The post Victorians*, with an Introduction by The Very Rev. W. R. Inge (London, Ivor Nicholson, 1933), p. 483.
4 CP, *Unshackled*, p. 20; ESP, TSM, p. 6.
5 T. W. G., In Bohemia, citizen Pankhurst, *Manchester City News*, 12 April 1913; ESP, *The life of Emmeline Pankhurst: the suffragette struggle for women's citizenship* (London, T. Werner Laurie Ltd., 1935), p. 18.
6 R. Pankhurst, The right of women to vote under the Reform Act, 1867, *Fortnightly Review*, September 1868, p. 254.
7 ESP, TSM, pp. 37–47.
8 CP, *Unshackled*, p. 21.
9 Death of Mr Robert Goulden, *Salford Reporter*, 30 April 1892. For Sophia Jane's early background see Purvis, *Emmeline Pankhurst* and P. Bartley, *Emmeline Pankhurst* (London, Routledge, 2002).
10 E. Pankhurst (hereafter EP), *My own story*, pp. 1 and 9.
11 EP, *My own story*, pp. 10–11; ESP, *Emmeline Pankhurst*, pp. 12–13.
12 CP, *Unshackled*, p. 17.
13 ESP, *Emmeline Pankhurst*, p. 14.
14 CP, *Unshackled*, p. 20.
15 ESP, TSM, p. 55.
16 Quoted in CP, *Unshackled*, p. 22.
17 ESP, TSM, p. 57.

18 EP, *My own story*, p. 13.
19 EP, *My own story*, p. 13.
20 CP, *Unshackled*, p. 23.
21 ESP, *TSM*, pp. 63–4.
22 ESP, *TSM*, pp. 58–9 and ESP's account in *Myself when young*, ed Countess of Oxford and Asquith (London, Frederick Muller, 1938), pp. 260–1.
23 ESP, *TSM*, p. 99.
24 ESP, *TSM*, pp. 65–6; ESP, *Emmeline Pankhurst*, pp. 18–19.
25 ESP, *TSM*, p. 66.
26 ESP, *TSM*, p, 67.
27 ESP, *TSM*, p. 67.
28 CP, *Unshackled*, p. 27.
29 ESP, *TSM*, pp. 66–7.
30 EP, *My own story*, p. 18.
31 ESP, *TSM*, pp. 83–4; CP, *Unshackled*, p. 25.
32 ESP, in *Myself when young*, p. 262; ESP, *TSM*, p. 85.
33 ESP, *TSM*, p. 102.
34 CP, *Unshackled*, p. 28.
35 ESP, *TSM*, pp. 84–5.
36 CP, *Unshackled*, p. 27.
37 ESP, Those elfin days in *Little innocents: childhood reminiscences* (London, Cobden-Sanderson, 1932), p. 39.
38 ESP, in *Myself when young*, ed Countess of Oxford and Asquith, p. 264.

2

GROWING UP IN AN ATMOSPHERE OF POLITICS

1889–91

Emmeline had determined that her new Emerson's should sell a more moderately priced version of the artistic furnishings and pretty wares found at the major department London store, Liberty's, just across the road from their new home in Russell Square. She employed an impecunious cabinet maker to make furniture decorated with fretwork, and bought lovely silks in bright colours, lamp shades, Chinese tea-pots, old Persian plates, Japanese embroidery, rugs from Turkey, cretonnes by William Morris and his imitators and Indian brasses. Many of the items in the shop were also to be found in the house. When Christabel, Sylvia and Adela came home on dark winter afternoons, they would find the warm welcoming glow from scarlet shades on lamp-stands or the bright vibrant colours of the beads of the Japanese blinds that Emmeline had put up herself. Christabel had watched her mother with admiration as she did all these tasks, often helping her. Her father, who liked to be in the library, lined with his own books, would declare that he was 'a helpless creature' as far as manual work was concerned. It was her mother who was the practical one in the family, the person who laid the carpets, made the curtains, upholstered the furniture and decided on the colour schemes. The large double drawing rooms on the first floor, soon to be used for political meetings, were painted yellow, Emmeline's favourite colour, and decorated by Mary with a frieze of purple irises. Tall brass standard oil lamps, with yellow shades, tastefully lit the room since Emmeline intensely disliked the modern gas lights.[1]

Once everything was shipshape, Cecil Sowerby, an artist whom Aunt Mary had known in her Paris schooldays, was engaged to tutor Christabel and her sisters. The only published accounts about the new governess are offered by Sylvia but her claim in *The suffragette movement* that Cecil Sowerby 'gave us no lessons, but read to us and took us to museums and places of interest' must be questioned.[2] A letter written in a clear, legible, neat hand from the eight-year-old Christabel to her father, who was away from home on a legal case, makes it clear that some lessons were taking place, however inadequate the teaching might have been:

My dear Father

When are you coming home? I am going to learn Latin with Miss Sowerby we are going to begin next Friday. We have got a new grammar which is much nicer than the other one. Do you think my writing is better than it was last time I wrote to you, Miss Sowerby thinks it is.

There is not anything more to tell you, because it is so soon after you went away that there was not much time for anything to happen.

We all send our love

I am

Your loving
Christabel[3]

Cecil Sowerby, whatever her failings, broadened the girls' horizons by taking them to the nearby British Museum, where they especially liked the Egyptian rooms and the mummies. And when the shy, artistic Sylvia, who was drawing constantly, asked about the human frame and begged to be allowed to see a skeleton, Miss Sowerby tried to arrange a visit to a medical museum, but found that children were refused admission. Richard initiated his disappointed and curious daughters into the mysteries of the human body by bringing home a cardboard anatomical man with a pink muscular system, coloured vital organs and finally a skeleton, all revealed by turning back successive layers.[4]

After Cecil Sowerby left the Pankhurst household to return to her painting, the girls were without a governess. The idealistic Richard suggesting sending the children to a Marxist international school established in London for refugee and destitute children. Emmeline was horrified. Richard then suggested that the local state Board School, attended by working-class children, where the fee might be as small as a few pence a week, might be appropriate. Emmeline would not agree to that either. They were 'too highly strung' and would 'lose all originality', she insisted, if put in a large class where children were taught by rote learning. Christabel and Sylvia spoke about the matter to Susannah who firmly squashed any idea that going to a Board School would be pleasant; they would have to mix with rough children from whom they would catch all forms of horrible illnesses as well as 'things' in the hair while the strict teachers would use the cane.[5]

The resourceful Christabel came up with an idea; instead of going to school, she and Sylvia should give each other lessons. Richard and Emmeline reluctantly agreed to the scheme since they had little money to spare to hire another governess; nor could they contemplate the fees for a private middle-class school for two daughters (Adela could not yet read). The girls' attempts at self-improvement were not always successful, however, especially in arithmetic. Sylvia remembered one puzzling incident when Christabel set her some sums to do, subtracting the greater from the lesser. Neither of the sisters could understand why the sum would not come right and were embarrassed when their mother explained the mistake.[6]

On another occasion, Christabel and Sylvia decided to give some lectures and spent several days reading about their respective subjects – Christabel on coal and Sylvia on tea. They carefully wrote out their speeches and were anxiously waiting for the moment when they could show their parents, two aunts and a second cousin, how well they had prepared. On the appointed day, Adela suddenly announced one hour before the event that she would give a lecture too, on the cat. In haste, the youngest Pankhurst daughter then hunted down the household puss and lay on the hearthrug, studying her. Christabel and Sylvia were disgusted and unsettled at this attempt to upstage their hard work. When Richard called upon his eldest daughter to begin, Christabel's confidence suddenly deserted her; she found it difficult to read her prepared script and stumbled, in an inaudible voice. Her father's pleas to 'Speak up' and 'Don't be self-conscious' only made her more nervous. The shy Sylvia followed, giving an even more halting performance. Then Adela, without notes, stepped forward and spoke briskly and clearly about the cat, to rounds of applause. Christabel felt humiliated.[7] But, ever optimistic, she soon regained her composure and a short time later was prepared to take the lead in asking her father some specific questions about religion.

The children were often in the kitchen with the servants and overheard gossip about whether their father was religious. In particular, Ellen, the cook, told them directly that since they were not taught to pray, bad luck would befall them in this world and they would 'burn in Hell fire' in the next. Christabel and Sylvia listened in stressful silence. Later, when they were on their own, they spoke to each other about their worries. 'I shall ask Father', said Christabel. The two went to Richard together. He explained kindly how he had not spoken to them on the subject since he wished them to make up their own minds, when they were older. Patiently, Richard explained the biblical version of Christ's life and, according to Sylvia, stated that he himself did not believe the supernatural interpretation. Then he took both daughters to his library, took down some books that discussed the issue and encouraged them to read and think for themselves. On many occasions as the girls grew older, Sylvia states that her father would say, 'If ever you go back into religion you will not have been worth the upbringing.'[8] Nonetheless, his encouragement to Christabel to investigate for herself, to question, to reason and think through the biblical story, was a maxim she never forgot.

By this time, a clear hierarchy had emerged among the Pankhurst children with Christabel accepted as the natural leader. Her position as the eldest child gave her a mature status of which she was tenacious. Although Richard often said that the children should take it in turns to accompany their parents to various events, it was usually Christabel alone who was selected for this honour. A bright, highly intelligent child, she felt special and secure from an early age since she knew she was her mother's favourite; in addition; her intellectual superiority gave her considerable advantage over her siblings. She was always reading, especially adult novels which the outspoken Harriot Stanton Blatch, daughter of the American suffragist Elizabeth Cady Stanton, told Emmeline was making her eldest daughter 'far too sentimental'.[9] But Christabel was reading a much wider range of literature than just novels, including the radical journals that came to Russell Square, such as the *Link* and *Review of Reviews*.[10] The clever Christabel was also healthy, and with her chestnut curls, rosy cheeks and flawless colouring was regarded by her parents and visitors alike as the prettiest of the Pankhurst girls. This was a situation that Sylvia, understandably, found difficult, feeling deeply wounded when her mother described her light hair as 'insipid'.[11] With her frequent headaches, weak eyes and pale complexion, Sylvia was considered not strong and her concerned parents did not encourage her to read.

As the eldest child, Christabel was expected to look after Sylvia since Susannah devoted most of her time to Adela and Frank. Christabel and Sylvia were inseparable companions. The older sister would spend long hours reading to the younger since Sylvia could not read until she was nearly eight years old. To be given so much attention and kindness only increased Sylvia's gratitude and admiration for the clever Christabel. 'It was a joy to me to walk beside her', she recollected, 'half a step in arrear, gazing upon the delicate pink and white of her face and neck, contrasted against the young, green plants coming up in the Square garden in the spring.'[12] And if Christabel suggested that the two of them should do something daring, Sylvia would follow.

Christabel was envious of the nice clothes that the other girls in Russell Square wore, especially the frilly white petticoats underneath their pretty dresses. She and Sylvia only had outdoor coats made from inexpensive, hard-wearing green serge, stocked at Emerson's, and navy blue serge dresses, with knickers to match. When their mother's old friend Noemie came to visit one day from Paris, she bought as presents for the girls white muslin pinafores decorated with tucks, ribbons and lace. A delighted Christabel quietly suggested to Sylvia that without letting any of the grown-ups know they should secretly wear the pinafores under their dresses, with the lace showing, so that they could be like the other girls. 'To such matters I was wholly indifferent', commented Sylvia, 'but as Christabel desired it, I agreed as a matter of course.'[13]

The two girls quarrelled just once in their childhood, over some minor matter, and a dejected Sylvia stood in the dusk of the landing outside the nursery door. When she heard Christabel's step, the fretful child ran with outstretched arms to her big sister, realising with great joy that Christabel had reached out her arms to take her in and hug her. 'She was our mother's favourite', wrote the adult Sylvia in later years in the influential *The suffragette movement*, 'we all knew it, and I, for one, never resented the fact. It was a matter of course; and I loved her too much to be jealous of her.'[14] But Sylvia's denial that she was jealous of Christabel must be questioned. Even a cursory reading of *The suffragette movement* reveals a tale of sibling rivalry whereby Emmeline's preference for her eldest daughter had a profound effect upon the way Sylvia shaped her memoir. It was Adela's view that Sylvia was of a 'jealous temperament'.[15]

Adela was usually excluded from the Christabel and Sylvia twosome. A weakness in her legs, from birth, had necessitated the wearing of splints so that she did not walk until she was three years old. As the youngest, smallest and most frail of the Pankhurst girls, she was pampered by the adults, becoming a solitary child who lived in a make-believe world of story-telling and plays in which she acted out all the characters.[16] Treated as the baby of the family, Adela was deeply conscious of the differences between herself and her elder sisters. 'My father treated his elder daughters as if they were grown up when they were only little children', she commented bitterly in later life. 'He gave them an exaggerated idea of their importance and made them intensively self-conscious. They were hurt and humiliated, beyond words and belief, if found fault with.'[17] Bobbing like corks on the tide of adult life, Christabel and Sylvia became immersed in the radical political interests of their parents.

The house in Russell Square soon became a centre for gatherings of men and women of progressive thought – socialists, Fabians, free thinkers, anarchists, suffragists and radicals of every kind. In particular, that summer of 1888 was memorable for the strike among women working in the Bryant and May match factories in London's East End, a protest into which Emmeline threw herself with enthusiasm – and about which the Pankhurst girls heard many stories. The match-makers, many only fifteen and sixteen years old, earned scandalously low wages that were subject to fines for such offences as lateness or dirty feet. They ate their food in their workrooms so that the dangerous phosphorous used in making the matches mixed with their meal and produced 'phossy jaw', a disease that rotted jaw bones and teeth. The strikers, who marched to the House of Commons in protest about their lot, were supported by an impassioned Emmeline who worked with Annie Besant, Herbert Burrows and the Women's Labour League to help the women form a trade union that pressed successfully for better work conditions.[18]

The significance of the Match Girls' Strike was not lost on the Pankhurst household. At a time when trade unions were mainly for skilled male workers, who were better paid, it had been shown that poorly paid working women could organise successfully, even taking their grievances to Parliament. Discussions about this 'new' trade unionism for women 'whirled' about the young ears of Christabel, Sylvia and Adela, 'mingling' with their 'childish interests' as well as talk about other radical political issues.[19] In particular, during the late autumn of 1888 a frequent topic of conversation in the Pankhurst household was the deepening divisions within the women's suffrage movement.

Matters reached a head in mid-December when a split occurred in the London-based Central Committee of the National Society for Women's Suffrage over whether women's political associations that had aims other than women's suffrage, such as the Women's Liberal Federation, should be allowed to affiliate with suffrage societies. Emmeline and Richard joined the majority group that accepted such an affiliation, soon to be known as the 'Parliament Street Society', after the address of its central office. The minority, which included Millicent Garrett Fawcett, were against such affiliation, fearing that it would destroy the non-party nature of their cause; this group became known as the 'Great College Street Society'. Another disagreement soon erupted among both groups of suffragists over the perennially vexed question of whether married women should have the parliamentary vote if they possessed the necessary property qualifications. Emmeline and Richard were strong supporters of including wives in all women suffrage bills and were bitterly disappointed when the leadership of the Parliament Street Society looked both ways and supported bills which explicitly excluded married women as well as those couched in terms of their equal claim with spinsters and widows.[20] Although Emmeline and Richard were increasingly moving in the socialist circles around the growing Labour movement, it was the enfranchisement of women and particularly the removal of the disabilities of married women that was becoming their cherished reform. Christabel listened to her pregnant mother's impassioned complaints that she was an individual in her own right, an employer of assistants in her shop, a tax payer – as well as a wife and mother – and should not be excluded from any parliamentary franchise reform.

Christabel remembered the joy in the household when her little brother, 'a fine, strong child', was born on 7 July 1889.[21] He was named Henry Francis, like little Frank, but soon became known as 'Harry'. Christabel, Sylvia and Adela took it in turns to hold the newborn Harry, so different in appearance from Frank, and were even allowed, on rare occasions, to share their bed with him. Mother and baby were doing well so Richard set off for another case in Manchester. Suddenly, the vigilant Susannah noticed that her mistress had severe haemorrhage and insisted that a doctor be called immediately. Christabel heard those words with terrible dread; her mother was dying and the family doctor lived too far away to attend quickly. 'We children were herded beyond hearing to the basement kitchen', she recollected. 'Aunt Mary came down, pale with dread, to be assailed with questions about a possibly ailing pet.'[22] Meanwhile, the ever-resourceful Susannah ran through the streets, cap-strings flying, knocking on front doors of houses displaying a doctor's brass plate. Eventually one agreed to attend Emmeline, despite the fact she was not his patient. Susannah had 'saved Mother's life', reflected a grateful Christabel in the 1930s, when she was writing her manuscript of the suffragette movement. 'To this day I draw breaths of relief – of thankfulness – that she was spared to us then.'[23]

On 23 July 1889, when Harry was just two weeks old, a meeting of a new organisation to champion the cause of married women, the Women's Franchise League, was held in Emmeline's bedroom. This new society had been founded by three women who moved in similar radical Liberal suffragist circles to the Pankhursts – Elizabeth Wolsthenholme Elmy, the League's first secretary, Alice Scatcherd its treasurer, and Harriet McIllquham, the first chair of its Council. Emmeline and Richard were members of the League's first provisional committee which took the advanced view that there could be no compromise on the vote for all women – married or single – or on a broader range of reforms that brought equal civil rights for women with men.[24] Another distinguishing feature of the new society was its policy of establishing international links, both with sympathisers with the earlier abolitionist movement in the USA but especially with members of the North American women's suffrage movement.

The celebrated American suffragist Elizabeth Cady Stanton became a corresponding member of the League, and her daughter, Harriot Stanton Blatch, married to an Englishman and living in Basingstoke, Hampshire, was an early member, as were others active in radical Liberal circles such as Florence Fenwick Miller. But the League went further than relying upon such traditional sources of support. It attempted to build links with interested men and women within the emerging Labour and socialist movements, primarily by providing speakers on women's suffrage for radical clubs and organisations such as the Women's Co-operative Guild.[25] When Ursula and Jacob Bright, old friends of the Pankhursts, later joined the League, however, the influence of Liberal women with loyalty to the Liberal Party began to grow, especially from the summer of 1890 when Ursula took a dominant role in the leadership. She began to forge stronger links with the Women's Liberal Federation, even persuading a sceptical Emmeline Pankhurst to join it.[26]

Christabel, Sylvia and Adela were not insulated from these debates. They heard their parents discussing such matters within the home but, more importantly, Emmeline and Richard considered the presence of their two eldest daughters at the Russell Square gatherings vital for their political education. Christabel and Sylvia had developed a lively interest in politics and were eager to help in arranging the chairs, distributing leaflets and taking the collection in pretty little brocade bags. Sylvia would print the notice 'To the Tea Room' while Christabel might help her mother arrange the lovely bouquets of bright flowers that decorated the drawing room. Often an entertainment of some kind would be included in the programme as a way to draw an audience for a meeting, such as songs sung by a contralto. But all this was a side-show compared to the serious speeches and lively discussions to which the sisters listened, absorbing what was said, seeking to know and to understand.[27] In particular, Christabel heard women's suffrage argued from a radical viewpoint, often interspersed with condemnation of the political parties, including the Liberal Party which was repeatedly thwarting the path of progress. A child who had no friends of her own age and who had few interests outside those of her family circle, she was old before her time. Precocious and confident, she saw herself as mature and often read the political literature that came to the house, especially Stead's *Review of Reviews*, one of her favourite journals. When she read in the latter an article claiming that after ten years of age the brain could make no more cells and was completed, the ten-year-old said to herself, 'My brain is fully formed! I have as much sense as anyone else! I will not be treated as a child anymore!'[28]

Christabel remembered from these days at Russell Square a number of the notable speakers and visitors, especially the 'ever-true' Member of Parliament, Jacob Bright, a staunch friend of the women's cause.[29] She never forgot Richard Haldane either, a radical Liberal MP, who promised much on women's suffrage and delivered little. The Women's Franchise League had adapted the Women's Disabilities Removal Bill, drafted by her father and first introduced to the Commons in 1870 by Jacob Bright, to expressly include married women in its suffrage demand; a keen Haldane agreed to sponsor the bill while another up-and-coming young Liberal, Sir Edward Grey, consented to back it. But although Haldane brought the bill before Parliament in 1889 and 1890, he did not bring it to a vote. When her mother, Ursula Bright and other disappointed League women confronted him in the Parliamentary Lobby, he coolly replied that the bill was simply a declaration of principle and had no chance of becoming law for at least fifty years. That evening, Christabel listened to the smouldering discontent voiced by her mother. Her father was no less indignant. 'Why are women so patient? Why don't you force us to give you the vote?' he said to his daughters. Then mimicking the actions of a cat, he clawed the air with his long fingers, playfully adding, 'Why don't you scratch our eyes out?'[30] The ten-year-old Christabel listened carefully. That a male Liberal MP who claimed to be a supporter of women's suffrage had envisaged 'no early enactment' of the League's suffrage bill was a valuable political lesson neither she nor her mother ever forgot.[31]

For Christabel, it was the uncompromising and strong-minded Women's Franchise League members, such as Alice Scatcherd and especially Elizabeth Cady Stanton, who impressed her, not unreliable politicians like Richard Haldane. The tall, bony Alice Scatcherd, active in women's trade unionism in her native Yorkshire as well as the organiser of the League in the north, was a frequent visitor to Russell Square as well as a regular speaker. The lively and outspoken wife of a wealthy factory owner, she was described by Christabel as 'a great nursery favourite'.[32] The Pankhurst girls were fascinated by the fact that, unlike their mother, Alice Scatcherd did not follow the common practice among well-dressed middle-class women of wearing a veil when going outdoors. Her strong feminist stance on this matter was complemented by a refusal to wear a wedding ring or to attend a wedding ceremony in the Church of England since she believed that the insistence that a bride should pledge her obedience to her intended helped to keep women in subjection.[33]

But of all the speakers at Russell Square, it was the radical American feminist Elizabeth Cady Stanton, a corresponding member of the Women's Franchise League, who 'greatly interested' Christabel.[34] By the time Elizabeth Cady Stanton made her final visit to Britain in 1890, in her seventies, she was a celebrated figure within the American women's movement, her name linked with her close working partner, Susan B. Anthony. Over fifty years earlier, in 1848, the visionary Elizabeth Cady Stanton had drafted with Lucretia Mott the famous 'Declaration of rights and sentiments', which she read out at the first women's rights convention, held in Seneca Falls, New York.[35] Her insistence that women must learn to work together, stand on their own two feet and be self-reliant was to be reiterated and adapted later by Christabel within the different context of the British women's suffrage movement.

Immersed in this discussion of radical politics, Christabel was also the key pin in publishing the *Home News*, a newspaper produced initially weekly and then monthly by herself and her sisters, for family circulation. She copied into the paper, in her own hand, letters on important subjects that Richard gave to her; she also helped Sylvia copy out her own various essays, including a series on 'Walks in London' which included descriptions of the House of Commons, the British Museum, National Gallery and the Tower of London. The six-year-old Adela, unable to read and write, was anxious not to be excluded from this enterprise; she dictated to Christabel stories about a little servant girl whom everyone bullied and about a poor widow with a large family whose lives were transformed by the kindness of a wealthy benefactor.[36] Christabel, the main contributor to the *Home News*, regularly wrote reports of meetings of the Women's Franchise League which included such observations as: 'Mrs Pankhurst looked elegant in a trained velvet gown', the 'Misses Pankhurst wore white crepe dresses with worked yokes' and 'the refreshments were delicious, the strawberries and cream being especially so'. Her impression of one meeting, held in May 1892, when she was eleven years old, is revealing:

> Mrs. Pankhurst held an At Home in her beautiful house on May 28th. There was a great number of people there. Dr. Pankhurst, as Chairman, said in his speech that if the suffrage was not given to women, the result would be terrible. If a body was half of it bound, how was it to be expected that it would grow and develop properly. This body was the human race and the fettered half, women. He then, with many compliments, called upon Mrs. Fenwick Miller to speak. Mrs. Fenwick Miller spoke of . . . the growing power of the Women's Franchise League. Some opponents tried to prove that women were naturally inferior to men, but our girls won degrees and honours at the Universities.[37]

The attentive Christabel, listening to adult discussions about injustices to women in late Victorian society, was being socialised into a feminist view of the world, a view that ran counter to the dominant Victorian ideology that women were inferior and subordinate to men and should, ideally, be located within the private sphere of the home as wives and mothers.[38] She was hearing that women could challenge, rather than accept, the dominant ideas about their place in society, and bring about change. When asked in 1908 by a reporter about the training that had enabled her to become 'so brilliant a leader' of the women's suffrage movement, Christabel replied, 'My father and mother were both political, and I grew up in an atmosphere of politics.'[39]

Christabel, tantalisingly, gives few details about other aspects of her childhood, although she remembered clearly the joy that music brought to their home:

> Mother had a moving contralto voice. Father hardly knew one tune from the other – but he loved to hear his wife sing. We children would be admitted to the drawing-room for a while, and even after banishment to bed we could still hear the music through open doors and fall asleep listening.[40]

It is Sylvia who recounts the picturesque London streets that she and her sisters could enjoy, when they were taken out for walks, the alluring smell of a French chocolate shop as well as the magnificent display that Snow, a stationer, had in the window at Christmas. Then there were the Scotsmen in their kilts, playing the bagpipes, and women selling bunches of lavender. Particular treats were the Punch and Judy show or the rare occasions when the children took a hansom cab. When they were out shopping with the proud Susannah, the shopkeepers usually made a fuss of her charges. 'Are they all yours?' was an oft-repeated question. The local butcher would even occasionally send sweetbreads as a present to 'the young ladies' as he called Christabel, Sylvia and Adela.[41]

During the summer, the girls were allowed to play outside in the Russell Square garden with its avenues of plane trees. They would walk the circular path in the garden, chattering away, and then creep into one of the small round enclosures at each of the four corners of the Square, places that adults never entered, secret magical areas to which they gave special names. The 'Froggety' was so named because Sylvia had found a toad there which the girls excitedly recognised from their picture books. The lawns in the Square garden were another place of delight where the sisters might sit making daisy chains while admiring the beautiful laburnums, pale-blue larkspur and flower beds of brilliant colour.[42] Usually the three girls were together, but one day Adela ventured into the Square on her own and was approached by some big boys whose questions and remarks frightened her so much that she told Susannah. When Emmeline heard about the alarming incident, she scolded Christabel and Sylvia for leaving their younger sister alone and discussed the matter with Richard. 'Father says I ought to talk to you', the anxious mother confided to her daughters, as she tried to open up the topic of sex education. But the talk went no further and the subject was never brought up again. Thereafter, when the children wanted to play outside they were confined to the safety of the narrow dark garden at the rear of the house, enclosed by a high wall.[43]

Now when the children were taken out by Aunt Mary, Adela was supposed to keep pace with her big sisters. But although the splints had been removed from her legs, they were still weak and the constant refrain of 'don't dawdle' became the daily misery of her life. Since the birth of Harry, she was no longer the baby of the family and became a lonely child who did not find her sisters friendly. She recollected how Christabel and Sylvia would whisper confidences and tell stories that they would not let her hear and even, on one occasion, complained loudly to their mother because she admired 'a small boy, Bertie Bernstein and actually, in the full sight of everybody, put my arms round him and kissed him'. In particular, the unhappy Adela remembered that Sylvia was a 'fearful "telltale" and would retell all the unpleasant things she knew against me to aunts and friends'. Christabel, on the other hand, was noted for her 'common sense'.[44] Such views have rarely been voiced in the dominant narrative about the childhood of the Pankhurst girls, that written by Sylvia herself in *The suffragette movement*.[45]

Another diversion from the 'atmosphere of politics' in which Christabel grew up were the occasional holidays to the Isle of Man, Clacton-on-Sea, Basingstoke or Aberdeen where Aunt Bess, her father's sister, lived. At Clacton, where the children stayed for a few months in 1891 with Susannah and Ellen, their parents visiting infrequently, they had their first experience of the squalid life of certain sections of the working class, something they had only previously read about in the novels of Charles Dickens. Many of the East End of London trippers who came to Clacton, on a cheap day return, got drunk and became loud and abusive. Ellen insisted one evening on taking the children to the railway station since she thought she might see a docker she knew. The sight of intoxicated women and men, cursing and fighting as they struggled to find an empty seat on the return train, horrified her middle-class charges.[46]

On another occasion, the sensible Christabel stayed on her own with Harriot Stanton Blatch and her husband in what was then rural Basingstoke, in Hampshire. For Christabel the visit offered a rare opportunity to play with someone other than her siblings, namely the Stanton Blatch's daughter, Norah, a few years her junior. This was the first time that Christabel had been separated from Sylvia, her constant companion, who felt hurt that she had not been included. The matter was soon put right when, a short time after Christabel's return back home, both girls were invited to Basingstoke for a summer holiday and told firmly by their mother to be on their best behaviour. The excited Sylvia was shocked by the antics of the tomboy Norah who, as soon as she and Christabel arrived, took them climbing up a wood-pile from which she dropped fir cones onto unsuspecting people walking in the road below while the perpetrators crouched down, out of sight. Christabel had willingly joined in the prank, much to her sister's astonishment. The mischievous Norah and Christabel planned another prank to take place in a few days' time during haymaking when Harriot Stanton Blatch would be in London. They confided to Sylvia how all three of them would avoid being sent to bed at the usual time by pushing over in the hay the maids who came to fetch them. Then they would run as fast as their legs could carry them across the fields, returning at an hour of their choosing. On the appointed day, Christabel, Sylvia and Nora put their plan into action. The good-humoured Mr Blatch kept an eye on the girls in a field nearby, letting them play late before bringing them back home to bed. The next morning, an angry Harriot Stanton Blatch came to the girls' bedroom and firmly scolded Christabel, saying that as the eldest she was to blame. When the girls were alone again, Christabel and Norah insisted they had done no wrong but the brooding Sylvia said nothing, fearful that they had disgraced their parents.[47]

Notes

1 ESP, TSM, pp. 89–90.
2 ESP, TSM, p. 107.
3 CP to Richard Pankhurst, Jill Craigie Collection (hereafter Craigie Collection) at The Women's Library at the London School of Economics (hereafter TWL). Unfortunately the top right-hand corner of the letter, probably containing the date, is missing.

4 ESP, TSM, p. 108.
5 Adela Pankhurst Walsh (hereafter Adela APW), My mother: an explanation & vindication, APWP, pp. 8–9; E. S. Pankhurst, TSM, p. 108.
6 ESP, TSM, p. 108.
7 ESP, TSM, p. 106.
8 ESP, TSM, p. 109.
9 ESP, TSM, p. 105.
10 ESP, TSM, p. 100.
11 ESP, TSM, p. 88; Adela suggests that Sylvia 'imagined my mother disliked her fair hair', APW, My mother, p. 12.
12 ESP, TSM, p. 99.
13 ESP, TSM, p. 98.
14 ESP, TSM, p. 99.
15 APW, My mother, p. 1.
16 ESP, TSM, p. 102.
17 APW, My mother, p. 4. It is interesting to note that Harrison, Sylvia Pankhurst, p. 15 states 'Tragically, Adela carried throughout most of her life the deep, terrible, unresolved and festering jealousies of childhood . . .' without any acknowledgement that such a statement might also apply to Sylvia.
18 A. Taylor, Annie Besant: a biography (Oxford, Oxford University Press, 1992), pp. 205–12; Purvis, Emmeline Pankhurst, p. 26.
19 ESP, TSM, p. 91.
20 S. S. Holton, Suffrage days: stories from the women's suffrage movement (London, Routledge, 1996), pp. 71–5.
21 CP, Unshackled, p. 28.
22 CP, Unshackled, p. 28.
23 CP, Unshackled, p. 28.
24 S. S. Holton, Now you see it, now you don't: the Women's Franchise League and its place in contending narratives of the women's suffrage movement, in The women's suffrage movement: new feminist perspectives, eds M. Joannou and J. Purvis (Manchester, Manchester University Press, 1998), pp. 15–36.
25 Holton, The Women's Franchise League, p. 25.
26 EP, My own story, p. 16.
27 ESP, TSM, p. 98; ESP, My elfin days, p. 41.
28 ESP, TSM, p. 100.
29 CP, Unshackled, pp. 28–9.
30 ESP, TSM, p. 97.
31 CP, Unshackled, p. 29.
32 CP, Unshackled, p. 29.
33 ESP, TSM, p. 97.
34 CP, Unshackled, p. 29.
35 E. Griffith, In her own right: the life of Elizabeth Cady Stanton (Oxford, Oxford University Press, 1984), p. 53.
36 ESP, TSM, p. 107; V. Coleman, Adela Pankhurst: the wayward suffragette 1885–1961 (Melbourne, Melbourne University Press, 1996), p. 15.
37 CP, Unshackled, p. 29.
38 On women's role in Victorian society see, for example, K. Gleadle, British women in the nineteenth century (Houndmills, Palgrave, 2001). For a feminist critique see C. Dyhouse, Feminism and the family in England 1880–1939 (Oxford, Basil Blackwell, 1989).
39 B. Hatton, Women's votes, a chat with Christabel Pankhurst, LL.B, Sunday Times, 8 March 1908.
40 CP, Unshackled, p. 30.

41 ESP, Sylvia Pankhurst, in *Myself when young*, ed the Countess of Oxford and Asquith, p. 264.
42 ESP, TSM, pp. 99–100.
43 ESP, TSM, p. 103.
44 APW, My mother, pp. 11–12 and 4.
45 Although Pugh in *The Pankhursts* does note that Adela regarded Sylvia as a persecutor who told tales on the young ones, he does not mention that she also spoke of Christabel's common sense. A similar omission is to be found in Harrison, *Sylvia Pankhurst*, p. 15. For an exception to this general rule that Adela's voice has rarely been heard see J. Liddington, *Rebel girls: their fight for the vote* (London, Virago, 2006), pp. 17–31; J. Purvis, Emmeline Pankhurst (1858–1928), suffragette leader and single parent in Edwardian Britain, in *Lone Mothers*: Special Issue of *Women's History Review*, eds T. Evans and P. Thane, February 2011, pp. 87–108.
46 ESP, TSM, pp. 110–11.
47 ESP, TSM, p. 112.

3

SISTERLY RIVALRY
1892–6

By autumn 1892 it was painfully apparent that Emerson's, described as an 'Art Furnishers and Decorators', was a costly burden. Additional financial worries emerged during that winter of 1892–3 when the ninety-nine-year lease of 8 Russell Square came to an end. Richard was presented with a heavy bill for the wear and tear of a century of tenants, including not only the strengthening of the balcony and the entire re-decoration of the interior but also the replacement of any missing items. He had already paid for the replacement of the old brick drains by a more modern system and the news of this new outlay, which he could not afford, came as a shock. Despite the fact that he was a lawyer, Richard had not checked the terms of the lease. After the bill for the dilapidations had been paid, Richard and Emmeline were stunned to hear that the repairs would not be undertaken since the house was to be demolished and a hotel built on the site.[1]

The worry of debt hanging over his head for many years to come caused Richard much anxiety, and his health began to suffer so that he spent a few weeks seeking a cure at Smedley Hydro in Southport, a hydropathic establishment where water was applied externally to the body of the patient. Although the water treatment did provide some relief, his stomach pains were not helped by the pressurised life he led. Richard had his chambers in London but most of his legal work was still on the northern circuit so that he was away a lot from the children and the wife he adored. Emmeline and Richard talked the matter over and came to the conclusion that they would have a better quality of life if they moved back to Manchester. The closing of her shop, however, with the shattering of her dream of earning enough money to support her husband's career in Parliament, made Emmeline ill so it was thought wiser to take a furnished apartment for a short time in the sleepy seaside resort of Southport, some forty miles from Manchester, where the bracing air would be beneficial not only for her health but also for Richard's.[2]

The children were excited with the news that they were moving to the seaside which, for Christabel, 'summed up all the joys of life for us'. The morning after they arrived at the apartment, Christabel and Sylvia were up before the others, walking on the deserted promenade before breakfast. Although Emmeline scolded the two for going out on their own, they sensed a whiff of freedom in the air. When living in Russell Square, they would never have dared to walk the streets without an adult present. This was not the only change of which the girls were conscious. The regime enforced by domestic servants had also disappeared since only the caring and faithful Susannah had been retained. Nor did the new apartment have a nursery where they might be tucked away and given their own special meals. Instead, their mother and father sat around the table with their children, eating the same food, an act that made Christabel and Sylvia feel very grown up. The one regret was that Aunt Mary was no longer living with them. Since Emerson's had been wound up, she had decided to take a new direction in life, training as a teacher of dress-making, an occupation followed too by her sister, Ada.[3]

Christabel missed Aunt Mary, as did the dejected Emmeline. Now confined to the home as a full-time wife and mother, without her shop, her political meetings and her sister, her mother's 'active spirit', commented Christabel in a characteristic understatement, 'was perhaps not wholly content'.[4] Yet despite her unhappiness, Emmeline realised that the time had come for the twelve-year-old Christabel and the ten-year-old Sylvia to have some formal schooling. Rather than send them to a small, middle-class establishment that taught their pupils to be ladylike wives and mothers, Emmeline and Richard settled on one of the newer, more academic schools for girls that were being established at this time, Southport High School for Girls. When Adela heard the news she pleaded to be allowed to be a pupil there too. A reluctant Emmeline finally agreed, despite her fears that her seven-year-old daughter was much too young.[5]

The three sisters entered Southport High School for Girls in January 1893 and stayed just one term. Adela loved it, despite the fact that their father had stipulated that none of his daughters should attend religious instruction, a request that made the sisters feel different, set apart from other more socially conventional pupils.[6] The teachers appreciated her abilities and encouraged her to do well. The fragile Adela was particularly happy that she had children of her own age to associate with, children who had not heard of high-minded causes.[7] Sylvia too applied herself to her studies with zest. Keen to prove herself to her mother and Christabel, she flourished in her small class of just nine pupils, being placed second in the class at the end of the term. Unexpectedly, Christabel's end-of-term report read less favourably since she was placed ninth out of a class of fourteen, revealing starkly the inadequacies of her previous unsystematic schooling. While she received the expected 'Excellent' for her reading, she was placed fifth in her class for Latin and grammar, sixth for geography, seventh for poetry and history, eleventh for her writing (described as 'Very poor'), and thirteenth for French and arithmetic, nearly the bottom of the class. However, her industry was said to be 'Very satisfactory' and her conduct 'Excellent'.[8]

Sylvia states in *The suffragette movement* how she was particularly proud of her class teacher's comment, 'A most promising pupil'. However, she makes no reference to the 'Very satisfactory' assessment for industry given to her big sister but states instead that it was said of Christabel 'that she could do better at her lessons if she tried, a reputation she carried with her throughout her school life'.[9] What is apparent, as emphasised earlier, when reading the differing accounts by the three Pankhurst girls of their childhood is that we find stories of sisterly rivalry so that other interpretations are possible than those offered in Sylvia's frequently cited text. In the latter, Sylvia makes no mention of the fact that the clever Christabel missed a substantial time off school during the term – five mornings as well as six afternoons – which hindered her academic progress. Whatever the reason for these absences – perhaps Christabel was ill or, much more likely, she stayed at home as a companion to her unhappy mother – Sylvia had no scruples about recording for prosperity derogatory comments about her sister that have been frequently recounted by subsequent writers as indicating that Christabel was lazy and lacking in commitment.[10] In contrast, Sylvia could admit to no faults of her own. She carefully omits to mention in *The suffragette movement* the thirteen times she arrived late at the high school.

During that summer of 1893 Christabel and her family moved home again, this time to rented rooms in a farm-house on the top of a hill in the pretty village of Disley, some sixteen miles south-east of Manchester. Although Christabel and Sylvia now shared a governess with two girls in the village, it was the country life that the children enjoyed, especially since it revived their mother's flagging spirit. A rejuvenated Emmeline helped with the hay-making and was keener than her children on black-berrying, urging them to reach high for the big berries, irrespective of the thorns, torn stockings and scratched limbs. She even hired a pony and trap and took her offspring out for the day. But it was the surprise present from their father of a donkey that enthralled Christabel and her siblings. Jack, as he was known, was incredibly stubborn and erratic and needed much coaxing before he would pull the trap.[11]

The children's hearts 'were heavy', remembered Christabel, when they heard they were to leave the countryside for sooty Manchester.[12] For a short time they lived at 173 High Street, Oxford Street, Manchester until Emmeline found a suitable residence – Lerne House, 4 Buckingham Crescent, Daisy Bank Road, Victoria Park, a residential area with tall, old trees. The spacious Buckingham Crescent house, to which the family moved in 1894, was a two-storey building in a block of four, facing fields. Although there was only a small, walled garden at the back of the house, the front had a substantial stretch of land that was undivided from the other dwellings. Since only one of the other three houses was occupied, the children roamed freely through the gardens of the empty houses in-between. The first big event in which Christabel, Sylvia, Adela and Harry were involved at 4 Buckingham Crescent was the marriage of Susannah to the keeper of Disley Gold Links. The children were fascinated by the fact that the bride-groom, an ardent teetotaller, refused to pop the cork of the bottles of champagne generously supplied by their parents for the wedding guests.[13]

In September 1893, Christabel, Sylvia and Adela had been enrolled at the Manchester High School for Girls. This time they stayed much longer than in their previous high school – Christabel until April 1897, Sylvia until July 1898

37

and Adela until July 1902. The Manchester High School for Girls, founded in 1874, had become under its first headmistress, Miss Elizabeth Day, one of the most prestigious of the new academic schools for girls, employing women graduates as specialised subject teachers. Miss Day, unimpressed by Richard Pankhurst's reputation as a republican and agnostic, had initially refused to admit his daughters, a decision that was over-ruled by the school governors after a character reference for each of the girls had been submitted.[14] Christabel was placed in the probationary class in the upper school, Sylvia in the lower school and Adela in the preparatory class. All three were regarded as quiet, well-behaved pupils – and all three wrote differing accounts of their own schooling and, in particular, about Christabel's.

Sylvia in *The suffragette movement* tells of how 'from the first' the mature, confident Christabel was a favourite with her class teacher and given at once the trusted position of monitor of her class. However, soon after this honour she was punished with a 'conduct mark' for speaking on the stairs, as the girls filed down, even though she was ignorant of the rule. Although her sympathetic class teacher explained to Miss Day that it was not a deliberate attempt to flout the school rules, the stern headmistress insisted that no exceptions could be made and that Christabel's monitor's badge must be forfeited. Sylvia remembered too how Christabel, who excelled in the private dancing classes that their parents had arranged for their two eldest daughters, was chosen by the French mistress to play the part of the dancing master in the school's Christmas production of Moliere's *Bourgeois Gentilhomme*. Unfortunately, Miss Day was present at one of the lessons when the budding actress omitted the last paragraph of her lines and insisted that another girl must have the part. Emmeline was so upset when she heard the news that Richard went to the school, to plead with Miss Day. It was all to no avail. Emmeline came to detest the school, and would now keep her daughters home on 'the slightest pretext', saying a week spent with her helping at a bazaar was of greater educational value than school attendance.[15]

But any honey comments that Sylvia makes about Christabel in *The suffragette movement* are usually mixed with vinegar. The unhappy Sylvia who, unlike her sisters, detested the Manchester High School for Girls, finding the pupils ignorant, the teaching dull and dry, the homework excessive and the discipline petty, would wait at playtime for Christabel to come down the stairs from the upper school with her class mates. The artistic Sylvia, who used every opportunity she could to introduce drawing into every lesson, was used to her big sister comforting her but now found that she was 'cold-shouldered' by Christabel and her friends 'as a little girl from the lower school . . . I ceased to wait for Christabel by the stairs. She accepted my withdrawal without comment'.[16] Sylvia recounts every small fault she can find with Christabel, telling how her sister made friends with the pretty Edith whose home life was a constant round of visits and entertainments. 'I was distressed to hear her presently praising Edith's home life at the expense of our own . . . at home, according to Christabel's view, there was "nothing but politics and silly old women's suffrage."'[17] While Christabel's own sparse memoir sheds no light on this particular remark she is alleged to have made, it seems out of character and contradicts what she herself remembers of her childhood. 'We never went to a boarding school and never wanted to, if only because it would have meant missing too much of Father and Mother', she writes about this time in Manchester. 'The attraction of two such personalities, and all the political and other interests and activities that centred in them, made home seem preferable to any school at a distance.'[18]

If Sylvia's picture in *The suffragette movement* of her big sister is open to question, so too must be her silence on Adela's experiences as a pupil at Manchester High. Adela recollects how at her new school, Sylvia's enmity towards her had not abated. 'How horrid your sister is', Adela's schoolmates commented. One such companion, Barbara Cattinach, an Irish girl, went up to Sylvia and passed sarcastic remarks. 'Your face would frighten a crow off its nest', and then something much worse, 'Go and boil your head and play with the gravy.' The startled Adela laughed at the comments, thinking them witty, but the bruised Sylvia rushed to tell her parents the story as soon as they all arrived home. Emmeline and Richard were shocked. Forbidden to play with her friends, the unhappy Adela grew fat and lost interest in her school work, despite the fact that Miss Day had told her mother that her youngest daughter had 'literary ability'. Worse was the baiting she received at home from her big sisters who teased and humiliated her, calling her thin hair 'rats tails' and shouting 'she is a lump – a lump – a lump'.[19]

Despite the sisterly rivalry among the Pankhurst girls, by the time she was fourteen the bookish Christabel was well read and seeking to answer broad philosophical questions, such as 'What is truth?' Indeed, she was supplementing her formal schooling by studying philosophy, especially the writings of John Stuart Mill.[20] Christabel had been introduced to his works by her father, and greatly admired Mill's support for women's suffrage as well as his logical thinking, his concern for social justice and his wish to make the world a better place. That Mill's books were readily available at home, in her father's library, gave the bright Christabel an opportunity to read them at her leisure and to explore the ideas he discussed. Indeed, in the 1950s, she told a correspondent that Mill had been a key formative influence on her early life:

> John Stuart Mill was my girlhood . . . I might say, my childhood ideal human being. My father admired him greatly and his books were consequently in our home. I was quite familiar with them all . . . except I think his large tome on Sir W. Hamilton's philosophy which I do not remember reading. Mill's book, 'Utilitarianism' was my Bible. His 'Subjection of Women' I did not bother about because to me all books in favour of women's enfranchisement were demonstrating the self-evident and labouring the obvious . . . I envied him his early education, thinking with him, as he expresses himself in his Autobiography, that it would be a very great advantage to get inside one all that information and knowledge at a tender age.[21]

Christabel's interest in philosophy and logic set her apart from her sisters, giving her an intellectual edge. Emmeline had always said that she wanted her daughters to develop 'their individuality' and this Christabel certainly did.[22] The proud Richard encouraged his clever daughter to think through and talk about difficult philosophical issues, rather than to be a quiet, submissive girl who knew her place in life. 'What was so fine about Father', recollected Christabel, 'was that he practiced [sic] his belief in the equality and rights of women in his home and this it was that did so much to make me confident in my argument and conflict with unjust men politicians.'[23] But it was not just in verbal skills that the eldest Pankhurst daughter excelled. Christabel surpassed everyone in the private dancing class she and Sylvia attended. The mastering of the various dance movements gave her a poise and grace that was to stand her in good stead during her suffrage years. A delighted Emmeline, happy to make the flowing dancing outfits for her beloved daughter, hoped that Christabel would become an accomplished dancer whom she could accompany when she performed in the great cities of the world. But, by the age of about sixteen, when Richard and Emmeline were discussing her future, Christabel had tired of the idea. 'People will say my brains are in my feet!' she confessed to Sylvia. Richard came up with another suggestion. 'Christabel has a good head', he pointed out, 'I'll have her coached; she shall matriculate!' Emmeline burst into tears on hearing such words, protesting she would not have her daughters brought up to be high school teachers.[24]

Concerns about schooling were always dwarfed for Christabel by the great social and political struggles in which her parents were actively involved. She and her sisters continued to attend Women's Franchise League meetings, especially when they were held in their home.[25] The League's Honorary Secretary, Ursula Bright, corresponded regularly with the much younger Emmeline Pankhurst, for whom she had a motherly affection, and it is not inconceivable that Christabel heard her mother read out sections of these letters at the breakfast table. In particular, during autumn 1893, Ursula regularly spelt out her worries about the forthcoming Local Government Bill, whether the right of married women to vote would be included, whether all their friends in Parliament who said they would support married women's rights would do so, whether the wrangling between the Tories and Liberals would destroy the bill, whether the bill would be shelved for want of time.[26]

Such stories about the struggle to find firm support for women's enfranchisement within the all-male parliamentary arena were not new to Christabel. Nor was her mother involved in just the Women's Franchise League. As soon as she moved back to Manchester, Emmeline had joined the Executive Committee of the Manchester National Society for Women's Suffrage which was enjoying a new lease of life under its new secretary, Esther Roper. During 1894 the re-energised Emmeline was busy helping to organise a large demonstration in the Manchester Free Trade Hall as well as speaking at both indoor and outdoor meetings alongside her husband and other activists.[27] However, although Emmeline's and Richard's enthusiasm for women's suffrage never wavered, it was into the developing socialist movement that they were being increasingly drawn, both having joined the Fabian Society in September 1890.[28]

Emmeline and Richard had been delighted when their close friend Keir Hardie was elected to Parliament in 1892 as an independent 'Labour' candidate for the constituency of West Ham South, London. Although there was no Labour Party at this particular point in time, Hardie's success helped to propel the formation of the Independent Labour Party (ILP) in Bradford in January 1893 and the emergence of the Labour Representation Committee (LRC) some seven years later.[29] From its inception, Emmeline and Richard were keen supporters of the ILP which Emmeline joined, believing that socialism would be the means of 'righting every political and social wrong', including votes for women.[30] In September 1894 she finally resigned from the Lancashire and Cheshire Union of the Women's Liberal Association, of which Ursula Bright was President. Despite Ursula Bright's dismay, Emmeline was glad to shed her association with the Liberal Party. She had never forgiven the great Liberal statesman William Ewart Gladstone for his opposition to women's suffrage and believed that the Liberal Party was a men's party that exploited the work of Liberal women for its own ends. The advice of Liberal leaders, that women could 'earn' their enfranchisement by allying with men, had been disastrous since the women 'left off working for themselves, and threw themselves into the men's work'.[31] That her father and now her mother had resigned from the Liberal Party, both holding it in disdain, was something that Christabel never forgot.

Richard wanted to follow Emmeline's lead and join the ILP but hesitated, knowing that close identification with such a radical organisation could bring professional disaster. But the hesitation did not last long. 'Gallant as ever, he held his head high and faced the new storm that broke upon him as the first man of his sort and standing in the city, perhaps in the whole country, to join the Labour movement', noted Christabel.[32] Clients began to drift away, while invitations to important civic functions were no more. Richard continued to give his services free to the trade unions and working people who sought his help. But such generosity did not pay the bills or clothe his family. The worry increased the severity of his stomach pains, which had not been cured by his stay at Smedley Hydro, although he carefully hid from Emmeline and their children the extent of his discomfort. Despite these problems, Richard would not abandon his political beliefs but rose earlier and worked later. In 1896, he became a member of the National Administrative Council (NAC) of the ILP, but did not stand for re-election the following year.[33]

Christabel and her sisters were now drawn by their parents into their work for the socialist cause and, in particular, saw for themselves the grim conditions of poverty in which many working-class families lived in the Manchester area. Often on a Sunday morning Christabel and Sylvia would accompany their father when he spoke in the poor districts of Manchester, urging the down-trodden men and women to join the ILP. And then, during the unemployment crisis in winter 1894, when both Emmeline and Richard took the lead in setting up a Committee for the Relief of the Unemployed, both girls helped their mother on Saturday mornings when she stood on a lorry distributing hot soup and bread to the hungry thousands waiting in the bitter cold in Stevenson Square or in the deprived districts of Ancoats, Gorton and Openshaw.[34] Their father and Leonard Hall, a doctor's son, were politically active in other ways, leading deputations to Manchester City Council and the Boards of Guardians and sending resolutions to the Government demanding that local authorities should be empowered to acquire land, machinery and materials that might provide work at trade union rates. At the height of this unrest, Christabel and her siblings heard on 17 December 1894 that their mother was successfully returned as the ILP candidate for the Chorlton Board of Guardians, news that was especially welcome since one month earlier Emmeline had been defeated when standing for election to the Manchester School Board.[35] This was the first post as a socialist and public representative to which Emmeline had been elected and she threw herself into the philanthropic work with typical zeal and earnestness. As Christabel observed, her mother hoped that through the Labour movement 'the grim problem of poverty might be solved'.[36]

For Christabel, who was close to her mother, Emmeline was an important role model in her devotion to public duty. So it is no surprise that Christabel too, with her well-developed social conscience, joined the ILP. She did not flinch when asked to dance at various ILP functions, sometimes performing an Irish jig with Sylvia. And she willingly accepted Robert Blatchford's request to teach dancing to poor slum girls, the 'Cinderella children', as they were called.[37] Many years later, Adela, reflecting on these years, spoke about the social consequences for Christabel of her involvement in the socialist movement, especially how it restricted her social life and the type of young men she might meet:

> Christabel, a pretty, lively girl, had a sensitive conscience; no doubt,
> there stirred in her a desire to live and enjoy living – but to do so would
> have been betraying the cause . . . Loyally, she joined the I.L.P. and cut
> herself off from all associations which might draw her away from the
> working class movement. No doubt, the I.L.P. young men adored her,
> but she never looked on them as possible life mates, for her education
> and training had been on middle class lines though we had no associa-
> tions in Manchester at the time, except with the Labor [sic] movement
> and, indeed we were almost too hard up to meet anyone else on equal
> terms.[38]

The socialists who now frequently visited the Pankhurst home at 4 Buckingham Crescent may have been less sophisticated than the audiences at Russell Square, but all were inspired by the writings of Karl Marx and united in their desire to lift the masses out of the hands of greedy and exploitative capitalists. Well-known national figures, such as Keir Hardie and Bruce Glasier and his wife, Katherine St John Conway, invariably stayed overnight when they were in the area. Christabel and Sylvia both admired Hardie, although Christabel was less reverential towards him than her sister. Other ILP members, such as Caroline Martyn and Ben Tillett, were also known to the Pankhurst children, as well as Tom Mann, at that time secretary of the ILP. Mann was their great favourite since he would play games with them. On one occasion, the mischievous Christabel came silently behind him and slipped around his neck a harmless grass snake bought recently at a local market. The startled man jumped through a nearby open window which, fortunately, was on the ground floor. The girls had a glimpse too of the aged German socialist leader Wilhelm Leibknecht who came to Manchester with Karl Marx's daughter, Eleanor, and her co-habiting lover, Edward Aveling.[39]

The talk about the evils of capitalism and about the necessity for class conflict as the means to bring about a socialist, egalitarian society flowed around the children's ears. Socialist journals such as the *Labour Leader*, edited by Hardie, Robert Blatchford's the *Clarion* and the Manchester *Labour Prophet*, as well as a number of smaller socialist publications, were in the house for Christabel, Sylvia and Adela to read, the *Labour Leader* being a particular favourite.[40] But, above all, Emmeline and Richard taught their children socialist principles by their example.

Christabel heard from her mother, now a Poor Law Guardian, about the horrific conditions she found in the Chorlton Workhouse, especially for women and girls. Aged women and men sat on backless benches that made their bodies ache and had no privacy, no possessions, not even a locker. The women, lacking even a pocket in their gowns, were obliged to keep any small treasures in their bosoms. The majority of them had led respectful lives in the past and lost their employment at a time of life when it was impossible to get work or had been full-time housewives who had become penniless when their husbands died. Then there were also in the workhouse young pregnant women, most of them unmarried and poor servants, doing the harshest physical work up to the moment of delivery. After confinement in hospital for just two weeks, they could either continue their harsh life in the workhouse, but separated from their baby, or face the bleak world outside with the baby but without money, a job or a home to go to. As sad as these cases were, it was perhaps the plight of the little girls of seven and eight years old, shivering with cold that winter as they scrubbed the stones of the long, draughty corridors, that most stirred Emmeline's compassion and that of her listening daughter. These girls, clad winter and summer in thin cotton frocks with short sleeves and low neck and the flimsiest of knickers, were even denied nightdresses. For these children, as for all the workhouse adults, the diet was dull and non-nutritious, consisting mainly of a daily weight of bread, served in one solid ration, as in prison.[41]

Christabel heard, with admiration, the story of how her compassionate yet practical mother did not ask for reform of workhouse conditions but demanded it, converting other Poor Law Guardians to support her view.[42] Within six months of Emmeline's appointment the elderly had wooden high-backed arm-chairs as well as lockers. The women and girls had new bonnets and dresses with pockets. The management of the hospital was reorganised, as well as the diet and, best of all, a decision had been made to remove the children to cottage homes in the country. Emmeline contended that her experiences as a Poor Law Guardian were 'potent factors' in her education as a suffragette militant. The parliamentary vote in women's hands, she believed, was not only a right but a desperate necessity.[43] Christabel listened intently and agreed.

It is highly probable that Christabel, as the eldest daughter, was taken by her mother to see the workhouse conditions for herself, including the notorious lock wards where the babies born to prostitutes with VD were kept. When the naïve Adela eventually made a visit to the workhouse, accompanied not by her mother but another Poor Law Guardian, she was distressed to be told that the babies in the lock wards had nothing before them 'but to cry their lives away', that they were 'diseased' and 'conceived in sin'. Returning home, it was to her big sister Christabel that the shocked Adela turned for information:

> I asked my sister Christabel the meaning of those words and it was then that I first learned of the Social Evil and of the wages of sin, visited on the children from generation to generation. Naturally, I got, also, the Socialist explanation of the necessity of this under Capitalism, that a certain proportion of women must sell themselves for bread and that the ruling classes, purchased for their base pleasures, the daughters of working men.[44]

The intellectual Christabel was steeped in feminism and socialism. She too wanted a socialist society where working women could earn a decent wage and no longer be exploited by capitalists.

That dream seemed a step nearer when, in July 1895, her father was asked by the ILP to stand as their parliamentary candidate for the Gorton District of Manchester. When Richard pointed out that he could not afford election expenses, the ILP offered to finance him. Richard had to make do with just £342 and the advertisement of meetings by the cheapest means possible, the chalking of pavements, a method later adopted in the suffragette movement.[45]

Christabel and Sylvia daily accompanied their mother to Gorton, speaking to voters and taking meagre meals in the homes of poor ILP supporters. It was all to no avail. Their father lost the election, winning 4,261 votes compared to 5,865 for his wealthy Conservative opponent. The disappointed girls and Harry went with their parents to the ILP meeting after the count where Richard gave a short speech announcing that the large number who had voted for him was a great victory for socialism and indicative of better times to come. Christabel, in charac-teristic manner, hid her sorrow but Sylvia could not contain her feelings. Despite her father's reassurance, 'There is life in the old bird yet!', she wept throughout. When they all arrived back home, Emmeline told Sylvia that she had 'disgraced the family'.[46]

The late spring and summer of 1896 were exciting times for the fifteen-year-old Christabel since her name and even her picture began to appear in the press in association with the struggle over free speech at Boggart Hole Clough, an uncultivated open space of some sixty-three acres where the ILP had been holding open-air meetings for some years. Manchester City Corporation had acquired the site that spring and the chair of its Parks Committee, Mr Needham, prohibited any further meetings in an attempt to stop the growing influence of the socialist 'rabble'. The prohibition was ignored and on Sunday, 17 May 1896, John Harker, a well-known ILP speaker, was given a summons for holding a meeting on the grounds that he was guilty of occasioning an annoyance. Richard Pankhurst immediately leapt to the defence, arguing that there was no by-law limiting the right of public meetings, and then gave notice of appeal when Harker was found guilty and fined. Christabel keenly followed the events since she and Sylvia were being taken by their parents, Sunday after Sunday, to join the other ILP protestors in the Clough. She was thrilled to be there, hearing the defiant speeches and engaging in a small act of defiance herself, namely helping with the collection for those who had been prosecuted. Although collections were not permitted at these meetings, her mother had ignored that ruling on 7 June when the crowd of about four thousand saw her stick the ferrule of her umbrella into the ground as a receptacle for those who could donate a few pennies. From that time onwards, Christabel and Sylvia had been helping with the collection each weekend.[47]

The drama of it all was vividly brought home to Christabel when her mother was summoned to appear before the police courts, along with Leonard Hall and seven other men believed to be associated with the meeting. Although there was much speculation that Richard might represent his wife, Emmeline, in her pretty pink straw bonnet, spoke in her own defence, defiantly announcing that she would pay no fine and would continue to speak at the Clough as long as she was at large. Two of the men who refused to pay their fines were sent to prison, but the case against Emmeline was continually adjourned; nor did the authorities dare reprimand her daughters. 'Dr. Pankhurst's two charming girls, Christobel [sic] and Sylvia, have been collecting each Sunday, but the Parks Committee have not yet got their courage up to the point of summoning them', commented the *Labour Leader*.[48]

But Christabel's name, although not Sylvia's, was taken at a Clough meeting on 21 June, along with that of her mother, Mrs Harker and two other women. The popular Emmeline, a key leader in the protests, had spoken to a large enthusiastic crowd of orderly people, possibly numbering 15,000. When her name had been taken in the usual manner, she had expressed her determination to go to prison rather than pay any fine.[49] The politically aware Christabel was glad to be included among the rebel women and especially to be linked to the Clough 'heroine', her defiant mother. She felt proud that her own name was considered important enough to be mentioned in the *Labour Leader*.[50] Sylvia in *The suffragette movement* makes no mention of her elder sister's early brush with the authorities. Keen to play down Christabel's socialist credentials, she portrays herself as 'the' Pankhurst daughter who fought for a better socialist world.[51]

45

On Sunday, 5 July 1896, a bright, sunny day, Christabel and Sylvia again accompanied their parents to the Clough, driving there in an open barouche that also included Keir Hardie and Aunt Mary. This time a crowd of about 50,000 people awaited them. As Emmeline and Hardie walked together to the meeting place, a loud cheer broke out which echoed and re-echoed around the ravine. The warning by a constable that the speakers were engaging in an illegal act was ignored. Again Christabel and Sylvia helped in the collection, which this time amounted to £20.2s. The following Saturday, a head-and-shoulder portrait of each girl appeared in the *Labour Leader*, together with that of their mother.[52] This was a heady experience for the nearly sixteen-year-old Christabel. As the Clough protests continued and men were arrested and then released, she and the rest of her family were involved in many of the various celebrations. The evening welcome for Leonard Hall on 11 July, after he had been released earlier in the day, included a brass band and procession that fell in behind a wagonette in which Emmeline sat next to the ex-prisoner. Then when Fred Brocklehurst was released on the morning of 18 July, all the Pankhurst family shared in the ceremonial welcome breakfast.[53]

Events took another turn in early August when Manchester City Council, realising the weakness of their case, passed a new by-law prohibiting public meetings in its parks unless express permission had been granted by the Parks Committee. All previous summonses for 'occasioning an annoyance' were also withdrawn, implying that the previous prosecutions had been illegal. The partisan nature of the new by-law angered the ILP, who ignored it with the consequence that new summonses were issued and court cases resumed. Eventually, the Home Secretary intervened; he refused to sanction the new by-law and put pressure on the City Council to frame a new one, which it did, permitting any reasonable request to hold public meetings in local parks.[54]

The Pankhurst family were delighted with this victory for the ILP and free speech, but for Christabel and Emmeline in particular, the dispute was a key aspect of their political apprenticeship. The Clough controversy exposed them to a more assertive range of tactics than those adopted by most of the suffrage societies of the day. ILP members had refused to accept legal rulings which they considered unjust and, on being found guilty before the police courts, had gone to prison rather than pay a fine. Further, the tactic of continuing protests when comrades were in prison, and of arranging welcome breakfasts as well as marches and parades when they were released, caught the attention of the public – and the media. Even the novel advertisement of meetings by chalking pavements rather than the more conventional expensive printing of leaflets had attracted inches of coverage in the local press. The effectiveness of these socialist tactics was not lost on Christabel. Some nine years later, she would deliberately seek imprisonment as a means to bring publicity to the women's cause as well as draw upon the publicity-seeking practice of pageants, processions and brass bands.[55]

Sometime shortly after the Clough controversy, Christabel was allowed to have a bicycle. She had been asking for one ever since the stay in Southport but her father would not agree, fearful that his eldest daughter might have an accident when riding in the traffic. However, the Clarion Cycling Club, which combined the spreading of the socialist message with physical exercise, was increasingly popular with young ILP men and women and Richard and Emmeline finally relented, saying that Christabel – and Sylvia – could join. The Clarion cyclists were out most Sundays, visiting villages or towns, selling socialist leaflets, singing songs from their song-book and collecting for the cause. In *The suffragette movement*, Sylvia tells how her mother and elder sister scanned the catalogues of bicycle makers, choosing for Christabel the most expensive Rudge Whitworth model costing £30, while she had to make do with a 'cheap little machine' of curious design, home-made out of gas piping, low-geared and too small for her. Sylvia portrays her elder sister as selfish in this respect while positioning herself as responsible, willing to accept an inferior bicycle since she had heard that their parents had financial worries. The familiar critical picture of an uncaring elder sister is drawn again. The impatient Christabel, writes Sylvia, would keep saying 'Come on!' when they were out cycling together, not bothering to check whether she was alright. Sometimes the athletic and fit Christabel, using the different gears for up hill and down dale, would be so far ahead that she arrived home one hour before her struggling sister. On the occasion when Sylvia was thrown over the handle-bars and badly shaken so that she had to walk some distance before re-mounting, Christabel just 'rode on, not noticing that I had ceased to follow'.[56] Sylvia nursed and nurtured these deep resentments against Christabel, storing them up for posterity.

Richard accepted but, like many parents, did not particularly like his daughters' new craze; he feared that the joys of cycling each Sunday were diversions away from the political and public work he valued so highly. He may also have harboured concern that the sexually naïve, pretty Christabel, sixteen years old on 22 September 1896, would be propositioned by more experienced, working-class men. The annual meeting of the Clarion Clubs, held in Chester, met about this time and Christabel persuaded Sylvia and her mother to accompany her there, Emmeline travelling by train, her daughters by bicycle. When the three met up in Chester, they were greeted by a number of socialist male colleagues, including the influential Robert Blatchford. Blatchford, with his tub-thumping style of writing, made socialism comprehensible to the ordinary man and woman. About 30,000 copies per week were sold of the *Clarion*, which he edited, while sales of his *Merrie England: a plain exposition of socialism, what it is and what it is not* had reached over 2 million.

Blatchford and his friends had booked the commercial room, the only comfortable room in the main hotel in Chester, and as Christabel, Sylvia and their mother passed by, he hastily ran out to greet them. He had never been able to strike up a satisfactory friendship with Keir Hardie, whose *Labour Leader* he disliked, seeing it as a rather earnest newspaper that identified with the ILP rather than with any broader inclusive approach to socialism that might include groups such as the Marxist Social Democratic Federation.[57] Knowing that the Pankhursts were close friends with Hardie, Blatchford tried to persuade Emmeline that the man could not be honest since his paper was losing money every week. Christabel and Sylvia grew increasingly angry as they listened to his words. When Blatchford then asked the three women to join him in the commercial room, Christabel interposed, 'Mother, do not go!'[58] She liked Hardie but, above all, he was sympathetic to the women's cause whereas Blatchford was not.

Notes

1 ESP, TSM, p. 112.
2 ESP, TSM, p. 113; CP, *Unshackled*, pp. 30–1.
3 ESP, TSM, p. 113.
4 CP, *Unshackled*, p. 31.
5 ESP, TSM, p. 114.
6 Coleman, *Adela Pankhurst*, p. 15 quotes Adela as saying, 'I think I was only about six when my father – a most revered person in my existence – assured me there was no God – and I knew inside me that he was wrong.'
7 APW, My mother, p. 13.
8 Reports from The Southport Proprietary School Co. Limited, The High School for Girls, for Christabel and Sylvia Pankhurst, First Term 1893, ESPA.
9 ESP, TSM, p. 114.
10 Mitchell, *Queen Christabel*, p. 34 merely repeats Sylvia's words. Pugh, *The Pankhursts*, p. 36 notes that Christabel 'showed herself reluctant to undertake systematic study. She enjoyed novels, but otherwise gave the impression of being rather self-indulgent, even lazy'.
11 ESP, TSM, pp. 114–15.
12 CP, *Unshackled*, 31.
13 ESP, TSM, pp. 115–16.
14 Manchester High School for Girls, Application for admission forms for Christabel, Sylvia and Adela Pankhurst, held in the Manchester High School Archives. Grateful thanks to Dr C. A. Joy, the High School Librarian, for supplying photocopies of these forms and other material.
15 ESP, TSM, pp. 123–4.
16 ESP, TSM, pp. 121–2.
17 ESP, TSM, p. 123.
18 CP, *Unshackled*, p. 31.
19 APW, My mother, pp. 15–16.
20 Miss Pankhurst talks on the Bible, *New York Times*, 4 May 1925, p. 14.
21 CP to Helen Pethick-Lawrence, 3 November 1951, Craigie Collection. I have corrected Christabel's typing errors (and mostly throughout this book – she was a poor typist) and have typed up this extract in one paragraph rather than following the practice she frequently used, in this letter and others, of one-sentence paragraphs.
22 Mrs Pankhurst, by the Pilgrim, *Labour Leader* (hereafter *LL*), 4 July 1896.
23 CP to Fred Pethick-Lawrence (hereafter FPL), 22 April 1957, P-L Papers.
24 ESP, TSM, p. 124.
25 A meeting was held at 173 High St, Oxford Road on Friday, 17 November 1893. One Women's Franchise League Minute Book (hereafter WFLMB) has survived, Special Collections, Northwestern University Library, Illinois, USA. Grateful thanks to R. Russell Maylone, the Curator, for arranging for a microfilm of these minutes to be sent to me.
26 See, for example, Ursula Bright to EP, 28 November 1893, ESPA.
27 E. Crawford, *The women's suffrage movement: a reference guide 1866–1928* (London, UCL Press, 1999), p. 648; Report of the Executive Committee of the Manchester National Society

for Women's Suffrage, presented at the Annual General Meeting, 20 November 1894 (Manchester, 'Guardian' General Printing Works, 1894), p. 8; Purvis, *Emmeline Pankhurst*, pp. 40–1.

28 F. W. Galton to ESP, 7 February 1929, ESPA.

29 See K. Morgan, *Keir Hardie: radical and socialist* (London, Weidenfeld and Nicolson, 1975), Chapter 4; C. Benn, *Keir Hardie* (London, Hutchinson, 1992), Chapter 4.

30 CP, *Unshackled*, p. 32.

31 EP, *My own story*, p. 15.

32 CP, *Unshackled*, p. 32.

33 ESP, *TSM*, pp. 120–1.

34 ESP, *TSM*, p. 129; CP, *Unshackled*, p. 33.

35 *LL*, 22 December and 24 November 1894.

36 CP, *Unshackled*, p. 34.

37 ESP, *TSM*, p. 128.

38 APW, The philosophy of the suffragette movement, APWP, p. 11.

39 ESP, *TSM*, p. 128.

40 ESP, *TSM*, p. 126.

41 EP, *My own story*, pp. 24–5.

42 ESP, *Emmeline Pankhurst*, p. 36.

43 EP, *My own story*, p. 28.

44 APW, The story of my life, n.d., p. 4, APWP.

45 ESP, *TSM*, p. 135.

46 ESP, *TSM*, p. 136.

47 ESP, *TSM*, p. 137; Purvis, *Emmeline Pankhurst*, p. 47; *LL*, 11 July 1896.

48 *LL*, 11 July 1896.

49 *LL*, 27 June 1896; Bruce Glaiser entry for 21 June 1896, Bruce Glasier Diaries, Sydney Jones Library, University of Liverpool.

50 *LL*, 27 June 1896.

51 In her description of the Clough free speech struggle, Sylvia does not mention that she was present either; see her *TSM*, pp. 137–8.

52 *LL*, 11 July 1896.

53 A. Rosen, *Rise up women! The militant campaign of the Women's Social and Political Union 1903–1914* (London, Routledge and Kegan Paul, 1974), p. 22.

54 ESP, *TSM*, p. 138.

55 Rosen, *Rise up women!*, pp. 22–3; J. Lawrence, Contesting the male polity: the suffragettes and the politics of disruption in Edwardian Britain, in *Women, privilege and power: British politics, 1750 to the present*, ed A. Vickery (Stanford, CA, Stanford University Press, 2001), pp. 201–26.

56 ESP, *TSM*, p. 140.

57 L. Thomson, *Robert Blatchford: portrait of an Englishman* (London, William Clowes and Sons, 1951), Chapter 10; Morgan, *Keir Hardie*, p. 67.

58 ESP, *TSM*, pp. 140–1.

4

YOUNG WOMANHOOD

1897–1902

Looking back on her life when sixteen years old, when she was immersed in feminist and socialist politics, Christabel reminisced:

> Those were the best of all the years. If politics and movements did mean forgoing some things that other people's children had, those other children had not our Father and Mother, our interesting life. Our lot contented us; we were proud of it.[1]

But such an assessment was not shared by all her siblings. The relentless, time-consuming involvement of Emmeline and Richard in political and public work made the younger children, Harry and Adela, feel neglected and unloved. '[T]hey were working for others', says Adela of her frequently absent parents, 'but for my little brother and myself the regime of servants without the wise and good Susannah . . . was disastrous.'[2] The seven-year-old Harry, a delicate child, was slow at learning and became a solitary figure, wandering off on his own. Harry failed to pair with any of his competitive sisters, the four-year age gap with Adela proving a barrier that was rarely breached while the twosome of Christabel and Sylvia seemed to shut him out. 'My sisters took little notice of him', recollected Adela. 'He was small and unimportant and they with their cycling and socialist interests, by this time nearly grown up.'[3]

Despite their grown-up status, Christabel and Sylvia were not beyond teasing the still desperately unhappy Adela. In her desire to be loved again, Adela pretended she was lame, a ploy that backfired. 'Why don't you dig a hole and bury yourself in it?' said the disgusted Christabel. Matters came to a head when, one day, Adela could not find a reading book she had brought home from Manchester High School for Girls. 'Sylvia, ever suspicious', she wrote, 'assumed I had stolen it and showed it to my mother who took it to her room intending to question me about it and had forgotten the whole thing.' When her teacher asked for the book to be returned, Adela could not find it. Afraid that both her teacher and her mother would think she was a thief, Adela decided to run away and live in the slums but was seen by a gardener as she changed out of her school uniform and into a poor girl's dress. The headmistress was contacted and the distressed pupil taken home. A doctor was sent for, but Adela refused to speak.[4] She was in the throes of a nervous breakdown and had to spend a year away from school, passing a rainy winter at home followed by a holiday with her Aunt Bess, in Aberdeen.[5]

Richard and Emmeline, deeply concerned about the vulnerability of their youngest daughter, asked Christabel and Sylvia to treat their sister with special care. Christabel needed no prompting; all 'the charm and sweetness of her nature' came to the fore.[6] But when Adela told her Aberdeen cousins about the teasing at home, and these tales got back to her father, Richard took a stiffer line with his elder daughters. Christabel was surprised that Adela had taken everything so seriously and endeavoured to be more careful in what she said while even Sylvia, who still 'regarded me with hostility', recollected Adela, 'moderated her tone'. Once back at school, Adela flourished under the watchful and encouraging eye of her new teacher, Miss Rhys, eventually becoming a member of the committee of the school magazine in which she published six stories as well as an account of a school party.[7]

In the immediate short term, however, the rivalry between the Pankhurst sisters did not fade away. Adela was selected to sing in the school's choral group and one weekend, when Emmeline did not get back in time from a political meeting to attend a concert, Christabel and Sylvia went on their own. They jeered so much at their younger sister's performance that Adela never had the courage to try to sing in public again.[8] The three Pankhurst girls were each talented in different ways – the confident Christabel was well read with a remarkable memory, the emotional Sylvia had artistic ability, while the fragile Adela showed strengths in literature and history. But the differing personalities of the sisters, as well as the competition between them, created tensions that spilled over into adult life.

It soon became apparent to Christabel that Adela's health was not the only worry facing her parents that spring of 1897. Her father's recent high-profile campaigning for the socialist cause had cost him the support of many potential clients, a situation that added to worries about his health. Emmeline decided that a stay in the fresh air of the countryside might help Richard recover and found a farmhouse at Mobberley, in Cheshire, from which he could travel to his chambers in Manchester each day. Once again, Christabel and her siblings were uprooted to live in temporary accommodation, until autumn 1897. Some six months earlier, in April, Christabel had left the high school which her two sisters still attended.

The sixteen-year-old Christabel was uncertain what she should do next. The range of jobs open to her was limited. Despite the expansion of opportunities for women in occupations such as clerical work, retailing and school teaching, the labour market was still strongly segregated by gender, with women being concentrated in low-status jobs that paid wages barely adequate for the maintenance of a respectable lifestyle. The articulate, well-read and serious-minded Christabel had no desire to be a clerk, or to teach or work in a shop.[9] It was decided that she would study French, logic and dressmaking, a rather strange combination that reflected her own interests and the prompting of Emmeline. Several times a week Christabel travelled with her father on the train to Manchester to attend her classes. Occasionally Richard would sit up sharp, as the pains in his stomach became severe, and then relax, as the spasm passed. However, he always reassured Christabel – and her siblings – that such attacks were nothing serious, only indigestion.

The time at Vale Wood Farm passed pleasantly and Richard's health seemed to improve. The socialist cause was not forgotten, however, particularly the obligation to help comrades who were in less fortunate circumstances, such as Leonard and Pattie Hall and their children, long-time friends and political associates. The Halls had fallen on hard times when Leonard, the breadwinner, was imprisoned over the Clough protests, and although the ILP had offered some financial help to his pregnant wife, it was woefully inadequate. Such troubles only added to Leonard Hall's anxieties so that when he was finally released, he became seriously ill. Emmeline, Richard and the children were determined to do what they could to help and so they planned a picnic tea, to be held at the farm on Whit Sunday 12 June 1897, at a charge of one shilling per head, all proceeds to go to the Leonard Hall Fund. It was hoped to attract at least one hundred members of the ILP and Clarion Cycling Club.[10] Later that month Christabel and Sylvia spent twelve shillings and sixpence each for shares in the Clarion Cyclists' Club House Company. The aim of the Company was the renting of a house at Bucklow Hill, near Knutsford, where refreshment, recreation and accommodation would be offered at a reasonable cost to Clarionettes from Bolton, Liverpool, Manchester and surrounding towns. Any profits from the venture were to go to the Cinderella Club for poor children, or some such similar scheme. Described as the 'first Socialist Guest House', Emmeline and Richard were among the promoters of the scheme and keen for their two eldest daughters to be involved.[11]

That autumn of 1897, Christabel and her family moved back to their Manchester home since her father seemed much better. Now seventeen years old, Christabel was still undecided as to the direction her life should take. Many years earlier, Emmeline and her school friend Noemie had agreed that if ever they should marry and have daughters, the girls would stay in the home of the other for a year, to perfect her French or English, as the case might be. It seemed a good idea to put that plan into action for Christabel. It was arranged that during the following June Emmeline would take Christabel to live with Madame Dufaux, who now resided in Geneva. Emmeline would stay a short while and then bring Noemie's daughter Lillie back to Manchester.

Soon Christabel and her mother were spending many hours together, making elegant clothes suitable for a young woman's stay on the European continent. Emmeline, a keen seamstress, wanted to show off her favourite, pretty daughter who had a slim, athletic figure and the poise of a ballerina. Christabel was less excited than her mother about the trip, fearing that it meant 'a final, irrevocable "growing up"'.[12] En route to Geneva, the travellers did some sightseeing in Paris. But the daughter was less enchanted with the city than the mother. 'Christabel takes it all with her usual calm', wrote a disappointed Emmeline to Richard, the devoted husband and adored father whom both women missed. 'If only Father could have been there', penned Christabel, 'all would have been perfect. It was a long time since Mother and he had been thus parted. Nineteen years, nearly they had been married, but his letters were more love letters than at the beginning.' Before they had left Manchester her father's passing words to Christabel were to remind her to be considerate towards her mother since she would miss him and the children she left behind.[13] They were the last words that Richard was to say to his eldest daughter.

The sixteen-year-old Sylvia had been entrusted with the task of looking after her father, Adela and Harry while their mother was away. The sisters left behind in Manchester were soon writing to Christabel, eager for news. They heard how she had had a studio photograph taken in Geneva, wearing an ankle-length pleated dress, her arms in a ballet-like pose, her chestnut curls piled high on her head. But by the time of Christabel's reply to Sylvia, on 1 July 1898, it was apparent that she was now in Corsier where her hosts had a lake-side holiday home – and enjoying a range of sports:

> All this morning we have been rowing in the boat. It is lovely & warm at present. Yesterday I went out on the tandem & when we were a long way from home (about 10 miles) the tyre burst. Armand & I walked home while Henri [Noemie's two sons] went on his machine to fetch the motor-car . . . Tomorrow we are going on a picnic.

Christabel also informed Sylvia that a piano had been hired and that she and their mother much preferred the holiday home to their host's house in Geneva:

> Mother says will you make a parcel of 'Studios' & put some drawings of your own in – some of your charcoal things etc. Also you must not ride too much on your bicycle . . . Love to Father and all of you.[14]

A few days later, at tea-time, when Christabel and her mother were sitting in the garden, a telegram came for Emmeline. It was from Richard. 'I am not well. Please come home.'[15] The news fell like a bombshell, Emmeline believing that it was a coded message from Richard saying that Harry was ill, worded in such a way to lessen her anxiety.[16] She decided that she must leave immediately while Christabel would stay in Switzerland, until sent for. En route from London to Manchester, on 5 July 1898, Emmeline was sitting in the railway carriage when someone entered her compartment, sat down and opened a newspaper. She saw the black border and read of her own husband's death. In deep shock, she cried out as the startled passengers tried to console her. The day after arriving back home Emmeline had the sad task of registering the death of her fifty-eight-year-old husband, from a gastric ulcer that had perforated his stomach.[17] Warm tributes to Richard Pankhurst were published in the local and socialist press, his funeral on 9 July attracting large crowds.

Knowledge about what was happening at home mainly came to Christabel through letters. She wept for her adored father, remembering his courtesy and loving ways with his children and his wife. 'Mother was queen – "Where's my lady?" – was always his first word . . . He never in our hearing addressed her by her first name, but always by some word of endearment.'[18] Christabel wanted to return home but Emmeline persuaded her to stay in Switzerland, to perfect her French. Besides, there was no one free in the Dufaux household to accompany Christabel and it would be unthinkable for her to make the journey on her own. 'I often think of the last thing that Father said to me', wrote the weeping daughter to her broken-hearted mother. '"Be nice to her; she will feel it at first", meaning that you would feel leaving him, and the other three. Dear darling, he did not know.'[19] Reflecting on her father's death, many years later, Christabel speaks of the devastating effect it had on their family. 'It was the collapse of our happy life, of our world as it had been.'[20]

While in Geneva, Christabel received many letters of condolence hinting that, as the eldest daughter, her role in life must be to help her mother in her hour of need. She did not need to be reminded of her responsibilities; she was well aware of them and waited to hear what Emmeline thought she should do. But being cast in the role of 'dutiful daughter', subordinating her own wishes to a parent, was not easy for a young woman who had been brought up to express her own individuality and treated as an adult. With her favourite daughter so far away, the grieving Emmeline sought comfort with Sylvia who became her closest confidante.[21]

Despite the fact that he was a lawyer of mature years, the idealistic Richard had left no will, or any money, only debts that he had been struggling for years to liquidate. His estate was estimated at £500, but after deduction for tax, solicitors' costs and some of his debts, only £40. 16s. 11d was left.[22] Emmeline was determined to pay the creditors and decided to move to a humbler house and sell whatever was of value, including furniture, pictures and books. Robert Blatchford, keen to help, printed an appeal in the *Clarion*, but Emmeline firmly rejected it, arguing that she did not wish working people to subscribe for an education for her children when they could not provide for their own. Instead she suggested that any money collected went towards the building of a socialist hall, in her husband's name.[23] Desirous of Christabel's view on the matter, Emmeline wrote to her, asking if she approved. 'Of course I did', remembered Christabel.[24] However, suggestions from some wealthier people for a 'Dr Pankhurst Fund' that would gather in subscriptions solely for the education and maintenance of the four dependent children were acceptable to Emmeline, nearly £935 being collected by 17 August 1898.[25] But the Fund was controlled by a committee of men who decided how and when the money should be spent, making her feel as though she and her children were objects of charity. Further, now that she was the main breadwinner in the family, with four dependent children as well as herself to support, she needed an additional source of income. The necessitous Emmeline decided to set up a dressmaking business.

Christabel was unimpressed with her mother's plans, thinking that a dress-making venture seemed a waste of her talents. 'You are so clever', she opined, 'that it seems strange that there is not something more suited to you.' But fearful that she might have been too dismissive of the scheme, the helpful daughter then asked, 'Have you any ideas about me yet? Madame Dufaux thinks I ought to go in for dressmaking too.' Emmeline agreed with Noemie; since her eldest daughter had no strong preference for what kind of employment she wanted to take up, it would be a good idea if Christabel became her 'right hand' in the business.[26] It was with great relief that Christabel soon heard that her mother had abandoned the dressmaking idea. But the alternative venture in which she was to help, namely another shop like Emerson's that would sell silks, cushions and artistic wares, did not appeal either to a young woman who had been raised in an atmosphere of politics. 'I felt no aptitude for business', Christabel confessed:

> But I could suggest no practical alternative. In any case, the time and circumstances were far too sad and grave for the assertion of likes or dislikes. Nothing seemed to matter very much, anyhow, and if one could be of some use that would be all to the good.[27]

In her letters home, Christabel tried to hide from her mother her stoical atti-tude about the new shop. She was glad to hear that Aunt Mary, now Mrs Clarke, had left her unhappy marriage and was once again living in the Pankhurst house-hold, helping to make goods to sell in Emerson's. Other news from home told of more far-reaching changes. Her mother had gladly accepted the offer, from the Chorlton Board of Guardians, of the post of Registrar of Births and Deaths in a working-class district of Manchester, a position that would bring a steady income together with a pension on retirement. A humbler house, with a room suitable for the registry, had been rented in a crowded neighbourhood near the sooty air of the city centre. 62 Nelson Street, off Oxford Road, was a semi-detached, two-storey red-brick house with a small lawn in front and a larger expanse of garden at the back. With little money to spare, Emmeline had sold all her solid mahogany furniture and various other goods and furnished the new residence with cheap American imports.[28] It was to 62 Nelson Street that the eighteen-year-old Christabel returned in autumn 1898.

The atmosphere of grief that Christabel found in the new house tugged at her heart:

> It had been midsummer when I went away. When I returned, summer had gone . . . All was now in the minor key, depressed, forlorn. Mother was . . . energetic in her doings, but wan, and with a tragic look that never quite left her through all the ensuing years.[29]

The distraught Sylvia clung to the bereft Emmeline while the sad Adela and Harry felt excluded and neglected. As the eldest child, Christabel tried to both support and rally her family, putting on a brave face. She too wept for her much-loved father, but out of sight, alone at night when only the faithful serv-ant Ellen heard her crying. Her 'rosy cheeks and smiling lips' the next day meant that her sorrow was largely unnoticed.[30] The changed financial circumstances in the family forced Emmeline to think about ways in which her daughters could earn a living. Adela, still at the Manchester High School for Girls, wanted to be a schoolteacher and so it was a great relief when a friend advised that training as a pupil teacher was offered free at the state-aided Ducie Avenue Higher Grade Board School.[31] Sylvia's future too seemed settled. She had been having private lessons with a local well-known artist, Elias Bancroft, and when Charles Rowley came to value the paintings Emmeline wanted to sell, he had viewed her drawings. Impressed with their quality, he sent the still-life groups to the Municipal School of Art who offered the talented sixteen-year-old a free studentship.[32] But for the eldest daughter, the studious Christabel, there was no such joy; she had to help support her family by working in their shop in King Street in central Manchester.

Early each morning Christabel travelled by tram to her place of employment. Emmeline would appear later, after her first stint of morning duties in the regis-try. 'My resolves were good', Christabel remembered, 'but as time went on I felt more and more unqualified for this avocation. Business was not good for me and I was not good for business.'[33] She became extremely unhappy. When her father was alive, the whole family had all been politically active in suffrage and socialist circles; now that he was dead, all that was gone. Her mother had lost heart and only kept a spark of her previous political involvement alive, particularly through her membership of the ILP and her place on its NAC.

However, the controversy over the outbreak of the Boer War in autumn 1889 suddenly changed matters and rekindled some of Emmeline's old enthusiasms. The early stages of the war went disastrously against British troops, who were humiliatingly defeated and besieged at Ladysmith, Kimberley and Mafeking, cre-ating a strong wave of patriotism at home. During Gladstone's time, Richard had taken the part of the Boer republics and Emmeline and her children now held to the same view, seeing Britain as an imperialist aggressor, attacking a small com-munity of Dutch settler farmers who were trying to defend their homes and land. However, the calls of the Pankhurst family for peace were not popular. Sylvia, at the School of Art, found that a fellow student threatened to break the windows of 62 Nelson Street. Adela, who had been unhappy at the bleak Dulcie Avenue Higher Grade Board School and was now back at the fee-paying Manchester High School for Girls, was struck in the face by a book thrown at her by another pupil while her teacher stood by, saying nothing. The sickly ten-year-old Harry was assaulted viciously by some of his class-mates outside the school gates of the small private boys' school he attended. His schoolmaster, Mr Lupton, found the unconscious boy in the road, and carried him home.[34]

These distressing incidents did little to lift Christabel's gloom. Mitchell criti-cally asserts that Christabel was at this time in her life living a 'witheringly aimless existence', a theme echoed by Pugh who states that she was continuing 'to drift languidly through life'.[35] But such negative assessments fail to appreciate how Christabel continued serving in the hated shop out of filial duty, enduring the work for another year. Emmeline finally came to the conclusion that she must do something to help her able, intellectual daughter and so suggested that she take some classes at Owen's College, Victoria University (later to become Manchester University). The situation was eased by the fact that Sylvia had persuaded her mother that she should take the lower-fee, part-time route for her second year at art college, spending half her week at Emerson's to give Christabel some days off.[36] Christabel was elated at this news, especially since her father had been a student and then an honorary teacher at Owen's. Since she was unable to attend full-time to study for a degree, she took part-time classes in logic, her favourite subject, and a couple of other courses, including literature. 'Those lectures were my gateway to a future so filled with inspiring thoughts and activity', she wrote enthusiastically, 'that I came to reckon myself the happiest person on earth.'[37]

On the late afternoon of 11 October 1900, Christabel attended a meeting of the Women's Debating Society at Owen's College. The principal of the College, Sir Alfred Hopkinson, gave a talk on 'The politics of the poets' and during the discussion that followed she found, to her surprise, she rose and nervously uttered a sentence or two. Hopkinson, impressed by her remarks, asked the graduate sitting beside him who the speaker was and then referred to these comments in his closing speech. After the meeting had ended, the chair of the Women's Debating Society, Esther Roper, came down from the platform to speak to Christabel, whom she had already met, and invited her home to meet her companion, Eva Gore-Booth. Esther and Eva were some ten years older than Christabel and from contrasting social backgrounds. Esther, born in Cheshire in 1868, was the graduate daughter of a factory hand who became a missionary while Eva, born in 1870 in Co. Sligo, Ireland, was one of five children of Sir Henry Gore-Booth, landowner and Arctic explorer.[38] From now until February 1902 Christabel took part in six further meetings of the society as her friendship with Esther Roper and Eva Gore-Booth developed.

Christabel was captivated with her new friends and threw herself with enthusiasm into many of the activities they pursued. She helped Eva run a dramatic group called the Elizabethan Society at the Manchester University Settlement, both women overseeing productions of two Shakespeare plays, *Macbeth* and *Romeo and Juliet*. Christabel also joined Eva's poetry class.[39] But, above all, Christabel was delighted that her new friends were actively involved with her two main political interests, women's suffrage and socialism. Esther Roper was the secretary of the North of England Society for Women's Suffrage, which was affiliated to the NUWSS on whose executive committee she sat. With Eva Gore-Booth, co-secretary with Sarah Dickinson of the Manchester and Salford Women's Trade Union Council, Esther was conducting something of a women suffrage revival as she insisted on the importance of the parliamentary vote for working-class women. Esther, Eva and their co-workers held open-air meetings in factory districts, spoke to women workers at the mill gates, distributed leaflets and canvassed homes in working-class areas in an effort to collect signatures for petitions to Parliament asking for votes for women.[40]

The argument about the necessity for the parliamentary vote for working women gained new force after 1901 since the newly founded Labour Representation Committee (LRC), which would later develop into the Labour Party, had arranged for its constituent organisations to finance parliamentary candidates. The issue became even more urgent when the textile trade unions became affiliated to the LRC in 1902; 4d. was to be levied annually on each member, women included, of which 1d. was for the maintenance of Labour MPs. Women trade unionists, therefore, were paying the election expenses of Labour candidates and their salaries, if elected to Parliament, but were denied the right to the parliamentary vote.[41]

Such anomalies were not lost on Christabel who was keen to participate in the various campaigns. She joined both the North of England Society for Women's Suffrage and the Manchester and Salford Women's Trade Union Council. In the various activities and discussions focused around these societies she found an exciting world which gave her the opportunity to make her debut as a speaker at the University Settlement, in late January 1901. 'Miss Pankhurst shows considerable promise as a speaker', waxed the *Labour Leader* eloquently. 'She is cool, and possesses keen critical faculties, and will maintain the traditional eloquence of her family.'[42] In her memoir, Christabel gratefully acknowledged the debt she owed to Esther Roper and Eva Gore-Booth, for all that they had taught her. 'This was a stage in my political apprenticeship of great and lasting value, and I owed much to the example and sympathy of these two friends.'[43] Christabel's participation in organised feminism in the Manchester area restored her confidence, boosted her faith in political action – and revived the interest of the Pankhurst family in women's suffrage.

At Easter 1901, Christabel attended the ILP conference at Leicester, arriving a few days later than her mother and Sylvia. She rebuked her mother for proposing to join a small group on the NAC who were planning to challenge the policy of the executive, pointing out that it ill became her, after two years' absence from conferences, to engage in such action. 'Mrs. Pankhurst accepted this ruling', noted Sylvia, 'as early evidence of her daughter's ascendency.'[44] This was a theme that Sylvia was to repeat throughout *The suffragette movement*, presenting her mother as weak and dominated by Christabel throughout the suffragette movement, which was far from the reality since the two women worked in unison. The fiery, passionate Emmeline always welcomed Christabel's advice, as on this occasion in 1901, since she knew that her eldest daughter had a cool head for politics. 'Christabel is not like other women; not like you and me', she would often say to Sylvia, 'she will never be led away by her affections!'[45]

While at the conference, the Pankhurst women met up again with Keir Hardie, a family friend who, much to their delight, had been elected to the House of Commons as a Labour MP in the 1900 general election. Hardie, who was keen to promote the speaking talents of the charming Christabel who he thought had a 'brilliant future', arranged for the eldest Pankhurst daughter to take the place of a delegate who was leaving early.[46] In her address, Christabel criticised a resolution made by Margaret MacDonald advocating that teachers and children should withdraw from state schools as a form of passive resistance to the Conservative Government's education proposals. She argued instead that such illegal action should be avoided and more constitutional methods adopted, such as the distribution of leaflets outlining the areas of concern.[47]

As Christabel was drawn more and more into feminist and labour politics, she found that the Pankhurst name was a useful asset. 'My political path was easy. "Dr. Pankhurst's daughter" was the passport to the friendship of one and all, in Lancashire, Cheshire, and Yorkshire, the sphere of action in my early suffrage days.' Indeed, she found that the executive committee of the North of England Society for Women's Suffrage, of which she became a member, was composed largely of her father's contemporaries, all members with him of the original committee for women's suffrage.[48] And of course the Pankhurst name was useful when she wanted to publish in the socialist press. The *Labour Leader* for August 1901, for example, published one of her letters in which she urged all socialists and delegates to the forthcoming Trades Union Congress to support a resolution sent in by the Wigan and District Weavers that the time had arrived when the parliamentary franchise should be extended to women on the same terms as men. Christabel pointed out that the request was not for the parliamentary franchise for all adult women since women did not ask for this until all adult men were also enfranchised. 'I believe', she continued,

> that the proposers wish not only to enfranchise a large number of women, but also to affirm that sex is not a disqualification for the enjoyment of full political rights. The recognition of this will enormously improve the position of the women of this country.[49]

These points – that enfranchisement for women should be on equal terms with men, that sex should not be a barrier to political citizenship, that recognition of women's electoral equality with men would bring wider social reform – were to be reiterated time and time again by Christabel during the forthcoming suffrage campaign.

Emmeline, spurred on by Christabel's enthusiasm, too became a member of the North of England Society for Women's Suffrage, although she only paid a five-shilling subscription in contrast to Christabel's ten.[50] She too was convinced that the parliamentary vote would raise women from their degraded position in society and be a means of reform. Her work as a Registrar in a working-class district had shocked Emmeline, even after her years as a Poor Law Guardian. 'I have had little girls of thirteen come to my office to register the births of their babies, illegitimate, of course', she wrote in sorrow. 'In many of these cases I found that the child's own father or some near male relative was responsible for her state.'[51]

Emmeline's election, as an ILP candidate, to the Manchester School Board in November 1900 had strengthened her feminist conviction. She had found that it was the male teachers who had all the advantages, including much higher salaries, while the women teachers, in addition to their regular class work, had to teach the girls sewing and domestic science for no extra pay.[52] Determined to do something to change this state of affairs, an issue that Emmeline often discussed with Christabel, at the 1902 Easter ILP Conference she moved a resolution that:

> in order to improve the economic and social condition of women it is necessary to take immediate steps to secure the granting of the suffrage to women on the same terms as it is or may be granted to men.

The motion was passed unanimously.[53] Christabel and her mother were of one mind on this issue.

By summer 1902, Emmeline was speaking alongside Christabel, Esther Roper and Eva Gore-Booth at open-air meetings in Lancashire, held under the auspices of the North of England Society for Women's Suffrage.[54] These gatherings were part of a campaign to get David Shackleton, sponsored by the LRC, elected to Parliament in the hope that he would continue there the fight for women's suffrage. The speakers were elated when Shackleton was returned for the Clitheroe division in August. Since voteless women formed over half of the 18,000 Clitheroe trade unionists who would be paying sixpence each into a fund for his salary, Christabel used the occasion to voice support for women's suffrage in a letter to the *Manchester Guardian*. The women's majority in the trade unions, she asserted, gave them great power over the Labour Party and would enable them to insist on efforts being made to secure women's suffrage.[55] She was soon to be disappointed on this score.

Christabel was making a name for herself as an outspoken advocate of women's rights, especially after the *Labour Leader* had published her article in May 1902 on 'the woman's point of view' of the Conservative education bill. The essay had ended characteristically with the statement, 'All other rights . . . depend on the right to vote, and the most important work in which women can engage is that of securing their own political enfranchisement.'[56] The news that some four weeks earlier women had been granted the right to vote for state elections in New South Wales, Australia gave Christabel an added focus. Australia was one of the first countries to grant suffrage to the majority of its female citizens, second only to New Zealand which had given women the parliamentary vote in 1893.[57] Yet in Britain, the 'mother' country, all women were still voteless. Already enrolled in her part-time adult education classes at Owen's College, Christabel could see no logic in the situation. Nor was she impressed with many of the male membership of the ILP. The ILP claimed to be in favour of sex equality but too few were doing anything about it. Her mother, on the other hand, still hoping that the ILP would support a women's suffrage measure, was a founder member that August 1902 of a new local ILP branch, Manchester Central.[58] But Emmeline, like Christabel, was becoming increasingly disillusioned by the dismissive attitude of too many male socialists who believed that a limited women's suffrage measure would only benefit the Conservatives.

Christabel and Emmeline lost no opportunity to voice their concerns when influential ILP members, such as Bruce Glasier, visited 62 Nelson Street. Glasier was to give a lecture in Salford on Sunday, 19 October, and arranged to stay overnight at their home. However, he was contemptuous of the arguments of his hosts and recorded his feelings in his diary:

> A weary ordeal of chatter about woman's suffrage from 10 p.m. to 1.30 a.m. – Mrs & Christabel Pankhurst belabouring me as chairman of the party for its neglect of the question. At last get roused and speak with something like scorn of their miserable individualist sexism: and virtually tell them that the I.L.P. will not stir a finger more than it has done for all the woman suffragists in creation. Really the pair are not seeking democratic freedom, but self importance.[59]

The following day the unsympathetic Glasier wrote even more waspish thoughts, especially about Christabel who had lost her eyebrows in an accident at the hairdresser and was now pencilling them in. 'Pankhursts somewhat contrite for last night's harpyism: but I feel tired of them. Christabel paints her eyebrows grossly and looks selfish, lazy and wilful. They want to be ladies, not workers, and lack the humility of real "heroism".'[60]

Christabel was beginning to lose faith in the ILP as a vehicle for supporting women's enfranchisement. Nonetheless, she continued trying to merge her feminism and socialism, working alongside some of the ILP supporters and continuing to speak on women's suffrage at various ILP branches, including Glasgow and Sheffield on 2 and 26 November 1902, respectively.[61] The trouble that her mother was having with the male administrators of the Dr Pankhurst Fund added further fuel to her thinking. Without any consultation, her mother had suddenly been informed that from 31 December 1902 the allowance for the maintenance and education of the children would be reduced to £50 per year, payable monthly. This was unacceptable to Emmeline who hotly discussed the issue with Christabel. They were all living on a shoestring since only Christabel, of the four Pankhurst children, was contributing to the family income. School fees had to be paid for both Adela and Harry while Sylvia, who had been awarded a travelling studentship that enabled her to study for a short time in Venice and Florence, had to be sent fifteen shillings a week. When the administrators of the fund suggested that priority should be given to Harry's education, both Emmeline and Christabel were outraged. 'I believe & my husband thought it too that it is quite as important to give opportunity of education to gifted girls as to boys', wrote the indignant Emmeline to Mr Nodal, one of the fund administrators. Refusing to bow to the administrators' wishes, she stated firmly, 'I cannot without a sacrifice of self respect accept any reduced sum. Rather will I try to do without it altogether.'[62]

Christabel was angry about the unjust treatment of her mother at the hands of insensitive men who treated women as subordinates rather than equals. Daughter and mother stood firmly together on this issue, just as they would be united on most other matters in the ensuing suffragette campaign. On Christmas Day 1902 another misfortune struck the Pankhurst household. Adela suddenly fell ill with diphtheria and scarlet fever. Since these diseases were contagious, Christabel and Harry had to hurriedly find lodgings while Adela was isolated at home. In addition to the worry about Adela's health, additional financial burdens fell on Emmeline's shoulders. There were the doctor's fees to be paid, the rent for the rooms where Christabel and Harry were staying, plus the cost of employing a nurse for £2. 2 shillings weekly to look after the sick patient.[63]

Notes

1 CP, *Unshackled*, p. 34.
2 APW, *My mother*, p. 14.
3 APW, *My mother*, p. 17. Sylvia, however, in her *TSM*, pp. 146–7 states, 'There was a tender bond between the little brother and me.' This is just one of the many contradictory statements made by the Pankhurst sisters and it is difficult for any researcher to evaluate and interpret the competing claims.
4 APW, *My mother*, pp. 20 and 16–22.
5 Coleman, *Adela Pankhurst*, p. 21.
6 APW, The philosophy of the suffragette movement, p. 18.
7 APW, *My mother*, p. 23; Manchester High School for Girls School Magazine for June 1899, February 1900, November 1900, July 1901, November 1901, March 1902, July 1902.
8 APW, *My mother*, p. 23.
9 ESP, *TSM*, p. 147 notes that she heard Christabel 'telling some friends at the Clarion Cycling Club that she wanted to find an easy job which would occupy her from about ten a.m. to four in the afternoon. I listened in consternation, hoping she spoke in jest'.
10 LL, 29 May 1897.
11 D. Pye, *Fellowship is life: the National Clarion Cycling Club 1895–1995* (Bolton, Clarion Publishing, 1996 reprint, first pub. 1995), p. 43.
12 CP, *Unshackled*, p. 35.
13 CP, *Unshackled*, pp. 35–6.
14 CP to ESP, 1 July 1898, ESPA.
15 ESP, *TSM*, p. 150, Sylvia states that her father dictated these words to her on Monday, 4 July 1898. Christabel in *Unshackled*, p. 35, offers a slightly different version of events, claiming that a telegram arrived saying, 'Father ill. Come', implying that Sylvia sent it. It is possible, of course, that two telegrams were sent, one from Richard and one from Sylvia.
16 ESP, *TSM*, p. 151.
17 Purvis, *Emmeline Pankhurst*, p. 52.
18 CP, *Unshackled*, p. 34.
19 CP, *Unshackled*, p. 36.
20 CP, *Unshackled*, p. 35.
21 ESP, *TSM*, p. 152; APW, *My mother*, p. 25.

22 Purvis, *Emmeline Pankhurst*, p. 54.

23 ESP, *TSM*, p. 153.

24 CP, *Unshackled*, p. 37.

25 Letter from W. H. Dixon and John J. Graham, Honorary Treasurer and Honorary Secretary of the Fund, *Manchester Evening News*, 23 July 1898; Dr Pankhurst Fund, List of Subscriptions to 17 August 1898, Purvis Collection.

26 CP, *Unshackled*, pp. 37–8.

27 CP, *Unshackled*, p. 38.

28 Purvis, *Emmeline Pankhurst*, p. 55. Dr Pankhurst Fund, the Hon. Treasurer's account of receipts and payments to December 31st, 1899, states that on 1 September 1899 payment of £317 16s. 2d. was made for 'Furniture purchased for use of Mrs. Pankhurst and Children', Purvis Collection.

29 CP, *Unshackled*, p. 38.

30 APW, My mother, p. 27.

31 APW, My mother, p. 25.

32 ESP, *TSM*, pp. 154–5.

33 CP, *Unshackled*, p. 40.

34 ESP, *TSM*, pp. 155–6; APW, My mother, p. 27. Emmeline was one of a group of fifteen people who later resigned from the Fabian Society, in March 1900, over its support for the war.

35 Mitchell, *Queen Christabel*, p. 42; Pugh, *The Pankhursts*, p. 87.

36 ESP, *TSM*, p. 157.

37 CP, *Unshackled*, p. 40.

38 See entries on Eva Gore-Booth (1870–1926) and Esther Roper (1868–1926) in Crawford, *The women's suffrage movement*, pp. 249–51 and 607–8, respectively. See also G. Lewis, *Eva Gore Booth and Esther Roper: a biography* (London, Pandora Press, 1988) and Sonja Tiernan *Eva Gore Booth: an image of such politics* (Manchester, Manchester University Press, 2012), both of which rely mainly on Sylvia's *The suffragette movement* and denigrate Emmeline and Christabel.

39 M. D. Stocks, *Fifty years in every street: the story of the Manchester University Settlement* (Manchester, Manchester University Press, 1945), p. 20; Teirnan, *Eva Gore-Booth*, p. 62; Lewis, *Eva Gore Booth*, p. 94.

40 Liddington and Norris, *One hand tied behind us*, pp. 82–3.

41 Rosen, *Rise up women!*, p. 26.

42 *LL*, 26 January 1901.

43 CP, *Unshackled*, p. 41.

44 ESP, *TSM*, p. 158.

45 ESP, *Emmeline Pankhurst*, p. 47.

46 *LL*, 23 March 1901.

47 ESP, *TSM*, p. 158.

48 CP, *Unshackled*, pp. 41–2.

49 Letter from CP to the editor, *LL* 31 August 1901.

50 Report of the Executive Committee of the North of England Society for Women's Suffrage, Presented at the annual meeting, 29 November 1901 (Manchester, Taylor, Garnett & Co.), p. 18.

51 EP, *My own story*, p. 32.

52 EP, *My own story*, p. 35.

53 *Manchester Guardian*, 2 April 1902.

54 Report of the Executive Committee of the North of England Society for Women's Suffrage, Presented at the annual meeting, 24 November, 1902 (Manchester, 'Guardian' General Printing Works), p. 10.

55 *Manchester Guardian*, 2 August 1902; Rosen, *Rise up women!*, p. 26.

56 CP, The education bill: the woman's point of view, *LL*, 31 May 1902.
57 J. Hannam, M. Auchterlonie and K. Holden, eds, *International encyclopedia of women's suffrage* (Santa Barbara, CA, ABC-CLIO, 2000), pp. 23 and 208. J. Adams, *Women and the vote: a world history* (Oxford, Oxford University Press, 2014), pp. 115–34. Australia's claim to be ahead of most other Western countries in this respect is compromised by the failure of Queensland and Western Australia to give Aboriginal men and women either the federal or state vote until 1962.
58 Liddington and Norris, *One hand tied behind us*, p. 169.
59 Entry for 18 October 1902, Glasier Diaries.
60 Entry for 19 October 1902, Glasier Diaries.
61 Report of the Executive Committee of the North of England Society for Women's Suffrage, Presented at the Annual Meeting, 7 December 1903 (Manchester, 'Guardian' General Printing Works), p. 9.
62 EP to Mr Nodal, 29 November 1902, Purvis Collection; Purvis, *Emmeline Pankhurst*, pp. 60–4.
63 Information gleaned from EP to Mr Nodal, 28 December 1902 and EP to Sir William Bailey, 7 January 1903, Purvis Collection; Purvis, *Emmeline Pankhurst*, pp. 60–4.

5

FOUNDATION AND EARLY YEARS OF THE WSPU

1903–4

The New Year of 1903 did not begin on a happy note for Christabel. She was still living away from home, in lodgings with Harry, when he suddenly fell ill. Since the doctor feared that Harry had caught the contagious diphtheria and scarlet fever that was threatening Adela's life, Christabel was advised to move immediately – and did so, this time staying with friends. After some anxious days, it was discovered that Harry had chicken pox. By the end of the month, both he and Adela had recovered from their illnesses and plans were afoot for Adela to continue her convalescence at her grandmother's, on the Isle of Man. Before Christabel and Harry could return back home, 62 Nelson Street had to be disinfected.[1]

Sylvia was still in Italy while all this was going on. Yet many years later she writes about these incidents in *The suffragette movement* as though she were present. And, unsurprisingly, she presents Christabel as an uncaring, heartless sister, telling untruths about why Christabel had to change addresses:

> Christabel had never been willing to act the nurse to any . . . human being. She detested sickness, and had even left home when Adela had scarlet fever and Harry had chicken-pox, on the first occasion going into hired lodgings, on the second to stay with friends.[2]

This was to be just one of many 'twists' that Sylvia gave in her supposedly 'authoritative' account of the Pankhurst family and the suffragette movement.

Now that Adela and Harry were fit again, Christabel began once more to spend time with Eva Gore-Booth and Esther Roper. One early spring day, when Emmeline was telling Esther about some women's issue that Christabel had dealt with, Esther replied, 'She ought to be a lawyer.'[3] Despite the fact that women were then barred from the legal profession, the proud Emmeline was thrilled at the idea. Christabel would be following in her father's footsteps, learning legal skills that would be an asset to the women's cause. The eager Christabel needed no persuasion that this was the right course for her. She loved her classes in logic and enjoyed arguing and debating a point. The financial implications of such a career move were discussed. It was decided that Sylvia, who had stayed in Italy long after her scholarship had expired, should return home and help in the shop so that Christabel could be coached for matriculation for entrance to Owen's College, where she would study for her law degree. An excited Christabel wrote to Sylvia with the news, saying how she hoped to become a barrister. Shortly after her sister's return to Manchester, Christabel left for a holiday in Venice, at the invitation of Esther and Eva.[4]

Once back home, Christabel continued to work for women's suffrage alongside Eva and Esther, but her growing disillusionment with the ILP was such that she voiced again her concerns in the Labour press. In an angry letter, published both in the *Labour Leader* and the *Clarion* in March 1903, she criticised the delegates at the recent LRC Conference, held at Newcastle, for making no condemnation of the injustice whereby thousands of workers were disfranchised 'merely because they happen to be women' and expressed 'no determination to work for the removal of that injustice'. Emphasising her point, Christabel concluded:

> It will be said, perhaps, that the interests of women will be safe in the hands of the men's Labour Party. Never in the history of the world have the interests of those without power to defend themselves been properly served by others . . . I hope the women of England will not have to say that neither Liberal, Conservative, nor Labour parties are their friends![5]

By highlighting how working men were discriminating against their own women-folk and opposed to women's interests, Christabel was emphasising that it was not just capitalists who had an interest in the subordination of women but socialist men too.

Her bravery in voicing such unpopular views attracted some private praise in Labour circles. At the 1903 Easter ILP conference, Isabella Ford, a prosperous Quaker suffragist from Leeds, joined Emmeline on the NAC. Although in public Isabella always spoke warmly about the ILP's support for women's political equality, privately she confided to the Pankhurst family that the executive members were 'no more than lukewarm' on the subject of votes for women.[6] Among the leadership, only Keir Hardie was committed to the women's cause while key figures like Philip Snowden and Bruce Glasier were actively hostile. This was no surprise to Christabel.

In May, John Hodge, Secretary of the Steel Smelters' Union, stood as an ILP candidate at the Preston by-election. He was not returned and afterwards wrote to the *Labour Leader* complaining how he had lost through the 'efforts of Miss Pankhurst and her friends to damage my candidature by the poster they issued'. Christabel was furious but replied calmly to the accusation, returning the personal attack. She pointed out that in Mr Hodge's first election meeting and in his election address he had said nothing about the franchise for the women workers of Preston. The poster of which he complained was issued by the North of England Society for Women's Suffrage which stated that in the county borough as a whole, women textile workers numbered 12,000 compared to only 8,000 men. 'These twelve thousand women', she asserted, were 'left out of Hodge's election address! Is this Labour representation?' It was not the poster that had lost Hodge the election but his own action. The uncompromising Christabel added an additional barb. Although she was aware that the Conservative candidate, Mr Kerr, was opposed to women's suffrage, there was:

> little to choose between an enemy and a friend who does nothing. It is not enough to have supporters who are merely 'in favour'. A majority of the House of Commons is 'in favour' now of giving political rights to women, but with no result. We want friends who will do something practical.

The women trade unionists who were contributing to the funds of the LRC were determined to have their enfranchisement made a trade union question in the same way that Labour representation was, as was shown by the ballot taken recently by the Bolton Weavers' Union.[7] The issues raised by Christabel were particularly pertinent since many women operatives in the Lancashire mill towns were now facing unemployment or substantially reduced working hours, due to a cyclical shortage of raw cotton.[8] By this time, Christabel had decided that 'the liberation of politically fettered womanhood' was going to be her aim in life. '[T]his vote question must be settled', she penned. 'Mine was the third generation of women to claim the vote and the vote must now be obtained. To go on helplessly pleading was undignified. Strong and urgent demand was needed.'[9]

Christabel would not be quiet about the ILP's apathy on the women's cause. In a leading article in the August 1903 issue of the *ILP News* she gave further vent to her frustration:

> As a rule, Socialists are silent on the question of the position of women. If not actually antagonistic to the movement for women's rights, they hold aloof from it. One gathers that some day, when the Socialists are in power, and have nothing better to do, they will give women votes as a finishing touch to their arrangements, but for the present they profess no interest in the subject . . . This attitude is very unsatisfactory . . . It is not at all impossible to have tyranny under Socialism . . . Why are women expected to have such confidence in the men of the Labour Party? Working-men are as unjust to women as are those of other classes.[10]

The article had barely been printed when another incident revealing the ILP's hostility to equality for women came to prominence.

Sylvia, who had been home for about six months now, had a commission to paint murals on the walls of Pankhurst Hall which had been built a few years earlier by the ILP in honour of her father. A couple of days before the re-opening ceremony, on Friday evening, 2 October 1903, Sylvia was astonished to learn that part of the hall was being used by a branch of the ILP that would not admit women as members. When she enquired further she was told that the reason for this state of affairs was because a social club, used by men and including non-ILP members but closed to all women, was attached to the branch. The Pankhurst family heard the news with indignation and disbelief. That a hall built in the memory of an adored husband and father who fought for women's rights should ban women from its premises was an insult to his memory. Christabel reproached her mother, saying she had allowed the cause of women's suffrage to become effaced. Emmeline bitterly agreed.[11] At the ceremony on 2 October Emmeline noticed that there were very few socialists present so that she felt 'almost ashamed' to have brought Walter Crane, an influential artist and illustrator, well-known socialist and former part-time director of design at the School of Art in Manchester, up from London to formally declare the hall open.[12]

The following day, when Philip Snowden came to Pankhurst Hall to give a lecture and attend a social, Christabel refused to speak to him. The disillusioned Emmeline, feeling that she had wasted her nine years of service in the Labour movement, even refused to contribute to the Keir Hardie wages fund of £150 per year which the ILP had voted as the minimum necessary amount to support him as an MP.[13] Declaring that she would do no more for Labour representation until women's interests were taken seriously, Emmeline discussed the matter with her daughters, especially Christabel. 'Mother and I arrived at the conclusion', recollected Christabel, 'that who would be politically free herself must strike the blow, and that women could not do better than pay the independent Labour movement the compliment of imitation, by starting an independent women's movement.'[14] Emmeline decided that the new women-only organisation that would campaign for votes for women and run parallel to the ILP rather than be formally affiliated to it, as so many historians have assumed, should be called the 'Women's Labour Representative Committee'.[15] But Christabel pointed out that Eva Gore-Booth and Esther Roper had already decided on a similar name for an organisation they were forming among women textile workers, and that an alternative had to be found. Party to her mother's plan to enlist local socialist women in the new venture, Christabel joined the Manchester ILP Branch on 6 October.[16]

Three days later, Emmeline said to these friends, 'Women, we must do the work ourselves. We must have an independent women's movement. Come to my house tomorrow and we will arrange it!'[17] The little group that joined Emmeline and Christabel at 62 Nelson Street on Sunday, 10 October 1903, mostly wives of ILP men, agreed with the name that Emmeline had chosen for the new organisation: the 'Women's Social and Political Union' (WSPU).[18] Like the NUWSS and the North of England Women's Suffrage Society, the purpose of the WSPU was to campaign for votes for women on the same terms as they were, or should be, granted to men, but unlike these two organisations which both admitted men, the WSPU was single sex. Further, as Christabel noted, the WSPU was established on an 'independent non-party, non-class foundation', important points that her mother also emphasised. Further, 'Deeds, not words', insisted Emmeline, was to be the WSPU's permanent motto.[19]

Christabel, now an undergraduate law student at Owen's College as well as a founding member of the WSPU, was still also on the executive committee of the North of England Society for Women's Suffrage. Here she worked not only alongside Eva Gore-Booth but also other well-known suffragists, such as Eleanor Rathbone, Sarah Dickinson, Bertha Mason, the Revd. S. A. Steinthal and Sarah Reddish.[20] Over the coming months, Christabel continued speaking for both societies. Thus on 8 and 22 November and then on 6 December 1903 she addressed the Leicester ILP, the Derby Socialist Society and the Liverpool ILP, respectively, on behalf of the North of England Society.[21] In mid-November, she was also a WSPU speaker at a public meeting in Sheffield, presided over by Edward Carpenter, sharing a platform with Isabella Ford from the NUWSS. On this occasion, although both speakers tried to persuade women to join the Sheffield Suffrage society, Christabel's message had a more defiant tone. She urged the women in the audience 'not to be divided . . . to join together on one question – the vote', to throw off 'party' allegiance. Isabella, on the other hand, spoke much more cautiously, urging women to stand together not for their own sake but for 'the sake of the children and for the sake of the nation'.[22]

Christabel was beginning to make an impact as a speaker, stressing the centrality of the so-called 'Woman Question' to the 'Labour Question'. We can see this in the first pamphlet she published, entitled *The parliamentary vote for women*, possibly delivered initially as a lecture. Taking as her text the Chartism slogan, 'Political Power Must Precede Social Regeneration', she outlined in sixteen closely argued pages her thoughts on the matter. 'The great social injustices', she began, are '*the subjection of labour and the subjection of women.*' Although they were co-equal manifestations of the 'spirit of tyranny', class subjection was not so complete as sex subjection:

> As a class, working men, possessing political rights, have influence and standing in the nation . . . The individual working man is the equal of his associates: in his private life he is no one's inferior. Women, on the other hand, are, as a class, without the power and prestige which the vote gives. As individuals they live with their social superiors, not with their equals. In marriage, law and custom give the husband a distinct advantage . . . That the children of a marriage belong in law to the husband gives him a very strong hold over their mother. The economic dependence, too, of married women does much to keep them in domestic subjection.[23]

In view of women's low political and social status, it was no surprise that their earnings were so much lower than those of men so that most lived in poverty, unable to afford sufficient food, warm clothing and comfortable lodgings. This was particularly so for those with dependants, such as widows with families, women with aged parents or invalid relatives to support, and wives whose husbands could or would not work. It was argued by some that women were paid less because they are unskilled. 'If most women are unskilled', Christabel contended, 'it is because of lack of opportunity.' No provision was made for their technical education, while it was contrary to custom and to the wishes of trade union organisations to apprentice them to skilled trades. Nor did parents give their daughters such advantages as were available, encouraging girls to place too low a value on themselves and to see women as taking second place. 'Until women regard themselves, and are regarded, as the equals of men, they will continue to be at a disadvantage in the industrial world.'[24]

There was only one cure for the industrial weakness of women, and that was for men to renounce all claims to authority over women, whether in social, political or domestic life, to recognise them as equals, to allow them equal rights, liberties and opportunities. The key factor in bringing about such equality was the granting of the parliamentary vote to women.[25] The Chartists said truly that political power must precede social regeneration. Political inequality involved social inequality. While the demand for political rights came first from middle-class women, working-class women through the Labour representation movement were now roused on the question. Yet despite this concerted effort by working women, most working men showed little desire to give to women the political rights they themselves possessed. Indeed, opponents of women's enfranchisement often suggested that the 'teaching of feminist and collectivist principles set sex against sex, and class against class'. The reply to this was that 'while the dominations of class and of sex exist, there must be conflict.' It is only when all men and all women 'stand on an equal footing' that their interests become the same:

> When we consider how much wiser and happier Humanity would have been if all the women and men of the past had been free, we see how important it is to break down the oldest and strongest of tyrannies – the tyranny of sex.[26]

Christabel's developing powers as a writer and especially as a feminist speaker were soon to be given full rein in the WSPU in which she would later hold the administrative post of Chief Organiser. But during these early months of the WSPU, both she and her mother considered it wise not to hold any office 'lest the Union be discounted as "just Mrs. Pankhurst and Christabel" and dubbed "a family party"'.[27] Mrs Rachel Scott, genial and full of humour, was the first honorary secretary while Mrs Helen Harker, serious and determined, was treasurer for a time. Weekly meetings were often held at 62 Nelson Street and occasionally in a small room above a warehouse in Portland Street. Although members gave what pennies they could afford to support the work, supplemented by the proceedings of various fund-raising events, such as jumble sales, sales of home-made jam and, at Christmas, a carol-singing collection, the bulk of the financial burden was borne by Emmeline who also received donations from sympathisers.[28] The dedicated Christabel also made her own contribution, making sure that she did not waste money – or time – on more frivolous matters:

All my own money went into the funds. Instead of theatres and dances – just the vote, and nothing but the vote . . . I . . . thought all else meaningless in comparison, and every penny really wasted that was not spent on the one great object.[29]

During the week, letters would be written from 62 Nelson Street asking if WSPU members could speak at various functions organised by the ILP, the trade unions, debating societies, Labour Churches, Clarion Clubs and women's guilds. Then Emmeline or Adela would usually bring to the weekly meetings a list of replies, including unsolicited invitations, and the speakers would be allotted; volunteers would also be sought to draw a crowd, at a fair, park, market or street-corner.[30] Initially, there were only five speakers – Emmeline, Christabel, Sylvia, Adela and Teresa Billington, a Manchester schoolteacher and agnostic who had first met Emmeline when she had been sent to see her, as a member of the Manchester Education Committee, in regard to her wish to be exempted from the teaching of religion. All were members of the same ILP branch, Central Manchester.[31] The early WSPU therefore depended largely upon ILP networks, even if it was not formally affiliated to it.

Teresa Billington remembered that in these early days of the WSPU, Emmeline Pankhurst was 'convinced . . . of her own importance and that of her close companion Christabel in carrying an accepted responsibility', seeing the campaign for women's suffrage as 'a duty laid on them'. Every member of the Pankhurst household upheld that the women's cause came first, above everything else. 'They believed in each other . . . had a large enveloping ambition for each other. There was no position so high but it might not one day be graced by Mother or Christabel.'[32] Harry and Adela prophesied that their mother would become Prime Minister and Christabel Chancellor of the Exchequer, a suggestion that the older WSPU members did not find incredulous, despite their laughter.[33]

In high hopes, one of the earliest political acts of the WSPU was to ask those men standing for election to Manchester City Council to support a resolution stating that the council would petition Parliament to make women also eligible as candidates in such elections. Although some favourable replies were received, nothing came of the issue.[34] Then, in December 1903, a deputation waited on John Hodge, chair of the LRC and Labour candidate for Gorton, asking him if he would support a women's suffrage measure, if elected to Parliament. Hodge replied that he was pledged to the Steelsmelters' Mill, and Tinplate Workers' Association, to give first place in private members' bills to the extension of the check-weighmen's clause, but that he would do 'all in his power' to ensure that one of the measures promoted in the House of Commons by the Parliamentary Labour Group should be for such a bill. The WSPU had more success, however, when they approached a Councillor Parker, from Halifax, also standing for election to Parliament, since he pledged to put votes for women 'first' on his programme.[35] But Parker was not returned – nor was Hodge.

Such setbacks were a disappointment for the WSPU membership, and especially Christabel. They told the *Clarion* that women in the past had been 'too apologetic for their existence, and too submissive'. Confidently, they published a bright-yellow pamphlet, probably written by Christabel, outlining their women's charter, 'That for all purposes connected with, and having reference to, the right to vote at Parliamentary elections, words in the Representation of the People Act importing the masculine gender shall include women.'[36] Such terms for women's enfranchisement, of course, were those that had been advocated by Richard Pankhurst over thirty years earlier.

While all this was going on, Christabel was also fighting a more personal battle. Her law course at Owen's College involved attendance of just two days a week, the other weekdays being spent either in articles with a solicitor or reading in chambers – but only if you were a male student. As a woman, Christabel was barred from such activity. Deeply aggrieved by such sex discrimination against her ambition to become a barrister, she decided to challenge the ruling, fully supported by her mother who asked Lord Haldane, as an avowed supporter of equal rights, to sponsor her daughter's application to become a law student at Lincoln's Inn. By mid-December Christabel was mobilising support for her cause, writing to various sympathisers, including the aged and long-time suffrage campaigner Elizabeth Wolstenholme Elmy, seeking assistance in forming a committee that would help secure the admission of women to the bar.[37] The younger woman greatly respected Wolstenholme Elmy's feminist ideals while the elder cherished Christabel 'almost as a granddaughter'.[38]

During the Christmas vacation from her university studies, a determined Christabel busied herself writing a flurry of letters. On 2 January 1904, she wrote twice to William Stead, the progressive editor of the *Review of Reviews* and supporter of the women's cause:

> May I offer you a little piece of news for your paper. I have posted today an application for admission as a student at Lincoln's Inn . . . Of course it will be refused this time but I think we ought to bombard the various Inns of Court with frequent applications. We shall be successful ultimately.[39]

Stead had obviously been impressed by Christabel since he had commissioned from her an interview with Keir Hardie, a copy of which she enclosed with her second letter to him, also dated 2 January. Apologising for the lateness of her article, she pointed out that Hardie had not only been travelling but also unwell so that he had been slow to reply to her questions.[40]

The following day, Christabel penned more letters, again to Elizabeth Wolstenholme Elmy and to two Benchers, Mr Haldane and Mr Hopkinson, who might be involved in considering her application to Lincoln's Inn. However, as she related to Mrs Elmy, she did not expect a positive reply from Mr Hopkinson, also the Principal of Owen's College. 'I don't hope for very much support from him for he is the man who when in Parliament voted once for & once against women's suffrage & declares himself to be a consistent person all the same.' Wondering how to advance her case, Christabel contacted Mrs Elmy once more. 'I am almost afraid to ask you to do this as you are so busy', she wrote apologetically, but would she be kind enough to write to another Bencher, Lord Hobhouse, who was supposed to be in favour of women barristers.[41] Elizabeth Wolstenholme Elmy, living in Congleton, a tireless worker for the women's cause, wrote not only to Lord Hobhouse but also to six other Benchers – and to William Stead, to whom she enclosed Christabel's letter.[42]

Christabel had judged Alfred Hopkinson's response accurately. A few days later he replied to her, expressing doubts that Lincoln's Inn 'would be willing to take what is, I believe, quite a new departure as regard the admission of students'.[43] Within two weeks, Christabel heard that her application had been refused, along with those of Ivy Williams LLD and Bertha Cave.[44] The socialist press took up Christabel's story. 'Miss Christabel H. Pankhurst is finding the obstinacy and selfishness of men a pretty formidable barrier in her path', opined Julia Dawson in the *Clarion* early in 1904. The Benchers of Lincoln's Inn refused her admission 'not on legal grounds, but purely as a matter of personal prejudice'.[45]

Deep disappointment and anger bubbled in the Pankhurst household. 'What rage we all felt when her application was refused', recollected Adela, 'and how proud of our pretty Christabel when her name and picture were in all the papers!'[46] For Christabel, the rejection of her application for legal training was a formative experience in her life, a further impetus to her feminist conviction that men discriminated against women because they were women, not on the grounds of their ability or talents. There was another galling fact to consider – even though her two sisters were younger than she was, they were both pursuing the careers they wanted. Sylvia had won a scholarship worth £50 a year to study at the Royal College of Art, in London, where she was now living. Adela was now earning £30 a year as a pupil teacher of poor working-class children in a state elementary school at Irmston, a job she loved since she believed she was redeeming humanity, working for others, serving socialism.[47] But for Christabel, there was no comfort that she could advance the legal career she wanted. Thwarted in her ambition, she knew that the only way forward was to campaign for the parliamentary vote for women. Once that had been won, other social reforms for the benefit of all women would follow.

An opportunity to air her views publicly on the matter soon presented itself when Christabel and Bertha Cave were invited to plead their case in a debate of the Union Society in London. Christabel was so persuasive in her argument that she won a majority vote in her favour. '[A]ll the law men I know admire her & wish her well', Jane Brownlow informed Elizabeth Wolstenholme Elmy, to whom Christabel had written a twelve-page letter about the event, as soon as she arrived home.[48] But admiration and good wishes did not bring equality for women or grant them entry to the legal profession. On 2 February 1904, Christabel wrote to Mr Wallis Grain, a barrister, who had spoken on her side, explaining that she believed that 'all artificial disabilities imposed merely on the ground of sex harmful and unjust. I want women to have complete equality with men of rights and opportunities not as regards the legal profession only, but in every other direction also'. Christabel opined:

> We stand most in need of political rights but to get a share in carrying on the business of the Courts is almost as important . . . We look forward to the day when women are allowed to serve on the jury and some of our judges are women, but the presence of female counsel in the courts will be a great step in advance.

In a postscript she added, 'I have of course a personal reason for wishing to enter the professions & that is that I believe it to be the one for which I am most fitted.'[49]

A few days later, Emmeline returned to Manchester, having been in London for a meeting of suffragists, mainly from the NUWSS, on 3 February. The women had waited patiently in a committee room of the House of Commons to press friendly MPs, including Sir Charles McLaren and Keir Hardie, to introduce a women's suffrage measure, as a private member's bill during the coming session. These annual meetings always followed the usual civilities, with the sympathetic MPs saying they would vote for a women's suffrage measure when they had the opportunity to do so, and the forlorn deputation leaving quietly, hanging on pledges that never brought the desired reform. The impatient Emmeline had not been asked to speak but was determined not to allow yet another occasion to pass without any concrete result. 'Sir Charles McLaren has told us', she abruptly began,

> that numbers of his colleagues desire the success of the women's suffrage cause . . . Will Sir Charles McLaren tell us if any member is preparing to introduce a bill for women's suffrage? Will he tell us what he and the other members will pledge themselves to *do* for the reform they so warmly endorse?[50]

The embarrassed Sir Charles was not prepared to say anything of the kind. The small group of women left in some anger, telling Emmeline she was 'an interloper, an impertinent intruder'. What right did she have to step in and ruin the good impression they had made? No one could tell how many friendly MPs she had 'alienated' with her 'unfortunate remarks'.[51] The unrepentant Emmeline arrived home, telling the story to her children. For some time, Christabel had been discussing with their mother the necessity for new methods of campaigning and she believed that the time had come to do something about it. 'How long you women have been trying for the vote', she said sorrowfully to her mother. 'For my part, I mean to get it.'[52] Vague pledges of support from influential MPs, who soon gave priority to party political issues, were pointless.

Christabel decided to press her case at the initial meeting of the Free Trade League to be held at the Free Trade Hall, Manchester, on the evening of

19 February 1904. Winston Churchill, a Conservative MP about to defect to the Liberals, was to give the address. She applied for a ticket and received one for the platform, which suited her plan well. After Churchill had spoken for an hour and a half, he proposed a resolution, which was seconded by others, that 'this meeting affirms its unshakable belief in the principles of Free Trade adopted more than fifty years ago'. Suddenly Christabel stepped forward and asked to be allowed to move an amendment on women's suffrage. The chair explained that he could not permit such a request since it contained words and sentiments on a contentious matter to which persons agreed on Free Trade might have difficulty giving their support. Christabel refused to give way, but finally conceded, amid loud cries of 'Chair'. Looking back on this incident, in later life, she recollected:

> This was the first militant step – the hardest to me, because it was the first. To move from my place on the platform to the speaker's table in the teeth of the astonishment and opposition of will of that immense throng, those civic and county leaders and those Members of Parliament, was the most difficult thing I have ever done.

As this statement makes clear, 'militancy' for Christabel meant challenging the conventional expectations about women being submissive and forcing the women's issue into male party politics. However, although Christabel felt she had 'imposed' upon the attention of political leaders and the public women's claim to the vote, she was disappointed that the issue soon faded from their view and reproached herself 'for having given way too easily'. Next time such a meeting was held, she decided, 'a mark should be made that could not disappear'.[53]

Christabel's action at the Free Trade Hall was taken on her own initiative and not a tactic of the North of England Society for Women's Suffrage. But the WSPU membership had decided not to be too submissive, or too polite, and there was a long tradition of such disruptive action by men in Labour politics – and by women in the Women's Franchise League. Nevertheless, Christabel's stand reveals an important aspect of her character: she was confident enough to act independently, just as her mother had done at her recent meeting at the House of Commons. Christabel and Emmeline now regularly took the initiative, each supporting and encouraging the other as bolder steps were taken. Nonetheless, despite their concerns about the lukewarm attitude of the ILP towards women's suffrage, the WSPU was still mainly centred in the local Labour movement as in early March 1904 when Christabel spoke on 'Labour representation for women' to a large audience at a meeting organised by the Liverpool ILP. She spelt out how the question was one of special importance to the Labour Party, because the lower remuneration that women received, for the same work that men did, tended to keep down the general standard of living. It also retarded the social intellectual development of women and, through them, of the whole race. A resolution was then passed, calling on local and Labour MPs to support a motion in the House of Commons, scheduled for 16 March, asking for the removal of the disabilities of women in regard to the parliamentary franchise. The motion was being proposed by none other than Sir Charles McLaren, with whom Emmeline had clashed the previous month.[54] Although the motion was carried on the appointed day by a majority of one hundred and fourteen, none of the Labour MPs took part in the debate. Christabel was disgusted. 'Why . . . were they all silent, leaving it to members of the other parties to give voice to the claims of women?' Even the 'vulgar attacks on women' made by two Liberal MPs, Mr Labouchere and Mr Cremer, 'did not rouse the members of the Labour party to speak. Not they'.[55]

Christabel's refusal to say nothing about such deplorable behaviour was making its mark in the national daily press and winning her praise from other feminists, not least the doughty Elizabeth Wolstenholme Elmy who visited Manchester later that month for a day of women's suffrage meetings. Elizabeth gave a friend all the news, explaining how soon after her various meetings had ended, at about five o'clock:

> Christabel Pankhurst came for me and I dined with herself, her mother & 2 sisters & Mrs. Scott . . . & had a most loving and hearty welcome. Christabel & Mrs. Scott travelled with me as far as Stockport as they were going to speak on WS at a great Labour meeting at Heaton Moor. Mrs. Pankhurst is immensely improved though she has nothing like the brain of her husband and oldest daughter. The other 2 girls are clever and sweet, but have not Christabel's force & originality. The boy [Harry], the baby I knew, is at school near London, so I did not see him.[56]

Mrs Elmy's astute assessment of Christabel was to prove accurate.

Emmeline was delighted that April when, at the ILP Conference at Cardiff, she successfully moved a resolution on women's suffrage and the NAC was instructed to prepare and introduce by its Labour MPs a bill that would grant equal voting rights to women. 'Socialist women in the country looked to their own Socialist party for a lead on this question', she emphasised.[57] The popular Emmeline Pankhurst was elected again to the NAC, a move that did not please everyone present, especially those such as Snowden who favoured adult suffrage. Glasier noted in his diary that at one of the NAC's Cardiff meetings, 'I have to urge Snowden to display some grace towards Mrs. Pankhurst.'[58]

Such grace was probably not forthcoming since a short time after the ILP Conference had ended, the forceful Christabel burst into an angry exchange in the *Labour Leader* with Snowden, highlighting their differing views about class and gender politics, as well as their differing approaches to the question of women's enfranchisement. In an article titled 'The I.L.P. and women's franchise', Snowden had argued against women's enfranchisement on the same property qualifications as men, saying that it would not serve the interests of the working class since a disproportionate number of the enfranchised would be wealthy and propertied women who would not support Labour candidates. 'We do not want to abolish class distinctions to raise distinctions of sex', he insisted.

'The evils we want to remove are not confined to one sex. They are common to both, and cannot be removed by approaching the work from its sex aspect.'[59] Always the fiercest feminist critic of Labour men who refused to consider that women's interests might differ from their own, Christabel retorted, 'Sex distinctions exist however, and it is not by ignoring them, but recognising and attacking them that we shall secure their abolition.' Further, while she admitted that the existing base of the parliamentary franchise was 'anything but satisfactory', by far the most serious defect was that by which a person, simply because she was a woman, was deprived of 'political existence'. So while the extension of the parliamentary franchise, on its present basis, would leave many women without votes, it would 'put an end to the rule of one sex by the other; it will strike the death-blow of the aristocracy of sex'.[60]

When Snowden sent a letter in response to Christabel's attack, she commented angrily again, this time criticising not only her protagonist but also the ILP leadership generally:

> As for adult suffrage the I.L.P. has always given preference to other questions. Bruce Glasier, for one, has said on platforms that 'we have votes enough. What we must do is to learn how to use them.' That is all very well for men who have two-thirds of a loaf, while we have not a crumb . . . Philip Snowden claims it as a merit that the I.L.P. has not advertised the position of women as being one of special hardship. He ought to be a woman for a while. As Miss Snowden he would never have been either a councillor or a Parliamentary candidate.[61]

As these comments make clear, Christabel feared that too many male socialists were refusing to emphasise women's oppression as a sex, fearful that it would expose the divisions in the working class between women and men and thus weaken the development of class solidarity.[62] Emmeline, as a member of the NAC, was mixing with these men and critical too of their support for adult suffrage since she knew that an adult suffrage bill would not enable women to vote, unless it expressly stated so.[63] But Emmeline kept hope longer than Christabel that the ILP leadership in particular would come round to their point of view.

The bitter debate between the adult suffragists and the women suffragists, aired publicly in the *Labour Leader* and the *Clarion*, also erupted in the *Manchester Guardian* and drew in Amy Bulley, Chair of the Manchester and Salford Women's Trade Council of which Christabel was a member. Amy Bulley had little patience with the women suffragists, arguing that the Council existed to unionise and protect working women, and not to concern itself with such matters. Christabel defiantly refused to accept such strictures. 'As a member of the Women's Trade Union Council I wish to dissociate myself from this expression of opinion regarding the industrial problem', she insisted. 'In common with modern trade-unionists, I hold the view that trade-unionism without political power and without political action is powerless to bring about a substantial and permanent improvement in the condition of the workers.' Women workers understood this only too well, 'as their petitions to Parliament demanding the franchise and the formation of the Women's Textile and Other Workers' Representation Committee shows. Every class of the community has found political rights necessary to their advancement'.[64]

Christabel hoped that by bringing the issue into public debate, the Manchester and Salford Women's Trade Union Council would be forced to accept her proposal, but at a special meeting called to discuss the question, it was decided by a large majority that the Council should retain its non-political status and focus on the organisation of women's labour.[65] Christabel resigned from the Council, as did Eva Gore-Booth and Sarah Dickenson.[66] Eva and Sarah now set about forming a new splinter organisation which would include women's enfranchisement in its aim, namely the Manchester and Salford Women's Trade and Labour Council. Christabel joined the new organisation which attracted seven unions and about two thousand members from the 'old' Council, now left with a powerless rump of just one hundred members. Most suffrage historians, writing from a socialist feminist perspective, 'blame' Christabel for this split, seeing it as a disastrous move for the Labour movement and for trade unionism.[67] But Christabel was approaching the issue from a women-centred perspective, highlighting how the interests of working women were not being served by socialists or by trade unionists. The new organisation was to prove popular with working women since, within a year, ten branches with a membership of three hundred each were established. These working women were to pressurise Labour MPs for their voting rights and were to meet considerable hostility from union leaders.[68]

During that July of 1904, when Christabel was criticising Amy Bulley's views, she was also busy in other activities that would advance the cause of women. In mid-July, Elizabeth Wolstenholme Elmy travelled to Manchester to form, with Christabel and a few other interested persons, a Committee to Secure the Admission of Women to the Legal Profession.[69] Christabel was appointed Honorary Secretary, and the address of the Committee was given as 30 King Street, Manchester. On 21 July, she wrote on the new society's official headed notepaper to Mr Wallis Grain, inviting him to join them and asking if he would be kind enough to send the names of any lawyers 'on our side' so that she could extend the invitation also to them. 'I want – in the Autumn – to arrange meetings to be addressed by an American woman lawyer who will be in England then', she continued. 'To see & hear a real, live woman lawyer might have a good effect on some of our opponents if they could be induced to attend.'[70] One week later, Christabel wrote again to Mr Wallis Grain, enquiring whether he thought it possible for her to argue her case before the Benchers:

> Have you ever heard of it being done? Your offer to represent me is very kind, though as far as they would consent to it, I should be wise I think to represent myself – just to show that a woman can do so.

Further, she wondered whether a debate on the political enfranchisement of women might be held since the vote was 'the key' to everything else, including the admission of women to the legal profession. 'Unless you think we are sure to be defeated . . . a debate on the subject would be helpful.'[71]

Although the Committee for Securing the Admission of Women to the Legal Profession was strategically important for any future hopes that Christabel held about a career in law, the highlight for her during this summer of 1904 was meeting again Susan B. Anthony, the distinguished American suffragist and social reformer, now eighty-four years old. Miss Anthony, breaking her homeward journey with a visit to Britain after attending the International Congress on Women in Berlin, was in correspondence with Elizabeth Wolstenholme Elmy who was keen for Christabel to meet the leading light of the American women's movement.[72] The North of England Society for Women's Suffrage arranged a garden party in Miss Anthony's honour, on 25 July, in the spacious grounds of Mrs Hylands' house, at Victoria Park, Manchester. On the day of the fete, the excited Christabel published in the *Daily Dispatch* a long essay about the distinguished visitor, praising her for her devotion to the women's suffrage and anti-slavery campaigns, pointing out how her support for these unpopular causes had brought her abuse and derision. Miss Anthony was still continuing her work since in only four States in North America did women enjoy political rights. She believed that a woman who has the vote becomes a 'vital force – declaring her will for herself, instead of praying and beseeching men to declare it for her'.[73]

When Susan B. Anthony met the pretty twenty-three-year-old Christabel at the garden party, she thanked her warmly for what she had written, and tucking Christabel's arm under her own, led her away for a little talk, inspiring, claimed one journalist, the younger woman to 'work harder and more courageously'.[74] Emmeline, the proud mother, recollected how after Miss Anthony's departure, Christabel spoke of her often, always with 'sorrow and indignation' that such a splendid worker for humanity was destined to die without seeing the hopes of her lifetime realised. 'It is unendurable', declared Christabel to her mother, 'to think of another generation of women wasting their lives begging for the vote. We must not lose any more time. We must act.'[75]

When Christabel returned to her undergraduate studies that autumn of 1904, she did not abandon her political work but continued with it, in her spare time. Thus in early October, together with Teresa Billington, she spoke one Sunday evening at Tib Street, Manchester, on the political disabilities of women and then, later that month, on the same theme, at Stockport Labour Church.[76] Christabel also made sure that she kept in contact with the seasoned campaigners from whom she could learn much, such as Mrs Elmy and the recently widowed Katherine Thomasson, a generous financial supporter of the women's movement and a fellow member of the executive committee of the North of England Society for Women's Suffrage. 'I am waiting here 5 minutes for the Manchester train', Elizabeth Wolstenholme Elmy wrote in pencil, from Congleton station on 15 October, to her friend Harriet McIlquham. 'Christabel meets me at the station, & I spend the night with her, Eva and Esther. We are sure to talk into the small hours.'[77]

Christabel was still, nominally, a member of the NUWSS which was holding its national convention in London on 25 and 26 November and she had arranged to attend, as a delegate from the North of England Society, travelling down to London with Elizabeth Wolstenholme Elmy. However, on 23 November she wrote to her aged friend, 'greatly disappointed' that she would be unable to travel with her the following day since she had to be in the registrar's office in the morning until half past ten, in place of her mother. Unfortunately, on 24 November the plan had to be changed again. 'I was not able to get away today', Christabel apologised regretfully to Mrs Elmy:

> Mother has not been very well & I wanted to stay here as late as I could. I leave at 8.30 in the morning & arrive 12.20. I shall take a cab & hope to be at the Convention before the morning sitting is over.

Although Christabel had already prepared her speech, she was keen to receive any advice that Elizabeth Wolstenholme Elmy might give:

> I hope there will be time before the afternoon sitting for you to tell me what (if anything) you think it would be well for me to say. I gather that you are to open the discussion of [the] plan of campaign so you will be able to sound the right note.[78]

Whether Mrs Elmy gave any advice we do not know, but Christabel's speech was considered important enough to merit coverage in the *Women's Suffrage Record*:

> You find the women of Cradley Heath working at chain-making for 2s. 6d., 4s., and 5s., a week; if you go to the shirt makers you will hear that their conditions are worse . . . in their industrial position women have rather gone back than forward . . . This is my claim to the franchise – that it will advance the industrial condition of women.

Further, the impassioned Christabel urged all party women in the audience, Conservative, Liberal or Labour, to be 'a thorn in the side of their respective parties' until women's enfranchisement was a part of the party programme.[79] She was certainly doing her part to perform such a role in the developing Labour movement.

Notes

1 EP to Mr Nodal, 26 and 31 January 1903, Purvis Collection; Purvis, *Emmeline Pankhurst*, pp. 63–4.
2 ESP, TSM, p. 164.
3 CP, *Unshackled*, p. 42.

4 ESP, *TSM*, p. 165.

5 *LL*, 13 March 1903.

6 ESP, *TSM*, p. 167; J. Hannam, *Isabella Ford* (Oxford, Blackwell, 1989), p. 91.

7 *LL*, 23 and 30 May 1903.

8 Rosen, *Rise up women!*, p. 29.

9 CP, *Unshackled*, p. 42.

10 CP, Women and the Independent Labour Party, *I.L.P. News*, August 1903.

11 ESP, *TSM*, pp. 167–8; K. Hunt, Why Manchester? Why the Pankhursts? Why 1903? Reflections on the centenary of the Women's Social and Political Union, *Manchester Region History Review*, xvii, i, 2004, p. 7 is sceptical about this story since she can find no evidence that 'North Salford ILP operated such a discriminatory policy at Pankhurst Hall which went against the whole spirit and rules of the ILP'. Hunt omits to note that while Sylvia in her *TSM* refers to the 'opening' of the hall, Bruce Glasier in his diary for 3 October 1903 refers to a 're-opening', perhaps after refurbishment or completion of the building.

12 Entry for 3 October 1903, Glasier Diaries.

13 ESP, *TSM*, pp. 167–8.

14 CP, *Unshackled*, p. 43.

15 See Fulford, *Votes for women*, p. 114. Holton, *Suffrage days*, p. 108 claims the WSPU was a 'ginger group within the ILP' and Coleman, *Adela Pankhurst*, p. 32 that the WSPU 'formed an independent group within the ILP'. The source for these claims is probably Sylvia's *TSM*, p. 168, yet a careful reading of Sylvia's book reveals that she does not state that the WSPU was affiliated to the ILP but that her mother intended it to be 'a women's parallel to the I.L.P.'.

16 Liddington and Norris, *One hand tied behind us*, p. 280, note 24.

17 CP, *Unshackled*, p. 43.

18 CP, *Unshackled*, speaks of '[w]e' at this initial meeting; that is, her mother, the socialist women and herself. Sylvia was not present, nor, it would appear, was the eighteen-year-old Adela.

19 CP, *Unshackled*, p. 44 and EP, *My own story*, p. 38. Sylvia in her *TSM*, p. 168 claims that her mother intended that the WSPU should be mainly composed of 'working women'. Neither Emmeline in *My own story* or Christabel in *Unshackled* repeat this assertion but emphasise, as noted here, that the WSPU was intended to be free of any social class or party political affiliation. Sylvia's account of the WSPU's foundation in *TSM* differs markedly from that given in her earlier 1911 book, *The suffragette*, p. 7, which accords with that of her mother and Christabel: 'Almost all the women who were present on that original occasion were working-women, Members of the Labour Movement, but it was decided from the first that the Union should be entirely independent of Class and Party.' In her even earlier account of the suffragette movement, in articles in *Votes for Women*, October 1908, Sylvia gives no information on the founding of the WSPU which indicates that she was not present.

20 Report of the Executive Committee of the North of England Society for Women's Suffrage, Presented at the annual meeting, 7 November 1903 (Manchester, 'Guardian' General Printing Works, n.d.), Lists of Officers.

21 National Union of Women's Suffrage Societies, Report of the Executive Committee of the North of England Society for Women's Suffrage, Presented at the annual meeting, 8 November 1904 (Manchester, 'Guardian' General Printing Works), p. 9.

22 *LL*, 14 November 1903; Hannam, *Isabella Ford*, pp. 92–3.

23 CP, *The parliamentary vote for women* (Abel Heywood & Son, Manchester, n.d., c.1903/4), p. 5.

24 CP, *The parliamentary vote for women*, pp. 9–10.

25 CP, *The parliamentary vote for women*, pp. 11–12.

26 CP, *The parliamentary vote for women*, p. 16.

27 CP, *Unshackled*, p. 44.

28 CP, *Unshackled*, p. 45; Rosen, *Rise up women!*, p. 31; Teresa Billington-Greig (hereafter TBG) Papers, Box 397, Folder A6, TWL; CP, My war chest: how we gathered and spent £100,000, *Weekly Dispatch*, 10 April, 1921, p. 5. Teresa Billington, who married Frederick Greig in 1907, wrote her notes in later life, long after her split with the Pankhursts.
29 CP, My war chest, p. 5.
30 TBG Papers, Early days. 1903–5: militancy in plan, in C. McPhee and A. Fitzgerald, eds, *The non-violent militant, selected writings of Teresa Billington-Greig* (London and New York, Routledge, 1987), p. 95.
31 Liddington and Norris, *One hand tied behind us*, p. 175.
32 TBG Papers, Emmeline Pankhurst, The home.
33 TBG Papers, Early WSPU, the Gore-Booth & Roper connection.
34 *Manchester City News*, 31 October 1903.
35 Rachel Scott, Letter to the Editor, *Clarion*, 4 December 1903.
36 Julia Dawson, Our woman's letter, *Clarion*, 1 January 1904.
37 See Elizabeth Wolstenholme Elmy (hereafter EWE) to H. McIlquham, 16 December 1903, Elizabeth Wolstenholme Elmy Papers, British Library (hereafter EWEP), Add Ms 47,453, f.212.
38 M. Wright, *Elizabeth Wolstenholme Elmy and the Victorian feminist movement: the biography of an insurgent woman* (Manchester, Manchester University Press, 2011), pp. 3 and 189.
39 CP to William Stead, 2 January 1904, William Stead Papers (hereafter Stead Papers), Churchill College, Cambridge.
40 CP to William Stead, 2 January 1904, Stead Papers.
41 CP to Mrs Elmy, 3 January 1904, Stead Papers.
42 This information is written in Elizabeth's hand on Christabel's letter to her, dated 3 January 1904, Stead Papers.
43 Alfred Hopkinson to CP, 5 January 1904, Letter Book of Sir Alfred Hopkinson, Vol. 2, 1902–6, VCA 5, John Rylands Library, University of Manchester. Thanks to Alex Robinson for bringing this letter to my notice.
44 On 9 February 1904, Bertha Cave wrote to Christabel, indicating that she did not wish her application to be seen as a 'feminist' act on behalf of other women: 'I was very pleased to receive your letter, but I wish it to be understood that I am in no way acting in concert with other women aspirants to the Bar', EWEP, Vol. V, Add Ms 47,453, f.239. Ivy Williams had obtained her LLD from London University in 1903 and like all women had to wait until the passing of the Sex Disqualification (Removal) Act of 1919 before being allowed admission to the legal profession. She was called to the Bar in June 1922 and was the first woman barrister in England.
45 J. Dawson, Our woman's letter, *Clarion*, 22 January 1904.
46 APW, The philosophy of the suffragette movement, pp. 19–20.
47 Crawford, *The women's suffrage movement*, p. 516; Coleman, *Adela Pankhurst*, pp. 28–9.
48 CP, *Unshackled*, p. 42; ESP, TSM, p. 179; J. Brownlow to Mrs Elmy, 19 February 1904 and Mrs Elmy to H. McIlquham, 21 January 1904, EWEP, Vol. V, Add Mss 47,453, fs.241 and 227.
49 CP to Dear Sir [Mr Wallis Grain], 2 February 1904, copy in DMC.
50 EP, *My own story*, p. 40.
51 EP, *My own story*, p. 40.
52 EP, *My own story*, pp. 35–6.
53 CP, *Unshackled*, p. 46. This broad definition of 'militancy' is used throughout this book; see Introduction, note 1.
54 *LL*, 12 March 1904.
55 CP, Letter to the Editor, *LL* and *Clarion*, 26 March and 1 April 1904, respectively.
56 EWE to H. McIlquham, 30 March 1904, EWEP, Add Mss 47,453, f.262.
57 *LL*, 9 April 1904.

58 Entry for 5 April 1904, Bruce Glasier Diaries.

59 P. Snowden, The I.L.P. and women's suffrage, *LL*, 16 April 1904.

60 CP, Letter to the Editor, *LL*, 23 April 1904.

61 Letter from CP quoted by J. Dawson, Our Woman's Letter, *Clarion*, 6 May 1904.

62 For an insightful analysis of the place of women in the ILP see J. Hannam, Women and the ILP, 1890–1914, in *The centennial history of the Independent Labour Party*, eds D. James, T. Jowitt and K. Laybourn (Halifax, Ryburn, 1992), pp. 205–28; and J. Hannam and K. Hunt, *Socialist women: Britain, 1880s to 1920s* (London and New York, Routledge, 2002), Chapter 5.

63 EP and I. Ford, Letter to the Editor, *LL*, 18 November 1904.

64 CP, Letter to the Editor, *Manchester Guardian*, 14 July 1904.

65 Liddington and Norris, *One hand tied behind us*, pp. 178–9.

66 Crawford, *The women's suffrage movement*, p. 249.

67 Lewis, *Eva Gore-Booth and Esther Roper*, p. 97, in a stinging indictment states, '[I]n 1904 Christabel tried to force Eva's hand in making the WTUC declare women's suffrage one of its aims to disastrous effects. From this year to the beginning of the war, Christabel caused the splitting of seven organisations.' Similarly, Liddington and Norris, *One hand tied behind us*, p. 179 comment that Christabel 'was prepared to take action independent of suffragists with whom she had previously worked closely and considered her friends, even if this entailed the risk of wrecking nearly ten years of patient trade union effort'.

68 S. Lewenhak, *Women and trade unions: an outline history of women in the British trade union movement* (London and Tonbridge, Ernest Benn, 1977), pp. 134–5.

69 EWE to H. McIlquham, 18 July 1904, EWEP, Add Mss 47,453, f.308.

70 CP to Mr Wallis Grain, 21 July 1904, copy in DMC.

71 CP to Mr Wallis Grain, 28 July 1904, copy in DMC.

72 EWE to H. McIlquham, 5 July 1904, EWEP, Add Mss 47453, f.303.

73 I. Husted Harper, *The life and work of Susan B. Anthony* (Indianapolis, IN, Hollenbeck Press, 1908), Vol. III, p. 1331; CP, Woman's rights, an American reformer in Manchester, *Daily Dispatch*, 25 July 1904.

74 Womanly Mrs. Pankhurst, *The Woman's Journal*, 30 October 1909.

75 EP, *My own story*, p. 37.

76 *LL*, 14 October 1904; Report of the Executive Committee of the North of England Society for Women's Suffrage, Presented at the annual meeting, 8 November 1904 (Manchester, 'Guardian' General Printing Works), p. 10.

77 EWE to H. McIlquham, 15 October 1904, EWEP, Add Mss 47,454, fs.25.

78 CP to Mrs Elmy, 23 and 24 November 1904, TWL.

79 Report of a national convention of the National Union of Women's Suffrage Societies, London, 25 and 26 November 1904, *Women's Suffrage Record*, 31 December 1904, p. 12.

6

CHRISTABEL AND ANNIE
GO TO PRISON

1905

Christabel's insistence that women's enfranchisement would particularly benefit working women did little to pacify working-class activists like Ada Nield Chew from Rochdale, a member of the ILP and Adult Suffrage League. Just before Christmas 1904, Ada had written angry letters to both the *Labour Leader* and the *Clarion*, complaining about the ILP's support for a Women's Enfranchisement Bill that would give votes to women on the same terms as men. If such a measure became law, she argued, 'wealthy men' would not stand idly by but would ensure that their wives, daughters and sisters had enough property to be enfranchised, so that Labour male voters would be swamped. Thus the 'entire class of wealthy women would be enfranchised' by this limited bill while 'the great body of working women, married or single, would be voteless still'.[1] Eva Gore-Booth and colleagues, on behalf of the Manchester and Salford Women's Trade and Labour Council, disagreed, pointing out that they welcomed any practical step towards the final aim of womanhood suffrage, a position also supported by the leadership of the Women's Co-operative Guild.[2] Christabel plunged into the controversy, challenging Ada Nield Chew in an acrimonious exchange of views that was to run through the spring and into March of 1905.

'Some of us are not at all so confident as is Mrs. Chew of the average middle-class man's anxiety to confer votes upon his female relatives', she commented acidly. Christabel continued:

> We who support that Bill know, if Mrs. Chew does not, that some of the worst enemies of the enfranchisement of women are to be found among the official Liberals, the very same men being warm supporters of the proposal to extend the franchise as regards men.[3]

An angry Ada Nield Chew replied that she would never support a bill based on property qualifications, which prompted Christabel to point out that her antagonist had 'misunderstood' the situation. The Women's Enfranchisement Bill, Christabel insisted, was not based on property qualifications but provided that all Acts of Parliament, present or future, which conferred the franchise should apply to women, the majority of whom would be 'working women'.[4] The heated exchange between these two strong-minded individuals became particularly strained after Christabel invited Ada to conduct a survey in her own town of Rochdale as to the proportion of working women to women of property who would be enfranchised by the bill. 'She will find', Christabel remarked coolly, 'that about 90 per cent will be workers.'[5] A sharp-tongued Ada Nield Chew turned down the invitation, insisting not only that she was too busy to spare the time but that '[w]orking women and the Labour Party have surely better work to do than to fight the battles of women rich enough and intelligent enough to do it for themselves'.[6] After Christabel re-asserted that the Women's Enfranchisement Bill had the support of socialists, the bitter exchange faded away.[7]

Christabel's resolve in this matter had been strengthened by events that had taken place at the LRC Conference two months earlier, in late January 1905. Her mother had tried to persuade the Conference to support the Women's Enfranchisement Bill, arguing along the same lines as Christabel, but the delegates supported instead an amendment in favour of adult suffrage, some four hundred and eighty-three for and two hundred and seventy against.[8] Christabel and Emmeline had been bitterly disappointed with this setback. 'I feel deeply grieved at our defeat', wrote Emmeline to Philip Snowden who, shortly to be married to suffragist Ethel Annakin, was unexpectedly supporting the Women's Enfranchisement Bill, seeing it as a way to concede the principle of sex equality and as an important step towards adult suffrage. 'If you knew how I long to get this *vote* question settled', penned Emmeline:

> I am so weary of it and long long years of struggle first against ridicule and contempt and now of indifference and apathy . . . how much my daughter and I felt your kind manner on Saturday morning and your understanding words of sympathy.[9]

There was one consolation, namely that Keir Hardie promised to introduce the bill in Parliament as a private member's bill, provided he was successful in the ballot due to take place on 21 February. Fearful that Hardie might not be lucky in the draw, Emmeline travelled to London about one week beforehand and day after day stood in the lobby of the House of Commons, with Sylvia and a few other suffragists, imploring MPs who professed to be supportive of women's suffrage to give priority to the women's bill if they were fortunate enough to be allocated one of the fourteen places. Not one agreed. Despair crept in when the news arrived that Hardie had not drawn a place. After frantic lobbying, the Liberal MP Bamford Slack, who held the fourteenth place and whose wife was a member of the executive committee of the NUWSS, was persuaded to introduce the bill.[10]

When Emmeline arrived back home at 62 Nelson Street, she complained bitterly to Christabel about the lethargy of the NUWSS women who had offered no help. Soon Emmeline was writing to the London-based Dora Montefiore. 'Is it possible to form a Women's Parliamentary Committee in London to do this lobbying work? The old-fashioned and official gang will never do it. I have no confidence in them.'[11] Christabel had no faith in the 'old-fashioned and official gang' either and so, together with her mother and Teresa Billington, she continued to speak in towns in Lancashire and Yorkshire time and time again, in support of the Women's Enfranchisement Bill.[12]

On Sunday, 23 April 1905, at a crowded meeting at the Free Trade Hall, Manchester, Christabel engaged in debate with Mrs Jennie Baker, from Stockton, a keen adult suffragist. 'Both did well', noted Bruce Glaiser, who presided. 'Miss P smarter.'[13] Even Sylvia recorded for posterity that her sister was the 'easy victor'.[14] The following day, the opening day of the ILP Conference, Christabel again put the case forcibly for women's suffrage, claiming that although she was an adult suffragist, the alternative to the bill was not adult suffrage but manhood suffrage. 'The Labour Party must settle this question', she insisted. 'It is a Socialist question, and the Labour Party cannot afford to neglect the appeal of their sisters in their hour of need.' Teresa Billington and Keir Hardie stood on the same platform, making their speeches in favour too, as did three other suffragists. The delegates were impressed so that the resolution in favour of the bill was overwhelmingly carried. For the *Labour Leader*, it was the charming Christabel, who spoke 'clearly and strongly, and met a flattering reception', who was the impressive figure.[15]

A 'thrill of excitement' ran through WSPU ranks and the older suffrage societies at the news that the Women's Enfranchisement Bill was set down to be presented in the Commons on 12 May 1905, the first women's suffrage bill in eight years.[16] Meetings were held and petitions organised as new life sprang into the movement. The energetic Christabel continued speaking at local trade councils while the hopeful Emmeline returned to Westminster. On 12 May, Emmeline, accompanied by Elizabeth Wolstehenholme Elmy, Isabella Ford and Dora Montefiore, was one of about three hundred women who thronged the Strangers' Lobby and surrounding areas on the House of Commons.[17] The Women's Enfranchisement Bill was Second Order of the day which meant that the anti-suffragists could, if they so wished, talk it out by prolonging discussion of the First Order measure, a bill to compel carts travelling along public roads at night to carry a light at the rear. Keir Hardie had pleaded to those promoting the latter, to no avail, to withdraw their bill so that the women's bill could have more time. The feared outcome happened. The debate about the Lighting of Vehicles Bill was deliberately spun out from noon to four o'clock as silly stories and foolish jokes were told. At four o'clock Bamford Slack rose to move the second reading of the women's bill and after half an hour, the aged Henry Labouchere, a fierce opponent of women's suffrage, rose to make a long anti-suffrage speech. 'It was the same speech that he has made so often before', an angry Emmeline later told *Labour Leader* readers. 'It contained the same jokes, the same coarse references to women, and it was received, as some women saw and heard, by the House with laughter and cheers.'[18] By such means, the bill was talked out since at half past five the House adjourned and no division could be taken.

Christabel was despondent but not in despair when she heard the news of the bill's defeat. A few days before the bill was 'talked out', she and the small band of WSPU women had begun holding joint weekly Sunday meetings with the ILP in Tib Street, Manchester, to publicise their cause.[19] Some months before, the ranks of the WSPU speakers had been swelled by the recruitment of two new working-class women, Hannah Maria Mitchell (nee Webster) and Annie Kenney, both of whom subsequently wrote their autobiographies.[20] But it was the arrival of Annie Kenney in particular into the membership of the WSPU that had far-reaching consequences for both Christabel and the suffrage campaign. Annie became not only a close friend but later rose to a leadership position within the Union, the only woman of working-class origin to do so. The warm friendship between Christabel and Annie would last through two world wars and span over fifty years, being broken only by Annie's death in 1953. It was the most significant friendship that Christabel was to form during her lifetime and one that she cherished, even in old age when the two lived on different continents, miles apart from each other.

Annie Kenney had been born in the Pennine village of Springhead, Saddleworth, in Lancashire, on 13 September 1879 and was therefore one year older than Christabel. The fifth of eleven children, she had grown up in a financially stretched but happy household where both parents worked in a cotton factory. At the tender age of ten, Annie began work as a half-timer, becoming a full-time factory hand three years later. She worked long hours, rising at five each morning so that she could be at the factory just before six, leaving at half past five each night. As a wage earner, Annie noticed that when her working brothers and sisters put their weekly wages into the family purse, the boys were given much more than the girls as pocket money. And when her parents came home after a day in the factory, her father would sit reading or go to a club or public meeting while her mother had to do various household chores till midnight.[21] Annie's feminist awareness of the injustices women experienced began to grow, as well as her religious conviction. She became a Sunday School teacher and, at the age of seventeen, was confirmed in the Church of England. At the age of twenty, her political education began when an interest in the Labour movement was kindled, largely through reading Robert Blatchford's articles in the *Clarion*.

However, the *Clarion* gave to Annie more than an introduction to socialism; it opened up for her a wider literary world in which she discovered a range of writers and poets such as Walt Whitman, William Morris, Edward Carpenter, John Ruskin and Charles Lamb. Keen to communicate her newly found enthusiasm for socialism and literature, she circulated the *Clarion* among her workmates at the Wood End Factory, as well as works of poetry, literature and art.[22] Unfortunately, Annie then found herself among the fifty or so women operatives who were laid off when the owner of the factory went bankrupt. It was not until about fifteen weary months later that she was hired again but then found that her new employer was paying women wages below the level to which they were entitled. She encouraged the women to strike until they received the wages that were their due, a request to which their employer agreed.[23]

Annie was deeply upset when her mother died, early in the New Year of 1905. Keen for new interests and companionship, she joined the Oldham Clarion Vocal Union and sang socialist songs. She became good friends with another singer, Jane Ogden, who was also a member of the Oldham Trades Council. And it was during that spring of 1905 that the Oldham Trades Council invited Christabel and Teresa Billington to speak. Annie, an active socialist, attended the meeting with her sisters, at Jane's invitation, not expecting much to happen. 'I had never heard about Votes for Women', she confessed. But she was soon converted to the women's cause. Although Christabel seemed the less impressive speaker, being 'more hesitating, more nervous' than Teresa, it was Christabel, with her zeal, who impressed her. Christabel spoke not of women's woes and helplessness, but of the need for young working women, especially women cotton factory workers, to be politically active, 'to rise up and fight for their rights'.[24] At the end of the meeting, the enthralled Annie and her sisters approached Christabel, asking if she would address an Oldham meeting of factory women if it was arranged for them. Christabel agreed.

The rapport between the twenty-six-year-old Annie and the twenty-five-year-old Christabel was instant. Annie had a presence about her that was appealing; with her striking physical appearance, especially her luminous blue eyes and her loosely dressed golden hair piled high on top of her head, she stood out from the other more drab-looking women in the audience. But it was what she said and how she said it that impressed Christabel, who 'hoped great things' from this first contact with the lively woman who was to become her closest friend.[25] Annie had a powerful although not melodious voice and spoke with a pronounced Lancashire accent. Chirpy, and with a great sense of humour, she spoke her mind. She had a pithy, vivid turn of phrase, enhanced by the fact that she 'could not speak grammar', as one suffragette later phrased it.[26] Christabel recognised Annie's potential both as a speaker and as a magnet to draw other working-class women to the suffrage cause. And so Annie was persuaded to say a few words at the Oldham meeting.

However, on the night in question, there was so little interest in women's suffrage that the choir and the speakers vastly outnumbered the audience of two. Undeterred, Christabel had soon arranged for Annie to give a longer speech at one of the Tib Street meetings. The intensely nervous and highly strung Annie, whose request for exemption was not granted, never forgot the way her middle-class friend helped to nurture her latent talent.[27] She adored the gifted and educated Christabel and would loyally follow her. Nonetheless, Annie became a charismatic figure in her own right, an inspiring speaker, strong-minded and capable of taking the initiative, when necessary.

Soon 62 Nelson Street became Annie's second home. Evening by evening, after her day's work, and on Saturday afternoons, she would take the train to Manchester, doing any work that was necessary for the WSPU. Hannah Mitchell would visit too and remembered meeting Annie there and her sister, Jenny. They were 'good-looking, well-mannered young women, wearing dark costumes of excellent quality, with white silk blouses. Both were fine examples of the self-respecting Lancashire mill girl, intellectual and independent'.[28] Bubbling with ideas and impatient to be useful, Annie suggested to Christabel that they should set up their platform in Lancashire villages on the Sunday before the annual fairs or wakes began.

That summer of 1905, Christabel, Annie and the rest of the small band of WSPU women passed from wake to wake in places such as Staley Bridge, Royton, Mosley, Oldham, Lees and Hyde, competing for an audience with quack medicine vendors, temperance orators or Salvation Army and other preachers. Sylvia often took the chair since she was home for the holidays. 'I have a young woman here to speak to you who has worked as a half-time hand in the cotton mill, and another young woman who wants to be a lawyer', she would begin.[29] After one meeting at Blackburn, an impressed trade union official asked Annie if she would help them to persuade local women to join the union. Christabel, seeing ready-made audiences for suffrage talks in such a clientele, advised her friend to accept the invitation. Annie went about her work with gusto so that after two weeks she had recruited more women to the local union than had joined in the previous year. Boosted by this success, she now followed another suggestion made by Emmeline and Christabel, that she further her political apprenticeship by standing for election to the all-male committee of the Lees card and blowing-room operatives, to which she belonged. Annie was duly elected.

She used the shilling paid to each member of the committee for being present at committee meetings to further her education by enrolling as a corresponding student in a course on trade unionism, run by Ruskin College, Oxford.[30] Her experience in local politics, dealing with rough working-class men, many opposed to women's enfranchisement, would stand her in good stead in years to come.

Annie's involvement in the WSPU 1905 summer campaign was restricted by the free time she had after her factory work and the few holidays that were her lot. Christabel, on vacation from her university studies, faced fewer limits. She threw herself into women's suffrage work in Lancashire and Yorkshire, speaking not only under the WSPU banner but also under the auspices of the North of England Society and the ILP. July in particular was a frantic month as she gave well over twenty speeches, at least seven being for the North of England Society where her friends Esther Roper and Eva Gore-Booth were active too.[31] Elizabeth Wolstenholme Elmy could not praise Christabel enough. 'How grandly dear Christabel & her mother are working for W.S. [Women's Suffrage]', she confided to a friend:

> It is C's holiday time just now, & she is speaking 3 or 4 times each week, & twice or thrice each Sunday . . . & Mrs. Pankhurst almost as often. The best work of W.S. is being done by the splendid workers outside the N.U. [NUWSS], which seems quite incapable of rising to the greatness of the question.[32]

Elizabeth also noted that 'in nine cases out of ten', Christabel and her mother had 'to pay their own travelling & other expenses, which is a very heavy pull on a small income'.[33]

Not all of Christabel's talks during this summer of 1905, however, were restricted to a women's suffrage theme. She was still a member of the Manchester Central Branch of the ILP and committed to a socialist programme of social reform. Thus on Sunday, 2 July, she spoke at West Salford ILP on 'What the Labour Party would do for children', while at the local Altrincham branch one week later her theme was 'Woman from a socialist standpoint'.[34] She also spoke at several meetings held to press on the Government the necessity of passing the Unemployed Workmen Relief Bill that had been introduced by Walter Long, the president of the Local Government Board. At the big Heaton Moor demonstration, organised by various Labour councils in the area, she shared a platform with W. E. Skivington, John Harker and Leonard Hall, among others, while Eva Gore-Booth was on the second platform and Emmeline on the fourth.[35]

Further national demonstrations in support of the unemployed bill were held in industrial towns throughout England. However, by late July, it seemed that this measure was fated not to be brought before Parliament that session, although the Government did find time for a bill dealing with a dispute between the Scottish Free Churches and the United Free Church of Scotland. When questioned in the House of Commons about this, the Conservative Prime Minister Arthur Balfour explained that a particular 'crisis' had made necessary the Scottish Bill, whereas it was not absolutely necessary to deal with the unemployed that session.[36] Such insensitive remarks acted like a lightning rod to many in the Labour movement. On 31 July, a protest by four hundred to five hundred and fifty unemployed, ragged men marched through central Manchester where a scuffle broke out with the police who used their batons. Four men were arrested. One of the leaders of the protest pointed out that the marchers 'were doing what Mr. Balfour had told them to do – to create a crisis'.[37] Within two weeks, despite denials that it was acting in response to the Manchester 'riot', the Government had found time to pass the unemployed relief bill. Keen to help, Emmeline suggested that the Labour group on the city council and the emergency committee of the ILP meet at her house to discuss how best to take advantage of the new relief provision.[38] That protests, demonstrations and arrests had created a 'crisis' that forced the Government to act was noted by Christabel, who carefully assessed the new militant mood in the ILP. Whatever its shortcomings on the women's issue, she was astute enough to realise that its methods bore fruit.

Some months earlier, Christabel and some of the other WSPU members had angrily confronted Keir Hardie with their complaints about the hostile attitude of too many ILP men towards women's suffrage. Hardie listened with great sympathy. The ILP must be brought into line, he retorted; votes for women on the same terms as men must be supported and a big campaign mounted. Give him the necessary data, he told the irate Christabel, and he would prepare a pamphlet and get the ILP to publish it. Christabel did such a thorough job in writing out the arguments and presenting the facts that all Hardie had to do was write a preface and conclusion. The pamphlet, titled *The citizenship of women: a plea for women's suffrage*, written during that summer of 1905, was published the following year but with only Hardie's name on it.[39] In this text, effectively her second major publication, Christabel summarised the case for women's suffrage, as had been advanced from the days of John Stuart Mill and her father Dr Richard Pankhurst, and also the adult versus women's suffrage controversy. 'The "half angel, half idiot", period is over in the woman's world', she asserted:

> She is fighting her way into every sphere of human activity . . . Sooner or later men will be compelled to . . . recognise her as a co-worker, and they could not begin better than by admitting her right to be a co-voter.[40]

Mrs Elmy continued to be impressed. 'Christabel speaks twice to-day in Albert Square, Manchester', she proudly informed Harriet McIlquham on 13 August. 'Last Sunday from 7,000 to 8,000 persons attended the meetings. They are <u>primarily</u> on the unemployment question, but she always works in W.S.'[41] Indeed, a few days later, under the auspices of the WSPU, Christabel spoke on women's suffrage when she addressed the Leigh Board of Guardians, the theme also of talks in mid-September in Hartlepool and West Hartlepool.[42] But she never lost her interest in socialist issues, speaking to the Middlesbrough ILP in late September not only on unemployment but also on a recent Government measure that had been passed, an Order for Underfed School Children.[43] Christabel was working hard to keep the socialist movement on her side, if possible.

She returned to Manchester and began the final year of her legal degree in a dejected mood. What was the point of campaigning so hard when the women's suffrage issue bore no fruit? The old tactics pursued by the NUWSS, the North of England Society and the WSPU of lobbying MPs to bring in a private member's bill were futile. Since 1870, nineteen such bills had failed to bring a women's suffrage measure, and now Bamford Slack's bill had suffered the same fate. It was an insult to women. Only a bill supported by the Government had any chance of becoming law. The Government, apparently, as revealed by the passing of the Unemployed Bill, responded to coercion. The protest by the Manchester unemployed had been quite 'a small and mild affair', Christabel believed, but had grown in the telling, becoming a 'riot' by the time it reached London's politicians. 'Militancy by the unemployed, *militancy that was only thought to have happened*, moved the Government to do what before they would not or could not do!' Christabel reasoned that the WSPU had to draw upon this male socialist tradition of radical protest and do something similar for a women's suffrage measure to be passed.[44] The time-honoured method of 'kicking up a row' was one way to move forward the slow procedures of parliamentary government. The WSPU was 'making no headway, our meetings were not reported . . . our work was not counting', Christabel later told one reporter. 'I knew that if a blow was to be struck for women's freedom the time had come to strike.'[45]

With that sharp political insight that was to serve her in good stead in the years to come, Christabel decided it was pointless to waste energy on the failing Conservative Government of twenty years and better to target those in the Liberal Party who were likely to be in office after the January 1906 election. The future Liberal leaders, soon to hold a major rally on Friday, 13 October, at the Free Trade Hall, Manchester, must be challenged on the fundamental principle of Liberalism – whether government of the people by the people included women – and a direct question asked as to whether the Liberals intended to enfranchise women. Christabel knew that the answer would not be in the affirmative and so intended this time that her protest should not be merely one of words but one of deeds, kicking up a row that would result in imprisonment. Imprisonment would bring publicity, force the women's cause into the public eye, be 'a proof of women's political discontent, a demonstration that the political subjection of women rested not on women's consent but on *force majeure* used to impose and enforce it'.[46]

Christabel discussed her new confrontational tactics in confidence with just a few trusted people – her mother, Annie and Teresa Billington. It was decided that Emmeline could not take part in the Free Trade Hall protest since it might jeopardise her work as Registrar of Births and Deaths, her main source of support for herself and her family. Instead, Christabel, Annie and Teresa would have the task of asking a question about votes for women when Sir Edward Grey, the main speaker, would outline future Liberal policy. The day before the event, however, the worried Emmeline pointed out that she thought it best if only Christabel and Annie went to the meeting, since she would find it difficult to deal with the organisation of protest meetings and letters to the press if all three were imprisoned. Teresa, as a newly paid ILP organiser who had pledged herself to organise branch meetings as part of the campaign, could not be spared.[47]

On the afternoon of 13 October, Christabel and Annie stood at the big dining room table at 62 Nelson Street making a small banner from a swatch of calico on which they painted, in black polish, 'Votes for Women'. They did their job so thoroughly that the stain seeped through the material, staining the table top with the bold letters.[48] That evening, with the banner tucked inside her blouse, Christabel bade her anxious mother farewell with the words, 'We shall sleep in prison tonight.' Calm, but with 'beating hearts', she and Annie took their seats at the back of the Free Trade Hall. After Sir Edward Grey had finished his speech, in which there was no mention of women's suffrage, Annie rose and asked the question that Christabel had phrased in advance – 'Will the Liberal Government give votes to women?' No answer was given and so Christabel jumped up, repeating the question while unfurling the banner. 'The effect was explosive!' she recalled. 'The meeting was aflame with excitement.'[49] Once the angry cries from the audience had died down, the Chief Constable of Manchester made his way to where the two were sitting and promised that if their question was put in writing, an answer would be given after the vote of thanks. Annie scribbled the question on a piece of notepaper which was taken to Sir Edward Grey. He smiled when he read it.

Christabel and Annie sat patiently, waiting, but found that Grey's response to the vote of thanks included not one word in answer to their question. Immediately Annie, with her loose hair flowing (she had taken off her hat), stood on her chair and asked the question again. The audience became a mob as hordes of angry men shouted and roared, shaking their fists while the stewards rushed to drag her down. The protective Christabel put one arm around her companion's waist and with the other warded off the blows. As she did so, the men scratched and tore at her arm and hand so that blood flowed down onto Annie's hat that lay upon the seat. The two women held together, shouting over and over 'The question, the question, answer the question!'

Soon six men, Liberal stewards and plain-clothes policemen, dragged Christabel down the central aisle into the anteroom of the Free Trade Hall, others following with Annie. As they passed the platform, the Liberal leaders sat in silence. While the men in the front seats shouted 'Throw them out!', those in the free seats at the back roared 'Shame!'[50] Christabel knew from her legal studies that simply disturbing a meeting would not result in imprisonment and so committed the technical offence of assault. According to the testimony given the following day by Inspector Mather, she spat in the face of Superintendent Watson before repeating the action in regard to himself, also striking him in the mouth. The two women were then ejected into South Street where Christabel struck him again. He asked the women to go away, but they refused, shouting excitedly and drawing a crowd. He had no choice but to conduct them to the police station. During the journey, he continued, Miss Kenney clung to Miss Pankhurst, treading on her skirt so that the garment lay on the pavement.[51] Arriving in a dishevelled state, the two were charged with obstructing a footway and assaulting the police. Both were released and ordered to appear in court the next day.

The next morning, before her court case, Christabel read the hostile newspaper accounts of their action, considered more appropriate to women of the slums. 'If any argument were required against giving to ladies political status and power, it has been furnished in Manchester', opined the *Daily Mail*. 'If Miss Pankhurst desires to go to gaol rather than pay the money, let her go', stated the *Evening Standard*, which thought that the two women had behaved like 'children in the nursery'. A crumb of comfort and offer of help came in a telegram from Keir Hardie. 'The thing is a dastardly outrage', he suggested, 'but do not worry, it will do immense good to the Cause. Can I do anything?'[52]

Up before the crowded police court, Christabel dared not explain the technical and symbolic character of her assault for fear of being discharged. Coyly she claimed that the supposed 'spit' was really only a 'pout', a perfectly dry purse of the mouth.[53] Listening in the court to the evidence against her, she did not dispute the charges. 'My conduct in the Free Trade Hall and outside was meant as a protest against the legal position of women today', she explained. 'We cannot make any orderly protest because we have not the means whereby citizens may do such a thing; we have not a vote; and so long as we have not votes we must be disorderly.'[54]

The magistrates returned a verdict of guilty for both women. For assaulting the police, Christabel was sentenced to a fine of 10s. 6d. and costs, or seven days' imprisonment, and a further 5s. or three days' imprisonment for obstructing a public highway, both sentences to run concurrently. Annie was only found guilty of obstruction and offered the choice of a 5s. fine or three days in jail. On hearing the sentences, Christabel responded defiantly, 'I shall pay no fine', to which Annie added, 'Hear, hear'.[55] The anxious Emmeline, sitting in the courtroom, hastily followed both women into the room into which they were ushered and told them she would pay their fines. But the resolute Christabel replied, 'Mother, if you pay my fine I will never go home.'[56] Emmeline did not disagree since she believed that her first-born had the finest political instinct.

Christabel's brilliant tactic of interrupting male political discourse and insisting that women were treated as active participants in the male sphere of public politics brought welcome publicity for the women's cause.[57] The incident was broadcast not only in the local press but also in national newspapers such as the *Times* and the *Globe*, as well as abroad. The *Manchester Guardian* carried a full report of the trial under the headline 'Miss Pankhurst and the Police' and also published an article about the WSPU by Teresa Billington who worked energetically, with Emmeline, to organise protest meetings and pen letters to the press.[58] Space was also given to the meeting protesting about the treatment of Christabel and Annie which, despite a cold, drizzling rain, attracted some one thousand men and women in Stevenson Square on Saturday evening, 14 October. The majority of the speakers were WSPU women, including Emmeline, Teresa and Hannah Mitchell. The fiery Emmeline said how proud she was to be the mother of one of the young noble women who had gone to prison in the endeavour to bring the question of women's rights to the forefront. She echoed the thoughts of many when she condemned the violence with which the two had been ejected from the Free Trade Hall.[59] Emmeline Pankhurst identified herself with the new tactics 'promptly and unreservedly', wrote Evelyn Sharp many years later, evidence not only of her perception but also of her 'perfect understanding' with Christabel. Mrs Pankhurst had many qualities that made her an exceptional woman, 'not the least of them was the vision that primarily enabled her to detect where the younger woman excelled in political acumen and freshness of outlook'.[60]

For Christabel and Annie in Strangeways Gaol, locked in their box-like cells dimly lit by high, small windows, furnished with plank beds, straw mattresses, tin utensils and an unhygienic wooden spoon, the hardships were barely noticeable. 'We were thinking of other things', remembered Christabel. People regularly came, offering to pay her fine, including a visiting magistrate, an old friend of her father's. Christabel even heard a rumour that the Liberal MP, Winston Churchill, who had shared Sir Edward Grey's platform, had sent an emissary with the very same purpose. 'We neither knew nor cared to know who had tried to release us before the day which the law and our own resolve had fixed. Annie and I knew that in the contest of wills our will must prevail.'[61] Yet the less robust Annie felt troubled by the strangeness of prison life, which brought out the protective side of her companion. When the two went to the prison chapel, Annie remembered how Christabel 'took my hand tenderly and just held it, as though I were a lost child being guided home . . . I saw that she had confidence in me and . . . [that] gave me confidence in myself'.[62] Released on the morning of 16 October, Annie was greeted by a sea of strange faces as well as members of the Clarion choir, two of her sisters, some factory women and Emmeline Pankhurst. 'Annie, as long as I have a home you must look upon it as yours. You will never have to return to factory life', said Emmeline warmly.[63] That evening Annie received an ovation from two thousand people assembled in Stevenson Square.

Meanwhile, Christabel was still in prison and doing all the things prisoners had to do, including scrubbing and cleaning her cell. Over a thousand persons stood outside the prison gates at eight o'clock in the morning of 20 October, ready to greet her, including her mother, Annie, Eva Gore-Booth, Hannah Mitchell and Sam Robinson, chair of the Manchester Branch of the ILP. But, as everyone came forward, 'one outstripped the rest', Christabel recollected. 'She was a complete stranger to me, but she gave me the first greeting. It was Flora Drummond. We were friends at sight. She became another pillar of the movement and one of its most notable personalities.'[64] Flora Drummond, manager of a typing pool in Manchester which she had now placed at the service of the WSPU, was born in 1879. She had experienced injustice early in her life when, having trained to work as a post mistress for the Post Office, she was refused admission because she was one inch below the regulation height. The rejection rankled with Flora who saw it as a discriminatory practice against women who were usually shorter than men. Both Flora and her husband, a journeyman upholsterer, were early members of the ILP and the Fabian Society, Flora also being a keen member of her local Clarion Club.[65] Good at organising and directing, Flora Drummond would soon be known, affectionately, as 'The General' because of her pugnacity and her habit of riding a horse at the head of the WSPU processions, dressed in a paramilitary uniform, complete with epaulettes and peak cap.

Flora was one of many sympathetic women who attended the big reception for Christabel and Annie in the Free Trade Hall which Teresa Billington and Sam Robinson had been planning for a week. The hall was packed to overflowing that evening of 20 October. On the platform sat a representative of nearly every woman's organisation in Manchester and district, as well as Elizabeth Wolsthenholme Elmy. The chair, Leonard Hall of the ILP, set the tone of the meeting by saying he wished there were a million women or men in England who had half the spirit of the two women they were honouring tonight. John Harker, President of the Manchester and Salford Trades and Labour Council, moved a resolution demanding the parliamentary franchise for women on the same terms as it is or may be granted to men. Then it was the turn of the heroines, who were each presented with bouquets. The audience gave the nervous Annie an ovation as she rose to deliver her speech but when Christabel was introduced, some boos could be heard among the cheers, an indication that not all those present approved of her tactics. Nonplussed by the mild dissent, Christabel spoke with passion and fire, describing how she and Annie had asked a question about votes for women at a Liberal Party meeting and were going to do the same at Tory meetings. Mr Balfour, a Tory and the current Prime Minister, wanted 'a crisis' before he would legislate. As far as the women in England were concerned, she concluded, to rousing cheers, 'there was a crisis'.[66] Then Keir Hardie spoke, condemning the 'brutal and unjustifiable treatment' that Miss Kenney and Miss Pankhurst had received. He was proud, he declared, to belong to a party which had in its ranks such fine women who would endure 'insult, and prison to get justice too long delayed'.[67]

Christabel knew that her militant tactics had worked. News of the Free Trade Hall protest had travelled far beyond Britain. The long years of press silence about votes for women which, by keeping women uninformed, 'had so largely smothered and strangled the movement', were gone, she noted. '[W]here peaceful means had failed, one act of militancy succeeded.'[68] 'I wish you had been at the meeting on Friday', she wrote to the Lancashire working-class suffragist Selina Jane Cooper and her husband, four days after the welcome celebration, as she thanked them for their note of congratulations. 'It was a great success & worth all the unpleasant times we had been through . . . I shall stop at nothing & all the Manchester ILP women seem ready for prison or anything else.' The two hecklers had been asked to address ILP branches at Oldham and Sheffield and so Christabel enquired if anything could be organised in the Coopers' district.[69] Then suddenly, without warning, Christabel's political activity was reined in.

The university authorities were aghast that one of their women undergraduates had served a prison sentence for disorderly conduct and threatened to expel her. It would appear that the Principal, Alfred Hopkinson, made a strong successful intervention on Christabel's behalf. Christabel was called to his office and it was agreed that she would not repeat the tactics she had used at Sir Edward Grey's meeting, although no restrictions were placed on her speaking. On the afternoon of 1 November 1905, Hopkinson read out to the Disciplinary Committee a pledge from Christabel to abide by these rules. 'Having regard to it and to what was said at the former meeting', he wrote to her that evening, 'we feel justified in allowing you to continue your attendance in the University and in taking no further action.'[70] Christabel was grateful for this 'friendly settlement', as she termed it, since she did not wish to abandon her undergraduate degree after nearly two and a half years' work.[71]

After these heady days, Christabel settled down to studying and also acted occasionally as Deputy Registrar for Births and Deaths when her mother was away on suffrage business or ill. On 6 November 1905, for instance, she registered the birth of Donald McMurray, born some six weeks earlier.[72] But women's suffrage was her main aim in life and her advocacy of confrontational methods caused some friction, not only with the other suffrage societies but also with some of her friends, especially the pacifist Eva Gore-Booth who cared little for violence and was intolerant of any embellishment in the story that the two prisoners told about their arrest. A troubled Eva asked Teresa Billington to tell Christabel that she should not 'fit her explanation to her audience. She either deliberately invited imprisonment or she was a victim; she either spat at the policeman or she did not. She can't tell one tale in Manchester & another in Oldham'.[73] The friendship between Eva and Christabel, of which Emmeline Pankhurst had always been jealous, now began to cool. Keen to work hard for her legal degree, Christabel no longer found the time to attend Eva's poetry classes.[74]

Christabel, like Eva, was still a member of the Executive Committee of the North of England Society for Women's Suffrage, and Esther Roper its Secretary. However, 'a Liberal gang' was now dominant in this organisation so that the very idea that some of its key personnel had approved the rowdy interruption of a Liberal Party meeting, and, worse, joined in celebrations organised with the ILP to welcome the prisoners, was viewed with horror.[75] Margaret Ashton, President of the Lancashire and Cheshire Union of the Women's Liberal Association, had taken great exception to what she saw as Labour attacks on Liberals, arguing that the ILP women had retarded rather than hastened the women's cause.[76] In late November 1905, Christabel resigned her membership of the North of England Society, after it had condemned her behaviour. Eva and Esther resigned too, as did a number of other well-known Labour women, including Sarah Reddish, Nellie Keenan and Sarah Dickenson.[77] Eva and Esther did not join Christabel in the WSPU, however, since they disliked intensely militant methods and did not wish to be 'mixed up with and held accountable as a class for educated and upper class women who kick, shriek, bite and spit'.[78] Instead they initially focused their suffrage campaigning through two other bodies in which they were key players and which adopted constitutional methods, namely the clumsily named Lancashire and Cheshire Women's Textile and Other Workers' Representation Committee and the Manchester and Salford Women's Trades and Labour Council.[79] Thus as the year was drawing to a close, it was apparent that there were pronounced differences in the kind of tactics favoured by the various women's suffrage societies.

On 4 December 1905 came the long-expected resignation of Arthur Balfour, the Conservative Prime Minister, and the calling upon Sir Henry Campbell-Bannerman, the Liberal leader, to form an administration until the results of a general election were known. Christabel immediately swung into action, with what Annie called her 'second act of statesmanship', namely a militant election policy.[80] This involved opposing all Government ministers unless a definite promise was forthcoming from the future prime minister, widely believed to be Campbell-Bannerman, that votes for women would be included in the King's Speech in the next parliamentary session. As noted earlier, Christabel had decided long ago that only a Government measure on women's suffrage, not a private member's bill, would bring success, and so it was on the Government that pressure had to be exerted. Since resources were limited, she decided to focus on the candidature for North-West Manchester of the Liberal MP Winston Churchill.

'It has been decided to oppose Mr. Winston Churchill at the General Election, on the ground that he is a member of the Liberal Government which refuses to give Women the Vote', she wrote confidently for the WSPU's election manifesto, the first by-election in which it was to campaign. 'The Government is anxious to have freedom for the Chinese in South Africa, but will not give political freedom to British Women . . . which they have been demanding for some half a century.' Christabel continued:

> Although Liberals profess to believe in political freedom the Liberal leaders have always been opposed to Women's Franchise. It was a Liberal Government in 1884 which refused to give votes to women when the male agricultural labourer was being enfranchised. The present Cabinet contains many enemies and no real friends of Women's Franchise.
>
> INHABITANTS OF NORTH-WEST MANCHESTER!
>
> If you believe that women ought to have political freedom, better wages, and fairer treatment all round, VOTE AND WORK AGAINST WINSTON CHURCHILL AS A MEMBER OF THE LIBERAL GOVERNMENT.[81]

The strategically minded Christabel set about planning how to make the WSPU's general election campaign newsworthy. It was decided that a votes-for-women question must be asked at the first great Liberal rally at the Albert Hall in London, on 21 December, when the Liberal leaders would outline their policy and appeal for national support. Annie and Teresa Billington were chosen to make the protest and since money was short, one of Sylvia's paintings was sold to pay for their fares. Once in London, Annie sent an express letter to Sir Henry Campbell-Bannerman, asking if the new Government would give women the vote. She would be in the hall that night, she pointed out, and if a favourable reply were not given to the question, she would feel obliged to protest. In the middle of the Prime Minister's speech that evening, the nervous Annie, dressed in disguise, asked the question and hung her banner over the private box in which she was sitting. '[E]verybody roared with laughter', she recollected, 'for it was upside down!' Then, from a high balcony, Teresa released her nine-foot-long banner. Pandemonium broke out. The two women were flung from the hall as an organist played loudly, trying to drown the noise.[82]

The following day, Annie, Sylvia and Teresa returned to Manchester for Christmas to find Christabel busy with plans for interruptions at Winston Churchill's meetings. That dry and fine Christmas Eve, they all went carol singing to raise some much-needed money for the WSPU, a grand total of 5s. 6d. being collected.[83] Sylvia attended the crowded opening night of Churchill's campaign and asked the necessary question while displaying a banner. During the uproar that developed, he told the audience that nothing would induce him to vote for giving women the franchise and that he would not be 'hen-pecked' into a question of such grave importance. The next day, the newspapers made much fun of these remarks, one commentator even writing a verse titled

'The Heckler, and the Hen-pecker'.[84] Christabel's youngest sister, Adela, now also began taking part in confrontations at the big public meetings while the fifteen-year-old Harry risked prosecution when, in the early hours of the morning, he pasted strips saying 'Votes for Women' across all the Churchill red and white posters.[85]

Christabel was keen to play a part in all this activity but had to keep her promise to the university authorities not to engage in such rough-and-tumble tactics. Unlike Sylvia, she was deeply sceptical about the support of Labour men for the women's cause and was willing to develop contact with Conservative MPs who professed to be sympathetic. One such man was the defeated Conservative leader, Arthur Balfour, who was fighting a losing battle to retain his East Manchester seat. He agreed to be interviewed at the local Queen's Hotel where he was staying and so Christabel led a small WSPU deputation of Annie Kenney, Flora Drummond and some others to meet him. During the course of the conversation, Balfour was asked why he and his colleagues had not granted women the parliamentary vote when they were in power. 'Well, to tell you the truth, your cause was not in the swim', he replied in his urbane manner. Knowing that there had been peaceful pleading for more than forty years on women's suffrage, the astounded Christabel left the hotel determined that, 'Never again should a political leader, whatever his party, make that the excuse for having refused or neglected to give votes for women.' Only militancy, she reasoned, would keep the issue in 'the political swim'.[86] That popular newspapers such as the *Daily Mail* were regularly covering the activities of the 'suffragettes', as they were now called, including her interview with Balfour, offered confirmation of the effectiveness of the new tactics.[87]

Soon after their departure from the hotel, Christabel and her companions noticed they were being shadowed by detectives. It had already been arranged that some of their group would travel immediately to Liverpool and heckle Sir Henry Campbell-Bannerman, the new Prime Minister, when he spoke there that evening. The detectives, suspicious that this might be the case, followed the women who tried vainly to throw off their pursuers. Eventually Christabel, who was not to be among the protestors, decided that a ruse was necessary to put the enemy off the scent. 'Come and see me off to Liverpool', she said in a very loud voice to her companions. They accompanied her to the station, the detectives shadowing at a distance. With wry amusement, Christabel boarded the train, one of the detectives leaping into the last carriage. After arriving in Liverpool, she walked about, looking in hat-shop windows, visiting large stores and exploring the most attractive parts of the city. Eventually the detective lost the trail and she returned home, to Manchester. Meanwhile, the hecklers, all unsuspected, had made their separate ways to the Sun Hall, Liverpool where each woman in turn repeated the question to the Prime Minister – 'Will your Liberal Government give votes to women?' All were thrown out of the hall without receiving a reply. 'No more ceremonious waiting for question time', reflected Christabel, 'because question time for women never came!'[88]

Notes

1 Ada Nield Chew, Letters to the Editor, *Clarion*, 16 and 30 December 1904. Ada later changed her view, becoming a women's suffragist in the 1910s and also an organiser for the NUWSS.

2 E. Gore-Booth, E. Roper, S. Reddish, S. Dickinson and N. Keenan, Letter to the Editor, *Clarion*, 30 December 1904; M. J. Bury, President, and M. Llewelyn Davies, Secretary of the Women's Co-operative Guild, and A. McLean, President and A. Buchan, Secretary of the Scottish Co-operative Women's Guild, Letter to the Editor, *Clarion*, 30 December 1904.

3 CP, Letter to the Editor, *Clarion*, 6 January 1905.

4 Nield Chew, Letter to the Editor, *Clarion*, 13 January 1905; CP, Letter to the Editor, *Clarion*, 20 January 1905.

5 CP, Letter to the Editor, *Clarion*, 10 February 1905.

6 Nield Chew, Letter to the Editor, *Clarion*, 17 February 1905.

7 CP, Letter to the Editor, *Clarion*, 3 March 1905.

8 Philip Viscount Snowden, *An autobiography, Vol. 1* (London, Ivor Nicholson and Watson, 1934), p. 283.

9 Quoted in Snowden, *An autobiography, Vol. 1*, p. 283.

10 Rosen, *Rise up women!*, p. 36; Purvis, *Emmeline Pankhurst*, pp. 70–1.

11 EP to Dora Montefiore, 19 February 1905, quoted in D. Montefiore, *From a Victorian to a modern* (London, E. Archer, 1927), p. 118.

12 18 March at Oldham Women's Political Union and Trade Council, 25 March Ashton-under-Lyne Trade Council and 20 March Stockport Trade Council, NUWSS, Report of the Executive Committee of the North of England Society for Women's Suffrage (Manchester, 1905), p. 8.

13 Entry for 23 April 1905, Glasier Diaries.

14 ESP, *TSM*, p. 182.

15 *LL*, ILP, annual conference, 28 April 1905.

16 EP, *My own story*, p. 42.

17 National Union of Women's Suffrage Societies, Report of the Executive Committee of the North of England Society for Women's Suffrage (1905), p. 9 notes that Christabel spoke at Hyde Trade Council and Accrington Trade Council on 2 and 9 May, respectively.

18 Mrs Pankhurst, The defeat of the Women's Bill, *LL*, 19 May 1905.

19 *LL*, 12 May 1905.

20 Mitchell, ed, *The hard way up*; A. Kenney, *Memories of a militant* (London, Edward Arnold & Co., 1924).

21 W. T. Stead, Miss Annie Kenney, the suffragette, *Review of Reviews*, June 1906, p. 584.

22 Kenney, *Memories*, pp. 18 and 22–3.

23 F. W. P. L. [Fred Pethick-Lawrence], Character sketch: Miss Kenney, *Labour Record and Review*, April 1906, p. 27.

24 Kenney, *Memories*, pp. 27–8; ESP, *TSM*, p. 186.

25 CP, *Unshackled*, p. 45.

26 ESP, *TSM*, p. 186; Emmeline Pethick-Lawrence to Jill Craigie, 23 September 1944, Craigie Collection.

27 Kenney, *Memories*, pp. 29–30.

28 Mitchell, ed, *The hard way up*, p. 127.

29 ESP, *TSM*, p. 187.

30 Kenney, *Memories*, pp. 31–2.

31 National Union of Women's Suffrage Societies, Report of the Executive Committee of the North of England Society for Women's Suffrage (1905), pp. 9–10 notes that Christabel spoke at Mexboro's Trade Council on 3 July, Darlington on the 5th, Barrow on the 12th, Leicester on the 18th, Bolton on the 19th, Blackburn on the 25th and Huddersfield on

the 27th. *LL*, 7 July 1905, p. 165 notes that she spoke at branches of the ILP for Manchester Central and West Salford, and also with her mother at an open-air women's franchise meeting organised by the WSPU.

32 EWE to H. McIlquham, 5 July 1905, EWEP, Add Mss 47,454, f.124.

33 EWE to H. McIlquham, 12 July 1905, EWEP, Add Mss 47,454, f.125.

34 *LL*, 7 and 14 July 1905.

35 *LL*, 7 July 1905.

36 House of Commons Debates (hereafter H. C. Deb.), 4s. Vol. 150, 26 July 1905, columns 256–7.

37 Quoted in Rosen, *Rise up women!*, p. 48.

38 *LL*, 18 August 1905.

39 ESP, TSM, p. 169.

40 J. Keir Hardie, *The citizenship of women: a plea for women's suffrage* (London, ILP, 1906), pp. 14–15.

41 EWE to H. McIlquham, 13 August 1905, EWEP, Add Mss 47,454, f.134.

42 *LL*, 18 August and 22 September 1905.

43 *LL*, 29 September 1905.

44 CP, *Unshackled*, pp. 48–9. On this point see K. Hardie, Women and politics, in *The case for women's suffrage*, ed B. Villiers (London, T. Fisher Unwin, 1907), p. 79 and, more recently, Lawrence, Contesting the male polity.

45 Hatton, A chat with Christabel Pankhurst.

46 CP, *Unshackled*, p. 48.

47 Plan period of study & teaching record, TBG Papers.

48 CP to Helen Pethick-Lawrence, 2 May 1957, Purvis Collection.

49 CP, *Unshackled*, p. 50.

50 ESP, *The suffragette*, pp. 27–8.

51 *Manchester Guardian*, 16 October 1905.

52 Quoted in ESP, TSM, p. 190.

53 CP, *Unshackled*, p. 52.

54 *Manchester Guardian*, 16 October 1905.

55 *Manchester Guardian*, 16 October 1905.

56 EP, *My own story*, p. 49.

57 Marcus, Introduction, p. 9.

58 *Manchester Guardian*, 16 October 1905.

59 *Manchester Evening News*, 16 October 1905; *LL*, 20 October 1905.

60 E. Sharp, Emmeline Pankhurst and militant suffrage, *Nineteenth Century*, April 1930, pp. 518–19.

61 CP, *Unshackled*, pp. 53–4.

62 Kenney, *Memories*, pp. 39–40.

63 Kenney, *Memories*, p. 41.

64 CP, *Unshackled*, p. 54.

65 Banks, *The biographical dictionary of British feminists Vol. 1*, p. 70; Crawford, *The women's suffrage movement*, p. 175.

66 *LL*, 27 October 1905.

67 *LL*, 27 October 1905.

68 CP, *Unshackled*, p. 55.

69 CP to Mr and Mrs Cooper, 24 October 1905, Selina Jane Cooper Papers, Lancashire Record Office, Preston.

70 Alfred Hopkinson to Miss Pankhurst, 1 November 1905, Letter Book of Sir Alfred Hopkinson, Vol. 2 1902–1906 (VCA/5), John Rylands Library, University of Manchester; Elizabeth Wolstenholme Elmy to Harriet McIlquham, 14 December 1905, EWEP, Add Mss 47, 454 f.180.

71 CP, *Unshackled*, p. 62.
72 Certificate of Registry of Birth, signed by C. H. Pankhurst, 6 November 1905, Department of Libraries and Theatres, Manchester Public City Libraries Archives.
73 Social and feminist awakening, TBG Papers.
74 Socialist feminist historians, unfairly, usually interpret Christabel's cooling friendship with Eva and Esther Roper as indicative of ruthlessness, the casting aside of people once important to her. See, for example, ESP, *TSM*, pp. 195–6; Lewis, *Eva Gore-Booth and Esther Roper*, pp. 97–8; Liddington and Norris, *One hand tied behind us*, pp. 195–8.
75 EWE to Harriet McIlquham, 14 December 1905, EWEP, Add Mss 47,454, f.180.
76 Margaret Ashton, Letter to the Editor, *Manchester Guardian*, 16 October 1905.
77 NUWSS, Report of the Executive Committee of the North of England Society for Women's Suffrage, Presented at the annual meeting, 24 November 1905 (Manchester, 'Guardian' General Printing Works), p. 3. Others who resigned included the Reverend S. A. Steinthal who had supported women's suffrage for well over thirty years.
78 Quoted in Lewis, *Eva Gore-Booth and Esther Roper*, p. 114.
79 Tiernan, *Eva Gore-Booth*, p. 93 also suggests that before the end of 1905 Eva and Esther had formed the National Industrial and Professional Women's Suffrage Society for those who did not wish to remain aligned to the North of England Society and were not directly related to trade unionists or factory workers.
80 Kenney, *Memories*, p. 49.
81 CP, *Unshackled*, pp. 57–8.
82 ESP, *The suffragette*, pp. 41–2; Kenney, *Memories*, pp. 46–7.
83 Kenney, *Memories*, p. 49.
84 ESP, *The suffragette*, p. 47.
85 Coleman, *Adela Pankhurst*, p. 36; ESP, *The suffragette*, p. 48.
86 CP, *Unshackled*, p. 58.
87 Mr Balfour and the 'suffragettes', *Daily Mail*, 10 January 1906.
88 CP, *Unshackled*, p. 59.

7

TO LONDON AS STRATEGIST
OF THE WSPU
1906

As the general election results came rolling in during late January 1906, the Pankhurst family heard the joyful news that Keir Hardie was one of twenty-nine Labour candidates returned to Parliament. But that was the only glimmer of hope. The Liberal Party had been swept to power with a majority of nearly one hundred in the House of Commons.[1] The prospect of a strongly entrenched Liberal Government being in power for a number of years, from whose 'unwilling grasp' the vote must be wrested, filled Christabel with foreboding. 'We must go to work in London now', she said to her mother. 'We can't afford it', was Emmeline's sharp reply, repeated to herself rather than to her daughter. 'Mother, the money will come', insisted Christabel. 'We cannot let these people escape us. Parliament is in London. Our fight must be made there too.'[2]

Christabel longed to go to London herself but knew that was impossible since her final undergraduate examinations were being held in June. She would have to be content with continuing her Sunday talks in Lancashire and Yorkshire, including a big suffrage meeting at Leeds in early February, when she would stay at Adel Grange, the home of socialist Isabella Ford.[3] So Christabel asked Annie, now living at 62 Nelson Street as one of the family, if she would go to London instead, to carry the WSPU campaign there. Emmeline, with motherly concern, warned Annie not to speak to any man in the street except a policeman. With such sound advice, Annie packed her wicker basket, put the £2 left in WSPU funds in her purse and began her journey to rouse London.[4]

The optimistic Annie went to 45 Park Walk, Chelsea, a small, shabby boarding house where Sylvia, who was living there, had taken a room for her so that they could work together.[5] With the help of suffrage supporters, including Dora Montefiore, Keir Hardie, journalist William Stead and Minnie Baldock, the wife of a fitter in East London's Canning Town, Annie was soon contacting poor women in the East End. And, remembering Christabel's advice about being bold, she audaciously planned with Sylvia to hold a WSPU meeting and a procession to the newly elected Parliament on the very day it opened, 19 February. Handbills advertising the Caxton Hall meeting and procession were distributed and the press, who were hovering around the boarding house in Park Walk, helped to keep the movement in the news.[6] When Emmeline Pankhurst came down to London and heard that a hall holding seven hundred people had been booked, she was aghast at the ambitious scale of the plans. Yet, despite her foreboding, the Caxton Hall meeting was filled to overflowing. 'Anyone who has ever heard Mrs. Pankhurst speak has heard one of the finest orators of the day', recollected Annie. 'The whole atmosphere became electric directly she started.'[7]

When news filtered through that there had been no mention of women's suffrage in the King's Speech, Emmeline led a march to the House of Commons of some three thousand women, many of them East End mothers carrying babies in arms. They waited in the cold rain outside the Stranger's Entrance, twenty at a time being allowed in to petition MPs who remained indifferent.[8] Meanwhile, within the Commons, Keir Hardie as the leader of the new Labour Party was replying to the King's Speech, condemning the way the Liberal Government had ignored the women's cause and expressing the hope that it would remove the disgrace of treating women no better than criminals and the mentally ill. His fellow Labour members did not rally to his side. They decided that the five places they drew for private members' bills should be devoted to various class issues in their party programme, such as old-age pensions, the feeding of destitute schoolchildren and the right of the unemployed to work. One place remained in doubt and Emmeline demanded that it be given to votes for women. The Labour MPs refused and decided it should be given instead to a relatively trivial matter, a checkweighing bill that would protect the earnings of workmen.[9] Emmeline felt betrayed. Accompanied by Sylvia, she went to Hardie's rooms at 14 Nevill's Court and wept, begged and implored her old friend to change the situation. She 'would not go back to Christabel in Manchester', telling her that the opportunity to bring forward a women's suffrage measure by the Labour Party 'had been refused'. A stone-faced Hardie explained that he was powerless to change the minds of his colleagues but promised that if he won a place for a bill or resolution, he would devote it to votes for women.[10]

Christabel heard the news with particular disdain since she had recently been elected Vice Chair of a Socialist Society founded by students at Manchester University, with Victor Grayson, the future Labour MP, being appointed as Chair.[11] Her mother and Annie were still in London when, on 1 March 1906, she wrote to Mary Gawthorpe, a working-class teacher active in labour politics in Leeds who had written supportively to her when she was in Strangeways prison. Christabel had welcomed Mary's pledge to go to prison herself, if it was necessary to win the vote, and now hoped that she would write to influential Labour men, asking what they intended to do for women's enfranchisement this parliamentary session. 'From what I have heard', she warned Mary,

> it is quite necessary to keep an eye on them . . . J. K. H[ardie] is the one who really wants to help. The further one goes the plainer one sees that men (even Labour men) think more of their own interests than of ours.[12]

The events in London, however, were not all bad news. There had been good coverage in the press of the first WSPU demonstration in that city and of her mother's historic appeal for justice for women, the *Daily Mirror* even publishing a photograph of women carrying a large banner inscribed 'Votes for Women'.[13] New members had joined the WSPU and a group of unemployed women from West Ham had voted to form the first London branch of the organisation, the Canning Town Branch. Christabel was particularly pleased with the name 'suffragettes', first coined by the *Daily Mail*, now being applied to WSPU members. 'There was a spirit in it, a spring that we liked. Suffragists, we had called ourselves till then, but that name lacked the positive note implied by "Suffragette". Just "want the vote" was the notion conveyed by the older appellation', she observed, whereas the hardening of the 'g' in 'the Suffragettes' said 'they meant to get it'.[14] In addition, Christabel heard that her mother had appointed a woman that neither of them knew as Honorary Treasurer of the WSPU, Emmeline Pethick-Lawrence, a person who was to become a close friend to the eldest Pankhurst daughter over the next eight years or so and become, with her husband, an influential force within the organisation.[15]

Emmeline Pethick-Lawrence (often called 'Mrs Lawrence'), a wealthy, radical socialist, had been recommended to Mrs Pankhurst by Keir Hardie who believed that her excellent administrative skills would be useful to the WSPU. Born on 21 October 1867 to middle-class, Nonconformist parents, Emmeline Pethick grew up admiring her father's 'passionate love of justice' and 'deep strain of religious mysticism', something she also shared.[16] As a young woman keenly interested in social reform, she took up, with the help of Mary Neal, settlement work for the West London Mission. Both came to accept the message of socialism and wanted closer contact with working-class people, especially working-class girls and young women. In 1895 they realised this ambition when they left the mission and founded the Esperance Girls' Club. Four years later, Emmeline Pethick met the suave Frederick William Lawrence, a wealthy, clever young man who was reading for the Bar at the same time that he was giving free advice on legal matters at Mansfield House, Canning Town, the settlement with which she was then associated. Born on 28 December 1871 into a prosperous Unitarian family, Fred had taken a Double First in mathematics and Natural Sciences at Trinity College, Cambridge. He fell in love at first sight with the handsome Miss Pethick, but it was not until October 1901 that they married. Aware that his wife did not want to subsume her own individuality within her marriage, Fred added her surname to his own and gave her, on their first anniversary, a key to her own garden flat on the roof of Clement's Inn, a building off Fleet Street in which they had leased a large apartment. The couple, who had no children, also had a country retreat designed for them by Sir Edward Lutyens, 'The Mascot', near Holmwood in Surrey.[17]

In the autumn of 1905, the Pethick-Lawrences were on a visit to South Africa when they read in the press the sensational story about the imprisonment of

Christabel and Annie after their Free Trade Hall protest. Since a general election was looming, they hurried back to England in January 1906, partly because Fred hoped he might be asked to contest a seat, which did not happen. The return of twenty-nine Labour MPs to the new Parliament brought hope to them both and they met up again with Keir Hardie who introduced them to Emmeline Pankhurst. Mrs Lawrence turned down the initial request to help develop the WSPU in London. The insightful Hardie, who had raised £300 to help the movement get started in the metropolis, sent Annie Kenney. A bowled-over Mrs Lawrence agreed to become the WSPU's Honorary Treasurer. 'There was something about Annie that touched my heart', she remembered. '[S]he seemed to have a whole-hearted faith in the goodness of everybody that she met.' Thus, she continued, it was by 'a very extraordinary sequence of incidents that I, who am not of a revolutionary temperament, was drawn into a revolutionary movement'.[18]

Christabel did not meet the new Honorary Treasurer of the WSPU until some months later since she was still studying in Manchester while also giving her regular Sunday suffrage talks. That March of 1906 she also comforted her aged friend Elizabeth Wolstenholme Elmy whose husband had died, attending the funeral at Manchester Crematorium with Esther Roper and two other friends. At the funeral service, Christabel spoke of Ben Elmy's fight for justice for women in such a warm manner that Mrs Elmy's Congleton friends found it hard to believe that the 'sweet, disarming young girl' at the graveside was 'the terrible Miss Pankhurst' so maligned by the press.[19]

The 'terrible Miss Pankhurst' was discreetly rejoicing in the news that a Central London Committee of the WSPU had been formed with Sylvia, who had been Acting Secretary of the small initial group, as Honorary Secretary, Emmeline Pethick-Lawrence as Honorary Treasurer and Annie as a paid organiser on a salary of £2 a week. Other Committee members included her mother and Flora Drummond, who were both soon to return to Manchester, Mary Neal, Mary Clarke (Emmeline Pankhurst's sister and Christabel's aunt), Lucy Roe (Sylvia's landlady), Nellie Martel and newly recruited member Irene Fenwick Miller. Within a week of her appointment, Emmeline Pethick-Lawrence had brought order and method to the WSPU's ramshackle financial affairs. Her friend Alfred Sayers, a chartered accountant, was appointed auditor while outstanding debts were met and initial expenses cleared by a donation made by Fred and by £100 collected by Hardie.[20] Christabel was impressed. The Honorary Treasurer had organisational skills that complemented the more intuitive gifts of herself and her mother. And that was not all. With her well-developed social connections, Mrs Lawrence would be a tremendous asset to the WSPU.

Christabel found it difficult to focus on her university studies that spring of 1906 since there were many distractions, especially in regard to what was happening in London. A deputation of about thirty women had called at 10 Downing Street on 9 March, and Annie, Flora Drummond and Irene Fenwick Miller had been arrested after refusing to leave. The three women were released without charge, however, on the orders of Prime Minister Henry Campbell-Bannerman, who said he would receive a deputation of all the suffrage societies on 19 May if application was made in a proper manner. The astute Christabel was suspicious, fearing that the Prime Minister was not to be trusted. 'I fancy the Libs. will promise to give us the vote before they next go to the country, in the hope of getting out of doing it in the end', she confessed to Dora Montefiore:

> Then would come the election, and a new Government, which would have the same old excuse that they could not, until the end of their term give us the vote – and so on *ad infinitum*. These men are as wily as serpents, and we must be wilier.[21]

A few weeks later, Christabel wrote to the WSPU London Committee, saying that she thought it advisable to visit the Liberal candidate in the by-election being held at Eye in Suffolk and intimate to him that, unless he obtained a pledge from his Government on votes for women, the suffragettes would oppose his return and take a similar course in regard to every future Government nominee. Annie Kenney, Teresa Billington and Mrs Lawrence duly went down to Eye but did not stay long, due to pressure of work in London.[22]

Suddenly news arrived that Keir Hardie had won a place to present in the Commons, on 25 April, a Resolution expressing the view 'That, in the opinion of this House, it is desirable that sex should cease to be a bar to the exercise of the Parliamentary franchise.' Christabel held no hope that the Resolution would be upheld; both she and her mother were convinced that anti-suffrage MPs would talk the Resolution out and so planned a protest, in advance. On the evening of 25 April, Emmeline, Sylvia, Annie, Teresa and some others sat in the Ladies' Gallery behind the heavy brass grille that screened them from the debating chamber below, listening to the insulting statements made by the anti-suffragist Mr Cremer and the laughter they evoked. At ten minutes to eleven, another opponent of women's suffrage, Mr Evans, was still talking against the Resolution, reiterating the all-too-familiar arguments that women's proper place was the home. Believing, erroneously, that the time had passed when a division of the House could be called, the disgusted WSPU members engaged in a noisy protest. 'Divide! Divide!' and 'We refuse to have our Bill [sic] talked out', they shouted.[23] The MPs, including Hardie, were appalled at the breach of decorum as the police rushed to clear the gallery. Once outside, the WSPU women met a hostile reception from ILP supporters, such as Ethel Snowden, who believed that such militant action had wrecked the chance of winning the support of the House.[24] But Christabel was firmly on her mother's side, condemning the old, familiar tactics of talking out as a 'dishonest practice which has so long disfigured and discredited Parliamentary life'. Not one member of the Liberal Cabinet, she insisted, had shown himself a friend to the women's cause. If the Prime Minister, who claimed to be in favour of women's suffrage, refused to grant the vote this parliamentary session, then suffragettes would be forced to carry on far more militant action than in the past.[25]

Campbell-Bannerman soon had an opportunity to express his views when he received at the Foreign Office on 19 May a deputation of suffragist MPs, whose spokesperson was Keir Hardie, and some four hundred women representing over half a million of their sex, including groups of suffragists, cooperators, temperance workers, liberals and socialists as well as a WSPU deputation led by Emmeline Pankhurst. Emmeline pleaded in the crowded room that the militant women felt the question so keenly that they were prepared 'to sacrifice for it everything they possess, their means of livelihood, their very lives, if necessary'.[26] The Prime Minister, in a long reply, professed to be in favour of women's enfranchisement but admitted that, since some of his Cabinet were opposed to it, he could make no pledge on the issue but only preach 'the virtue of patience'. A murmur of disappointment rang around the room at this phrase, only stopping when Keir Hardie spoke. Then Mrs Elmy, in a frail voice, told how she had been working for the cause since 1865. Annie, in her clogs and grey shawl, gave vent to her frustration by jumping on a chair and shouting, 'Sir, we are not satisfied! The agitation will go on!' Campbell-Bannerman's parting advice to the women, which Christabel later heard about, amused her greatly – 'Go on pestering people!'[27]

Christabel and her mother had been determined that the part played by the WSPU on this day should be far more ambitious than what the NUWSS had planned: merely the holding of a meeting at Exeter Hall. Teresa Billington was appointed as a second WSPU London paid organiser specifically for the purpose of organising a procession and demonstration in Trafalgar Square, the traditional meeting place for the discontented and oppressed. By half past three in the afternoon the protestors were in the square where a predominantly male audience of seven thousand was assembled. This was the first large open-air WSPU demonstration held in London. The speakers included not only Emmeline Pankhurst, Annie Kenny, Keir Hardie, Teresa Billington and Dora Montefiore, but also the Lawrences and Selina Cooper.[28]

Christabel viewed all these protests with satisfaction, observing that militancy had now begun to take hold in London. Campbell-Bannerman's fruitless response to the deputation confirmed her belief that no progress would be made on women's suffrage unless all Cabinet members were converted to the cause, a change that could only be brought about by putting pressure on the Government. '[T]he only way for either men or women to get what they want is to interfere with the peace of mind of the Government', she wrote in an uncompromising pamphlet. 'Men can do this by means of their Parliamentary vote. Women, because they have no vote, must adopt some other means of making their wishes felt.'[29]

Concerns of a more personal nature now arose in the Pankhurst family. Sylvia had told her mother that she wanted to relinquish the post of Honorary Secretary of the London branch of the WSPU. The two years of her scholarship were near its end and she needed to build a portfolio that would help her get employment as an artist. Emmeline insisted that Sylvia retain her position until Christabel had completed her studies and would be free to come to London and make her own selection for the post. Sylvia refused.[30]

Christabel sympathised with their angry mother. Her final law examinations were fast approaching and she had to put a stop to all WSPU work. 'Panic prompted concentration and I withdrew from human society to that of my books.'[31] However, the suffrage drama was still played out around Christabel, even in the city of Manchester. The twenty-year-old Adela disguised herself in their mother's 'best hat and silk coat' to enter a Liberal meeting held at nearby Belle Vue Gardens. She was arrested with Hannah Mitchell and Alice Morrissey for interrupting proceedings and served a week in Strangeways, her two companions being in for just three days.[32] The imprisonment of the frail Adela, who looked much younger than her age, worried both Emmeline and her 'kind and friendly' big sister, as Adela called Christabel. 'Neither mother nor Christabel wished me to throw up my [teaching] position to go to gaol again, but when I had done so and was taken on as an [WSPU] organiser, they accepted it with a good grace.'[33]

There was much rejoicing in the Pankhurst household when the news came that the clever Christabel, the only woman on her course, had passed her law degree with First Class Honours, a distinction shared with one other student, Harry Finklestone. But the joy was also tinged with some sad remembrance. '[W]e thought of Father, his Owens College days', Christabel recollected, 'his interest in the University and his thoughts about my taking to law.'[34] On 30 July 1906, a hot summer day, Christabel met Elizabeth Wolstenholme Elmy and her son Frank at Manchester railway station in the morning and then travelled with them to the university, before going home to dress for the graduation ceremony. The proud Emmeline and Adela, as well as Esther Roper, were also in the audience. As Christabel stepped forward for the conferment of her degree, someone shouted out, 'Why have you not brought your banner?'[35] The faint booing was soon drowned out by overwhelming cheering. Later that day, when Mrs Elmy saw Christabel again, she thought she looked 'a little fagged as well she may, having lived <u>two</u> strenuous lives for 2 years past that of a diligent student, & that of an active political agitator'.[36] Annie, looking back on this day some eighteen years later, still wondered how Christabel had managed to attain such high academic honours. 'Where she studied, how she studied, when she studied, is to me still a mystery. She was working for the movement the whole of the day and practically every night.' Christabel, she reflected, was always modest too, never flaunting her academic qualifications. 'She never spoke of her degree, never used the letters that she was entitled to. This was Christabel.'[37]

Sylvia in London that June was also near the closing days of her college term. Facing a precarious future, she expected a letter from her mother, but none arrived. Emmeline was still angry with her second daughter. Facing financial hardship, she had closed down Emerson's, always a drain on her resources, and was busy arranging the move to a cheaper family home at 66 Upper Brook Street where her brass plate as Registrar for Births and Deaths was to be mounted by the front door. 'We were no longer a family', Sylvia recollected bitterly; 'the movement was overshadowing all personal affections . . . my last letter unanswered,

I ceased to write at all, except on matters of importance.' Having resigned the post of Honorary Secretary of the WSPU, Sylvia was also acutely aware of developing political differences between herself and her elder sister and of the greater influence that Christabel held over their mother; whatever the favoured Christabel decided, she wrote in *The suffragette movement*, 'eventually always swept Mrs. Pankhurst along with it'.[38]

However, what Sylvia omits to mention in her influential memoir is another reason that may have influenced her decision to resign her post. Shortly after moving to London she had begun an affair with Keir Hardie, twenty-six years her senior, a married man and an old family friend. Secrecy was of the utmost importance since any public knowledge about their relationship would damage Hardie's political career and bring censure on his much younger lover. Hardie, a deeply conventional man, had no intention of leaving his wife, Lily, who lived in faraway Scotland. For some years there had been gossip in socialist circles that the Labour MP was having an affair with the beautiful, widowed Emmeline Pankhurst, but it was Sylvia, not Emmeline, with whom Hardie was emotionally involved.[39] Their affair, which lasted for most of the suffrage campaign, had a lasting impact on Sylvia's relationship with her relatives since it deepened her socialist conviction. After Sylvia resigned her WSPU post that summer of 1906, two suffragettes who were also members of the ILP were appointed joint Honorary Secretaries in her place: the wealthy, sixty-two-year-old philanthropist Charlotte Despard, an adult suffragist at heart, and the thirty-one-year-old Edith How Martyn, BSc, the first woman Associate of the Royal College of Science and close friend of Teresa Billington. When Emmeline Pankhurst, still resident in Manchester, heard the news she feared that 'divided counsels' would result from these appointments, a prediction that proved to be accurate.[40]

Amidst these worries, it was a great relief to Christabel to be able to move to London and become the WSPU's Chief Organiser on a salary of £2.10s. per week. She took up residence not with Sylvia, who was shortly moving from Park Walk to unfurnished rooms at 120 Cheyne Walk, Chelsea, but with the Pethick-Lawrences whose flat at Clement's Inn had become the centre of WSPU activities. Christabel was to live with the Lawrences for six years, becoming, like Annie, a daughter to the childless couple. The wealthy Pethick-Lawrences, who liked to live in comfort and in beautiful surroundings, believed not only in hard work but also in relaxation and holidays. They could afford to take Christabel and Annie on expensive continental trips and entertain them, as well as other suffragettes, at their country home, 'The Mascot', in Holmwood. Guests spending weekends at The Mascot would discuss politics, browse through the books, sit in the garden with its apple and pear trees, play leisurely games such as croquet, be taken for drives in their hosts' car and attend occasional entertainments, such as a performance of old English folksongs and dances by the Esperance Girls' Club. The generous and hospitable couple looked after Christabel so that it is no surprise that she gratefully acknowledged their support, noting how her hosts were the people who first made her 'really enjoy' a holiday.[41]

But holidays were yet to come; what was important now was work. Christabel had arrived in London in time to witness the sentencing on 4 July of Annie, Teresa Billington, Jane Sbaroro, an elderly seamstress, and Adelaide Knight, a small, lame woman, to six weeks' imprisonment. They had been part of a deputation to the Cavendish Street home of Herbert Asquith, the Chancellor of the Exchequer and the most entrenched of the anti-suffragists in the Cabinet. The women were sent to Holloway, the first of many suffragettes to enter that jail, a move that evoked much publicity.[42] 'Sympathy with the prisoners and indignation with the Government drew more women into our ranks', Christabel noted.[43] Following the court proceedings, she chaired a protest demonstration of about two hundred women in Hyde Park, at which Teresa also spoke.[44] Weekly meetings were now being held regularly in Hyde Park, near the Reformer's Tree, serving as a recruiting ground for the WSPU. Two other new members who joined about this time and became influential in differing ways were Hertha Ayrton and Mabel Tuke.

Hertha Ayrton, an electrical scientist and a Vice President of the NUWSS, attended a meeting at Clement's Inn that summer of 1906 and was converted to the militant cause by the 'beautiful young . . . Christabel Pankhurst' who 'in her short speech impressed me profoundly with her clear judgment and her keen political insight'.[45] Hertha, occupied with her research into electric arc carbons, rarely engaged in militant actions herself but generously contributed to WSPU funds, offered hospitality to members of the Union and, above all, vigorously defended militant tactics. Mabel Tuke, who was to become close to Christabel and her mother, had met the Pethick-Lawrences on their homeward voyage from South Africa and was returning to England after the recent death of her husband, an army officer. The Pethick-Lawrences invited Mabel to join them and Christabel for lunch. 'She came, still in mourning, gentle and beautiful, the last woman in the world, it might have been supposed, to join a militant movement', Christabel remembered:

> Yet when, after luncheon, I remarked: 'I must go now and chalk pavements for a meeting' (for leaders were still at the chalking stage), what did she say but 'I'll come and chalk pavements too!' . . . From that day onward she was one of us.[46]

Mabel Tuke, an accomplished pianist, was known to her friends as 'Pansy'. Her close friendship with Christabel was to last long after the women's suffrage campaign, into old age.

Now that she was established in London, Christabel was keen to re-assert her position as the key strategist of the WSPU. She assessed the situation and decided that there was too heavy a reliance on poor women from the East End of London who regularly turned out for Labour demonstrations, thus making their involvement in WSPU agitation too predictable and less newsworthy than it might be. Members of Parliament, she believed, saw such demonstrators, unjustly, as a 'stage army'. Christabel wanted 'a movement based on no class distinctions, and including not mainly the working class but women of all classes'. Shrewdly, Christabel estimated that the House of Commons, even its Labour members, 'were more impressed by the demonstrations of the feminine bourgeoisie than of the feminine proletariat'.[47]

Christabel was determined to break the WSPU's reliance on the Labour movement and to mobilise women from all sections of society, including aristocratic and middle-class women who were more likely to vote Conservative and Liberal. The WSPU, she reasoned, should not become 'a frill on the sleeve of any political party', but 'rally women of all three parties and women of no party, and unite them as one independent force'.[48] What was critical in election campaigning was for voteless suffragettes to act independently of parties and encourage electors not to vote for Government candidates but rather to support the candidate, whether Liberal, Conservative or Labour, who appeared most in support of women's suffrage. Such an anti-Government policy had been used to great effect by male Irish politicians, such as Charles Parnell, to press their case for Home Rule. It was the key way, Christabel reasoned, to make women work for their own cause as well as to demonstrate the unpopularity of a Government that refused women their democratic political right. And now was the critical time to push for women's enfranchisement, before the well-known Liberal anti-suffragist Herbert Asquith became Prime Minister, as was expected in a few months' time.

Christabel soon had an opportunity to launch her bold anti-party – and therefore anti-Government – policy. A by-election had been announced at Cockermouth, in Cumberland, a constituency held by the Liberals with only a small majority in the last election when they had faced a Conservative opponent. The fight now was three-cornered since the Labour Party were also fielding a candidate, Robert Smillie, a miners' leader, whose presence threatened to split the narrow Liberal majority. Smillie, an adult suffragist, did not even mention women's suffrage in his election pamphlets and was regarded as lukewarm in his support for the women's cause.[49]

Not knowing anyone in the constituency, Christabel wrote to the secretary of the Cockermouth ILP branch, asking if arrangements could be made for her coming. She did not, however, forewarn him about the change in WSPU policy. When she arrived alone in Cockermouth, she was put up in the home of a prominent ILP member who assumed, as did Smillie, that she had come to support the Labour candidate.[50] Christabel set about preparing for the first WSPU meeting. She sold handbills from a market stall and contacted the local newspapers to inform them that she and her two companions, Teresa Billington and Marion Coates Hansen, a Poor Law Guardian from Middlesbrough, would be the speakers. At the appointed hour in the evening, Christabel was waiting for her friends to turn up when a telegram arrived, saying they were delayed. Facing the large, friendly crowd on the lorry she had hired for a platform, Christabel showed no nervousness as she apologised for their absence. Then with her usual charm, enthusiasm and wit, she begged the electors to vote against the Liberal candidate and made no mention of support for Smillie. 'Miss Pankhurst, one of the notorious band of lady suffragists . . . was certainly an object of interest', noted the local press, 'and had to encounter a considerable amount of interruption, but was equal to the occasion.'[51] Her host was less pleased. Christabel left his home, either at his bidding or on her accord, and moved to the more expensive option of a hotel.[52]

Christabel held the fort alone for three days, addressing the big crowds until Teresa and Marion eventually arrived. That all three were members of the ILP and not actively supporting the Labour candidate led to much condemnation in socialist circles. 'No hope of winning', penned an angry Bruce Glasier in his diary. 'Great indignation at the conduct [of the women].'[53] For a number of socialist feminists, too, such as Mary Gawthorpe, the non-party position of the WSPU created uncomfortable political choices. She had gone to Cockermouth representing the Women's Labour League, specifically in support of Smillie. Although not yet a WSPU member, the suffragettes asked her to abandon the Labour platform and speak with them instead. 'I could not see my way to join the W.S.P.U.', she reminisced, 'for I had not yet grasped either the virtue or value of the tactics: "Keep the Liberal out", if it meant – *at any cost*.'[54] When the poll was declared on 3 August 1906, the Liberals lost the seat to the Conservative candidate, Sir John Randles, who won 4,593 votes while Smillie trailed last with just 1,436. The ILP blamed the disastrous result on the suffragettes who had encouraged women to put the struggle for the vote 'above the interests of our movement', as Glasier angrily termed it.[55]

The controversy rumbled on with Christabel insisting that the success of the WSPU campaign against the Government candidate had depended upon the maintenance of an 'impartial attitude' in regard to the Labour and Conservative candidates.[56] In a letter to the *Labour Leader* Christabel and Teresa made it clear that they stood together on the issue, speaking with one voice. 'Labour M.Ps tell us candidly that they are sent by the Trade Unionists to the House of Commons to promote reforms which must take precedence of women's suffrage', they wrote. 'This being so, women are obliged to take such means of forcing their question upon the attention of the Government, as that adopted at Cockermouth.'[57] Marion Coates Hansen, who presided at the enormous meetings where the two women spoke, was also forthright in her support. The WSPU '*may* have members who are members of the I.L.P.', she insisted, 'but its policy is clear and defined. It wants "Votes for Women" as its primary object. It is allied to *no* political party.'[58]

Matters came to a head when the Manchester and Salford ILP requested that the Manchester Central Branch, to which Christabel and Teresa belonged, demand their immediate resignation. 'The Manchester Central Branch . . . is not the least likely to do anything so babyishly silly', predicted Elizabeth Wolstenholme Elmy.[59] And she was right. Teresa Billington, campaigning in Scotland, was unable to attend the meeting held on 4 September 1906 at the Portland Street Café, Manchester. But Christabel was present, as well as her anxious mother, keen to defend and support her eldest daughter. In a long statement to the committee, Christabel confirmed that she had written to the Cockermouth ILP, asking for accommodation during their stay, but found out, shortly after her arrival, that they did not want her to mention women's enfranchisement during the campaign. An astounded Christabel replied that the object of her political life was the enfranchisement of women and that the only way to obtain it was through fighting the Liberals, a strategy which the Labour members could not endorse. In her concluding remarks, Christabel said that she believed that the strategy adopted by the WSPU was 'promoting the highest interests of true labour representation' and refused to give any pledge binding future WSPU election policy. A long, heated discussion then ensued during which both Christabel and her mother defended their corner. Eventually, towards ten in the evening, a motion was carried, by eighteen votes to eight:

> That this branch meeting does not approve of the resolution of the M/C & Salford I.L.P., inasmuch as in their opinion, the two members have simply endeavoured to carry out the immediate extension of the Franchise to Women which is included in the official program of the party as one of its objects.[60]

Christabel was delighted with the outcome. She had stood firm and faced down her critics. And there was a further spinoff. Her success in vindicating her actions consolidated her position as the key strategist of the WSPU and also attracted more recruits to her cause. '[L]ess than 3000 is a *small* meeting now', Elizabeth Wolstenholme Elmy noted joyfully.[61] Even Sylvia Pankhurst in her 1911 book *The suffragette* praises Christabel for the independence of party tactics she had developed at Cockermouth, pointing out that MPs of all political persuasions would abandon any pledge on women's suffrage at the bidding of their party leaders. That Christabel had followed this path, when many on the WSPU Committee doubted her wisdom, was evidence of 'that keen political insight and that indomitable courage and determination which are so essential to real leadership'.[62] Sylvia insists too that, at Cockermouth, the socialist candidate Smillie 'had not been attacked'.[63]

However, in *The suffragette movement*, published twenty years later, Sylvia changes her tune, now condemning her sister, labelling the anti-party stance as anti-socialist. 'Christabel was most pointed in emphasizing to the electors that she cared not a straw whether they voted Tory or Labour. Coming from I.L.P. women, these tactics were a shock to the Labour Party.' Further, since Christabel's popularity and fame soared after Cockermouth, Sylvia in *The suffragette movement* also engages in bitter character assassination:

> Christabel had the admiration of a multitude; hundreds, perhaps thousands of young women adored her to distraction . . . To those who had known the lethargic Christabel in the days of Emerson's, and remembered the schoolgirl who could always have done much better if she would, her activity was a marvel.

Sylvia continues bitterly, 'Mrs. Pankhurst upheld her as an oracle, the Pethick Lawrences lauded her political genius . . . As for me, I detested her incipient Toryism.'[64] Most suffrage historians have followed Sylvia's analysis, seeing the 1906 Cockermouth by-election as the final split between the WSPU and socialism.[65] But such judgements are made through a socialist rather than a feminist lens. Many suffragettes, especially in the regions, continued to be *both* WSPU and ILP members.[66]

Brimming with enthusiasm after her Cockermouth success, Christabel came back to London in time to open another WSPU by-election campaign, this time in the Battersea constituency of John Burns. Burns was considered a particularly suitable target since he had accepted office in the Liberal Government, despite being elected as a Labour MP, and considered votes for women as votes for 'ladies'. The eager Christabel chalked pavements to advertise meetings and then, near the appointed time, summoned a crowd by ringing a big hand-bell at factory gates at the lunch break or at street corners in the afternoon or evening. People would rush forward to hear the charismatic, articulate young woman standing on a chair or other platform. 'Now', she would say, in her assertive, confident voice, 'I'm going to tell you about our tactics!'[67] Her talks were always informative since Christabel read voraciously, studying the speeches of great political orators, works on constitutional history and Parliament. And every morning, before her day's work began, she devoured the daily newspapers so that she could link political issues of the past and present as she offered a scathing denunciation of the Liberal Government's policy. Yet, despite Christabel's learning and erudition, Emmeline Pethick-Lawrence remembered that she always had the common touch with the ordinary people, having 'neither the appearance nor the manner of "the highbrow" . . . her speeches were full of wit, and a kind of challenge that suited her pretty, youthful appearance'.[68] Even the jealous Sylvia captures something of the fascination that Christabel held for a crowd:

> That she was slender, young, with the flawless colouring of a briar rose, and an easy grace cultivated by her enthusiastic practice of the dance, were delicious embellishments to the sterner features of her discourse. Yet the real secret of her attraction was her audacity. Fluent in its assurance . . .[69]

Christabel's role as the key strategist of the WSPU was widely accepted among the membership and confirmed by the new arrangements made for her in September 1906 when two adjoining rooms on the ground floor of Clement's Inn were acquired for the London headquarters; whereas the large room served as a general office, where the busy throng of the press located in nearby Fleet Street might gather, the smaller one became Christabel's private office where she soon had the services of her own secretary. The smooth running of the organisational side of the WSPU had been considerably aided by the appointment of a general office manager, Harriet Roberta Kerr, a red-headed Scot from Aberdeen who had owned a secretarial agency. Beatrice Sanders, a member of the ILP, whose husband was a Fabian Society lecturer, later became the financial secretary while Mary Home, a pale young woman with a hare lip, the only daughter of a retired Indian army doctor, kept newspaper cuttings and research material. The learned, eloquent and thin Aeta Lamb, born in Demerara where her father had been a botanist, often helped with speech writing.[70]

This network of women supported Christabel as she prepared her many talks and in her general work as Chief Organiser of the WSPU. But it was especially Jessie Kenney, the youngest of the Kenney daughters and secretary to Emmeline Pethick-Lawrence, who became another trusted friend. Christabel often asked Jessie to see a prominent MP or Cabinet Minister and to point out the man in question from the range of photos kept on the main office mantelpiece. Jessie too would take some of the pressure off Christabel's shoulders when anxious parents called at Clement's Inn, worried about imprisoned daughters.[71]

With all these developments, the conduct of WSPU business was put on a more regular footing. Soon the large office was being used for weekly At Homes, held on Monday afternoons, where members and prospective members gathered to hear the leaders speak. The slim Christabel, usually clad in green, would mount a chair and with a sheaf of papers and cuttings in one hand give the news for the week. Annie watched with admiration:

> No one will ever surpass Christabel for tactics. Not a word was lost, not a movement overlooked. The politicians, the public, the Press, were like an open book to her, and we were all placed as though she were playing a serious game of political chess, her opponent being Parliament.[72]

Since Christabel's role in developing WSPU strategy was so pivotal, it was generally assumed that she should not place herself in a position where she would risk prison again. Thus she helped to plan a demonstration on 23 October 1906, to coincide with the autumn opening of Parliament, but did not take part. Emmeline Pankhurst led the deputation to the Commons where only about thirty well-dressed women were admitted to the Lobby, a separate contingent of working-class women being turned away. On hearing that a women's suffrage measure would not be considered that session, Mary Gawthorpe sprang up onto a settee to address the weary crowd and was roughly dragged down by the police. Amidst the scuffling and shouting, another suffragette took her place and then another in that most hallowed of male spaces. Emmeline Pankhurst, who was flung to the floor, was not arrested, and nor was Charlotte Despard, but ten others were – Annie, Adela, Emmeline Pethick-Lawrence, Mary Gawthorpe, Teresa Billington, Minnie Baldock, Irene Miller, Dora Montefiore, Edith How Martyn and Annie Cobden-Sanderson, a well-known socialist and daughter of the great Richard Cobden, a radical leader for the repeal of the Corn Laws. The next day, the women appeared before the Westminster police court whose authority they noisily refused to recognise. The irritated magistrate ordered the women to keep the peace for six months or be imprisoned for two months in the Second Division. All chose prison. The women protested, making speeches and clinging to the court rails until they were ignominiously dragged away, leaving behind shreds of clothing, hats, hairpins and papers strewn along the floor. 'Never was such a scene in a Court of Justice before', opined the *Daily Mirror*, a view echoed by many commentators.[73] That the husband of Annie Cobden-Sanderson as well as her two well-connected sisters, Mrs Cobden-Unwin and Mrs Cobden-Sickert, each donated £100 to WSPU funds, while Fred Pethick-Lawrence promised £10 for each day that his wife was in Holloway, only added to the glare of publicity.

Christabel had determined that the WSPU should not be dependent on the protest of working-class women, and now the wisdom of her strategy bore fruit. There was widespread uproar that women of well-known positions outside suffrage circles should be treated in this way. The *Daily News* asserted that no class had ever got the vote 'except at the risk of something like revolution', while the *Daily Mirror* asked, 'By what means, but by screaming, knocking, and rioting, did men themselves ever gain what they were pleased to call their rights?'[74] But it was the treatment of Annie Cobden-Sanderson, brought up in a Liberal family but now a member of the ILP, married to a bookbinder who had founded the famous Doves Press and close friend of renowned socialist William Morris, that aroused the deepest indignation. The playwright George Bernard Shaw in a letter to the *Times* condemned the Government's action, claiming that 'one of the nicest women in England [was] suffering from the coarsest indignity and the most injurious form of ill-treatment that the law could inflict on a pickpocket'. Another correspondent, the suffragist Florence Fenwick Miller, the anxious mother of imprisoned Irene, asserted angrily, 'You have taken, and are treating as a felon, a daughter of the great Cobden, the man who gave you the cheap loaf.' Why, she asked, were these women not treated as political offenders and placed in the First Division, where male political offenders such as Charles Parnell had been placed in the past? Male political offenders had books and the use of writing materials, lived in decent rooms and were allowed to receive letters and occasional callers. 'But your women political prisoners are being treated like the commonest of criminals, merely for protesting in the hearing of your legislators against the inequality of men and women under our Constitution.'[75] For the first time, Millicent Garrett Fawcett, president of the NUWSS, who had known Annie Cobden-Sanderson for thirty years, publicly supported the suffragettes:

> I hope the more old-fashioned suffragists will stand by them . . . far from having injured the movement, they have done more during the last 12 months to bring it within the region of practical politics than we have been able to accomplish in the same number of years.[76]

Christabel and Emmeline were delighted when, on 31 October, the Government announced that all the prisoners would be transferred to the more comfortable First Division. 'We are at last recognised as a political party . . . and are a political force', rejoiced Emmeline.[77] The public outcry over the way the women had been treated, as well as pressure from Keir Hardie and other MPs for amelioration of prison conditions, had forced the Government's hand. Both Annie and Adela, who had been in prison before, seemed to cope well but Emmeline Pethick-Lawrence, a first-time offender, found confinement in Holloway very difficult.[78] On the verge of a nervous breakdown, she was released early, on 28 October, giving the necessary undertaking to keep the peace for six months. For Sylvia Pankhurst, too, her first experience of prison was harrowing. However, on transference to the First Division she claimed the right to send for drawing-paper, pen, ink and pencils so that she could record the scenes around her. Christabel, as Chief Organiser of the WSPU, had instructed suffragettes not to write about prison conditions, for fear it would divert attention away from their primary cause. But Sylvia, ever a rival to her sister, thought it would be good publicity for the WSPU to take up the cause of prison reform and so gave dozens of interviews to the press, as well as sketches for publication.[79] Christabel was soon to come around to Sylvia's way of thinking on this issue.

The events of October and November 1906 had an important impact on Christabel's position as Chief Organiser of the WSPU. As she herself acknowledged, the fact that Annie Cobden-Sanderson had decided to go to prison for the cause not only aroused public sympathy and interest but also encouraged a large number of women, especially middle-class women, to join the organisation.[80] The success of her strategy strengthened Christabel's self-conviction and confidence. At long last the WSPU was being fashioned as the women-only, cross-class, non-party militant organisation she wanted. Women of all political sympathies and social classes were joining the WSPU and developing a sex solidarity, a sense of their own distinctiveness. The way was open for wealthy women, who were more likely to vote Conservative, to support their sisters and sponsor an organisation that was not tied to the emerging Labour Party.

Ironically, the demonstration of 23 October also brought a man much more into the leadership of the WSPU: Fred Pethick-Lawrence. While his wife was in prison, Fred took on her duties as Honorary Treasurer of the WSPU, in which capacity he continued to act while the fragile Emmeline recuperated in Italy. He set about reorganising the accounting side of WSPU funds, separating off the literature sales section into a trading department called the Woman's Press. Alice Knight, a shopkeeper, was brought in to look after the new section while Beatrice Sanders, wife of Alderman Sanders, afterwards a Labour MP, became financial secretary and keeper of the books. Although Fred never held a formal position within the WSPU, from now on he devoted most of his time to its financial and legal affairs, being particularly well known for instructing suffragettes on how to deal with their defence when in court, arranging their bail and calming their worried relatives. He also became the person with whom the police were glad to deal, especially later in the movement when large numbers were arrested.[81]

As a man within a women-only organisation, Fred Pethick-Lawrence's position was somewhat problematic but made easier by the fact that he did not work in direct militant action but behind the scenes. Male sympathisers for the women's cause, 'suffragettes in trousers', as Israel Zangwill termed them, usually embodied a particular notion of masculinity. The Cambridge-educated, upper-middle-class Fred Pethick-Lawrence, in his well-cut suits, was very much the 'English gentleman' who believed in fair play and courage, a man with a vote who wished chivalrously to defend and protect women campaigning for their constitutional right.[82] But, above all, Fred's 'honorary' role within the WSPU was generally accepted because he and his wife were close to Christabel, who lived in the spare room in their flat, at their invitation. The Pethick-Lawrences had faith in Christabel, believing that she could accomplish great things for the women's cause. Yet even though Christabel was just nine years his junior, Fred was content that she call him 'godfather', just like the working-class folk-dancing women that he and his wife knew. Although there is no evidence that Fred loved any woman other than his wife, he did worship Christabel, confessing that he found her 'quite irresistible'.[83] Emmeline Pethick-Lawrence was equally fulsome in her praise. 'Miss Pankhurst and I talk over all WSPU business, she told another suffragette, 'and are of one mind concerning everything.'[84] However, Emmeline Pankhurst never liked Fred. They 'never got on', recollected Jessie Kenney; there was always 'an "atmosphere" between them'.[85]

Christabel, as the Chief Organiser of the WSPU, was always busy, planning by-elections, devising new strategies, delivering uplifting speeches and also engaging in the more mundane but essential tasks of advising and helping new members. In early November 1906 she wrote to Annot Wilkie, a teacher and ILP member, and also the first secretary of the Dundee branch of the WSPU, praising her for the excellent work she was doing in that town, as well as offering some advice:

> Do not write to Miss Billington at the prison, but send your letter here and we will embody it in a long one from this Office. If you send a let-ter to her she can receive no more letters for a fortnight therefore it is better that one long letter giving everybody's messages should be sent from here.[86]

And then there were by-election campaigns to organise, this time in Huddersfield. Ever agile in her thinking about courting publicity for her anti-party/anti-Government propaganda, Christabel had changed her mind about the value of suffragettes speaking about their prison experiences, and so was delighted when the Holloway prisoners were released early, on 24 November. They could come to Huddersfield and tell their stories while placards saying 'Electors, oppose the Government that imprisons women' were displayed.

Christabel and a cheering crowd greeted Annie and Mary Gawthorpe when their train arrived at Huddersfield, two hours late. Then arm-in-arm the three women, guarded by policemen and followed by applauding hundreds, made their way into the station square where a meeting was in progress. All the suf-fragettes in Huddersfield – including Emmeline Pankhurst, Nellie Martel and

Teresa Billington – were working hard, holding over seventy meetings, enrolling two hundred new members and speaking to over 100,000 people.[87] The strain took its toll. Mary Gawthorpe had a nasal haemorrhage while the usually robust Christabel became ill through overwork. 'We are all hoarse and tired, but we are happy. We are confident that we have done such harm to the cause of the Liberal candidate that he has no hope of winning', Christabel told one journalist. 'Never have we had such a reception as we have had here. Men, as well as women, listened to us earnestly, and there was an absence of those silly interruptions and heckling we experienced in Hyde Park.'[88]

Christabel's optimism was misplaced: Arthur Sherwell, the Liberal candidate, was returned but with a substantially reduced majority of just three hundred and forty over his Labour rival who also polled fewer votes than in the last election.[89] While Keir Hardie praised the 'cordial relations' between the women's and labour movements at Huddersfield, other Labour members were dismayed, blaming the suffragettes for the fall in their own vote.[90] The press, however, focused on the reduced majority of the Liberal candidate, attributing it to WSPU intervention. 'When the Suffragettes began their campaign they were mistaken for notoriety hunters, featherheads, flibbertigibbets', opined the *Daily Mirror*. 'Now they have proved that they are in dead earnest, they have frightened the Government, they have broken through the law, they have made votes for women practical politics.'[91]

Christabel was heartened by the Huddersfield election but not too impressed by the decision of Millicent Garrett Fawcett to hold a 'complimentary banquet' in honour of the released prisoners, at the Savoy Hotel on 11 December, at which the Aeolian Ladies' Orchestra would play. '[T]he non-militants gave a dinner to our prisoners', she recollected. 'We highly appreciated this act of solidarity and moral support. Had they shared our fare in prison, it would have meant still more.'[92] Adela was the only one of the Pankhurst family who attended the lavish banquet with its champagne toasts and many speeches, although she later claimed that she was too much of a socialist to be impressed by such bourgeois trappings.[93] Adela was accompanied by Annie and Mary Gawthorpe after Emmeline Pethick-Lawrence had come to the rescue, asking Pansy to take them shopping to find something suitable to wear. Annie chose a green silk Liberty dress while a crepe skirt and crepe-de-chine blouse with a low cowl collar was considered just right for Mary.[94]

The banquet was soon overshadowed by further arrests of another twenty militants who made forays into Parliament Square. On 21 December 1906, Christabel was present at the court case of one such protest, led by the amiable Flora Drummond who was sentenced, with her comrades, to two weeks in Holloway.[95] On their release the women, who had spent Christmas away from their families in cold prison cells, were entertained at a social gathering of WSPU members at Caxton Hall, Westminster. Christabel optimistically claimed, '[N]o other women would ever have to spend another Christmas in gaol for the suffrage, for by next Christmas women would have the vote.'[96] She was to be repeatedly disappointed on that score. Soon after this social event, Emmeline Pethick-Lawrence hit on the idea of organising welcome breakfasts for released prisoners, an initiative that Christabel eagerly endorsed. Welcome breakfasts would emphasise not only the sisterhood between all members of the WSPU but also serve as useful publicity, reminding the public of the Government's inhumanity against those who fought for their democratic right of citizenship.

Notes

1 Fulford, *Votes for women*, p. 132.
2 CP, *Unshackled*, p. 61.
3 See *LL*, 9 and 16 February 1906, pp. 541 and 561, respectively.
4 Kenney, *Memories*, p. 58.
5 Kenney, *Memories*, p. 59; ESP, *TSM*, p. 197. Montefiore, *From a Victorian to a modern*, pp. 50–1, questions Sylvia's version of events, claiming that when Annie arrived in London, she went straight to her house in Hammersmith, saying that she wished to get in touch with working women in East London.
6 ESP, *TSM*, pp. 197–8.
7 Kenney, *Memories*, p. 70.
8 *Daily Mirror*, 20 February 1906.
9 ESP, *Emmeline Pankhurst*, pp. 55–7.
10 ESP, *TSM*, p. 204.
11 *LL*, 9 March 1906. The Society was founded on 22 February.
12 CP to Mary Gawthorpe, 1 March 1906, cited in M. Gawthorpe, *Up hill to Holloway* (Penobscot, ME, Traversity Press, 1962), p. 210.
13 *Daily Mirror*, 20 February 1906.
14 CP, *Unshackled*, pp. 62–3.
15 The Pethick-Lawrences did not hyphenate their surname until after the First World War but throughout I have hyphenated their name for simplicity.
16 Emmeline Pethick-Lawrence (hereafter EPL), *My part in a changing world* (London, Victor Gollancz, 1938), pp. 44, 38, 42.
17 EPL, *My part*, pp. 112, 121–31; F. Pethick-Lawrence (hereafter FPL), *Fate has been kind* (London, Hutchinson & Co., 1943), pp. 51–6; B. Harrison, Emmeline and Fred Pethick-Lawrence in his *Prudent revolutionaries: portraits of British feminists between the wars* (Oxford, Oxford University Press, 1987), p. 246.
18 EPL, *My part*, pp. 147–8.
19 EWE to H. McIlquham, 7 March 1906, EWEP, Add Mss 47,454, f.227.
20 EPL, *My part*, pp. 148, 152.
21 CP to Dora Montefiore, 22 March 1906, quoted in Montefiore, *From a Victorian to a modern*, p. 116.
22 ESP, *The suffragette*, p. 66.
23 *LL*, 4 May 1906; Rosen, *Rise up women!*, p. 66.
24 Hannam, *Isabella Ford*, p. 116.
25 CP, The story of women's franchise, *Labour Record*, May 1906, p. 52.
26 EP, *My own story*, pp. 64–5; *Labour Record*, June 1906, p. 85.
27 ESP, *TSM*, p. 212; CP, *Unshackled*, p. 65.
28 *LL*, 25 May 1906; ESP, *The Suffragette*, p. 65; Rosen, *Rise up women!*, p. 67.
29 CP, Why we protest at Cabinet Ministers' meetings, pamphlet published by NWSPU, n.d., c. October 1907.
30 ESP, *TSM*, p. 215; Raeburn, *Militant suffragettes*, p. 24.
31 CP, *Unshackled*, p. 66.
32 Mitchell, ed, *The hard way up*, p. 142; Liddington, *Rebel girls*, p. 61.

33 APW, My mother, p. 33.
34 CP, Unshackled, p. 66.
35 Manchester Guardian, 2 July 1906.
36 EWE to H. McIlquham, 3 July 1906, EWEP, Add Mss 47454, f.275.
37 Kenney, Memories, pp. 51–2.
38 ESP, TSM, pp. 215–16.
39 Romero, Sylvia Pankhurst, p. 37 claims that Sylvia's affair with Hardie began in 1906, although Winslow, Sylvia Pankhurst, p. 4 dates it from 1904.
40 ESP, TSM, pp. 215–16.
41 Kenney, Memories, p. 77; ESP, TSM, p. 214; Gawthorpe, Up hill to Holloway, p. 250.
42 See ESP, The suffragette, pp. 84–6; see Daily Mirror and Daily Graphic, 28 June 1906, for accounts of the initial trial.
43 CP, Unshackled, p. 66.
44 Morning Advertiser, 5 July 1906.
45 Evelyn Sharp, Hertha Ayrton 1854–1923: a memoir (London, Edward Arnold, 1926), pp. 192–3.
46 CP, Unshackled, pp. 67–8.
47 CP, Unshackled, pp. 66–7.
48 CP, Unshackled, p. 69.
49 Rosen, Rise up women!, p. 70.
50 Letter from R. Smillie to the Editor, LL, 24 August 1906.
51 Raeburn, The militant suffragettes, pp. 22–3.
52 CP, Unshackled, p. 68.
53 Entry for 2 August 1906, Bruce Glasier Diaries.
54 Gawthorpe, Uphill to Holloway, pp. 222–7.
55 Entry for 8 August 1906, Bruce Glasier Diaries.
56 CP, Letter to the Editor, LL, 24 August 1906.
57 CP and Teresa Billington, Letter to the Editor, LL, 17 August 1906.
58 Marion Coates Hansen, Letter to the Editor, LL, 17 August 1906.
59 EWE to H. McIlquham, 28 August 1906, EWEP, Add Mss 7454, f.299.
60 Minutes of Manchester ILP Central Branch Meeting, 4 September 1906, Manchester Public City Libraries Archives.
61 EWE to H. McIlquham, 6 September 1906, EWEP, Add Mss 47454, f.303.
62 ESP, The suffragette, p. 96.
63 ESP, The suffragette, p. 94.
64 ESP, TSM, pp. 220–1.
65 Liddington and Norris, One hand tied behind us, p. 207 speak of Christabel's 'arrant disloyalty'; Pugh, The march of the women, p. 178 asserts that at Cockermouth, Christabel 'appeared to support the Conservative' through her 'insistence on moving to the right'.
66 See, for example, Cowman, 'Incipient Toryism'?
67 ESP, TSM, p. 220.
68 EPL, My part, pp. 160–1.
69 ESP, TSM, pp. 220–1.
70 ESP, TSM, p. 224; Crawford, The women's suffrage movement, p. 331; K. Cowman, Women of the right spirit: paid organisers of the Women's Social and Political Union (WSPU) 1904–1918 (Manchester and New York, Manchester University Press, 2007), Chapter 4.
71 Rosen, Rise up women!, p. 21; David Mitchell interview with Jessie Kenney, 24 March 1964, DMC.
72 Kenney, Memories, p. 101.
73 Daily Mirror, 25 October 1906; see also Times, 24 and 25 October 1906. The Illustrated London News, 27 October 1906, referred to the suffragettes' 'latest absurdity'.
74 Daily News and Daily Mirror, 25 October 1906.

75 Letters from George Bernard Shaw and Florence Fenwick Miller to the Editor, *Times*, 31 and 29 October 1906, respectively.
76 Letter from Millicent Fawcett to the Editor, *Times*, 27 October 1906.
77 *Daily Mirror*, 1 November 1906.
78 Kenney, *Memories*, pp. 105–6; APW, Thoughts in prison, *Labour Record*, November 1906, p. 236.
79 ESP, *TSM*, p. 238.
80 CP, *Unshackled*, p. 71.
81 EPL, *My part*, p. 189.
82 S. S. Holton, Manliness and militancy: the political protest of male suffragists and the gendering of the 'suffragette' identity, in *The men's share? Masculinities, male support and women's suffrage in Britain, 1890–1920* (London, Routledge, 1997), pp. 110–34.
83 FPL, *Fate*, p. 70.
84 EPL to Miss Marsden, 1 December 1909, Jennie Baines Papers, Fryer Library, University of Queensland.
85 Interview with Jessie Kenney, 2 July 1965, DMC.
86 CP to Miss Wilkie, 9 November 1906, Manchester Public City Libraries Archives.
87 *Daily News* and *Daily Mirror*, 27 November 1906.
88 *Daily News*, 27 November 1906.
89 *Labour Record*, December 1906, p. 219.
90 J. Keir Hardie, The Huddersfield contest, and Bruce Glasier, How we fought Huddersfield, LL, 30 November 1906, pp. 441 and 413, respectively.
91 *Daily Mirror*, 1 December 1906.
92 CP, *Unshackled*, p. 83.
93 APW, The story of my life, p. 5. Emmeline Pankhurst had not yet been to prison and so was not invited.
94 Kenney, *Memories*, p. 106; Gawthorpe, *Uphill to Holloway*, p. 252.
95 *Tribune*, 22 December 1906.
96 LL, 4 January 1907.

8

RAPID GROWTH OF THE
WSPU AND SPLITS

1907

The dawn of the New Year 1907 saw Christabel writing to Elizabeth Robins, eighteen years her senior, an author and ex-actress, especially renowned for her portrayal of Ibsen heroines.[1] Elizabeth Robins greatly admired the militants and had written a suffrage novel, *The Convert*, as well as a play titled *Votes for Women!* which would be performed later in the year. The suffragette heroine in the play, Vida Levering, was a single woman who in the past had had an abortion when she became pregnant by a family friend. Initially she had been called 'Christian', which worried both Christabel and her mother. 'Now Christabel has no past', the anxious Emmeline had written earlier to Elizabeth, 'still many people might connect the imaginary with the real & say that Christian's story is Christabel's.' Always protective of her favourite daughter, Emmeline pleaded, '[O]ur work is so difficult as it is without paragraphs in the papers when the play appears suggesting that this person or that is the original of the heroine.'[2] Elizabeth Robins duly changed the name of the heroine to Vida Levering, and Christabel and Emmeline increasingly sought to bring the renowned and charismatic Miss Robins, who moved in elite Liberal circles, into the WSPU.

The well-connected Elizabeth Robins, whose close friends included liberal-minded lawyers and Government politicians, such as Sir Edward Grey, was a useful contact since the WSPU needed to keep up pressure on the Liberal Party. But, as her biographer makes clear, she was determined not to become 'simply a conduit for relaying information' to the persistent Pankhursts. Although Sylvia Pankhurst states that Elizabeth Robins 'fell in love' with Christabel, Angela John points out that she was not 'as dazzled' by the Chief Organiser of the WSPU as Sylvia claims but found Christabel 'very persuasive and admired her mind and utter commitment'.[3] Elizabeth Robins was not the only suffragette who felt this way; she was merely one of a network of women who supported Christabel during the strenuous years of campaigning. Although not as close to Christabel as Annie Kenney, she nonetheless was a loyal supporter of the WSPU, keeping up an exchange of letters with its Chief Organiser for many years.

Such webs of friendship and comradeship, which cut across class and status, were critical to the successful working of the WSPU and, in particular, to Christabel's role within it. As she was never tired of explaining, the WSPU was a woman's movement that took in 'the highest and the lowest, the richest and poorest. The bond is womanhood!'[4] The demands made on her in trying to bring women to work together to press for their citizenship rights were enormous. Yet Christabel's self-assurance and confidence as a leader, as well as her unshakeable belief that her cause was right, meant that she did not hesitate to give instructions to her followers, as she thought necessary. We see this trait in her character time and time again, including later that January of 1907 when she wrote to a WSPU member, giving help and advice about working up a meeting. 'You shall have the bills [posters] you want. They are leaving today', she wrote to Mrs. Louise Cullen who was involved in forming a Hammersmith Branch. 'A meeting in your district timed for some day after 1st wd be advisable. I am hoping to see you tomorrow & we will have a good talk.'[5]

Christabel would often appear too on a platform with a new speaker, leading by example, helping the protégé to understand the importance of standing firm, especially when the audience was antagonistic, as Evelyn Sharp found out when she made her maiden speech early in 1907 at a stormy meeting at Fulham Town Hall. The mainly male audience, overwhelmingly drawn from the Marxist Social Democratic Federation, was hostile since they saw the votes for women campaign as a bourgeois movement. Christabel, who opened the proceedings, made no attempt to placate her foe, with some amazing results. 'She won every one of the women who sat mutely on the front benches and had never seen a woman stand up to a man in public', recollected Evelyn. Apart from Christabel's 'political insight', that was her great asset:

> to put fight into women and make them demand as a right what they were inclined to beg as a favour . . . her attitude drove the men in the audience, who also had never previously encountered this sort of thing in a woman, to a frenzy.[6]

Christabel, who had developed her speaking skills in the rough and tumble of the socialist movement, knew how to handle an audience.

The hostility of socialist men to women's suffrage never failed to amaze her. She was not surprised when she heard that at the Labour Party Conference in Belfast that January, which her mother attended, a motion to support a Women's Enfranchisement Bill, strongly backed by Keir Hardie, was overwhelmingly defeated in favour of an adult suffrage measure. A dejected Hardie waited till the end of the conference to drop his bombshell. If the motion that had been carried was intended to bind the action of the Labour Party in the House of Commons, then he would have to seriously consider whether he should remain a member of that Party which he had largely created – and that had been his life's work.[7] The stunned audience sat in silence. A few weeks later, the executive of the Labour Party dealt with the crisis by giving MPs a free vote on the women's issue, and by re-electing Hardie as leader. Christabel was unimpressed. She felt Hardie had abandoned the women's franchise for party political manoeuvring. But, above all, she was angry that the Labour Party had gone back on its word; it claimed to be in favour of sex equality and now wanted to support adult rather than women's suffrage. Not a person to be deflected from her cause, Christabel argued her case again in the socialist press, pointing out how in the past every campaign for adult suffrage had ended in a compromise where women had been excluded. 'It is what happened in the Chartist movement in this county, and is what would happen again . . . Adult suffrage can only be obtained by first bringing about the enfranchisement of women.'[8]

Disillusioned with socialist men, Christabel pressed on with her aim of bringing women of all political persuasions into the WSPU. Knowing that many Liberal women were horrified at the rough treatment suffragettes experienced at the hands of hooligans in their own party, a party that was now in Government and doing nothing to help women's enfranchisement, she spoke about these matters with Elizabeth Wolstenholme Elmy. Ever eager to help her protégé, Mrs Elmy wrote to Harriet McIlquham in early February, seeking her help, asking if Christabel could address a set of Liberal women in Bristol. 'She is anxious to get more & more in touch with Liberal women & especially to address WLAs [Women's Liberal Associations].'[9] How successful this new direction was at this particular time for Christabel is difficult to determine, but it is probable that some Liberal women were among the audience who attended the WSPU Conversazione, held at the London rooms of the Royal Society of Artists on Tuesday evening, 12 February 1907, when she and Annie, among other suffragettes, gave their five-minute speeches.[10]

Earlier that Tuesday, a new session of parliament had met, with no mention of votes for women in the King's speech. Christabel, a brilliant strategist, had anticipated this. As 'Men's Parliaments' excluded women who could not even vote for them, she had carefully planned for a 'Women's Parliament' to be held the following day, with more to follow. The inauguration of these 'Women Parliaments', assemblies gathered with the specific aim of discussing votes for women and then taking immediate militant action by women who were willing to go to prison, was a major policy initiative in WSPU campaigning in 1907.

Tickets for the first Women's Parliament, held at three o'clock on 13 February at Caxton Hall, had been sold in advance and the Exeter Hall was hired to take the overflow. Amidst great excitement, a resolution was passed condemning the omission of women's suffrage from the King's speech and demanding that the Commons give immediate facilities. With the cry 'Rise up women!' Emmeline Pankhurst proposed that a deputation carrying the resolution take itself immediately to the Prime Minister. The elderly Charlotte Despard led about four hundred, most working women, from the hall into the street where they broke up into smaller groups to which had been appointed a leader, distinguished by a badge or article of dress. The first contingent faced fierce resistance as it neared Westminster Abbey. Foot police punched and dragged them into the road, mounted police reared their horses. Hour after hour more contingents tried to reach the Commons. Bruised and injured women were arrested and released, pending a trial.[11]

Christabel, presiding at a meeting held that evening in Caxton Hall to welcome the heroines of the afternoon, encouraged those who had not been arrested to follow their example. Urging her audience to insist on their right to enter the Commons, she advised her listeners 'not to be afraid of the police, to link arms, not to break up their ranks, and if they lost sight of their leaders to become leaders themselves'.[12] The women left the hall, including one group numbering between two and three hundred led by Christabel herself. The women held fast, as best they could, but by 10 p.m. the struggle had ended. Overall sixty arrests had been made, including Christabel, Sylvia, Mary Gawthorpe, Charlotte Despard, Nell Kenney (sister of Annie and Jessie) and Frances Rowe. Fred Pethick-Lawrence arranged the £2 bail for Christabel and all the other women.[13]

Next morning the newspapers gave extensive coverage to the previous day's events, condemning the violence the police had used to suppress a peaceful demonstration. Typical were the headlines in the *Daily News*, 'Raid by 700 Suffragettes. March on the Commons – 60 Arrests. Charge by Mounted Police. Women Trampled upon and Injured. Free Fight in Palace Yard'.[14] Such accounts were eagerly devoured by Christabel before she appeared with the other women, at ten o'clock in the morning, at Westminster Police Court. Hatless and wearing a green cloak, she asked, as organiser of the demonstration, to be tried first. Her speech from the dock gave her an opportunity not only to cross-examine Inspector Lewis who had given the order to use mounted police, but also to place responsibility for the violence upon the shoulders of the Government which refused to give women their democratic rights and had instructed the police to use every measure to clear the women away.[15] Mr Curtis Bennett, the magistrate, briskly intervened to say that the women themselves were responsible for the disorder, by the tactics they adopted, and that they had to be stopped. 'It can be stopped', retorted Christabel, 'but only in one way.' The prompt reply was 'twenty shillings or fourteen days'.[16] Christabel chose imprisonment, as did fifty-three other women. This time, after the public outcry about the treatment of Annie Cobden-Sanderson, Christabel and most of the other prisoners were put in the First Division in Holloway.

This was Christabel's second imprisonment and placement in the First Division brought some advantages including wearing her own clothes and being supplied, if she wished, with meals, newspapers and books from outside. But despite these privileges, she found prison life 'inimical' to leadership since 'planning and directing action' became impossible.[17] For some months now she had been writing a series of articles for the *Penny Magazine* on 'The Adventures of a Suffragette' and shortly after her release an essay was published in that journal, describing her time in Holloway. The lack of hygiene was highlighted as one of the most objectionable features of prison life. Prisoners were allowed only a small quantity of water for washing each day while only cold water was used for cleaning purposes so that soup and other food of very inferior quality were served in unclean tins. Worst of all, meals had to be eaten with 'a very unwholesome wooden spoon' which was handed down from one prisoner to another and could, therefore, be the means of transferring disease.[18]

When Christabel and most of the other prisoners were released two weeks later, they were greeted by a large crowd before being accompanied to Eustace Miles Restaurant, a vegetarian eating place, for a celebration breakfast.[19] Sylvia, on the other hand, still had another week to serve. Keir Hardie had written to her twice, sent her some books to read and advised her to do as much sketching and writing as possible. 'I have you often in my thoughts & shall be happier when you are again free', he penned.[20] Christabel, on her release, was still unaware of the strong emotional bond between her sister and their old family friend. Besides, she had other matters on her mind, namely the welcome news that, for the first time ever, a member of parliament who had drawn first place in the private members' ballot had decided to introduce a Women's Enfranchisement Bill. Christabel was hopeful that Mr Dickinson, a Liberal, might be able to carry the Commons with him but was never over-confident that such a measure would pass. 'If they kill this Bill policies will change', she warned. 'If we do not get the vote, it will mean revolution amongst women.'[21] Emmeline Pankhurst too had already uttered a similar message. 'We shall not shrink from death if necessary for the success of the movement', she had told her followers. 'We are not playing at politics in this agitation. If the Government brings out the Horse Guards, and fires on us, we will not flinch.'[22]

The date for the second reading of the Dickinson Bill had been set as 8 March but four days beforehand, Emmeline Pankhurst received a stern warning from her employer, the Registrar General, saying that if she continued to take part in any further political agitation for women's enfranchisement in the 'indiscreet manner' she had hitherto adopted, he would 'consider seriously' whether she should be allowed to retain her post as Registrar for Births and Deaths.[23] Emmeline's job was based in Manchester, where she still lived, and was the sole source of income for herself and Harry, still a schoolboy. Since she did not want to lose her only means of livelihood, she had been careful only to engage in constitutional work for the WSPU, so as to minimise the risk of imprisonment. Mary, her sister, deputised when she was absent from home.

Emmeline confided in Christabel and the Pethick-Lawrences. Christabel thought the Registrar General was being unfair. 'Mother ... used to take the most extraordinary measures to get back, by night trains, in order to be in her office during the hours officially appointed for her attendance. No shadow of complaint had ever reached her.'[24] The Pethick-Lawrences begged Emmeline to resign her official appointment so that she could devote her energies full time to the WSPU. They pointed out that funds were sufficient to guarantee her, the star speaker, an income of £200–300 per annum. The WSPU had grown considerably so that it now had forty-seven branches with district organisers outside the London region, seven rooms at its headquarters at Clement's Inn and an income for the fiscal year from 1 March 1906 to 28 February 1907 of £2,959 4s.[25] Emmeline decided to delay her decision until 8 March when the outcome of the Dickinson Bill was known.

The Ladies' Gallery at the House of Commons was closed to women on that day; since the so-called 'Raid' on the House, the police had orders to prevent any women entering parliament, unless personally accompanied by an MP. So Christabel and her mother went to the offices of the *Daily Mirror* instead to read the details of the debate in the House as they came through on the telegraph tape. After five hours, their worst fears were confirmed. The bill was talked out. At a meeting held at Exeter Hall that evening, Christabel rallied the women present to:

> forget party politics and to rise up united in strenuous opposition to the Liberal Government, which having come into power by professing to stand for freedom, insulted the women of the country by refusing them the elementary rights of citizenship.[26]

Her call was heeded. On 20 March hundreds marched to parliament again, including about forty Lancashire factory women recruited by Annie and Adela, and ten Yorkshire lassies, all dressed in clogs and shawls. Christabel urged the women to 'get inside the . . . House itself, sit down next to Sir Henry Campbell-Bannerman . . . [and] seize the mace', that symbol of parliamentary male authority, of male elective democracy.[27] Seventy-five women and one man were arrested. The following day Emmeline Pankhurst resigned her post as Registrar of Births and Deaths knowing that her WSPU fees would not cover the loss of her salary and pension.

The press contacted the WSPU about the matter, Christabel explaining that her mother's resignation had practically been forced upon her by a clique of Manchester Liberals who strongly opposed her opposition to the Liberal Government.[28] The Manchester home now had to be given up and provision made for Harry's future by apprenticing him to a builder in Glasgow. Christabel's Aunt Mary offered her services to the WSPU, as an organiser. From now until the end of the militant campaign, Emmeline Pankhurst never had a settled home but led an itinerant life, travelling around the country, leading the by-election campaigns and speaking at endless meetings. She lived in hotels, rented flats or stayed at homes of friends eager to accommodate their much-loved leader. When in London she did not stay with the Pethick-Lawrences and Christabel but often at the Inns of Court Hotel, on the corner of High Holborn and Lincoln's Inn Fields.[29]

While Emmeline travelled around the country, Christabel was based at WSPU headquarters, although she too was a frequent speaker, sometimes at a distance. Her long hours of work also included selecting potential recruits prepared to go to prison, a task she shared with Mrs Pethick-Lawrence. Naomi Jacob, a young underpaid schoolteacher and secretary of the WSPU Middlesbrough branch, was one such applicant. Christabel, whose brown hair was inclined to be wispy, was wearing a red tam o' shanter on the day Naomi was interviewed, and tapped the desk with a pencil all the time Naomi was speaking, weighing up accurately the weaknesses of the young woman before her. 'No, you can't go!' was the final decision. When asked why, Christabel replied, 'Because you would make a joke of it all, and play the fool.' Later, taking Naomi aside, Christabel advised her, 'You might be quite a useful person if you could overcome your idiotic love of popularity, Jacob.'[30] Naomi later claimed that she never did.

The long hours of toil took their toll on Christabel's health so that she occasionally fainted.[31] Nor was that the only concern. Charlotte Despard and Annie Cobden-Sanderson, members of both the WSPU and ILP, were voicing again old grievances about WSPU policy at Cockermouth and planned to raise the matter at the ILP Conference to be held in Derby in early April. Although still a member of the Manchester Central Branch of the ILP, Christabel was not prepared to attend the Conference and argue her case, yet again. Nor was Teresa Billington. Emmeline Pankhurst decided to take that task upon her shoulders. 'I have greater claims in the forbearance & regard of the Party than they have', she informed the chair of the Manchester Central Branch, '& am I believe more disposed to make allowances than the younger women.'[32]

The Pethick-Lawrences decided it was time to take the overworked Christabel, Annie and Mary Gawthorpe away for an Easter holiday on the Italian Riviera. 'I am going away on Wednesday to Bordighera', Christabel wrote to Elizabeth Robins on Monday 25 March, '& I return just in time for the first performance of the play. It is very nice of you to arrange about seats for Mother and me.'[33] En route to their destination, the travellers stayed for a short time in Paris before catching the express train to their destination. On the same train, in the restaurant car, was the British Prime Minister, Henry Campbell-Bannerman, who was asked by Annie and Mary about votes for women. The embarrassed Campbell-Bannerman explained that he was going away for a rest and trusted they would make no fuss. When he alighted a few stations before theirs, he stood on the platform, waving his hat and wishing them all a pleasant holiday.[34] The irony of the situation was not lost on Christabel and her companions, or by the press who later wrote about the encounter.

While all this was going on, Emmeline Pankhurst, back in England, was attending the ILP April Conference. In a tense atmosphere, a resolution was debated condemning the actions of the WSPU women at Cockermouth and Huddersfield as 'detrimental to the party' and claiming that 'loyalty to the constitution and policy of the party' was an essential condition of membership. An emotional Emmeline rose to the occasion and gallantly defended Christabel's policy. 'We are not going to wait until the Labour Party can give us a vote', she declared. 'It is by putting pressure on the present Government that we shall get it. We have opposed nobody but Government nominees, and in that we have followed the tactics of the Irish Party.' In a trembling voice she announced, 'If you think my conduct inconsistent with my membership I will resign.'[35] There were cries of protest she should stay in the ILP and some deafening cheers of support – and then later the encouraging news that she was popular enough to be elected again as delegate for the next Labour Party Conference. A chirpy Emmeline believed that such action showed that 'our enemies are defeated & we have only to go on with our work. The best of the men will back us up'.[36]

Christabel had originally planned to be back in London by 9 April, so that she could accompany her mother to the opening night of Elizabeth Robins' play. However, by 8 April she was still in Bordighera, writing apologetically to Miss Robins from the Grand Hotel du Cap and explaining:

> We did not get away from London till two or three days after we meant originally to leave . . . we therefore added a little to the holiday at the other end . . . Mother is in London & will be at the theatre tomorrow of course. That makes me feel I shall not be absent in a way. She & I are very much one you know . . . I hope your holiday did you good. I feel very much better for mine – quite eager for work again. I felt just a little jagged before & am so much looking forward to seeing you again.[37]

When a refreshed Christabel returned home, it was straightaway back into WSPU work. A public luncheon was held at the Holborn Restaurant on Saturday 20 April, to welcome the released prisoners. Elizabeth Robins had been billed to chair the meeting but was unable to attend since she did not feel well. Her absence was probably strategic, tied in with the decision to divide equally between the WSPU and the NUWSS a quarter of her royalties for the highly successful *Votes for women!* which, during the first week of production, amounted to £7 4s 10d (£7 24p) each.[38] Both Mrs Lawrence and Christabel were keen to keep the high-profile celebrity on their side and each wrote to her separately after the lunch. 'It was a great disappointment not to have you with us today', penned Christabel, 'I hope you won't be ill – you looked far from well the other day.' She continued, 'Mrs Lawrence & I had such a happy time with you last Monday except that I was in one of the muffled moods which sometimes pervade me – you will excuse that won't you?'[39]

The ink of Christabel's pen barely had time to dry before she travelled up to Manchester where she was due to speak at several meetings with her mother, Annie, Emmeline Pethick-Lawrence and Elizabeth Wolstenholme Elmy.[40] Indeed, Emmeline Pankhurst had journeyed north to Manchester a few days earlier, seizing the opportunity to sort through her few meagre possessions at 66 Upper Brook Street. Christabel helped her mother gather most of the family papers to give them for safe keeping to her aunt Ada Goulden Bach, her mother's sister, now married and living in London.[41] Once the Manchester home was given up, Christabel travelled back to London and to her usual round of duties. 'Many thanks for the cheque. I enclose treasurer's receipt', she penned in a hand-written letter to WSPU member Maud Arncliffe Sennett who had responded promptly to an appeal for funds.[42] Then, towards the end of April, when one of the most crowded and rowdy of the Hyde Park meetings to date took place, Christabel was given a hearing although Mrs Rowe and Flora Drummond were drowned out.[43]

About this time an edited book titled *The case for women's suffrage* was published for which Christabel and her mother had each written a chapter. The editor, Brougham Villiers, observed that in 'less than three years the movement for the enfranchisement of women has made greater strides than in the century before' so that the discontent among women 'has at last found voice'. The WSPU, he asserted, had provided the 'electric spark' which had turned 'woman the suppliant into woman the rebel'.[44] Christabel's essay discussed a subject dear to her heart, the legal disabilities of women, chief among which was the lack of the parliamentary vote. However, in her wide-ranging discussion she revealed how the WSPU was concerned not just with the vote but a much broader agenda of social change. Many of the disabilities that women experienced in her day, she pointed out, were not based on law but on custom. For example, there was no Act of Parliament barring women from judicial office but some previous judicial decisions. Undoubtedly drawing upon her own painful experiences, she commented that the Benches of the Inns of Court 'have the right to regulate admission to the Bar, and their power of rejecting applicants is virtually absolute'. The fact that the legal profession was closed to women rendered impossible the appointment of a woman lawyer or judge. Even juries were men only so that the 'old principle that accused persons must be tried by their peers was violated every time that a woman is brought forward for trial'.[45]

The assumption that women would get married and be financially dependent upon their husbands rather than financially independent through their own employment shaped the inferior educational provision that girls received and the employment market, so that employers were in the habit of dismissing women employees on marriage. It was married women in particular who experienced greater disabilities, Christabel insisted, due to the old legal rule that the husband and wife were one. Wives faced special disabilities in regard to ownership of property, laws of inheritance, maintenance by husbands, control of children and the obtaining of credit. 'How does such a condition differ from slavery?' It was especially the double sexual standard upheld in divorce cases, a standard set by men, that Christabel attacked. A husband could secure a divorce on the sole ground of his wife's adultery, but adultery on a husband's part gave his wife no right to obtain a divorce:

> To obtain a divorce from him she must prove, in addition to adultery, bigamy, cruelty, or desertion for two years and upwards. The decision as to whether the acts proved amount to legal cruelty, rests with a male judge who is apt to take a lenient view of a fellow-man's shortcomings.[46]

Christabel acknowledged that many of the injustices which women experienced in 1907 would, in the course of time, be removed by Parliament. But, as industrial society grew complex, there were increasing demands on its time so that Parliament was too busy attending to the demands of enfranchised men to have time to spare for the needs of unenfranchised women. She warned that if the danger of unfair industrial legislation for women – imposed as much to protect men from competition as to protect women from exploitation – was averted, then new injustices would arise.[47]

The publication of Christabel's essay did nothing to ease the tensions within the WSPU – which now also included murmurings that it was run autocratically so that the rank-and-file were merely informed of policy, not active participants in its formation. Christabel considered Teresa Billington-Greig (she had married earlier in the year and added her husband's surname to her own) the prime malcontent. There had always been competitive tension between the two strong-minded women so they were never easy in each other's company. Christabel did not trust Teresa, the first woman national organiser for the ILP, while Teresa, for her part, complained that Christabel was 'consistently elusive', even in WSPU meetings.[48] In the autumn of 1906, Teresa had been sent to Scotland, to recruit new WSPU members and to form branches. She resented the move, not least because it allowed Christabel's star to shine more brightly and lessened her own influence. Keen to curb the power of the leaders of the WSPU, Teresa had drawn up a constitution which recognised members as enfranchised voters and declared that the annual conference of delegates was the ultimate governing power.[49] Against Christabel's better judgement, the constitution had been adopted that autumn.

By May 1907, the atmosphere between Christabel and Teresa was decidedly cool, yet Christabel had little time to ponder long on the matter since she was extremely busy. There were the regular WSPU meetings in Hyde Park on Sundays, the At Homes, and rallies in places such as Birmingham where, on 10 May, she spoke with Nellie Martell and Jennie Baines, a working-class woman married to a boot and shoe maker. Above all, there was always the necessity of trying to think of new sensational tactics to attract the attention of the press and public, the unfailing support to be given to new WSPU organisers and voluntary workers – and the interminable correspondence. 'I am so very anxious that we shall have a crowd of women in these meetings', Christabel wrote in her scrawling hand in early May to Jennie Baines, a voluntary worker in Birmingham whose out-of-pocket expenses had to be paid. 'I hear there were not enough at Southampton. Now do not stint in anyway in getting tickets & money. If you are short of money send to Mrs. Lawrence.'[50]

Soon Christabel was writing again to Jennie, apologising for her absence at one gathering and then, two days later, sending another letter, this time typed, indicating that at long last she no longer felt that it was necessity to write personally in her own hand but to use the services of her secretary. 'I approve of your plans', she noted encouragingly. There followed advice about whom to contact for permission for the use of land for an open-air meeting, as well as suggestions for speakers for the At Home. 'Perhaps Mrs. Pankhurst may be able to come, but it is quite doubtful where she will be at that time.' Christabel herself or Mrs Martel or both of them could attend if it was held on the Friday rather than the Monday. 'Monday is a very bad day for us to be out of London, as the London

"At Home" is held then.'[51] Then there was correspondence with Caroline Phillips, Honorary Secretary of the Aberdeen branch of the WSPU as well as with Maud Arncliffe Sennett, a rank-and-file member who wrote to the Chief Organiser of the WSPU suggesting that more should be done to convert men to their cause. 'I quite see the importance of converting the men . . . but I want most to appeal to the women even more in our general work', replied a diplomatic Christabel. 'It is just because they are so guided by men that we must try to emancipate them by telling them that they must work out their own salvation.'[52]

By June the disgruntled Teresa Billington-Greig had resigned as an organiser for the WSPU, although she still continued to work for the organisation in a voluntary capacity. Keen to give the new provincial branches in Scotland more autonomy and boost her own importance, Teresa established a semi-autonomous Scottish Council with its own treasury and with herself as Honorary Secretary.[53] Nor was that all. Disturbing rumours were reaching Clement's Inn that Teresa, Charlotte Despard and Edith How Martyn, all ILP members who were very critical of Christabel's anti-party policy, intended a coup against the leadership, a move that would take place at the annual conference planned for 12 October.

Christabel and her mother listened to the rumours with concern, but were unsure of the exact details of the plan. In 19 June, on the train to Portsmouth, a worried Christabel sent Sylvia a letter, asking if she could find out more:

> Dearest Sylvia
>
> I wonder if you can discover exactly what Mrs. Wells has heard & what she thinks is brewing . . . the more we know the better . . . Please write result to me at the <u>Mascot Holmwood Surrey</u>. I go tomorrow afternoon at 2 & stay till Friday noon so as to consult Mrs. Lawrence.
>
> I am sorry to worry you about my affairs. You poor child have not had much family assistance in your worries. This is more than my affair tho' – it concerns the Union as a whole. T.B. [Teresa Billington-Greig] is a wrecker . . . Love C.[54]

Emmeline Pankhurst wrote to Sylvia too, pointing out, '[W]e have just to face her [Teresa] & put her in her place. She has gone too far this time.'[55] Matters were not helped by the fact that Teresa seemed to be gaining support among some WSPU members. At a recent meeting to welcome her back from Scotland, she had been greeted with a storm of cheers and a standing ovation.[56]

While considering how to best deal with the rising tensions, Christabel continued with her heavy workload, trying hard to bring women of all political persuasions into the WSPU, especially organisers and speakers who would go 'into the towns and villages'.[57] An occasion to attract recruits, as well as raise funds for the recently launched £20,000 appeal, came on 28 June when she and Emmeline Pethick-Lawrence spoke at a Garden Party, held at 56 Kenninghall Road, Clapton, under the Auspices of the Central Society for Women's Suffrage, the North Hackney Women's Liberal Association, as well as the WSPU.[58] Then there were the At Homes at which Christabel regularly spoke, as well as two meetings in Bournemouth from where she wrote to Elizabeth Robins, giving her details about influential Liberals she had met, on Elizabeth's recommendations. 'I am very sorry that I have not written sooner, but I have been very busy', she confessed. Keen to broaden the appeal of the WSPU to all women, irrespective of political affiliation, she then asked Elizabeth if she knew Lady Gwendolen Cecil, a Conservative, who was a member of the executive committee of the Ladies Grand Council of the Primrose League. 'I am trying to get an interview with her as the P. League is disgracefully inactive in the matter of WS [women's suffrage].'[59]

For some weeks Christabel had been active in arranging for a suffragette presence at the by-election in the Colne Valley, a Liberal stronghold, where the dashing Victor Grayson, about her own age, was standing as an independent Social and Labour candidate. Grayson, a member of the Manchester Central Branch of the ILP, was known to the Pankhurst family and, in his election address, had championed the women's cause. Although Christabel had by now lost much of her faith in socialist men, she knew that this by-election was particularly important; if WSPU members worked hard for Grayson to win, it would vindicate her policy of 'keep the Liberal out' and force the Government's hand. 'I hope you are ready for the Colne Valley election', she wrote to on organiser on 6 July 1907. 'We must make a very good show there. I am trying to persuade London workers to go and help.'[60] Adela, Mary Gawthorpe and Nellie Martell also arrived to assist local activists while Emmeline Pankhurst made a flying visit. On 19 July a poll returned Grayson with a one hundred and fifty-two majority, a victory that made headline news. In his acceptance speech he thanked the women for what they had done to keep the Liberal out and expressed his determination to do all he could to bring about votes for women.[61] A delighted Christabel lost no time in optimistically claiming that her tactics were effective. 'By the defeat of the Government at Colne Valley our movement is brought a stage nearer to success . . . We have only to pursue with unflagging energy our by-election policy, and victory is certain.'[62] But victory was not certain. It came as no surprise to Christabel that Grayson, now elected to Parliament, soon forgot about votes for women and directed his energies towards the unemployed.[63] For Grayson, as for so many socialist men, women's rights were secondary to the class struggle.

By August the Scottish WSPU branches had passed resolutions demanding a limitation on the number of paid organisers on the WSPU's National Executive Committee – who had all been appointed by Christabel or Emmeline Pethick-Lawrence.[64] Some of the London membership were also supportive of those who argued that the central committee should be democratically elected and involve members from provincial branches.[65] Christabel was aghast. 'It was as though in the midst of battle the Army had begun to vote upon who should command it, and what the strategy should be.'[66] She believed, as did her mother, that charismatic leadership was the best way for a militant organisation such as the WSPU to operate since then decisions could be made quickly, in response to changing circumstances, without the cumbersome bureaucracy of a lengthy democratic process that included a multitude of committees, the making and carrying of resolutions, the proposing and acceptance of amendments.

Emmeline Pethick-Lawrence wholeheartedly agreed with Christabel and her mother. She greatly admired the young woman sharing her home, believing that Christabel, who had conceived the militant campaign, 'possessed in a high degree a flair for the intricacies of a complex political situation'. Such a quality was especially necessary since so many of the new women 'pouring into the Union' were 'quite ill-informed about' political realities.[67] Mrs Lawrence did not hesitate to speak bluntly to Christabel and her mother about the WSPU's internal crisis, stressing that she had come into the movement because she had confidence in their policy and did not want to see Mrs Pankhurst's leadership 'watered down or diminished or even thwarted by some system of committee control enabling others, without the same vision, to share the leadership'; unless they continued to lead, she would have to reconsider her position.[68] With such an endorsement, the way ahead was clear.

Christabel and her mother decided what they would do; they would hold a central committee cabal before the members' meeting at which they could tear up the 1906 constitution and re-enforce their control. These decisions would then be announced to the membership without a vote being taken. The plans were made in secret over a couple of weeks, although Emmeline Pankhurst confided the details to Sylvia who was now in the North of England, studying the conditions of life for working-class women and painting their portraits.[69] When Sylvia read her mother's letter she replied immediately, condemning the plans as ill-judged. 'Do not fear the democratic constitution. You can carry the Conference with you', she pleaded.[70]

Meanwhile, Jennie Baines wrote hurriedly to Christabel, giving her more information about the dissidents. 'It is very sad that such a spirit as you tell me of should be growing up in the Union', Christabel replied, 'but as you say the oldest & best members are sound and true.'[71] Although this was not an entirely accurate assessment, Christabel began to put the secret plan into action, sending a letter to all London (but not provincial) members, inviting them to a meeting on 10 September where 'important business' would be discussed.[72] Keen to have well-known protagonists on her side, she had already sent two letters to Elizabeth Robins. 'I am so glad that you are willing to come on the 10th Sept.', she had written. '[W]e . . . are so proud to have you with us.' But Elizabeth was somewhat reluctant to commit herself, not least because she was busy working on the proofs of her novel, *The convert*. Christabel persisted. On 30 August she sent Elizabeth a prepaid telegram, asking if it was convenient for her mother to call that afternoon. When no reply was received, she penned another letter to Elizabeth expressing the hope that she would attend the members' meeting. 'I am not going away next week [for a holiday] after all as there is too much to keep me here', she added. 'I sympathise with you in yr agitated feeling for I am feeling just a <u>little</u> so.'[73] Christabel visited Elizabeth the following day, and she agreed to later join the central committee.

At the National Executive Committee meeting of the WSPU held in the afternoon of 10 September, Emmeline Pankhurst announced that the annual conference planned for two days' time was abolished, the constitution annulled and that a new central committee would be elected immediately from those present. Charlotte Despard, both a WSPU and ILP member, supporter of adult suffrage and one of the Honorary Secretaries of the WSPU (the other was Caroline Hodgson), asked on whose authority such changes were made. Emmeline Pankhurst promptly replied that she was responsible and boldly announced that the governing power would be vested in a central committee chosen and appointed by herself. The names of the new committee members were read out – Mary Gawthorpe, Annie Kenney, Nellie Martel, Mary Neal, Elizabeth Robins and Elizabeth Wolstenholme Elmy, with Mrs Lawrence as Honorary Treasurer, Christabel as Organising Secretary and Mabel Tuke and Emmeline herself as the new Honorary Secretaries. All the edicts were presented by Emmeline as resolutions and passed by all present, only Charlotte Despard and Caroline Hodgson dissenting.[74]

That evening, at the members' meeting at Essex Hall, Emmeline skilfully presented the changes as a *fait accompli*. She then called upon all present to give her their loyalty, which the majority did. However, Charlotte Despard, Teresa Billington-Greig, Caroline Hodgson, Edith How Martyn and other disaffected members refused to do so. Claiming that they were *the* WSPU, the 'pro-democracy' group soon found they could not secure the WSPU's offices or finances and so, two months later, called themselves the Women's Freedom League (WFL), Charlotte Despard becoming their elected president.[75] Although Emmeline Pankhurst had resolved that 'her' organisation should now be called the National Women's Social and Political Union, that name was soon dropped in favour of the more familiar WSPU.

Once news about the September split became public, the press began swarming into the WSPU's general office, seeking information about those who had formed a rival organisation. An upbeat Christabel told the *Morning Post*:

> We shall expect every member joining us in future to take this pledge: 'I hereby undertake not to support the candidate of any particular party at Parliamentary elections until women have obtained the Parliamentary vote.' By such a pledge we preserve the solidarity of the Union. Mrs. Despard gave her word that she would never work in elections except for Labour candidates. She is very much in favour of votes for women, but she seems to favour the Labour movement more, whereas our Union places votes for women before anything else.[76]

Emmeline Pankhurst too was confident about the split, despite the fact that the secession was supported by twelve branches. 'All our best workers are with us', she informed Elizabeth Robins. 'They are most enthusiastic about future work free from intrigue & wire pulling.'[77]

Mrs Lawrence, with over-flowing heart, was totally supportive of the way in which her two comrades, 'born leaders', as she termed them, had acted. 'I cannot sufficiently admire the courage with which the Founder of this Movement & her heroic daughter – our beloved Christabel – have dealt with the enemy within the ranks', she wrote to Elizabeth Robins. 'I would sell all that I have if need were, to follow them to the victory they are going to win. My heart is full of admiration & love for them – and I think it the privilege of my life to serve them.'[78] Elizabeth Wolstenholme Elmy also approved of the prompt and vigorous way in which Christabel and her mother had acted. 'London is the very hot-bed of intrigue & treachery & I have been expecting something of this kind ever since it was made headquarters', she confided to Harriet McIlquham. 'Mrs. Pankhurst's so-called autocratic action was of the nature of a desperate remedy to meet a desperate situation', she suggested. 'The whole intrigue is to make Mrs. Despard the despot of the movement, to put Mrs. Pankhurst & the rest of us under her rule.'[79] Christabel for her part expressed no regret at losing her one-time friends and colleagues; nor did her mother. For both women, it was not individuals but ideals that were important. 'Mrs Despard & the rest – may do what they please – we shall argue with them no more', Christabel told Elizabeth Robins. 'Internal troubles have made the real work of the movement very difficult – but now we are at peace.'[80]

Nonetheless, the leaders felt it necessary to visit all WSPU branches, which had a considerable degree of autonomy, and explain what had taken place.[81] Not all such visits were welcome. When Christabel planned to attend a Scottish Council meeting in September, Helen Fraser promptly telegrammed to say that her presence 'will not be necessary'. Christabel attempted to smooth the ruffled feathers here and elsewhere. 'Unity is all that is required now to take us through the little difficulty in which we stand', she wrote to Mary Phillips in Aberdeen.[82] Before long Christabel herself would be taking part in a demonstration in Edinburgh of women's suffrage societies and, despite any reservations she had, speaking on the same platform with Charlotte Despard and Teresa Billington-Greig.[83]

Now that the bitter disagreements within the WSPU about its political independence had been finally settled, Christabel wrote to the secretary of the Manchester Central Branch of the ILP on 13 September, resigning her membership, 'at least until such time as women have obtained the Parliamentary vote. My position as one of the leaders of the W.S.P.U. demands the strictest political independence'. She expressed her 'heartfelt thanks' for the services that the branch had given to the women's cause in the past, knowing that it would continue that support in the future. The following day, Emmeline Pankhurst followed her daughter's lead and sent in her resignation too, but in terms that expressed an affinity with socialism:

> I am still a Socialist and in sympathy with the objects of the Party but I am convinced that until women are men's political equals my first duty is to work independently of party for the political freedom of my sex.[84]

Meanwhile, the *Labour Leader* welcomed the 'determination' of Charlotte Despard and her friends to work with the Labour Party as 'far as they can consistently do so' in the cause of women's enfranchisement.[85]

Although both Adela and Sylvia were unhappy about the resignation of their relatives from the ILP, it was especially Sylvia who was condemnatory. In *The suffragette movement*, she blames Christabel rather than their mother for such action, commenting bitterly that whatever interest Christabel 'had ever possessed in the Socialist movement, in which she had been reared, she had shed as readily as a garment'. But what really irked the middle Pankhurst daughter was that the 1907 split increased Christabel's influence in policy making. '[T]he main work and policy of the W.S.P.U. was directed by Christabel and the Pethick-Lawrences. Mrs. Pankhurst was usually in the provinces, moving from campaign to campaign, lodging to lodging.'[86] What Sylvia failed to acknowledge was that her mother was always consulted on all major policy matters. It was the everyday executive control of the WSPU, in which her mother had little interest, that passed to Christabel and the Pethick-Lawrences (known as the 'triumvirate').

Adela, on the other hand, had a more pragmatic approach to feminist politics than Sylvia. She was now a WSPU organiser and, despite some reservations, showed her support for her mother and Christabel by joining the newly formed Young Hot Bloods (YHB), a tight-knit group of single WSPU members under the age of thirty (married women could not become members) who became devoted to Christabel and Emmeline Pankhurst. All members had to sign a pledge not to divulge the meaning of the letters 'YHB' and to be ready for danger duty. Meetings were usually held in a tea shop in the Strand, Emmeline Pankhurst being the sole older WSPU member who was allowed to attend. Adela was a member of its General Committee, as were Vera Holme, Elsa Gye, Jessie Kenney, Charlotte Marsh and Vera Wentworth.[87]

Christabel always rated highly the friendship, love and steadfastness that this group and other suffragettes gave to her and her mother. So when she heard that the proofs of Elizabeth Robins' novel *The convert* included a less than flattering picture of one such suffragette, immediately recognisable as Nellie Martel, she did not hesitate to write to the author in stern terms:

> I have been quite worried & am still about the lady in the book who <u>is</u> founded on fact. You & she belong to the same committee & she is quite as well intentioned as any of us. I wish she could have been left out or made unrecognisable. It would be easy to draw an ugly picture of any of us you know . . . The person is helping very much in the present crisis.[88]

While Christabel did not fret about losing the friendship of Teresa Billington-Greig, she could be protective of those who were loyal to her.

Meanwhile, Fred Pethick-Lawrence had not been idle but was using his money and journalistic expertise to help the WSPU launch its own journal. *Votes for Women*, edited by himself and his wife, appeared in October 1907, shortly after the split. Initially a monthly journal costing three pence, the paper became within six months an affordable one-penny weekly with a circulation of nearly 30,000 by 1909. 'Votes for Women/Price one penny/Articles by Annie Kenney/ Mrs. Lawrence-Christabel/Other Suffragettes as well' the newspaper sellers might chant as they stood in the gutter (they were prohibited by law from standing on the pavement in case they obstructed pedestrians). *Votes for Women*, with all its news, including Christabel's regular articles on policy and the national campaign, became a very effective medium for branding the WSPU throughout the UK, as well as keeping members in touch.[89] It helped to consolidate Christabel's power as the key strategist, as well as forge a sense of sisterhood and community among its regular supporters.

The unsigned leader in the first issue of *Votes for Women*, titled 'The Battle Cry', undoubtedly written by Christabel, spelt out the WSPU's message loud and clear:

> To women far and wide the trumpet call goes forth, Come fight with us in our battle for freedom . . . Come and join us, whatever your age, whatever your class . . . If you are tied to any men's political party you must break that tie before you come into this movement . . . those who come must come as soldiers ready to march onwards in battle array . . . We fight for nothing less than the emancipation of one-half of the whole human race.[90]

As this statement makes clear, the WSPU was never waging just a single-issue campaign for the parliamentary vote. It wanted the emancipation of the female sex. Although military language was used to describe its organisation and its activities, the WSPU was organised and led 'much the same as the Salvation Army under General Booth', asserted Christabel.[91]

For some time now Christabel had been pondering upon a comment made by Israel Zangwill, the novelist, in a speech supporting women's enfranchisement when he had pointed out that in one of his early novels female suffrage had been passed by a Conservative Government. 'I warn Sir Henry Campbell-Bannerman that, unless he hurries up, my words will come true', he joked.[92] The reprinting of the talk in the Brougham Villiers edited volume in which Christabel too had a chapter reminded her that this might be an avenue worth exploring. In early October 1907 Christabel began a private correspondence with the former Conservative Prime Minister, Arthur Balfour, an alleged supporter of votes for women, enquiring whether when 'next in office' he would extend the parliamentary franchise to women. Since such a declaration would be useful to the WSPU as a stick with which to taunt the Liberals, Christabel was wise enough to suggest that any formal meeting with Balfour could be deferred until such time that he felt able to make a positive commitment. But ever the tactician, she appealed to him as a Conservative wanting to extend his party's share of the electorate by pointing out how a positive statement on his part would prevent 'the threatened alliance' between a large section of the women's suffrage movement and the Labour Party:

> I am very anxious that the whole women's suffrage movement (and not our own society alone) shall remain independent of the Labour Party because I am far from being persuaded that the Labour party can or will take effective action upon their pledge. A favourable declaration from you will be of far greater importance and will have the effect of prevent-ing a Labour-Suffrage alliance.[93]

While awaiting a reply, Christabel went about her work as usual, speaking at meet-ings, formulating strategies and writing supportive letters to organisers, voluntary workers and friends alike.[94] On Saturday 12 October she also met up with Annie, now an organiser in the west of England, based in Bristol, for an 'At Home' at the Portman Rooms, in celebration of the second anniversary of their first imprison-ment in Strangeways. The event was attended by seven hundred women.[95] Annie was one of the few people to whom Christabel confided the news about her let-ter to Balfour whose evasive six-page reply, marked 'Not for publication', was received nearly a fortnight later. Balfour, a 'fence-sitter by temperament', stated that he was not convinced that there was a strong feeling among the mass of women that they wanted to be included in the electorate. Further, as leader of the Conservative Party, he could not give his support for women's suffrage without consulting his colleagues.[96] Despite the disappointment, Christabel thought it best to keep open such a channel of communication. 'I thank you very much for your kind reply', she replied in late October, in a friendly manner, and continued:

> The demand for the vote on the part of women is far stronger than peo-ple imagine. If only you would say what you would regard as a proof, that a demand exists! I know that we can fulfil any condition that you may lay down . . . I wish I could put into words the desire that the women of my generation have for this thing. It is very hard and such a waste of energy to spend the best years of one's life in working for what ought to be ours by right.[97]

The regret expressed in this letter about spending the best years of one's life fighting for a just cause did not appear to linger. Christabel had 'changeable moods', remembered suffragette Mary Richardson. 'Hers was an amazing charac-ter, capable of alternating between storm and sunshine in the space of moments.'[98] Christabel was soon writing a more cheerful letter to Elizabeth Robins, hoping she could come to a speech she was giving in Brighton on 30 October. Elizabeth Robins frequently wrote articles on the British suffrage movement for both English and American journals, and had recently published a pamphlet for the WSPU titled *Woman's Secret?* in which she argued for a greater understanding by men, the dominant sex, of women's views. 'Have I told you how very much

I like "Woman's Secret"?' Christabel enthused to its author on 29 October. 'Are you better & stronger? We are getting on better than ever. Yesterday's At Home was crowded.'[99]

That very evening, after writing to Elizabeth Robins, Christabel was at Romford Parliamentary Debating Society, defending the WSPU's militant tactics. Then in early November she took part in a similar discussion, with Annie and Emmeline Pethick-Lawrence, this time at the Clifton Debating Society, Bristol, before travelling to speak at Southampton. The women's campaign in Bristol, opined the *Daily Chronicle*, was particularly interesting since Bristol had been the scene of so much former agitation when men had been demanding their enfranchisement. '[T]he militant Suffragists are not intending to burn down houses and halls, to pull Bishops out of their carriages, and so on, though they were advised by a Cabinet Minister only a few days ago to behave like men', it noted.[100]

The advice to behave as men fighting for their enfranchisement was not forgotten by Christabel who was well versed in franchise history. The issue was particularly pertinent that autumn of 1907 since it was rumoured that the Deputy Leader of the Liberal Party, Herbert Asquith, Chancellor of the Exchequer and a fierce opponent of women's enfranchisement, would be the next Prime Minister. 'Argument and patient services are quite lost upon such as man as he is', Christabel warned readers of *Votes for Women*. 'Nothing but hard political fighting will break down his opposition to the emancipation of women.'[101] Asquith was due to address a Liberal meeting at Nuneaton on Saturday 16 November, and so none other than Christabel, together with Flora Drummond and Jessie Kenney, turned up to organise the heckling. 'Votes for women!' and 'The women of England want justice!' about thirty women shouted at intervals throughout his speech. 'Shame!' and 'Chuck her out!' came from other sections of the room as each woman in turn was ejected roughly from the building.[102]

Christabel was keen for such interruptions to continue at other gatherings at which Asquith spoke, including those held in his own constituency in East Fife, Scotland. On 12 November she had written to Mary Phillips, who was helping Helen Fraser in Glasgow, asking if she could organise a rousing campaign there, as well as in the East Fife constituency. 'We have in London a band of voluntary workers who are prepared to organise on behalf of the Union in various parts of the country on payment of out-of-pocket expenses', she explained. 'I want you, if you can do so, to do the same great service in Scotland.'[103] Mary agreed to help over the next four weeks or so. 'I feel it is a very great advantage to have your assistance', replied Christabel, enclosing with her letter some leaflets on why the suffragettes protested at Liberal meetings.[104]

At such a meeting held at Aberdeen in mid-December Asquith, as expected, made no reference to women's suffrage in his long speech. When pressed at question time, he said that he was prepared to withdraw his opposition to women's enfranchisement when he was satisfied of two things, 'first, that the majority of women desire to have a Parliamentary vote, and next, that the conferring of a vote upon them would be advantageous to their sex and the community at large'.[105] Christabel observed that Asquith was attempting to lay down for women conditions never imposed in the case of men's agitation for the vote. 'Men have never been called upon to prove that the majority of those for whom enfranchisement was sought really desired it.'[106]

The heckling of Asquith and other Cabinet Ministers upset their Liberal supporters so much that the latter began to attend open suffrage meetings and cause pandemonium. This was so at a WSPU meeting held at Birmingham Town Hall on 20 November, at which Christabel, Emmeline Pankhurst, Nellie Martel and Emmeline Pethick-Lawrence were billed to speak. About two hundred students took possession of the gallery facing the platform, and armed with hooters, rattles, whistles and a variety of noise-producing instruments, created so much disturbance that no one could be heard. Christabel, who opened proceedings, appealed to them as a fellow-student, all to no avail. When she said that one or two of them were 'not yet quite out of the nursery', the response was the singing of the National Anthem. Emmeline Pankhurst then attempted to say something and a youth immediately started playing a cornet. As a fight broke out, the police arrived to quell the disturbance.[107] A similar pandemonium occurred in Nottingham on 2 December when between two and three hundred young men made a concerted din as Christabel tried to speak. She stood her ground pluckily, for over an hour. At one point, mice were released onto the platform. While several of the women ran in fright, Christabel picked up a few of the creatures and handed one down to a reporter. 'We can afford to smile at these little occurrences – at the thoughtlessness of young fellows', she declared. Although cheers greeted this incident, it did not obtain her a hearing.[108]

Rowdy scenes such as this convinced Christabel of the need to educate the public about the aims and methods of the WSPU. Consequently she had been busy writing informative leaflets for general distribution. 'I have sent to you today 4,000 leaflets explaining why we protest at liberal meetings', she wrote to Jennie Baines after the Birmingham fiasco. Jennie was staying at the Salvation Army Home in Liverpool and shortly to travel to Sunderland. Christabel advised her not to make a stir in the town before the meeting but to keep an element of surprise. 'I am writing to my sister Adela to send women and will you please discuss the matter with Miss Kenney'. Christabel suggested to Jennie:

> You can stay with Mrs Harwin, Palace Temperance Hotel, High Street, Sunderland and mention that Mrs Drummond who stayed with her on Tuesday has sent you. As soon as the Sunderland meeting is over, will you please hurry back to your work in Lancashire as time is short.[109]

Jennie Baines, now an organiser on a salary of £2 week, was considered by Christabel to have done 'excellent work'.[110] Soon she was asking for a postcard of herself to be made, presumably to be sold at meetings or in suffrage shops alongside the postcards of the leaders and other organisers. The request was passed to Mrs Lawrence who fretted, '[W]e are spending an awful lot of money just now, and your poor Treasurer has sleepless nights.'[111]

Christabel put a brave face on the recent rowdyism she had encountered, telling readers of *Votes for Women* that it was difficult 'to injure a good cause' and that 'more good than harm' had come from the encounters.[112] The University of Birmingham Debating Society accepted her challenge to debate the motion 'That the methods of the Women's Social and Political Union are best calculated to advance the cause of Women's Suffrage.' However, the good-humoured debate which took place on 5 December ended with the motion being lost.[113]

Soon Christabel was back in London, speaking at West Kensington, Chiswick Town Hall and Clapham, among other places.[114] And there were the usual administrative and rank-and-file queries with which to deal. 'I do not know whether the Secretary has written to you about the proposed Drawing room meeting in your house', she wrote on 7 December to Mrs Holroyd Chaplin, 2 Holland Villas Road, London. She explained that since her correspondent could not provide an audience, she did not know whether they could avail themselves of her 'very kind offer, but later on we may be in a position to do so'.[115] To another willing helper, Mrs Grinling, Christabel sent handbills announcing the main London meetings during 1908, encouraging her to advertise the events and to bring her friends. 'At the Caxton Hall in February and at the Albert Hall on March 19th', she added, 'many women will be present from the Provinces for whom we are anxious to provide accommodation. We shall be very glad to know if you can provide hospitality for any of our friends on either of these occasions.'[116] There was also another letter from Balfour to answer; it had arrived just as Christabel was leaving to campaign against the Government nominee in a forthcoming by-election in mid-Devon.

Christabel was pleased that at a recent Conservative Conference in Birmingham a woman suffrage resolution had been carried.[117] 'I have told you before how much more friendly & polite the Tories are nowadays', she commented to Elizabeth Robins.[118] Keen to nurture any political advantage that might arise from such a situation, she replied to Balfour in mid-December giving him, as he had requested, her views about the employment of married women. John Burns, the one-time socialist who many thought had 'sold out' to the Liberals by becoming President of the Local Government Board, had recently argued that wives should be excluded from employment. Christabel informed Balfour that she strongly disagreed with Burns' view and asserted that he was 'quite incapable of taking any save the masculine view of things'. Pressing home the point about reactionary views held by many Labour men, she mentioned that in Huddersfield, when a number of married women working in the mills had asked for a crèche to be established, so that their children might be cared for during the day, the proposal had been 'rejected by the Town Council, Labour members voting against it'. Explaining to Balfour that she was going to the London School of Economics the next day, to examine the latest publications on the wages of married women, a list of which she would send to him, Christabel concluded, 'From my knowledge of the lives of my working women friends, I am convinced that to exclude married women from industry will involve great hardship & will lower their domestic status.'[119]

Christmas was fast approaching and so it was decided to spend it at Teignmouth, one of the places in the mid-Devon by-election where Christabel was campaigning. The Liberal majority at the last general election had been just 1,219, so she was hopeful that when the poll was returned in the New Year, the Government candidate could be defeated. On Saturday 21 December, Christabel spoke at Teignmouth and Newton Abbott before dashing back to London for her regular Monday 'At Home', then rushing down again to Teignmouth where her mother joined her.[120] Christabel and Emmeline asked Sylvia and Mary Gawthorpe to come and spend Christmas with them. Mary gladly accepted but Sylvia refused, saying she needed some time on her own, not telling her relatives why. Still a member of the ILP, Sylvia had avoided quarrelling about the split in the WSPU and had recently returned to London where she found a letter waiting for her. It was probably from Hardie, suggesting that they end their relationship. 'I was so utterly miserable', she told Mary over twenty years later. 'My heart was almost broken. I was very near ending my life!'[121] After three days on her own, Sylvia wanted desperately to find some relief from her unhappiness and so hastened down to Teignmouth on Christmas Eve. It was dark when she arrived and a fierce gale was blowing. When she found her relatives and Mary Gawthorpe 'as merry as crickets', she instantly regretted that she had come. On Boxing Day, feeling that she could no longer keep up appearances, she insisted on returning to London, much to her mother's disapproval.[122] Sylvia's unwillingness to talk openly to either her mother or Christabel about what was troubling her undoubtedly helped to create a situation where the middle Pankhurst daughter was seen as 'difficult'.

After Sylvia left that Boxing Day of 1907, Christabel sat down to write to Balfour again. Her visit to the library at the London School of Economics had not been particularly fruitful in regard to the topic of the prohibition of wage-earning by married women since so little had been written on it. After more expansion on the theme, she concluded her letter with a gentle reminder:

> By this post I am sending you cuttings from the 'Aberdeen Free Press' showing that we are gaining ground. You told us in Manchester in 1906 that we were 'not in the swim'. Very helpful were your words on that subject. We have tried very hard to get into the swim – and we think we are succeeding.[123]

Notes

1 CP to Miss Robins, 4 January 1907, Elizabeth Robins Papers, Harry Ransom Humanities Research Center, University of Texas at Austin (hereafter HRHRC).
2 EP to Miss Robins, 19 November 1906, Robins Papers, HRHRC.

3 Angela V. John, *Elizabeth Robins: staging a life, 1862–1952* (London and New York, Routledge, 1995), p. 156; ESP, *TSM*, p. 221.
4 CP to Henry Harben, 7 August 1913, Harben Papers, BL.
5 CP to Mrs Cullen, 25 January 1907, Suffragette Fellowship Collection, Museum of London (hereafter SFC).
6 E. Sharp, *Unfinished adventure: selected reminiscences from an Englishwoman's life* (London, John Lane, Bodley Head, 1933), p. 131.
7 *LL*, 1 February 1907.
8 CP, The truth about adult suffrage, *Labour Record*, February 1907, p. 270.
9 EWE to Dearest Friend, 5 February 1907, EWEP, Add Ms 47,455, f.49.
10 Conversazione at the Rooms of the Royal Society of Arts on Tuesday, February 12th, 1907, 8.30 to 11.00, leaflet, ESPA; *Daily Chronicle*, 13 February 1907.
11 Rosen, *Rise up women!*, p. 80.
12 *Times*, 14 February 1907.
13 *Times*, 14 February 1907; *Daily News*, 15 February 1907. Sylvia in her *TSM*, p. 253 claims that as she was leading a small band of women she was 'surprised to see Christabel slip quietly . . . behind me. She told me later that she thought it would necessary for her to go to prison in London, and on the spur of the moment she had decided to take this opportunity while sentences were short'. But the contemporary records comment on plans that were well laid and made no mention of Sylvia leading a group – see *Daily News* and *Daily Chronicle*, 14 February 1907. Nor does Sylvia in her earlier book *The Suffragette* pp. 139–42, repeat the same storyline that she later spun.
14 *Daily News*, 14 February 1907.
15 *Times*, 15 February 1907.
16 ESP, *The suffragette*, p. 143.
17 CP, *Unshackled*, p. 76.
18 CP, The adventures of a suffragette: VI. In prison for the vote, *Penny Magazine* No. 445, Vol. XXV [1907], pp. 163–4.
19 When in prison, suffragettes invariably chose vegetarian food since it was of better quality than non-vegetarian.
20 Hardie to Sylvia, 27 February 1907, ESPA.
21 Raeburn, *The militant suffragettes*, p. 36.
22 *Daily Telegraph*, 18 February 1907.
23 Chief Clerk at General Registrar Office to Madam [EP], 4 March 1907, Craigie Collection.
24 CP, *Unshackled*, p. 79.
25 CP to ESP, 3 August 1957, cited in R. Pankhurst, Suffragette sisters in old age: unpublished correspondence between Christabel and Sylvia Pankhurst, 1953–57, *Women's History Review*, 10, 2001, p. 498; WSPU, *First annual report, including balance sheet and subscription list for the year ending February 28th, 1907* (London, Clement's Inn, WSPU [1907]).
26 *Daily Chronicle*, 9 March 1907.
27 *Daily Mail*, 21 March 1907; Liddington, *Rebel girls*, p. 123.
28 *Daily Chronicle*, 23 March 1907.
29 Purvis, *Emmeline Pankhurst*, p. 92.
30 N. Jacob, *Me: a chronicle about other people* (London, Hutchinson, 1932), p. 199.
31 Mrs Rowe to Harriet McIlquham, 24 March 1907, TWL.
32 EP to Sam Robinson, 2 March 1907, Hannah Mitchell Papers, Manchester Public City Libraries Archives.
33 CP to Miss Robins, 25 March 1907, Robins Papers, HRHRC.
34 Kenney, *Memories*, pp. 117–18.
35 Independent Labour Party, *Report of the fifteenth annual conference, Temperance Hall, Derby, April 1st and 2nd 1907* (London, ILP, May 1907), pp. 47–8; *LL* 5 April 1907.
36 See EP to Helen Fraser, 3 April 1907, SFC.

RAPID GROWTH OF THE WSPU AND SPLITS

37 CP to Miss Robins, 8 April 1907, Fales Library, Elmer Holmes Bobst Library, New York University.
38 EPL to Miss Robins, 19 April 1907, HRHRC; John, *Elizabeth Robins*, p. 148.
39 CP to Miss Robins, 20 April 1907, HRHRC.
40 *LL*, 19 April 1907.
41 Richard's tender letters to Emmeline during their courtship were carefully kept by his widow and on her death passed to Christabel who refers to them in *Unshackled*. Unfortunately, they are no longer extant. Most of the other family papers Emmeline eventually gave to Sylvia, probably in 1912, hoping she would write a biography of Richard, ESP to FPL [early July 1959], P-L Papers.
42 CP to Mrs Arncliffe Sennett, 23 April 1907, Maud Arncliffe Sennett Collection, BL Vol. 1 (hereafter MASC).
43 *Times* and *Daily Chronicle*, 29 April 1907.
44 Brougham Villiers, Introduction to his edited *The case for women's suffrage* (London, T. Fisher Unwin, 1907), p. 17.
45 CP, The legal disabilities of women, in Villiers ed, *The case for women's suffrage*, pp. 86–7.
46 CP, Legal disabilities of women, pp. 95–6.
47 CP, Legal disabilities, pp. 97–8.
48 TBG, 1906 Stevenson Square meetings, TBG Papers, Box 398, 7/TBG2/B62.
49 L. Bell, The woman's movement and democracy, and M. Phillips, Woman's point of view, *Forward*, 2 November 1907; T. Billington-Greig, The difference in the women's movement, *Forward*, 23 November 1907; Rosen, *Rise up women!*, pp. 88–9.
50 CP to Mrs. Baines, n.d., Jennie Baines Papers, Fryer Library.
51 CP to Mrs Baines, 13 and 15 May 1907, Baines Papers.
52 CP to Miss Phillips, 14 May 1907, Watt Collection, Aberdeen Art Gallery and Museum; CP to Mrs Arncliffe Sennett, MASC, Vol. 1, c121 g1.
53 *Women's Franchise*, 27 June 1907, p. 7. See L. Leneman, *A guid cause: the women's suffrage movement in Scotland* (Aberdeen, Aberdeen University Press, 1991), pp. 50–1 and S. Pedersen, *The Scottish suffragettes and the press* (London, Palgrave Press, 2017), pp. 97–8.
54 CP to ESP, 19 June 1907, ESPA.
55 EP to ESP, 22 June 1907, ESPA.
56 *Women's Franchise*, 27 June 1907, p. 8.
57 CP, The movement week by week, *Women's Franchise*, 27 June 1907, p. 6.
58 Invitation for a Garden Party, Friday, June 28th 1907, John Johnson Collection, Women's Suffrage, Box 3, Bodleian Library, Oxford.
59 CP to Miss Robins, 11 July 1907, Robins Papers, HRHRC.
60 CP to Mrs Baines, 6 July 1907, Baines Papers.
61 *Daily Mirror*, 20 July 1907; *Women's Franchise*, 25 July 1907, p. 50; Liddington, *Rebel girls*, pp. 147–56.
62 *Women's Franchise*, 25 July 1907, p. 48.
63 ESP, TSM, p. 367.
64 The organisers on the National Executive were Annie Kenney, Mary Gawthorpe, Minnie Baldock, Nellie Martel, Adela Pankhurst and Flora Drummond.
65 See Mrs Rowe to Mrs McIlquham, 1 August 1907, TWL.
66 CP, *Unshackled*, p. 82.
67 EPL, *My part*, pp. 175–6.
68 CP to Lord Pethick-Lawrence, 25 May 1957, P-L Papers; Sylvia Pankhurst to CP, 10 July 1957, Craigie Collection; CP, *Unshackled*, p. 82.
69 Sylvia's travels were probably prompted by the fact that Hardie, who had been ill earlier that summer, was no longer in London but had embarked on a world tour that would not end until spring the following year.
70 ESP, TSM, p. 264.

71 CP to Mrs Baines, 28 August 1907, Baines Papers.

72 CP to Miss Thompson, 31 August 1907, SFC.

73 CP to Miss Robbins, Telegram, 30 August and letters 27 and 30 August 1907, Robins Papers, HRHRC.

74 Rosen, *Rise up women!* pp. 90–1. There are conflicting accounts of the 1907 split. In a letter dated 13 September 1907, to be sent to various newspapers, C. Despard claimed that C. Hodgson, but not herself, signed the new 'pledge' in Christabel's presence, Harriet McIlquham Papers, TWL.

75 For accounts of the Women's Freedom League see, for example, C. Eustance, Meanings of militancy: the ideas and practice of political resistance in the Women's Freedom League, 1907–14, in *The women's suffrage movement,* eds Joannou and Purvis, pp. 51–64; H. Francis, 'Dare to be free!': the Women's Freedom League and its legacy, in *Votes for women,* eds Purvis and Holton, pp. 181–202; Crawford, *The women's suffrage movement,* pp. 720–4.

76 *Morning Post,* 13 September 1907.

77 EP to Miss Robins, Robins Papers, HRHRC.

78 EPL to Miss Robins, 15 September 1907, Robins Papers, HRHRC.

79 EWE to H. McIlquham, 13 September and 11 October 1907, EWEP, Add Mss 47455, fs.111 and 121.

80 CP to Miss Robins, 15 September 1907, Robins Papers, HRRC.

81 See EP to Miss Thompson, 17 September 1907, SFC.

82 CP to Miss Phillips, 20 September 1907, Watt Collection.

83 *LL,* 11 October 1907.

84 Minutes of Manchester ILP Central Branch Meeting, 17 September 1907, Manchester Public City Libraries Archives. A number of WSPU members, such as Flora Drummond, also resigned from the ILP.

85 *LL,* 20 September 1907.

86 ESP, *TSM,* pp. 247–8, 265–6.

87 Copy of Y.H.B. Statement, Rex V. Kerr & Others File, Schlesinger Library, Radcliffe College, Massachusetts, USA.

88 CP to Miss Robins, 26 September 1907, Robins Papers, HRRC.

89 Raeburn, *The militant suffragettes,* p. 44; M. DiCenzo, Militant distribution: *Votes for Women* and the public sphere, *Media History,* Vol. 6, No. 2, 2000, pp. 115–28; J. Mercer, Making the News: *Votes for Women* and the mainstream press, *Media History,* Vol 10, No. 3, 2004, pp. 187–99; M. E. Tusan, *Women making news: gender and journalism in modern Britain* (Urbana and Chicago, IL, University of Illinois Press, 2005), pp. 153–5.

90 *Votes for Women* (hereafter *VFW*), October 1907, p. 6.

91 CP, *Unshackled,* p. 83.

92 I. Zangwill, One and one are two, speech delivered at Exeter Hall, 9 February 1907, reprinted in Villiers ed, *The case for women's suffrage,* p. 206.

93 CP to Mr Balfour, 6 October 1907, A. J. Balfour Papers, BL Mss Add 49793, f.17–18.

94 See, for example, CP to J. Baines, 16 October 1907, Baines Papers and CP to Miss Robins, 22 October 1907, HRHRC.

95 *Daily News,* 14 October 1907.

96 Mitchell, *Queen Christabel,* p. 113; A. J. Balfour to CP (copy), 23 October 1907, Balfour Papers, Add Mss 49793, f.19.

97 CP to A. J. Balfour, 28 October 1907, Balfour Papers, Add Mss 49793, f.31.

98 M. Richardson, *Laugh a defiance* (London, Weidenfeld and Nicolson, 1953), p. 63.

99 CP to Miss Robins, 29 October 1907, Robins Papers, HRHRC.

100 *VFW* [Supplement], 24 October 1907, p. xii; Dobbie, *A nest of suffragettes,* p. 13; *Daily Chronicle,* 2 November 1907.

101 *VfW* [Supplement], 7 November 1907, p. xviii.

102 *Daily Mirror,* 18 November 1907.

103 CP to Miss Phillips, 12 November 1907, Mary Phillips Papers, Linton Park Plc, Linton, Maidstone (hereafter Mary Phillips Papers).
104 CP to Miss Phillips, 28 November 1907, Mary Phillips Papers.
105 *VfW*, January 1908, p. 58.
106 *VfW* [Supplement] 26 December 1907, p. xlvi.
107 *Daily Telegraph*, 21 November 1907.
108 *Daily Chronicle*, 3 December 1907.
109 CP to Mrs Baines, 28 November 1907, Baines Papers.
110 CP to Mrs Baines, incomplete letter, n.d., Baines Papers.
111 EPL to Mrs Baines, 14 November 1907, Baines Papers.
112 *VfW*, 5 December 1907.
113 *Daily Chronicle*, 6 December 1907.
114 *VfW*, 5 December 1907.
115 CP to Mrs Holroyd Chaplin, 7 December 1907, TWL.
116 CP to Mrs Grinling, 18 December 1907, Craigie Collection.
117 *VfW*, December 1907, p. 38.
118 CP to Miss Robins, Robins Papers, HRHRC.
119 CP to Mr Balfour, 16 December 1907, Balfour Papers, Add Mss 49,793, f.39.
120 *VfW* [Supplement] 19 December 1907, p. xliv.
121 ESP to Mary Gawthorpe, 10 May 1929, Mary Gawthorpe Papers, Tamiment Library, New York University.
122 ESP, TSM, p. 272.
123 CP to Mr Balfour, 26 December 1907, Balfour Papers, Add Mss 49,793, f.42.

9

GREATEST LIVING SPEAKER
OF HER DAY

1908

Since both Balfour and Asquith had asked for proof that there was widespread demand from women for the vote, Christabel announced at the beginning of the New Year 'a comprehensive campaign' that would prove that very point. Women's Parliaments would meet in the Caxton Hall, Westminster, on 11, 12 and 13 February. This would be followed, on 19 March, by the first ever demonstration in support of women's suffrage to be held in the large and imposing Albert Hall. Then on Sunday 21 June, the WSPU would organise a mass meeting in Hyde Park. It was also pointed out that the Union's work had expanded so much that six additional rooms had now been taken over at Clement's Inn while the Monday 'At Homes' were so overcrowded that they would now be held in the Portman Rooms which could accommodate about 400.[1]

Although large meetings that enlisted the support of the public were to be a key feature of WSPU activity in 1908, the year began for Christabel with the usual round of much smaller local meetings, including speaking twice to Jewish associations in Manchester.[2] Then she crossed over the Pennines to Leeds, and travelled south to speak at the invitation of the Women's Liberal Association in Brighton, before journeying up to Birmingham.[3] The person most frequently at her side at this time was Mrs Lawrence. Emmeline Pankhurst, leading the by-election campaigns in the provinces, was listed only once to speak on a platform with her favourite daughter this January, a pattern that was to become increasingly common over the next few years.[4] She often felt 'almost an outsider' during her brief stays in London and resented Christabel's work and friendship with the Pethick-Lawrences in whose home she lived.[5] This resentment was to grow steadily over the next four years.

Christabel was overjoyed in mid-January when she heard that the Liberal candidate had been defeated in favour of the Conservative at the turbulent Mid-Devon by-election in Newton Abbot. But mob-law had reigned when the verdict was announced as a group of young men who supported the ousted Liberal attacked Emmeline Pankhurst and Nellie Martel with clay, rotten eggs and snowballs packed with stones.[6] Keen that their ordeal should not be in vain and that the Conservatives should acknowledge the contribution made by the WSPU, Christabel sent Balfour copies of newspaper reports that claimed that the suffragettes had influenced the voters. 'Some of us have worked a bit of our lives into the work of defeating the Government in Devon – indeed my mother & Mrs Martel went near to losing theirs outright', she told him, 'so that we do not like other people to claim all the credit.' If Balfour could not mention the suffragettes in this connection then perhaps, when castigating the Government for their misdeeds, he could refer to their attitude to the women's issue.[7] The problem with Cabinet Ministers, Christabel confided to another correspondent, was that they 'can't move with the times & that they think the women of the younger generation will submit to the kind of treatment meekly submitted to by their mothers'.[8]

Meanwhile, Christabel found that her brother Harry had suddenly arrived in London. The building firm where he worked was in financial difficulties and so he had travelled to the metropolis, to stay with Sylvia. A decision about his future was delayed until their mother returned to London. Emmeline Pankhurst was concerned to hear that her only surviving son was not settled in an occupation. Christabel pointed out tactfully that an outdoor life in all weathers was not really suitable for her brother's delicate health and suggested instead an office job, as a secretary. Emmeline eagerly embraced this idea, offering to pay for weekly classes in shorthand and typing, a reader's ticket at the British Museum, as well as an allowance of £1 per week. With the matter settled, she left again for the provinces. With their mother out of the way, the practical Christabel and Sylvia arranged for Harry to have an eye test so that the spectacles he so badly needed, and which their mother had discouraged, could be ordered. But Harry Pankhurst, like his sisters, was not interested in the dull work of an office job. Soon he was working for the WSPU, chalking pavements, heckling Cabinet Ministers, speaking at street corners and pushing around barrows of suffrage literature.[9]

As on previous occasions, the Women's Parliaments of 11–13 February were held just after the King's Speech which, as predicted, included no reference to votes for women in the Government's forthcoming programme. Christabel thought up a new ruse for the opening day, something that would vividly emphasise women's right to enter the Houses of Parliament. At about a quarter to four in the afternoon, a furniture removal van, full of suffragettes, stopped outside the St Stephen's entrance to the Commons. The back doors of the van flew open and the women rushed forward. The police, although warned to be ready for a suffragette protest, were so surprised by the manoeuvre that two of the women rushed through the entrance before being stopped. Meanwhile, at Caxton Hall, Christabel, Annie and Emmeline Pethick-Lawrence were organising a deputation that would carry a resolution to the Commons. While the rank-and-file tried unsuccessfully to reach the St Stephen's entrance, forcing their way through crowds and police barriers, their leaders urged them on from the relative safety of wheeled vehicles, Christabel's cab nearly overturning. That evening, another unsuccessful attempt was made to enter the Commons. By the end of the day, fifty women had been arrested, but not Christabel. In court the following morning, all the women, with three exceptions, were given six-week sentences in the Second Division in Holloway because they refused to undertake not to repeat their action. The magistrate warned that if ever they offended again, he would revive the Tumultuous Petitions Act, dating from the reign of Charles II, which forbade the petitioning of his Majesty or parliament by more than ten persons.[10]

At a Caxton Hall meeting later that day, a defiant Christabel announced that she could find twelve women or more, even a hundred, to test this Act. '[T]he present struggle', she insisted, 'was a trial of strength between modern women and a number of old men who could not move with the times.'[11] Meanwhile, Emmeline Pankhurst, still limping from an ankle injury sustained at Newton Abbott, had returned from Leeds to London to attend the last day of the Women's Parliaments. She led a deputation of thirteen women to the Commons and was one of ten arrested for 'obstructing the police'. Christabel, Sylvia and the Pethick-Lawrences managed to gain admission to the crowded police court where the women were tried. The sentence was the same as on the previous occasion, six weeks in the Second Division.[12]

The press covered the events of the Women's Parliaments in detail, giving special prominence to the eye-catching 'Pantechnicon Raid of Parliament', as it became known, which was likened to a Trojan horse.[13] Christabel's clever ruse was praised in witty verse by one of the prisoners who managed to smuggle a pencil into her cell. The piece, to be sung to the tune of the popular nursery rhyme 'Sing a song of sixpence', soon appeared in the *Daily Mail* – 'Sing a song of Christabel's clever little plan/ Four and twenty Suffragettes packed in a van/ When the van was opened they to the Commons ran/ Wasn't that a dainty dish for Campbell-Bannerman? Asquith was in the treasury, counting out the money/ Lloyd George among the Liberal women speaking words of honey/ And then there came a bright idea to all those little men/ "Let's give the women votes", they cried, "and all be friends again."'[14]

Christabel became concerned about her mother who, while in prison, had had a migraine attack and been sent to the prison hospital.[15] 'I hope all our prisoners go through their term without suffering in health', wrote the anxious daughter on 16 February to Sam Robinson, the secretary of the Manchester Central Branch of the ILP to which she had once belonged. Shortly after the parliamentary session had opened, H. Stanger, the Liberal MP for Kensington, won a place in the private members' ballot for a women's enfranchisement bill. The date for the second reading of the bill was set as 28 February. Christabel hoped that Sam Robinson could use his influence with the Labour Party to ask them to support Stanger's bill. 'The Parliamentary Labour party have now a chance to redeem themselves & wipe out their bad record in regard to woman suffrage', she emphasised. 'I believe Mother's imprisonment may have made a little impression on them, hardened as they are.'[16] The Stanger Bill did pass its second reading, by two hundred and seventy-one votes to ninety-two, but was then blocked. Instead of being sent to a Standing Committee where the various committee stages could have been taken uninterrupted by ordinary business, it was sent to a committee of the whole House, where it could go no further unless the Government set aside time to discuss it. 'You see that the Government have once more tricked the women by shelving their Bill', Christabel wrote regretfully to Jennie Baines. 'Well, never mind, we must grow stronger, and one day very soon we shall be strong enough to be a match for them.'[17] All hopes were now placed on the large meeting to be held in the Albert Hall in March and the big demonstration scheduled for 21 June. Such meetings were now particularly necessary since women were beginning to be barred from events where Lloyd George was speaking, unless they had a special pass.[18]

Christabel's fame was such that she had celebrity status and was courted in a variety of ways. In early March, the *Sunday Times* published a long interview with her, while Madame Tussaud's famous waxworks asked her to sit for them.[19] And in mid-March, the prestigious *Vanity Fair* published an article by Christabel on the history of the women's suffrage campaign.[20] A few days later, the charismatic and quick-witted Christabel spoke at Gray's Inn Hall at the annual ladies' night of the distinguished Hardwicke Society, a club of eminent lawyers. She had been invited to take part in a debate on the motion 'That the grant of suffrage to women has been indefinitely postponed by the violent methods of some of its supporters'. She opposed the motion – and won, by one hundred and ninety-one notes to one hundred and sixty-five. Lady Frances Balfour, meeting Christabel for the first time, was highly impressed with the young woman with the 'peculiarly resonant voice, sweet in tone and far reaching'. She had her opponent:

> well in hand, when she suddenly turned on him and called him a 'popinjay'. The word was so unexpected that even the victim laughed and though I would not have liked to have said it, the occasion was so perfectly fitted to the term.

Christabel, Frances Balfour believed, was, like the rest of her family, 'a born debater'.[21]

The WSPU's Albert Hall meeting, the first woman suffrage meeting ever held there and the largest indoor gathering in the history of the women's movement, drew an audience of seven thousand. The meeting had been preceded by further new forms of eye-catching publicity. 'The suffragettes certainly show no lack of ingenuity in their methods of calling attention to their demands', opined the *Daily Mirror* when it covered the whole of its front page for Saturday, 7 March 1908 with a photograph of a large kite, flying over Parliament, bearing the message 'Votes for Women, Albert Hall, March 19'. The Self-Denial week, 15–22 February, designated by Emmeline Pethick-Lawrence to raise funds, also attracted media attention. Women gave up luxuries and birthday presents, sold marmalade, flowers and toys, rattled collecting boxes, held drawing-room meetings and tea parties, swept road crossings, sung in the streets and sent jewellery and valuables to Clement's Inn to be sold, while sympathetic male authors, such as John Galsworthy and Henry Nevinson, donated autographed copies of their books.[22] The amount collected would be announced at the Albert Hall meeting.

On the night in question, Christabel, Annie, Emmeline Pethick-Lawrence, other WSPU officials and ex-prisoners were greeted with a thunder of applause as they came on to the platform. Among the chairs on the stage was one bearing a large placard reading 'Mrs. Pankhurst's Chair'; she was still in prison and not due to be released until the following day. Christabel opened proceedings by welcoming everyone, and then telling them that her mother and those imprisoned with her had been released unexpectedly that afternoon. Tremendous cheering broke out. Emmeline Pankhurst, waiting quietly in the wings until the other speakers were seated, then walked on to the platform and took her seat, to wild applause. Meanwhile Fred Pethick-Lawrence was operating a large scoring clock, which registered the amount collected during Self-Denial week and the amounts donated that evening, the grand total reaching nearly £7,000.[23]

It was after this excitement that Christabel rose to speak, a great cheer greeting her. She referred to the comments made by Herbert Gladstone, the Home Secretary, in February that argument alone was not enough to win women's suffrage, that the time comes when 'political dynamics are more important than political argument'.[24] Christabel took up his challenge:

> We know that arguments alone are not enough . . . It is because we are recognised to-day as women who are ready to *act* that the movement stands where it stands now . . . The effect of our tactics has been to rouse the conscience of the nation, to stir within women a new sense of self-respect, a new sense of the dignity of their sex, and a new hope for the future, to rouse in men a feeling of truer respect for womanhood than this generation of men has ever known . . . the Government . . . are always telling us to wait for the vote, because other matters are important. We are deaf to that argument now . . . Now, women, it depends upon us, and upon how we fight how soon we win.[25]

Christabel's stirring call impressed her audience. The journalist Nevinson, one of the few men at the Albert Hall that evening, had no doubt that Christabel was the 'greatest living speaker' of her day.[26] He later elaborated that it was particularly the 'dignity of womanhood' that she sought to establish, the equality of women with men:

> She could have played on men with all of the feminine arts, had she chosen; but all those supposed advantages of sex . . . she entirely rejected. Women must stand on the fair, open, and level ground, recognised as possessing their legal and constitutional position in the control of their own and their country's destiny.[27]

In her speech at the Albert Hall on 19 March, Christabel had mentioned that the WSPU was fighting the Government at the pending by-election at Peckham, close to the Union's headquarters. When the poll was returned, a crushing blow was delivered to the Government; a Liberal majority of 2,339 at the last election had been converted into a Conservative majority of 2,494. 'The men and women of Peckham have stood by us in our determination that no Liberal shall be returned so long as the Government is false to its principles', announced a triumphant Christabel. Even the successful candidate, Mr Gooch, agreed that much of his success was due to the untiring activity of the suffragettes.[28] The charming Christabel, an accomplished speaker with a ready wit and repartee, captivated her working-class audiences, and captured the heart of many a journalist. Christabel was magnetic, claimed one such reporter, because 'She is so every inch alive . . . She is saturated with facts, and the hecklers find themselves heckled, twitted, tripped, floored. I think they like it. She does, and shows it.'[29] The Liberal press, pontificating on why they lost the by-election, were flooded with replies about the effectiveness of suffragette tactics. Mr St John G. Ervine, in a letter to the editor of the Liberal organ *The Nation*, commented, 'You, Sir, cannot realise the influence which a speaker like Miss Christabel Pankhurst, fluent of speech, quick-witted, good-humoured, can exert on that great army ever present in each constituency which is always on the wobble.' Is it not time, he asked, that Mr Asquith gave up minimising the importance of the suffragettes? It was certainly time for the Liberal Party to do something for the women.[30]

Early in April 1908, the ailing Sir Henry Campbell-Bannerman resigned as Prime Minister, on the grounds of ill health (he died later that month). Asquith, who had held the reins of power for some time, took his place. It was the news that Christabel had been dreading. Campbell-Bannerman had been personally in favour of giving women the vote, though restrained from doing so by the bitter opposition of other members of his Government, and when he resigned the WSPU had to 'fight a harsher foe'.[31] Prior to Asquith taking office, there had been feverish discussion in the press about the most important Cabinet changes with accurate predictions that Winston Churchill would be promoted to the Cabinet as President of the Board of Trade in succession to Lloyd George who would take over from Asquith as Chancellor of the Exchequer. Since Churchill, whose constituency was North-West Manchester, was a newcomer to the Cabinet, the constitutional law of the time stipulated that he and others in the same situation would have to seek re-election.

Christabel eagerly followed the press reports. 'In today's "Morning Post" there is a long article about the possibility of an early by-election in North West Manchester', she confided to Jennie Baines on 1 April:

> I hope, therefore, that you will spend as much time as you can in the constituency, holding open air meetings and rousing up the people . . . When Mr. Churchill's By-Election does come, it will come very quickly, so we must do plenty of work beforehand.[32]

Christabel personally took charge of the by-election team of forty women who held, on average, twelve meetings a day, including large gatherings in the

Queen's Theatre and Cheetham Hill Public Hall. 'Miss Pankhurst is suffering from hoarseness but never missed a meeting', observed one newspaper.[33] A total of nine by-elections were now being held, including one at Dewsbury to which Christabel made flying visits with Nellie Martel as well as trips to London, to speak at the Portman Rooms.[34]

While Christabel was campaigning in Manchester, *Throne and Country* published an interview Mr Whiteley Ward had conducted with her, in a series titled 'Women of the Hour'. He had gone to Clement's Inn, resolved to see the woman whose name was prominent in the press, and was surprised to find that the 'Prime Minister of Women's Suffrage', as he called her, was a 'young girl, obviously quite good-looking, obviously on the hither side of two and twenty – a girl with "energy" written in every feature of her youthful face'. Whiteley Ward was curious as to why the WSPU was opposing a Liberal Government that was sponsoring a temperance reform Licensing Bill, which would also prohibit the employment of women as barmaids. 'We are simply trying to get the vote', explained an impatient Christabel, 'we have refused to subordinate the interest of our cause to that of the Licensing Bill, or any other measure.' Was the votes for women movement only the thin end of the wedge, leading to the next demand, that women become MPs? 'There is no authority for any such statement', replied Christabel diplomatically. 'But if experience proves that male representation does not give us sufficient voice in public affairs then, no doubt, a claim will arise for the presence of women in the House of Commons.'[35]

The Licensing Bill was not the only issue being debated at the North-West Manchester by-election; tariff reform, the future of the House of Lords and Home Rule for Ireland were also on the agenda. Christabel found that Liberal women were not supporting Churchill but standing aloof, one of the most prominent, Margaret Ashton, stating that she would work for the Liberal Party no more until they gave her a vote. A desperate Churchill pleaded, to no avail, 'Trust me, ladies, I am your friend and will be your friend in the Cabinet.'[36] The sceptical Christabel hit back immediately, stating that she attached no importance to his statement. Sir Henry Campbell-Bannerman was in favour of votes for women, yet even he, as Prime Minister, could not induce his colleagues to take action, and where his influence failed Mr Churchill's was not likely to succeed. The WSPU would be satisfied with nothing less than a definite undertaking from Mr Asquith and his Government that the women's enfranchisement bill now before the Commons would be carried into law without delay.[37]

Despite the heavy snow on polling day, 24 April 1908, 89% of the male electorate turned out. Churchill was defeated by his Conservative opponent, William Joynson-Hicks, a lawyer, teetotaller and temperance supporter.[38] During the campaign, Joynson-Hicks had written to Christabel, asking for fair play for Churchill; she had promptly replied that this matter could only be decided by the Union's leaders. Although Joynson-Hicks readily acknowledged 'the assistance' he had received 'from those ladies who are sometimes laughed at . . . on having taken some part in the victory', the *Morning Leader* attributed Churchill's defeat to all the forces ranged against him, including the Licensed Victuallers' Associations who were furious at the suggestion that their huge profits from the sale of alcohol should be limited in any way. Christabel told a different story. '[W]ithout our opposition, Mr. Churchill would certainty have been re-elected.'[39]

A dejected Churchill was soon standing in a safe Liberal seat, at Dundee, where Emmeline Pankhurst took charge of the campaign, Christabel arriving to take part in the later stages. This time he was returned, as were the other Liberal candidates in Scotland. Christabel acknowledged that this was 'a distinct setback' for the WSPU whose election progress was checked for the time being since party allegiance was stronger in Scotland than South of the border.[40] Nonetheless, although the other ministerial by-elections also returned Liberal candidates, overall the Liberal vote was down by 6,663. At Wolverhampton East where a Liberal majority of over 2,800 at the general election was reduced to just eight, the suffragettes had a 'great influence', claimed the *Daily Mail*, Christabel Pankhurst being the 'star turn' at a meeting of over two thousand. 'Best speech I ever heard in my life', said one elderly working-class man, 'Can't see why the Liberal Government holds out against her . . . look 'ere, I pay 4s. a week rent, and next door to me is a woman who pays 8s.; yet I've got a vote, and she ain't; no sense in it.'[41]

Throughout May Christabel continued to address the 'At Homes' at the Portman Rooms, as well as speak in a range of poor and more affluent London locations, including Battersea, Bowes Park, Walthamstow, Richmond, Muswell Hill and Camberwell.[42] On 20 May, as expected, Asquith refused to give facilities for the Stanger Bill. He did say, however, that he would introduce an electoral reform measure for men only that would be worded in such a way as to admit a women suffrage amendment, if any MP moved it, provided that the amendment was framed along democratic lines and had behind it the support of the women of the country, as well as that of the male electors. The following day the *Times* published Christabel's letter condemning Asquith's comments:

> He reverts to the old Liberal Policy of delay, the fruits of which we have seen so often before . . . Nothing short of a definite pledge of action this Session will satisfy the National Women's Social and Political Union, and unless this is given we shall continue to bring effective pressure on the Government.[43]

She also wrote to Balfour, hoping that he might be tempted to outflank the Prime Minister by receiving a WSPU deputation.[44] But Balfour was not so easily hooked.

Christabel's hopes were now set on the big Hyde Park demonstration to take place on Sunday, 21 June as a way of showing that men and women from all parts of the country were prepared to come together to support the suffragette demand for the parliamentary vote. 'It will be remembered that on the famous occasion in Hyde Park, when the men pulled down the railings [and won the vote], 67,000 men demonstrated', she proclaimed. '[W]e are confident of being able to double that figure.'[45] The astute Emmeline Pethick-Lawrence, with her flair for publicity, asked the women to wear favours of purple or green on their white dresses, a branding exercise that unified the suffragettes, the colours forever more becoming identified with the WSPU. White stood for 'purity' and green for 'hope', while purple represented 'dignity . . . and self-respect which renders acquiescence to political subjection impossible'.[46] Suffragettes wearing the colours engaged in a flurry of activity to advertise the big event, chalking pavements, distributing handbills, carrying posters and sandwich boards through the streets, and canvassing houses. Items in the colours were soon on sale, including shantung motor scarves and ribbons while 'Votes for Women' was worn on buttons, hats, rosettes and even on the trimmings of baby bonnets. Flora Drummond, who was organising the Hyde Park demonstration with military precision, manned the megaphone on a decorated steamer that sailed down the Thames; as it passed the terrace at the House of Commons at 3.45, she called on the MPs having afternoon tea with their guests to come to Hyde Park.[47] Meanwhile, Christabel was not idle. She wrote to the chairs of the twenty platforms that would hold eighty speakers, suggesting that those with the strongest voices should make the longest speeches, and penned various articles for the press and *Votes for Women*.[48] She also warned that 'if, after our demonstration in Hyde Park . . . the Government are still obdurate, we shall take it as a signal that further militant action is required to wring from them the necessary reform'.[49]

On Sunday, 21 June, Emmeline Pankhurst, accompanied by the seventy-year-old Elizabeth Wolstenholme Elmy, led the seven colourful processions of about 42,000 women who converged in Hyde Park, attracting crowds of about half a million.[50] Several bands played and seven hundred beautifully embroidered banners fluttered above the heads of the crowd, gleaming in the brilliant sunshine. Christabel, in her academic robes over a green tussore silk dress, together with Emmeline Pethick-Lawrence, headed the procession from the Embankment. A crowd surged around Christabel's platform, young men with straw hats initially jeering at her, shouting in chorus 'We want Chrissie'. But Christabel, undismayed, proceeded with her speech, discarding her cap and gown in the heat of the day, and winning the admiration of nearly all her listeners even if not all carried her conviction. 'If you want to know why this once most derided of movements has emerged from obscurity to brilliant popularity', opined the *Daily News*, 'you have only to stop and listen to Christabel Pankhurst. Her hair loosened in the breeze, her eyes sparkling with the fighting spirit, her face shining with confidence . . . She was born to command crowds.'[51]

The twenty-two-year-old Grace Roe, an art student, was in Hyde Park that day, having gone there with her aunt and brother. She was feeling ill, but was determined not to leave until she had seen the young woman everyone was talking about. The graceful Christabel, trained in the ballet, 'had lovely hands and a wonderful way of using them', she remembered:

The crowd were very restless . . . singing a parody of some popular song . . . But she soon had them quiet and eating out of her hand. I said to myself, 'She's all sincerity from the top of her head to her fingertips. This is the woman I want to follow'.[52]

By October Grace had joined the WSPU. H. W. Massingham, the editor of the *Nation*, was also in the crowd and so fascinated by Christabel that he told Nevinson one could take '50 snapshots of her gestures & all wd be beautiful'.[53]

'Woman's Sunday', as it became known, had extensive glowing coverage in the press. 'Never, in the estimation of the most experienced observers, has so vast a throng gathered in London to witness a parade of political forces', commented the *Daily Chronicle*. At the closing of events at five o'clock, a resolution was passed, calling upon the Prime Minister to grant women's suffrage without delay. That evening, Christabel wrote to Asquith, asking what action the Government intended to take in response to the demand. Next day he sent a reply saying he had 'nothing to add' to his recent statement on the subject.[54]

The massive demonstration in Hyde Park on 21 June 1908 was a critical turning point for the WSPU since its leaders felt, in Emmeline Pankhurst's words, that they had 'exhausted argument'.[55] Christabel opined, 'Besides revealing the popularity of our movement, the Hyde Park demonstration has proved finally and beyond all doubt that it is impossible to win the vote by peaceful methods alone.' Mrs Lawrence agreed. 'We have touched the limit of public demonstration . . . Nothing but militant action is left to us now.'[56] Asquith's provocation on this and subsequent occasions meant that militancy became a '*reactive* phenomenon', each shift in militant tactics being a reasoned response to a yet more 'repressive treatment of feminist women' by an obdurate Government.[57] From now on, militancy, which had always involved non-violent tactics, such as civil disobedience, verbal harassment of Liberal MPs and peaceful demonstrations, gradually began to include acts of deliberate violence, initially in the form of 'undirected, uncoordinated individual acts of window-breaking'.[58]

Keen that the Government should see the immense following that the suffragettes attracted, Christabel, her mother and Emmeline Pethick-Lawrence invited the public to join a large demonstration to be held in the hallowed ground of Parliament Square on the evening of 30 June. This was contrary to regulations and the Commissioner of Police immediately issued a proclamation warning the public not to assemble, although he also declared that the approaches to Parliament must be kept open. The afternoon of 30 June, Union members gathered in Caxton Hall from where Emmeline Pankhurst, accompanied by twelve other women, marched to Parliament carrying a women's suffrage resolution. Asquith refused to see them. Meanwhile, Christabel was addressing the audience left in the hall, telling them that sometimes one had to be 'a law-breaker before one could be a law-maker'. She cited the great Victorian radical politician and orator John Bright who, when advocating the extension of the franchise in 1866, had pointed out that Parliament had never been hearty for reform. He had advised the men at that time 'to fill the streets with people from Westminster Bridge to Charing Cross. The women were now proposing to do the same thing, and to fill Parliament Square with people who wanted votes for women'.[59]

At eight o'clock that evening, women in twos and threes attempted to reach the House of Commons by venturing into the vast crowd that had gathered in the square. 'Parliament was guarded by police as against some dangerous and terrible enemy', Christabel later wrote, 'one thousand, six hundred and ninety-four extra constables were on duty.'[60] A few suffragettes, such as Jessie Stephenson, managed to enter the House but were ejected at once. Others clung precariously to the iron railings of Palace Yard, attempting to make a speech until the police pulled them down, flinging them into the swaying, excited crowd that mingled cheers and jeers. Enraged by the violence shown to their comrades, Edith New and Mary Leigh marched down Downing Street and flung stones through several of the windows of Asquith's official residence. They were among the twenty-nine women arrested who also included Jessie Kenney and Mary Clarke, Christabel's aunt.[61] This was the first wilful act of violence in the Union's history and so Mary Leigh and Edith New sent a message from the police court to Emmeline Pankhurst saying that, having acted without orders, they would not resent repudiation. Far from scolding the women, both Emmeline and Christabel approved their actions. 'Everyone must admire the courage and devotion which promoted the act', noted Christabel, 'and recognise the surprising fact to be, not that the thing has been done now, but that it was not been done before.'[62]

The freelance militancy of Edith New and Mary Leigh throws light upon the so-called 'autocratic' rule of the WSPU leadership and necessitates a questioning of the popular representation of rank-and-file members as puppets who followed the orders of the leadership. As Christabel later told a police superintendent, 'We cannot always control our women. It was not part of our programme to break windows in Downing-street. It was not prearranged. It was done by individuals on their own initiative.'[63] As Morley and Stanley point out, the WSPU was a loose coalition of women whose opinions, analyses and actions differed enormously so that 'militancy' changed its form and was often located within the webs of friendship among feminist activists.[64] This independent judgement was an aspect of militancy that Christabel strongly encouraged and supported since she saw it as 'a forward step in self-emancipation'.[65]

Soon after the Hyde Park demonstration, it had been announced that there would be WSPU open-air demonstrations held throughout the country in the coming weeks. During this oppressively hot summer of 1908, large crowds gathered at these events at which Christabel and Emmeline Pankhurst usually spoke together with Mrs Lawrence, Annie and Nell Kenney, Mary Gawthorpe, Flora Drummond and suffragettes drawn from the local region. At Heaton Park, Manchester, on Sunday 19 July, a crowd of 150,000 were present while at Woodhouse Moor, Leeds, the following Sunday, 100,000 assembled.[66] In between these large gatherings, Christabel would travel back to London to speak at the

'At Homes'. Although the suspension of the latter during August gave her the opportunity to take a short break at a German spa, copy for *Votes for Women* was still produced, as well as a series of articles for the *Weekly Dispatch*.[67] Edith New and Mary Leigh were due to be released on 22 August and Christabel, with great difficulty, persuaded her fifty-one-year-old mother not to tax her energies by returning to London for the event but to extend her holiday with Flora Drummond in Scotland.

When the two prisoners were released at eight o'clock on the morning of the 22nd, Christabel, Emmeline Pethick-Lawrence and a group of supporters greeted them affectionately. A band played as the ex-prisoners were led to the decorated waiting carriage where the horses were taken out of the shafts and six women, dressed in the WSPU colours, harnessed in their stead, the two WSPU leaders walking at the side. A good-humoured crowd joined the novel eye-catching procession as it marched to the ceremonial breakfast at the Queen's Hall, to the strains of the 'Marseillaise'.[68] At the breakfast Christabel, who presided, received prolonged applause as she rose to speak. The two women had been treated with the greatest possible severity, she said, to try to crush their spirit. 'It had taken women 40 years to think of throwing stones; it did not take men 40 minutes.' Those women still languishing in prison for their political convictions 'were doing more to serve the interests of the nation than all the Cabinet Ministers put together'.[69]

Elsie Howey, Vera Wentworth, Florence Haig, Maud Joachim and Mary Phillips were due to be released within a month. Knowing that the publicity surrounding the welcome breakfasts brought in a harvest of converts, Christabel set about trying to get the well-known Elizabeth Robins involved in the next one. 'Can you come to the Breakfast on 16th Sept?' she wrote in early September. Elizabeth agreed.[70] However, before then, the by-election in Newcastle, at which her mother was campaigning, engaged Christabel's time. 'I hear from Mother that there will be a tough fight in Newcastle', she wrote to organiser Jennie Baines. 'I wish you could be there; I am sure you would be a great help.' The difficulty was that Jennie was already organising a meeting in Lancaster. 'We have not got your Lancaster address in the office', Christabel continued anxiously. 'As far as possible, do not ever leave us in any doubt as to where you are, so that we can get in touch with you at a minute's notice.' Then there was Miss Hamilton Scott in Newcastle to write to, regarding who might be available to help. 'Miss Gye leaves for Newcastle tomorrow', Christabel informed her, 'and I hope the other two whom you name may join you later on.'[71]

Christabel, Mrs Lawrence and Elizabeth Robins made flying visits to support the work of Emmeline Pankhurst, Una Dugdale and Nellie Martel in Newcastle. However, not all of the local working-class women welcomed the 'posh' suffragettes from 'down South'. Lisbeth Simm, an ILP member who had faced an uphill struggle when attempting to organise local women in the Women's Labour League, was appalled at the amount of money the suffragettes raised in poor areas of Newcastle. When she attended a WSPU meeting on 14 September where a further £30 was collected in addition to the entrance fees of 6d, 1s and 2s, she 'wished she'd had her shilling back'. Lisbeth felt that the suffragettes had little idea of the hardship their fundraising produced, nor did she like what she saw as their airs and graces. '[H]ow very theatrical they are', she lamented.[72] Such views reveal some of the tensions, already discussed, between local ILP women and the suffragettes. However, this was not a uniform pattern since in many local branches, suffragettes were also members of the ILP.[73] Although Christabel, like her mother, wanted the parliamentary vote for women as part of a wider pro-gramme of social reform, she always emphasised the solidarity *between* women rather than class differences, and welcomed women of all political persuasions into the WSPU.

Indeed, Mary Phillips, a Scottish woman and WSPU organiser currently in Holloway, was regarded as one of the 'keenest socialists'.[74] Mary's release was supposed to take place on 16 September but was delayed for two days for the minor offence of writing to her anxious mother. Christabel thought highly of Mary Phillips, and on the day of her release wrote to the WSPU organiser in Aberdeen informing her, 'We gave a fine Scottish welcome to Miss Phillips this morning'.[75] Flora Drummond and the other Scottish suffragettes who greeted Mary Phillips wore tartan and Glengarry caps which adorned the released pris-oner too, once outside the prison gates. Bagpipes played while the carriage in which she was drawn was decorated with purple heather and thistles. Flora Drummond marched alone at the head of the women, then came Christabel and Emmeline Pethick-Lawrence.[76] That evening in the Portman Rooms, the five ex-prisoners were presented with an illuminated address, designed by Sylvia and signed by Emmeline Pankhurst. It expressed the 'deep sense of admiration' for the courage of the women in enduring a long period of private and solitary con-finement in prison for the cause of votes for women. After the five ex-prisoners had expressed their determination to continue with their protests, Christabel gave a stirring speech.[77]

With this event ringing in her ears, Christabel then travelled down to the West of England the following day, a Saturday, where she, her mother, Mrs Lawrence, Nellie Martel, Mary Gawthorpe, Edith New, Dorothy Pethick (sister of Mrs Lawrence), Jessie Kenney and Gladice Keevil, among others, spoke from seven platforms at a large demonstration organised by Annie Kenney at Durdham Downs, Bristol. A crowd of 10,000 gathered. When one heckler asked Christabel about the WSPU's militant methods, she replied that the women were only doing the kind of lawbreaking that Bristol men had done in the past, to win the vote.[78] But such matters aside, it was a great joy for Christabel to see Annie again. She stayed in Bristol for the weekend, attending one of Annie's At Homes where over £70 was collected. Perhaps it was during this time that Christabel gave to Anne a gold bracelet, inscribed with the words 'Christabel Pankhurst Hyde Park June 21st 1908 To dearest Annie with all my love & in recollection of our great day out'.[79] Annie was always to be Christabel's closest friend, even when time and distance separated them, as it would do in the future.

For the rest of that September, Christabel stayed mainly in London, rejoicing when she heard that a Liberal majority of 6,481 votes in Newcastle had been turned into a majority of 2,143 for the Conservatives. She did, however, keep her promise to Jennie Baines to speak at Lancaster Hippodrome, on Sunday, 27 September.[80] Two days later, when Nevinson heard her speaking at Crouch End Assembly Rooms in London, he recorded that she was 'most exquisite in grace & quite friendly'.[81] But Christabel also had steely purpose. In early October, she and her mother were awaiting a reply to a polite letter sent to Asquith, asking him if he intended to carry in the forthcoming parliamentary session, beginning 12 October, Stanger's women's enfranchisement bill which was still before the Commons.[82] A negative reply was soon received. Effort was now put into planning a WSPU demonstration in Parliament Square the day after the opening of parliament, the anniversary of the first imprisonment of Christabel and Annie. Both Christabel and her mother wanted to mobilise the people, to make votes for women a popular protest.

For some time Christabel had been discussing which new words might be used to advertise such an event. 'Give me a fresh word', she said to Mabel Tuke one day, 'to storm, or besiege or invade the House of Commons . . . was not exactly right.' Mabel suddenly suggested 'Rush'.[83] Thus the famous handbill was printed which was to give Christabel fame and notoriety throughout the land – 'Men & Women Help the Suffragettes to Rush the House of Commons on Tuesday Evening, 13th October, at 7.30'. Women who were willing to go on the demonstration, to plead their case in person, were asked to send their names to Christabel. 'We are afraid of nobody, neither crowds, policemen, nor Cabinet Ministers', she told the press. 'The audacity that we are accused of is the one quality that is going to win the battle for us in the long run.'[84]

On Sunday afternoon, 11 October, at a mass meeting in Trafalgar Square, Christabel, Emmeline Pankhurst and Flora Drummond distributed thousands of the handbills to the vast crowds. The police were present, taking note of what was said, and soon a summons was issued to all three women to appear at Bow Street Station the following day, on a charge of inciting to riot. The three did not go but went, instead, to the usual weekly gathering at Queen's Hall. The anxious audience were expecting arrests but the magistrate, Henry Curtis Bennett, had adjourned the hearing until the 13th, the day of the 'Rush'. Audaciously, Christabel, her mother and Flora decided to appoint their own time and place for arrest. On the morning of the 13th, Christabel sent a message to the police, 'We shall not be at the office, 4, Clements Inn, until six o'clock to-day, but at the hour we shall all three be entirely at your disposal.' Furious at the snub to his authority, Curtis Bennett ordered an immediate arrest, only to discover that the culprits could not be found at WSPU headquarters. Flora was elsewhere, while Christabel and Emmeline had retreated to the roof-garden of the Lawrences' private flat at Clement's Inn. Here, under the soft blue of the autumnal sky, they spent most of the day preparing for what might be a long absence. At six p.m. sharp they walked downstairs and met Flora Drummond.

The journalists who had been hovering in WSPU headquarters all day suddenly had their story. Flash photographs of the women being arrested, before being taken to Bow Street police station, were on the front page of many newspapers the next day.[85] Bail was refused and so the three faced the prospect of spending the night in the bleak police cells, unable to join the crowd of about 60,000 gathered in the vicinity of Parliament Square which had been cordoned off by the police. Five thousand constables were on duty and, as on previous occasions, groups of women from Caxton Hall tried to push past their lines and were arrested.[86] By the end of the evening, twenty-four women – including Christabel, Emmeline Pankhurst and Flora – had been arrested, and ten people taken to hospital.

In her police cell, Christabel was becoming increasingly anxious. She was to act as lawyer for the three the following day, but there was no table on which to write and only a narrow wooden bench for a bed which would prevent a good night's sleep. Her mother came up with a solution. She telegraphed Sir James Murray, a sympathetic Liberal MP who was also father-in-law of one of the younger suffragettes. He immediately 'brought life, cheer, and comfort to that dreary, foul place', recollected Christabel. 'Beds from the Savoy were brought . . . A table was spread and delicious foods and fruits appeared. Our gaolers, now all interest, lent a hand.' Then a breathless Lady Constance Lytton, not yet a signed-up WSPU member, arrived with Mrs Lawrence, both carrying blankets and rugs. 'With heartfelt thanks we fed and slept', recalled Christabel, 'and woke refreshed and ready for all that might betide.'[87]

Next morning, at Bow Street police court, the three principal prisoners entered the dock first. Christabel stunned the magistrate by asking for trial by jury rather than the case being dealt with summarily. Curtis Bennett merely smiled and said such a request was not applicable in this case. Christabel then asked for an adjournment in order that they may be properly advised and was told that the case must be heard first before any decision could be made. There was a flutter in the courtroom as the slender, pretty Christabel rose to cross-examine Superintendent Wells. 'Was there a Cabinet Minister present at the Trafalgar-square meeting?' she asked. 'One', came the reluctant reply. 'Was he Mr. Lloyd George?' Christabel inquired, as laughter broke out among the women sitting at the back of the room. 'I may have to call him as a witness.'[88] Indeed, several Cabinet Ministers besides Lloyd George had observed events the previous night, including Herbert Gladstone, John Burns and Richard Haldane. But that was not all. Christabel knew that the law was not impartial in respect of women; the suffragette leaders had been arrested for inviting the people to 'rush' the House of Commons while Will Thorne, MP, who had called upon the unemployed to 'rush' the bakers' shops, was a free man. Keen to expose the Government's double standards, she asked both Superintendent Wells and Inspector Jarvis whether the Government intended to prosecute Will Thorne. Under pressure, Wells was obliged to admit that Thorne might be.[89] The preliminary examination over, Curtis Bennett granted one week's adjournment, with bail, to prepare the case.

The sharp and witty manner in which Christabel had conducted the case led the *Evening News* to call her 'Suffragette Portia', a reference to Shylock's able daughter who disguised herself as an advocate in Shakespeare's play *The Merchant of Venice*.[90] It was a name that was to stay with her during further legal proceedings within a week's time.

During the adjournment week, Christabel published an article titled 'Why we raided the House', asserting that the Government had 'declared war upon the women who claim political liberty' since it refused to grant them their democratic rights.[91] But it was especially at a crowded public meeting at St James's Hall on 15 October, where several MPs were among the audience, that she expounded her views. Christabel looked back to the fight in 1215 between King John and the Barons which resulted in Magna Carta, the charter which stated clearly that an English king could not govern as he wished, but must govern according to the law. If the king broke that law, then his people could use force to make him behave properly, to establish constitutional Government; that is, Government according to law. 'We must make Mr. Asquith as much afraid of us as King John was of the Barons', she insisted. Far from militant methods alienating the people, the sight of women fighting for their rights, although 'unladylike', had 'touched the hearts of the people, and finally won them over to our cause'.[92]

However, the majority of the press did not see it that way. 'No self-respecting community can accede to the demands of people who seek to gain their ends by such dangerous methods', announced the *Daily Express*. 'The time for dealing gently with the idle, mischievous women who call themselves "militant suffragettes" has gone by'. The *Times* believed that the suffragettes were becoming 'a public nuisance . . . piling up evidence of their unfitness to take part in the framing of laws', while the *Globe* condemned the 'shrieking sisterhood' for bringing the 'good name of their sex into such disrepute'.[93] Millicent Garrett Fawcett, leader of the NUWSS, was deeply concerned that many of the newspapers were using the word 'suffragist' when speaking of the suffragettes. Although she did not want to attack publicly the WSPU, fearing that 'the enemy' wanted to divert suffragists from their proper target, she had soon changed her mind. By mid-November she was openly dissociating the NUWSS from the WSPU, emphasising that the suffragists upheld only law-abiding constitutional methods.[94]

Meanwhile, Christabel was preparing for the forthcoming trial on 21 October. She wrote to both Lloyd George and Gladstone, asking them to attend as witnesses. When both prevaricated, she applied for a subpoena to compel their attendance.[95] It was a brilliant move which added greatly to the enormous interest in the trial. A few days before she was due in court, a chirpy Christabel wrote to Elizabeth Robins, 'We want to keep the proceedings going as long as we possibly can. We shall never have a better opportunity of having a thoroughly good trial.'[96] In the crowded court room on the 21st, the slim Christabel in a white muslin dress with a broad band of purple, white and green stripes around her waist, her wispy brown curls with a hint of gold in them piled on her head, cut a fresh, feminine and graceful figure. But more than her appearance, her sparkling wit, biting sarcasm, good humour and the depth and force of her arguments impressed all who listened as she stated the case for the defendants, teasing out the meaning of the word 'rush' and cross-examining the two Cabinet Ministers.[97] In particular, it was her exchanges with the reluctant Lloyd George, the Chancellor of the Exchequer, who had been present at the Trafalgar Square meeting ten days earlier that delighted the court room:

> Miss Pankhurst: Now this word 'rush' . . . [w]hat does it mean? – I understood the invitation from Mrs. Pankhurst was to force an entrance to the House of Commons. Miss Pankhurst: No, no. I want you to keep your mind centred on the bill. Let us forget what Mrs. Pankhurst said. What did the bill say? – I really forget what the bill said. Miss Pankhurst: I can refresh your memory. The bill said, 'Help the Suffragettes to rush the House of Commons'. – Yes: that's it. Miss Pankhurst: I want you to define the word 'rush'? – I cannot undertake to do that.[98]

Christabel's sharp cross-examination of Lloyd George and his many evasions made him and the Liberal Government look very foolish. That Lloyd George had trained as a lawyer and was known for his political flair only added to her mastery of the situation. Keen to establish that the crowd that been peaceful on the night in question, and that the WSPU leaders had not advocated any form of violence, Christabel continued questioning further.

Lloyd George was clearly uncomfortable in the witness box and frequently glanced at Curtis Bennett, perhaps expecting some help. Unknown to Christabel, earlier that month Curtis Bennett had visited the Home Office with the police commissioner Sir Henry Edward, expressly to discuss the 'rush' leaflet. He had not hesitated to say that he thought the leaflet was a 'direct incitement to violence' and so was not an impartial magistrate in the police court, as Christabel suspected.[99] On this day, however, with intense press interest, he could not be seen offering any direct help to Lloyd George. Knowing that Lloyd George had taken his six-year-old daughter with him to watch the scene on the evening of the 13th, Christabel used that knowledge to support her contention that the crowd was orderly. 'You thought it was quite safe for a child of those tender years to be amongst the crowd?' Her witness snapped back, 'I was not amongst the crowd.'[100]

Curtis Bennett was fast running out of patience, especially when Christabel asked leave to call another witness before Herbert Gladstone, namely Marie Brackenbury. Marie had spent six weeks in prison and been told privately, by Horace Smith, the magistrate who sentenced her, that he merely carried out Home Office policy in suffragette cases.[101] After questioning Marie, and exposing how the law was not impartial to women, the cross-examination of Herbert Gladstone, the Home Secretary, held few surprises. Christabel established that Gladstone in some of his past speeches had said that political argument alone was not enough for men to win their political enfranchisement and that *force majeure* had been used. 'Why don't you give us the vote then?' she pertinently asked, much to the amusement of the court room.[102] The proceedings had begun at ten in the morning and went on till 7.30 in the evening, when an irritable Curtis Bennett asked how many further witnesses Christabel proposed to put into the box. 'About fifty', she replied. 'We are sorry to take up the time of the court, but we are fighting for our liberty.'[103] Without further ado, Curtis Bennett adjourned the case for three days, until 24 October.

Although Emmeline Pankhurst and Flora Drummond had also asked some questions in the police court on the 21st, the day was Christabel's. The *Daily Graphic* included on its front page a drawing of Christabel conducting her 'clever' examination of Lloyd George, while many other papers also gave extensive coverage to 'Portia in the Dock'.[104] But it was the critic Max Beerbohm who gave the most flattering portrait of the twenty-eight-year-old female counsel for the defence:

> Miss Pankhurst . . . has all the qualities which an actress needs . . . Her voice is charmingly melodious . . . And her face . . . is as vivid and as variable as her voice . . . Her whole body is alive with her every meaning; and, if you can imagine a very graceful rhythmic dance done by a dancer who moves not her feet, you will have some idea of Miss Pankhurst's method.

As she stood there, 'with a rustling sheaf of notes in one hand, her other hand did the work of twenty average hands . . . [she] seemed as comfortable and self-possessed as Mr. Curtis Bennett on the bench'.[105]

Despite the fact that Christabel was the darling of the press, the strain was beginning to tell on her. Nonetheless, she continued with the case, trying to prolong it as much as possible to get maximum publicity for the women's cause. There was another worry. What would happen to the WSPU if, as seemed likely, she and her mother were both sent to prison? The impending crisis was discussed and it was decided that the burden on Emmeline Pethick-Lawrence could best be relieved if Sylvia stepped in, to take Christabel's place, and the charming Elizabeth Robins helped her.[106]

When the trial resumed on Saturday 24 October, Christabel was not in top form. Not only was she under considerable strain, she had agonising period pains. Sylvia and a friend had been rushing backward and forwards to the chemist for various pills to relieve the discomfort.[107] Christabel had only cross-examined two witnesses when Curtis Bennett sternly brought a halt to proceedings, asking the defendants to deliver their closing statements. As the person who had to make the leading speech for the defence, Christabel rose to the occasion, making another defiant, brilliant speech, delivered quickly and with great emotion. She accused the police court and the Government of corruption since one of the witnesses, under oath, had told how one of the justices was coerced by the Government into making a charge of guilty before the evidence was heard. 'The Liberal Government have outdone the monarchs of old times in their attempt to corrupt the fountain of British justice', she thundered. '[T]hey dare not see this case before a jury . . . they have removed this case to what we can only call a Star Chamber of the twentieth century.'[108] This reference to earlier times, when English monarchs interfered with the legal system and established their own courts to rule as despots, was not lost upon those in the court room. The Star Chambers, although abolished in 1640, was a byword for tyranny and oppression and part of an 'old collective memory'.[109]

Christabel went further, asserting that the charge that should have been made against the defendants was that of illegal assembly which would have meant trial by jury. Instead, the Government preferred to send suffragettes to the police courts which they controlled, and which dealt with common criminals, not political offenders. The Government had 'practically torn up' Magna Carta, the cornerstone of the liberties of the individual in English society. Women were denied both their legal and constitutional rights. The law of the land was that taxation and representation must go together, and the suffragettes were seeking only to enforce 'the observance' of that law.[110] Women had a constitutional right to go themselves in person to lay their grievances before the House of Commons, and this the suffragettes had done.

A reporter listening to Christabel came to the conclusion that she 'was not quite her usual self . . . that she might break down at any moment'.[111] And she did. Although Sylvia in *The suffragette movement* later claimed that her sister 'wept with rage', contemporary sources contend that Christabel broke down in tears when she enlarged upon the hopelessness of the thousands of prisoners who had been brought before that very court.[112] But ever resourceful and resilient, and conscious of the responsibility upon her shoulders, she quickly regained her composure, reminding her audience that violence had preceded progress in regard to the enfranchisement of men:

> The Reform Bills were got by disorder. We are told that, prior to 1832, the Mansion House, the Custom House, the Bishop's Palace, the Excise Office, three prisons, four toll-houses, and 42 private dwellings and warehouses were burnt. There was a general rebellion, but as a consequence the Reform Bill of 1832 was won. Then we have the Reform Bill of 1867. That was won in consequence of the breaking down of the Hyde Park railings. In 1884 we had the Aston Park riots. They made it impossible for the legislators or any section of them to withstand the enfranchisement of the agricultural labourers.[113]

If the defendants went to prison, Christabel warned, then they would come out ready to issue another bill calling upon the public 'to compel the House of Commons and compel the Government to do us justice'.[114]

The extensive press coverage of the Bow Street trial was a publicity gift to the WSPU, like a suffrage meeting 'attended by millions'.[115] Yet, despite Christabel's brilliance at the Bow Street trial, on the last day it was her mother who stole the show as her poignant oratory brought tears to the eyes of her listeners. Christabel was always more cerebral in her speeches, keener to develop an argument. Emmeline, twenty-two years her senior and an extempore speaker, always spoke from the heart. 'Sir, I want to endorse what my daughter has said, that in my opinion we are proceeded against in this Court by malice on the part of the Government. I want to protest as strongly as she has done.'[116] Despite the eloquence of Emmeline's moving oratory as she drew upon her experience of life, pointing out how the marriage, divorce and guardianship of children laws were all 'abominable, atrocious, and unjust' to women, Curtis Bennett showed no mercy. He found the three women guilty of inciting to riot and ordered that they be bound to keep the peace for twelve months, in default of which Emmeline Pankhurst and Flora Drummond would serve three months, and Christabel ten weeks, in the Second Division. All three chose imprisonment and were sent to Holloway. The press now expressed censure of the Government rather than criticism of the suffragettes. 'To punish a political offence as though it were a vulgar crime is . . . unjust', proclaimed the *Manchester Guardian*. 'This is not British liberty', announced the *Woolwich Pioneer*. 'It is an importation from . . . the Czar of Russia.'[117]

Emmeline Pankhurst had defiantly stipulated when entering Holloway that the suffragettes would no longer tolerate being treated as common criminals and would therefore refuse to be searched and made to undress in front of wardresses. Further, as a political offender she claimed the right to speak to her fellow political prisoners during exercise or whenever she came into contact with them. The Governor granted the three new prisoners permission to undress in private, but would not relax the silence rule: Mrs Pankhurst's claim to be treated as a political offender, with all its associated privileges, would have to be sent to the Home Secretary.[118] Living in a small, bare, airless cell with a narrow plank for a bed had a particularly depressing effect on Christabel.[119] Although she was placed in a cell adjoining that of her mother, and Flora Drummond was close by, communication was restricted. Then all too soon both of her companions were removed to the prison hospital – Flora Drummond, in the early stages of pregnancy, felt unwell, while Emmeline had a severe attack of migraine. Flora was released early, on 3 November, on grounds of ill health, but there was no such respite for Christabel and her mother.

The knowledge that her mother was too ill to assume her leadership role jolted Christabel into action. Fred Pethick-Lawrence visiting Christabel on an afternoon in late October found her 'full of life' and with her usual 'indomitable spirit'. Christabel passed to Fred a rallying message to read out at the WSPU meeting to be held that evening, the second to be convened in the Albert Hall.[120] Although Sylvia was taking Christabel's place in the WSPU, she knew her limitations and was devoting herself only to organisational matters, the large correspondence and getting letters and articles into the press, rather than speaking on a platform. At the Albert Hall meeting, chaired by Emmeline Pethick-Lawrence, it was Fred who took Christabel's place as an exponent on militant policy.[121]

Meanwhile, in Holloway, Christabel and Emmeline heard that the Home Secretary had refused the request to be treated as political offenders, and in particular the privilege of speech with fellow prisoners. On the cold, cheerless autumn day of Sunday, 1 November, at the afternoon exercise, Emmeline suddenly called to Christabel and bade her stand still till she came up to her. Mother and daughter then linked arms and talked in low tones. Emmeline was immediately seized by a wardress and returned to her hospital cell, the other suffrage prisoners cheering her action. For refusing to abide by the rule of silence, both Christabel and her mother were put in solitary confinement for one day, without exercise or chapel.[122] Emmeline then heard, incorrectly, that Christabel was ill and, in desperation, applied to the Board of Visiting Magistrates to be allowed to see her. The application was again refused, with the advice that another request could be made in a month. Emmeline became severely depressed. When Christabel heard this news, she was deeply concerned and applied twice, without success, to see her mother.[123]

News about the situation filtered outside Holloway. Questions were asked in parliament, including a request by Keir Hardie for the WSPU leaders to be treated as first-class misdemeanants. Incensed by the treatment of their imprisoned leaders, WSPU members were determined to let them know they were not forgotten. On Saturday afternoon, 14 November, they marched to Holloway, thousands of ordinary men and women joining them on the way. The procession, about half a mile long, circled twice around the prison. Flora Drummond stopped at the prison gates and called for three cheers for the prisoners. The crowd then joined in the singing of the Women's Marseillaise, played by two brass bands, and put their own words to popular tunes such as John Peel, Men of Harlech and John Brown's Body.[124]

Shortly before this event, the Literary Agency of London had tried, unsuccessfully, to get in touch with Christabel; a London publisher was keen for her to write a short book on the women's movement, while she was in prison, for an advance of £100 plus royalties. Fred Pethick-Lawrence dealt with the matter, informing the agency that Christabel was not allowed, under present prison regulations, to undertake the work. Nonetheless, he also wrote to Herbert Gladstone, the Home Secretary, with regard to obtaining permission, as did Sylvia and Keir Hardie.[125] However, Gladstone was ill and an aide at the Home Office who dealt with the request was furious:

> For cool impudence this seems to be unsurpassed by anything they have done . . . She desires to write a book in prison because 'as soon as she was released she would undoubtedly be busy otherwise.' That is to say her <u>entire</u> time when she chooses to come out will be occupied in arranging further breaches of the peace.

As Gladstone was unavailable, the aide showed the enclosures privately to Geoffrey Howard, Secretary of the Liberal Members' Suffrage Society, who told him that he believed the Government would have the 'entire support of Liberals here favourable to the suffrage if we refused the request and the matter was made public'.[126]

The matter was made public in the press not by the Home Office but by Sylvia.[127] *Votes for Women* reprinted the information too, also conveying the news that Gladstone had refused to allow the Pankhursts to be transferred to the First Division in Holloway and to receive visitors.[128] The Home Secretary was getting increasingly exasperated with the WSPU leaders and the stream of angry letters and visits from influential women pleading their case while NUWSS members, such as Lady Frances Balfour, were increasingly worried about the growth in membership in the militant wing and how that was damaging the constitutionalist case. 'I dined with the Home Secretary last night', she confided to Millicent Garrett Fawcett:

> He was rather a keen suffragist, but I see his trials with the militants have a good deal upset him. He had just seen Mrs Cobden Sanderson, 'a terrible, an awful woman', sd Herbert making large eyes. She wanted an interview with the Pankhursts wh. he denied.

Frances Balfour was told that Christabel and her mother were suffering from 'cerebral excitement', one doctor reporting that after their outside life of excitement and tension 'they can't stand prison life . . . He [Home Secretary] . . . thinks the Government are crushing the whole movement'. The anxious Frances Balfour formed the impression that Gladstone would do his best to persuade his Government colleagues to receive a deputation from the constitutionalists, despite the fact that he knew he had 'no influence' in the Cabinet and found Asquith 'uninterested' in the woman question. 'There is no doubt just now', Lady Balfour lamented, 'militarism [sic] has injured us.'[129]

By 21 November, Christabel had served one month in Holloway and so was allowed to write one letter, which was presumably vetted by the authorities. She chose to write to Mrs Lawrence (as did her mother), knowing that extracts would be published in *Votes for Women*. 'I cannot tell you how stirred . . . we are by Saturday night's demonstrations', Christabel penned. 'I am simply delighted by the progress the movement is making . . . By being in prison we are doing as much as we can to embarrass the Government.' She went on to say that she had been reading Ruskin and Tolstoy's *War and peace*:

> One really learns in prison the value of things . . . [a] book . . . a newspaper or a walk, things one takes for granted outside, are the highest privileges here. Please tell the members of the Union how happy we feel and how contented to be here, because of what they are doing outside.[130]

That evening another WSPU procession took place although this time the police, one thousand strong, diverted the route so that the women could not approach within a quarter of a mile in front of the prison where the WSPU leaders were held. Pausing at the nearest point to the back of the prison, the women, led by Mrs May with a megaphone, shouted out 'Mrs. Pankhurst!' and then 'Christabel!'[131] Sylvia was helping too, but in a different way. On 11 December she wrote to C. P. Scott, the influential Liberal editor of the *Manchester Guardian*, asking for his help. Scott persuaded the Home Secretary to let him visit Emmeline Pankhurst and managed to arrange for Christabel to spend an hour with her each day. Both the prisoners were also allowed two newspapers a day, a concession that Keir Hardie had obtained.[132]

News reached Christabel about the uproar that broke out at a Women's Liberal Association meeting held at the Albert Hall on 5 December, at which Lloyd George spoke on women's suffrage. During the heckling of the speaker, a man stubbed out the lighted end of his cigar on the wrist of Helen Ogston, a graduate from St Andrew's University, while another struck her in the chest and stewards knocked her down. Helen wielded a dog whip against her attackers, an act that attracted much notoriety in the press. Lloyd George had offered nothing new on the woman question, but merely reiterated his faith in Asquith's proposed Electoral Reform Bill which, he said, would surely include women.[133] Shaken by the experience, Lloyd George shortly announced that in future all women would be excluded from his meetings. 'Though women were excluded from the hall', observed a cynical Christabel, 'their question was not.' Thus at Lloyd George's first 'womanless public meeting', in Liverpool, the women stood in the building opposite the hall shouting out 'Votes for Women' through a megaphone, a call heard by the speakers on arrival as well as their audience waiting inside. And within the meeting, sympathetic men 'risked insult and broken heads, and even their livelihood, by challenging delinquent Liberal leaders on the issue', a protest they continued for much of the campaign.[134]

Meanwhile, special preparations were being made for Christabel's release on 22 December. 'We are anxious that the events of this day should be memorable', Emmeline Pethick-Lawrence announced, 'because of the great joy it will bring us.' Keen that the talented young woman who shared her home should receive her due, she urged all who could do so to wear the WSPU's uniform of a purple or green skirt, a white jersey golf coat and a felt hat of purple or green, which could be purchased at the Union's shops or elsewhere in honour of a 'a beloved and wise General' who had led them 'again and again to victory'. Those wearing the uniform would walk in front and immediately behind Christabel's carriage, while those who found it impossible to wear the colours would form in the rear. 'We shall secure not only first-class bands, but they will be larger than those used on ordinary occasions', promised the Honorary Treasurer of the WSPU.[135] For Emmeline Pethick-Lawrence, Christabel was the 'Maiden warrior!' who, like the young Siegfried, took the broken pieces of the weapon of destiny and welded them into a magic sword to break the curse of a terrible domination. It was Christabel with her 'spirit of dauntless and conquering youth, strong, joyous, and confident, and untouched by the shadow of fear' who would bring deliverance for women.[136]

Mrs Lawrence was not the only WSPU member preparing for Christabel's return. Mabel Tuke was also busy, organising a special fund so that a silk tricolour flag, engraved with key days in the history of the WSPU, could be given to Christabel and a decorative chain and pendant, wrought by hand in the colours of the Union, with amethysts, pearls and green agate could be presented to Mrs Pankhurst on her release in the New Year.[137]

The carefully laid plans were suddenly thrown into disarray when Christabel and her mother were released about six o'clock on the evening of Saturday 19 December, together with Mary Leigh. No one was waiting outside Holloway to greet them apart from a representative of a record company who had arranged for Christabel to make a recording titled 'Suffrage for women'. Christabel and her mother were taken to the recording studio where she delivered her statement in a measured, rhythmical style that conveyed nothing of the vitality and passion that made her such a popular speaker in the flesh.[138] The task completed, the two then travelled to Holmwood to join the Lawrences. The warm welcome that Christabel received soon brought the colour back to her cheeks while long country walks helped her to regain her 'usual liveliness'.[139] 'They are all quite well & looking bonny', wrote a cheerful Mrs Lawrence to Mary Phillips.[140] Earlier that Sunday, a happy Flora Drummond and four of the organisers had been driven down to Holmwood to greet the released prisoners and to re-schedule the welcome celebrations.

22 December 1908, 'Christabel Pankhurst's Day', as it became known, began with a breakfast at a quarter to ten in the morning at the Inns of Court Hotel. Five hundred women and men, drawn from all parts of the country, assembled in the rooms which were decorated with evergreens and the banners and flags of the Union. As the released prisoners arrived, rapturous cheering broke out following by hearty singing of 'For they are jolly good fellows' and 'Britons never will be slaves'. Bouquets of flowers in the Union's colours were given to the ex-prisoners, Christabel's spray of violets and lilies of the valley being presented to her by Mrs Sanders on behalf of the staff at Clement's Inn and the London organisers. Emmeline Pankhurst gave a heartfelt speech of thanks for all the support the prisoners had received and then Christabel delivered a rousing address, expressing the belief that the New Year would bring votes for women.[141] That her mother spoke first was the natural order for Christabel. Although she was the key strategist of the WSPU she always acknowledged that her mother was its leader, the inspirational figurehead.[142]

After breakfast, the triumphal procession set out through the West End to Clement's Inn. A happy Christabel and her mother sat among a mass of flowers in an open landau inscribed with a banner saying 'To Victory' and pulled by four white horses, led by four suffragettes dressed in the colours. Charlotte Marsh, a member of the YHB, headed the procession, as colour bearer, followed by Emmeline Pethick-Lawrence, Flora Drummond, the Kenney sisters and the organisers. Other suffragettes, some mounted on milk-white steeds, followed behind the landau. As the procession advanced, the bands struck up the

Marseillaise and 'See the Conquering Hero Comes'. The crowds of sightseers, impressed by the colourful spectacle, were unusually silent.[143]

However, the climax of the celebrations was the great meeting that evening in the Queen's Hall. When Emmeline Pankhurst, wearing purple, and Christabel, in a pale green silk dress, appeared on the platform the cheering and clapping was deafening. It had been decided that Annie would present to Christabel the flag mounted on an aluminium staff on which were inscribed the dates in Christabel's life which coincided with the key dates in the history of the WSPU. '[W]ith our love and with our admiration we present to you the colours of our Union', said the proud Annie. The great crowd took up her cry of 'One, two, three, Christabel!' over and over again, until they were hoarse. Once the noise had subsided, a glowing Christabel, in her turn, paid tribute to her dearest friend, Annie Kenney. 'She and I had the honour, of which we will be proud to the very last day of our lives, of being the first two militant Suffragists. There are a great many of you now.'[144] After more cheering, Christabel was called upon her to address the audience. Another five minutes of deafening enthusiasm followed, the entire audience singing 'For she's a jolly good fellow', before Christabel spoke.

For over an hour, she defended militant methods, pointing out how they were critical not just for winning the parliamentary vote but for the emancipation of women:

> Friends . . . our militant campaign has been thought out with the utmost care . . . We are fighting for the emancipation of women . . . We are working for the bread of women, we are working that women may not go hungry, we are working for what is even more important – the dignity of women . . . You know the old methods of working for the vote are futile, and not only futile, but humiliating, unworthy of you . . . [R]evolt is a great and glorious thing . . . when injustice has to be broken down. Therefore, we do not apologise for our methods . . . they are right in themselves . . . the rightness of our militant methods does not depend upon success. You may resist injustice and fail . . . and still you have done right. When you are confronted by oppression, when you are confronted by the forces of evil, then you must go and do battle against them . . . We are going to win because we have right on our side.

Rallying the women to follow her, Christabel cried, '[T]he women in this Union are the happiest people in the world! We have the love of our comrades . . . the respect of our enemies . . . the support of the people.'[145]

When the ecstatic support for Christabel had died down, Emmeline Pankhurst rose to speak, but only briefly since she did not want to overshadow her brilliant daughter on this, her special day. 'Friends', she began,

> I have not any longer that physical vigour of youth, which has just filled me with so much maternal pride . . . [but] I have come out of prison with as much youthful spirit as the youngest girl in the hall.[146]

Emmeline's decision to let Christabel be centre stage that evening was indicative of her absolute faith in her daughter, and of her generosity in acknowledging the vital part the younger woman played in the suffrage struggle. 'It was a night of hero worship, and Miss Christabel Pankhurst was the heroine', opined the *Daily News*. 'It was a really wonderful sight to see the crowds of mature men and women, many with hair tinged with grey, fervently idolizing that little erect figure.'[147] And Christabel herself looked back on 22 December 1908 as one of the 'happiest days in the whole movement'.[148] At the peak of her fame, she was courted by the press and loved by her followers.

Notes

1 *VfW*, January 1908, p. 53.
2 *VfW*, 9 January 1908, p. liv.
3 *VfW*, January 1908, pp. 54 and 50, 6 February 1908, p. lxx.
4 *VfW*, January 1908, p. 50.
5 Jessie Kenney, Notes on Ethel Smyth, Mrs Pankhurst and Christabel, Kenney Papers, University of East Anglia, KP/5; ESP, TSM, pp. 266–7.
6 *Times*, 20 January 1908; EP, *My own story*, pp. 92–3.
7 CP to Balfour, 20 January 1908, Balfour Papers, f.44.
8 CP to Sir Alfred Turner, a retired Major General who supported women's suffrage, 26 January 1908, Purvis Collection.
9 ESP, TSM, 273–4; Richardson, *Laugh a defiance*, p. 1.
10 *Daily Mirror*, 12 February 1908; *Evening Standard and St. James's Gazette*, 12 February 1908.
11 *Daily Telegraph*, 13 February 1908.
12 *Daily Mirror*, 14 February 1908.
13 *Daily Chronicle* 12 February 1908 headline was 'Raid By Women, 50 Arrested Outside the House. Troy Horse Ruse', that of the *Daily Telegraph* for the same date 'Suffragist Raid on the House of Commons. In A Pantechnicon Van. New Trojan Horse'.
14 Quoted Raeburn, *The militant suffragettes*, p. 49.
15 EP, *My own story*, pp. 99–103; ESP, *Emmeline Pankhurst*, p. 76.
16 CP to Mr Robinson, 16 February 1908, Manchester Public City Libraries Archives.
17 CP to Mrs Baines, 29 February 1908, Baines Papers.
18 CP to Mrs Arncliffe Sennett, 28 February 1908, MASC, Vol. 2; *VfW* [Supplement], 12 March 1908, p. xcvi.
19 Hatton, Women's votes, a chat with Christabel Pankhurst; *The Sketch*, 11 March 1908.
20 CP, Women's votes: the history of a crusade, *Vanity Fair*, 18 March 1908.
21 Lady F. Balfour, *Ne obliviscaris dinna forget* (London, Hodder and Stoughton, 1930), Vol. II, p. 152.
22 *VfW*, February 1908, p. 66; Rosen, *Rise up women!*, p. 100.
23 *VfW*, April 1908, pp. 112–13.
24 ESP, TSM, p. 278.
25 *VfW*, April 1908, pp. 101–2.
26 Henry Woodd Nevinson Diaries, Entry for 19 March 1908, Bodleian Library, Oxford.
27 H. Woodd Nevinson, *Fire of life* (London, James Nisbet & Co. in association with V. Gollancz, 1935), pp. 253–4.
28 *VfW*, April 1908, pp. 104–5.
29 ESP, *The suffragette*, pp. 214–15.
30 *The Nation*, 28 March 1908.
31 CP, *Unshackled*, p. 92.
32 CP to Mrs Baines, 1 April 1908, Baines Papers.

33 Raeburn, *The militant suffragettes*, p. 54; *VfW*, 30 April 1908, p. 130.
34 *VfW*, 30 April 1908, p. 132, and 16 April, p. cxiv.
35 G. Whiteley Ward, Women of the hour, 1. Miss Christabel Pankhurst, *Throne and Country*, 18 April 1908, p. 517.
36 ESP, *TSM*, p. 280.
37 *Manchester Guardian*, 20 April 1908.
38 *Daily News*, 25 April 1908.
39 *VfW*, 30 April 1908, p. 130; Mitchell, *Queen Christabel*, p. 123; *VfW*, 30 April 1908, p. 127.
40 CP, *Unshackled*, p. 91.
41 *Daily Mail*, 1 May 1908; *VfW*, 7 May 1908, pp. 150–1.
42 *VfW*, 7 May 1906, p. 156.
43 *Times*, 21 May 1906.
44 CP to Balfour, 21 May 1906, Balfour Papers, f.48–9.
45 *VfW*, 30 April 1908, p. 108.
46 EPL, The purple, white & green, in *The Women's Exhibition 1909 Programme* (London, NWSPU).
47 *Daily Chronicle*, 19 June 1908.
48 See, for example, CP to Mrs Baines, 17 June 1908, Baines Papers; CP, What we women want, *Daily Mail*, 13 June 1908.
49 Letter to the Editor, *Times*, 21 May 1908.
50 *Times*, 22 June 1908; *Daily Chronicle* for the same date claims crowd numbered 300,000.
51 *Daily News*, 22 June 1908.
52 Interview with Grace Roe, 22 September 1965, DMC.
53 Entry for 21 June 1908, Nevinson Diaries.
54 CP, *Unshackled*, p. 96.
55 EP, *My own story*, p. 106.
56 *VfW*, 25 June and 2 July 1908, pp. 265 and 280.
57 Morley with Stanley, *Emily Wilding Davison*, p. 153.
58 Holton, *Suffrage days*, p. 134.
59 *VfW*, 2 July 1908, p. 282.
60 CP, *Unshackled*, p. 97.
61 *Daily Mirror*, 1 July 1908.
62 *VfW*, 9 July 1908, p. 297; EP, *My own story*, p. 118–19.
63 *Times*, 15 October 1908.
64 Morley with Stanley, *Emily Wilding Davison*, p. xiii.
65 FPL, *Fate has been kind*, p. 101. M. Vicinus, *Independent women: work and community for single women 1850–1920* (London, Virago, 1985), p. 262 emphasises this point.
66 *VfW*, 23 July and 30 July 1908, pp. 321 and 349 respectively.
67 See CP, Women's fight for the vote, *Weekly Dispatch*, 26 July, 2 August, 9 August, 16 August 1908.
68 *Daily News*, 24 August 1908; *VfW*, 27 August 1908, p. 404.
69 *VfW*, 27 August 1908, p. 405; *Daily Graphic*, 24 August 1908.
70 CP to Miss Robins, 3 and 7 September 1908, HRHRC.
71 CP to Mrs Baines, 8 September 1908, Baines Papers; CP to Miss Scott, 7 September 1908, Craigie Collection.
72 D. Neville, *To make their mark: the women's suffrage movement in the North East of England 1900–1914* (Newcastle upon Tyne, Centre for Northern Studies, University of Northumbria, 1997), p. 22. EPL to Miss Scott, 15 September 1908, notes that £100 was raised among local women in Newcastle, Craigie Collection. For a fascinating account of the diverse range of women from all social classes who joined the WSPU see D. Atkinson, *Rise up women! The remarkable lives of the suffragettes* (London, Bloomsbury, 2018).

73 Holton, *Suffrage Days*, Chapter 5; Hannan and Hunt, *Socialist women*, Chapter 5 and Cowman, 'Incipient Toryism?'
74 Leneman, *A guid cause*, p. 52.
75 CP to Miss Phillips [Caroline], 18 September 1908, Watt Collection.
76 *Daily Mirror*, *Daily Telegraph* and *Daily Graphic*, 19 September 1908.
77 *VfW*, 24 September 1908, pp. 471–2.
78 *VfW*, 24 September 1908, p. 476.
79 Bracelet in Purvis Collection.
80 *VfW*, 24 September 1908, p. 467.
81 Entry for 29 September 1908, Nevinson Diaries.
82 *VfW*, 8 October 1908, p. 17.
83 CP, *Unshackled*, p. 104.
84 *Sunday Times*, 11 October 1908.
85 For example, *Daily Graphic*, 14 October 1908.
86 *Daily Dispatch*, 18 October 1908.
87 CP, *Unshackled*, p. 105; C. Lytton and J. Warton, Spinster, *Prisons and prisoners: some personal experiences* (Heinemann, 1914), p. 28; L. Jenkins, *Lady Constance Lytton: aristocrat, suffragette, martyr* (London, Biteback, 2015), p. 102.
88 *Evening News*, 14 October 1908.
89 *VfW*, 22 October 1908, p. 58.
90 *Evening News*, 14 October 1908.
91 CP, Why we raided the House, *VfW*, 15 October 1908, p. 41.
92 CP, *The militant methods of the N.W.S.P.U., being the verbatim Report of a Speech by Christabel Pankhurst, at the St. James's Hall, on October 15th, 1908* (London, Woman's Press, n.d.), pp. 14 and 11.
93 *Daily Express*, *Times* and *Globe*, 14 October 1908.
94 D. Rubinstein, *A different world for women: the life of Millicent Garrett Fawcett* (Hemel Hempstead, Harvester Wheatsheaf, 1991), p. 163.
95 CP, *Unshackled*, pp. 107–8.
96 CP to Miss Robins, 19 October 1908, HRHRC.
97 ESP, *The suffragette*, p. 283.
98 *VfW*, 29 October 1908, p. 68.
99 I. C. Fletcher, 'A star chamber of the twentieth century': suffragettes, Liberals, and the 1908 'Rush the Commons' case, *Journal of British Studies*, 35, 1996, p. 515.
100 *VfW*, 29 October 1908, pp. 68–9.
101 Quoted in Fletcher, 'A Star Chamber', p. 520.
102 *VfW*, 29 October 1908, p. 72.
103 *VfW*, 29 October 1908, p. 72.
104 *Daily Graphic*, *Daily Mirror* and *Daily News*, 22 October 1908.
105 M. Beerbohm, Miss Christabel Pankhurst, *Saturday Review*, 24 October 1908, pp. 509–10.
106 EP to Miss Robins, 23 October 1908, HRHRC.
107 Harrison, *Sylvia Pankhurst*, p. 100.
108 *VfW*, 29 October 1908, p. 77.
109 Fletcher, 'A Star Chamber', p. 521.
110 *VfW*, 29 October 1908, pp. 77–8.
111 *Daily Telegraph*, 26 October 1908.
112 ESP, TSM, p. 290; *Daily Telegraph* and *Daily News*, 26 October 1908.
113 *VfW*, 29 October 1908, p. 80.
114 *VfW*, 29 October 1908, p. 81.
115 EPL, *My part in a changing world*, p. 205.
116 *VfW*, 29 October 1908, pp. 81–2; Purvis, *Emmeline Pankhurst*, pp. 116–17.

117 *Manchester Guardian* and *Woolwich Pioneer*, 28 and 30 October 1908, respectively.
118 Purvis, *Emmeline Pankhurst*, p. 117.
119 EPL, My *part*, p. 205.
120 *VfW*, 5 November 1908, p. 97.
121 *VfW*, 5 November 1908, p. 97.
122 EP, *My own story*, p. 132; *Times*, 18 November 1908.
123 *VfW*, 19 November 1908, p. 126.
124 *VfW*, 12 November 1908, p. 109; *Sunday Times*, 15 November 1908.
125 Mr Perris to FPL, 2 November 1908, Viscount Gladstone Papers, BL Add 46066, f.97; Mr Cazenove to FPL, 4 November 1908, Gladstone Papers, f.99; FPL to Mr Perris, 4 November 1908, Gladstone Papers, f.98; K. Hardie to Gladstone, Gladstone Papers, 5 November 1908, f.95; *Sunday Times*, 15 November 1908; *VfW*, 19 November 1908, p. 121.
126 Home Office minute, 5 November [1908], Gladstone Papers, f.100.
127 *Sunday Times*, 15 November 1908.
128 *VfW*, 19 November 1908, p. 127.
129 Lady Frances Balfour to Mrs Fawcett, 11 November 1908, TWL.
130 *VfW*, 26 November 1908, p. 148.
131 *VfW*, 26 November 1908, p. 155.
132 ESP, TSM, p. 292; ESP to Mr Scott, 11 December 1908, *Manchester Guardian* Archive. Adela had been allowed to visit her mother before she had been sent to solitary confinement.
133 *Daily Graphic, Times, Daily News, Daily Chronicle* and *Daily Telegraph*, 7 December 1908.
134 CP, *Unshackled*, pp. 117–18.
135 *VfW*, 10 December 1908, p. 179.
136 *VfW*, 17 December 1908, p. 200.
137 *VfW*, 10 December 1908, pp. 178–9.
138 CP to Helen Pethick-Lawrence, 17 April 1957, Craigie Collection; *The blaze of day: the suffragette movement* (CD, Pavilion Records, 1992) states incorrectly that the recording took place on 18 December 1908.
139 Raeburn, *The militant suffragettes*, p. 82.
140 EPL to Mary Phillips, 20 December 1908, Mary Phillips Papers.
141 *VfW*, 24 December 1908, pp. 217–18.
142 See CP, *Unshackled*, pp. 74 and 119 where she refers to her mother as 'queen of the movement' and 'as supreme commander of our forces', respectively.
143 *Daily News* and *Daily Mirror*, 23 December 1908; Raeburn, *Militant suffragettes*, p. 83.
144 *VfW*, 31 December 1908, p. 230. See also *Daily News*, 23 December 1908.
145 *VfW*, 31 December 1908, p. 234.
146 *VfW*, 31 December 1908, p. 232.
147 *Daily News*, 23 December 1908.
148 CP, *Unshackled*, p. 118.

1 Christabel as a baby, c.1881.
  © Mary Evans Picture Library

2 Richard Pankhurst, 1879. Institute
  of Social History, Amsterdam

3 Sylvia, Adela and Christabel
  Pankhurst, c.1890. Institute of Social
  History, Amsterdam

4 Emmeline Pankhurst with Harry,
  c.1897. Institute of Social History,
  Amsterdam

5 Christabel aged seventeen, summer 1898, studio portrait taken in Geneva. Her mother hoped that she might become a ballet dancer. © Mary Evans Picture Library

6 Annie Kenney. Author's collection

7 Annie Kenney and Christabel Pankhurst, 13 October 1905. Author's collection

8 Christabel graduates with First Class Degree in Law, July 1906. Author's collection

9 Christabel, Jessie Kenney, Nellie Marrel, Emmeline Pankhurst and Charlotte Despard, Clement's Inn, 1906. Author's collection

10 Christabel inviting crowd to 'Rush the House of Commons', Trafalgar Square, 11 October 1908. © Heritage Image Partnership Ltd/Alamy Stock Photo

MR. AND MRS. PETHICK LAWRENCE AND MISS CHRISTABEL
PANKHURST GOING TO BOW STREET, OCTOBER 14, 1908.

The National Women's Social and Political Union,

11 Fred and Emmeline Pethick-Lawrence and Christabel, going to Bow Street Trial,
    14 October 1908. Author's collection

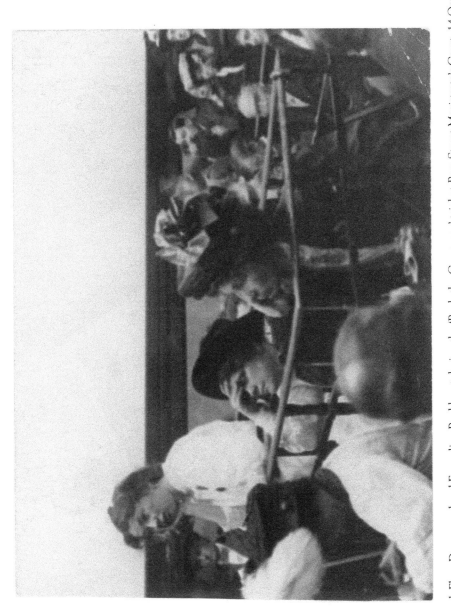

12 Christabel, Flora Drummond and Emmeline Pankhurst during the 'Rush the Commons' trial at Bow Street Magistrate's Court, 14 October 1908. © Mary Evans Library

13 Emmeline Pankhurst and Christabel in prison, October 1908. © The March of the
Women Collection/Mary Evans Picture Library

14 Welcome to Christabel Pankhurst, Mary Gawthorpe to her right, January 1909. Author's collection

15 Christabel in her office in Clement's Inn, c.1910. Author's collection

10

'REMEMBER THE DIGNITY OF YOUR WOMANHOOD'

1909

Having spent a joyful Christmas at Holmwood, the refreshed Christabel then travelled with the Lawrences to the small village of Villars in the Rhone Valley for a New Year break. But when the English visitors in the resort discovered that 'Miss Pankhurst' was in their midst, they sent a special invitation to her to give them an address on votes for women. Some four hundred people attended the event, a number of them expressing their intention of following up the subject when they returned to England.[1]

Back in Britain, the New Year had barely dawned when WSPU organiser Mary Phillips published an article to the 'Dear, brave, noble women!' who had recently been released from Holloway. Her praise for Christabel and Emmeline Pankhurst was indicative of the affection and admiration that members of the WSPU felt for their leaders. Emmeline was applauded for her 'splendid courage' in 'fighting for us and with us' in the women's cause so that she had earned an 'unassailable' place in the hearts of those who knew her best, a place that would be 'hers for ever'. The Chief Organiser of the WSPU, the same age as Mary, was spoken of in equally fulsome terms:

> Christabel, can we too strongly express our gratitude to and admira-
> tion for her – our brilliant politician, our gifted orator who so fearlessly
> exposes the tricks and shams of the men who misrule the country, who
> has thought out and carried through unflinchingly the most perfect and
> successful policy on which a reform movement has ever been fought,
> who, above all, led the way to freedom through prison bars, treading the
> thorny path and bearing cheerfully all the misunderstanding and the
> abuse that falls to the lot of the pioneer.[2]

Such openly expressed faith in and devotion to the charismatic Christabel boosted her confidence, enabling her to become one of the most respected and popular leaders of the women's movement in Edwardian Britain. Yet such welcome approval in no way detracted from the affection that many suffragettes also felt for the inspirational leadership of her mother.

Early in 1909 Christabel, in her powerful role as key strategist of the WSPU, tried to bring to heel the Aberdeen branch which, contrary to Union policy, had close links with the local Liberal Party and did not favour dictates from London. On 5 January she sent a peremptory telegram to Aberdeen's organiser, stating, 'Sylvia Pankhurst arrives Thursday morning to take charge of local work. Thursday's meeting had better be abandoned.'[3] Sylvia stayed in Aberdeen for a month, trying to put affairs in order with the help of a new organiser, the relatively inexperienced Ada Flatman. That both Sylvia and Ada were Englishwomen was not welcomed by the maverick branch which left the WSPU within five months. The appointment of Ada brought the total number of paid organisers to thirty, double that of the previous year, as revealed in the WSPU's annual report. The flourishing WSPU now occupied nineteen rooms at Clement's Inn, compared with thirteen a year earlier, while income had virtually tripled from £7,546 to £21,214. Eleven regional offices had been established – in the West of England with offices in Bristol and Torquay; in Lancashire with headquarters in Manchester and branches in Preston and Rochdale; in Birmingham, Leeds and Bradford, Newcastle, Glasgow, Edinburgh and Aberdeen. The Monday afternoon At Homes, now held in the Queen's Hall, were attracting about one thousand people every week while *Votes for Women* had become a twenty-four-page weekly with a 16,000 circulation.[4]

Such progress confirmed Christabel's belief that the militant methods she had initiated were bearing fruit. She, her mother and Mrs Lawrence all believed that victory was near and shared the general expectation that the unpopular Liberal Government would soon be forced to call a general election – which it would not win. Such an expectation made it imperative, Christabel insisted, that votes for women was included in the current parliamentary session, otherwise a discredited Liberal Government would court disaster at the polls. This was the theme of her short talk on 14 January, the evening when the WSPU celebrated the release of her mother and Mary Leigh from prison.[5] On this occasion, when Emmeline was presented with a beautiful necklace in the Union's colours, it was Christabel's turn to stand aside, to let her mother take centre stage. 'Mother as supreme commander of our forces delivered to the Government her ultimatum for 1909', remembered the dutiful daughter.[6]

Three days later, Christabel travelled to her home town of Manchester to speak at a crowded meeting at the Free Trade Hall. The event had been advertised in a novel and inexpensive way by Mary Gawthorpe, the District Organiser for Lancashire, who had arranged for ten suffragettes to each carry one letter in the name 'CHRISTABEL'. 'I deny the right of any Minister of the Crown to refuse us the right to self-expression at the ballot box', the defiant Christabel told her audience. She told, amid much laughter, the amusing story of the Minister for War who on a recent visit to Halifax was afraid to meet the suffragettes: he left his train four miles short of the distance he had to go, travelling the rest of the way by motor car.[7] Determined to press her case with the Government, Christabel wrote a polite letter to Asquith on 20 January, asking him to receive a small deputation on the subject of women's enfranchisement.[8] Asquith refused, pointing out that he did not think such a deputation would serve 'any useful purpose'. 'Are women to sit down quietly when receiving such an answer?' asked an indignant Christabel.[9]

The WSPU's reply came on 25 January, the day the Cabinet met for the first time in the New Year. A small deputation of women, including Mary Clarke, Christabel's favourite aunt, walked passed the police officer on duty in Downing Street, rang the bell at No. 10 and asked to see the Prime Minister. When they refused to go away they were arrested, four of them being later sentenced to one month's imprisonment.[10] The harsh treatment of the women, simply for 'knocking on the door of Number 10', a symbolic reminder of their subordinate status, angered many of their sex. Later that day, Christabel penned a letter to one such women, Muriel Wallis from Nottingham:

> I am told that you are seriously considering the question of going to prison for Votes for Women. I do hope you will decide to take this course. It is the very most effective thing that can be done for the cause.[11]

Similarly, when Caroline Townsend, Joint Honorary Secretary of the Lewisham branch of the WSPU, informed Clement's Inn that she wanted to participate in the next deputation, Christabel sent a letter of encouragement. 'We are delighted to hear from you that you are ready for active service . . . Perhaps you would like to call and see us here before then, to talk matters over?'[12]

Such personal letters of encouragement were an important aspect of Christabel's work but, inevitably, given the nature of her job, much of her correspondence was with the organisers to whom she gave directions, advice and general information. On 31 January she wrote to Mary Phillips, informing her that she would have to continue the work in Newcastle for some time longer since Edith New, the new district organiser, was unable to be there at present. Mary at this time was an itinerant organiser and so was not attached to any one region or place but travelled around the country, as directed. Now in Newcastle, she had recently sent a diary detailing her work to Clement's Inn, tucking inside it some letters, presumably to save postage. 'By the way don't enclose letters in the diary', Christabel advised, 'as they may not be read so promptly as when sent in the ordinary way.' Anxious that Mary's expenses should not get out of hand, Christabel also wanted the final veto on any additional expenditure that might be incurred. 'Send for the ventriloquist if you can use his services to advantage', she added in a postscript. 'If he requires a fee however write to me again before definitely settling to have him or if time presses telegraph "fee so much".'[13] Although Emmeline Pethick-Lawrence, as the WSPU's Treasurer, had a key responsibility for levels of expenditure while Beatrice Sanders, the financial secretary, scrutinised all expenses, Christabel too played a role in sanctioning how organisers spent Union monies.

By early February, Mary Phillips was back in her native Scotland, in Forfar where a by-election was pending while Christabel, in London, was engaging in a rare event for her; accompanied by her mother and the Lawrences, she was one of two hundred and thirty guests who attended a subscription ball organised by Una Dugdale and held at 92 Lancaster Gate, kindly lent by Mrs Albert Hughes. The ball was organised in great style, with the WSPU colours evident not only in the decorations but also in the pale green and pale mauve frocks of the ladies. Even the menus were hand painted with sprays of purple and white heather and showed a choice of 'Crème de Sole a la Suffragette' or 'Langue froide a l'anti-Suffragette', while Laurence Housman's beautiful banner of 'Woman passing from Prison to Victory' graced the ballroom where Ernest Gilchrist's band played.[14] The ball, which raised £108 for the WSPU, reminded Christabel of how important dancing had once been in her life. But never sentimental, she knew those days had gone. Her life's work now was to win votes for women and she was soon in contact again with her organisers, that effective network of women that made possible the expansion of the WSPU.

On 7 February, three days after the ball, Christabel penned another letter to Mary Phillips, this time congratulating her on 'the excellent plans' she had made at Newcastle. 'Much of the success of the protest was due to your efforts.'[15] Such encouragement was essential to the success of the WSPU. Yet the task of overseeing the organisers was not easy, especially since there were too few of them and Christabel sometimes lacked understanding when time off was needed, perhaps for ill health or domestic reasons. The itinerant organiser Jennie Baines, a working-class wife and mother with dependent children, had been suffering with repeated attacks of chorea (St Vitus's dance). 'Will you let me know on what date you will be free to resume full work', Christabel enquired anxiously in early February. 'I want to know because of all these by elections.' Keen not to lose the expertise of this effective organiser, fourteen years her senior, Christabel softened her question by adding, 'Of course I don't want to hurry you and you must get yr teeth properly done.' The tone of her letter to Jennie in early March was similar. 'It is good news that you are better, but I am sorry your progress is slow. How long does the doctor think it will be before you are ready for active service once more?'[16] Sacrifice for the higher purpose of the women's cause was always the key priority for the WSPU leaders so that an organiser's return to post rather than to full health was a common concern. Nonetheless, Christabel always warmly acknowledged the great debt the WSPU owed its organisers who, '[s]corning delights . . . lived laborious days . . . ready at any moment to risk possible injury from politically excited mobs or to face arrest and imprisonment'.[17]

That February of 1909, Christabel continued her talks in London at the weekly At Homes, together with meetings held further afield, with Mary Gawthorpe at her side, at Liverpool, Southport and Preston.[18] Then she spent a short time on the by-election circuit, joining her mother, Adela, Flora Drummond and a number of other suffragettes in Glasgow and Edinburgh.[19] The plight of Ada Flatman in the troublesome Aberdeen branch was a constant headache so that Christabel kept regularly in touch with her. 'As to what you say of some of the local members, you will find that the discontented ones had better be left alone for the time being', she advised on 16 February. Ada was also informed that the suggested change of day for the evening At Home was a good idea but the planned afternoon At Home, once a month, would 'not be very useful from a business point of view as the interval is too long'. Three days later another letter was sent to Ada telling her that Mr Murray, a Liberal MP sympathetic to women's suffrage, was leaving for Aberdeen and would be a useful contact in regard to the big meeting she was planning. 'Do make a point of seeing him', Christabel urged, 'as he will give you invaluable assistance'.[20] But Ada's appointment was not a success and within two months she had returned to England.

Since nothing was said about women's suffrage in the King's Speech, when Parliament reconvened, the WSPU decided to hold another Women's Parliament, on 24 February, from which a deputation led by Emmeline Pethick-Lawrence would sally forth. The day before, Mrs Lawrence informed Asquith of her intentions but, yet again, he declined to receive the deputation, adding that he had an engagement elsewhere at the time appointed.[21] Christabel thought up a humorous ploy. She had recently discovered that a regulation in the Post Office Guide stipulated that postmasters could arrange for the conduct of a person to an address by an express messenger. Why not post 'human letters' to 10 Downing Street? She asked Jessie Kenney if she could find two women who would be prepared to take on the task. 'Miss [Daisy] Soloman and Miss [Elspeth] McClelland were highly amused when I told them about Christabel's idea', recollected Jessie, 'but fell in with it.'[22] On 23 February, Christabel 'dispatched' the two women from Clement's Inn. One carried a poster with Asquith's name and address, the other a placard stating that a deputation would wait on the Prime Minister at the House of Commons the following day. Flora Drummond took the women to the East Strand Post Office where Jessie paid the threepenny postage and secured the services of a telegraph boy. The party walked to their destination but Asquith's butler refused to receive the women or to sign the official form of receipt. '[Y]ou must be returned: you are dead letters', he firmly announced.[23] The large crowd that had gathered found the incident very amusing, as did the press, which next morning gave extensive coverage to the event.

Daisy Soloman was among the twenty-nine women arrested during the deputation to parliament the next day, as well as Emmeline Pethick-Lawrence, Constance Lytton, Una Stratford Dugdale and Helen Watts, the deaf daughter of a Nottingham vicar who had great difficulty in making people understand what she was saying. Christabel, her mother, Mabel Tuke, Jessie Kenney and Fred Pethick-Lawrence were among those who visited the women in the police cells. 'Christabel came & told me that two telegrams came for me & had got mislaid', wrote the undaunted Helen Watts to her anxious parents.[24] Constance Lytton who, before the deputation, had lunched with the WSPU leaders at Clement's Inn, recalled with pride how Christabel had visited her at the police station and said 'Thank you'. She 'seemed grateful for my share in the day's work', recollected the Earl's daughter. 'This was a most unlooked-for honour and joy.'[25]

Christabel, her mother and Fred Pethick-Lawrence, in Bow Street court the following day, offered support to the defendants, Christabel giving 'smiling encouragement' to the successive women who appeared in the dock.[26] Twenty-eight of the defendants, including Mrs Lawrence, were sentenced to up to two months' imprisonment. A few days later, Mary Clarke and two other suffragettes were released from Holloway. Mary, unhappily married and living apart from her husband, was exceptionally fond of her sister Emmeline and her niece Christabel and regarded them as her closest relatives. Since Emmeline was campaigning in the provinces, Christabel made sure she was at the prison gates to greet Aunt Mary on her release, the supportive Fred at her side. Reflecting on the day's events, Christabel was conscious that more needed to be done to attract more middle-class Northern women, like her aunt, into the WSPU. Perhaps the charming Elizabeth Robins, with her celebrity status, might be just the person to help. 'Is there any hope of getting you to deliver your lecture in Leeds & Bradford?' Christabel enquired of the actress and author. 'We do want to get the leisured women in these places to be more active in this cause. From what people tell me, I gather that your lecture is just the thing for them.'[27] At this time Christabel was enjoying some 'celebrity' of her own since Ethel Wright, an exhibitor at the Royal Academy, had been painting her portrait.[28] Christabel had also modelled for Madame Tussaud's Waxworks. However, such pleasures were soon marred by worrying news about her brother, Harry.

The nineteen-year-old Harry, who was back at the Fels' farm in Essex, had suddenly taken ill with serious inflammation of the bladder and been brought to London, to the Pembridge Gardens nursing home of Sisters Gertrude Townend and Catherine Pine. His mother was distressed by this news, especially when Dr Mills informed her that Harry would need an examination under chloroform. As usual, she turned especially to Christabel, her favourite daughter, for comfort. The generous and kind-hearted Fred Pethick-Lawrence suggested that bracing sea air might be good for the ailing Harry and so offered to take him, his mother and Christabel to a hotel in Margate for the weekend. The anxious Emmeline Pankhurst, keen to do the best for her boy, wrote to Dr Mills on 1 April, enquiring whether they could re-arrange Harry's weekend appointment. '[We] are entirely in your hands in the matter.'[29] Harry rallied and so Dr Mills postponed the appointment.

Back in London again, Christabel had to deal with WSPU business. That Emmeline Pethick-Lawrence had been sentenced to two months' imprisonment whereas Charlotte Despard, leader of the Women's Freedom League, was to serve just one month, for the same offence of leading a deputation to parliament, had caused much consternation at Clement's Inn and considerable comment in the press.[30] The embarrassed Government conceded some minor concessions. 'Mr. Pethick Lawrence has just gone to Holloway to see Mrs. Lawrence', Christabel informed Ethel Birnstingl on 6 March. 'The Home Secretary has been very unwilling to give permits, but he has yielded at last and this morning the necessary permit came.'[31] Emmeline Pethick-Lawrence was coping much better with this imprisonment, her second, even though she spent most of her time in the hospital wing. Christabel began elaborate preparations for her release and, in the meantime, gave fine tributes to the woman who had raised £20,000 for the WSPU during the past year. Mrs Lawrence is someone who stands in the very front 'as a friend, as a leader, as a fighter for womanhood', she told one Queen's Hall audience which gave generously to the cause while their treasurer was in prison. The gallant Fred marked £8,000 on the score board as the sum that had been raised from a Self-Denial week.[32] The 'love and companionship' of our 'beloved treasurer', Christabel said on another occasion, lightens 'our burdens and give[s] us joy in the big political fight we have undertaken'.[33]

A crowd of over one thousand people stood outside the prison gates in sparkling sunshine on Friday, 16 April, when Emmeline Pethick-Lawrence was released, the cheers drowning the music of the band. Her mother, Fred, Christabel, Emmeline Pankhurst, Annie Kenney and Mary Gawthorpe greeted her warmly before she was whisked away to the Criterion Restaurant for a welcome breakfast. But it was the colourful procession in her honour the following day that included tributes Christabel thought she would appreciate that stirred the public's imagination. Elsie Howey, a clergyman's daughter, headed the procession as Joan of Arc, the warrior maid – Mrs Lawrence's favourite heroine. Dressed in glistening armour with purple, white and green plumes on her helmet, Elsie Howey rode a huge white charger, leading the half-mile-long contingent all the way from Marble Arch to the Aldwych Theatre. Once inside the theatre, Emmeline Pethick-Lawrence expressed her deep appreciation of the warmth shown to her, including the present of a motor car, an Austin painted and upholstered in the Union's colours.[34] Nevinson found her speech 'much too long' but described Christabel's as 'most charming & concise'.[35] Christabel was her charming self again some nine days later when she welcomed Elizabeth Wolstenholme Elmy to a Monday At Home, praising her aged friend for her work in 'the uplifting of the womanhood of this country'.[36]

The last speaker at this meeting was Helen Kangley, one of the delegates from Washington to the International Women Suffrage Alliance (IWSA) whose fifth Congress, held in London, had begun that very day, 26 April. The Congress attracted representatives not just from the United States but also seventeen European countries, as well as Australia, Canada and South Africa. Christabel was keen to make contact with such delegates for the women's cause. She and her mother had been planning for some weeks to emphasise the worldwide aspects of their work by inviting the international delegates to participate in a WSPU meeting to be held at the Albert Hall on 29 April. 'We are often so bound up with our struggle here, with our little by-elections . . . that we are apt to lose sight of the world-wide significance of the movement', *Votes for Women* reminded its readers. 'It is not the women of Great Britain we are fighting for, it is the womanhood of the world.'[37] The WSPU leaders were particularly anxious to explain the importance of militant methods to the delegates since their application, in 1906, to join the IWSA had been turned down, opposed by the NUWSS, a charter member. Although sympathy for the suffering of the suffragettes had been expressed at various congresses since then, the IWSA stuck to its policy of one national organisation per country, only admitting WSPU members as 'fraternal delegates'.[38] Like British women, Alliance members were divided on the 'appropriateness and wisdom' of militant tactics.[39] That April it was Millicent Garrett Fawcett, as usual, who represented England at the Congress, not Christabel or her mother.

Nearly two hundred international delegates attended the WSPU mass meeting at the Albert Hall on 29 April. Emmeline Pankhurst spoke movingly, stressing that no people enslaved ever had freedom given to them; they always had to win it for themselves. But it was Christabel's words that were long remembered. Although violence was sometimes right, the suffragettes would never use it until driven to it, she insisted. Nothing could stop women demanding the vote and the suffragettes said to other women who were content with words, not deeds, 'Remember the dignity of your womanhood; do not appeal, do not beg, do not grovel, take courage, join hands, stand beside us, fight with us.'[40] After such stirring speeches, suffragettes who had been to prison mounted the platform where Emmeline Pankhurst presented to each a 'Holloway' brooch and illuminated scroll, both designed by Sylvia. Although *Votes for Women* described the event as 'one of the most enthusiastic meetings ever held by the Union', many IWSA delegates were unimpressed.

Rosa Manus, from the Netherlands, described how when the ex-prisoners seated on the platform heard Emmeline or Christabel Pankhurst speak a word of which they approved they '*all* called out together – here! here!! [hear hear!] or if they disapproved – shame – shame. It is a ridiculous way'. Although in her view the suffragettes did 'no end of harm by the way they act and go about in their noisy ways', she was ambivalent about it, also acknowledging that they did 'a great deal of good as through them a lot is spoken about women'.[41] Whether such ambivalence was conveyed to Christabel is debatable. But by 1909 she was conscious of how the 'peaceful side of our work – the indoor and outdoor meetings, correspondence, distribution of literature, paper-selling, processions, demonstrations, interviews, by-election campaigns' was downplayed by commentators and the 'historically false impression given' that 'our movement was only militant, while the constitutional and educational work for the women's vote was done by others'.[42]

The constitutional aspects of the campaign often involved what Christabel termed 'comic touches', something that was put to good use now that suffragettes were banned from making legitimate protests at Liberal public meetings. New and ingenious ways, rich in humour, were found to continue the pestering of Cabinet Ministers. At Bristol, where an evening meeting was to be held, two women managed to slip into the hall unobserved during the afternoon and hide among the organ pipes where they could see everything, including the police searching for them, without themselves being visible, before shouting out 'Votes for Women!' as soon as the speeches began.[43] At Liverpool, where honorary degrees were to be bestowed on two Cabinet Ministers, Mary Phillips gained admission to the hall the day before, and spent the whole night hiding under the platform before uttering the infamous words in support of the Liverpool suffragette, Patricia Woodlock, who had been given a long prison sentence of three months.[44] For Christabel, such humorous aspects of their campaign were to be encouraged since they 'eased the strain and burden of the solemnities, the hardships . . . the sadness' that came of dwelling on the ill-results of the disenfranchisement of women.[45] 'We are all delighted by the splendid protest made in Liverpool, and we congratulate you very heartily on your pluck and ingenuity', she wrote cheerfully on 10 May to Mary Phillips. 'I hope you will soon have another Cabinet Minister in Liverpool.'[46] And, of course, Christabel visited Patricia Woodlock, a prisoner who particularly needed the support of the WSPU leadership since she was now the only suffragette left in Holloway.

For some time now the WSPU had been planning a grand bazaar or 'Exhibition' to be held at the Prince's Skating Rink, Knightsbridge, from 13 to 26 May, to raise money for the cause. Sylvia, who had been asked three months earlier to decorate the hall in the colours, had embarked upon an ambitious scheme to cover the walls with twenty-foot-high murals painted on wood. Together with seven ex-students from the Royal College of Arts, she worked with great enthusiasm to complete the project and did so, on time.[47] The week before the opening of the Exhibition, various novel ways of advertising the event took place, including marches by the newly formed fife and drum band in their smart military uniforms of purple, white and green, led by drum-major Mary Leigh carrying a handsome silver mace. The band continued to parade the streets every evening until the bazaar ended and even made several appearances marching around the hall.[48] Those who attended the Exhibition found a variety of entertainments, including short, one-act suffrage plays performed by the Actresses' Franchise League, Morris-dancing displays and a demonstration on self-defence by Edith Garrud, the first British woman jiu-jitsu instructor. Popular exhibits were the two replica prison cells that showed the contrasting conditions experienced by the male political offender, in surroundings of comfort and ease, and the much smaller suffragette Second Division cell. The various stalls offered a range of goods for sale including needlework, leather work, word carving, cakes, books signed by the author, toys, ice cream soda and flowers. But more than this, to the delight of Christabel, the sickly Harry was well enough to attend the Exhibition. Her tall, slender, convalescent brother, so shy and gentle and so like his father in his support for the women's cause, was frequently seen standing by their happy mother's side. Proud of all his mother had achieved and, as the only man in the family solicitous for her comfort, Harry helped as best he could.[49]

Many of the best hat-makers in London contributed to the goods for sale at the Exhibition and the gallant Fred Pethick-Lawrence bought a hat for Christabel – as well as for his wife and all the Clement's Inn staff. He also purchased a volume of Shelley's poetry for Christabel and of Keats for Annie, while Jessie was given a copy of Oliver Goldsmith's *The deserted village*.[50] Although grateful for such kindness, Christabel was ever the tactician, never letting her attention slip from the women's cause. While the Exhibition was in full flow she published a call for volunteers to send in their names for the next deputation to the Prime Minister, on 29 June, and also engaged in other pressing business.[51] Recently, John Burns, President of the Local Government Board, had called suffragettes 'female hooligans' and 'vulgar creatures' when they interrupted his speech at the opening ceremony at the Children's Infirmary, Carshalton. Christabel was not prepared to let such comments pass. On 16 May, at a Sunday afternoon meeting in Hyde Park, she reminded her audience that Burns, the ex-socialist militant who had been imprisoned in the past, had been 'far worse' in his time than the militant suffragettes who were fighting for a great cause.[52] And there was another pressing issue to confront.

Another Liberal Minister, Winston Churchill, was to receive a deputation from the Manchester Liberal Federation on electoral reform which might lead, Christabel feared, to votes for women being ignored, especially since the Liberal Government had introduced a wide range of social reforms of benefit to the working classes. She believed that the influential newspaper editor C. P. Scott would be a member of that deputation and, in a forthright manner, wrote to him, pressing her case:

> It is hardly necessary, I know, to remind you of the point, but I hope that in discussing this question [of electoral reform] with Mr. Churchill, you will not forget Woman Suffrage . . . the women's position ought to be made secure before the Reform Bill is introduced.

Christabel continued:

> We hope to be able to show them [the Government] that whatever else they do – in spite of Old Age Pensions, Labour Exchanges, and other measures of this kind which they may introduce, they cannot win the by-elections unless they give votes to women.[53]

While preparing for the release on 16 June of Patricia Woodlock, an organiser in Liverpool, and for the deputation of 29 June, Christabel continued her busy schedule of writing her weekly *Votes for Women* column and giving talks to a wide range of groups to work up popular support. Thus in early June she addressed businesswomen at Winchester House, Old Broad Street and on Sunday afternoons spoke in Hyde Park where she attracted enormous and ever-increasing crowds.[54] However, the work and sacrifice of individual Union members were never forgotten. On the day of Patricia Woodlock's release Christabel published a profile of her, praising the only woman who had been to prison four times for the cause:

> In Patricia Woodlock we have one of those who are the great strength of the women's movement, for she is fearless, loyal, unselfish, ready to do the smallest or greatest service, as a speaker, and, above all, as a fighter.[55]

The forthcoming deputation, to publicise the right to petition as guaranteed by the 1689 Bill of Rights, was to be the largest held so far and so Christabel was kept busy answering correspondence from intending participants and sending out instructions.[56] Evelyn Sharp, a Kensington WSPU member who made her living as a journalist and writer, expressed her regret at being unable to volunteer. Christabel understood Evelyn's predicament and, on 14 June, sent her a sympathetic reply:

> How sweet & dear of you to write to me as you do about the deputation. Please don't think that we expect you to join . . . We realise that just now . . . you can't. I want to take this opportunity of thanking you for all you do . . . for I know what a professional woman's life & difficulties are.[57]

Despite the warm tone of this letter, the pressure of her workload was taking its toll on Christabel's health. Three days later, she was in touch again with Elizabeth Robins, enquiring about the cost and effectiveness of a health cure she had tried in Germany. Discreetly, Christabel did not say the cure was for herself. 'A Suffragette wants to know of a place where they cure people of indigestion & run-downness.'[58]

Health problems or not, the work of the WSPU had to continue. At the crowded At Home on 28 June, the day before the deputation, all three leaders of the WSPU were present. Christabel explained clearly the legality of deputations, quoting from historical documents to show that throughout history those who denied the right of the subject to present a petition were considered tyrannical and unjust. She also promised the Government the 'time of their lives' during the forthcoming Budget campaign.[59] An opportunity to press her point came sooner than she envisaged, indeed that very evening. Tickets for a Government reception at the Foreign Office, in honour of the King's birthday, had just been handed in at Clement's Inn. They had been given to the husband of a suffragette who had persuaded him to pass them to WSPU headquarters. Theresa Garnett, who had just returned from campaigning in the provinces, happened to be there when the tickets arrived and the quick-thinking Christabel pounced on her. 'Now you could do it – if anyone could get away with it, you could.' Theresa's plea that she did not have an evening dress was silenced by Una Dugdale who offered to lend a gown belonging to her sister Daisy. A 'husband' was found for the intruder, a young man just down from Cambridge, and the 'couple' went to the reception where Theresa delivered a short speech on votes for women and was promptly arrested for disturbing the peace. The following day, the story was broadcast in the newspapers.[60]

The deputation of eight women that Emmeline Pankhurst led on the evening of 29 June through crowded streets to the Commons, the thirteenth attempt to present a petition to the Prime Minister, ended less peacefully. Although the women reached the entrance to St Stephen's Hall, where Chief Inspector Scantlebury handed Emmeline a note from the Prime Minister saying he was unable to receive them, three thousand police, some on horseback, guarded every approach to Parliament. Other small groups of women made desperate dashes from Caxton Hall only to find they were surrounded by a vast mob of shouting and swaying humanity. In protest against their brutal treatment, another small group broke the windows of the Home Office and other Government buildings. They delivered the petition by wrapping a copy of it around each stone and then tying it with string so that it could be swung against a window and dropped through the hole, without hurting anyone. Fourteen men and one hundred and eight women, including Emmeline Pankhurst and the Hon. Evelina Haverfield, daughter of Lord Abinger, were arrested.[61] Although window breaking had been undertaken without the knowledge of the leadership, Christabel subsequently described it as 'essentially right, appropriate, and fitting'. For months, she continued, the WSPU had been trying to show that its members had a constitutional right to petition the Prime Minister, and that in withholding that right the Prime Minister was acting in violation of the law.[62] Keen to win support from those in the legal profession who were sympathetic to her case, she also wrote to Mr Grain, the lawyer, asking him to circulate to his legal friends a paper outlining her argument.[63]

Christabel was one of those who decided that the case of Emmeline Pankhurst and Evelina Haverfield should be treated as test cases for the right to petition. On 9 July the magistrate ruled that he considered a Member of Parliament could not be compelled to receive those who wished to petition him but, nonetheless, also stated that he was willing to ask for a higher court judgement on the matter, provided Mrs Pankhurst made no further attempt to send a deputation to Parliament until the case was decided later that year. Mrs Pankhurst agreed.[64] The case of the fourteen women charged with stone throwing was adjourned until Monday, 12 July.

In between the deputation of 29 June and the trial of the stone throwers, something happened, Christabel later wrote, 'destined to have far-reaching influence on the militant movement'.[65] On 2 July, Marion Wallace-Dunlop, an artist and illustrator, was sentenced to one month's imprisonment in the Second Division for having defaced St Stephen's Hall by stencilling on a wall an extract from the Bill of Rights. On reaching Holloway, she applied to the Home Secretary to be placed in the First Division, as befitting a political offender. Her request was refused. Three days later, without the foreknowledge of the WSPU leadership, she went on hunger strike. After fasting for ninety-one hours, she was released.[66] Yet again, a new WSPU tactic – the hunger strike – had been initiated without the prior authorisation and knowledge of the leadership. Yet Sylvia Pankhurst in *The suffragette movement* claimed that 'Christabel . . . when not actually the instigator, was, as a rule, aware of every intended militant act, down to its smallest detail', a statement that is clearly untrue.[67] Indeed, Sylvia is inconsistent on this point since in her earlier book, *The suffragette*, she does not accredit such powers to her elder sister.[68] Window breaking and the hunger strike, both inaugurated independently by rank-and-file women, were to become two of the best-known militant suffragette activities.

As Christabel had always insisted that the independent judgement of the rank-and-file was one of the main purposes of the movement, a step forward in self-emancipation, she was cautiously delighted with this new turn of events.[69] Here was yet another way to circumvent Government control. When she heard that the fourteen stone throwers convicted on 12 July were considering following Marion Wallace-Dunlop's example, she wrote the following day to C. P. Scott, hoping he would use his influence with the Government to prevent the terrible suffering this would entail.[70] That very day, 13 July, the fourteen stone throwers, as prearranged if political prisoner status was not granted, refused to wear prison clothes or to clean their cells; since their poorly ventilated cells were stifling in the intense midsummer heat, they also broke their cell windows. Early that morning, one of their number, Gladys Roberts of Leeds, a former solicitor's clerk, was delighted to find an inscription to Christabel scratched by a former inmate on her tin knife – 'Glorious Christabel/ Courage! Brave heart, victory is sure/ Help comes to those who work and endure.' Someone in a cell lower down to Gladys called for three cheers for Mrs Pankhurst, then Christabel, then Annie Kenney.[71] Christabel was prevented from visiting the prisoners but thought out what the *Daily Mirror* termed 'an ingenious plan'. Together with Mabel Tuke and two photographers, she waved and signalled to the prisoners from a house that overlooked Holloway while the inmates waved back, through their broken window panes.[72] Within hours, all the women were on hunger strike.

Christabel was confident that the hunger strikers would not be detained long since legal advice to Clement's Inn had confirmed that any resort by the authorities to forcible feeding would be illegal. On 20 July, after six days of fasting, all the women were released.[73] 'We are proud of having destroyed the Government's weapon of coercion', a high-spirited Christabel wrote to Balfour on 22 July:

> They will never in future be able to keep us in prison more than a few days, and this power we shall use – unless, of course, the Government prefer to let us die. I hardly think, however, that even they will adopt so extreme a course, if only for the reason that it would not pay them politically to do so.[74]

Similar sentiments were expressed to C. P. Scott.[75] In *Votes for Women* Christabel captured the mood of all Union members when, in biblical language, she described the hunger strikers as 'martyrs' and 'heroic comrades' for whom the spirit triumphed over physical suffering:

[O]ur comrades who are carrying through the 'hunger strike' . . . are fighting their way out of prison. The spiritual force which they are exerting is so great that prison walls are rent, prison gates forced open, and they emerge free in body, as they have never for an instant ceased to be in soul.[76]

To critics who argued that the stone throwers should not be regarded as political offenders because they committed acts of violence, Christabel replied that the violence committed was 'purely technical, the damage caused being quite nominal, and the stones . . . thrown when no injury to persons was possible'. Citing legal precedence, she pointed out that whether an offence was political or not depended not upon the character of the act, but upon the motive with which it was done. The WSPU reserved the right to use the hunger strike 'because, while it is undoubtedly wrong to deny to Suffragists the privileges of political offenders, by far the greater and the more fundamental wrong is to imprison them at all'.[77]

For some weeks now Christabel had been asking for volunteers for the next deputation, as well as appealing for workers for the summer holidays. So there was still plenty of work to do before she herself could take a break. 'Your offer to join the next deputation is most welcome', she wrote to Ethel Birnstingl, on 24 July, 'and I admire your courage and determination in thus resolving to make another approach to the Prime Minister.'[78] And there was the usual round of letters to write to those who were organising protests, including Louise Cullen to whom Christabel sent for distribution one thousand leaflets denying the accusation made by Herbert Gladstone in the House of Commons that some of the WSPU prisoners had kicked and bitten the wardresses.[79] 'I am pleased to be able to tell you that 3 or 4 [suffragettes] are going from London to Norwich by the 3.20 train from Liverpool Street Station on Monday', she had informed Louise the day before. 'In case they cannot get the late train back to London, do you think the Labour men would offer them hospitality? Will you send a reply by return of post to Mr. Rutter, 67, Chancery Lane, W.C.'[80] Such statements indicate clearly that there were still strong links between the WSPU and the Labour movement, refuting the claim of most socialist historians that there was a sharp break between the two organisations after Christabel and her mother resigned from the ILP in 1907.[81] Christabel's correspondence reveals that she was still in touch with Labour men who were willing to support the suffragettes, especially now that heckling at Liberal public meetings became difficult as women were either excluded or restricted from entry. 'I am writing to the I.L.P. to say we shall send someone about the middle of next week, and whoever goes will be prepared to address their Sunday meeting', she told Louise.[82] Every Liberal rally now became a battleground as with ingenuity and courage suffragettes hid under platforms, scaled roofs, descended through skylights or found other inventive ways to shout 'Votes for women!' Arrests and hunger striking followed.

As arranged, Christabel now spent the rest of August at Lahmann's Sanatorium, Weissen Hirsch near Dresden, Germany, seeking a cure for her indigestive and bowel problems and general tiredness. It had been agreed among the leadership that this was the best time for her to go abroad since her mother was still in the country, scheduled to attend summer campaign meetings and then to have a holiday in Scotland. By seeking a cure now, Christabel would be back well before her mother left for her American tour in the autumn, which she had helped to arrange.[83]

Christabel found her inactive life at the spa somewhat tedious, but nonetheless stayed the full course, writing regularly to her mother and friends, including Elizabeth Robins. 'I often think of you & imagine you in these surroundings', she told Elizabeth. 'A neighbour of yours at Henfield, Miss Mack, is here. We sit at the same table & talk together a good deal.' Christabel continued:

> I am very glad to have come here for it has stopped the dwindling process which had been going on that brought me to a thin & rather weak condition. Also one gets useful ideas as to how to live when at home. Here I am vegetarian & their vegetarian food is certainly (with the exception of that which you provide) the best I know.

Explaining that there were said to be eight hundred people at the crowded health centre, very few of whom were English, Christabel informed Elizabeth that she would leave for Dresden on 4 September and then, two days later, join the Lawrences who were to spend a week at Oberammergau. 'After 6 weeks exile, however pleasant, it will be very nice to see home & friends again. This do-nothing life is so different from one's ordinary existence that sometimes it is quite tiring.'[84] Two more letters from Weissen Hirsch followed, since Elizabeth had asked for Christabel's advice on an article she had written about women's suffrage. The second letter was particularly long and expansive. 'I don't at all regret the use of a little violence by women', Christabel informed Elizabeth, 'because it shows that they are not servile & overawed by the idea that men are physically stronger.'[85]

By 8 September Christabel was back at her desk in WSPU headquarters and writing to Elizabeth again, trying to arrange a time when they could meet. 'It is delightful to be home again', she enthused. 'I have had such a welcome from the dear Clements Inn people & am fully the happiest person alive. There is no place like home & nothing like work.'[86] While she had been away, the press and *Votes for Women* had been full of stories about the hunger strikers whose militancy had not impressed all WSPU members. Elizabeth Wolstenholme Elmy, who had worked for forty-four years for women's enfranchisement, feared the executive of the WSPU was 'disgracing itself' by supporting the stone throwing and delaying, not advancing, the women's cause.[87] Emily Blathwayt of Eagle House, Batheaston, a village on the outskirts of Bath, who regarded Annie Kenney as one of her own family, was of a similar view. She wrote to Clement's Inn, resigning her membership. The amiable Colonel Linley Blathwayt, her husband, who often drove suffragettes to and fro in his motorcar, expressed his disapproval in a letter to Christabel. Anxious not to lose the support of a family which provided warm hospitality for so many WSPU workers, Christabel immediately sent a long reply to the Blathwayts. 'She writes very sweetly but thinks their methods right', recorded Emily in her diary on 10 September:

> She hopes someday I shall be able to join again and I hope I shall when all this trouble is over. She appeals to L[inley] as a soldier, but he . . . wants to know . . . where would be the limit to the means she would allow. If stone throwing fails would she go on to bombs etc.[88]

Christabel had made no mention of bombs, nor did the topic arise when Annie came up to London to discuss the situation. But Christabel in her article in *Votes for Women* on 17 September made it clear that the Government's exclusion of women from Liberal public meetings and the Prime Minister's refusal to receive a women suffrage deputation had 'driven women to the point of revolution', making a change in suffragette tactics necessary. Obedience to honour and liberty – which women valued as fiercely as men – must be defended 'no matter though social order and harmony be for a time destroyed'.[89]

The very day that Christabel's article appeared, Asquith was due to give a Budget Speech at Bingley Hall, Birmingham. Christabel had already been in touch with Jennie Baines, hoping she could organise a protest and, if possible, get the support of university students.[90] But organising a protest was not easy since women were banned from attending the meeting. '[W]e realize from your letter . . . what great difficulties you and the others have to cope with', Christabel wrote encouragingly to Jennie on the morning of the 17th, 'but we know that if it is humanly possible to make a protest you will do it . . . we shall think of you to-night and how eagerly we shall wait for news.'[91] Earlier that day, Mary Leigh and Charlotte Marsh had climbed onto the roof of a house near Bingley Hall and loosened tiles. When Asquith's car appeared at the appointed hour, they threw slates at it, taking care not to hit the Prime Minister or his chauffeur. A hose pipe was turned on the two women and stones thrown at them in an attempt to force them down. Eventually they were led away in their drenched clothes and stockinged feet, blood streaming from their wounds. Eight other women were also arrested. The following day Christabel and Emmeline Pethick-Lawrence rushed to Birmingham, but were refused permission to consult with the prisoners. Mary Leigh and Charlotte Marsh were sentenced to three months' imprisonment, both with hard labour, while the other women, who had broken windows, received shorter sentences.[92]

Neither Christabel nor the other two leaders of the WSPU had advocated the attack on Asquith's car. However, they had little choice but to endorse it. The Birmingham protest, an optimistic Christabel confided to Jennie Baines, was 'one of the biggest successes we have had'. She continued with kind words, only too aware of the strain the event had placed on this hard-working itinerant organiser:

You can rest on your laurels for the next fortnight. Don't worry about anything, but just have a quiet time with your husband & children who must be very happy to have you with them once more. My best wishes please to Mr. Baines who is making his sacrifice too for the movement in sparing you.[93]

But few in the country saw the Bingley Hall protest as a 'success'. There was a chorus of criticism from the public, from MPs, such as Walter Long, and from the press. Christabel stoutly defended the tactics. 'It is this Government who are to blame', she informed Mr Long:

They refuse to give us the vote & then attempt to render futile one form of agitation after another . . . we are prevented from making our protest at Cabinet Ministers' meetings and the Prime Minister refuses to receive woman suffrage deputations.[94]

Christabel took the same line in a letter to the *Times*, arguing that it was the Government who had driven women to use methods which, 'because they savour of violence', were repugnant to them.[95] The two other leaders of the WSPU were in complete agreement with her. Emmeline Pethick-Lawrence reiterated that suffragettes were engaged in a revolution that had been 'forced' upon them while Emmeline Pankhurst told the press there was nothing to choose between the Prime Minister and the Tsar of Russia since the will to oppress and tyrannise was in both men.[96]

During the midst of this exchange of views, Christabel had her twenty-ninth birthday, on 22 September. Among the greetings and presents she received from her family, the Lawrences and close friends were gifts from WSPU members. 'You are very kind to remember my birthday & to send me your good wishes & such a charming present', she wrote to Mary Phillips. 'Your request shall be attended to though to say which is my favourite flower is no easy matter.'[97] But, with women on hunger strike in Winston Green Gaol, there was little time to linger on such sentiments. 'Thank goodness for the hunger strike', Christabel wrote optimistically to Jennie Baines on 23 September, 'but for that the women sentenced at Birmingham would, in view of the long sentences with hard labour, have to undergo a very severe punishment for their brave action.' The prison authorities were trying to find ways of breaking the hunger strike, she told Jennie, and informed her that the legal advice the WSPU had received was that forcible feeding was 'illegal and, moreover, it cannot be done with any real effect if the prisoners make a resistance'.[98]

Christabel's optimism was misplaced. She had barely finished writing to Jennie Baines when dreadful news arrived at Clement's Inn – hunger-striking suffragettes in Winston Green Gaol, Birmingham, were being forcibly fed. Food had been poured into rubber tubes that had been forced up nostrils (the most common method) or down throats and into the stomach (the more painful operation) after a steel or wooden gag had prised the mouth open.[99] A horrified Christabel and her mother hurried with their solicitor to Birmingham, intending to take legal action on the prisoners' behalf, but were firmly refused contact with the women. Together with Mabel Tuke, the three leaders of the WSPU issued a joint letter condemning the 'brutality' of the Government which had 'violated' the bodies of women with the 'horrible outrage of the gag and feeding tube'.[100] Although the word 'rape' was not used, the instrumental invasion of the struggling body, accompanied by overpowering violence, humiliation and suffering, was seen as akin to it. The fact that the tubes may not have been new or clean, but used previously on the diseased or mentally ill, only added to the feelings of abuse, dirtiness and indecency that the women felt.[101]

An indignant Emmeline Pankhurst begged Keir Hardie to ask questions in the Commons which he duly did at the first opportunity, on Monday, 27 September 1909. Mr Masterman, in speaking for the Home Secretary, justified forcible feeding as 'ordinary hospital treatment' that was given to those who refused food. At various stage of the discussion, there was 'laughter' from many MPs.[102] Although disgusted at this turn of events, Christabel was still hopeful that the Government could be beaten legally if the WSPU took 'the firmest possible stand' and other protestors also joined the hunger strike.[103] She also circulated WSPU organisers and supporters, asking them to collect signatures from as many doctors as possible to support a memorial to Asquith, organised by Dr Flora Murray, who condemned forcible feeding as an 'unwise and inhumane action' that presented the 'gravest risks' to the health of the person. The memorial was signed by one hundred and sixteen doctors, including prominent men such as Victor Horsley, F.R.C.S., W. Hugh Fenton, M.D., M.A., C. Mansell Moullin, M.D., F.R.C.S. and Forbes Winslow, M.D.[104]

Christabel willingly stood aside to let her mother, who professed to be incompetent with a pen, write a passionate article for *Votes for Women* readers that condemned 'a Liberal Government in Free England' for torturing women who were campaigning for their citizenship rights.[105] The article added to the burning resentment that so many suffragettes felt about women's subordinate position in Edwardian society. Webs of friendship and solidarity became firmer as many became more determined to follow the militant path, wherever it might lead. The strong condemnation of forcible feeding was not confined to the WSPU and some in the medical profession. A stream of indignant letters were published in the press. H. N. Brailsford and Henry Nevinson, leader-writers for the *Daily News*, resigned their posts in protest against their editor's support for the Government. 'We cannot denounce torture in Russia and support it in England', they wrote in a much-discussed letter in the press.[106] By early December, the courts ruled that the WSPU's legal challenge to the Government, based on Mary Leigh's case, could not be upheld; the verdict favoured the defendants who argued that forcible feeding was necessary to save her life and that only minimum force had been used.[107] From now on, forcible feeding became the Government's response to hunger-striking suffragettes, doctors administering it to punish, rather than treat, the hunger strikers.[108]

The anxious Christabel travelled to Birmingham to greet the first hunger striker to be released, Laura Ainsworth, a schoolteacher and daughter of a school inspector. The ailing Laura, liberated at 6.50 a.m. on the morning of 5 October, was in such a serious condition that she had to be taken to a nursing home. She spoke to Christabel about her ordeal, telling how four or five wardresses held her down twice a day while a tube about two feet long was pushed down her throat so that she felt she was choking; when the tube was pulled out, she was sick. Christabel immediately made the news public and denounced the Liberal Government for its 'campaign of violence against women'.[109] Soon leaflets about the experiences of the forcibly fed suffragettes were published by the WSPU, as well as a poster depicting the gruesome operation in some detail. The Government, Christabel thundered at a WSPU rally at the Albert Hall on 7 October, would have no peace:

> We have at last got up steam and tasted the joy of battle. Our blood is up. Are we going to stop? Never, never! We will not betray the women in prison . . . Our methods are morally right . . . in a struggle for our rights as human beings things may be done which would not be right in another cause . . . for the weak to use their little strength against the huge forces of tyranny is divine.[110]

The two other leaders of the WSPU also gave passionate addresses. Emmeline Pankhurst stressed that it was the duty of women to make 'the greatest sacrifices' that women and children might be born 'free and equal'. Emmeline Pethick-Lawrence claimed that the women's war was a 'holy war', a crusade 'to free the body and soul of woman from the desecration of sex domination'.[111] The grand sum of £2,300 was raised that evening, including £250 donated by Fred.

For some weeks Christabel had been asking for women to join a protest at Newcastle on 9 October where Lloyd George was due to speak about his 'People's Budget' which aimed to impose new methods of taxation upon the wealthier classes to improve the standard of living of those who were poor. Christabel's quarrel with Lloyd George was not over his proposed reforms but over the Government's refusal to grant women the vote.[112] The Newcastle protest differed from that at Birmingham in that it was much more carefully planned, in secrecy, since the Special Branch of the Metropolitan Police had recently established a section to deal specifically with the suffragettes.[113] Aware that the activities of the WSPU were now being closely observed by the authorities, Christabel wrote to Jennie Baines, informing her that she had advised the Newcastle organiser, Annie Williams, not to divulge their plans in letters to Clement's Inn since any correspondence might be opened at the post office.[114]

Lady Constance Lytton was one of the suffragettes who volunteered to join the Newcastle protest and on 8 October Christabel accompanied her to that city. During the train journey, Constance became impressed with:

the wonderful character, the imperturbable good temper, the brilliant intellect of my companion . . . I showed her some letters and papers on which I wanted her advice . . . Whether they were print, typewritten, or manuscript, she had read them all in a moment, so as to discuss them with me afterwards.

After the two had reached their destination and deposited their luggage in a hotel, they went to a meeting in a lodging house where there were twelve other women, including Kitty Marion, Dorothy Pethick, Emily Wilding Davison, and Jane Brailsford, wife of the Liberal journalist who had recently resigned his position on the *Daily News* staff. '[W]e were all intending stone-throwers', recollected Constance, 'and Christabel was there to hearten us up and to go into details about the way in which we were to do it.'[115] That evening, when Christabel addressed a crowd of four thousand in the Drill Hall, a gang of local college students made a disturbance with bells, whistles and other noisy instruments. After twenty-five minutes of trying to make herself heard, the good-tempered speaker merely lowered her voice and spoke only to the journalists so that her speech was reported in the London dailies as well as the local papers. The following day, when Constance threw her stone at what she thought was Lloyd George's car – Sir Walter Runciman was in it – she aimed it low to avoid injuring the chauffeur or anyone else. Arrested and sent to prison for a second time, she was soon released because of her social position, as was Jane Brailsford. Both women had been on hunger strike and the prison doctors had been alerted about Constance's weak heart.[116]

Emmeline Pankhurst's impending lecture tour in the USA had been creating a stir in the North American press, some newspapers even reporting incorrectly that her 'able second and lieutenant . . . her daughter Christable [sic]' would accompany her.[117] But Christabel had never contemplated joining her mother on this trip; she was needed in England, holding the WSPU's reins of power while her mother was out of the country. The stir about Emmeline's impending tour revolved around the question of whether she would be barred, under immigration regulations, from landing in America because of her prison convictions in England. Her old friend, Harriot Stanton Blatch, had invited her to speak under the auspices of the New York Equality League of Self-Supporting Women, a suffrage society of working women that Harriot had founded in 1907 with the aim of attracting working-class industrial women workers as well as their college-educated sisters in the professions. Once Harriot had elicited from the immigration authorities that Emmeline's convictions were political rather than criminal, the plans had been set on a firm footing, although moderate American suffragists, such as Carrie Chapman Catt, feared that the charismatic Mrs Pankhurst might produce a 'deluge of suffrage anarchy'.[118]

Emmeline's trip, managed by the J. B. Pond Lyceum Bureau, was primarily to enable her to earn some money to ensure the best medical care for Harry.[119] A single parent, with the delicate Harry to support, her only source of income was the money she was paid as a WSPU speaker.[120] During the summer, she had sent her boy back to the farm after his last bout of illness since she believed, mistakenly, that an active, outdoor rural life would help him to grow stronger. A few days before she was due to sail to New York on 13 October, the devastating news arrived that Harry was paralysed from the waist down. His worried landlady had brought him in her car to the Pembridge Gardens nursing home of Catherine Pine and Gertrude Townend. Christabel and her mother, both in Newcastle at the time, immediately sent a telegram to Sylvia who was in Kent, with her easel and paints, since she could reach Harry's bedside much quicker than they could. Dr Mills advised the family that they would have to wait until the inflammation abated before it would be known if Harry would regain the use of his limbs. The sight of the gentle Harry in great pain, unable to use his legs, greatly distressed his kin. Fearing he would need expensive treatment and might even become an invalid, and assured by Dr Mills that the patient would have the very best of care, Emmeline decided that she had no choice but to undertake her lucrative lecture tour. Harry was left in the skilled hands of Dr Mills and Nurses Pine and Townend, and under the overall charge of his Aunt Mary and his sisters. Since Mary Clarke was an organiser in Brighton, Adela was in Scotland and Christabel held the post of Chief Organiser of the WSPU, the main brunt of the responsibility fell upon Sylvia's shoulders.

Christabel, accompanied by Sylvia, Emmeline Pethick-Lawrence and Mabel Tuke, bid her anxious mother farewell at Waterloo station on the 13th. For Christabel, her mother's trip was '[n]erved by necessity', but for the embittered Sylvia, writing *The suffragette movement* some twenty years later, their mother was condemned as heartless, implying that she was responsible for Harry's eventual death:

> So ruthless was the inner call to action, that . . . she persevered with her intention . . . there was never a moment of doubt as to where she should be substituted – on the platform or by the bedside of her son. The movement was paramount.[121]

Adela was particularly close to Harry but Sylvia failed to tell her that he was seriously ill until much later. When, in 1933, she read Sylvia's account of these events, she was shocked. 'Dear Harry . . . would surely be hurt to know that Sylvia used the opportunity which his dependence on her in the last few months of his life gave her to make money by trying to blast his mother's reputation.'[122] But Sylvia herself did not consistently tell the same story. In her later account of their mother, she claimed that Emmeline 'steeled herself to persevere with her journey . . . the fees to be earned by her lectures would be of utmost value in providing for the boy's needs'.[123]

After seeing her mother off on the boat-train at Waterloo on 13 October, Christabel hurried back to her office where there was the usual correspondence to answer as well as various WSPU activities to organise. 'Our boy is in for a long tedious illness', she confided to Jennie Baines who had enquired about Harry, 'but the doctors seem encouraging. So we hope all will go well . . . The laddie is so patient & unselfish.'[124] With her mother away, Christabel felt it was particularly important that she was visible and so continued with her planned speaking schedule, interspersed with time spent with Harry. When she stood on a platform on 16 October with Laura Ainsworth and Jane Brailsford at Bermondsey, where a by-election was soon to be held, Nevinson thought she was in superb form. 'Christabel . . . is at her best with working crowds, knowing instantly whether to answer their interruptions or not. The audience was full of enthusiasm for her . . . But there was much noise & disruption too.'[125] The hooligans at her address at Chigwell, Essex, three days later, soon grew tired of being laughed at by the audience and listened peacefully. Perhaps the presence of the chair of the meeting, Mr Ballie Weaver, a member of the Men's League for Women's Suffrage, helped to calm proceedings. He patiently explained why women wanted the vote. To him and all other men who supported their cause, Christabel gave grateful thanks. 'Great courage was needed by these truly chivalrous men', she penned, 'for they were treated with little mercy by those mortified by failure to silence the Suffrage demand.'[126]

Winston Churchill, when receiving a deputation from the Women's Freedom League on 18 October, claimed that the cause of women's enfranchisement had marched backwards during the last four years because of the 'tactics of silly disorder and petty violence' of the WSPU. If suffragists had continued with 'constitutional . . . dignified tactics', he suggested, women's enfranchisement would have stood a 'good chance' of being included in the programme of any great political party at the next general election.[127] Christabel was furious. If votes for women were not an issue at the next general election, it was not because active suffragists had been too militant, but because they had not been militant enough, she replied. 'Members of the present Government must learn that neither their violent and coercive measures nor their inconsequent and abusive utterances will have the effect of checking the militant campaign.'[128] The work of the Union all over the country had been given a stimulus by the Government's latest outrage of forcibly feeding hunger-striking suffragettes. Churchill was due to speak in Bristol in mid-November and Christabel was determined that the suffragettes would make a protest. However, private family matters were again impinging on her public work.

'Harry is making good progress', she wrote on 21 October to Mrs Badley who had enquired about the effectiveness of his medical care. 'When Mother returns, if he is not making the progress he ought I shall feel very much inclined to try the treatment you suggest, & shall urge the change of treatment upon her.' Four days later, Christabel reported optimistically that Harry had 'less pain & sleeps better'. His 'present doctor is <u>very good</u> & is very fond of Harry & gives him his best care'.[129] Such private worries intruded into her thoughts as she desperately tried to exert pressure on the Government to stop forcible feeding of hunger

200

strikers, a task in which Jennie Baines helped by collecting certificates of support from sympathetic doctors. 'It was not necessary for Dr. Greenhouse to say that the women wished to protest against forcible feeding, what we wanted him to say was whether or no[t] he thought forcible feeding would be safe', Christabel chided Jennie. 'I am writing to Dr. Greenhouse myself to explain the point.' Not content with trying to get the support of certain doctors in the medical profession, Christabel also wrote in late October to C. P. Scott, who had spoken out against forcible feeding in a leader in the *Manchester Guardian*, urging him to see Herbert Gladstone privately on the matter.[130] That week's issue of *Votes for Women* included a reprint of a by-election poster showing the horrors of forcible feeding with the stark message 'TORTURING WOMEN IN PRISON VOTE AGAINST THE GOVERNMENT'.[131]

During November, Christabel spoke regularly at meetings to celebrate the release of forcibly fed prisoners from Birmingham and Newcastle, and also at the At Homes, usually with Emmeline Pethick-Lawrence at her side. The pace of her life was not leisurely. She spoke not only in London but also Northampton, Derby, Brighton and Bristol over a two-week period and then travelled up to Glasgow for the beginning of December. But the failing health of Harry cast a bleak shadow over everything so that even the defeat of the Government nominee in the Bermondsey by-election brought little joy.[132] Dr Mills had told Christabel and Sylvia that their brother would never walk again. 'I know that you give him love as well as skill and if the two things together can prevail, then what we fear won't happen', Christabel confessed apprehensively to Dr Mills on 4 November. 'At moments I can't help hoping although the letter you read out told me how very serious & dark the outlook is.' As the eldest daughter, Christabel felt a special responsibility towards her mother, and worried about how she could convey the news to her. 'As to Mother', she confided, 'I want things to be made as easy as possible. At the very best it will be very terrible I am afraid.'[133] A short time later, Christabel wrote thanking both Mrs Mills and her husband for their kindness towards herself and Sylvia 'in thinking out how to meet this great trouble'.[134] The two sisters talked it over and decided that the bleak news about Harry should be held back from their mother, until she returned.

Meanwhile, Christabel continued to hammer out WSPU policy in the weekly pages of *Votes for Women*. Asquith had called a general election since the House of Lords had defiantly vetoed the People's Budget, a move that had strengthened his hand. His hypocrisy in presenting himself as a defender of the freedom of the democratically elected Commons over the unrepresentative Lords should be exposed, she expounded, since 'he himself has no right to tax the women of the country, whom he and his followers in the House of Commons in no way represent'.[135] Similar views were expressed at a meeting at Portsmouth Town Hall on 20 November where Christabel attracted an orderly crowd of over two thousand men and women. However, a talk at Bristol four days later, where Annie took the chair, ended in disaster. 'The students through [sic] flour over Annie and Christabel and made their hair quite white', noted Mary Blathwayt. 'Not a word could be heard all the evening.'[136]

Interspersed with all this writing of articles, travelling and giving speeches was the usual round of WSPU business, including overseeing the organisers, to make sure everything was running smoothly. The way in which the Newcastle organiser, Annie Williams, had handled the release of Kitty Marion, who had been forcibly fed, was a cause for concern. 'Just that things may go right in future', Christabel firmly told Annie,

> I want to say that it was unwise to leave Miss Marion alone with the reporters. It is very difficult for a released prisoner to know what to say & what to leave unsaid. The organiser in charge . . . ought to see the prisoner & talk over her experiences with her & help her to put her story into shape.[137]

And directions had to be sent to other organisers, such as Jessie Baines, who was working in Lancashire. 'I shall be glad . . . if you can go to Oldham, Crewe and Bolton without delay for the purpose of spying around and making preliminary plans and arrangements', Christabel wrote on 22 November. 'The Christmas holiday this year cannot be very long because of the coming General Election', she penned the following day,

> but we think it should be possible for everybody to begin their holiday on Thursday, 23rd December, and to get back to their respective districts on Thursday, December 30th. Mrs. Pethick Lawrence wants all the organisers to dine with her on the 28th or 29th December, but you will get a personal note from her very shortly.[138]

Christabel also wrote to the petite, unpredictable Dora Marsden, an organiser in Southport, Lancashire, asking her to secure volunteers for a protest. 'Southport is the last resort of degenerates and I have only got one definite promise', replied a perky Dora.[139] Through all these difficult weeks, when Harry was ill, her mother in North America and her workload heavy, Christabel had the loyal Mrs Lawrence by her side. 'Miss Pankhurst and I talk over all . . . things . . . and are of one mind concerning everything', Emmeline Pethick-Lawrence told one organiser. 'Miss Pankhurst and I . . . must spend the Sunday together talking over the week's decisions and the week's work', she wrote to another. 'I do not think you can realise the immense responsibility . . . of this whole national campaign and how difficult it is for us to run about the country.'[140]

With the forthcoming general election so near, Christabel wrote to Balfour again, asking for a meeting since the WSPU wanted to know if, as leader of the Conservative and Unionist Party, he would extend the franchise to qualified women:

> Until we have explained to you what we should like the next Government to do for us and until we have heard what you have to tell us in reply, it is not possible for us to complete our arrangements for the General Election.[141]

But Balfour's position within his own party had been weakened since he had made no attempt to stop the Tory majority in the Lords from vetoing the People's Budget. And, significantly, he was regarded as being too soft on women's suffrage, constantly under pressure from his suffragist sisters-in-law, Lady Frances and Lady Betty Balfour, as well as besieged by Lady Constance Lytton, another in his social circle.[142] Balfour's reply to Christabel was short and to the point:

> The question of Women's Suffrage is one on which there are very deep divisions of opinion . . . which do not follow Party lines. The policy, therefore, of granting or withholding the Parliamentary vote to women, in existing circumstances, is no portion of the official programme of the [Conservative and] Unionist Party. Each member of it is at liberty . . . to express what view he pleases upon the subject without derogation from his Party loyalty.[143]

This disappointing news for Christabel was soon compounded by more. On Tuesday, 7 December, the Lord Chief Justice delivered his verdict about the appeal of her mother and of Evelina Haverfield, namely that while he recognised the right to petition the Prime Minister, he did not recognise the right of deputation to him. Christabel challenged this judgement, hammering home her defiant message in that week's *Votes for Women* that although the right of petitioning, the only constitutional weapon available to the voteless citizen, had been rendered null and void, the policy of the WSPU would remain 'unchanged'. As soon as the new Parliament assembled, a deputation would go to Westminster to petition the Prime Minister.[144]

When Emmeline Pankhurst returned to England on 8 December, Christabel braced herself to tell her mother the painful truth about Harry. When Emmeline heard that her only son would never walk again, she wailed in despair, 'He would be better dead!'[145] Since Sylvia, unlike her sisters and Aunt Mary, held no official position in the WSPU, it was decided that she would stay with Harry until he was stronger, and then resume her artistic career. On 9 December, Christabel stood by her mother's side at a special meeting at the Albert Hall to welcome home the much-loved leader of the WSPU. Emmeline did not speak of her personal sorrow but merely said how the women's movement was 'impersonal' and went on with or without her. As many beautiful flowers were presented to her, the audience cheered again and again, Mrs Lawrence hailing her as the 'Liberator of women'. In another stirring moment, hunger strikers marched onto the platform to be presented with medals. It was left to Christabel, the eldest daughter who was so protective of her grief-stricken mother, to outline the policy of the WSPU during the general election. Cries of 'Bravo!' erupted when she promised they would fight the Liberal Government. Prime Minister Asquith, she insisted, was an 'enemy of popular liberty, a Constitution wrecker, a cruel ruler'. Over four hundred and fifty women had gone to prison 'for liberty' during his term of office.[146]

Appearances on a public platform hid the personal turmoil Christabel felt about Harry whose condition had rapidly worsened as his old bladder problem flared up again. Dr Mills called in consultants who confirmed that there was no hope of recovery. Christabel could not believe that Harry was dying; nor could her mother or sisters. One night, when Sylvia was sitting by Harry's bedside, he confided that he had fallen in love with Helen Craggs, a young woman of his own age whom he had met when campaigning in Manchester the previous year. He had lost touch with her and desperately wanted to see her again. Sylvia was determined to grant Harry his wish. Helen was found and came immediately to Harry's bedside. 'Think of him as your young brother', Sylvia begged. 'Tell him you love him; he has only three weeks to live.'[147] There was no need to plead. Many years later, Helen confided to Grace Roe that Harry was her first and only love.[148] Helen sat with Harry all day and, at night, slept on a sofa to be near the telephone in case she was summoned.

Out of a deep sense of public duty to the wider women's movement, neither Christabel nor her mother wanted personal affairs to interfere with WSPU business, an attitude that all their followers understood and appreciated. It was a quality especially rare in women, indicating their realisation of the part they were playing as leaders in the women's cause. Whatever her private feelings, Christabel kept to her speaking schedule and continued to deal with queries from organisers and part-time volunteers alike. 'I have carefully thought over your letter offering to help at the General Election', she wrote to Ethel Birnstingl, 'and have come to the conclusion that you will help most by being at the office for the special purpose of making banners, etc.' To Mary Phillips, Christabel penned a note congratulating her on the success of her reception in Bradford for Lady Constance Lytton, 'I have heard from her how well organized it was'. To Theresa Garnett, who had been forcibly fed in prison after accosting Churchill in Bristol with a whip in her hand, she expressed the Union's warm appreciation for her 'pluck & determination. Your protest stirred everybody up & had made Cabinet Ministers distinctly nervous. Annie Kenney will tell you all about what has been going on in Bristol'.[149]

Christabel was still in close contact with Annie, who suddenly decided to write to Balfour, probably to help ease some of the burdens on Christabel's shoulders. 'I have not told our Leaders I have written, I have not told a single person', Annie penned in her untutored hand. 'I wish you would receive me on another deputation. I want to put our case before you . . . I know I am uneducated, but I love my Country and I love the people and I long to see Women free.' Balfour, in his dispiriting reply, pointed out that while he had no sympathy 'whatever with those who think that men have political rights by some divine ordinance, while women have none', he nonetheless doubted whether the enfranchisement of women would bring about any great improvement in their social and industrial condition.[150]

That Christmas of 1909, spent with Harry in the Pembridge Gardens nursing home, was the most distressing Christabel had ever experienced, not least because her mother, jealous of the growing tenderness between Harry and Helen, complained that Helen was taking from her 'the last of her son'.[151] For Christabel, despite the deep sadness in her heart, pressing WSPU business had to be dealt with, namely the brutal treatment of Selina Martin and Lesley Hall, working-class suffragettes in Walton Gaol, Liverpool who, contrary to the treatment for remand prisoners, had been forcibly fed. In particular, Selina's refusal to comply with the prison authorities had led them to throw her on the floor, handcuffed with her hands behind her back. After being kept in chains at night, she was carried by the arms and legs up a flight of stairs, face down, her head bumping on each stone step, where the forcible feeding took place. Once the operation had been performed, she was handcuffed again, flung down the steps and dragged back to her cell. That it was contrary to the law to treat untried prisoners in this way deeply angered Christabel, who immediately took action. 'Enclosed is a copy of the statement sent this morning to the press on the subject of the treatment of Miss Selina Martin and Miss Leslie Hall while on remand', she wrote to Jennie Baines on 30 December. 'A leaflet addressed to the electors dealing with the same subject is being printed and will be ready tomorrow . . . this terrible story should be made the chief feature of an appeal to the electors and to women.'[152]

A copy of the leaflet was also sent to the Home Secretary, Herbert Gladstone. 'At one time it would not have been thought possible that such things could happen in this country', wrote an indignant Christabel. 'Certainly it is high time that this deplorable state of affairs should be brought to an end, and that a strong protest should be made against the Government's action in regard to the Woman Suffrage question.'[153] The heavy demands of her workload at a time when she was in deep distress over the plight of a much-loved brother gave Christabel little rest. She did not write her usual end-of-year assessment of the Union's activities for *Votes for Women*, with its hopes for the future. That task was left to Fred Pethick-Lawrence.[154]

Notes

1 *VfW*, 7 January 1909, p. 253.
2 *Forward*, 2 January 1909.
3 Telegram from CP to C. Phillips, 5 January 1909, Watt Collection.
4 Quoted in Rosen, *Rise up women!*, pp. 114–15.
5 *VfW*, 21 January 1909, p. 278.
6 CP, *Unshackled*, p. 119.
7 *VfW*, 28 January 1909, p. 292.
8 *Times*, 21 January 1909.
9 *Daily Chronicle*, 26 January 1909.
10 *Times* and *Daily Chronicle*, 26 January 1909.

11 CP to Miss Wallis, Folio Album complied by Miss Muriel Wallis, Craigie Collection.
12 CP to Caroline Townsend, 9 February 1908, SFC.
13 CP to Mary Phillips, 31 January 1909, Mary Phillips Papers.
14 VfW, 11 February 1909, p. 341.
15 CP to Mary Phillips, 5 February 1909, Mary Phillips Papers.
16 CP to Mrs Baines, 6 February and 2 March 1907, Baines Papers.
17 CP, Unshackled, p. 126.
18 VfW, 11 and 18 February, pp. 322–3 and 363, respectively; Liverpool Courier, 13 February 1909.
19 VfW, 11 February 1909, p. 336.
20 CP to Miss Flatman, 16 and 18 February 1909, SFC.
21 Times, 24 February 1909.
22 J. Kenney, The flame and the flood, np.
23 Daily Mirror, 24 February 1909; Raeburn, Militant suffragettes, p. 89.
24 Helen Watts to Mother and all, 25 February 1908, photocopies of Helen Watts Papers, Nottinghamshire County Record Office.
25 Lytton, Prisons and prisoners, pp. 35 and 58.
26 Daily Telegraph, 26 February 1909.
27 CP to Miss Robins, 28 February 1909, HRHRC.
28 VfW, 12 March 1909, p. 422; this painting now hangs in the National Portrait Gallery, London.
29 EP to Dr Mills, 1 April 1909, TWL; ESP, TSM, p. 306.
30 See EP to Mr Scott, 8 and 11 March 1909, Scott Papers.
31 CP to Miss E. Birnstingl, 6 March 1909, Craigie Collection.
32 VfW, 26 March 1909, p. 474.
33 VfW, 16 April 1909, p. 552.
34 Daily News, 19 April 1909; VfW, 23 April 1909, pp. 574–5; Raeburn, Militant suffragettes, p. 94.
35 Entry for 17 April 1909, Nevinson Diaries.
36 VfW, 30 April 1909, p. 606.
37 VfW, 23 April 1909, p. 565.
38 M. Bosch with A. Kloosterman, eds, Politics and friendship, letters from the International Woman Suffrage Alliance 1902–1942 (Columbus, OH, Ohio State University Press, 1990), pp. 44–5.
39 J. Rupp, Worlds of women: the making of an international women's movement (Princeton, NJ, Princeton University Press, 1997), p. 137.
40 VfW, 7 May 1909, p. 634.
41 VfW, 7 May 1909, p. 634; Bosch with Kloosterman, eds, Politics and friendship, pp. 83–4.
42 CP, Unshackled, pp. 125–7.
43 VfW, 7 May 1909, p. 634.
44 VfW, 14 May 1909, pp. 653–4.
45 CP, Unshackled, p. 99.
46 CP to Miss Phillips, 10 May 1909, Mary Phillips Papers; see also CP to Ada Flatman, 24 May 1909, SFC.
47 ESP, TSM, p. 304.
48 VfW, 21 and 28 May 1909, pp. 693 and 723, respectively.
49 National Women's Social & Political Union, The women's exhibition 1909 programme (London, The Woman's Press, n.d.); Raeburn, Militant suffragettes, pp. 96–7; ESP, TSM, p. 306.
50 Raeburn, Militant suffragettes, p. 97; J. Kenney, The flame and the flood, np.
51 VfW, 21 May 1909, p. 695.
52 VfW, 21 May 1909, p. 704.

53 CP to Mr Scott, 21 May 1909, Scott Papers.
54 *VfW*, 4 and 18 June 1909, pp. 755 and 826, respectively.
55 *Christian Commonwealth*, 16 June 1909, pp. 649–50.
56 CP to Dear Friend, 23 June 1909, form letter, SFC.
57 CP to Miss Sharp, 14 June 1909, Evelyn Sharp Nevinson Papers, Bodleian Library, Oxford.
58 CP to Miss Robins, 17 July [sic] 1909, Robins Papers, HRHRC.
59 *VfW*, 2 July 1909, p. 873.
60 Raeburn, *Militant suffragettes*, pp. 102–3.
61 *Daily News, Daily Telegraph* and *Daily Chronicle*, 30 June 1909; *VfW*, 2 and 9 July 1909, pp. 872–9 and 907–11, respectively.
62 *VfW*, 9 July 1909, p. 920.
63 CP to Mr Grain, 1 July 1909, DMC.
64 *VfW*, 16 July 1909, pp. 935–42.
65 CP, *Unshackled*, p. 129.
66 *VfW*, 16 July 1909, p. 934.
67 ESP, *TSM*, p. 316.
68 ESP, *The suffragette*, p. 96.
69 See FPL, *Fate*, p. 101.
70 CP to Mr Scott, 13 July 1909, Scott Papers.
71 Raeburn, *Militant suffragettes*, pp. 106–7.
72 *Daily Mirror*, 15 July 1909.
73 *VfW*, 23 July 1909, pp. 971–2.
74 CP to Mr Balfour, 22 July 1909, Balfour Papers. Ms Add 49793, f.52.
75 CP to C. P. Scott, 22 July 1909, Scott Papers.
76 CP, Coercion defeated, *VfW*, 23 July 1909, p. 986.
77 *VfW*, 23 July 1909, p. 977.
78 CP to Miss Birnstingl, 24 July 1909, SFC.
79 CP to Mrs Cullen, 24 July 1909, SFC; WSPU leaflet, *A false accusation* (London, n.d.).
80 CP to Mrs Cullen, 23 July 1909, SFC.
81 Garner, *Stepping stones*, p. 29; Pugh, *March of the women*, p. 221; Pugh, *The Pankhursts*, p. 158.
82 CP to Mrs Cullen, 17 July 1909, SFC.
83 See CP to Miss Robins, 17 July 1909, Robins Papers, HRHRC.
84 CP to Miss Robins, 22 August 1909, Robins Papers, HRHRC.
85 CP to Miss Robins, 1 September 1909, Robins Papers, HRHRC.
86 CP to Miss Robins, 8 September 1909, Robins Papers, HRHRC.
87 EWE to H. McIlquham, 17 September 1909, EWEP, Add Mss 47, 455, f.270.
88 Dobbie, *A nest of suffragettes*, p. 34.
89 *VfW*, 17 September 1909, p. 1181.
90 CP to Mrs Baines, 10 September 1909, Baines Papers.
91 CP to Mrs Baines, 17 September 1909, Baines Papers.
92 *VfW*, 24 September 1909, p. 1210.
93 CP to Jennie Baines, 19 September 1909, Baines Papers.
94 CP to Mr Long, 20 September 1909, Suffrage Papers, Linton Park Plc.
95 *Times*, 21 September 1909.
96 *VfW*, 24 September 1909, p. 1205; *Daily News*, 25 September 1909.
97 CP to Miss Phillips, 22 September 1909, Mary Phillips Papers.
98 CP to Mrs Baines, 23 September 1909, Baines Papers.
99 See J. Purvis, The prison experiences of the suffragettes in Edwardian Britain, *Women's History Review*, 4, 1, 1995, pp. 103–33; J. Purvis, The power of the hunger strike, *BBC History Magazine*, June 2009, pp. 36–40.
100 *Times*, 29 September 1909.

101 Tickner, *Spectacle of Women*, p. 107; Purvis, Prison experiences, p. 123.
102 *VfW*, 1 October 1909, pp. 1 and 4.
103 CP to Mrs Baines, 29 September 1909, Baines Papers.
104 *VfW*, 8 October 1909, p. 19.
105 EP, The fiery cross, *VfW*, 1 October 1909, p. 8.
106 *Times*, 5 October 1909.
107 *Times*, 10 December 1909.
108 See J. F. Geddes, Culpable complicity: the medical profession and the forcible feeding of suffragettes, 1909–14, *Women's History Review*, 17, 1, 2008, pp. 79–94.
109 *VfW*, 8 October 1909, pp. 20 and 24.
110 *VfW*, 15 October 1909, p. 43.
111 *VfW*, 8 and 15 October 1909, pp. 24 and 43, respectively.
112 See her letter in *Newcastle Daily Chronicle*, 11 October 1909.
113 B. Porter, *The origins of the vigilant state: the London Metropolitan Police Special Branch before the First World War* (London, Weidenfeld and Nicolson, 1987), p. 198 gives the date as 11 September 1909.
114 CP to Mrs Baines, 22 September 1909, Baines Papers.
115 Lytton, *Prisons and prisoners*, pp. 203–4.
116 Lytton, *Prisons and prisoners*, pp. 223–31; *VfW*, 15 October 1909, p. 36.
117 Two militant English suffragists who come to aid cause in America, *Fort Wayne Journal Gazette*, 18 October 1909.
118 *VfW*, 27 August 1909, p. 1115; E. C. Dubois, *Harriot Stanton Blatch and the winning of woman suffrage* (New Haven, CT and London, Yale University Press, 1997), p. 113.
119 Mrs Pankhurst (New York, J. B. Pond Lyceum Bureau, n.d.), National American Woman Suffrage Association (hereafter NAWSA) Papers, Library of Congress, Washington DC; CP, *Unshackled*, p. 147.
120 See J. Purvis, Emmeline Pankhurst (1858–1928), suffragette leader and single parent in Edwardian Britain, *Women's History Review*, 20, 1, 2011, pp. 87–108.
121 CP, *Unshackled*, p. 147; ESP, TSM, p. 320.
122 APW, My mother, pp. 47–8.
123 ESP, *Emmeline Pankhurst*, pp. 93–4.
124 CP to Mrs Baines, 13 October 1909, Baines Papers.
125 Entry for 16 October 1909, Nevinson Diaries.
126 CP, *Unshackled*, p. 135.
127 *VfW*, 22 October 1909, p. 54.
128 CP, Mrs Winston Churchill, *VfW*, 22 October 1909, p. 56.
129 CP to Mrs Badley, 21 and 25 October 1909, TWL.
130 CP to Mrs Baines, 22 October 1909, Baines Papers; CP to Mr Scott, 29 October 1909, Scott Papers.
131 *VfW*, 29 October 1909, p. 68.
132 *VfW*, 29 October 1909, p. 70; 5 November 1909, pp. 82 and 91.
133 CP to Dr Mills, 4 November 1909, TWL.
134 CP to Mrs Mills, 18 November 1909, TWL.
135 CP, Lords, Commons and suffragettes, *VfW*, 12 November 1909, p. 104.
136 *VfW*, 26 November 1909, p. 132; Dobbie, A nest of suffragettes, p. 38.
137 CP to Miss Williams, 15 November 1909, Craigie Collection.
138 CP to Mrs Baines, 22 and 23 November 1909, Baines Papers.
139 Dora Marsden to CP, 28 November 1909, Baines Papers.
140 EPL to Miss Marsden, 1 December 1909 and EPL to Mrs Baines, 24 November 1909, Baines Papers.
141 CP to Balfour, 3 December 1909, Balfour Papers, Ms Add 49793, f.55.

142 Constance Lytton to Balfour, 7 and 8 October 1909, Balfour Papers, MS Add 49793, fs.146 and 148.
143 Balfour note, 'To be sent to various women suffrage organisations & to Miss Pankhurst Dec. 1909', Balfour Papers, Ms Add 49793, f.59.
144 CP, The right of petition, VfW, 10 December 1909, p. 168.
145 ESP, *Emmeline Pankhurst*, p. 94.
146 VfW, 17 December 1909, p. 181; *Times*, 10 December 1909.
147 ESP, *TSM*, p. 323.
148 Jill Craigie interview with Grace Roe [1975?], Craigie Collection.
149 CP to Miss E. Birnstingl, 11 December 1909, SFC; CP to Miss Phillips, Mary Phillips Papers; CP to Miss Garnett, 13 December 1909, Craigie Collection.
150 A. Kenney to Balfour, 18 December 1909, Balfour Papers; A. Balfour to Miss Kenney, 3 January 1910, Kenney Papers.
151 ESP, *TSM*, p. 323.
152 CP to Mrs Baines, 30 December 1909, Baines Papers.
153 CP to Gladstone, 1 January 1910, Gladstone Papers, BL, Add 46066, f.211.
154 VfW, 31 December 1909, p. 216.

11

PERSONAL SORROW
AND A TRUCE

1910

On 5 January 1910, the gentle Harry Pankhurst died at the Pembridge Gardens nursing home, his family and Helen Craggs at his side. He was just twenty years old. Emmeline Pankhurst was inconsolable. Although Sylvia in *The suffragette movement* gives the impression that she was the only sister who grieved for Harry and for whom Harry himself cared, this was not so. Christabel too felt keenly Harry's death, remembering how her brother 'had grown so like his father, in his support of the women's cause, in his way with his mother and sisters, and in his attitude towards all women'. And Adela, who had been her brother's constant companion in their childhood, had always been particularly close to her Harry. 'My dear brother's illness was kept from me to the last', she wrote bitterly and resentfully many years later. 'Sylvia did not inform me of it.'[1] Helen Craggs coped with the loss of her first love by spending many nights after Harry's death riding round on the Inner Circle line of the London underground, until dawn, determined never to marry any other young suitor.[2]

For Christabel, despite her sorrow, there was no escape from the long hours of work she had to undertake as Chief Organiser of the WSPU, especially since her mother was stricken low with grief. As Geraldine Lennox, one of the office staff at Clement's Inn, recollected:

> When her [Christabel's] brother died a General Election campaign was on. Christabel was billed to speak at many meetings in outlying parts of London where tubes and 'buses were difficult to get. Knowing all that she had gone through and the little rest she had had, two or three of us arranged to have taxis to fetch her home – these were paid for out of our own pockets. The second night of this arrangement Christabel thanked us for our thought but insisted that as the other workers had to find their way home by 'bus and tube, 'bus and tube were good enough for her.[3]

A brief appreciation of Harry soon appeared in *Votes for Women*. '[H]e was unselfish, devoted to the public good . . . a fighter in the great cause of justice to women.' At the end of the epitaph was a short statement saying that Mrs Pankhurst, on behalf of herself and her daughters, gratefully acknowledged the kind expressions of sympathy from so many friends who, she felt sure, would understand her inability to thank them personally as she would wish to do. For some weeks, this task fell to Christabel. 'Please give to all our comrades at Liverpool our loving thanks for their messages of sympathy in the loss of our darling boy', she wrote to organiser Ada Flatman. 'You may imagine how precious we feel the affection of the members of the Union to be. Harry talked often during his illness of the women in prison & felt so much for them.'[4] For Harry's broken-hearted mother, her ability to subordinate her private sorrow to the demands of the women's movement came to the fore again.[5] 'If you can arrange it I would be grateful if Bradford friends would just behave to me as if no great sorrow had come to me just now', wrote a sad Emmeline Pankhurst to Mary Phillips on 9 January. 'It breaks me down to talk about it although I am very grateful for sympathy. I want to get through my work & know that you will help me to do it.'[6] Christabel's maternal uncle, Herbert Goulden, stepped in to help the grief-stricken family by buying Harry's cemetery plot and paying the funeral expenses.[7] Harry was buried on 10 January.

The bereavement in the family took its toll on Christabel who, as the eldest and favourite daughter, felt a special responsibility for family misfortunes, especially her mother's welfare. But like her mother, she subordinated her private sorrow to the demands of the women's movement. On 12 January 1910, just two days after the funeral and clothed in black mourning dress, she spoke at a WSPU meeting in Ladbroke Road. Nevinson noted that she looked tired and pale. But two days later, at a large meeting at Fulham Town Hall with an overflow of two or three thousand, she had regained some of her old charm. 'Christabel was received with splendid favour . . . She spoke superbly. I have never heard her finer – slim, in thin black, in perfect temper, never at a loss. She completely conquered them.' On 21 February, when Nevinson was at the Duke of York's theatre to see Galsworthy's *Justice*, there were 'cheers for Shaw [George Bernard] & for Christabel who was in an upper box with the Lawrences'.[8] Other well-known figures, such as the poet John Masefield, knowing of Christabel's plight under heart-wrenching circumstances, also made contact with her. 'It would be a great pleasure to me to meet you some day', he wrote to Christabel. 'I have been at your side, in spirit, so often, that I feel as though we were not quite strangers.'[9]

For the January 1910 general election, Christabel had written a leaflet titled *Militant methods* in which she justified the tactics of the WSPU and its opposition to the Liberal Government.[10] While the campaign was in full swing, Lady Constance Lytton was arrested on 14 January and forcibly fed. Ashamed of the preferential treatment she had received on hunger strike in October 1909, when her release had been ordered after only two days in prison, on the ground that her heart was weak, she had been determined to test whether the prison authorities would exercise the same leniency if they were unaware of her aristocratic status. Disguised as 'Jane Warton', a plain working woman with spectacles, and dressed in a long, green, cheap coat with portrait badges of the WSPU leaders pinned to the collar, Constance protested outside Walton Gaol, Liverpool, against the treatment of its suffragette prisoners, and was arrested. Sentenced to a fortnight in the Third Division, she went on hunger strike. Constance had told Ada Flatman, the organiser for Liverpool, about her plan and Ada promptly informed Christabel. 'Do not tell a soul about our friend', Christabel confided. 'It had better go on till the end. She is willing we know.'[11] 'Jane Warton' did not tell the authorities about her heart condition, nor did a perfunctory examination detect it. Forcibly fed eight times, it was only when the press informed her brother, Lord Lytton, that there was a rumour that his sister was in Walton Gaol that her real identity was discovered. The Home Office immediately released her, on 23 January, just eight days into her sentence.[12]

Christabel went into the attack, stigmatising the Liberal Government as 'snobs' who distinguish between people and accusing Herbert Gladstone, the Home Secretary, of 'sheer and deliberate untruthfulness'.[13] She made similar points in a private letter to George Bernard Shaw, enclosing also a copy of Constance's description of her experiences. 'We hope that the revelations . . . of the way in which our prisoners are treated will do a great deal toward putting an end to the practice of forcible feeding.'[14]

The appalling treatment by a Liberal Government of Lady Constance Lytton, a peeress of the realm, caused a public outcry and undoubtedly influenced many male voters. As Liberal seats began steadily falling to the Tories, Christabel claimed it was a victory for the WSPU.[15] On 24 January, she wrote to Betty Balfour, Constance's sister, 'You will feel unhappy and anxious about your sister, I know . . . We do love her for what she has done.' Speculating optimistically about the Tory Government to be, she continued, '[T]here will be less for the women in this Union to suffer in the new Government. I have already four promises from Unionist Members to ballot for the Women's Enfranchisement Bill.'[16] Christabel's hopes were high, despite Balfour's refusal to pledge his party to a women's suffrage measure which, she had told him, was based on 'party convenience'.[17] But it was Asquith, not Balfour, who formed the new Government. Although the Liberals had been returned with no overall majority, polling two hundred and seventy-five seats against two hundred and seventy-three for the Conservatives, they were supported by eighty-two Irish Nationalist and forty Labour MPs.[18] Realising that the new political situation might be useful to the women's cause, Henry Brailsford set about forming a Conciliation Committee for Women's Suffrage, eventually composed of fifty-four MPs across the political spectrum, who would compose and promote an agreed women's suffrage bill. Christabel, her mother and Mrs Lawrence were initially doubtful about the new proposal, but ultimately agreed to support it.

At the Queen's Hall on 31 January 1910, a frail Emmeline Pankhurst announced that until further notice, the WSPU would suspend all militant action, only peaceful and constitutional methods being used, even when carrying on its anti-Government policy. For Christabel, 'the truce', as it became known, was a shrewd tactic since it allowed her to quietly take stock of the effectiveness of militancy and also to replenish the energies of her followers, as well as her mother and herself who were emotionally drained over Harry's death. Writing in her autobiography over twenty years later, she recollected the factors that had propelled her to support such a decision:

> My own strongest, but unspoken reason, for welcoming the Conciliation movement was that it might avert the need for stronger militancy . . . Mild militancy was more or less played out. The Government had, as far as they could, closed every door to it, especially by excluding Suffragette questioners from their meetings . . . a pause in militancy would give time for familiarity to fade so that the same methods would be used again, with freshness and effect . . . [Further,] our women were beginning to revolt against the one-sided violence which they experienced in the course of their attempts to petition the King's Prime Minister . . . They were arguing that the W.S.P.U. respect for human safety ought to apply to themselves as well as to everyone else. They were questioning whether, for the sake of others dear to them, or even for their own sake, they had any right to risk personal injury, if a little damage to panes of glass would have the same, and indeed more, effect.[19]

Militancy would remain suspended until 21 November 1911, apart from one week in November 1910.

The truce announced on 31 January had barely begun when Christabel received an indignant letter from suffragist Eleanor Rathbone, a member of the NUWSS and fierce critic of militant tactics, suggesting that the women in Walton Gaol had been treated more considerately than the WSPU suggested. The impatient Christabel sent a curt reply:

> [T]hose who have not had personal experience of forcible feeding and prison conditions generally, and have never had any personal intercourse with those who have been in prison, are not really qualified to express any opinion upon the matter. Certainly they are not entitled to write to the newspapers, in defence of the authorities.[20]

But the public outcry against the treatment of Lady Constance was on Christabel's side. On 19 February, Christabel was feted as the honoured guest at a large gathering of the New Vagabond Club, at the Hotel Cecil. Shortly afterwards, she addressed meetings in London before travelling in early March to the Ilkeston by-election, Derbyshire, where she joined her mother for a weekend's campaigning. This was followed by a speech at Bristol, where she met up with Annie, and then a trip to Dublin at the invitation of the Irish Women's Franchise League.[21]

Some welcome news that indicated the Government was prepared to improve the prison conditions of the suffragettes arrived on 15 March 1910 when Winston Churchill, now Home Secretary in the new Liberal Government, introduced a new rule that would come into effect in a month's time. Rule 243a permitted the Secretary of State to approve 'ameliorations . . . in respect of the wearing of prison clothing, bathing, hair-cutting, cleaning of cells, employment, exercise, books, and otherwise' for any Second or Third Division offender whose 'previous character is good' and who had been convicted of, or committed to prison for, 'an offence not involving dishonest, cruelty, indecency, or serious violence'.[22] Christabel cautiously hailed the reform 'as a sign that better counsels are beginning to prevail, and as a triumph for those comrades of ours who have risked health and life in defence of the rights of political prisoners'. Nonetheless she was quick to point out that the treatment of suffragette prisoners involved 'something more than . . . the provision of mere physical comforts', namely their recognition as political offenders. 'In this regard, as in others, we claim that there shall be the same law for women as for men.'[23] In view of the changed prison conditions, Christabel, her mother and Mrs Lawrence advised their WSPU members that the hunger strike was now 'inapplicable' and, if ever resorted to again, 'must be organised as a political policy with utmost deliberation'.[24]

The big WSPU meeting at the Albert Hall on 18 March, the sixth that had been held there, had a feeling of victory, both in the speeches and among the audience. Medals were presented by Emmeline Pankhurst to all those brave women who had been forcibly fed during the past few months, and over £1,650 collected. The forthcoming spring programme, which would include a Self-Denial week and a great Women's Demonstration on 28 May, was also announced. In a rousing address, the charismatic Christabel gave her followers a message of hope, saying that although the worst of the battle might be over, they still had militant methods in reserve. In particular, she stressed the importance of women being confident of victory, and of having faith in the human spirit which could overcome all obstacles:

> So long as the women in this country are self-respecting, are determined, and are brave – nothing, absolutely nothing, can deprive them of the certainty of early enfranchisement . . . We know we shall win . . . Our experience has given us absolute confidence, but there is something more that is given to us . . . our complete power of the human spirit . . . and we shall allow ourselves to be an instrument of that force in the future just as we have done in the four or five years of this campaign.[25]

Perhaps Christabel was thinking, as she spoke, about her late grandmother Sophia Jane Goulden who had died of double pneumonia that spring. As a resident of the Isle of Man, which was independent of Britain, Grandmother Goulden had had a parliamentary vote.[26] The news of her passing, coming so soon after Harry's death, hit the Pankhurst family hard. Although Grandmother Goulden had had a stroke some years ago, she had recovered sufficiently to lead an active life and to continue following, with the greatest pride, the exploits of her eldest daughter and her granddaughters in the women's suffrage movement.[27] At the end of March, Christabel went on a much-needed holiday with Annie to Sark, in the Channel Islands, all expenses paid by the Pethick-Lawrences. It was not only Christabel who was exhausted. Annie was tired from all the dashing about she had undertaken during the general election. As often happened when Christabel was away, Fred wrote an article for the page she usually filled in *Votes for Women*.[28]

In the meantime, the Conciliation Committee had come into being with Lord Lytton as chair and Brailsford as secretary. The committee decided to sponsor a private member's bill which was deliberately drawn along narrow lines to win the support of the Tories. Thus the Bill to Extend the Parliamentary Franchise to Women Occupiers did not seek to give the parliamentary vote to women on equal terms with men, but to extend it to women possessed of a household qualification or of a £10 occupation qualification; however, a wife could not be qualified in respect of the same property as her husband.[29] All the suffrage societies, including the WSPU, decided to support the bill, at least in public, the truce enabling the Union to follow more conventional forms of propaganda. During the past year the WSPU had held more than 20,000 meetings, and now that militancy was suspended, a time of even greater effort in building up the organisation and extending its educational work could be entered upon.[30] However, privately both Christabel and her mother were concerned that the bill was too narrow and would be seen as a Tory initiative since it favoured property-owning women who would be more likely to vote Conservative. Nonetheless, Christabel believed that the present parliamentary session offered the best opportunity in fifty years of agitation for securing a women suffrage measure.[31] 'The new Bill does not give us all we want', she wrote publicly in *Votes for Women*, 'but we are for it, if others also are for it.'[32]

Christabel worked behind the scenes, trying to enlist the support of influential men supposedly in favour of votes for women, such as Arthur Balfour, leader of the Conservatives. 'Mr. Churchill, last night, gave a list of measures which the Liberal Government are desirous of carrying and this list includes Electoral Reform', she wrote to Balfour on 13 April. 'Will it be possible to ask in the course of your speech whether this scheme of Electoral Reform is to include Woman Suffrage?' Christabel was delighted when Balfour did raise the issue of women's suffrage in a parliamentary debate and wrote immediately to thank him. 'How kind it was to refer as you did . . . to our question. What you said will make people think and will do very much good.' A further letter of praise was sent five days later.[33] Determined that nothing should go wrong, she also wrote to C. P. Scott, the influential editor of the *Manchester Guardian*, and also to Elizabeth Robins, asking her if she would join one of the platforms at the demonstration on 28 May. 'You will do your best with such Cabinet Ministers as you know, will you not!' she entreated Elizabeth. 'Can you get for us <u>names</u> for the procession', she added in a postscript. 'If well known people march – others follow suit.'[34] Christabel was pleased when Elizabeth agreed to join the procession but turned down the invitations to join the former actress on holiday in June since it was not a convenient time of year to be away. 'At Whitsuntide

Mrs. Tuke & I shall be staying at Billingshurst', Christabel continued, '& we want to motor to Henfield to see you. May we? If so, what is the best day: Sat, Sunday or Monday are available.'[35]

Despite Christabel's optimism, the crisis between the House of Lords and the Commons had still not been resolved. There was talk of another general election which could mean that the women's franchise bill would not get a hearing. However, the sudden death of King Edward, in early May, changed the mood of Parliament which felt that controversies should be suspended in the nation's hour of mourning. The canny Christabel immediately realised the importance of the changed political situation. On the front page of the 13 May issue of *Votes for Women* appeared a photograph of the widowed Queen Alexandra, edged in black. Inside it was announced that, in view of the universal sorrow occasioned by the King's death, the demonstration planned for 28 May would be postponed until 18 June, the only available alternative date the Albert Hall could offer. 'All Suffragists are especially and profoundly moved by the death of King Edward', Christabel wrote. 'In him as Sovereign was personified the nation, to serve which, through their citizen power, is the dominant aspiration of modern womanhood.' But more than this, Christabel emphasised that Edward's successor had a responsibility to the women of Britain, namely to grant them the parliamentary vote so that they could work for the good of the Empire:

> [T]he new King rules not over these Islands alone, but over vast dominions beyond the seas. In some of these dominions, women are numbered among the citizens and hold equal voting rights. But while they are enfranchised, and thus enabled to take part in shaping the Empire's destiny, the women of the Mother Country, the heart of the Empire, are denied the right and privilege of British citizenship. This is, surely, the time for relieving them of this stigma, and for setting free their hands to build for the prosperity and honour of the race and of the Empire![36]

Like so many middle-class feminists of her time, Christabel Pankhurst was appropriating imperial ideology and rhetoric to justify British women's right to equality.[37] On the front page of the following week's *Votes for Women*, a picture of the new Queen, Mary, was reproduced:

> [T]he young and gracious Queen, who has already enthroned herself in the hearts of the people . . . was from her babyhood a bonny, typically English girl, blessed with a strong sense of humour, and a happy, cheery nature, simply and sensibly trained by a wise father and mother.[38]

For the embittered Sylvia Pankhurst, writing nearly twenty years later, in *The suffragette movement*, it was all too much. 'Christabel, daughter of Republican Dr. Pankhurst, vied with the Conservative organs in her expressions of devotion to the Throne.'[39]

But Christabel was more than this barbed criticism. Unlike her socialist sister, she wanted to unite all women, irrespective of their social status or political affiliation, since she believed that the subordination of women to men was more significant than class oppression. For Christabel, the priorities of aristocratic men in regard to their womenfolk were no different to those of working-class men – both were concerned with protecting their own interests. Consequently she emphasised how the forthcoming procession of 18 June was a key moment for all women to stand together, in sisterhood, united in their demand for the vote:

> June 18 will be something more than a political demonstration; it will be a festival at which we shall celebrate the sisterhood of women. According to the old tale of men's making, it is not in women to unite and to work with one another. Women have only now discovered the falsity of this, and they are rejoicing in their new found sisterhood.[40]

By early June, the optimistic Christabel was commenting that the prospects for the women's franchise bill seemed 'very bright', a view that was echoed by many suffragettes and suffragists, including the veteran campaigner Elizabeth Wolstenholme Elmy.[41] 'Women are going to get the vote now', Christabel told a loudly applauding audience on 3 June at the Royal Victoria Pavilion, Ramsgate, one of the towns she was visiting on her East Kent tour. The local reporter was entranced. 'This remarkable leader . . . with her pleasant girlish figure and appearance, allied to wonderful ability and a splendid gift of oratory, seemed untiring in her espousal of the cause, and spoke with indomitable courage and unfailing hopefulness.' There was nothing of the 'blue stocking' about her, despite her law degree. 'Her charm of manner, the frank, open face and winning smile, together with the determined mouth and chin, expressive eyes and brilliant ability, make in Miss Pankhurst an ideal leader of the cause which she so valiantly champions.'[42]

Even if Christabel read such flattering commentary, there was no escape from her duties as Chief Organiser of the WSPU. Together with Emmeline Pethick-Lawrence, she had to make sure that the local branches ran well and deal with any problems that arose. Lily Nourse had recently resigned as Honorary Secretary of the Marylebone WSPU branch and Christabel felt obliged, on the very day she was speaking at Ramsgate, to write to her personally, expressing her regret at the news. 'I hope that the private claims upon your time will not prevent you from still doing much for the Union', she wrote encouragingly. 'Just now everyone is so greatly needed . . . So do help us all you can . . . Thanks for all you have done.[43] And, of course, as the key strategist of the WSPU, Christabel never took her eye off the necessity of keeping in touch with sympathetic powerful men. Once back in her office at Clement's Inn, she wrote to C. P. Scott again, expressing the hope that the WSPU would be able 'to rejoice in Mr. Asquith's friendship and the certainty of victory'.[44]

Peaceful campaigning in places such as East Kent was a critical aspect of WSPU policy to win popular support for the bill. However, it was not only the local press that admired the Chief Organiser of the WSPU. *The Week End*, a London-based popular newspaper, described Christabel Pankhurst as 'the' popular leader of the suffragists, both its 'slave and darling'. Few people had any idea 'of the amount of hard work which this young lady puts in at Clement's Inn and elsewhere. Twelve or fourteen hours a day is her usual stretch'. The well-respected *Vanity Fair*, which usually featured public male figures, honoured Christabel too, as 'A Woman of the Day', complete with a cartoon by Spy. 'She has courage and charm, and would make more enemies if she was less gracious' the comment ran.[45]

14 June had been set as the date for the introduction of the women's franchise bill in the Commons. Two days before that, Christabel sent another chirpy letter to Balfour:

> I am so happy in the thought that we have your support for the plan of carrying a suffrage bill this year . . . When you so kindly saw me a few weeks ago you made me realise how easy, from the practical, House of Commons point of view, it would be to carry the bill this year. Since then everything has moved forward so smoothly and well. With your help, we shall in a few days have the assurance of enfranchisement. I can't quite put into words what that means to us, but if you have ever so longed and worked for anything as we have for this, you will understand.[46]

The great suffrage procession to the Albert Hall on 18 June, organised by the WSPU but including over one hundred and thirty suffrage groups, militant and non-militant, had been planned with military precision. Spirits were high since four days earlier the first reading of the Conciliation Bill, introduced by Labour MP Mr D. J. Shackleton, as a private member's bill, had been unopposed in the Commons. With the theme 'From Prison to Citizenship', the 10,000 women who marched from the Embankment at 6.30 p.m. on that fine June evening took over two hours to reach their destination. The marchers, accompanied by forty bands, included all ages, ranks and occupations of women – aristocrats, housewives, factory women, box makers, shirt makers, musicians, writers, civil servants, pharmacists, nurses, actresses, clerks, sanitary inspectors, health visitors, schoolteachers, stenographers, shop assistants and churchwomen. Detachments from the Colonies, France, America, Germany, Sweden, Denmark, Holland, Norway and Italy also took part, illustrating international support for the women's cause in Britain. Seven hundred banners of all colours, sizes and designs floated above the marchers, the recently formed Men's Political Union for Women's Enfranchisement carrying the heavier ones. Of particular interest was the six hundred and seventeen-strong Prisoners' Pageant headed by Christabel and her mother, Emmeline Pethick-Lawrence, Lady Constance Lytton and Annie Kenney. Each of the ex-prisoners, dressed in white, carried a silvered wand tipped with a silvered arrow which glittered in the evening sunshine. Cheers were raised too for the contingent of university graduates in their red and black academic robes, velvet caps and mortar boards. 'It takes a good deal to astonish a London crowd', commented the *Daily Telegraph*, 'it is doubtful if the metropolis has ever before witnessed such a remarkable demonstration.' 'It was a thing of sheer beauty', opined the *Morning Leader*, 'the applause of a vast concourse of onlookers followed it right along its nearly three miles route.'[47]

When the procession arrived at the Albert Hall, Emmeline Pankhurst gave a short speech that opened with the phrase, 'One word: Victory!' She then read a resolution calling upon the Government to grant facilities for the women's franchise bill this session. Christabel issued a warning. '[I]f facilities are refused . . . if Mr. Asquith ventures . . . to flout the opinion of the Commons, and through them the opinion of the people, then *something must be done*; and if revolution is needed, there must be revolution!'[48]

Christabel was right to be cautious about Asquith. Faced with three major problems, namely a revolt from the House of Lords, Home Rule for Ireland and trade union militancy, he was not prepared to give time to an issue he personally opposed and considered marginal. In this he was supported by many MPs, including the Irish Nationalists. At a Cabinet meeting on 23 June, it was agreed that the Conciliation Bill would be allowed a second reading but that no further facilities would be granted that parliamentary session.[49]

When the decision was announced in the Commons, the WSPU leaders were bitterly disappointed. Christabel immediately wrote to Balfour, asking if she may see him. 'Mr. Asquith's statement . . . has greatly dissatisfied us, but before taking any action I want your advice if you will be so very kind as to give it to me.' Balfour's reply, marked private, was terse:

> You want my 'advice': but I am afraid you are very unlikely to take it! . . . If rumour is to be believed, the Government is not only divided on the question of Suffrage, but those who are in favour of Suffrage are divided as to the <u>kind</u> of measure which they will consent to support. If this is so, their and our difficulties will be increased . . . I have no advice to offer but patience . . . advice not very likely to be taken![50]

Christabel was not crushed by Balfour's tone. Although polite in her reply, she stood her ground, saying that if:

> the Prime Minister refuses . . . to reconsider his decision, we shall be obliged if only for self respect's sake to express our indignation and dissatisfaction by means of militant action. To show patience would we consider be to condone the Government's destruction of the bill.[51]

On 30 June, Asquith announced that two days, 11 and 12 July, would be set aside for the second reading of the Conciliation Bill. Christabel again wrote to Balfour, 'I think you must have had a great deal to do with bringing about this change of attitude on his part . . . Many and grateful thanks to you for all that you are doing for us.'[52] The second reading of the bill was carried by the considerable majority of one hundred and nine votes. However, the Commons also voted to refer the bill to a committee of the whole House which meant that it would not be brought up for its committee stage unless given special facilities, which effectively extinguished its survival. '[A]nother hope is killed', recorded Nevinson in his diary.[53] But Christabel refused to accept defeat. 'To get the bill into Committee will be a struggle', she confessed to C. P. Scott, but added optimistically that it could be done 'if all who want the bill stand firm'.[54]

Asquith and key Cabinet members such as Churchill and Lloyd George had voted against the Conciliation Bill. The duplicitous Asquith, in the parliamentary debate, had argued that no suffrage measure would be 'satisfactory' which did not give women votes on the same terms as men. In a barbed reference to the militants, he pointedly stated that those who take the sword shall perish by the sword. A cause, he continued, which 'cannot' win its way to public acceptance by persuasion, by argument, by organisation, by peaceful methods of agitation is a cause which already and in advance pronounces upon itself a sentence of death.[55] The angry WSPU leaders responded that Asquith's pronouncements should be directed against himself and his Government which had been 'the aggressors in the conflict', getting the police force out to prevent women approaching Parliament.[56] It was particularly the opposition of Churchill and Lloyd George that upset Christabel. '[I]nstead of directly and openly attacking the principle of Woman Suffrage, they adopted the less honourable method of pretending to believe in Votes for Women, while attacking the . . . Bill . . . on the ground that it is "undemocratic".'[57] These two Government Ministers, she believed, were 'false friends' who 'cloak their opposition by saying that they want to give us a measure of adult suffrage which we ourselves do not ask for'.[58]

Nonetheless, despite these obstacles, Christabel still clung to the slim hope that facilities for the Conciliation Bill would be granted. Brushing off Asquith's opposition in a light-hearted way, she told her followers:

> Another such crisis arose when the Prime Minister declined to fix an early or any date for the Second Reading of the Bill. After one week of agitation he reconsidered his decision and appointed two days . . . Let us now repeat and redouble the effort which produced so great a result.[59]

Christabel's stand was supported by the WSPU membership at a crowded mass meeting at St James's Hall where the names of Lloyd George and Churchill were received with storms of hisses and cries of 'Traitors'.[60]

A great number of peaceful demonstrations in support of the bill were being held in large towns throughout the country, such as Manchester, Liverpool, Southport, Sheffield, Leicester, Nottingham and Edinburgh. The WSPU built on this success by planning another big peaceful procession to be held in Hyde Park, on 23 July, the anniversary of the successful working men's agitation for the vote, thirty-four years ago. 'Let me remind you that on July 23rd, 1866, the famous Hyde Park Demonstration, at which the railings were broken down, took place', Christabel informed all one hundred and fifty WSPU speakers in a circular letter, sent the day before the rally. Hoping that tomorrow's peaceful demonstration would have the same satisfactory result, she asked the women if, in the course of their speeches, they would lay particular stress:

> upon three matters of supreme practical importance – (1). The audience should be told about the 'Votes for Women' paper, and should be urged to read it regularly . . . (2). The address of our headquarters, 4. Clement's Inn, should be given. (3) The women present in the audience should be urged to join the Union.[61]

A number of suffrage groupings joined the WSPU demonstration on 23 July, including the Actresses' Franchise League, the Irish Suffragists, the Women's Freedom League, the Men's Committee for Justice to Women, the New Union for Men and Women, the Men's League for Women's Suffrage, the Fabian Society, the New Constitutional Suffrage Society, the Men's Political Union for Women's Enfranchisement and the International Women's Franchise Club, as well as contingents representing New Zealand and Australia, university women, teachers, musicians, nurses, midwives, businesswomen, gardeners and florists.[62] However, the NUWSS refused to participate since the WSPU leadership had given no guarantee that they would refrain from a resumption of militant tactics before the procession.[63] Since the number of marchers was so large, the police had suggested that two processions be formed which would meet in the Park.

In brilliant sunshine, banners waving in the breeze, bands playing and silver bells giving out a tinkling sound as they were blown by the wind, Christabel and Emmeline Pethick-Lawrence led the East Procession, headed by Flora Drummond in her green riding costume and smart felt hat. Christabel wore her academic gown and cap. The West Procession, which began at Shepherd's Bush, was headed by her mother, dressed in a long white cloak, with Mabel Tuke walking by her side.[64] 'Held down Christabel's dress as she climbed down the ladder', wrote the gallant Nevinson, 'and made a path for her to her platform . . . Saw . . . [her] borne away by a rushing mob of admirers.'[65] Christabel presided over one platform, as did other members of her family – her mother, her Aunt Mary and her sisters Adela and Sylvia. A network of close female friends and women she worked with were also chairs of other platforms including Annie, Emmeline Pethick-Lawrence, Charlotte Marsh, Flora Drummond, Georgina and Marie Brackenbury, Ada Flatman, Rachel Barratt, Dora Marsden, Lady Constance Lytton, Mary Leigh and Rosamund Massy. At 6.30 p.m. a resolution was passed, calling upon Asquith to provide facilities for the women's franchise bill to pass into law during the present parliamentary session. But even though about a quarter of a million people assembled in Hyde Park that day, there was 'no noisy enthusiasm', claimed the *Clarion*. Without any new spectacle to excite the crowd, most 'watched in silence'. Nonetheless, the colourful procession impressed all who saw it, not least the American Anna Shaw who wrote that it was a 'wonderful sight'.[66]

Throughout the rest of the summer, Christabel worked hard to influence the parliamentary process in regard to the women's franchise bill. In various talks and in articles in *Votes for Women* she again emphasised that it was the responsibility of Members of Parliament to 'compel the Government to make way for the Suffrage Bill'.[67] She also wrote to Balfour again and pressurised various influential friends to do all they could to help the women's cause.[68] 'Excuse pencil for this is written on the platform at St. James's Hall where we meet today as the Queen's Hall is being "done up"', she wrote to Elizabeth Robins on 25 July:

> We want to get writers to help by sending us articles answering anti suffrage arguments. Will you write one? If so we will announce it in the coming issue of the paper [*Votes for Women*]. Enclosed is a stamped telegraph form. May we have your reply saying whether you can write for us & if so when we may expect the article.

Christabel continued her letter with more personal news, namely that all August would be a holiday time when she would not go abroad for any 'cure' but visit various places in England:

> Some time ago I was to have stayed a night with you at Henfield. If you are to be there any part of August & if you have not made other plans which prevent, I could come . . . But don't say yes to this unless it is absolutely convenient.[69]

Three days later, Christabel was writing to Elizabeth again, thanking her for agreeing to write the article and informing her that she would be 'in Scotland from 15th to 23rd August and then for two days at the office. After that I cd join you', she added chirpily.[70] However, before she travelled to Scotland, she would spend a few days in early August in the Sussex countryside. 'Today I go to the Miss Becks, Duncan's Farm, Billinghurst, Sussex', Christabel hastily informed Elizabeth on the day of her departure, '& I have telegraphed to Clement's Inn . . . to send your Ms [to me] which it will be a pleasure to read.'[71] The vegetarian sisters Ellen and Edith Becks, keen supporters of the WSPU and devotees of Mrs Pankhurst, would travel up to London from the Sussex farm each week to attend meetings. They were delighted that the Chief Organiser of the WSPU would stay with them for a short time, enjoying the country air. Christabel had only been at the farm a day when she informed Elizabeth that she had read and despatched her manuscript to Clement's Inn. 'I like very very much what you have written . . . Very best thanks to you.'[72] Once back home with the Pethick-Lawrences, at the end of her holiday, Christabel wrote to Elizabeth again in warm, flattering terms:

A word to tell you what a happiness it was to see you again. My holiday has been a very delightful one & one of its best bits is the time spent with you. Don't forget to tell me whenever you have time to see me in London or at Henfield because even an hour together is worth while . . . Here I am in a nest of Kenneys – Annie & Jessie & two other sisters. It is nice to be with them. Annie was delighted to have your message & hopes to see you one of these days.[73]

Refreshed from her holiday, Christabel was soon immersed in WSPU work again. Together with Emmeline Pethick-Lawrence and Lord Lytton, she spoke at the first autumn WSPU meeting held on 3 October. Astounded by the recent proposal to give MPs a salary, Christabel announced defiantly, 'Women were certainly not going to pay to keep members in Parliament when they had no voice in their election. Let the men who elected them do that!' She ended her speech by calling upon WSPU members to not only join the forthcoming deputation to the Commons, when Parliament reassembled on 22 November, but also to engage in a form of passive resistance, namely a refusal to pay taxes.[74] Nevinson, who was in the audience, thought that none of the speakers were at 'their best . . . a rather weary air overall, as though all had been said & done'. But three days later, he noted that Christabel was in her stride again, 'much better than before & very charming'.[75]

What Nevinson did not know was that there was disagreement within the WSPU inner circle over the extent of its financial support for Mary Gawthorpe, a member of the Central Committee and one of the organisers for Manchester and district, who had been ill for some time. Christabel was keen to brief Elizabeth Robins, also a member of the Central Committee, on the subject and on 11 October suggested that she and Mrs Lawrence motor over to Henfield the following Sunday, if convenient, to discuss the matter. The meeting appears to have been brief and, subsequently, Emmeline Pethick-Lawrence felt obliged to give more details, including copies of relevant correspondence. The Finance Committee, she wrote, would be very ready to meet expenses for any medical treatment that Mary needed, if doctors so advised:

> In the absence of any need for special treatment we think £143 is an adequate salary for a year off-duty. There are many people in the Union who would be delighted to have Mary & nurse her, and Union friends have looked after her for the past six months. In the present case it seems to us that all due & adequate provision has been made.[76]

The matter, which was quietly resolved when Mary retired from the WSPU, shows how Christabel and Mrs Lawrence were concerned for the welfare of their employees. However, other organisers in the North West, such as Dora Marsden and Rona Robinson, would soon present a different range of challenges.

For some months now there had been industrial unrest with strikes called among certain groups of railwaymen, textile workers in Lancashire and Yorkshire, miners in Wales and Northern England and ship workers on the Clyde. Christabel was concerned that fear of a workers' rebellion would lead the Liberal Government to focus on that issue and abandon any support for the Conciliation Bill. Adopting a feminist analysis that put the power relationships between voteless women and voting men at the core of her argument, she pointed out that any political settlement between employers and striking employees posed a great danger:

> to our five millions of women workers, who have not between them so much as a single vote. This great body of unrepresented labour is utterly defenceless against the encroachments of self-interested employers and working-men competitors. Their claim to a living wage, even their right to work, are absolutely at the mercy of the privileged, because enfranchised, male classes of the community.[77]

For Christabel, women's suffrage was the key to ending the evils of women's low pay and subordination position in the labour market. In focusing here upon women in industry, she showed her support for working-class women as she did in other occupations in which they might be found, such as elementary school-teaching which was predominantly a female profession where the average pay for women was lower than that for men. Thus during a talk at the Memorial Hall, Farringdon Street, London, that October, she appealed especially to women schoolteachers to join the WSPU. The present unemployment in the teaching profession was a 'woman's question', she insisted, and 'voteless' women teachers were not 'armed with political power'.[78] Despite Christabel's support for working-class women, Sylvia in her influential book *The suffragette movement* ignored such statements, claiming that her sister had abandoned the working class and 'entered now into aristocratic Conservative circles'.[79]

The threat of industrial unrest was not the only problem the Liberal Government faced that autumn of 1910: Irish Nationalists were demanding Home Rule and the constitutional crisis between the House of Lords and the Commons was still rumbling on. There was talk about devolution to regional parliaments not only in Ireland but also in Scotland, Wales and England as a way to lighten the burden of parliamentary business at Westminster, with a central Imperial Assembly to deal with matters relating to the United Kingdom and the British Empire generally. Such ideas prompted the eager Christabel to ask, in *Votes for Women*, 'Will Women Get Home Rule?':

> [I]f the Constitution is to be made over again, women will clamour for admission with more insistence than ever before. If there is to be self-government for England, for Ireland, for Scotland, for Wales, there must be self-government for women too ... If, under a brand-new Constitution, the powers and functions of the Imperial Parliament are to

be defined and settled anew, women will not consent to being left out of consultation. If all Britain's self-governing dominions are to be given a voice in Imperial government, then the women of the Mother Country must have the vote, for they cannot any longer be held in political servitude while the women of Australia and New Zealand are free to share in the Imperial counsels.[80]

As this statement makes clear, Christabel is basing her claim for votes for women not only upon the grounds of equality with men in the British nation but also, as noted earlier, upon equality with those women in the Empire who were already enfranchised. Suffrage support for enfranchised women in the British Empire was not only part of the WSPU's rhetoric but also a response to the active anti-suffragism in Britain of prestigious male imperialists.[81]

Christabel and her mother hoped that the peaceful campaign of the WSPU during the year would encourage the Government to grant facilities for the women's franchise bill when Parliament reconvened, on 18 November.[82] Ever the strategist, Christabel had already warned, in early August, that she was planning another deputation to the Commons if the Prime Minister still refused to grant their just demand.[83] One of the many women who had volunteered for the deputation was the Indian princess Sophia Duleep Singh who lived at Hampton Court Palace and had been brought up as a member of the British aristocracy – and had joined the WSPU in 1908. Emmeline Pankhurst warmly accepted Sophia's offer, asking if she would walk by her side. Perhaps Sophia met Sushama Sen, who had travelled from India to spend four months in London that year and had been invited, by Emmeline and Christabel, to join an earlier demonstration.[84]

While names of those willing to take part in the November deputation, should it be necessary, were pouring into Clement's Inn, Christabel spoke at Edinburgh on Friday, 4 November, before travelling down the following day to the Bristol area for a brief weekend of relaxation. She was delighted to see Annie again, as well as the Lawrences and Mabel Tuke who had travelled all the way to Bristol to see the Saturday afternoon performance of Cecily Hamilton's *A Pageant of Great Women*. The small group, together with the suffragette Mary Allen, all sat in a private box at the Prince's Theatre watching the play which depicted Woman being torn, by male Prejudice, from the presence of blind Justice. Representative women of the past, including learned women (such as Jane Austen), artists (such as Angelica Kauffmann), saintly women (such as Elizabeth Fry), heroic women (such as Grace Darling), rulers (such as Queen Elizabeth I) and warriors (such as Joan of Arc), were called up to plead Woman's cause, although the play and actresses changed as the production moved around the country. This particular afternoon, the cast included the producer of the show, Edith Craig, an active member of the Actresses' Franchise League, as the painter Rosa Bonheur, and Lady Constance Lytton as the nursing pioneer Florence Nightingale.

'Congratulations the play went off *splendidly*', wrote an excited Annie to Edith Craig. 'You have done as usual wonders in a short time.'[85] The next day,

Sunday, 6 November, Christabel spent with Annie at the home of the Blathwayts, at Batheaston, where a suffragette arboretum had been developed by the Colonel in an adjacent field. Christabel, like visiting suffragettes before her, was invited to plant a tree. 'Christabel has planted her cedar of Lebanon by the pond', noted Emily Blathwayt, in her diary; 'it was raining all the time.' Softening her attitude about militancy, perhaps because the WSPU was now following peaceful, legal tactics, Emily observed, 'There is a wonderful charm about Christabel; she looks sweet and not like her photo. She is very quiet and retiring.'[86]

Christabel's outer calm and charm concealed an uncompromising aspect of her character, namely her determination to win the parliamentary vote for women. At another mass meeting at the Albert Hall, on 10 November, in support of the Conciliation Bill, she stood on the platform alongside her mother, Emmeline Pethick-Lawrence and Israel Zangwill, the novelist and staunch supporter of the women's cause. In a rousing speech, Christabel lampooned the unwilling Liberal Government for not granting women the parliamentary vote:

> The women of this Union are not prepared to be hoodwinked. We say to the Government, 'Carry this measure now if you are prepared to see it become law, and if you refuse to carry it now we shall take that refusal as a sign of hostility to our claim.' We make no apology for renewing hostilities with the Government . . . Are we likely to listen to counsels of cowardice, which tell us to submit? No! A thousand times, no! . . . it is a fight for liberty, it is a fight for the freedom of our spirit . . . Do they really think that the womanhood of this country in the twentieth century can be kept any longer in submission?[87]

Such fighting rhetoric might appeal to women who had hitherto not dared to join the WSPU. But other people, such as Henry Brailsford, secretary of the Conciliation Committee, was not impressed. Although he was not at the Albert Hall that evening, he had already told Nevinson that he was becoming increasingly irritated by Christabel's and Emmeline Pankhurst's repeated threats of renewing militancy, claiming they were 'wrecking all his diplomacy'.[88] But Brailsford's faith in diplomacy was misplaced and Christabel's assessment accurate since, as noted earlier, a decision had already been made by Cabinet Ministers not to grant facilities for the women's bill that session.

On 12 November, Sir Edward Grey, one of the pro-suffragists in the Cabinet, announced publicly that it would not be possible for the House of Commons to give time this year for the passage of a women's suffrage bill. 'His statement shows us exactly where we are', announced an exasperated Christabel at a Queen's Hall meeting two days later. The women's deputation had originally been planned for 22 November but the political impasse between the House of Lords and the Commons had reached crisis point and it was expected that Parliament, which would reconvene on 18 November, would be dissolved immediately and a general election called. Fearful that the Government would wind up parliamentary business without making any commitment about the future of the Conciliation Bill, the WSPU leaders decided to bring the deputation date forward by four days, so that a promise of facilities could be extracted from Asquith before he dissolved Parliament.[89]

When Parliament reconvened on 18 November, Asquith told the Commons that he had advised the King to dissolve Parliament. In the intervening days before the dissolution would take place, on 28 November, priority would be given to Government business. No mention was made of the Conciliation Bill. Christabel was not at the large gathering in Caxton Hall on 18 November where her mother was speaking; after discussion with her mother and Mrs Lawrence, it had been decided that she should stay out of the way, with Jessie Kenney, at Clement's Inn. When Emmeline Pankhurst heard of the Prime Minister's announcement she immediately led from Caxton Hall to the Commons a deputation of over three hundred women divided up into smaller contingents of twelve. Her own contingent included not only Princess Sophia Duleep Singh, but some well-known, aged suffragists, such as Elizabeth Garrett Anderson, the pioneer woman doctor and twice Mayor of Aldeburgh, Hertha Ayrton, the distinguished scientist, Annie Cobden Sanderson, Georgiana Soloman, widow of the Governor General of South Africa, and Dorinda Neligan, former Head Mistress of Croydon High School. Despite some jostling from the crowd, a path was made for them and they reached the doors of the Stranger's Entrance at about half past one. But the contingents that followed every few minutes later were treated with exceptional brutality by the police, many of them burly men recruited from the East End, since the Home Secretary, Winston Churchill, had given orders to force the women back rather than arrest them.

On 'Black Friday', as the day became known, the women were battered and pushed, their arms and thumbs twisted, dragged by their hair, thrown from one policeman to another, many of the latter being in plain clothes, then kicked and flung to the ground.[90] Members of the Men's Political Union, such as Hugh Franklin, were standing behind the women in Parliament Square, unable to help them. Jessie Kenney remembered vividly how some of them ran to Clement's Inn with the dreadful news. 'Suddenly some members of the Men's Political Union came rushing in . . . "It's terrible", they gasped, "this is not like any other deputation we've had." And they began to tell Christabel – and Christabel went quite pale.'[91] Later, when Brailsford and Dr Jessie Murray published a report about Black Friday (and about the smaller deputations on 22 and 23 November) based on testimonies of women who took part and on evidence volunteered by eyewitnesses, almost all of the one hundred and thirty-five statements described acts of sexual assault. Skirts were lifted high and knees thrust between legs and underwear torn. The most frequently voiced complaint was 'twisting round, pinching, screwing, nipping, or wringing the breast', an action that caused intense pain and was often accompanied by indecent language.[92] Among those who suffered such sexual abuse on Black Friday were Cecilia Haig, Henria Williams, Ada Wright and Christabel's Aunt Mary who was seriously injured as she lay in the road.[93]

After six hours of struggling, one hundred and fifty-five women and four men were arrested. The following day, the charges against most of those arrested were withdrawn after the prosecutor announced that the Home Secretary had decided that 'no public advantage would be gained by proceeding with the prosecution'.[94] One woman, a mother of eight grown-up children, told the magistrate, '[W]e consider it better to protest by breaking a pane of glass, worth a few shillings, than to have our own bodies broken.' Other women who suffered physical injuries told Emmeline Pankhurst, 'We cannot bear this.'[95] That many of the press reports implied that the women themselves were responsible for the sexual abuse of their own bodies only added to the strong feelings of injustice. Christabel remembered clearly many years later that the Black Friday struggle made the women 'think again that property, rather than their persons, might henceforth pay the price of votes for women'.[96] Such thinking had an important influence upon future forms of militancy that became focused away from street deputations to attacks on property where the militant knew that she had a good chance of arrest quickly, if at all, without the violent manhandling that damaged her body. However, for the time being, a defiant and indignant Christabel kept her counsel, announcing in *Votes for Women*, 'Negotiations are over. War is declared.'[97]

At an enthusiastic meeting on 21 November, Christabel's fighting speech was received with cheers as she said the discharge of the one hundred and seventy-seven women arrested in Parliament Square was a great victory for the women's cause.[98] She was also present the following day at the Caxton Hall meeting which she had urged all WSPU members to attend since they would await Asquith's promised statement with regard to women's suffrage.[99] It was Emmeline Pankhurst rather than Christabel who read out the disappointing news; the Prime Minister announced that after the general election a Liberal Government would, if returned to power, give facilities in the next Parliament for a bill that would be so framed as to admit of free amendment. Yet again, no mention was made of the Conciliation Bill. A stunned silence fell in the hall that 22 November as the women realised that no facilities had been promised this parliamentary session and that a free amendment sometime in the future would have no chance of being passed.

Christabel hastily rose to explain the significance of Asquith's trickery. 'The promise for next Parliament is an absurd mockery of a pledge. It is an insult to common sense . . . We . . . declare war from this moment.'[100] The decisive Emmeline Pankhurst immediately announced a deputation of protest, and led her followers to 10 Downing Street. During the violent struggle that ensued, she was arrested. Further arrests took place that evening as windows were broken in Government buildings. Christabel's Aunt Mary immediately travelled up to London and went to Canon Row Police Station where the women were being held pending trial the following day. However, the police refused Mary's request to see her sister. The determined Mary broke some windows in the station, and was promptly arrested. The next day, Emmeline Pankhurst and her sister appeared in court among the one hundred and fifty-nine women and three men defendants. Emmeline was discharged since no evidence was brought against her but the ill Mary, much to the consternation of her relatives, was sentenced a few days later to one month's imprisonment. 'The real offenders are the Government who deny justice and drive women to rebellion', she told the magistrate.[101]

In the midst of this furore Christabel had to defend WSPU members from accusations of assaulting the Prime Minister, whose car windows had been broken, and kicking Augustine Birrell, the Chief Secretary for Ireland, during 'The Battle of Downing Street', as the protest on the 22nd became known. The encounter with these Cabinet Ministers was 'trifling', Christabel told the press, 'proved by the fact that the police were in sight of what occurred, and did not arrest the women'.[102] Indeed, Birrell told C. P. Scott that a body of about twenty suffragettes swarmed around him:

> pulled me about and hustled me, 'stroked' my face, knocked off my hat and kicked it about and one whose unpleasant features yet dwell in my memory harangued me with 'Oh! You wicked man; you must be a wicked man not to help us' and so forth.

He was not kicked, he insisted, but in the struggle to get free twisted his knee and slipped the knee-cap.[103] Such skirmishes with Asquith and Birrell angered Millicent Garret Fawcett since she believed that they undermined the NUWSS's efforts to build support for a suffrage measure among Cabinet members. 'I do think these personal assaults perfectly abominable and above all extraordinarily silly', she wrote condemningly to Lady Frances Balfour:

> The P.M.'s statement on the 22nd was not just exactly all we wanted but it was better than anything that had ever been offered us before . . . And then these idiots go out smashing windows and bashing ministers' hats over their eyes.[104]

Liberal opinion seemed to rally behind the Prime Minister after 22 November while the members of the all-male Conciliation Committee, including Lord Lytton and Henry Brailsford, condemned the WSPU's action, arguing that conciliation and militancy could not go hand in hand. However, the confident Christabel dismissed such criticism. The brutality of the male police against defenceless women engaging in peaceful protest strengthened her belief that men were the enemy, waging a sex war against women. In another stirring speech in the Queen's Hall on 28 November, she spoke of our 'men friends' and of the 'men who are prepared to fight with us', but also said:

> The Conciliation Committee have been giving us good advice. They have been giving us a scolding. Well, we have been scolded and advised so often during the last five years that we are pretty well hardened to both things . . . [W]hen we find ourselves at variance with the

Conciliation Committee we are bound to prefer our own opinion and our own judgement. One thing we lay down here definitely and finally: this is a woman's movement, led by women, and we are not prepared to surrender the leadership of this movement to men, however well meaning, however earnest, and however devoted.[105]

Such thinking greatly upset Brailsford who liked to tell the leaders of the WSPU what they should do. He told Nevinson that he was:

much distressed at the W.S.P.U. distrust of him & their action agst his advice. They have even refused his letter to <u>Votes [for Women]</u> on behalf of the Conciliation Com & their sudden first raid entirely wrecked his diplomacy with Asquith.[106]

Yet it is extremely doubtful if there was anything to be gained from meeting with the entrenched anti-suffragist Prime Minister.

Now that campaigning for the general election was in full swing, the WSPU used only constitutional methods as it campaigned in fifty constituencies with the message, 'Vote Against the Government and Keep the Liberals Out'.[107] There was little time for other activities but Christabel joined in the good wishes sent to Elizabeth Wolsthenholme Elmy on the occasion of her seventy-seventh birthday on 1 December, together with a gift of £500 collected as a tribute of admiration and gratitude.[108] Then there was personal correspondence to deal with, including a letter from Elizabeth Robins who was having trouble with her eyes. 'Is there any hope of seeing you while you are in London?' Christabel enquired. 'How sad about your eyes – I had not an idea that they were wrong. They always <u>look</u> so everything that eyes ought to be.'[109] A trip with the Lawrences to the Aldwych Theatre to see a John Mansfield play was another welcome distraction.[110] But Christabel's speaking schedule, combined with her duties at Clement's Inn, kept her busy – an afternoon talk at the Skating Rink, Holloway Road on 3 December followed by an evening address at Tomer's Institute, Euston, a speech at South Lambeth on the 5th, a brief word of welcome to released prisoners in London on the 7th, before travelling to Glasgow to deliver a lecture the following day which had been advertised all week by the novel means of an elephant walking the streets, displaying on his howdah the WSPU electioneering poster. Then it was back down to Southport, Cheshire, to speak to another gathering.[111]

The energetic Christabel was in good form during the election campaign. When Nevinson heard her speak at Euston, interrupted by drunks and hostile Liberals, he described her as 'superb . . . broad enough for the audience & conquering them by audacity playing over charm'.[112] While converting the general populace to the women's cause was always one of Christabel's key aims, she could never forget that the suffragettes might need to resort to militant action in the future. In a rallying call in early December, at a welcome breakfast for released prisoners, she said:

We are going to get votes next session, and we are going to put on all the pressure we can . . . Ladies, the truce was all very well, but there is nothing like militancy! We glory in this fight because we feel how much it gives to us, how much it strengthens us . . . We fight to win, but we appreciate the battle while it goes on, because we know it is a magnificent school . . . I thank you, dear prisoners, on behalf of all of us at Clements Inn who have felt how much the cause was advanced by your tremendous courage and loyalty.[113]

Yet, despite all the efforts of the WSPU and its leaders, the new House of Commons was much the same as before, with the Liberals and Conservatives both winning two hundred and seventy-two seats each, the Irish Nationalists eighty-four and Labour forty-two. The Liberal Party again formed a Government, in coalition with the Irish Nationalists and Labour, and Asquith again became Prime Minister.[114] Nonetheless, *Votes for Women* gave an optimistic picture of the situation, claiming that the Liberal Party would have won some thirty or forty more seats but for the opposition shown by the WSPU. Further, it was calculated that there were now four hundred and seven MPs who were prepared to vote for a women's suffrage measure on the lines of the Conciliation Bill.[115]

Two days before Christmas, Christabel attended a festive welcome luncheon, complete with crackers decorated in purple, white and green, for another group of released Holloway prisoners, including her Aunt Mary. Mrs Lawrence was also present although Emmeline Pankhurst presided over proceedings. The shy Aunt Mary gave a brief address. 'She was very much loved by our members', recollected Christabel,

and their feeling for her was expressed that day by another of the prisoners, Mrs. Massy, who spoke of what her presence in prison had meant to them. Aunt Mary was, for all her gentleness, eloquent in an intense and very moving way, and brave.[116]

But Christabel and her mother were worried about Mary's health which had deteriorated since her injuries on Black Friday and during her recent imprisonment. They begged her not to travel to Brighton that evening for a welcome meeting there, but the frail Mary felt obliged to return to the city where she was a WSPU organiser. She came back to London on a busy Christmas Eve to the home of her brother, Herbert Goulden, who had invited his sisters, Christabel and other family members to spend the festive season there. They were all seated at the midday meal on Christmas Day when Mary quietly left the room, saying she felt very tired and wanted to lie down. Shortly afterwards Emmeline went upstairs and found her sister dead. Mary had burst a blood vessel in her brain.[117]

The Pankhurst family were devastated by the news. 'This year has seen the breaking for me of three of my closest bonds to this world, my boy, my mother & my dearest sister', wrote the grieving Emmeline to C. P. Scott. 'Can you wonder that today I want beyond all other things to end this fight quickly & get rest."[118] For Christabel too the death of the kind, thoughtful and loving Aunt Mary was a sad blow since she had been a second mother to the Pankhurst children. Yet again Christabel comforted her mother, as did Sylvia, who had not been at the Christmas lunch but alone at her studio at 42 Linden Gardens, Kensington, revising the final chapters of her forthcoming book, *The suffragette*, before she sailed to America where the volume was to be published.[119]

Notes

1 ESP, TSM, p. 324; CP, *Unshackled*, p. 147; APW, My mother, p. 48.
2 S. Walker, daughter of Helen, email to June Purvis, 1 October 2002. In 1914, Helen married Dr Duncan Alexander McCombie, twenty years her senior. After his death, she supported her two young children by running a business making jigsaw puzzles. In 1957 she became the second wife of Fred Pethick-Lawrence.
3 G. Lennox, Letter to the Editor, *Everyman*, 5 March 1931, p. 186.
4 *VfW*, 14 January 1910, p. 242; CP to Miss Flatman, 7 January 1910, SFC.
5 Sharp, Emmeline Pankhurst, p. 516.
6 EP to Miss Phillips, 9 January 1910, Mary Phillips Papers.
7 Romero, *Sylvia Pankhurst*, p. 51.
8 Entries for 12 and 14 January, 21 February 1910, Nevinson Diaries.
9 John Masefield to Miss Pankhurst, 31 January 1910, Craigie Collection.
10 CP, *The militant methods of the N.W.S.P.U.* (London, Woman's Press, n.d.).
11 CP to Miss Flatman, 19 January 1910, SFC.
12 *VfW*, 28 January 1910, pp. 274, 276.
13 *Times*, 25 January 1910.
14 CP to Bernard Shaw, 27 January 1910, G. B. Shaw Papers, BL, Add Mss 50515, f.317.
15 *VfW*, 21 January 1910, p. 264.
16 CP to Lady Betty Balfour, 24 January 1910, in Balfour, *Letters of Constance Lytton*, pp. 192–3.
17 CP to Balfour, 1 January 1910, Balfour Papers, Ms Add 49793, fs.61–6.
18 Rosen, *Rise up women!*, p. 130; Morgan, *Suffragists and Liberals*, p. 64.
19 CP, *Unshackled*, pp. 153–4.
20 CP to Eleanor Rathbone, 4 February 1910, Eleanor Rathbone Papers, Sydney Jones Library, University of Liverpool.
21 *VfW*, 4 March and 11 March 1910, pp. 352–3, 360, and 373, respectively.
22 Rosen, *Rise up women!*, p. 134.
23 *VfW*, 18 March 1910, p. 390.
24 EPL, Hunger strike, n.d. [late March 1910?], Hugh Franklin/Elsie Duval Papers, TWL.
25 *VfW*, 25 March 1910, p. 410.
26 The Isle of Man has its own Parliament and gave the vote to single and propertied women in 1881.
27 ESP to Mrs Norah Walshe, 18 October 1928, DMC.
28 Raeburn, *Militant suffragettes*, p. 142; *VfW*, 25 March 1910, p. 408.
29 Rosen, *Rise up women!*, p. 134.
30 ESP, *The suffragette*, p. 489.
31 *VfW*, 29 April 1910, p. 498.
32 *VfW*, 27 May 1910, p. 564.
33 CP to Mr. Balfour, 13, 14 and 19 April 1910, Balfour Papers, Ms ADD 49793, f.71–3, f.74 and f.76–8, respectively.

34 CP to C. P. Scott, incomplete letter, n.d. [5 June 1910?], Scott Papers; CP to Miss Robins, 29 April 1910, Robins Papers, Fales Library.
35 CP to Miss Robins, 2 May 1910, Robins Papers, HRHRC.
36 VfW, 13 May 1910, p. 536.
37 On this point see, for example, A. Burton, *Burdens of history: British feminists, Indian women, and imperial culture, 1865–1915* (Chapel Hill, NC and London, University of North Carolina Press, 1994).
38 VfW, 20 May 1910, p. 546.
39 ESP, *TSM*, p. 337.
40 VfW, 20 May 1910, p. 550.
41 VfW, 3 June 1910, pp. 580 and 577.
42 'The eve of victory', Miss Christabel Pankhurst in Thanet, *East Kent Times*, 6 June 1910.
43 CP to Mrs Nourse, 3 June 1910, Purvis Collection. The Honorary Treasurer, Lizzie Morris, had also resigned.
44 CP to Mr Scott, 6 June 1910, *Manchester Guardian* Archive.
45 *Week-End*, 14 July 1910; *Vanity Fair*, 15 June 1910, p. 753.
46 CP to Mr Balfour, 12 June 1910, Balfour Papers, Ms Add 49793, f.78–81.
47 *Daily Telegraph* and *Morning Leader*, 20 June 1910; see also the reports for that day in *Times*, *Daily News*, *Daily Chronicle* as well as *VFW*, 24 June 1910, pp. 628–30.
48 VfW, 24 June 1910, p. 635.
49 Rosen, *Rise up women!*, p. 136.
50 CP to Mr Balfour and Balfour to CP, 23 and 27 June 1910, respectively, Balfour Papers, Ms Add 49793.
51 CP to Mr Balfour, 28 June 1910, Balfour Papers, Ms Add 49793.
52 CP to Mr Balfour, 10 July 1910, Balfour Papers, Ms Add 49793, f.95.
53 Entry for 12 July 1910, Nevinson Diaries.
54 CP to Mr Scott, 14 July 1910, *Manchester Guardian* Archive.
55 Quoted in *VfW*, 15 July 1910, p. 691; see Atkinson, *Rise up women!*, p. xi.
56 *Globe*, 13 July 1910; *VfW*, 15 July 1910, p. 678.
57 VfW, 15 July 1910, p. 688.
58 CP to Mr Long, MP, 15 July 1910, Suffrage Papers, Linton Park Plc. Christabel added, '[Y]ours is the speech which of all the anti suffrage speeches pained us least because it did not express that disrespect for women which many anti suffragists undoubtedly feel . . . we prefer an honest opponent.'
59 VfW, 15 July 1910, p. 688.
60 VfW, 22 July 1910, p. 718.
61 CP to Miss Flatman, 22 July 1910, SFC.
62 VfW, 22 July 1910, pp. 711–14.
63 Mrs Fawcett to Societies affiliated to the NUWSS (marked confidential), 16 July 1910, TWL.
64 *Daily News*, *Times*, 25 July 1910; *VfW*, 29 July 1910, pp. 724–5.
65 Entry for 23 July 1910, Nevinson Diaries.
66 *Clarion*, 29 July 1910; Raeburn, *Militant suffragettes*, p. 150; A. Shaw to Dr Jacobs, 5 August [1910], in Bosh and Kloosterman, eds, *Politics and friendship*, p. 113.
67 VfW, 29 July 1910, p. 730.
68 CP to Balfour, 29 July 1910, Balfour Papers, Ms. Add 49793.
69 CP to Miss Robins, 25 July 1910, Robins Papers, HRHRC.
70 CP to Miss Robins, 28 July 1910, Robins Papers, HRHRC.
71 CP to Miss Robins, 3 August 1910, Robins Papers, HRHRC.
72 CP to Miss Robins, 4 August 1910, Robins Papers, HRHRC.
73 CP to Miss Robins, 28 August 1910, Robins Papers, HRHRC.
74 VfW, 7 October 1910, p. 4 and CP, No votes, no taxes, 7 October 1910, p. 8.

75 Entries for 3 and 6 October 1910, Nevinson Diaries.
76 CP to Miss Robins, 11 October 1910 and EPL to Miss Robins, 17 October 1910, Robins Papers, HRHRC.
77 *VfW*, 16 September 1910, p. 814.
78 *VfW*, 14 October 1910, p. 26; for the lowly social origins of women in elementary school-teaching see H. Kean, *Deeds not words: the lives of suffragette teachers* (London, Pluto Press, 1990), p. 2; A. Oram, *Feminist teachers and feminist politics 1900–39* (Manchester, Manchester University Press, 1996), pp. 14–44; D. Copelman, *London's women teachers: gender, class and feminism 1870–1930* (London, Routledge, 1996), p. 32. See also Atkinson, *Rise up women!*, p. xi.
79 ESP, TSM, p. 339.
80 *VfW*, 21 October 1910, p. 40.
81 J. Bush, *Women against the vote: female anti-suffragism in Britain* (Oxford, Oxford University Press, 2007), p. 110; I. C. Fletcher, Laura E. Nym Mayhall and Philippa Levine, eds, *Women's suffrage in the British Empire: citizenship, nation and race* (London and New York, Routledge, 2000); Burton, *Burdens of history*, p. 204.
82 See Form letter from EP to Dear Friend, 27 October 1910, SFC.
83 *VfW*, 5 August 1910, p. 742.
84 A. Anand, *Sophia, princess, suffragette, revolutionary* (London, Bloomsbury, 2015), pp. 227 and 247; Sushama Sen, *Memoir of an octogenarian* (Simla Anjali, 1971), p. 117. Grateful thanks to Sumita Mukherjee for this latter reference. See S. Mukherjee, *Indian Suffragettes: female identities and transnational networks* (Oxford, Oxford University Press, 2018).
85 K. Cockin, *Edith Craig (1869–1947): dramatic lives* (London and Washington, DC, Cassell, 1998), p. 98.
86 Dobbie, *A nest of suffragettes*, p. 44.
87 *VfW*, 18 November 1910, pp. 102–3.
88 Entry for 9 November 1910, Nevinson Diaries.
89 *VfW*, 18 November 1910, p. 101; Raeburn, *Militant suffragettes*, p. 152.
90 *Daily Express, Daily Mirror, Daily News*, 19 November 1910; *VfW*, 25 November 1910, pp. 120–1.
91 Raeburn, *Militant suffragettes*, p. 154.
92 *The treatment of the women's deputations by the Metropolitan Police, Copy of evidence collected by Dr. Jessie Murray and Mr. H. N. Brailsford, and forwarded to the Home Office by the Conciliation Committee for Women's Suffrage, in support of the demand for a public enquiry* (London, The Woman's Press, 1911), pp. 9, 33, 28–9. C. R. Jorgensen-Earp, ed, *Speeches and trials of the militant suffragettes: the Women's Social and Political Union, 1902–1918* (Cranbury, NJ and London, Associated University Presses, 1999), p. 122 notes that physical injury to the breast was at this time considered a primary cause of breast cancer.
93 Raeburn, *Militant suffragettes*, pp. 154–5; Richardson, *Laugh a defiance*, p. 10.
94 *VfW*, 25 November 1910, p. 117.
95 WSPU leaflet, *Plain facts about the suffragette deputations* (London, The Woman's Press, n.d. [1910]), p. 4; *VfW*, 24 May 1912, p. 534.
96 CP, *Unshackled*, p. 166.
97 *VfW*, 25 November 1910, p. 126.
98 *VfW*, 25 November, p. 123.
99 Form letter from CP to Dear Friend, 19 November 1910, MASC.
100 *VfW*, 25 November 1910, p. 127.
101 *VfW*, 25 November and 2 December 1910, pp. 128 and 142, respectively. See *Daily New, Times, Daily Telegraph*, 23 November 1910.
102 *VfW*, 25 November 1910, p. 127.
103 T. Wilson, ed, *The political diaries of C. P. Scott 1911–1928* (London, Collins, 1970), pp. 35–6.

104 Millicent Garrett Fawcett to Lady Frances Balfour, 28 November 1910, TWL.
105 *VfW*, 2 December 1910, p. 148.
106 Entry for 29 November 1910, Nevinson Diaries.
107 *VfW*, 2 December 1910, p. 139.
108 *VfW*, 9 November 1910, p. 168.
109 CP to Miss Robins, 2 December 1910, Robins Papers, HRHRC.
110 Entry for 4 December 1910, Nevinson Diaries.
111 *VfW*, 2 December 1910, p. 138; 16 December, p. 138, 9 December, p. 161.
112 Entry for 3 December 1910, Nevinson Diaries.
113 *VfW*, 9 December 1910, p. 161.
114 *VfW*, 23 December 1910, p. 193.
115 *VfW*, 30 December 1910, p. 207.
116 CP, *Unshackled*, p. 170.
117 ESP, *TSM*, p. 346; CP, *Unshackled*, p. 170.
118 EP to C. P. Scott, 27 December 1910, Scott Papers.
119 ESP, *TSM*, p. 346.

12

'RISE UP WOMEN!'

1911

The task of writing an appreciation of Aunt Mary fell not to Christabel but to Emmeline Pethick-Lawrence:

> Mrs. Clarke is the first woman-martyr who has gone to death for the cause. And quickly upon her footsteps has followed Henria Williams, another victim of Black Friday. How many more lives must be laid down . . . before an elementary act of justice and reparation is done to the womanhood of the country?[1]

Christabel and Adela accompanied their grieving mother to Aunt Mary's funeral, Una and Joan Dugdale being among the small band of suffragette mourners. Shortly afterwards Christabel wrote to the Blathwayts, thanking them for the kind offer to have a tree planted in Aunt Mary's name. 'She took a very big part in our great battle and devoted to the service of the movement all the powers that came from a very earnest, unselfish, sweet, brave nature.'[2]

Adela had come down to London for her aunt's funeral. The WSPU organiser for Sheffield and district, her work was not flourishing and she was regarded with increasing suspicion by the leadership, especially the WSPU's Treasurer, Emmeline Pethick-Lawrence, since she was not a good fund raiser.[3] Such unwelcome scrutiny put her under considerable pressure and she felt her family were not supporting her enough. On the few occasions when her mother visited, Adela found her 'affectionate and encouraging', praising her suffrage work. But her sisters were another matter. 'Sylvia invariably took headquarters' views', Adela recollected. 'She never suggested that Christabel ought to give me any more prominence or that my mother ought to be kinder to me. She never wrote to me from one year's end to another or asked me how I was.' Nor did Adela feel close to her eldest sister. 'Christabel grew suspicious of rivals', she recollected. 'Someone said I was the best speaker in the family and this remark was repeated several times. Christabel, I think, took it into her head that I would use my talent to form some faction against her.'[4] The unhappy Adela did not agree with the direction of militant policy, especially the violence, and tried to voice her misgivings to her eldest sister. Some fifty years later she could still remember clearly Christabel's reaction:

[U]nfortunately she took it amiss – was even persuaded I was about to found a counter-organisation with myself as a leader. This was so far from my intention that the suggestion when it was put to me deprived me of speech!

The years of poor health and hard work, and the death of Harry and now Aunt Mary, brought Adela to breaking point. She tried to resign from the WSPU but Emmeline Pethick-Lawrence persuaded her to stay on for what Adela described as 'another miserable year'.[5]

The WSPU leadership considered Adela's criticisms both unfair and ill-timed. Her mother was in low spirits, her faith in British justice and in men having been seriously undermined. And the hard-working Christabel was exhausted. The Lawrences persuaded Christabel to take, rather than cancel, the planned two-week holiday to Engelberg, Switzerland. Rangeley Hemsley, a member of the WSPU, accompanied Christabel and tried to teach her to skate. Rangeley had been swept off her feet some months before by Christabel's oratory at a Queen's Hall meeting to which her mother had taken her. The two holiday companions soon became firm friends, a friendship that continued into old age. 'She had everything', recollected the eighty-one-year-old Rangeley in the 1970s of the Chief Organiser of the WSPU, 'warmth, cleverness, sense of humour, charm. She could have been a success in anything she turned her hand to.'[6] The tired Christabel slept a great deal that holiday and exercised gently, returning to Clement's Inn refreshed and full of energy.[7]

The deaths of two suffragettes as a consequent of violence suffered at the hands of the police had strengthened Christabel's resolve, and she quickly became absorbed in her WSPU work again. Esther Knowles, the youngest member of the office staff at Clement's Inn, recollected that Harriet Kerr, the general office manager, became so anxious about the long hours that the absorbed Christabel spent at her desk that cold winter that she was asked to make sure the Chief Organiser's office was kept warm:

When she [Christabel] was engrossed in writing her leading articles . . . she used to become so oblivious of anything else around her, that she forgot all about creature comforts. One cold winter's morning Miss Kerr went into her room to find her literally blue with cold. The office was icy and the fire dead out. From that day it became my specific job quietly to slip into C.P.'s room at intervals, make up her fire as silently as I could and creep out again. This I did without C.P. ever seeming to be aware of my presence.[8]

Christabel had come back home to find that Teresa Billington-Greig had published in the *New Age* the first of three articles attacking bitterly the WSPU and, in particular, its leadership. The furious Teresa, who had announced her resignation as secretary of the Women's Freedom League (WFL) in protest against the 'conspiracy of silence' which prohibited anyone from criticising Emmeline Pankhurst's methods of 'emancipation in a hurry', was scathing about the 'trinitarian dictatorship', as she termed it, of 'Mrs. Pankhurst, Miss Pankhurst and Mrs. Pethick Lawrence'. They imposed, she argued:

> a yoke of emotional control by which the very virtues of the members are exploited; they produce a system of mental and spiritual slavery. The women who succumb to it exhibit a type of self-subjection not less objectionable than the more ordinary self-subjection of women to men.

Further, the WSPU had suppressed free speech, gradually edged out the working class in its ranks and become 'socially exclusive, punctiliously correct, gracefully fashionable, ultra-respectable, and narrowly religious'.[9] Despite the widespread coverage given in the press to the attack by 'Tess of the Suffragists', as Teresa was called, Christabel, her mother and Emmeline Pethick-Lawrence kept a discreet silence, at least in public, as did the leadership of the WFL.[10]

'Mother arrives on Thursday morning at 8', Christabel wrote on 16 January 1911 to new WSPU recruit Ethel Smyth, a well-known modern composer of a *Mass in D* as well as three operas, who had decided to put herself and her musical talent at the service of the women's cause for two years. 'I am going tomorrow to take her meetings [&] on Wed aft & evening & also on Thursday evening.'[11] Although Nevinson dismissed Teresa Greig-Billington's attack on the Pankhursts and the whole militant movement as 'treacherous . . . [m]ere jealous vanity & hatred, but harmful outside, not inside', his assessment was not entirely accurate.[12] In particular, there was a small but growing number of WSPU members in the Manchester district, including Dora Marsden, Rona Robinson and Grace Jardine, who were not entirely happy with the style of leadership and the direction of militant policy. In mid-December 1910, Rona had complained about the scope of her workload – and been summoned to Clement's Inn to talk things over with Christabel.[13] A month before, Christabel had chided the petite Dora Marsden, an organiser for Southport, about the poor preparations for the large bazaar she planned to hold in that town. 'I have consulted with others, and we adhere to the decision that a political shooting gallery is not desirable, and must not be undertaken', wrote Christabel sternly. 'It will be quite useless to write and ask the Countess de la Warr to open the Bazaar as she certainly will not do this.'[14] That Dora had not submitted her plans for the bazaar to Clement's Inn and was unwilling to follow instructions and a poor book-keeper only added to the tensions.

Christabel was ever the stoic about such matters. That January of 1911 she dealt with usual WSPU business as the friction between Dora and Clement's Inn mounted. On the 21st she attended the social evening to welcome released prisoners at Suffolk Street Galleries, Pall Mall, at which new recruit Ethel Smyth presented to Emmeline Pankhurst a tune she had composed for the WSPU, words contributed by Cecily Hamilton. 'The March of the Women' was received with such great enthusiasm that an encore was given by the choir, Ethel inviting the audience to join in the singing.[15] The new stirring song became the anthem of the WSPU, replacing the 'Women's Marseillaise'.

At the packed Queen's Hall meeting the following Monday, Christabel told her audience that her job as a recruiting sergeant was considerably easier these days since volunteers were coming in fast for the next deputation which would number one thousand. 'We are not waiting for any hand to deliver us, to cut our bonds', she insisted, 'we are ready to do that for ourselves.'[16] A return to more mundane administrative business included writing to Hugh Franklin, a member of the Men's Political Union for Women's Enfranchisement and recently released from prison. Hugh was wondering how he could get back the dog-whip with which he had attacked Winston Churchill who, as Home Secretary, he had held responsible for the police violence against suffragettes on Black Friday. 'A little advertisement for the movement is always helpful', replied the practical Christabel. 'At the same time, I do not think you would get very much Press notice of this, and it would not be worth while spending much money or a great deal of time.'[17] The advice had barely been sent when Dora Marsden sent in her resignation, taking her friends Grace Jardine and Rona Robinson with her.[18] Some five years later, Dora claimed that they all had been 'S.O.S. – Sick of Suffrage . . . weary of the interminable reiteration of threadbare arguments and the unending donkey work'.[19]

Christabel acted quickly. She contacted Jessie Stephenson who was willing to move to Manchester, as the new organiser. Soon Christabel was writing wistfully to Elizabeth Robins:

> It is so very long since we heard from you & saw you. I wonder what you are doing and thinking these days . . . One of our newest & nicest recruits is Ethel Smyth, the composer. Perhaps you know her. Her energy & kindness & spirit delight us all. What an old friend you are compared to her & so many others! . . . I wish you were more here . . . Come to London soon. I want to see you.[20]

Whether the evasive Elizabeth Robins came to London to see the Chief Organiser of the WSPU we do not know, but Nevinson was arranging for Christabel to meet the well-known Japanese artist and writer Mr Yoshio Markino, a keen observer of the peculiarities of English life. 'I should much like to meet Mr. Markino', Christabel replied to Nevinson in early February, 'because I admire his writing & the personality that beams through it. What frank expression he will give of his opinions & impressions of me I rather tremble to think.' Lunch, she explained, was the most difficult time for her to get away.[21] Eventually a time was set aside for Markino's visit to Clement's Inn. 'You see, everything is done by women here!' exclaimed the proud Christabel as she led her guest through the labyrinth of busy offices, many of which had notices saying 'Please keep silence in this room'. Markino sketched some of the staff as they went about their daily tasks.

'This is our most important room', Christabel commented when she came to the treasurer's office.[22] Although Markino was enchanted with all he saw, Christabel's thoughts were primarily focused on the fate of the Conciliation Bill and how to campaign for its successful passage into law.

As noted earlier, the new Parliament, which first met on 6 February, was very much the same as before, with Asquith again as Prime Minister. During the course of the King's Speech, no reference was made to any woman suffrage measure. However, shortly afterwards the first three places in private members' ballots were drawn by MPs who were members of the Conciliation Committee and Sir George Kemp, a Liberal who secured first place, announced he would sponsor a woman suffrage bill.[23] The Conciliation Bill was now revised; the £10 occupation qualification, to which Lloyd George among others had objected, was dropped and only the household qualification retained in the hope that it would make amendment possible and win wide support.[24] Edward Goulding, a Conservative MP who had secured second place, declared his intention of taking the second reading of the bill. Since Goulding was a member of the Conciliation Committee, Christabel was upbeat. '[T]he Bill is in the hands of one of the best friends of the Suffrage cause, and it commands a strong majority in the House of Commons', she informed *Votes for Women* readers.[25] But privately she was more circumspect because Asquith had declared that all available time during the present parliamentary session would be devoted to Government business, thus leaving no opportunity for discussion of bills initiated by MPs themselves.[26] 'We are thinking hard how best to frustrate the Government's knavish tricks', she informed Nevinson.[27]

Nonetheless, on 9 February, Kemp introduced the Second Conciliation Bill when it was technically read a first time. News about the divisions within the Cabinet dampened Christabel's hopes. '[T]here is the rumour that they will drop the Reform Bill altogether & content themselves with a Plural Voting Bill minus an "opportunity" for us', she told Elizabeth Robins the following day. 'Lloyd George is a rascal & Sir Edward Grey is culpably weak. Unhappy the country whose affairs are in such hands!'[28] Later that day, Friday 10 February, while travelling on the train to Leicester where she was to speak that evening, Christabel hurriedly wrote to Mary Phillips in Bradford. She was keen for Mary and some of her colleagues to cheer Keir Hardie's speech on women's suffrage, scheduled to be given at Shipley on Sunday afternoon. 'Do any of our Bradford members write shorthand & will they take a verbatim account & send it to us for *Votes for Women*?' she enquired. 'Get the reporting done voluntarily if you possibly can. If absolutely impossible you might give a reporter a few shillings for a verbatim report of that part of the speech only which refers to the Conciliation Bill.'[29]

Since the second reading of the Second Conciliation Bill had been set for 5 May, there was no time to lose. 'Let us work for the Bill as we have never worked in our lives before!' Christabel exhorted the suffragettes in a leading article in *Votes for Women* on 17 February. 'Our extraordinary success in the ballot for

Parliamentary bills has generated the feeling of optimism and confidence needed to sweep always all obstacles and to carry the Bill into law.' The bill, she reminded everyone, gave the vote simply to women householders:

> of whom it is estimated that there are something like a million . . . women of all classes, from the richest to the very poorest. Therefore, whatever else might be alleged against the Bill it cannot, by any stretch of the imagination, be described as undemocratic.[30]

Christabel had barely finished putting the final touches to this essay when she hastened to the by-election campaign in West Wiltshire. Here she met up with her mother, Emmeline Pethick-Lawrence and Annie. 'Miss Pankhurst's address was quite brilliant, and her replies to numerous questions drew forth the admiration of the audience', opined the *Bath Daily Chronicle*.[31]

However, Christabel's success on the political platform hid a secret worry. Her mother was not well. Emmeline's hectic campaigning schedule, so soon after her sister's death, was taking its toll. The anxious daughter asked Constance Lytton if she would be kind enough to take over Emmeline's next tour, and Constance agreed. 'Thousands of thanks for taking it', wrote a grateful Christabel to Constance on 1 March:

> Mother was really not fit to do the meetings & then go through her personal share in the protest . . . The little time of quiet has done her so much good. You must take care of your precious self now.[32]

Once back at Clement's Inn, Christabel soon found she had another thank-you letter to write. 'My hyacinths are a great satisfaction to me', she happily penned Ethel Birnstingl, a back-room worker in the Woman's Press in Charing Cross Road who had given the Chief Organiser a bowl of these highly scented flowers for her office. 'Thanks for them.'[33]

For a few months, the WSPU had been asking for a public inquiry into the conduct of the police on 18, 22 and 23 November last year. In response to a question in the Commons on 1 March 1911, the Home Secretary, Winston Churchill, denied the claim that the police had instructions which led them to terrorise and maltreat the women. The defiant Christabel attacked Churchill's statement, saying that it was 'a matter of everyday and universal knowledge' that the women who went to Westminster in November 1910 'were brutally and in many cases indecently ill-treated by the police acting under the orders of the Home Secretary'.[34] The furious Churchill immediately enquired whether Christabel or the *Times*, which reported the story, could be prosecuted criminally for libel.[35] The matter was quietly dropped, even though the Chief Organiser of the WSPU denounced Churchill's 'methods of barbarism', as she called them.[36] Christabel continued working hard for the Second Conciliation Bill, issuing the cry of 'Rise Up Women!' as she rallied supporters.[37]

Sometime earlier, Vida Goldstein, President of the Women's Political Association of Victoria, Australia, had written jointly to Christabel, her mother and Annie Kenney, expressing her 'reverent appreciation' of their fight for women's suffrage in Britain and contrasting the English and Australian situations.[38] After repeated invitations from Christabel and Emmeline to visit England, Vida finally arrived during spring 1911 to attend the big Albert Hall meeting on 23 March. At the initial opening ceremony that evening, Emmeline Pankhurst presented to Ethel Smyth a baton for the services she had rendered in composing and presenting to the Union the 'March of the Women'. Ethel Smyth, ostracised and rejected by the British musical establishment, was regarded as an eccentric figure. Although she never referred to herself as a 'lesbian' in any of her seven volumes of autobiography, Ethel often developed passions for women – and men – that were not reciprocated. She was soon to become close friends with Emmeline and to fall in love with her. Ethel often dressed in a mannish style that evoked an androgynous appearance, and being by temperament an enthusiast for any cause she espoused, embraced the colours of her WSPU in her everyday dress, often wearing a tie of the brightest purple, white and green or a purple cotton jacket.[39] However, this evening Ethel was resplendent in her academic robes, conducting the choir in a singing of the new anthem, all the audience joining in.

After the noise had died down, Christabel waited for her turn to speak as first her mother, then Emmeline Pethick-Lawrence and Vida Goldstein held the stage. Vida Goldstein, an enfranchised woman, was admired by Christabel. She was not only credited with having won the parliamentary vote for her sex in her native Victoria, in 1908, but five years earlier she had stood, unsuccessfully, as a candidate in the Australian Federal Elections, the first woman candidate in the British Empire ever to stand for Parliament. The presence of such a distinguished guest fired Christabel's enthusiasm as, in her own fighting speech, she condemned the dishonourable and unprincipled tactics whereby successive governments had deprived women of the parliamentary vote, and then called on all engaged only in constitutional methods to join the militants in one united force:

> Women, our call to you is this: Be united. Make yourselves a great conquering army. Let us be so many, so strong, so brave, so proud that nothing outside matters, no hostile forces . . . the strength of women . . . [is] the greatest human force in all the world.[40]

The enthusiastic response to this speech and all that happened that evening resulted in donations and promises totalling £5,000, raising the WSPU fund to a total of £96,500.[41]

'The Albert Hall meeting was a great success', Christabel wrote joyfully to Elizabeth Robins soon after the event, '& now tickets for the next meeting on June 17th are selling as quickly as anything.' But Christabel was much more evasive about Elizabeth's invitation to spend some of her Easter holiday with her, at Henfield:

I think a night at Henfield will fit in with my Easter plans (we have a week's holiday then) but I am not sure for a day or two. I may be spending days here & there in Surrey & Sussex, in which case I can visit you or I may go much further away in which case I can't.

Not wishing to antagonise her friend, Christabel quickly added, 'I want to see you very much then or some other time. When are you coming to London – to meetings & things?'[42] No mention was made to Elizabeth of Teresa Billington-Greig's recently published book which incorporated her articles attacking the WSPU. 'Mrs. Pankhurst is more frank and self-revealing than her daughter . . . the elder woman is the more lovable', wrote the angry Teresa. 'Miss Christabel Pankhurst is of harder stuff, not greater. The mother is a natural product, the daughter an artificial one.' And in a barbed comment about Christabel's leadership, Teresa asserted that the militant movement had encouraged its supporters:

> to act as though they believed that women were the superiors of men . . . The cultivation of distrust in all men because they are men is as evil as the cultivation of contempt for all women because they are women . . . By such forces are women turned into sexual prigs.[43]

Since there was a truce between the WSPU and the Government, Christabel was keen that the suffragettes extend their constitutional work and adopt additional forms of protest, such as tax resistance and Census evasion, tactics that the Women's Freedom League favoured. The new passive resistance tactics had been announced in February. On 24 March, Christabel made her own personal stand on tax resistance when she informed the Inland Revenue:

> I have decided to pay no income-tax until such time as the law permits me to qualify as a voter. Any proceedings that you may take for the recovery of the money will be quite in vain, as I shall decline to pay the amount claimed.[44]

More generally, Christabel argued that Census evasion provided an 'immediate opportunity for recording our protest as women against a Government that legislates without consent'.[45]

Census night was Sunday, 2 April 1911 and all the suffragettes were encouraged to attend various evasion gatherings throughout the country so that they could not be enumerated as resident at any particular address. In London, the 'Census Programme', as it was called, began the evening before with a concert at the Queen's Hall in honour of Ethel Smyth who conducted some of her own compositions, ending with 'The March of the Women'. Nevinson was there, enchanted by it all, especially at the close when he met Christabel leaving the building with Ellis Griffith, MP, leader of the Welsh party and a member of the Conciliation Committee. '[S]he turned to greet me & held my hand to lead her

243

through the crowd – that little hand so eloquent, so vital.'[46] The following night, Christabel joined about three hundred other suffragists in Trafalgar Square until the police cleared the area at twelve o'clock. Then it was to the Aldwych Skating Rink where Emmeline Pankhurst presided over a musical and theatrical entertainment, mainly provided by members of the Actresses' Franchise League. Since it was a Sunday night and the Rink was not licensed for music, each artiste was called upon for a 'speech' rather than a song or other turn. The WSPU leadership joined in the entertainment, Christabel receiving hearty applause for her address, given about half-past three. While Emmeline Pankhurst and Ethel Smyth then left the gathering, Christabel, Mrs Lawrence and a few friends retreated to the nearby Gardenia restaurant for coffee and a light breakfast. Here they talked long with Nevinson.[47]

Back in her office later that day, Christabel was unhappy with the press coverage of the evasion tactics of Census night, especially the suggestion that the protest had been a failure. A renewed effort had to be made, she decided, to attract more public support. 'The manner in which the Press boycotts all our Constitutional work, and distorts and misrepresents our militant action, is proving to be a most serious hindrance to the progress of our work', she told WSPU member Mrs Badley, of Petersfield, Hampshire, in early April:

There is no way out of the difficulty save that of increasing the circulation of our paper, 'Votes for Women' . . . With this end in view, we are writing to our most active & enthusiastic members, asking them to act as 'Votes for Women' agents . . . We hope that you will do this service for the cause as far as Petersfield is concerned.[48]

By now, Christabel had finalised her Easter holiday plans. She informed Elizabeth Robins that she would be spending the time at Holmwood, with the Lawrences, but if still convenient, she could dine and stay a night with her, at her nearby home. Elizabeth was content with this arrangement. 'Tuesday 18th I will be with you', responded Christabel. 'On 19th April I must be in London . . . What heaps we have to discuss!'[49] However, before she left Clement's Inn, Christabel had composed another personal letter, of a very different kind, to Hugh Franklin, recently released from prison. 'A word of welcome to you and thanks to you for your brave stand . . . We are very proud of our men friends who are fighting so bravely for us.'[50]

By now, Sylvia had arrived back home from her first American tour, with tales of all her adventures. In America, the five states that had granted women the vote – Wyoming, Idaho, Utah, Colorado and Washington – were in the West of that vast country. She had travelled widely, often speaking at two or more meetings a day. The extensive press coverage, which placed her rather than her mother or Christabel at the centre of attention, boosted her self-confidence, eventually helping her to break away from her relatives; the small income that her speeches and published writings generated helped her to remain independent of them.[51] Sylvia found life in the States 'a whirl, with harsh, rude extremes, rough and unfinished, yet with scope and opportunity for young people and with more receptivity to new ideas that is found in the old countries'. Indeed, she was so impressed with all she saw that she wondered if one day she might become an American citizen.[52] What she did not tell Christabel, and certainly not their mother, was that while she was away she had been writing tender love letters and poems to Hardie. 'Oh, Dearie, I do wish I were with you. How is my Darling?' the lonely Sylvia penned in mid-February. She constantly complained that Hardie, who addressed her as 'my little sweetheart', did not write enough and that his letters never arrived in time at their intended destination. In one poem, Sylvia wrote of wanting to feel Hardie's kisses on her mouth, the clasping of his arms and his dear lips pressing on her until 'my breath comes short . . . each touch/ Every caress, your breaking under your voice'.[53] Both Christabel and her mother would have been horrified if the content of Sylvia's correspondence had been made public. This was a particularly sensitive time for the WSPU. The scandal of a Pankhurst daughter having an affair with a married man old enough to be her father would capture newspaper headlines and possibly derail support for the passing of the Second Conciliation Bill. But no news of the affair leaked out. On 1 May, Sylvia played her expected part as she shared the platform at the London Pavilion with Emmeline Pethick-Lawrence and Christabel, a rare occurrence for the two sisters.[54]

Christabel received some encouraging news; widespread support for the Second Conciliation Bill had been expressed by eighty-six city and town councils, including Birmingham, Liverpool, Manchester, Sheffield, Leeds, Glasgow, Edinburgh, Dundee, Dublin and Cardiff.[55] But nothing could be left to chance. In particular, while she was certain that the bill would pass its second reading, she also knew that it had to pass all its stages that parliamentary session before it passed into law, something she was anxious about. She feared that the Government would try to trick the women again by delaying facilities for the bill until 1913. So in addition to speeches and articles stressing the importance of granting facilities now, she also became very energetic in petitioning supportive politicians and friends alike who might be able to influence the process.[56]

'This letter is inordinately long and you must forgive me', Christabel wrote apologetically to Balfour on 26 April, at the end of a ten-page communication. 'One is so anxious not to leave a single word unsaid which might show how very greatly we need your help.' Christabel asked Balfour if he would say in the House of Commons that the Prime Minister's pledge on women suffrage:

> could be fulfilled and ought to be fulfilled this year . . . Your appeal for fair-play would be echoed by Sir Ellis Griffith for the Welsh Party, by the Labour Members and by a great many Liberals and Irish Members . . . if you do not give a lead, then after all we may fail just because there is no one of influence equal to yours to claim that we be dealt with honestly.[57]

The reluctant Balfour, who had led the Conservative Party through two unsuccessful general elections in 1910, had other matters on his mind. He had made no attempt to control the Conservative majority in the House of Lords from rejecting Lloyd George's budget and, as a result, was becoming increasingly unpopular with his own backbenchers who wanted him to resign as their leader. Nonetheless, both Constance Lytton and Betty Balfour, his sister-in-law, pressed him to support women's suffrage and to see Annie Kenny. Balfour agreed. 'When your little friend from Manchester yesterday gave me, after you left the room, a flower wrapped in paper as a token of her regard', he wrote to Betty, 'I was deeply and even painfully moved, because I am sure that she thought that my sympathetic attention to her fervent pleading, meant not merely the will but the power greatly to further her objects.'[58] Balfour had already signed a petition in favour of women's suffrage, presented to him at the East Lothian by-election.[59]

Christabel also wrote to Ellis Griffith, hoping he would find many to support him in his championship of the Second Conciliation Bill.[60] And then there was Elizabeth Robins, that friend who moved in influential Liberal circles. '1913 is not good & the only object of offering facilities then wd be to "dish" us', Christabel confided to Elizabeth in a letter written while on a train journey back from by-election campaigning in Cheltenham. 'In view of this possibility I have written the article which you will find in "Votes for Women" . . . I wonder', she continued tactfully,

> if you feel disposed to cut the article out & send it with a personal note to Sir. E. Grey or any of your Cabinet Minister acquaintances. Or if you think it wise not to send the article perhaps you wd write anyhow.[61]

On Friday, 5 May 1911, the Second Conciliation Bill passed its second reading with little difficulty, by two hundred and fifty-five votes to eighty-eight. The majority of one hundred and sixty-seven exceeded the majority of one hundred and twenty-six by which the Government held office. As in 1910, the sponsors of the bill moved that the measure be referred to a committee of the whole House which meant, yet again, that it would not be brought up for its committee stage unless given special facilities. Asquith had pledged, on 22 November 1910, that the Conciliation Bill would be given facilities in the next Parliament and so Christabel, cautiously, took him at his word. At a vast meeting at Kensington Town Hall that Friday evening, after the prolonged and enthusiastic cheers had died down, she gave a rallying speech:

> If the anti-suffragists were discouraged before this [parliamentary] debate, what are they tonight? The game is in our hands . . . Men had to fight for their liberty, and it is well for us that we have to fight for ours . . . It has taught us the wonderful lesson of self-reliance.[62]

Privately, the anxious Christabel again importuned Elizabeth Robins for her help. 'Indirectly I hear that Asquith said in conversation with Lady Lewis (your friend) that we would be damned before we shd get the vote while he is at the heart of affairs.' Could Lady Lewis and her husband be asked to talk to Asquith?[63] A dinner party at the Lawrences on 16 May, at which the guests included not only Christabel but also Vida Goldstein, Markino and Nevinson, was a sub-dued affair since the brooding Christabel was thinking about how she could influence the political process.[64] Five days later she wrote to Lady Betty Balfour suggesting that Balfour might have a 'quiet word in private' with Asquith about his wish that the bill should be carried. Then, on 21 May, Christabel was again in communication with Elizabeth Robins. 'Can we meet & consult?' she impor-tuned. 'I shall ring you up this evening.' Christabel explained that matters were now urgent since she had learnt that the final Cabinet meeting to decide whether facilities for the Second Conciliation Bill would be granted this par-liamentary session would be in two days' time.[65] Eight days later, she heard the news she had been dreading: Lloyd George announced that the Government could not, owing to pressure of other legislation, allot time for the women's suf-frage bill this session. Next session, after the bill had been again read a second time, the Government would give a week to its further stages.[66]

The news was received with indignation by all WSPU members, including Maude Sennett who immediately wrote to the Union's Chief Organiser. 'There will be vigorous questioning in the House of Commons, we hope, today and tomorrow', Christabel replied, 'as many of our friends in the House seem to be anxious to compel the Government to make some definite undertaking.'[67] The cautious Christabel did not immediately call for a resumption of militancy since she had been told, privately, that Sir Edward Grey was to make another state-ment of clarification.[68] Nonetheless, the following day she sent a precautionary letter to all those who had volunteered for the next WSPU demonstration, to be held on 17 June, asking them to enrol more recruits and stating that if negotia-tions with the Government on behalf of the women's bill failed, then 'we as a Union will again have to shoulder full responsibility'.[69] Grey's statement later that day, stipulating that the week allotted for the bill would be 'elastic' and that the opportunity offered for the passing of the bill was a real one, restored some hope.[70] But nothing could be taken for granted. 'Sir Edward Grey's speech not-withstanding', Christabel wrote to Balfour,

> we still claim this Session is the appropriate time . . . Why shd we have to raise another £80,000 (the amount expended annually in the Suffrage agitation) and why should we be sentenced to another year's hard labour when the opportunity for carrying the Bill is now![71]

In Votes for Women, Christabel placed the issue in a comparative perspective. 'Our Colonies and America are leaving the United Kingdom behind in the matter of women's freedom. Norway and Finland have enacted woman suffrage, and now . . . Portugal . . . Our own country creeps along in the rear.'[72] When rumours reached her ears that the Government were intending to carry a Plural Voting Bill that parliamentary session, Christabel denounced it as 'an unpardonable insult to women' and asked those who believed in militancy to 'volunteer for action'.[73] Victor Duval, the founder of the Men's Political Union for Women's Enfranchisement, got in touch to ask how he could help, particularly in regard to questions he should ask at a forthcoming Liberal Party meeting. 'The Govt want stirring up', replied Christabel, '& so the more fuss you can make the better.'[74] Hope was again re-kindled when, on 16 June, Asquith wrote to Lord Lytton saying that Grey had accurately expressed the Government's intentions:

> The Government, though divided in opinion on the merits of the Bill, are unanimous in their determination to give effect, not only in the letter but in the spirit, to the promise in regard to facilities which I made on their behalf before the last General Election.[75]

Lord Lytton immediately let Christabel know the good news. '[H]ow much relieved we are by the Prime Minister's message', she merrily replied. 'What immense progress has been made! We may all feel happy I think. A thousand thanks to you.'[76]

The news made the prospect of the impending Women's Coronation Procession, which Christabel had been planning for some time and in which twenty-eight other suffrage groupings were to take part, a particularly joyous occasion. The procession was a response to the King's Coronation celebrations, planned for 22 and 23 June, which would overwhelmingly represent the 'manhood of the Empire', with no place for women. The Women's Coronation Procession of between 40,000 and 50,000 women who marched from the Embankment to the Albert Hall on Saturday, 17 June 1911 was the largest, most spectacular, harmonious and representative of all the suffrage demonstrations. On that bright but cool day, Flora Drummond on horseback led the way, followed by the colour bearer Charlotte Marsh. Then came Marjorie Annan Bryce, gallantly mounted as Joan of Arc, then a group of new crusaders, followed by Christabel, Emmeline Pankhurst, Emmeline Pethick-Lawrence and Mabel Tuke. Marching five abreast, the other participants walked in contingents as seventy bands played and banners and pennants fluttered in the breeze. The Prisoners' Pageant, seven hundred strong, was followed by the Historical Pageant which illustrated the political power held by women in the past. The Empire Pageant included representatives from India, the African colonies and protectorates and Fiji and the Western Pacific. The International Contingent included women not only from the USA and France but also Russia and Romania. The Women's Freedom League, the Church League for Women's Suffrage, the Catholic Women's Suffrage Society, the Women Writers' Suffrage League, the Men's Political Union for Women's Enfranchisement, as well as the National Union of Women's Suffrage Societies all took part. The Conservative and Unionist Women's Franchise Association organised a colourful Pageant of Queens. Elizabeth Wolstenholme Elmy, who had worked for the women's cause for forty-six years, reviewed the seven-mile-long procession from a balcony in St James' Street decorated with the banner 'England's Oldest Militant Suffragist Greets Her Sisters'. As the women walked past her, they saluted then dipped and raised their pennants.[77]

It was the 'greatest Suffragette procession every organised' opined the *Daily Mail*, a view echoed in most of the national press.[78] The crowds flocking to the Albert Hall that day were so great that an overflow meeting was hastily arranged at the Empress Rooms where Christabel, Annie and Vida Goldstein later spoke. At the main event, at the packed Albert Hall, the leaders of the WSPU all addressed the audience as well as Annie Besant, now living in India where she was establishing schools for girls. 'There is nothing that should be closed against a woman which a woman is able to do', advocated this formidable pioneer in the birth control movement. 'The churches should open to your women, the learned professions.'[79] Christabel, for her part, made a tactful speech in which the word 'militancy' was not used. 'We stand today speaking with a most certain hope than we have ever had before of the early triumph of our cause', she announced, confidently. '[I]t is the first time in human history that politicians have made a pledge to women and undertaken to fulfil it in the spirit!' Nonetheless, she warned:

> It may be yet that before we see this Bill of ours on the Statute Book more fighting will have to be done . . . Well, if that should be so, we are ready for the fighting. Fighting is a joy to us, and submission is a thing that we have forgotten all about![80]

Christabel's conciliatory tone was part of her attempt to portray the suffrage movement as an international movement where women of all races, cultures, religions and classes stood together, shoulder to shoulder, in their demand for women's suffrage. Nonetheless, her support for the limited women's suffrage measure contained in the Second Conciliation Bill puzzled some of the women visitors from other countries, as well as many socialist feminists, such as her sister Sylvia. But for Christabel, the main issue was to break down the sex discrimination women faced in being denied the parliamentary vote rather than how many women would be qualified under any bill; although her long-term aim was always universal suffrage for men and women, she believed that fighting for limited suffrage for women was realistic at this particular historical point in time and would attract cross-party support. Accordingly, new instructions were now given to suffragettes to suspend the anti-Government policy in by-elections and to ask instead of each parliamentary candidate whether they would support the Second Conciliation Bill or vote for any amendment that would widen its terms. Those who supported the bill as it stood were endorsed by the WSPU while those who favoured widening it were bitterly opposed.[81]

Christabel left no stone unturned in her desire to get cross-party support for the bill as it stood. On 25 June she telephoned Lord Robert Cecil, a Conservative peer, asking him not to support any amendments. 'Whether this is due to hostility to Lloyd George or to a desire to keep the Bill as it is I do not know', Cecil confided to his sister, Maud Selborne. 'But she wishes us to strengthen her hand.'[82] And, of course, Christabel had to brief the regional organisers on the new policy and offer advice. 'I am enclosing the list of Members of Parliament for Gloucestershire and Herefordshire', she wrote to Ada Flatman. 'You will see that Mr. Henry Terrell voted for the Bill in 1910 and against it in 1911. I hope you will be able to get him on the right side again.' The difficulty with the Liberals, she continued, was that:

> they want to vote for widening amendments in defiance of the bidding of the Conciliation Committee, and what I hope you will be able to do will be to get a promise from each one of them that they will be loyal to the Conciliation Committee and to vote against amendments which the Committee deem to be dangerous.[83]

Amid such activity, Christabel always had to arrange cover for her mother if Emmeline had one of her migraine attacks, from which she suffered all her life, or was otherwise unwell. In late June, when Emmeline was ill, the dutiful daughter took her mother's place at a meeting in the country.[84]

Once back in London, Christabel began campaigning in the constituencies of Bethnal Green and North-West Ham, where the two respective Liberal candidates, Mr Masterman and Baron de Forest, supported an adult suffrage measure rather than the limited franchise of the Second Conciliation Bill. The anxious Christabel contacted Victor Duval, asking him to make sure that the local members of the Men's Political Union in West Ham obtained from de Forest a promise that he would vote against any widening amendment.[85] But no such promise was forthcoming, or from Masterman in Bethnal Green. 'I am in favour of Women's Suffrage, but I will not support a Bill to give the vote to wealthy women of property', Masterman declared, advancing the typical argument of many in his party. 'I want to see this Bill amended so as to include the best women, the wives and mothers of poor working men.' Christabel denounced such thinking, telling the local electors in the constituency that one thousand women would be enfranchised by the bill, nearly everyone from the working classes. In the face of this, it was absurd to say the bill was undemocratic.[86]

That hot July of 1911 Christabel spent mainly in London, speaking or chairing the Monday afternoon meetings held at the London Pavilion for which she managed to secure, on two separate occasions, two Liberal MPs Sir Alfred Mond and Walter Roch.[87] She was pleased that her mother was going campaigning in Wales and Scotland since it would give the tired Emmeline at least some opportunity, however small, for rest and enjoyment of fresh rural air. And Christabel herself was looking forward to her own short holiday, once again at Duncans Farm in

Billinghurst. 'I shall to the Becks on August 5th', she told Elizabeth Robins, 'and if you are at home & not too busy I shd like to visit you on my way to them.'[88] When at the farm, Christabel again wrote to Elizabeth, giving her all the news:

> The Becks are watching & praying for rain but otherwise very cheerful . . . Every day we are to have a giddy round of country festivities including a cattle sale. Wednesday I shall spend in London motoring there & back so it won't be too much of a break in the holiday . . . Now I come to the real point of this letter which is that I enjoyed very, very much being with [you] again and talking with you abt the things that interest us.[89]

But the issue of the Second Conciliation Bill was never far from Christabel's mind and so, while on holiday at the comfortable old farm house, she wrote to sympathetic MPs such as Ellis Griffith, continued to produce her copy for the weekly *Votes for Women*, travelled regularly up to London and back to oversee WSPU business – and gave the occasional talk.[90]

Such activity sometimes involved more personal concerns, especially for suffragettes who fell seriously ill. The working-class Minnie Baldock, a stalwart London worker for six years, had recently been operated upon for cancer, usually a killer disease in those days. Christabel kept in touch with Minnie's worried husband, penning a comforting note when his wife first entered the New Hospital for Women. By mid-August, when Minnie was recovering from her ordeal, Christabel wrote her a warm letter:

> My dear Mrs Baldock
>
> Just a word to say how happy I am to hear that you are doing well. I hope you will very soon be about again & stronger than ever. Your doctor & nurses must be pleased with you for making such good progress. I am in London just to attend to some business & then I go away for another instalment of my holiday. Mother is in Scotland now addressing meetings & motoring from place to place.
>
> My love to you
>
> > Yours ever
> > Christabel Pankhurst[91]

Before Minnie went to recuperate in Brighton, at the home of Minnie Turner at 13 Victoria Road, Christabel visited her in hospital.[92] But such caring action always had to compete with the more mundane but necessary administrative business of the WSPU, including an enquiry from Una Dugdale, who was accompanying Emmeline Pankhurst on her Scottish tour, about the postponement of a meeting in Helensburgh. The tour was not running smoothly. Una was in Aberdeenshire and had obviously not received Emmeline's letter sent from

Skelmorlie, Ayrshire giving details of a change of plan and the problems encountered, especially in raising funds for travelling by car. The diplomatic Christabel replied to the anxious Una, 'I expect Mrs. Pankhurst will be writing to you direct or perhaps you will be seeing her.'[93]

Meanwhile Lloyd George, who had allied himself with Asquith and Churchill against the Second Conciliation Bill, told a meeting of Liberal suffragist MPs on 16 August that facilities promised for the bill should be used for a wider measure. Christabel instantly denounced his treachery since she suspected that the slippery Chancellor of the Exchequer saw the granting of women's suffrage purely in terms of his party's advantage, knowing that a wider party measure would not appeal to the majority of the House of Commons and could not be carried that parliamentary session.[94] Christabel had summed up the situation correctly. Lloyd George was soon writing privately to the Liberal Chief Whip, the Master of Elibank, that the Conciliation Bill 'would on balance add hundreds of thousands of votes throughout the country to the strength of the Tory Party'. He feared that through 'sheer drifting, vacillation and something which looks like cowardice' the bill was likely to get through Parliament. 'Say what you will, that spells disaster to Liberalism'.[95] Even without knowledge of such private correspondence, Christabel's fears were not soothed when another letter from Asquith to Lord Lytton, on 23 August, re-affirmed 'the promises' made by the Government for giving facilities for the Second Conciliation Bill. Instead she reminded suffragettes of the importance of being prepared for 'militant action' until the bill became law.[96]

More private worries now engulfed the Pankhurst family again. Adela, the organiser for Sheffield and district, was suffering from nervous exhaustion. The worried Emmeline Pankhurst met up in Scotland with her disillusioned twenty-six-year-old daughter who was accompanied by WSPU member Helen Archdale who looked after her. Helen, some ten years Adela's senior, had two children but was now estranged from her husband, an army officer who lived in India. 'I feel that Adela may not remain doing organising work in Sheffield & that since she is not well there could not be a better time to end that arrangement than now', Emmeline confided to Helen after their meeting. The unsettled Adela had told her mother that she wanted to study full time and Emmeline thought that the university college at Aberystwyth, Wales, which had a good reputation, was by the sea and within her financial means, would be a good choice. 'I do hope you will help me to get Adela to see that it is best for her to be working in a healthy unexciting place', Emmeline pleaded:

> I really am anxious about her future. She is very clever in many ways but a child in others & is not physically strong. I shall not be happy or comfortable until I feel she is better equipped to make her own way in the world and more self reliant.

The worried Emmeline told of her fear that she could not leave Adela financially independent and that, unless she married, she would have to earn her living.[97]

After meeting Adela again, Emmeline wrote to Helen telling her that she did not think her daughter was well enough to take the stiff entrance examination for Aberystwyth since there were 'many signs of nerve weakness'.[98] Emmeline was further troubled when Helen informed her that the term was due to begin on 19 September which she considered much too soon. 'Could she enter at the half term & so have a longer holiday. Or at Xmas . . . Let me know what you think and what Adela feels about it.'[99] The anxious mother, still emotionally raw after the death of Harry, did not want to risk the health of another of her children, even if it meant having to raise money during her forthcoming Northern American tour to support Adela during her time as a student. 'I feel . . . that Sheffield affairs should be settled as soon as possible & have written to Christabel to say so', Emmeline informed Helen in early September. 'She [Christabel] is away in Ireland but I hope will write to Adela very soon.'[100]

Christabel had been planning her tour of Ireland for some time. In mid-August she had written to one WSPU member asking for 'definite facts' about wages, hours and conditions generally of the women workers in Belfast. 'Also have you any knowledge of whether any direct effect upon public morals can be traced from these conditions. Has any estimate been made, for example, of the number of prostitutes in the city?'[101] But it was not just the possible link between the economic conditions of Irish women workers and prostitution that interested Christabel. She and Emmeline Pethick-Lawrence had travelled to Ireland that early September primarily to meet the committee of the Irish Women's Franchise League which was pressing for changes to a proposed Home Rule Bill, namely that it should include women as well as men voters for an Irish Parliament, specifically those women who were qualified to vote based upon the Local Government Register. Christabel and Mrs Lawrence motored to various places before arriving in Dublin, their final stop, from where Christabel wrote to Elizabeth Robins, asking if she could speak at a WSPU Monday afternoon session in October. 'I wonder if you know Ireland', Christabel enquired. 'I love it & the Gael in me feels very much at home.' Elizabeth turned down the invitation, claiming she had been ill again.[102] Once back in London, Christabel, the dutiful daughter, carried out her mother's wishes and contacted Adela about leaving her organiser's post, a process that was completed by mid-October. Shortly afterwards the unhappy Adela came to London where she lived for several months with Helen Archdale who was made prisoners' secretary, a post that included finding hospitality for those who came to London from around the country, helping them with any personal worries, attending court when they were tried and arranging bail.[103]

That autumn of 1911, the leadership of the WSPU was mainly in Christabel's capable hands since her mother sailed, on 4 October, for her fund-raising tour of North America. 'The voyage there and back always rests me', Emmeline Pankhurst told her eldest daughter; Christabel later commented that this was almost 'the only rest' her mother ever got.[104] Since Emmeline Pankhurst, the much-loved figurehead of the WSPU and its key orator, would be out of the country at this critical time, Christabel had suggested that the popular Annie

Kenney, her trusted friend, should be brought much more into national work. The suggestion had been readily endorsed by her mother and Mrs Lawrence. Before Emmeline Pankhurst sailed for North America, the willing Annie was withdrawn from her role as organiser for the West of England.[105]

By early October, if not before, Christabel was well aware of Lloyd George's machinations against the Second Conciliation Bill and, in *Votes for Women*, angrily condemned his activities:

> [T]here exists a conspiracy of wreckers and reactionaries who are bent upon carrying widening amendments in Committee in the hope of destroying the majority for the Bill . . . it is led by the Chancellor of the Exchequer . . . The particular amendment which Mr. Lloyd George intends to promote is one to give a vote to the wife of every elector, in virtue of her husband's qualification. This provision would apply to no less than six million women, so that the Conciliation Bill, instead of enfranchising one million women . . . would enfranchise *seven* million.

This particular amendment was of such 'magnitude' that it had no chance of becoming law. Lloyd George's object was not, 'as he professes, to secure to [for] women a wide measure of enfranchisement, but to prevent women from having the vote at all'.[106] That the Chancellor of the Exchequer claimed to be in favour of votes for women, yet was so unprincipled as to remain a member of a Cabinet that refused women their democratic right, was regarded as treacherous. Suffragettes now regularly punctuated Lloyd George's meetings with shrill cries of 'Give us the vote!', 'Resign!', 'Traitor!' and 'Wicked man!'[107]

The energetic Christabel continued her campaigning, making major speeches in Birmingham, Glasgow, Norwich and Ipswich, as well as Nottingham where the meeting was held under the auspices of the Free Church League for Women's Suffrage, where her fellow speakers included the Rev. T. Rhondda Williams, the Rev. E. J. Barren and Mrs. E. T. Holman.[108] Nor did Christabel neglect the Irish women's suffrage fight. 'I enclose two documents which I think will be of interest to you', she wrote to Alfred Gardiner, the editor of the *Daily News*, on 14 October:

> One is a copy of the resolution adopted by the Irish Women's Franchise League & sent to us for publication in the English Press. The other is a statement by the W.S.P.U. in which we express our determination to support the Irishwomen in their demand.[109]

Christabel also wrote articles on the subject herself and in mid-October travelled to Ireland again to give major addresses at Dublin and Galway.[110] Margaret Cousins, of the Irish Women's Franchise League, remembered how Christabel took Dublin by storm. 'She came; we heard and saw; she conquered.' The Rotunda, which held three thousand people, was packed:

She disarmed criticism. Young, slight, fair, pretty, well-dressed, with a clear and telling voice, one imagined her of the kind of Joan of Arc and other women who made history. She was very clever, with a natural flair for politics and political strategy.[111]

From Dublin, Christabel hastened back to London where on 20 October she spoke at the Gardenia Restaurant to the Irish Parliamentary Branch of the United Irish League of Great Britain.[112]

Christabel's emphasis upon the solidarity between English and Irish women, however, was not welcomed by all Irish suffragists, some of whom believed that she did not 'care one whit' about Irish independence from the British state and if it had to suffer for women's suffrage to succeed, then so be it.[113] Nonetheless, Christabel was politically astute enough to give time to the Irish question. She knew that the Irish Nationalist MPs at Westminster, led by John Redmond, could prevent the enfranchisement of both Irish and English women since they could side with Asquith against the Conciliation Bill in return for support for the Home Rule Bill.[114] As on previous occasions, Christabel sought the help of Elizabeth Robins, asking her if she would bring to the notice of 'Cabinet Ministers & others directly & indirectly connected' with the Government the importance of the WSPU's arguments.[115]

The Prime Minister suddenly announced, on 7 November, that the Government would introduce in 1912 its own bill that would extend the franchise to all adult male citizens currently excluded; the measure would be open to amendment so that, if the Commons so desired, women could be included.[116] The astonished Christabel first knew of this proposed new bill when she saw it advertised on newspaper stands. 'Manhood Suffrage is to be brought in', she hastily informed Elizabeth Robins. 'I saw it on the posters when I left you under the name of Adult Suffrage . . . Most serious.'[117] Once back at Clement's Inn, where the staff had already heard the devastating news, Christabel cabled her mother in America. Emmeline Pankhurst's 'first wild thought' was to return home but, knowing that Christabel would not compromise but fight for the Second Conciliation Bill, she decided to continue with her tour, cabling back, 'Protest imperative!'[118] Mrs Lawrence agreed. The Manhood Suffrage Bill was 'an affront to our intelligence . . . Submission is unthinkable'.[119]

That afternoon of 7 November, posters with messages such as 'Lloyd George Betrays the Women's Cause' and 'No Manhood Suffrage for Us' were carried by a number of women around Parliament Square. When Brailsford visited Clement's Inn that evening he described the occupants as 'livid with rage & deaf to reason'.[120] Lloyd George told his brother, 'The Pankhursts are furious' and boasted that the announcement about the new bill was 'entirely my doing'.[121] But Christabel was mobilising the suffragettes. The following day, Flora Drummond sent out a letter to the secretaries of all the WSPU local branches announcing that the anti-Government policy would be resumed and asking for volunteers for a deputation to Westminster on 21 November. Usually Christabel organised this kind of activity but recently she had devolved much of the central administration in regard to the local branches to Flora so that she could concentrate upon her political work.

In *Votes for Women* on 10 November, the uncompromising Christabel condemned again the treachery of the Liberal Government and its Chancellor of the Exchequer:

> War is declared – declared by the Government upon women! . . . The statement that a Franchise Bill is to be introduced which gives no place to women is . . . an outrage upon women's dignity. The insolence of the proposal is intensified by the fact that the Manhood Suffrage Bill is not put forward in response to any demand . . . it is simply an expedient for wrecking Woman Suffrage . . . The Government's latest attempt to cheat women of the vote is, of course, inspired by Mr. Lloyd George. The whole crooked scheme is characteristic of the man and of the methods he has from the first employed against the Suffrage cause.[122]

The Tory press, hostile to women's suffrage, nonetheless largely agreed with this analysis. 'There are plenty of men inside Parliament and outside . . . who would think it bare justice to enfranchise females who are ratepayers and tax-payers, and see no harm in adding a million women so qualified to the registers', opined the *Evening Standard*. 'But when it comes to throwing ten millions in at one stroke, to giving the franchise to every labourer's wife, every scullery maid and matchbox-maker and street flower-seller who has passed her twenty-first birthday, they will draw back.' The *Pall Mall Gazette* pointed out that adult women suffrage would mean a 'female majority in every constituency . . . something to which the most degenerate House of Commons would never set its seal', a view largely echoed by the *Times*. Even the Liberal *Daily Chronicle* had to admit that the Government's policy may 'cut the ground from under the Conciliation Bill, while, on the other, reducing the support at present available for the cause of Women's Suffrage'.[123]

Christabel continued to be an outspoken critic, both in her speeches and articles, of the machinations of 'Oily George', as he was known by the suffragettes.[124] Privately, she also vented her dislike of the man, again to Elizabeth Robins, and confided to Ellis Griffith, 'Lloyd George is indeed a traitor'.[125] Brailsford told C. P. Scott that Christabel 'envisaged the whole suffrage movement . . . as a gigantic duel between herself & Lloyd George, whom she desired to destroy'. He also informed Nevinson that he considered 'Christabel's services were almost at an end' and that he had decided to break with the WSPU, urging Nevinson to do the same.[126] But Brailsford was not an impartial observer. Despite the fact that he found Lloyd George 'slippery', the latter had secured his 'partial cooperation', meeting him on a few occasions around the time of Asquith's crucial announcement on 7 November.[127] 'Brailsford has Lloyd Georgeitis', Christabel remarked sarcastically to Sylvia.[128] She had barely uttered those words when surprising news arrived: Asquith had agreed to meet a delegation of nine suffrage societies, including the WSPU, on 17 November.

On 16 November, Christabel was upbeat when she spoke at a large Albert Hall meeting. Joined on the platform by Annie, Emmeline Pethick-Lawrence and Vida Goldstein, who was shortly returning to Australia, she urged her followers to stand firm and for all women to join the WSPU:

> Our minds turn back at such a time as this to Joan of Arc, the greatest woman in human history. She was reviled, she was denounced, she was done to death . . . and yet she was certain she was right. Remember her words as she died amongst the flames: 'My Voices *were* of God.' Everyone who fights in a great cause can say that too. Our Voices are of God. They *are* of God! Now, if one woman had the courage to save France and die for doing it, surely we, who are so many. . . shall find it very easy to laugh to scorn the people who do not understand! . . . Ours is a great crusade . . . join us. March under our banner. Share the victory that is before us.[129]

The strong religious theme in Christabel's speech, equating militancy with a spiritual quest, aimed at winning justice for women, did not impress Nevinson who found annoying what he termed Christabel's 'strange lapses into cheap gallery appeal'. Nor was he impressed by what he called Fred Pethick-Lawrence's 'rather theatrical style that disgusted even [Victor] Duval who sat next me'; Fred had announced that although he had intended to give £100 to the women's cause, the amount was now £1,000 because 'the Prime Minister had tried to trick the women'.[130] Yet the audience in the Albert Hall obviously disagreed with Nevinson's jaundiced assessment since over £4,000 was raised, as well as gifts of valuable jewellery.

The following day, with the applause of the previous evening still ringing in their ears, Christabel and Emmeline Pethick-Lawrence led the WSPU delegation of Annie Kenney, Mabel Tuke, Lady Constance Lytton and Elizabeth Robins in the deputation of all women's suffrage societies that Asquith had agreed to receive. Christabel stepped out to impress, in a smart long coat with wide lapels in satin stripes in the colours of the WSPU which the critic Nevinson considered 'fine – but a little overdone for the morning'.[131] When she arrived at 10 Downing Street, she found the portly Asquith in good humour, 'rosy-faced and smiling. He might have been Father Christmas with votes for women in his bag of presents'. Lloyd George, on the other hand, was pale and gloomy.[132] Millicent Garrett Fawcett briefly introduced the deputation and then Christabel gave a long statement, calling on the Government to abandon the Manhood Suffrage Bill and to introduce an equal franchise measure for men and women.

After all the other representatives had spoken, Asquith replied, denying that the Liberal Government intended any trickery. Although his remarks were flowery with compliments to those who had addressed him, he noted that 'Miss Pankhurst' had 'talked in terms of peace, presenting, I must say, a pistol in one hand and a dagger in the other'. In regard to Christabel's demand for equal suffrage, he replied, 'I am the head of the Government, and I am not going to make myself responsible for the introduction of a measure which I do not con-scientiously believe to be demanded in the interests of the country.' The pert Christabel, with a wave of her hand, instantly replied, 'Then you can go, and we will get another head', to which Asquith retorted, 'I may go if you like. If you can get rid of me'. The exchange did not stop there. 'We are not satisfied', said the spirited Christabel, to which Asquith replied very blandly, 'Oh, I didn't expect to satisfy you.' Helena Swanwick, one of the NUWSS representatives present, was unimpressed; she considered Christabel impertinent and her performance gener-ally ineffective since she had 'read most of her very halting speech and defiance does not read well'.[133] Perhaps this was why the loyal Annie suddenly confronted Asquith with the announcement, 'I'm a Militant, and we all hate and distrust you. Do you call yourself a statesman?' The startled Asquith refused to discuss the question. Seeing Annie at daggers drawn with the Prime Minister, the protective Christabel interjected, 'Don't fret yourself about him, he is not worth it. Our fight will be on public ground.'[134]

The preparations for the WSPU protest on 21 November were well in hand. On that fine frosty evening, Christabel presided over a meeting in Caxton Hall before Emmeline Pethick-Lawrence led the deputation to Parliament Square. Meanwhile another smaller group of a hundred and fifty women, armed with bags of stones and hammers supplied by Clement's Inn, smashed windows of not only Government offices but also the National Liberal Federation, the Guards' Club, the Daily Mail and Daily News, Swan and Edgar's, Lyon's Tea Shop, Dunn's Hat Shop, two hotels, as well as some small businesses. Mrs Lawrence was among the two hundred and twenty-three arrested.[135] Christabel had said nothing in her speech to encourage window breaking. Nonetheless, she stoutly defended this direction of militant policy, namely attacks on private as well as public property. At a meeting at the Savoy Theatre two days later, amid applause and loud cheers, she reiterated her views, telling her audience that men had got the vote by riot and rebellion, and that was how women must get it too. The window-smashing suffragettes had nothing to be ashamed of.[136]

On 24 November, at a meeting of the National Liberal Federation in Bath, Lloyd George gave a provocative speech. He declared himself in favour of women's suffrage and then asserted that the Second Conciliation Bill had been 'torpedoed' by the Manhood Suffrage Bill which would make way for a broad and democratic amendment that would enfranchise not a limited class of women to suit the Tories, but also wives of working men.[137] The indignant Christabel retorted, 'We shall never believe that Mr. Lloyd George is a genuine supporter of a democratic franchise for women until he secures that it be made a Government measure.'[138] In Votes for Women Christabel published a key article titled 'Broken windows' which outlined the WSPU's new policy of attacking public and private property, as a way to force the Liberal Government to grant women the vote:

There are in every community people who are a law unto themselves . . . criminals and reformers . . . They differ only in their motive. The criminal breaks the law to the injury of the State and for his own profit; the reformer breaks the law to his own injury, but for the salvation of the State . . . Our very definite purpose is to create an intolerable situation for the Government, and if need be, for the public as a whole . . . Militant Suffragists would, of course, be glad if an attack on Government property were sufficient to attain their purpose. But the present policy of the Government proves that these measures are not powerful enough to produce the effect desired . . . That is why private property has now been attacked . . . ordinary private individuals . . . are citizens, and, as such, the masters and employers of Cabinet Ministers. They have allowed their servants to deal in disgraceful fashion with the question of women's enfranchisement. Are they not, therefore, to be held responsible? . . . Remembering the injuries and insults done to the Deputation on Black Friday, we say that we prefer a thousand times the window-breaking of the 21st of November.[139]

The article, with a few additions, was shortly thereafter published as a leaflet.[140]

When Lloyd George breakfasted with C. P. Scott in early December, both men inevitably discussed the leaders of the WSPU. '[T]hey must be mad', opined Lloyd George. 'They are mad, Christabel Pankhurst has lost all sense of proportion and of reality', replied Scott. 'It's just like going to a lunatic asylum and talking to a man who thinks he's God Almighty', commented the Chancellor of the Exchequer. 'Yes, very much like that.'[141] But Christabel was not mad. She had logically and carefully thought out the strategy for the WSPU, namely forcing a crisis so the Government would grant votes to women. Her mother in America, with whom she kept in close contact, agreed with this strategy, as did Emmeline Pethick-Lawrence.

For some weeks, Votes for Women had been giving notice of a new journal that would soon appear, The Freewoman, and wishing well its two editors, Dora Marsden and Mary Gawthorpe, both former WSPU members. However, when the first issue appeared on 23 November 1911, Clement's Inn was shocked. The editorial contained a blistering attack on the WSPU, particularly on Christabel's leadership. Contesting the collective emphasis upon feminism as a political movement, it was argued instead that feminism was about the development of the freedom of the individual woman and her spiritual separateness, a set of ideas that had gained some limited currency in early twentieth-century Britain and America and has been termed 'avant-garde feminism'.[142] 'Freewomen' who thought and acted for themselves could be contrasted with 'bondwomen' who merely complemented and rounded off the personality of some other individual, rather than creating or cultivating their own.[143] Thus the suffragette movement, with its emphasis upon self-sacrifice for the cause and upon the surrender of autonomy to its leaders, was scorned. '[W]e do not regard the vote in itself as even a symbol of freedom, nor do we understand those who do.'[144]

'Miss Pankhurst has lost her political balance', it was acidly claimed. Although she had created a widespread women's movement, she was:

lacking political insight and even common sense. The recent call for a resumption of militant tactics when women's suffrage was on the eve of success was based on flimsy grounds, just as two years ago she called a truce on a flimsy pretext. Does she believe that, whatever form militancy may take, it will induce the Government, with Mr. Asquith as its head, to introduce a bill to give votes to women? Does she believe that whatever form militancy may take, the Liberal Party will demand the resignation of Mr. Asquith? If her reply to these questions is in the negative, she has utterly no case for militancy; and if she replies in the affirmative, she stands convicted of political ineptitude.[145]

The caustic criticisms, read by staff in WSPU local offices and even in the USA, made Christabel anxious. The volatile Dora Marsden had never been a team player; however, alarmingly Mary Gawthorpe was an old friend. Christabel did not respond publicly to this most personal of attacks, but other suffragettes were not prepared to remain silent. The following week, the *Freewoman* published a selection of the furious letters with which it had been inundated. 'Your vile attack on Miss Pankhurst fills me with amazement and disgust too deep for expression', wrote one unnamed correspondent. 'I consider that a public and acrimonious attack on a prominent militant leader is ill-judged and likely to harm the Suffrage Cause', complained Edith Zangwill who wished to clearly disassociate herself from a journal to which she had contributed an article. 'I much regret your onslaught upon Miss Pankhurst's leadership', wrote a 'disgusted and disappointed' Lilian Dove Willcox. 'It shows a petty spirit and belittles your literary venture.' Catherine Corbett taunted:

Having read your article on Miss Pankhurst, I certainly do not intend to subscribe to a paper for whose editors I have no respect. To turn round and stab in the back those who have shown us all a thousand kindnesses may be the goal of a 'Feminist', but will not be the ambition of the 'Suffragette'.[146]

The controversy about Christabel's leadership of the WSPU continued to rumble on in *The Freewoman*, drawing in the disgruntled Teresa Billington-Greig who fully supported the attack on her old rival's 'personal dictatorship', as she termed it. Katharine Douglas-Smith, on the other hand, pointed out that as far as the WSPU was concerned, 'all of us who serve under that banner do so of our own free will; for us no press-gang has existed, and we can leave at any moment'.[147]

While the controversy continued Christabel, buoyed up by her supporters, focused on her suffrage work. In mid-December, some lighter relief arose when she attended the WSPU's Christmas Fair and Fete in the Portman

Rooms which Sylvia had decorated, at Emmeline Pethick-Lawrence's request. The ever-resourceful Sylvia had reused the Prince's Skating Rink decorations, adding an eighteenth-century architectural setting of a village fair; she also designed the period costumes of the stall holders which included gentlewomen, workers of all sorts and a gipsy fortune teller. On this festive occasion, the elusive Elizabeth Robins delighted Christabel by presiding over proceedings on the second day, together with Ruth Cavendish Bentinck. A profit of £3,000 was raised from the event.[148]

However, that very day, 15 December, militancy took a different turn when, unknown to Christabel, Emily Wilding Davison was arrested for trying to force a piece of lighted linen saturated in paraffin through the slot of a letter box just outside Parliament Street post office. She told the detective who arrested her that she had set fire to two other pillar boxes in London earlier that day, and also to another, the previous Friday. 'I did this entirely on my own responsibility', she insisted.[149] Before the court one week later, Emily explained she had acted as she did as a protest against the vindictive two-month sentence passed upon 'my comrade, Mary Leigh'. In the agitation for reform in the past, 'the next step after window breaking was incendiarism' in which she had engaged 'to draw the attention of the private citizen' to the fact that women's suffrage was their concern as well as that of women.[150]

Christabel was taken aback by this first act of incendiarism by a WSPU member which received coverage only in a short paragraph on the back pages of *Votes for Women*.[151] Although Emily Wilding Davison had initiated this tactic within the context of feminist friendship and concern about the fate of one particular comrade, she had overstepped the mark.[152] Christabel had always encouraged the suffragettes to take their own independent action but within the overall policy direction set out by the leadership. But then, as she knew well, Miss Davison was a freelance rank-and-file militant who always went her own way rather than following directives.

Notes

1 VfW, 6 January 1911.
2 Dobbie, A nest of suffragettes, p. 46. An embroidered flag in WSPU colours, hermetically sealed, was later placed on her grave at Southgate, VfW, 1 September 1911, p. 773.
3 APW, My mother, p. 37.
4 APW, My mother, pp. 36–7.
5 APW to Helen Moyes, 11 February 1961, SFC.
6 Interview with Mrs Stride (nee Hemsley), 25 August 1975, DMC.
7 CP to Miss Robins, 1 February 1911, Robins Papers, Fales Library.
8 E. Knowles, Born under a lucky star, Calling All Women, 1975, p. 9.
9 Daily Express, 17 January 1911; Anti-Suffrage Review, February 1911, p. 29; Times, 19 January 1911.
10 The story often ran as front page news – see the Daily Express 17 and 18 January 1911.
11 CP to Ethel Smyth, 16 January 1911, Myrna Goode, Private Suffrage Collection.
12 Entry for 17 January 1911, Nevinson Diaries.

13 Unsigned letter from Rona Robinson to Dora Marsden, 15 December 1910, Dora Marsden Papers, Princeton University.

14 CP to Dora Marsden, 14 November 1910, Marsden Papers.

15 *VfW*, 27 January 1911, p. 272.

16 *VfW*, 27 January 1911, p. 278.

17 CP to Mr Franklin, Hugh Franklin/Elsie Duval Papers, TWL.

18 Dora Marsden to Mrs Pankhurst, 27 January 1911, Marsden Papers.

19 *Egoist*, 15 June 1914.

20 CP to Miss Robins, 1 February 1911, Robins Papers, Fales Library.

21 CP to Mr Nevinson, 6 February 1911, Evelyn Sharp Nevinson Papers.

22 Y. Markino, *My idealised John Bullesses* (London, Constable, 1912), pp. 151–2.

23 First place had been drawn by Mr Phillips, an Irish MP who, owing to the decision of the Irish Nationalists not to introduce any bill that session, withdrew his claim which had been secured under a misapprehension.

24 Rosen, *Rise up women!*, p. 146; Pugh, *The march of the women*, p. 140.

25 *VfW*, 10 February 1911, p. 308.

26 CP letter to editor, *Times*, 6 February 1911.

27 CP to Mr Nevinson, 6 February 1911, Evelyn Sharp Nevinson Papers.

28 CP to Miss Robins, 10 February 1911, Robins Papers, HRHRC. Plural voting, which was not abolished until 1948, is the practice whereby one person might be able to vote in more than one constituency.

29 CP to Miss Phillips, 10 February 1911, Mary Phillips Papers.

30 *VfW*, 17 February 1911, p. 324.

31 *VfW*, 17 February 1911, p. 320.

32 CP to Constance Lytton, 1 March 1911, SFC.

33 CP to Miss Birnstingl, 7 March 1911, Craigie Collection.

34 *Times*, 2 and 3 March 1911.

35 E. Troup to Mathews, 4 March 1911, Winston S. Churchill Archives, Churchill College, Cambridge.

36 CP, Churchill's methods of barbarism, *VfW*, 10 March 1911, p. 372.

37 CP, Rise up women!, *VfW*, 17 March 1911, p. 388.

38 Quoted in B. Caine, Vida Goldstein and the English militant campaign, *Women's History Review*, 2, 3, 1993, p. 367.

39 M. Vicinus, Fin-de-siecle theatrics: male impersonation and lesbian desire, in *Borderlines: genders and identities in war and peace 1870–1930*, ed. B. Melman (London and New York, Routledge, 1998), p. 182; E. S. Pankhurst, TSM, p. 377. The words of 'March of the Women' were written by Cecily Hamilton, who worked as an actress before becoming a writer and dramatist. She was a member of the Actresses' Franchise League and co-founded, with Bessie Hatton, the Women Writers' Suffrage League. For a short time, Hamilton was a member of the WSPU and then, for somewhat longer, of the Women's Freedom League. For further discussion about Smyth's collaboration with Hamilton and the role of music more generally in the suffragette movement see K. Cockin, *Edith Craig and the theatres of art* (London, Bloomsbury, 2017), pp. 104–12 and J. DeVries, Sounds taken for wonders: revivalism and religious hybridity in the British women's suffrage movement, in *Material religion in modern Britain*, eds T. Willem Jones and L. Matthews-Jones (New York, Palgrave Macmillan, 2015), pp. 101–23. For discussion about the Actresses' Franchise League see especially J. Holledge, *Innocent flowers: women in the Edwardian theatre* (London, Virago, 1981) and N. Paxton, *Stage rights! The Actresses' Franchise League, activism and politics 1908–1958* (Manchester, Manchester University Press, 2018).

40 *VfW*, 31 March 1911, p. 421.

41 *VfW*, 31 March 1911, p. 417.

42 CP to Miss Robins, 30 March 1911, Robins Papers, Fales Library.

43 T. Billington-Greig, *The militant suffrage movement: emancipation in a hurry* (London, Frank Palmer [1911]), pp. 198, 166–7.
44 *VfW*, 31 March 1911, p. 429.
45 *VfW*, 24 February 1911, p. 340. On Census evasion see Jill Liddington, *Vanishing for the vote: suffrage, citizenship and the battle for the census* (Manchester, Manchester University Press, 2014).
46 Entry for 1 April, 1911, Nevinson Diaries.
47 Entry for 3 April 1911, Nevinson Diaries.
48 CP to Mrs Badley, 3 April 1911, TWL.
49 CP to Miss Robins, 4 and 7 April 1911, Robins Papers, Fales Library.
50 CP to Mr Franklin, 7 April 1911, TWL.
51 Winslow, *Sylvia Pankhurst*, p. 25.
52 ESP, *TSM*, p. 350.
53 Harrison, *Sylvia Pankhurst*, pp. 118–20; Winslow, *Sylvia Pankhurst*, p. 24.
54 *VfW*, 28 April 1911, p. 498. The three shared a platform again on 8 June, *VfW*, 2 June 1911, p. 595.
55 Metcalfe, *Woman's effort*, p. 171.
56 See, for example, CP, Fair play for our bill, and Carry the bill, *Votes for Women*, 28 April and 5 May 1911, respectively, pp. 494 and 512.
57 CP to Mr Balfour, 26 April 1911, Balfour Papers, Mss Add 49793.
58 Balfour to Betty Balfour, 8 May 1911 and Constance Lytton to Balfour, 3 May 1911, Balfour Papers, BL, Ms Add 49831 and 47973, respectively.
59 *VfW*, 28 April 1911, p. 490.
60 CP to Mr Griffith, 27 April 1911, Sir Ellis Jones Ellis-Griffith Papers, National Library of Wales.
61 CP to Miss Robins, 28 April 1911, Robins Papers, Fales Library.
62 *VfW*, 12 May 1911, p. 532.
63 CP to Miss Robins, 8 May 1911, Robins Papers, Fales Library.
64 Entry for 16 May 1911, Nevinson Diaries.
65 CP to Lady Betty, 21 May 1911, Balfour Papers, BL Add Ms 49831; CP to Miss Robins, 22 May 1911, Robins Papers, Fales Library. Lady Betty promptly sent Christabel's letter to Balfour.
66 *Times*, 30 May 1911.
67 CP to Mrs Arncliffe Sennett, 30 May 1911, MASC.
68 Entries for 30 May and 1 June 1911, Nevinson Diaries.
69 Form letter from CP to Dear Friend, 1 June 1911, MASC.
70 *Times*, 2 June 1911; entry for 2 June 1911, Nevinson Diaries.
71 CP to Balfour, 2 June 1911, Balfour Papers, BL Add Ms 47993; see also CP to Mr Duval, 31 May 1911, Purvis Collection, asking Victor not to interrupt Grey's speech since he had announced in advance he would speak on women's suffrage.
72 *VfW*, 9 June 1911, p. 596.
73 *VfW*, 16 June 1911, p. 606; entry for 12 June 1911, Nevinson Diaries.
74 CP to Mr Duval, 15 June 1911, Purvis Collection.
75 The letter was published in the *Times*, 17 June 1911.
76 CP to Lord Lytton 16 June 1911, Knebworth House Archives.
77 *VfW*, 23 June 1911, pp. 625 and 632; *Manchester Guardian* and *Daily News*, 19 June 1911.
78 *Daily Mail*, 19 June 1911.
79 *VfW*, 23 June 1911, p. 629.
80 *VfW*, 23 June 1911, p. 630.
81 ESP, *TSM*, p. 353.
82 Quoted in G. E. Maguire, *Conservative women: a history of women and the Conservative party, 1874–1997* (Houndmills, Macmillan, 1998), p. 57.

83 CP to Miss Flatman, 4 July 1911, SFC.
84 EP to Alice Morgan Wright, nd. [26 June 1911], Sophia Smith Collection, Northampton, Massachusetts.
85 J. Kenney to Mr Duval, 29 June 1911, Purvis Collection.
86 VfW, 28 July 1911, p. 704.
87 VfW, 7 and 14 July 1911, pp. 657, 664, 671.
88 CP to Miss Robins, 20 July 1911, Robins Papers, Fales Library.
89 CP to Miss Robins, 6 August 1911, Robins Papers, Fales Library.
90 For example, she spoke at an At Home organised by Lady Downshire at Easthampstead Park, Berkshire, VfW, 25 August 1911, p. 760.
91 CP to Mrs Baldock, 17 August 1911, SFC.
92 Crawford, The women's suffrage movement, p. 29 notes that Minnie Turner, who knew Minnie Baldock, paid her expenses. Mrs Baldock died in 1954.
93 CP to Miss Dugdale, 21 August 1911 and EP to Una Dugdale, 18 August 1911, Purvis Collection.
94 VfW, 18 and 25 August 1911, pp. 746 and 758, respectively.
95 Lloyd George to The Master of Elibank, 5 September 1911, Elibank Papers, National Library of Scotland, Edinburgh.
96 VfW, 25 August 1911, pp. 754, 759.
97 EP to Mrs Archdale, nd. [August 1911], Craigie Collection.
98 EP to Mrs Archdale, nd. [early September 1911], Craigie Collection.
99 EP to Mrs Archdale, 6 September 1911, Craigie Collection.
100 EP to Mrs Archdale, nd. [early September 1911], Craigie Collection.
101 CP to Miss Irwin, 14 August 1911, Purvis Collection.
102 CP to Miss Robins, 11 and 15 September 1911, Robins Papers, Fales Library.
103 VfW, 20 October 1911, p. 46; Macpherson, Betty Archdale, p. 42.
104 CP, Unshackled, p. 186.
105 VfW, 6 October 1911, p. 11.
106 VfW, 6 October 1911, p. 8.
107 P. Rowland, Lloyd George (London, Barrie and Jenkins, 1975), p. 257.
108 VfW, 20 October 1911, p. 47.
109 CP to Mr Gardiner, 14 October 1911, Papers of Alfred George Gardiner, 1865–1946, Journalist, Editor of Daily News 1902–19, British Library of Political and Economic Science, London School of Economics and Political Science.
110 VfW, 20 October 1911, pp. 41–2; 27 October, p. 53; 3 November, p. 72; C. Murphy, The women's suffrage movement and Irish society in the early twentieth century (Hemel Hempstead, Harvester Wheatsheaf, 1989), p. 65.
111 J. H. Cousins and M. E. Cousins, We two together (Madras, Ganesh, 1950), pp. 171–2.
112 VfW, 27 October 1911, p. 53.
113 Murphy, The women's suffrage movement, p. 65.
114 VfW, 20 October 1911, p. 41.
115 CP to Miss Robins, 21 October 1911, Robins Papers, HRHRC.
116 Toye, Lloyd George & Churchill, p. 80.
117 CP to Miss Robins, 7 November 1911, Robins Papers, HRHRC.
118 EP, My own story, p. 201: ESP; Emmeline Pankhurst, p. 101.
119 Form letter from EPL to Dear Colleague in the Woman's Movement, 15 November 1911, SFC.
120 VfW, 10 November 1911, p. 84; entry for 8 November 1911, Nevinson Diaries.
121 Quoted in Toye, Lloyd George & Churchill, p. 80.
122 VfW, 10 November 1911, p. 88.
123 Quotes from VfW, 10 November 1911, p. 83.

124 See her article, The Manhood Suffrage Bill, *VfW*, 10 November 1911, p. 88, and her speech at the London Pavilion 13 November, *VfW*, 17 November 1911, p. 101.
125 CP to Miss Robins, 10 November 1911, Robins Papers, HRHRC; CP to Mr Ellis Griffith, 7 November 1911, Ellis-Griffith Papers.
126 C. P. Scott Diary, entry for 16 November 1911, C. P. Scott Papers, BL Mss 50901; entry for 31 October 1911, Nevinson Diaries.
127 Toye, *Lloyd George & Churchill*, p. 81.
128 ESP, *TSM*, p. 360.
129 *VfW*, 24 November 1911, p. 119.
130 Entry for 16 November 1911, Nevinson Diaries.
131 Entry for 17 November 1911, Nevinson Diaries.
132 CP, *Unshackled*, p. 188.
133 *VfW*, 24 November 1911, p. 117; H. M. Swanwick, *I have been young* (London, Victor Gollancz, 1935), 214.
134 Kenney, *Memories*, p. 170.
135 *Daily Express*, 22 November 1911.
136 *VfW*, 24 November 1911, p. 114; *Standard*, 24 November 1911.
137 Extract from Lloyd George's speech, Bath, 24 November 1911, John Johnson Collection, Women's Suffrage, Box 1, Bodleian Library, Oxford.
138 *VfW*, 8 December 1911, p. 160.
139 CP, Broken windows, *VfW*, 1 December 1911, p. 142.
140 CP, *Broken Windows* (London, WSPU, c.1912).
141 Wilson ed., *The political diaries of C. P. Scott*, p. 58.
142 L. Delap, *The feminist avant-garde: transatlantic encounters of the early twentieth century* (Cambridge, Cambridge University Press, 2007).
143 Bondwomen, *The Freewoman: a weekly feminist review* (hereafter *FW*), 23 November 1911, p. 1.
144 *FW*, 23 November 1911, p. 3.
145 *FW*, 23 November 1911, p. 4.
146 *FW*, 30 November 1911, pp. 23, 30–1.
147 *FW*, 14 December 1911, pp. 70, 72.
148 *VfW*, 15 December 1911, pp. 169, 171, 177; ESP, *TSM*, p. 354.
149 *The Standard*, 15 December 1911.
150 *VfW*, 29 December 1911, p. 212.
151 *VfW*, 22 December 1911, p. 196; CP, *Unshackled*, pp. 193–5.
152 See Morley with Stanley, *Emily Wilding Davison*, p. 153.

13

ESCAPE TO FRANCE

January 1912–end of June 1912

Christabel spent a welcome New Year holiday in Switzerland with the Lawrences and Annie. Arriving back at Clement's Inn, she found an abundance of letters from volunteers for the next protest demonstration.[1] Her joy at such enthusiasm was soon tempered by the news that a six-month imprisonment had been passed on Emily Wilding Davison. Despite the severity of the sentence, Christabel was determined that it should not cast a shadow over the forthcoming wedding of loyal WSPU member Una Dugdale, to Victor Duval, founder of the Men's Political Union for Women's Enfranchisement. In view of the 'admiration & esteem' in which the two young people were held, the Central Committee of the WSPU, on behalf of the Union, gave a wedding gift of a silver tea service.[2] Una and Victor, both from upper-class families with liberal credentials, had decided to make a feminist point at their wedding ceremony, to be held at the Royal Chapel of the Savoy on 13 January 1912. Una would not say the word 'obey' in her marriage vows, a move that pleased Clement's Inn – and attracted much notoriety in the press. However, on the day, the bride had to conform to tradition since the sympathetic chaplain officiating found out that if 'obey' was not included in the service, the marriage would be invalid.

Despite this setback, Una and Victor were able to make another small feminist protest; after Una's father, Commander Edward Stratford Dugdale, had led his daughter up the aisle, the section of the service concerned with the giving away of the bride, as though she was a chattel, was omitted.[3] Christabel was delighted at this small act of defiance against the subjection of women, undoubtedly a subject of conversation at the wedding reception, held at the Dugdale home at 13 Stanhope Place, Marble Arch. She, Emmeline Pethick-Lawrence and Constance Lytton were among the many suffragettes present.[4] Although Emmeline Pankhurst was due back home from North America just two days after Una's wedding, her arrival was delayed and so Christabel took her mother's speaking engagements at Ipswich and Norwich on 17 January. The following day, the much-loved figurehead of the WSPU arrived at Tilbury Docks determined on more serious militancy, a view that had already been aired by Christabel in her defence of the broken-windows policy. Always at one with her eldest daughter on the direction the WSPU should take, Emmeline Pankhurst now had the words, 'Sedition!' and 'The Women's Revolution' upon her lips.[5]

As soon as the opportunity arose, Christabel discussed with her mother her conflicting doubts about Fred Pethick-Lawrence – would he succumb to the charms of his old friend Lloyd George, who had recently asked to see him?[6] More seriously, Fred, a dull speaker, was becoming much more prominent on WSPU platforms and had a following in the Men's Political Union. Would the WSPU be able to contain this man within its women-only ranks? In addition, Christabel was becoming bored with having to fit in with the Lawrences' social routine, including rounds of dinner parties, which wasted valuable time that could be spent working for the cause. Christabel concluded that the only solution was to leave their home and take a flat of her own, become more independent; after all, she was thirty-one years old. Emmeline Pankhurst listened patiently to her favourite daughter's concerns and eagerly supported her plan. She had never liked Fred, or got on with him, believing he would go his own way. A possessive mother, she was always jealous of the ties of affection between Christabel and her hosts. A conversation with Jessie Stephenson, the organiser in Manchester, settled the matter. Jessie agreed to sublet to Christabel her flat in Staple Inn, close to Clement's Inn. By mid-February, Christabel had moved in.[7]

However, before the move, Christabel engaged in a busy round of WSPU duties. On 22 January, she presided at the London Pavilion welcome home meeting for her mother. Although this was her mother's day, when the much-loved Emmeline Pankhurst spoke about the Prime Minister's 'gross betrayal' to women, Christabel said something too. Aware that many ILP branches were condemning the Government's plan for a Manhood Suffrage Bill and calling for an equal franchise for both men and women, she seized the opportunity to call upon the Labour Party to take up that fight.[8] An answer came sooner than expected when, at the Labour Party Conference held at Birmingham just four days later, a resolution was passed by a large majority calling for both adult men and women to be included in the Government's forthcoming reform bill.[9] Millicent Garrett Fawcett was so impressed by this move that she abandoned the NUWSS's non-party positioning and sought an electoral alliance with the Labour Party, offering suffragist support when Labour candidates stood in three-cornered elections. The new NUWSS strategy became known as the 'Election Fighting Fund'.[10] Christabel, however, was more circumspect. The demand for an equal franchise, she argued, should be backed by 'vigorous and uncompromising action . . . Labour Members of Parliament . . . form part of the Government's majority . . . and . . . having the power of making and unmaking the Government, are responsible for the Government's action'.[11] Nonetheless, holding such views did not stop her from sharing a platform with Keir Hardie at a demonstration in Glasgow on 31 January.[12]

A few days later, Christabel was feted again in Northern Ireland where she addressed the Belfast Women's Suffrage Society. Enthusiastic applause broke out when she seconded the motion calling upon the Government to abandon the Manhood Suffrage Bill and to introduce, in its stead, a measure giving equal voting rights to men and women. Laughter erupted when, at the beginning of her speech, Christabel noted that she did not think she need apologise in Ireland for the militant methods used by the suffragettes. Women's suffrage was now widely discussed in the press, and militant action had made women stronger. When the history of this period came to be written, Christabel predicted, 'the most important question would be the revolution on the part of women, whereby they set themselves free from the subjection of centuries, and . . . won their position as the equals and partners of men'.[13]

After her return to London, Christabel moved into the flat she had sublet from Jessie Stephenson. But she was not completely at ease with the situation. Jessie Kenney remembered that Christabel 'was unhappy, distressed, not herself at all, though she did not speak about it'.[14] The Lawrences had been piqued that she wanted to leave their home in Clement's Inn. How would the WSPU fare without the three of them working in close proximity? Christabel, ever the tactician, tried to calm their fears, pointing out that Scotland Yard had been watching WSPU headquarters in Clement's Inn for some time; under such circumstances, it was much better if the leaders lived at separate locations, in case any of them was arrested. Life continued much the same as usual, at least for about a month or so. On 13 February, Christabel attended the adult suffrage meeting held at the Albert Hall, under the auspices of the Labour Party, the ILP and the Fabian Society, her mother and Mabel Tuke sitting by her side.[15] The following day, during the course of the King's Speech, the Government announced that it would introduce a reform bill for men only. 'A strong militant protest on the part of women is the inevitable reply to this insulting and menacing proposal', thundered the weary Christabel. 'Women must now fight for their political lives . . . Self-reliance is our watchword.'[16]

Christabel, her mother and Emmeline Pethick-Lawrence met to discuss what direction the WSPU should take. For the last six years the suffragettes had fought and suffered for the women's cause, all with no success. The weapons of the WSPU were not forceful enough and a women's revolution was needed. All three leaders agreed that attacks on private as well as Government property were now necessary, despite the fact that such attacks and their incitement would inevitably court arrest. And all three agreed that if this threat loomed, Christabel, as the key strategist, should avoid arrest so she could lead the movement.[17] The task of outlining the new tactics fell not to Christabel but to Emmeline Pankhurst, the acknowledged figurehead of the WSPU.

On 16 February 1912, at a dinner to welcome the November stone-throwers on their release from prison, Emmeline Pankhurst drew up the lines of engagement for the next demonstration on 4 March, which she was going to lead. '[T]he argument of the stone, that time-honoured official political argument . . . that is the weapon and the argument that we are going to use', she calmly announced. With carefully chosen words, she explained why the new course of action was necessary:

Why should women go into Parliament Square and be battered about and be insulted, and, most important of all, produce less effect than when they use stones? We have tried it long enough . . . We should not have minded if that had succeeded, but that did not succeed, and we have made more progress with less hurt to ourselves by breaking glass than ever we made when we allowed them to break our bodies.

As her supporters cheered, Emmeline told her audience that those who joined her on the next protest would be attacking private property on a much larger scale than previously, although she insisted '[w]e only go as far as we are obliged to go in order to win'.[18]

Christabel and Mrs Lawrence expected Emmeline Pankhurst to be arrested for delivering such a speech, as did the speaker herself. But this was not so, despite the fact that the talk was widely covered in the press and universally condemned. Ironically, at the same time that Emmeline Pankhurst was speaking, a member of the Liberal Government, Charles Hobhouse, a Cabinet Minister, had been addressing an anti-suffrage meeting in Bristol, saying that in the case of votes for women there had not been the kind of popular uprising which accounted for the burning of Nottingham Castle in 1832, or the tearing up of Hyde Park railings in 1867, prior to the passing of reform bills in these two years. Hobhouse's pro- vocative speech infuriated the WSPU leaders.[19] As Emmeline Pethick-Lawrence observed, the holding up to women of the example of men's methods of winning the vote in 1832 and 1867 indicated that he took 'the very grave responsibility of inciting them to serious forms of violence in comparison with which Mrs. Pankhurst's exhortation is mildness itself'.[20] Christabel agreed, claiming that the 'sensational challenge to women by a responsible Minister of the Crown had a decisive effect on the future course of the woman suffrage movement'.[21]

On 20 February, Christabel sent another letter to Lloyd George, seeking clar- ification of his statement on 17 November the previous year that during the present parliamentary session, several million women would be granted the fran- chise. A reply came three days later, in Lloyd George's speech at the Albert Hall. Christabel was sitting in the audience as she heard him announce that any sug- gestion that the Government proposed not to introduce a reform bill, or if they did, not to persevere with it or to draft it in such a way as to give opportunity for a women's suffrage measure, was 'an imputation of deep dishonour, which I decline to discuss'.[22] While Millicent Fawcett expressed in the *Times* her gratitude to Lloyd George for his 'fine speech', Christabel was unimpressed by his evasive- ness. She wrote to the suffragettes, entreating those who had volunteered for the protest of 4 March to avoid arrest before then, otherwise the planned demonstra- tion could be less effective. The only hope now, she insisted, was 'our fight for a Government measure'.[23]

Meanwhile, the strain of suffrage work was taking its toll on Emmeline Pankhurst's health. With Christabel's blessing, her mother had retreated to recuperate at Coign, Ethel Smyth's country cottage at Hook Heath, near Woking in Surrey. A deep friendship had developed between Emmeline and Ethel so that Emmeline became a frequent visitor to Coign, a quiet sanctuary where she could talk over any anxieties and relax. On this particular occasion, when she wanted to be fit for the planned deputation on 4 March, there was a problem – she had never thrown a stone before and was worried she would miss her target. Ethel came to the rescue; she taught her guest the necessary skill.[24] However, Emmeline Pankhurst's willingness to engage in stone throwing was not shared by all rank-and-file members, as some of the district organisers informed Christabel. Jennie Baines complained that she had 'tramped for miles' but secured only two volunteers from Rossendale Valley. Lilias Mitchell, the organiser for Aberdeen, warned that not only was the fare to London too expensive for many members of her branch but that paying travelling expenses was not an option since there were 'one or two mischief making members who might make out that we are paying people to go'.[25]

When Emmeline Pankhurst returned to London she met up with Christabel, and the two decided on a change of plan about which Emmeline informed Ethel Smyth in a letter which was never posted but later found, when police raided Clement's Inn. 'C. and I have talked it over', Emmeline explained:

On Friday [1 March] there will be an unannounced affair, a sort of skirmish, in which some of our bad, bold ones will take part, an unadvertised affair. I shall take part, but not in the way I told you of – that is off.[26]

While suffragettes were busy handing out leaflets inviting the public to take part in the protest of 4 March, Christabel was writing her weekly editorial. The article appeared on 1 March and made no mention of any unannounced skirmish but did warn that the public might find they did not 'altogether escape the uncomfortable consequences of the warfare between women and the Government'.[27] Later that day, at half past five in the afternoon, the unannounced 'skirmish' began when Emmeline Pankhurst, Mabel Tuke and Kitty Marshall (the spouse of the WSPU solicitor) took a taxi to 10 Downing Street and broke two windows. During the following hour, small relays of well-dressed women, hammers hidden in their muffs, smashed plate-glass windows in fashionable shops and department stores in London's West End, causing about £5,000 worth of damage. Emmeline Pankhurst was among the one hundred and twenty-one arrested.[28]

The WSPU had forced its new tactics onto a public stage just as a strike by coal miners, for improved wages, was soon to be settled. That evening a defiant Christabel told a journalist that the miners were getting the legislation they wanted because they had made themselves a nuisance, a message that was a direct incitement to women to endeavour to obtain a similar privilege. 'We are persuaded that the Government will not do anything until they are forced. As they do not yield to the justice of our demand we have been practically forced into adopting these tactics.'[29] Yet again, press condemnation was universal, the *Manchester Guardian* echoing the general consensus when it described the stone-throwers as 'unbalanced women' and Christabel's words as 'really farcical'.[30] On Monday, 4 March, further unannounced window smashing in London's West End took place and another ninety-six women were arrested, including Ethel Smyth. However, a protest in Parliament Square, planned for the evening, was reduced to a series of isolated incidences because of a heavy police presence.[31] At an afternoon meeting at the London Pavilion that day, the spirited Emmeline Pethick-Lawrence had voiced her strong support for the new tactics, announcing that members of the Liberal Government had 'found out their mistake' when they thought that 'the women of this country were inured to political subjection . . . The worm has turned at last'.[32] Christabel went further:

> If it is necessary, we shall not hesitate to burn a palace, and in doing so we shall be but following in the footsteps of the wise men who have preceded us. If Friday's methods are not strong enough we will terrorise the whole lot of you . . . In a great issue like votes for women, money and property count for nothing.[33]

The Liberal Government decided to act. Shortly before ten o'clock on the evening of 5 March, the police swooped on WSPU headquarters with a warrant for the arrest of the Lawrences and Christabel – 'WANTED, for conspiracy, under the Malicious Damage to Property Act, Christabel Pankhurst, aged about twenty-six; height about 5ft. 6in; fresh complexion, eyes dark, hair dark brown; usually wears a green tailor-made costume and a large fashionable hat'. Also charged with conspiring to incite others to commit malicious damage to property were the already imprisoned Emmeline Pankhurst and Mabel Tuke. Despite an extensive search, the police only found the Lawrences at Clement's Inn. Christabel was in her top-floor flat, writing an editorial for *Votes for Women*.[34]

Absorbed in her work, she was startled by a knock at her door. Evelyn Sharp stood there, hurriedly sent by Fred Pethick-Lawrence to warn that the police had a warrant for her arrest and to ask for her countersignature to a cheque so that WSPU funds could be transferred to Hertha Ayrton's bank account. After Evelyn left, Christabel barricaded her locked door but then heard footsteps ascending. To her relief it was another WSPU member, with a note from Jessie Kenney, warning that the Lawrences had been arrested.[35] 'We had anticipated that such action on the part of the Government would be directed against the leaders of the movement', Christabel later told one journalist, 'and we had arranged, in the interests of the movement, that I was to stand aside and not be arrested if I could avoid it.'[36] Christabel hastily packed a small suitcase and, finding no police outside the door, got away by cab. She was unsure where to go and but then remembered that Nurses Townend and Pine, both suffragettes, had jokingly said to her one day that she could hide in their nursing home if ever she wanted to escape from the police. At eleven o'clock that evening, a pale-faced Christabel arrived at their nursing home in Pembridge Gardens, seeking shelter and some space to think out a plan of escape. As she sat drinking warm milk, Catherine

Pine arranged for the fugitive to spend the night in an unknown supporter's flat nearby while Gertrude Townend dressed her in a nurse's uniform. The WSPU leader's well-known broad-brimmed hat was thrown onto the fire.

At one o'clock in the morning, Christabel slipped out of the nursing home accompanied by Catherine Pine, observant of the instruction that, if stopped by the police, she was to say she had been summoned to attend a patient. Police were walking the streets, including some who were searching a house not far away, but the two reached their destination uninterrupted. Unable to sleep, Christabel remembered from her legal studies how a political offender could escape to a foreign country and not be liable to extradition. So she resolved to go to Paris and from there to 'control the movement . . . keep the fight going, until we won!'[37] France was a logical choice. Christabel and her mother had met Parisian suffragists on various visits and holidays, as well as welcomed them to WSPU demonstrations. *Votes for Women* often carried information about French suffrage journals and feminists such as Madeleine Pelletier, while *La Suffragiste* included in its columns notice about WSPU activities. Indeed, in 1908 when Mlle Laloë had stood unsuccessfully for election as a municipal councillor in Paris, she had been referred to as 'The French Miss Pankhurst'.[38]

Now that she had formulated a plan, Christabel could barely wait till the morning to tell her hosts. 'But first I had one vital thing to do', she recollected. 'That was to write to Annie Kenny telling her that if I failed to escape she was to take control of our policy until I should be set free.' The deep and unwavering friendship between Christabel and Annie was at the heart of Christabel's decision, a firm foundation which she knew would never be shaken. 'Annie was, by her strength of character, her singleness of purpose, her strong tuition, and her perfect loyalty marked out for command if my attempt to escape should fail.'[39] Such reliance upon her trusted friend was particularly important to Christabel since she feared that another suffragette wanted to take control of the WSPU and sign a compromise peace with the Government.[40]

On the morning of 6 March, the anxious Christabel took a cab to Victoria Station to catch the boat train, leaving behind with her hosts the note for Annie. Her disguise included a long grey coat and a little dark hat with the brim turned down. Tied around her waist was £100 in gold sovereigns. While her companion bought the tickets, Christabel purchased some large glossy women's fashion magazines. On board the crowded train, Christabel took a seat in the far corner of a compartment, screening her face with her reading material. The woman sitting opposite, who had been looking at her intently every now and again, suddenly shouted 'Policeman!' as they neared their destination. 'My heart stopped! But she merely asked a railway policeman to post a letter for her!'

Christabel and her companion entered the ladies' cabin on the boat but since the sea was rough, the worried companion was advised not to accompany the WSPU's Chief Organiser to France but to return to London and give Annie a letter, asking her to visit as soon as possible. Seasick throughout the journey,

Christabel was glad when she could finally put her feet on French soil. Using the name 'Mary Barton', she hastily sent a cable to her hostess of the night before containing a message for Clement's Inn. 'Arrived. Tell them that Mary will control our paper and all other business from Paris.' The train ride to Paris was of unutterable relief. 'Saved! . . . the Union and the cause . . . As the train rushed forward I wrote my first notes and instructions to those at home and posted them when I got to Paris.'[41] Christabel found a small, cheap hotel near the Arc de Triomphe and waited for Annie to arrive.

Meanwhile, back in Britain the worried Annie had received the hurried note Christabel had written before her flight:

> I have decided to escape. If I fail and the Government are able as they think to deprive the Union of all leadership, I give to you full charge of the policy of the Union. I do this because I trust your intuition as regards our policy and your determination and courage to act bravely and to be relentless and uncompromising where policy is concerned.

Nonetheless, Christabel warned Annie that leading the WSPU was not easy:

> You will be deluged with advice by people thinking themselves to be 'intellectuals' . . . but I trust to you with your simple and straight way of looking at things more than to those who may profess to know more of political life than you do, but have not got your special qualities.[42]

Annie kept the note close to her, reading it again and again. The strong intellectual set in the WSPU included the talented Evelyn Sharp, a novelist and rebel journalist, and close friend of Henry Nevinson.

Annie, as second in command, would try hard to make sure that activism rather than intellectualism reigned. But what she yearned for most was news of the whereabouts of Christabel. Where was she? What Annie did not know was that Christabel was communicating through an intermediary, Lady Sybil Smith's governess in Chigwell, Essex. Esther Knowles would collect the letters from her and then hand them to staff at Clement's Inn.[43] On 8 March, Christabel's long-awaited letter arrived:

> Beloved Annie
>
> The bearer of this note is a good friend of the Cause. She, with another friend, helped me to escape. She will tell you where I am and give you an address that will find me. Keep this a secret . . . Come quickly, and bring with you a member who understands the language of the country that I am sheltering in. Disguise yourself, and watch closely for Scotland Yard men. Let your friend do all the talking, as you are so well

273

known . . . Press on and give all our loyal ones my love and my faith that each one will obey orders that will be sent through you by me, and by unity we shall win through. Come to me at the first possible moment.

Christabel.[44]

Only a few close friends knew Christabel's address, including her mother and Ethel Smyth who had got word to the influential Princesse de Polignac, an important figure on the Parisian avant-garde musical scene, that Christabel might welcome some help in getting settled. This was particularly important since Christabel, unlike her mother, was not a fluent French speaker. Winnaretta Singer-Polignac, a widow, used her considerable fortune, derived from the sewing-machine empire of her father, Isaac Singer, to support the arts, sciences and letters, and especially music. Her salon was a gathering place for luminaries of French culture such as Proust, Cocteau, Monet, Diaghilev and Colette, but especially a venue where the new work of struggling composers might be performed. Winnaretta had many lovers, including the society hostess Olga de Meyer and the artist, Romaine Brooks. Ethel Smyth, who had first met her in 1903 and become infatuated with her, was one of several women composers she supported. And so it was a matter of course that Christabel met the American-born Winnaretta who had an interest in women suffrage, although her energies were directed more towards women's creative accomplishments than political causes.[45]

During her first few days in Paris the tense Christabel did a lot of walking as she tried to relax – and to think. Would the suffragettes in Britain be loyal to a leader 'over the water'? What were the logistics of leading a movement when you did not live in the country of your followers? On the Sunday after her escape to France, she walked through the Bois de Suresnes and, on the balcony of a little riverside restaurant, ate her solitary luncheon. That very day, Annie arrived in France disguised as a widow and accompanied by Miss James, a Bristol suffragette who spoke several languages. But when she called at Christabel's hotel she found her out. The exhausted Annie waited patiently and was deep in slumber by the time Christabel returned. The two friends talked for many hours before Christabel accompanied Annie to her own hotel where Miss James had secured rooms. The talking continued the following day, mainly 'very serious', wrote Christabel, 'but enlivened by our sense of the humour of the situation. How we laughed over the police advertisement for the fugitive! How we revelled in the Government's comical discomfiture'.[46]

When Christabel asked Annie whom she wished as her second in command, the immediate reply was Rachel Barrett, an old acquaintance. Rachel, a former teacher and district organiser, with an external degree from London University, was considered by Annie to be 'an exceptionally clever and highly educated woman . . . who reasoned out everything, and analysed every point, and drew her conclusions carefully and with extreme caution'. Further, she was 'a devoted worker' who had 'tremendous admiration for Christabel' and could, therefore, be expected to be loyal. Christabel was pleased with Annie's choice, but again warned her to be on her guard against those who might wish to undermine her.[47]

Christabel feared that astute members of Asquith's Cabinet, in the absence of recognised WSPU leaders, would approach those suffragettes they thought had influence in the movement and weaken their determination to continue the militant fight. Another worry was that the idea of an elected committee to determine policy, which had split the WSPU in 1907, would find favour again. Indeed, Christabel believed that '[d]esperate attempts' would be made 'to destroy Annie's influence' and 'to shake her loyalty to me'.[48] That prediction came true sooner than anticipated. When Annie arrived back at Clement's Inn, she found a takeover being planned:

> Had I delayed, I should have found a small Committee who were going to decide policy by separating the funds which were to be used for con- stitutional and for Militant work. A small sum only was to be set aside for Militancy.

Annie managed to persuade the enthusiastic group not to do anything until she had seen the leaders in prison and visited Paris once more, to put their ideas to Christabel. 'Needless to say, there was no Committee', she noted; 'we were still a revolutionary party.'[49]

The exhausted, strained Christabel needed to replenish her strength and energy. 'C[hristabel] told us of all your kindness and generosity, which thrills us', wrote a grateful Ethel Smyth to Winnaretta. 'You *are* a brick, and I think Mrs. P.'s greatest comfort is to know she has friends like you.'[50] But the busy cultural scene around the Princesse de Polignac's salon in Paris was not to Christabel's liking. She needed rest and anonymity to keep her whereabouts secret until she was completely assured she would not be extradited. Although she periodically returned to Paris – and from mid-September established her base there – during these early months in France she settled in a little hamlet near Boulogne on the northern coast, close to England. 'The bracing climate and complete change accomplished wonders', she told one reporter, 'for I had been working very, very hard, and when I stepped ashore in France I was on the verge of a nervous breakdown.'[51] Here, when the weather was fine and the sky unclouded, the lonely Christabel would sit on the cliffs and gaze across the English Channel to her native land.

Annie visited every weekend, reported to Christabel and returned to London on Sunday, fully briefed about policy and with Christabel's articles (unsigned for six months) for her weekly column in *Votes for Women*. Rough notes about policy were the only form of documentation that Annie could make at these meetings, in case of arrest, and the notes had to be cryptic so that only she or those in close touch with her could understand them. By the time Annie arrived back home, Christabel had sent a bulky letter, containing all the additional important mat- ters she had thought of after Annie had departed.[52]

This warm, deep friendship between Christabel and Annie, at the very heart of the WSPU's organisation, was not just critical to Christabel's leadership of the WSPU. It also boosted Annie's self-confidence, helping to sustain her political activism:

> Christabel's vitality was good for me. She was fresh, virile, energetic. I would arrive sick, tired to exhaustion, and yet on Sunday morning I felt refreshed and ready for the labour awaiting me. She has the most vital-izing personality that I had ever met . . . The Saturdays in Paris were a joy. We would walk along the river or go into the Bois, or visit the gardens . . . [with] stacks of newspapers, pockets stuffed with pencils, and always a knife to sharpen them . . . arm in arm, talking incessantly.[53]

When the Lawrences were arrested, they had asked Evelyn Sharp to take over the editorship of *Votes for Women*. This Evelyn did with a group of helpers, ini-tially including Henry Nevinson.[54] 'It was a thousand joys to get the paper – like rain on parched earth to a poor exile', wrote the delighted Christabel to Evelyn when *Votes for Women* arrived in mid-March. When the paper had appeared on 8 March 1912, immediately after her escape, there had been a number of blank spaces, including that reserved for her own article, because the printers had sup-pressed content considered inflammatory.[55] But there were no blank spaces in the copy Christabel had just received. 'This is of course a very anxious time for all of you at Clement's Inn', Christabel commented kindly. 'I hear how wonderful you all are. The Govt no doubt expected that panic & chaos & disorganisation of every kind wd reign supreme!' She informed the new editor that her articles for the next few weeks would focus on the parliamentary situation, particularly the Second Conciliation Bill, due to have its second reading on 28 March, and the Home Rule Bill. There would be plenty of focus on militancy in the news columns, Christabel pointed out, since the law did not forbid publication of trial proceedings and so the editorial staff should feel no alarm about this:

> I think that if the Govt propose to take any further repressive action we shall get some hint of it. I feel that the tide is turning in our favour now that we are getting out of the stormy atmosphere that is always created by new militant developments.

Nonetheless, Christabel warned, '[W]e ought to foresee the possibility that at some point <u>all</u> ordinary printers will refuse to do anything for us.' Under the worst scenario:

> the paper may have to be printed abroad under even worse difficul-ties . . . A slight change in the name of the paper is enough I fancy to enable us to get round . . . the authorities shd the paper be suppressed. We cd call it Votes <u>to</u> Women.[56]

276

However, despite her gratitude that *Votes for Women* was in such capable hands, Christabel had a niggling worry that it might become more literary than militant. And since Evelyn Sharp had a literary background, she had asked Annie to be responsible for everything that appeared in the paper. This was a somewhat daunting task for an ex-mill girl who was not highly educated and had no experience of newspaper work. But Annie, with her keen intuition, considered herself to be a competent censor, detecting 'an article or sentence, even a word' that might show a weakening of militant policy.[57]

Christabel read in the English papers that she bought in France the fervent speculation about her whereabouts. The Government were pondering the question too, the Foreign Office even receiving a telegram from the Consul General in New York suggesting that the WSPU leader was in that city. The suffragettes themselves, the vast majority of whom did not know where she was hiding either, made merriment out of the situation. They poked gentle fun at the police who, in their desperate efforts to locate the missing person, searched the homes of Christabel's friends (such as Elizabeth Robins) and tapped the telephones at Clement's Inn.[58] 'Miss Christabel Pankhurst . . . was sighted in America', teased *Votes for Women*, 'we think in Massachusetts, but it may have been Brazil . . . [or] the more homely locality of Margate.'[59]

At a packed WSPU rally held in the Albert Hall on 28 March, when a record £10,500 was raised, Annie opened proceedings by reading out a stirring message from the missing Christabel:

> My very heart and soul are with you at this great meeting of rejoicing . . . The Government have struck us a hard blow but we rise stronger and more triumphant than ever before . . . until a measure giving equal voting rights to women is actually on the Statute Book, we as self-respecting women cannot and will not be at peace with the Government.[60]

Loud cheers reverberated around the room. When they had died down, speaker after speaker continued the amusing speculation about the whereabouts of the absent one. '[A] leader with the power of making herself invisible to all her enemies and very present to all her friends – that spirit of air and fire called Christabel' had obviously been in Persia or China, announced the emboldened Elizabeth Robins. 'A great deal has happened in three weeks since Christabel Pankhurst rode away on a broomstick to the back of beyond', said a humorous Evelyn Sharp. A gallant Israel Zangwill, when enquiring the whereabouts of 'our departed Christabel', suggested, 'Gentlemen of the police, she is here – in our hearts.'[61]

Meanwhile, in France, Christabel was making friends with a range of influential people, including Monsieur Jean Finot, editor of *La Revue Mondiale*. But she was especially close to the well-connected Madame la Baronne de Brimont who was married to an army officer and a keen supporter of the WSPU. The Baronne de Brimont not only frequented the exclusive salons of such luminaries as Madame Henri-Germain, la Comtesse de Fitzjames, Edith Wharton and Natalie Barney, but also moved in elite political and social circles, both in Paris and London where the Asquiths were among her social contacts. She advised Christabel on many matters, occasionally acting as a WSPU courier on trips to England. When an attempt was made to persuade the French Government to extradite Christabel, it was the Baronne de Brimont's influence that made the application a failure. Because of the sensitive nature of her work, her name was always kept secret by Christabel and known only to her closest associates.[62]

Despite the presence of such a loyal friend in Paris, Christabel looked forward eagerly to visits from Annie and any other suffragettes who made the journey across the English Channel. On the morning of 28 March, the day the Second Conciliation Bill was to have its second reading, the *Times* published a long letter from Sir Almroth Wright, MD, a distinguished biologist, in which he claimed that the 'militant hysteria' of the suffragettes was a result of the physiological changes that accompanied menopause. Every doctor knew, he insisted, that 'the mind of woman' was affected by 'the change of life' and this was especially so among spinsters, which explained why there was so 'much mental disorder' in the women's movement. 'The recruiting field for the militant suffragists is the half million of our excess female population – that half million which had better long ago have gone out to mate with its complement of men beyond the sea.'[63]

Christabel was not the only person to condemn Almroth Wright's statement. Suffragists of every shade rallied to support the militants against such deeply misogynist views. Later that day, the Second Conciliation Bill failed to pass its second reading by fourteen votes. This did not surprise Christabel. Although a number of MPs claimed to have voted against the bill because of militant tactics, she believed it had been sunk in advance by party politics. Lloyd George's support for the alternative male suffrage measure meant the loss of many Liberal and Labour supporters, while forty-one Irish nationalists, despite a previous commitment to women's suffrage, now opposed the bill to avoid the possible resignation of Asquith at a time when they hoped to win independence for Ireland from British rule. A large numbers of Labour MPs, twenty-five out of a total of forty-two, were absent on the day, considering their various negotiations regarding industrial disputes as more important. But while the support of the Labour Party for the bill had been weak, it was the turnabout of the Irish MPs that had killed it off.[64] Christabel, with her intricate knowledge of parliamentary politics, was soon working on a WSPU manifesto which was published in the *Times* and *Standard* shortly after the bill was defeated. The WSPU had had private knowledge for 'many months past', she claimed, that the Irish nationalists had intended to wreck the Conciliation Bill in the interests of Home Rule:

> This knowledge was a prime cause of the refusal of the Women's Social and Political Union to trust any longer to the Conciliation Bill or any other private member's proposal . . . The only way . . . is to secure a

Government measure for women's suffrage. The Nationalists will, of course, vote for this in order to prevent the defeat of the Government and the consequent loss of Home Rule.[65]

Annie had vowed to Christabel that she would 'never colour any event' when describing it to her, 'but stick to unadulterated facts'.[66] The news about the health of Emmeline Pankhurst, a convicted offender serving a two-month sentence for stone throwing and also a prisoner on remand, waiting to be charged with the more serious offence of conspiracy, was not good and soon to be the subject of a long letter by Ethel Smyth to the *Times*, as well as a WSPU pamphlet.[67] Christabel knew that her mother was going through the menopause and suffering from many of its unpleasant hormonal changes, but she was distressed to hear that she had developed bronchitis in her damp prison cell. It was a relief when she heard that her mother and the Lawrences were released on bail on Maundy Thursday, 4 April, and Mabel Tuke acquitted.

The date for the conspiracy trial, to be held at the Central Criminal Court, the Old Bailey, was set for 24 April. Although Emmeline Pankhurst was too ill to travel to France, Christabel was often in her thoughts as in mid-April when, en route to the Lawrences' country retreat, she penned a letter to the frail Constance Lytton:

I go to Holmwood this afternoon for the week end & am looking forward to long talks with my co-conspirators. Much as I should wish the absent one to be there also I am glad that she is free to direct the ship even from a distance as she is doing in 'V for W'. What a fine article hers is this week.[68]

Similar sentiments were expressed a few days later in a warm letter to Mrs Billinghurst who had kindly sent a cheque towards the cost of the conspiracy trial. 'Whatever happens to us', wrote the proud Emmeline, 'we "conspirators" know that the movement will go on & that our splendid members will be loyal to my daughter[,] Annie Kenney & Mrs Tuke who will guide the ship in our absence.'[69] Again, at a reception for the 'conspirators' before their trial, Emmeline Pankhurst asked her followers to remain steadfast and not to listen to advice from friends outside the movement – which Nevinson considered a veiled reference to Brailsford. Without naming Christabel or Annie, Emmeline said firmly:

Read the paper [*Votes for Women*]. Take your political instructions from the leading articles. Consult those who remain at Clement's Inn to be consulted with regard to policy and with regard to work, and if you do that, whatever they do to us will not matter one jot.

Someone in the audience called out 'Christabel!' There was great and prolonged applause. When the noise had died down, Emmeline said in an emotional voice,

'Christabel sends you her love!' The applause became louder, then subsided as someone shouted out, 'We all send our love to Christabel.'[70]

This absolute faith that Emmeline Pankhurst had in Christabel's political flair never wavered, and was the foundation stone of their joint leadership of the WSPU. As noted earlier, Emmeline had often told Sylvia that 'Christabel is not like other women; not like you and me; she will never be led away by her affections!'[71] And that was a trait in her character that Christabel herself recognised, that she could be 'hard-headed' whereas her mother would be guided by emotion and feeling:

> I could not depend on any of the others to stay abroad through thick and thin. Least of all could I depend upon Mother to do it! I knew her ardent spirit too well. I knew that if I were to return to England and she were to stay in Paris, and if I were to find myself in prison, as I certainly should, Mother would soon be back in London and we should meet in Holloway, both prisoners, and both disabled for command.[72]

But Christabel's assessment of her own abilities did not find favour with Sylvia. In particular, her frequent claim that she and her mother were in such close harmony that they were like two sides of the same coin grated with the middle Pankhurst daughter. The old rivalry between the two sisters was about to erupt again.

Sylvia had returned on 8 April from her lecturing tour in the USA to find suffragettes being mobbed in London streets while WSPU meetings were thronged. She had heard about the mass window smashing with dismay, as did the American suffragists she met. In *The suffragette movement*, she writes how this was a critical moment in her life; she decided that she would devote her energies to winning the vote, rather than undertake any other artistic project since other people's prejudices would always overshadow her attempts to secure commissions. And in a veiled yet barbed reference to Christabel, she wrote, 'I neither could nor would now withdraw to another country.'[73] No acknowledgement was made to the fact that it was Christabel and not Sylvia herself who was charged with conspiracy.

Sylvia assessed the new situation – Christabel in France and their mother and Mrs Lawrence likely to be given long prison sentences – and saw it as her chance to take her eldest sister's place. As a socialist and supporter of the Labour Party, she wanted to bring the WSPU back to its socialist links and to encourage the working class to join in the suffrage struggle. That Christabel and their mother had tried on a number of occasions to mobilise public support for the women's cause, Sylvia conveniently ignored. That the WSPU did attract a large number of socialist and working-class women, she did not acknowledge. Sylvia was particularly happy that a women's suffrage resolution had been passed by the Labour Party at its annual conference earlier in the year but was disappointed that it was the leadership of the NUWSS, not of the WSPU, that engaged in an electoral alliance with the left. But the person who had acted as mediator in the negotiations for the NUWSS to support Labour candidates in three-cornered elections was none other than Henry Brailsford, long regarded with suspicion by Christabel and her mother.[74]

Sylvia resolved to visit Christabel (now known as 'Miss Amy Richards') in France. She called on Catherine Pine and was told, in great secrecy, her sister's Paris address. Dressed in a nurse's uniform, Sylvia crossed the Channel. There is only one account of her meeting with Christabel, in her book *The suffragette movement*, written some twenty years after the event. Sylvia claims that she found Christabel:

> entirely serene, enjoying the exciting crisis of the W.S.P.U. and her life in Paris, the shops and the Bois. After the strenuous office routine of Clement's Inn – correspondence, meetings, interviews – Paris meant relaxation. Her articles dashed off at great speed, she was ready for sight-seeing, for which I had no heart, keyed as I was for the struggle, and awed by the suffering for so many in imprisonment and loss of health, friends, employment.

Sylvia asked Christabel what she might do to help. 'When those who are doing the work are arrested, you may be needed, and can be called on', was the reply. Since their mother was facing a conspiracy charge, Sylvia considered the answer ludicrous. When she pressed further on the matter, Christabel suggested, 'Well, just speak at a few meetings.' The crushed Sylvia realised she was not wanted in the WSPU leadership. Christabel was 'so absolutely convinced that her own policy was the only correct one', wrote the disappointed sister, 'so intensely jealous for it, that instinctively she thrust aside whoever might differ from her tactics by a hair's breadth . . . it was clearly evident to me that I too might become superfluous in her eyes'. Since no particular service was asked of her, Sylvia felt free to go her own way. But the younger sister said nothing to Christabel about this and offered no argument. 'I made no comment. I had always been scrupulous neither to criticize nor oppose her, to show no open divergence of opinion in relation to the movement.' Christabel then insisted, Sylvia claimed, that the two of them should go to an art gallery. Sylvia suggested the Pantheon. 'From thence I accompanied her to a favourite little shop, where she purchased a dress, and I yielded to her pressure to do the same. Then I left by the night boat, unable to endure another day.'[75]

Even allowing for the sisterly rivalry that had existed for some years between Sylvia and Christabel, the account that Sylvia has written about this encounter does not ring entirely true. Christabel is not only presented as autocratic, which she was, but as a frivolous rather than serious-minded person, someone more interested in buying clothes than the fate of suffragettes in England. No consideration is given to the possibility that Christabel may have been trying to lighten Sylvia's worries by taking her to an art exhibition or a shop. For Sylvia, Christabel was still the selfish, ruthless older sister who made decisions for her own advantage, knowing that she was their mother's favourite. But other accounts offer a differing story.

Geraldine Lennox, who worked in the editorial department at WSPU head-quarters from 1909 until 1913, first as a clerk and later in a more important position, claimed:

> [I]t was the wish of all that she [Christabel] should go free, for on her depended everything. Prison was faced cheerfully, knowing that she was 'outside' to carry on. And she never let us down. She was the balanced, clear-sighted brain of the Movement.[76]

Such positive views about Christabel's time in France have become lost in time as Sylvia's autobiographical narrative in *The suffragette movement* became the dominant reading of events.

What is clear is that Sylvia had misread the situation about her own importance to the WSPU in this time of crisis. Contrary to the impression that she gives in *The suffragette movement*, she was not at the centre of power. She had never held an official position, nor was she regarded as an effective speaker. Her major talents lie in artistic work and in writing, and in these respects she made an important contribution to the suffrage movement. But, above all, the socialist Sylvia saw the women's suffrage struggle in class terms and wanted to ally the WSPU to the Labour Party rather than maintain its political independence. Emmeline and especially Christabel, on the other hand, were convinced that male Labour MPs could not be trusted, evident in their weak support for the Second Conciliation Bill. And both now knew that Sylvia was having an affair with a Labour MP, their old family friend, Keir Hardie. Consequently, it was not to Sylvia but Annie Kenney that Christabel had turned in this leadership crisis. Unlike Sylvia, Annie had 'no personal ties that would impose upon her a divided loyalty'.[77] However, the snub to Sylvia only served to increase further the gulf between her and Christabel and their mother.

Emmeline Pankhurst, who stood staunchly behind Christabel on this matter, was soon to conduct her own defence at the forthcoming trial. Yet she was still not well and anxious about how effectively she could prepare her case, due to begin on 24 April. Fortunately, her third application for postponement of the trial was successful.[78] The Old Bailey conspiracy trial, opening on 15 May and covering six days, received widespread publicity in the press. Sir Rufus Issacs, the Attorney-General, presenting the case for the prosecution, told the jury that although there were only three persons in the dock they would hear much about 'Miss Christabel Pankhurst', who had not surrendered yet was included in the indictment since she was 'a prominent person taking a very active part in this conspiracy'. Indeed, during the proceedings, sections from Christabel's speeches and articles were read out, including:

> They say we are going to get heavy sentences. All I can say is, we might as well be hung for a sheep as a lamb. Let them give us seven years' penal servitude . . . We shall do our bit, even if it is burning down a palace.[79]

Fred Pethick-Lawrence, at this Old Bailey trial, valiantly defended Christabel's advocacy of militant methods, pointing out that militancy had only been adopted because of the 'trickery and chicanery' of politicians. But his precise, blunt and orderly address was no match for the passionate defence offered during the closing days of the trial by the great orator Emmeline Pankhurst. 'I will try to make you understand what it is that has brought a woman no longer young [she was fifty-three years old] into this dock', she began poignantly. As Emmeline told her life story, explaining how she wanted political reform to help those wretched women and children less fortunate than herself, she praised the absent Christabel, ever close to her heart:

> [T]here is another defendant, who is not here to-day, and I want to say . . . that perhaps, if I had not had that daughter who is not here today, I might never have found the courage to take the decision which I took in the course of the years 1903, 1904, and 1905.

Keen to stress how Christabel had spurred her into action, and acutely aware of mounting criticisms about her beloved daughter's escape to a foreign country, the mother went further to defend the absent leader. Emmeline Pankhurst told the court about the time in 1906 when she had been hesitant, because of the financial implications, of moving to London and expanding their work. Christabel had said:

> 'Never mind, Mother, go on, and the money will come' . . . when I heard that from that girl – who is not in the dock to-day, not because of any lack of courage, not because of any unwillingness to share our position, but because she has a sense of public duty . . . I felt inspired with the courage to go on.[80]

In summing up her case, Emmeline claimed it was not the defendants who had conspired but the Government which had conspired against the defendants, to crush their just war. Yet, despite the power and poignancy of Emmeline's oration, the all-male jury found the defendants guilty, although they also recommended that 'the utmost clemency and leniency' be shown, in view of the 'pure motives' of the suffrage agitation. The judge ignored such pleading, pronouncing the heavy sentence of nine months in the Second Division with Emmeline Pankhurst and Fred Pethick-Lawrence being ordered to pay the prosecution costs.[81] In her unsigned article in Votes for Women a defiant Christabel claimed that the three sent to prison should be placed beside those great people in history 'who, by defying laws and Governments, have carved out the liberties of the British people'.[82]

Soon Emmeline Pankhurst and Emmeline Pethick-Lawrence were back in Holloway while Fred was sent to Brixton. All three protested again to be treated as political prisoners and placed in the First Division, a request that was supported by memorials to Asquith and Reginald McKenna, the new Home Secretary, from a wide cross-section of British society – including Oxford dons, various branches of the ILP and the NUWSS, the Union of Ethical Societies and the Church Socialists. Protest meetings in support of the WSPU leaders were held in many towns and cities. Keir Hardie asked questions in the Commons while Asquith received petitions signed by a number of international figures, including Madame Curie, Prince Kropotkin, Upton Sinclair, Ellen Key, Olive Schreiner, Walter Bruno, the conductor at the Opera House in Vienna, and M. Jean Jaures, a member of the Chamber of Deputies in Paris.[83] Trying to find a way out of the dilemma, the Home Secretary asked to see Esther Knowles, telling her that he needed written confirmation that the defendants would not directly or indirectly indulge in any militancy while in prison.

Esther promised to give him an answer, as quickly as possible, before he was due to speak in the Commons on Monday, 10 June, at three o'clock. The Saturday before she travelled to Boulogne and met Christabel, who had journeyed there from Paris. Next day Christabel gave Esther a written form of undertaking which the defendants might sign. Once back in England on that fateful Monday, Esther hastened to Holloway and then Brixton, all three defendants signing the document. She then handed in the document to the Home Office before making her way to the House of Commons. McKenna read out the undertaking to his fellow MPs. 'It would not be without a sense of humour', remembered Esther, 'that a document . . . prepared by a fugitive criminal in exile for whom there was a hue & cry, should be openly and unconsciously read out in the High Court of Parliament by one of His Majesty's Ministers.'[84]

Emmeline Pankhurst and the Lawrences were duly placed in the First Division. However, when it was learnt that the other seventy-eight rank-and-file prisoners in Holloway, Winson Green, Aylesbury and Maidstone had not been granted political offender status, it was decided that all WSPU prisoners, including the leaders, would hunger strike. On 19 June, the protest began. Two days later, when forcible feeding was due to begin, Sylvia and Adela tried unsuccessfully to visit their mother. The anxious Adela, who had decided to train as a gardener, had hoped that she could use the money her mother had carefully saved from her last American tour to finalise the payment of her £200 enrolment fee at Studley Agricultural College in Worcestershire.[85] But the financial transaction had to wait until a more convenient time. Emmeline Pankhurst, weakened by her hunger strike, was lying in her bed when she heard screams from Mrs Lawrence, in the cell next to hers, as she struggled against being forcibly fed. When the doctors stood on the threshold of her own cell door, Emmeline Pankhurst's indomitable spirit triumphed over her physical frailty as she found the strength to grab a heavy earthenware jug from a nearby table and threaten to defend herself. The intruders retreated.[86] The prison authorities would never again attempt to forcibly feed Emmeline Pankhurst or Mrs Lawrence. Both women, as well as Fred Pethick-Lawrence who had been forcibly fed five times, were released on 24 June. The ill Emmeline Pankhurst stayed only a short time at Clement's Inn before retreating to a quiet place in the country. Needing complete rest, she sent out a letter announcing that until her health was completely restored, she would take no further part in suffrage work or accept responsibility for the agitation as conducted by others.[87]

The day after the release of the leaders, the impassioned George Lansbury, an ardent pacifist Christian and supporter of women's suffrage, strode up the floor of the House of Commons and pointing a finger at Asquith, shouted angrily, 'You will go down in history as the man who tortured innocent women.' Nor was Lansbury impressed with his fellow MPs. 'I tell you the Commons of England, you ought to be ashamed of yourselves.' After the Speaker had called on him three times to withdraw, Lansbury eventually walked out of the Chamber.[88] The historic scene was widely reported in the press and praised by the WSPU, Annie immediately writing to Lansbury:

> Thank God we have one man in the House of Commons who feels the sufferings of the Women who are being Tortured in Prison and is not afraid to bring a bit of real humanity in that dead alive place. Will you speak at the Pavilion meeting next Monday.[89]

The worried Christabel was relieved when her mother, travelling under the name of 'Mrs Richards', felt well enough to visit her. This was the first of many trips to France where Emmeline would discuss militant policy with her daughter, seek rest and take various cures for her poor health. 'Mother could relax; she revived her schoolday memories, explored Paris, looked at the shops. It was a happy interlude for both of us', recollected Christabel, 'in which, for a brief moment, we could prepare for the hard fight yet to come.'[90] Annie and Mabel Tuke, the Joint Honorary Secretary of the WSPU, also visited regularly.

Notes

1 *VfW*, 12 January 1912, p. 239.
2 EPL to Miss Dugdale, 11 January 1912, Purvis Collection'; *VfW*, 19 January 1912, p. 255.
3 *VfW*, 19 January 1912, p. 255.
4 Entry for 13 January 1912, Nevinson Diaries.
5 *VfW*, 26 January 1912, p. 264; ESP, *Emmeline Pankhurst*, p. 103.
6 Sylvia claims that Christabel told her that Lloyd George had asked to see Fred 'but that it would never do, she confided to me: "Mr. Lawrence could never stand up against Lloyd George!" Indeed it was clear she did not believe anyone in the world, save herself, could be trusted to negotiate with the "Welsh Wizard" ', ESP, *TSM*, p. 361.
7 Interviews with Jessie Kenney, 31 July 1964 and 2 July 1965, DMC; entry for 15 February 1912, Nevinson Diaries.
8 *VfW*, 26 January 1912 and 22 December 1911, pp. 262 and 189, respectively.
9 *VfW*, 2 February 1912, p. 274.
10 Holton, *Suffrage days*, pp. 176–7.
11 *VfW*, 26 January 1912, p. 266.
12 *Manchester Guardian*, 1 February 1912.
13 *VfW*, 9 February 1912, p. 289.
14 Interviews with Jessie Kenney, 31 July and 2 July 1965, DMC.

15 Entry for 13 February 1912, Nevinson Diaries.
16 *VfW*, 16 February 1913, p. 308.
17 How I escaped. Miss C. Pankhurst's dramatic story, *Daily Chronicle*, 13 September 1912.
18 Mrs Pankhurst, The argument of the broken pane, *VFW*, 23 February 1912, p. 319.
19 ESP, *TSM*, p. 373.
20 EPL, Inciting to violence, *VfW*, 23 February 1912, p. 325.
21 CP, *Unshackled*, p. 198.
22 Copy of letter from CP to Lloyd George, 20 February 1912, TWL; *VfW*, 1 March 1912, p. 336.
23 Draft of letter from Millicent Fawcett to Lloyd George, 24 February 1912, TWL; CP to Dear Friend, 24 February 1912, SFC.
24 Smyth, *Female pipings*, pp. 208–9.
25 Jennie Baines to CP, n.d. [February 1912] and Lilias Mitchell to CP, 16 February 1912, The National Archives (hereafter TNA), DPP 1/19, Exhibit 137 and 141, respectively.
26 Quoted in prosecution evidence presented 14 March 1912, *VfW*, 22 March 1912, p. 389.
27 *VfW*, 1 March 1912, pp. 340–1.
28 *Times*, 2 March 1912.
29 *Daily Telegraph*, 2 March 1912.
30 *Manchester Guardian*, 2 March 1912.
31 *Times*, 5 March 1912.
32 Quoted *VFW*, 22 March 1912, p. 389.
33 *Daily Chronicle*, 5 March 1912.
34 *VfW*, 8 March 1912, p. 359; CP, *Unshackled*, p. 202.
35 CP, My escape to Paris, *Weekly Dispatch*, 8 May 1921; CP, *Unshackled*, pp. 203–4; Sharp, *Hertha Ayrton*, pp. 234–5. There are some inconsistencies about this particular event in the various accounts.
36 How I escaped arrest. Miss C. Pankhurst's dramatic story, *Daily Chronicle*, 13 September 1912.
37 CP, My escape to Paris; CP, *Unshackled*, p. 204.
38 *VfW*, 14 May 1908, p. 161; see also 7 May 1908, p. 155; 23 July 1908, p. 327.
39 CP, My escape to Paris.
40 CP to ESP, 3 August 1957, cited in R. Pankhurst, Suffragette sisters in old age, p. 501.
41 CP, My escape to Paris.
42 CP, My escape to Paris.
43 Reminiscences of Esther Knowles, n.d., Craigie Collection.
44 Kenney, *Memories*, pp. 174–5.
45 See M. de Cossart, *The food of love: Princesse Edmond de Polignac (1865–1943) and her salon* (London, Hamish Hamilton, 1978), p. 109; S. Kahan, *Music's modern muse: a life of Winnaretta Singer, Princesse de Polignac* (Woodbridge, Boydell and Brewer, 2003), p. 172.
46 CP, My escape to Paris. Christabel's recollection of this meeting is slightly different to Annie's in *Memories*, pp. 176–7.
47 Kenney, *Memories*, p. 179; CP, My escape to Paris.
48 CP, My escape to Paris.
49 Kenney, *Memories*, pp. 176–7.
50 Ethel Smyth to Winnaretta Singer-Polignac, 13 April 1912, quoted in Kahan, *Music's modern muse*, p. 173.
51 How I escaped arrest, *Daily Chronicle*, 13 September 1912.
52 Kenney, *Memories*, pp. 182–3.
53 Kenney, *Memories*, pp. 183–4.
54 Nevinson was called to help with the paper on 6 March 1912. On 30 March 1912 he notes 'Agreed I was not wanted more on paper at present as a regular thing', Nevinson Diaries.
55 *VfW*, 8 March 1912, p. 351.

56 CP to Miss Sharp, n.d. [March 1912], Evelyn Sharp Nevinson Papers.
57 Kenney, *Memories*, p. 180.
58 TNA, FO 373/405, 92124, note dated 20 March 1912; *VfW*, 22 March 1912, p. 386.
59 *VfW*, 29 March 1912, p. 402.
60 *VfW*, 5 April 1912, p. 424.
61 *VfW*, 5 April and 13 September 1912, pp. 424–5 and p. 797, respectively; *Times*, *Standard* and *Daily News*, 29 March 1912.
62 Jessie Kenny to David Mitchell, 19 January 1965, DMC; autobiographical notes, Baronne Renee de Brimont Papers, Bibliotheque Marguerite Duran, Paris.
63 *Times*, 28 March 1912.
64 Rosen, *Rise up women!*, pp. 160–1; ESP, TSM, pp. 380–1.
65 *Times* and *Standard*, 1 April 1912.
66 Kenney, *Memories*, p. 183.
67 E. Smyth letter to editor, *Times*, 19 April 1912; WSPU pamphlet, Mrs Pankhurst's treatment in prison, statement by Dr Ethel Smyth (London, WSPU, n.d.).
68 EP to Lady Constance, 12 April 1912, TWL.
69 EP to Mrs Billinghurst, 18 April 1912, ESPA.
70 *VfW*, 26 April 1912, p. 469; entry for 20 April 1912, Nevinson Diaries.
71 ESP, *Emmeline Pankhurst*, p. 47.
72 CP, *Unshackled*, p. 217.
73 ESP, TSM, pp. 382–3.
74 Purvis, *Emmeline Pankhurst*, p. 184; Holton, *Suffrage days*, pp. 176–7.
75 ESP, TSM, p. 383–4.
76 G. Lennox, letter to editor, *Everyman*, 5 March 1911, p. 186.
77 CP, *Unshackled*, p. 208.
78 Purvis, *Emmeline Pankhurst*, p. 186.
79 *VfW*, 17 May and 24 May 1912, pp. 517 and 514, respectively.
80 *Suffrage speeches from the dock: conspiracy trial, Old Bailey, May 15th–22nd, 1912* (London, Woman's Press), pp. 9, 33–4.
81 *Standard*, 23 May 1912.
82 *VfW*, 24 May 1912, p. 540.
83 *VfW*, 24 May, 7 and 14 June 1912, pp. 535, 580 and 596–7, respectively.
84 Reminiscences of Esther Knowles.
85 TNA, PCOM 8/175, minutes dated 21 June 1912; APW, My mother, p. 39.
86 EP, *My own story*, pp. 251–2; *VfW*, 5 June 1912, p. 648.
87 *Standard*, 25 June 1912; *Daily Chronicle*, 27 June 1912.
88 *VfW*, 28 June 1912, p. 633; *Globe*, 25 June 1912.
89 A. Kenney to Mr Lansbury, n.d. [25 June 1912], George Lansbury Papers, British Library of Political and Economic Science, London School of Economics (hereafter Lansbury Papers).
90 CP, *Unshackled*, p. 217.

14

BREAK WITH THE LAWRENCES
July 1912–end of December 1912

In early July, Christabel and her mother moved to Boulogne, partly to escape the hot Paris summer and partly because it was easier for visitors from London. They stayed at the Hotel de Paris. On 10 July the Lawrences, still rather weak from their prison ordeal, came for a few days, on their way to spend a fortnight in Switzerland. Prior to their arrival, Christabel and her mother had assessed the future direction of the WSPU. With the imprisonment of the leaders, and now their necessary period of recuperation, the organisation was faltering. Although the loyal Annie was aided by a band of gifted helpers, her personal leadership was not strong enough to challenge powerful intellectual women, such as Evelyn Sharp, who were beginning to take control of WSPU affairs. The office staff at Clement's Inn, receiving conflicting directions from Annie and Evelyn, became slack so that the organisation in the various districts drifted too.[1] Emmeline Pankhurst suggested Grace Roe as the ideal person to help the struggling Annie. Grace, who had been a district organiser, with Helen Craggs, had worked with Emmeline during the December 1911 general election and had displayed not only sound organisational skills but also strong leadership potential. From now on, at Christabel's instigation, Grace trained as Annie's understudy.[2]

Christabel and her mother decided that the WSPU had to widen the secret attacks on public and private property, as a way to force the Government to concede, just like men had done in the past to win their own enfranchisement. Emmeline Pankhurst wrote to the Lawrences, asking them to break their journey to Switzerland at Boulogne, so that the future direction of WSPU policy could be discussed. Neither Emmeline nor Christabel recorded details of this meeting, although both the Lawrences did, many years later.

According to Fred, a discussion took place while the four of them were walking along the cliffs that lie between Boulogne and Wimereux. He and Christabel, a little apart from the two Emmelines, soon discovered that they held strongly opposing views. Although Fred admired what he termed Christabel's 'political genius', he was never averse to telling her exacting what he thought, and did so now, saying that the suggestions for future policy were totally misguided and based on 'second-hand' impressions that did not accord with the facts. The recent window-smashing raid had aroused a new popular opposition because it was an attack on private property. If graver acts of violence were to be committed, there had to be 'a sustained education campaign' to explain to the public the reasons for such extreme action. Fred also took it for granted that Christabel would return to London and resume her leadership of the campaign there. This would place the Government in the awkward predicament of having to choose between repeating the conspiracy trial in her case or declining the challenge to do so. Whichever course she adopted, Fred insisted, it would 'enhance her position and that of the W.S.P.U.'. Christabel strongly disagreed, arguing out that any opposition that might arise to the new policy was not different to that which, over and over again, had appeared when other new forms of militancy had been introduced. The best way to overcome this opposition was to repeat and intensify the attack in the early autumn. She also suggested that since the new policy was 'revolution-ary', it was necessary for her to remain outside the reach of Government so that she could continue to 'direct it'.[3]

The two Emmelines, seated a short distance away, hearing the heated dis-cussion, came and joined in. Mrs Lawrence considered the new policy sheer madness. In her memoir, she blamed Emmeline Pankhurst for the proposed 'civil war', claiming that excitement, drama and danger were the conditions in which Mrs Pankhurst's temperament flourished:

> While Christabel lived with us she agreed that we had to advance in militancy by slow degrees in order to give the average person time to understand every move and to keep pace. But since her escape to Paris, Christabel had gone completely over to her mother's standpoint.

Fred too, in his autobiography, takes a similar stand:

> Mrs. Pankhurst, as a born rebel, was even more empathic than Christabel that the time had come to take sterner measures. She appeared to resent that fact that I had even ventured to question the wisdom of her daughter's policy.

Next morning, 'after a friendly talk with Christabel', the Lawrences departed for Switzerland.[4]

Shortly after the Boulogne meeting, without the knowledge of Christabel or her mother, the first serious arson attempt was undertaken by Helen Craggs, Harry Pankhurst's first love. On 13 July, in the early hours of the morning, she was one of two women apprehended at the country residence near Oxford of Lewis Harcourt, one of the Government's leading 'Antis'. In the basket and satchel she had been carrying was found not only incendiary material but also a note addressed to 'Sir' in which she explained, 'When Cabinet Ministers tell us that violence is the only argument they understand, it becomes our duty to give them that argument. Therefore I have done my duty.'[5] Later, in a speech made to the WSPU, Emmeline Pankhurst announced that Helen Craggs (who had been sentenced to nine months' hard labour) had acted 'solely on her own responsibility'.[6] A few days after Helen had tried to fire Nuneham House, Sylvia Pankhurst claimed that a message came from Christabel, asking her to burn down Nottingham Castle (which angry male mobs had set alight in 1831, after the House of Lords had rejected a Reform Bill which would extend the parliamentary franchise to certain categories of men).[7] Whether the story is true or not, we do not know. However, what is clear from other sources is that firing buildings was not a coherent WSPU strategy at this time. When fires were started, the WSPU leadership did not know in advance.[8]

On 18 July, for example, Mary Leigh and Dorothy Evans travelled to Dublin to make a protest against the proposed Home Rule Bill which made no provision for women; they set fire to the curtains of a theatre box at the Theatre Royal where the Prime Minister had just seen a performance. Later, as Asquith drove to his hotel with the Irish leader, John Redmond, Mary Leigh dropped a hatchet into their carriage. The two women were subsequently sentenced to five years in prison but after prolonged hunger strikes and forcible feeding, served but sixteen weeks.[9] Christabel had no prior knowledge about the specific protests these two women would undertake but later noted that:

> Mother and I were determined to stand by them . . . They would respect life and hurt no one unless it were themselves . . . It was a rule we had laid down that none of our women had broken, and none of them ever did.[10]

When Mary Leigh was released in September 1912, Christabel praised her courage, rallying the WSPU membership by saying that 'spiritual force has once again triumphed over physical force . . . As women cannot be governed by the feeding-tube, they must be governed with and through their consent'.[11] But one suffragette to whom this rhetoric did not appeal was Christabel's youngest sister, Adela.

While the middle Pankhurst daughter, Sylvia, was taking an ever-expanding role in the WSPU, including organising the campaign in the August by-election in North West Manchester, Adela had decided to retire from suffrage politics. With the blessing of Christabel and their mother, the desperately unhappy Adela, worn out and weary but not defeated, made her participation in this by-election her swansong. She doubted the effectiveness of militant tactics and, like Sylvia, was a committed socialist who disliked the feminist politics of her mother and eldest sister.[12]

A few weeks before, Christabel had received a letter from Harriet Kerr, manager of the WSPU London office, saying that Mabel Tuke ('Pansy') was suffering with nervous exhaustion and had been admitted to Catherine Pine's nursing home. That very same day, a letter arrived from the patient herself. The gentle and kind Mabel, particularly close to Christabel and Emmeline Pankhurst and a member of their inner circle, had never had a robust constitution. Although after her release in April she had made a few trips to Paris, such happy interludes had not halted the deterioration of her health. The worried Christabel, using her pseudonym 'S.A.L.', immediately wrote a warm and affectionate reply to 'My dear & darling Pansy':

> You have just overdone your dear and precious self . . . It is time for us to take care of you now and more than time. I am glad that at any rate you are in the haven of a Pembridge Garden . . . I hope darling that you will have nice books and everything that can make you feel content & comfortable & that you will not think a worrying thought or do a stroke of work until you are perfectly well again . . . A little course of Paris when you are well enough to come wd do you a great deal of good. The food agrees with you so well and a little time with your own S.A.L. wd not be injurious perhaps. We cd look at shops but talk none.
>
> My own brave and dear, take care of yourself because you are very precious to us.[13]

The bonds of love, loyalty and friendship between Christabel, Mabel Tuke, Annie Kenney and other suffragettes were an integral part of their feminist politics and a key force in enabling Christabel to function as a WSPU leader living abroad. Like Emmeline Pankhurst, Mabel and Annie had undoubting confidence in Christabel's ability to lead the suffragette movement to a successful conclusion, and Christabel, for her part, had undoubting faith in her devoted friends. As Annie affectionately observed, Christabel was:

> the idol, the loved and honoured one, who gained their hearts as well as their heads . . . a big person with big ideas who had . . . implicit trust in the wisdom and courage, of those who followed her . . . she was the woman of the age . . . she alone could lead us to the land of political freedom.[14]

That Christabel was the object of such inspiration says much about her own personal qualities, including her gift for warm friendship. Jessie Kenney always insisted that Christabel was 'much warmer and more loyal' than Emmeline Pankhurst, although the contrary was usually believed by those who had an image of Christabel as remote and cold.[15] Christabel never lost her affection for Annie, Mabel and Jessie and even in old age kept in contact with them.

During late August, Mabel Tuke felt well enough to spend a few days with Christabel in Boulogne before travelling with Emmeline Pankhurst and Ethel Smyth to Evian les Bains, near Geneva, to take the cure.[16] When the treatment had ended, the party of three journeyed back to Boulogne to see Christabel again who had decided to make her main base in Paris. On 9 September, Emmeline Pankhurst informed a friend that she and Mabel were accompanying Christabel to Paris, for just a few days, 'to find rooms & see her settled'.[17] For about five months now Christabel's whereabouts had been kept secret, a key reason being the fear that, if known, influential Antis in England would approach the French Government and appeal for her extradition. Christabel and Annie had interviewed one of the leading legal men, as well as other influential French people, on the question. 'We had a definite pledge that such a course would not be adopted', recollected Annie, 'and though later an appeal was made in our British Parliament for her deportation, no notice was taken of it . . . Christabel's French friends kept their promise.'[18] Now that the fear of extradition had gone, it was no longer necessary to keep secret Christabel's place of residence. Further, if WSPU members were to be motivated to rally to the new militant policy, then it was critical that the location of their absent leader was known.

On 17 September 1912, *Votes for Women* ran on its front page snapshots of Christabel with the headline 'The Elusive One in Exile' while inside it was explained that she now lived in Paris:

> [N]ot for one single week since the arrest of the leaders . . . has Miss Pankhurst failed to supply the leading article and the political notes . . . to act, in a word, as Political Editor . . . In future, the articles will be signed; that will be the only change.[19]

That very same day, many newspapers published interviews with Christabel who had taken rooms at the Hotel de la Cité Bergeré, in the heart of Paris. The *Daily Sketch* and the *Standard* also ran photographs of the slim, fashionably dressed WSPU leader, strolling and shopping in the capital city, pictures soon reprinted in *Votes for Women*.[20] Most of the press coverage was brief, explaining how Christabel had lived in France for six months but now intended to settle in Paris, so that she could conduct the suffrage agitation from there. But to the *Daily Chronicle*, a paper that had always been more sympathetic to the suffrage cause, Christabel gave an extended interview in which she spoke not only of her dramatic escape to France but, rarely, expressed her personal feelings about living in that country and about her mother:

> [A]t times I was terribly unhappy, especially about my mother, whom some people had accused me of having deserted at a critical moment. Such a charge is grossly unfair. Still, I had not much time to be lonely, for I had work to do and I was seldom left alone. Scores of staunch friends made week-end flights from England to see me in exile. And then came the day which brought my mother to my arms again. Oh, the joy of that meeting! It did much to compensate for the pain and suffering that has passed before.[21]

During that summer of 1912, Christabel and Emmeline Pankhurst had heard that the WSPU's rented rooms at Clement's Inn, leased in Mrs Lawrence's name, would soon be reclaimed by the landlord. Emmeline Pankhurst made a brief trip to London to find alternative accommodation, and chose the palatial Lincoln's House, Kingsway, five stories high, built in Portland stone in Italian Renaissance style. With its grand hall, arched windows, tiled staircase and oak panels, as well as an electric lift, this large new building could house all the WSPU's growing central staff, and do justice to the importance of the Union's work.[22] Since the Lawrences were extending their holiday by visiting relatives in Canada, Emmeline Pankhurst was in control of all the arrangements. And she liked it. The new headquarters could be fashioned as she wished, her 'own' domain, a place where she would no longer be an 'outsider' from the provinces. Neither she nor Fred had paid the costs levied by the conspiracy trial. While Emmeline herself had no assets that the Government could seize in default of payment, Fred was wealthy and his country home, Holmwood, had already been occupied by bailiffs. Emmeline feared that the Government would strip the Lawrences of their fortune, thus putting pressure on the WSPU to curb militancy. Nor was that all. Sympathetic suffragettes would raise funds to help Fred and his wife, thus diverting necessary income from the WSPU. In short, Emmeline Pankhurst reasoned that the wealthy Lawrences had become a liability.

On returning to Boulogne, Emmeline discussed the matter with Christabel who had torn allegiances. Although fond of the Lawrences, Fred was becoming a problem, particularly in his insistence that he should no longer have a back-seat role in the WSPU but more recognition, including speaking on the platform with the leaders. Christabel was startled by his lack of awareness not only of his limitations as a speaker, but also of his anomalous position as a man in a women's movement. As Jessie Kenney recollected, 'the temperature of the platform and the meetings went down' when Fred spoke at length. 'Too many facts and figures, too dull, and nothing like the sparkle that Christabel and Mrs. P. L., my sister Annie and Mrs. P would bring.' Christabel always 'looked so bored' on these occasions.[23] All this, plus the fact that Fred had recently sided with his wife in disagreeing strongly with the proposed new direction of militancy, made Christabel assess the Lawrences in a different light. As Annie observed, once people questioned policy with Christabel, 'her whole feeling changed towards them'.[24] Christabel and her mother asked Annie Kenney and Mabel Tuke if they would come to Boulogne to discuss the situation.

On 8 September Emmeline Pankhurst wrote a warm but firm letter to 'Mrs. Lawrence' outlining the result of the deliberations. 'We [,] Mrs Tuke [,] Annie [,] Christabel and I have . . . had a long talk & as a result I write you this letter which embodies our views. I want you to regard it as a business letter' which 'concerns the situation as it seems to us to affect you and Mr. Lawrence, and your position in the Union as treasurer.' Emmeline Pankhurst went on to outline the fears about how the Government could strip Fred of all his worldly possessions and, in the process, weaken the WSPU. 'This is what we suggest after long & anxious thought', she continued:

It is a way of retaining your active participation in a great Imperial movement which is just beginning . . . Will you for a time lead the Imperial Suffrage Movement in Canada? It is a great mission & a great role . . . Please show my letter to Mr Lawrence & discuss it with him & believe that I have left unwritten many expressions of affection & appreciation which we all feel very deeply.[25]

Christabel hoped the Lawrences would accept the proposal since it was the only way for them to avoid hurt and embarrassment. 'The Government would have ruined Mr. Lawrence and he would not have liked it', she later told Sylvia.[26] But it was not to be. On 22 September, Emmeline Pethick-Lawrence sent to 'Mrs. Pankhurst' a polite, cool reply. 'Perhaps you are not aware that the present situation does not take my husband or me by surprise.' Completely ignoring the suggestion that they move to Canada, she continued:

Our answer today is . . . the answer which you yourself would give if asked to choose between the Movement (which you and we have in so large a measure jointly built up) and any other possession in life however dear and precious . . . we shall continue to be jointly responsible with you in the future as we have been in the past.[27]

The blunt rebuttal was not welcomed by Emmeline Pankhurst who was 'very much the great lady' and showed no gratitude, 'even irritation', at the way the administrative machinery of the WSPU was efficiently organised by the Lawrences. Emmeline Pankhurst decided to expel the Lawrences from the WSPU. '[I]t did not worry her', recollected Jessie Kenney, 'but it did Christabel.'[28] Nonetheless, Christabel accepted the inevitable. She knew that the departure of the Lawrences would mean the loss of the newspaper they had founded, *Votes for Women*, currently the WSPU's official organ, and so secretly set about founding an alternative, *The Suffragette*, which she would edit from Paris. With her own newspaper, Christabel believed she could offer more effective leadership in the new militant policy, something *Votes for Women* was failing to do.

On 2 October the Lawrences arrived back in Britain and were greeted by a friend who warned that they had been ousted from the WSPU. 'I don't believe it! Impossible! Incredible! You are dreaming!' exclaimed Emmeline Pethick-Lawrence.[29] The couple went to the new WSPU headquarters at Lincoln's Inn and found that no office space had been allocated to either of them. Worse, as they traversed the passages, conversations abruptly stopped as they approached. The next day, Emmeline Pankhurst invited them to her room and, in the presence of Mabel and Annie, told them that she had decided to sever their connection with the WSPU. The stunned Emmeline Pethick-Lawrence turned to Mabel and Annie, but both remained silent. 'My husband and I were not prepared to accept this decision as final', she later recollected. 'We felt that Christabel, who had lived for so many years with us in closest intimacy, could not be a party to it.'[30]

But the determined Emmeline Pankhurst was resolute; she ended the meeting by inviting the bewildered couple to meet her a few evenings later at a house in the west of London. In great haste, Emmeline Pankhurst journeyed to Paris to bring Christabel back to London. The following day, 6 October, Christabel and her mother sailed to England. To avoid detection, Christabel travelled in disguise as a second-class passenger while Emmeline had a first-class ticket. 'I did not feel it right that Mother should not have me with her on that very serious occasion', Christabel later wrote:

> So I decided to make a brief and, of course, secret visit to London. It was misty when I arrived, and I walked under cover of the mist to the same quiet abode which had sheltered me on the night before my first escape.[31]

That Christabel had risked detection to speak to the Lawrences brought them little comfort since she told them that she and her mother 'were absolutely united in this matter'.[32] Christabel made it clear that she had 'no further use for us', wrote an embittered Emmeline Pethick-Lawrence many years later:

> The sole reason given for her decision was that she intended to direct the Union from Paris. She said that we could speak as announced in the forthcoming meeting in the Albert Hall if we chose, but in that case neither Mrs. Pankhurst nor any other official of the Union would be there. She suggested that we should continue to edit Votes for Women, but it would be no longer the organ of the W.S.P.U.[33]

The shattered Lawrences listened in disbelief. Emmeline Pethick-Lawrence, like her husband, was convinced that their dismissal from the WSPU was the work of the fiery and impetuous Emmeline Pankhurst who, she told Nevinson, was regarded as an 'enfant terrible'.[34] She wanted to resist 'the ultimatum', as she termed it, but Fred dissuaded her, pointing out that it would split the movement and drag the issue into public controversy; after all, they had both supported Mrs Pankhurst as 'the acknowledged autocrat of the Union' and could not dispute it now.[35]

A final meeting to draw up the terms of the separation was held in Boulogne, in a small hotel facing the quay. The memo, signed by the foursome, stated, 'At the request of Mrs Pankhurst, Mrs Pethick Lawrence resigns all connection with the WSPU & Mr Pethick Lawrence resigns control of the Woman's Press.' Control of Votes for Women, which was running at an annual loss of about £2,000, would revert to the Lawrences who would 'retire from participation' in the Albert Hall meeting planned for 17 October. To release the Lawrences from all liability, the WSPU, with assets of about £10,000, would find 'another guarantor' in place of the proposed guarantorship of Mr Pethick-Lawrence, for Lincoln's Inn House, '& also set aside & place in the hands of a trustee a sum of £2,000 to meet any of the liabilities for which Mr & Mrs Pethick Lawrence are at present responsible'. Further, the Lawrences would devote 'such of the various sums promised by themselves to the funds of the WSPU as are not yet paid' to the working expenses of *Votes for Women*.[36] A statement about the split was prepared for later publication.

Thus the close friendship between Christabel and the Lawrences came to an abrupt end. The pain the separation caused the Lawrences was never forgotten, even if it lessened with the passing of time. 'From that time forward I never saw or heard from Mrs. Pankhurst again, and Christabel, who had shared our family life, become a complete stranger', wrote Emmeline Pethick-Lawrence over twenty-five years later. There was, she suggested bitterly, 'something quite ruthless about Mrs. Pankhurst and Christabel where human relationship was concerned . . . Men and women of destiny are like that'. Fred too penned similar sentiments in his memoirs published in the early 1940s. Christabel, he observed, shared with her mother an:

> absolute refusal to be deflected by criticism or appeal one hair's breadth from the course which they had determined to pursue . . . Many men and women who have made history have been cast in a similar mould . . . They cannot be judged by ordinary standards of conduct.[37]

However, at the time, shortly after the split, the bitterly hurt Fred had been less philosophical and had told Grace Roe, 'No one, not even you or the Kenneys, have been so close to Christabel as I have.'[38] And that was another reason why Emmeline Pankhurst had wanted the Lawrences out of the WSPU. She was 'always jealous' of the intimacy that had arisen between them and her eldest daughter and, in particular, had never got on with Fred who seemed 'almost infatuated' with Christabel.[39] With the wealthy couple out of the way, Emmeline Pankhurst could regain her lost companion, her favourite daughter, the brilliant strategist who would win votes for women. Together, mother and daughter could take forward the WSPU, founded in their own home and which they had led for the last seven years. There would be no need in the future to discuss policy with the Central Committee of the WSPU which Emmeline felt obliged to call to a meeting on 14 October, to formally ratify the ousting of its Honorary Treasurer and her husband. At that meeting, two members of the Central Committee who sided with the Lawrences resigned in protest – Mary Neal and, more significantly, Elizabeth Robins, one of Christabel's friends who had secretly visited her in Paris a few months earlier.[40] Even though it was Emmeline Pankhurst who had taken the lead in the expulsion of the Lawrences, Sylvia in her influential *The suffragette movement* predictably blamed the 'sweet-tongued and cool, although immovable' Christabel for the split. However, she told a different story in a later, less well-known book where the blame is firmly placed on her mother's shoulders.[41]

In her memoir, Christabel shines no further light on the matter.[42] However, two months after the split, she trusted Elizabeth Robins enough to confide why the separation had taken place:

It is not the case that we (Mother & I) have changed of late. We are just the same in our point of view as we were before & were prepared to go on in partnership with the Ls. But <u>they</u> changed especially after the arrest in March. The delicate-balance there had once been was destroyed before the October separation came. Mr L's point of view & his theory as to his own position in the movement underwent a transformation . . . You know what men are & this one though dear in his best aspect is difficult.[43]

Further, in a letter later sent to Harriet Kerr, Christabel implies that she had found Emmeline Pethick-Lawrence somewhat tiresome as the Union's Honorary Treasurer since she would make such a '<u>fuss</u>' about finance, causing 'a rippling of the waters'.[44] Once the split occurred, it would appear that Christabel thought it was the best outcome for all concerned. 'I think she sincerely felt that they [the Lawrences] did not feel they could give their all', Jessie Kenney recalled; 'their position, their money was at stake and that is why they would go no further.'[45]

Christabel now energetically set about, in secret, founding a new WSPU newspaper, *The Suffragette*, a paper she could mould as she wished. However, although she was to be the editor of the new publication, she needed trusted staff in London who would help her put the first issue together, ready for the planned publication date, 18 October 1912. She chose Geraldine Lennox as a subeditor. Geraldine had once been on the staff of *Votes for Women* but, after the split, had come over to the Pankhursts. In early October, Christabel wrote to her, praising the 'splendid way' in which she had approached the task, and also giving further instructions:

> I enclose a memorandum dealing with the arrangement of news for next week's paper. I think you will find it quite clear . . . Miss Kenny [sic] will have been talking to you about some of my ideas. We must give the paper a character of its own and I hope to get some outside advice on that point for my mind and I expect yours also has been so long on the 'Votes for Women' paper groove that a little help in getting out of that groove may be good.[46]

The news of the new weekly paper was only made public when a subscription leaflet was enclosed with a letter, dated 16 October 1912, sent by Emmeline Pankhurst to all WSPU members, explaining that the Lawrences were 'no longer working with us as colleagues'.[47] The Lawrences were not only infuriated by the fact that the news of the split had been leaked before it was published in *Votes for Women*; they felt betrayed by 'the long underground preparation' that had obviously been going on in founding *The Suffragette*, without their knowledge.[48] The following day, 17 October, the formal notice about their severance could be read in *Votes for Women* and *The Suffragette*, which both appeared one day before their official publication date:

At the first re-union of the leaders after the enforced holiday, Mrs. Pankhurst and Miss Christabel Pankhurst outlined a new militant policy, which Mr. and Mrs. Pethick Lawrence found themselves altogether unable to approve. Mrs. Pankhurst and Miss Christabel Pankhurst indicated that they were not prepared to modify their intentions, and recommended that Mr. and Mrs. Pethick Lawrence should resume control of the paper, Votes for Women, and should leave the Women's Social and Political Union. Rather than make schism in the ranks of the Union, Mr. and Mrs. Pethick Lawrence consented to take this course.

In these circumstances, Mr. and Mrs. Pethick Lawrence will not be present at the Royal Albert Hall Meeting on October 17.[49]

Christabel used the launch of her new suffrage paper to clearly articulate her feminist thinking and to rally the membership for militant action. She explained in the foreword to The Suffragette that she had chosen that title because it was a name that stood for 'the independence, courage, public spirit, and . . . humour, which are the attributes of the really womanly woman. The Suffragettes are . . . the advance-guard of the new womanhood'.[50] In a rallying editorial, she outlined the new WSPU policy:

The militancy sanctioned by the Women's Social and Political Union consists in defiance of legal enactments and in attacks upon property. The only limit that the Union puts to militancy is that human life shall be respected . . . Now, if ever, self-respecting women are stirred to rebellion . . . Each militant will now prepare such militant action as her individual conscience approves . . . Some of the greatest evils in the world come from having one standard of morality and conduct for men and another standard for women. The attacks upon the militancy of the W.S.P.U. are founded on this double standard. If the Suffragettes were men fighting for their political liberty they would be honoured and admired by the very people who to-day denounce them. If a woman fights by her husband's side for the freedom of her country or for the rights of men even, she is honoured. It is only when women fight side by side with women and for women that criticism is levelled against them.[51]

In this first issue of The Suffragette Christabel also continued her attack upon the parliamentary Labour Party which, through a coalition with the Irish Nationalists, kept the anti-suffrage Liberal Government in power rather than seeking to overthrow it for the sake of votes for women. The Labour Party, she pointed out, 'is not even prepared to vote unitedly against the third reading of a Manhood Suffrage Bill from which women are excluded'. The official excuse, that Labour members were not numerous, was hollow since their votes counted eighty-four on a division. As a result, a women's war upon the parliamentary Labour Party was inevitable, although it should be clearly understood that the WSPU attack was not made 'upon Labour and Socialist principles'. Thus Christabel reminded all suffragettes that 'from now onwards' Labour candidates as well as Liberal should be opposed at elections.[52]

The majority of the rank-and-file had had no inkling that there had been a division in the WSPU leadership and were deeply shocked by the news of the split. When Emmeline Pankhurst appeared on the platform at the Albert Hall that evening of 17 October, she had to draw upon all her powers of oratory to present the *fait accompli* as a favourable move and to offer her full support for Christabel's rallying calls in *The Suffragette*. Indeed, Emmeline opened proceedings by reading out a message from Christabel – 'We must fight as never before, and give no quarter to the enemy' – which was received with much applause. After calling for unity of purpose and of policy, Emmeline spoke with great pathos in her voice as she explained how militant women were the victims rather than perpetrators of violence, including sexual violence against little girls, and how this, and the White Slave Traffic worldwide, would continue until an equal moral code for men and women was established. Then, with impassioned oratory, she led to the main point of her talk, an endorsement of the new militant policy that she and Christabel had agreed, namely secret attacks on public and private property:

> There is something that Governments care for far more than they care for human life, and that is the security of property . . . and so it is through property that we shall strike the enemy . . . Be militant in your own way. Those of you who can express your militancy by going to the House of Commons and refusing to leave without satisfaction, as we did in the early days – do so. Those of you who can express their militancy by facing party mobs at Cabinet Ministers' meetings, and remind them of their unfaithfulness to principle – do so. Those of you who can express your militancy by joining us in anti-Government by-election policy – do so. Those of you who can break windows . . . those of you who can still further attack the sacred idol of property so as to make the Government realise that property is as greatly endangered by women as it was by the Chartists of old days – do so.
>
> And my last word is to the Government. I incite this meeting to rebellion.[53]

Emmeline's defiant note that she would fight alone, if need be, touched a chord in her appreciative audience who clapped and cheered. George Lansbury then rose to speak, warning that he would not be party to keeping in office any Government that refused by any kind of subterfuge to see that justice was done to women during the present parliamentary session. Mabel Tuke also briefly addressed the audience, followed by Annie Kenney who reiterated Christabel's call to oppose Labour candidates as well as Liberals at all by-elections.[54] But it was Emmeline Pankhurst's powerful and moving oratory that carried the meeting.

Yet despite the enthusiasm of her listeners, just £3,600 was taken in the collection and promises of further donations, an indication perhaps of divided loyalties.[55] But there was no disagreement between Christabel and the speakers at the Albert Hall that night. In particular, Emmeline Pankhurst's sentiments were a verbal embellishment of what the daughter had written more starkly in print. Christabel and Emmeline Pankhurst were in perfect accord on the new direction of WSPU policy, just as they balanced each other in their leadership of the WSPU; the older woman more guided by emotion and feelings, the younger by logic and reason.

The WSPU membership now had to decide whether, as *Punch* put it, they were 'Peths' or 'Panks'.[56] Such a choice meant, yet again, that individual suffragettes had to exercise their own independent judgement. Those who joined the 'Panks' knew they would be breaking the law and, as new developments in militancy arose, that they would have to consider their position again. For Christabel, such a process was a step towards 'self-emancipation' which, as noted earlier, she had always insisted was one of the key purposes of the movement.[57] Nonetheless, a number of influential members of the WSPU decided they would not become law-breakers and withdrew from the Union while an intellectual, left-leaning group, that included Evelyn Sharp, joined the Lawrences who formed a new organisation titled the 'Votes for Women Fellowship'. This Fellowship aimed, through the content of *Votes for Women*, to find a common meeting ground between all suffrage societies, whether militant or non-militant.[58] However, not many women left the WSPU to join the new organisation. Nor, at least publicly, did Emmeline Pethick-Lawrence want to cause such a schism.[59] Christabel and her mother were hopeful that enough of the WSPU membership would stay with them, and they did, particularly the younger members who were fired with enthusiasm about the injustices to their sex.

Annie Kenney's loyalty to Christabel earned her the nickname 'Christabel's Blotting Paper' by those WSPU members who were horrified at what had happened. The title 'neither flattered nor depressed me', reflected Annie many years later. 'I knew that blotters were useful things, and I had no ambition but to be of use to the only one I firmly believed could ever win the Vote.' Although Christabel had 'never questioned' but assumed which side her trusted friend would join, Annie was unhappy in having to make a choice at all. Nonetheless, she remained loyal to Christabel, declaring at one WSPU At Home, 'If all the world were on one side, and Christabel Pankhurst on the other, I would walk straight over to Christabel Pankhurst!'[60] Such a response was typical of those who sided with the Pankhursts. As Rachel Barrett enthusiastically told Nevinson, 'the Lawrences are just the Lawrences & this is the movement'. Similarly, Margaret Walker disagreed with those who criticised the autocratic rule of the Pankhursts. 'The members of the W.S.P.U.', she argued, 'regard themselves as soldiers in warfare, and we do not have conferences and dictate a policy to our leaders any more than soldiers would do in a campaign. We trust to the political sagacity of our leaders.' Overall, as Jessie Kenney observed, after the 1912 split loyalties became 'even fiercer'.[61]

The immediate effect of the Lawrences' departure was a change in the organisational structure of the WSPU. Emmeline Pankhurst now became Honorary Treasurer, and left the by-election campaigning to others. Mabel Tuke retained on her own, rather than jointly with Mrs Pankhurst, the post of Honorary Secretary. The Central Committee of the WSPU was disbanded. Christabel in Paris set the broad outlines of policy in consultation with her mother and trusted friends who visited her, especially Annie, Flora Drummond and later Grace Roe. While some experienced organisers such as Laura Ainsworth resigned their posts, as well as Dorothy Pethick and Nelly Crocker, sister and cousin, respectively, to Emmeline Pethick-Lawrence, the London headquarters attracted additional young women loyal to Christabel, many of whom had none of the experience in working-class movements that the earlier WSPU organisers had possessed. Yet matters were not always entirely clear cut. Although Elizabeth Robins had resigned from the Central Committee, she does not appear to have relinquished her WSPU membership; nor did Nelly Crocker, who still listed herself as a WSPU member in 1913.[62]

Christabel and her mother had anticipated that an incitement to attack property would deter all but the most committed – and that such law-breaking would inevitably drive the movement largely underground. So shortly after Emmeline's Albert Hall speech on 17 October, arrangements were made to lessen the effects of police arrests and raids by keeping the books in duplicate, by arranging for clerical staff to work in private homes as well as at the known London headquarters, and by changing the auditors.[63] Such developments were not always fully welcomed, even by those most loyal to Christabel. Looking back to the 1912 split, Annie Kenney reflected sadly, 'The old days were over . . . Christabel won . . . but the Movement, as a Movement, lost. The two [the Lawrences] had gone who had been the creative geniuses of the constructive side of a world-famed fight.'[64]

Christabel, now living at 9 Rue Roy in Paris, was determined to make a success of the restructured WSPU and put a lot of effort that autumn into establishing *The Suffragette* as its new official voice. 'Will you let me know what special articles you have in hand', she wrote anxiously to Geraldine Lennox on 30 October, as she worried about the content and layout of the paper:

> I understand that Mrs Tuke has written to various people asking them to write articles . . . Dr Ethel Smyth promised that she would get someone to write an article about the performance of her works [in] Vienna on Nov. 3rd. The article will be written in German, and so we shall have to get it translated.[65]

Over the next few days, more letters followed with further instructions, as well as concerns about printing errors in recent issues and the quality of the paper being used.

Sylvia had decided to settle in the East End since it had a long history of political activism on which she wanted to build. Her mother agreed to her request for

WSPU headquarters to be responsible for the shop she rented in Bow while the Kensington, Chelsea and Paddington branches agreed to act in a similar capacity for the shops opened in Bethnal Green, Limehouse and Poplar. Together with Zelie Emerson, a wealthy young American woman whom Sylvia had recently met in Chicago and who had followed her to London, Sylvia organised a number of meetings at which the speakers included not only herself but also her mother and Flora Drummond. But Christabel's suspicions about Sylvia's wish to ally the WSPU to the socialist movement were never far below the surface, and she became unhappy about the amount of coverage Sylvia was getting in these early issues of *The Suffragette*. 'With regard to the East End campaign. This must really be got into <u>half a page</u>', Christabel told Geraldine Lennox sternly on 3 November. Another concern was soon voiced by the frustrated Christabel. 'I quite see that it was necessary to print the end of my article on another page', she wrote on 8 November, however:

> It is disappointing that it is not signed, because it would have been a good thing for our readers to realise that the Editor is in such a position as to be able to comment on the important affairs of the week . . . I wonder how the mistake arose?

Later that day, while waiting for Annie to arrive, Christabel penned another letter to Geraldine, explaining that she would also be discussing the content and layout of the paper with her trusted visitor. Annie undoubtedly brought news from the London office which necessitated a third communication from Christabel to the worried subeditor in London. 'Mr. Sapte . . . a journalistic expert . . . will take temporary charge in order to develop the paper and get it on the right lines', Christabel explained. 'While he remains he will be over everybody in the Editorial Office.'[66]

Shaping *The Suffragette* along the 'right' lines was a critical task for Christabel since events had taken a different turn in London. On 5 November, when Philip Snowden's women's suffrage amendment to the Irish Home Rule Bill had been unsurprisingly defeated, a window-smashing raid had taken place in London's Bond Street.[67] The Labour Party, led by Ramsey MacDonald, had not supported the amendment as official policy; only twenty-seven of its MPs voted for it while five voted against and nine were absent.[68] Christabel was not impressed by such action from the only political party that claimed to be pro women's suffrage! Further, the Labour Party was at odds with numerous branches of the ILP that had backed a resolution, framed by George Lansbury, to vote constantly and relentlessly against the Government until they were either driven from office or compelled to introduce votes for women on equal terms with men. Christabel regarded Ramsay MacDonald as sex prejudiced and Janus faced, someone who claimed to support women's suffrage while also declaring that it was 'not men who have stood in the way of the enfranchisement of women, but a small section of the women themselves', namely the members of the WSPU.[69] In particular,

Christabel repudiated the claims levelled against the suffragettes that they were 'selfish' in asking the Labour Party to constantly vote against the Government. '[I]t is the Labour Party who are selfish', she insisted, 'in their determination to sacrifice the fundamental rights of women to questions of secondary importance framed in the interests of men who are voters already', namely Welsh Disestablishment, Home Rule and Trade Union Bills.[70]

George Lansbury, who sided with Christabel, was promptly informed by the Labour Party that since it had paid part of his election expenses and he had won his seat under their sponsorship, he should follow their policy or leave. On 9 November, he crossed the English Channel to confer with Christabel and her mother. Although Emmeline Pankhurst advised him not to resign his parliamentary seat of Bow and Bromley but to get resolutions of confidence in him passed at meetings in his constituency, Lansbury felt it was impossible to compromise on votes for women.[71] He resigned his seat, thus forcing a by-election in which he stood for re-election as an independent socialist, campaigning specifically for women's suffrage.

Christabel and Emmeline offered Lansbury their full support. This was the first time that a parliamentary seat would be fought solely upon a women's suffrage ticket and the first time that the WSPU had sponsored a candidate. 'The election in Bow and Bromley marks a turning-point in the movement for Votes for Women', wrote an optimistic Christabel in *The Suffragette* on 15 November. 'Work and money will not be stinted to ensure victory.' And again, in a private letter to Mary Phillips, she sang Lansbury's praises, claiming that if every Labour MP followed his example and voted against the Liberals, votes for women could be won:

> Have you noticed that . . . the Labour members are prepared to vote against the Govt on the Welsh Disestablishment Bill now that the Trade Union Bill may be dropped? So you see they can vote against the Govt on one question for the sake of another. It is when the <u>women's</u> interests are to be sacrificed that they are so true to the Government.[72]

A few days later, Christabel was writing to Mary again, wistfully wishing she could be working with her at the Bolton by-election and explaining that her mother would be with Mary, if at all possible, and that it was not only the Lansbury election that was keeping her away. '[A] great deal falls to her to do nowadays especially as our dear Mrs Tuke is having to rest for a bit and there is more work to be done now than ever there was.'[73] Mabel Tuke, socially well connected, who had worked hard behind the scenes to expand the WSPU London 'At Home' meetings, was in poor health again. Early in the New Year she would embark on a recuperative sea voyage to South Africa, returning to England later in 1913 and frequently visiting Christabel in Paris.

The increased workload that Christabel and her mother faced that autumn of 1912 included finding an organiser for Lansbury's election campaign. Christabel appointed the trusted Grace Roe rather than Sylvia, her socialist sister, much to

Sylvia's annoyance. Christabel and her mother may have been nervous about giving Sylvia such a prominent role, fearful that her affair with Keir Hardie, a friend of Lansbury, might become public and thus have a devastating impact on Lansbury's candidature. Since Emmeline Pankhurst was known for her plain speaking, she may already have told her 'troublesome' daughter that if she was to take on a more prominent role in the WSPU, she would not tolerate the liaison. This may help to explain why Sylvia's affair with Hardie began to fade after she began her work in the East End.[74] Be this as it may, undoubtedly the ideological differences between Christabel and Sylvia played a key part in Sylvia's displacement. Sylvia later wrote in *The suffragette movement* that the 'proper course for the W.S.P.U. was to place itself in contact with and work under the local Labour Party which was responsible for Lansbury's candidature'. But Grace Roe, loyal to Christabel, had no intention of working 'under' the Poplar Labour Representation Committee. According to Sylvia, Grace Roe was mainly concerned with upholding 'the superiority of her organization, resentful of advice, ignorant of election methods . . . had no sympathy with the Labour movement' and was critical of men.[75] But that is not the whole story since Sylvia herself admitted that the Trades Council and Labour representatives were 'none too friendly' towards the suffragettes while Joe Banks, Lansbury agent, was 'bitterly hostile'.[76] The lack of cooperation between the various organisations and individuals claiming to speak on Lansbury's behalf led to a range of differing policies being articulated. 'Best wishes from an absent friend to Mrs Lansbury and yourself for success', wrote an optimistic Christabel to Lansbury as polling day neared. 'Whatever the result the fight has been gloriously worthwhile and has done untold good.'[77] On 26 November, a wild and blustery day, polling took place. Lansbury lost by seven hundred and fifty-one votes to the Unionist candidate, Reginald Blair; his previous majority had been eight hundred and sixty-three.

After the announcement of Lansbury's defeat, suffragettes secretly poured acid, ink and tar into pillar boxes in London and a host of provincial cities and towns – including Nottingham, Newcastle, Ilkeston, Bristol and Worthing.[78] In an editorial in early December, Christabel defended the 'grave-revolutionary act' of the letter burners. Those who complained that such action interrupted 'commercial intercourse' should remember that strikes by working men who were miners and railway workers had inflicted much greater damage on the business world. And then in words that echoed her mother's important speech at the Albert Hall nearly two months earlier, Christabel articulated the wider reformist aims of the militants:

> What is the object of the letter-burners? It is to abolish White Slavery. It is to put an end to hideous assaults on little girls. It is to stop the sweating of working women. Whoever has lost a letter in the protest has at least the knowledge that his letter has been burned on the altar of freedom, and if he is a wise man he will insure himself against all such loss in future by compelling the Government to give votes to women.[79]

As such statements make clear, Christabel's aim was never, as her sister Sylvia claimed in *The suffragette movement*, the narrow one of an 'absolute and vigorous concentration on the vote, and on that alone'.[80] Christabel wanted a broad range of social reforms that would bring equality for women, including working women. In particular, a concern with sexual morality now became much more marked in her pronouncements as she pressed for an end to the double moral standard that disadvantaged women. The demand for a single moral standard for men and women had been central to the women's movement from the 1880s.[81] What was new, in the autumn of 1912, was the notion that the time for trying to win public support for the women's cause had passed, that militant action by women, such as burning letters, was seen as the way to *coerce* the Government to grant women their demands. As Christabel explained in *The Suffragette*, the purpose of the unpopular act of 'burning and otherwise destroying letters' was:

> to make the electors and the Government so uncomfortable that, in order to put an end to the nuisance, they will give women the vote . . . Women will never get the vote except by creating an intolerable situation for all the selfish and apathetic people who stand in their way.[82]

Christabel had been very disappointed when Lansbury was defeated. As she justly pointed out, the very people for whom he was fighting, namely women, were not allowed to vote for him and secure his return while the male voters could always be bought off by making the main issue questions which concern men.[83] The election defeat illustrated only too well the futility of using legal and constitutional means to win women's enfranchisement, as well as the deep prejudices against women's suffrage among Labour supporters. In a key article in *The Suffragette*, Christabel expounded her views at some length, praising Lansbury for his stand but criticising the Labour electors who would not vote for him and the Labour Party who condemned him:

> [W]hereas the best and most highly evolved men . . . will put the cause of Votes for Women first, a great mass of men are still so corrupted and led astray by party politics that to depend simply on the help of the electors to secure the enfranchisement of women is a grave and fatal mistake.

Women, she concluded, 'must work out their own salvation' by following a policy of militancy.[84]

Nonetheless, Christabel was keen to retain Lansbury's support and in a private letter told him that she had gladly accepted the offer of the left-wing *Daily Herald*, a populist newspaper he had helped re-launch, to have a column each day for WSPU business. 'I do hope that you will have great success in inspiring and gathering around you a band of people who will honestly try to give effect to the best Labour and Socialist ideals', she wrote. '<u>We</u> are supposed to be autocratic', she continued, 'but if we are, we take the full responsibility of the consequences of what we do', unlike Ramsay MacDonald, the leader of the Labour Party, a man both Christabel and Lansbury detested. MacDonald, Christabel insisted, 'is an autocrat when it is a question of having all his own way, and a democrat when it is a question of putting responsibility for mistakes and for failures upon the shoulders of the rank and file'. Hoping that Lansbury would continue to speak on suffragette platforms, Christabel queried:

> Miss Kenney would like to know how much time you can put at the disposal of the W.S.P.U. and then she can arrange that your meetings are held at the places where it is most important that you should speak.[85]

True to his word, Lansbury supported the WSPU over the next year or so, being once imprisoned for the cause and going on hunger and thirst strike.[86] But although Christabel was willing to accept his support, she did not wish to ally the WSPU to a male-dominated socialism, or to a male-dominated Labour Party. And so after Lansbury's election defeat, a decision was made by Christabel and Emmeline to cease WSPU activity in the East End and to close the WSPU shops. This upset Sylvia who persuaded her mother to change her mind, pointing out that she could organise a deputation to parliament of East End working women. Soon it was announced that such a deputation would take place in the New Year but that it would be national rather than regional, and be led by Flora Drummond rather than Sylvia.[87]

During the Lansbury election campaign, Christabel had renewed contact with Henry Nevinson and Elizabeth Robins. Nevinson had called on Christabel in Paris on 23 November and found her 'more charming, vivacious & happily tempered than ever'. Christabel talked to him about the split with the Lawrences but said nothing about what she would soon confide to Elizabeth Robins, namely that Fred had been insisting that he take a more central role in WSPU affairs. Nevinson merely recorded that Christabel spoke:

> with utmost enthusiasm of both, espec. of her. In him she missed humour & imagination, but praised him as a critic who let nothing pass without objection. She was much moved & cd not always quite steady her voice, but refused to regret anything.

Christabel informed Nevinson that she did not miss speaking on a public platform since 'she thought nothing of her speeches, good or not . . . but she did believe in her duty & power in steering the movement and holding the rudder'. After dinner in the Palais Royal, the conversation continued in Christabel's flat where Christabel spoke of 'the error of supporting the Labour Party . . . the uselessness of committees, and . . . rather disapproved of men's intimate concern in the movement'. Soon after nine o'clock, Annie arrived with news about the progress of the Lansbury campaign in Bow and Bromley. Nevinson left, his 'usual deep admiration renewed'.[88]

In contrast to Nevinson, the admiration that Elizabeth Robins had held for Christabel seemed to diminish after the ousting of the Lawrences. When she had resigned from the Central Committee of the WSPU, in protest over the split, Elizabeth had explained to Emmeline Pankhurst that her action did not mean that she relinquished 'any smallest part of my affection for you & Christabel'.[89] But affection for Christabel did not blunt Elizabeth's critical powers. Indeed, her resignation emboldened the often-elusive Miss Robins to be more assertive, to say what she thought about the WSPU leadership.

During November and December Elizabeth Robins wrote regularly to Christabel, criticising the way the WSPU was run. 'As to remoteness and legendarism, I don't worry about that for many reasons', replied Christabel in mid-November in a rebuttal to Elizabeth's criticism of her decision to live in Paris:

> One reason is . . . that the wonderful & miraculous loyalty of those at L.I.H. [Lincoln Inn's House] makes me feel as much there as ever I was. Another is that I really am in full & complete touch with what is going on. Another is that I am able by being here to give those who are there a feeling of greater security.

Above all, Christabel explained that she remained in Paris 'because I know that is best for the movement.'[90] Elizabeth Robins could not agree with this analysis and, on 23 November, sat down and wrote sixteen pages of blistering critique, of 'things that I've thought – not said to any other soul.' Elizabeth asked a number of probing questions. Can you wisely be sole judge of what is best? What does the loyalty of those in charge of the WSPU in London amount to if they are just blindly obedient? Elizabeth used the example of Geraldine Lennox, the subeditor of *The Suffragette*, to illustrate her point, arguing that the paper needed instead someone, unlike Miss Lennox, who was highly skilled and educated. The membership of the WSPU, Elizabeth insisted, needed 'binding together', all the more necessary now that women were leaving. 'Nobody has the power you & your mother have as public speakers', she pointed out as she stressed the need for leadership from the platform. 'Your following is melting away . . . you won't get it back by writing articles for the Suffragette.'

The angry Elizabeth went further; she criticised some of those dearest to Christabel:

> When I saw yr. mother last I begged her to have a strong council . . . Yr. mother said: 'I have Mrs. Tuke & Annie K.' These two, especially Annie K, are good helpers & fitted to carry out policies framed by stronger wits. They cannot contribute a jot of the force I covet for the W.S.P.U.

Taking into account the views of other strong-minded people on the Central Committee of the WSPU, Elizabeth dared to suggest, would mean that the leadership had to carry that Committee with it; this would make it easier to carry the rank-and-file, and ultimately the public. She also informed Christabel that she had asked Mrs Pankhurst about 'her theory of leadership' and been told that the WSPU functioned liked the Salvation Army. Elizabeth could not agree with the analogy since the emancipation of women made 'no appeal to superstition' but was a 'rationalistic faith' that could not call upon 'that great mass of ignorance & sentimentality' that served the Salvation Army.[91] Having penned such a scathing attack, Elizabeth Robins suddenly lost her courage and decided not to send the letter – but informed Christabel of its existence. 'I am sorry you did not send me the letter', wrote a chirpy Christabel on 28 November. 'The greatest disservice you can do me is to "spare me" in any way . . . don't wrap me in cotton wool after all these years. What have I done to deserve that!!'[92] The hesitant Elizabeth Robins hesitated no more and finally posted her letter.

Christabel was taken aback by Elizabeth's criticisms and composed an even longer reply, logically debating specific points that had been raised. She defended her position as the key strategist and policy maker of the WSPU. 'I always <u>have</u> been sole judge . . . and why should any change be made now? It was always understood that I decided political matters.' While she agreed with Elizabeth that the women's suffrage question was complex, Christabel argued she did not want 'people jogging my elbow'. Offended by Elizabeth's tone, she continued, 'There may be other ways of dealing with the situation & if so, let these wiseacres deal with it in their own way instead of standing round & criticising other people's way.' Repudiating the assertion that neither she nor her mother were ever at hand to support new enthusiastic recruits, Christabel argued, 'It is literally & physically impossible that Mother or I shall interview every new person on their first appearance . . . There are only 16 hours in the day available for work you know.' Besides, she continued:

> We are more at hand & more able to decide & act quickly than the controlling people in any other Society whatsoever (with their committees they have to be got together) & what is more, we have helping us more effective, efficient people than any of the other Societies have, as was proved last March when at a moment of great crisis & difficulty the ship sailed on & things were managed in a way that surprised everybody.

However, Christabel did agree with Elizabeth's claim that she alone could not make *The Suffragette* into a good-quality paper – 'Quite true!' – but then added a more barbed comment, 'But with others helping me, I can (e.g. if Miss Elizabeth Robins will write something sometimes).' She readily admitted that not everything was right with the new organ of the WSPU since its setting up had been rushed. But while confiding that she was still looking for a first-class woman with an instinct for journalism to manage the paper, Christabel stoutly defended the valuable contribution of the loyal Geraldine Lennox. 'Miss Lennox . . . came to the "Suffragette" out of desire to help the Union . . . she is such a good soul.' However, no conciliatory tone was adopted in regard to Elizabeth's suggestion that the WSPU needed a strong central council for collective decision-making. 'The world is our council', Christabel replied glibly. 'Why shd we pick out a selected few! . . . And what wd this council <u>do</u>? Put on the brake as far as I understand.' Musing on the general tone of Elizabeth's criticisms, Christabel added, 'All this that you say in your letter you say for the first time. Have you been thinking it all these years or is it the separation from the Lawrences that has put it into your mind?'[93]

Such comments did little to ally Elizabeth Robins' fears. Nonetheless, she wrote a 'nice' reply which encouraged Christabel to respond. 'There is so much that a letter can't explain about what makes me feel it right to be an "autocrat" – though you know I am not so regarded by the people who work with me', Christabel replied, in a more conciliatory tone. She also confided that she was concerned that funds for the WSPU might dry up:

> I am doing what I can here to make new friends who may now or here-after help us. If you know any people in Paris that you think it wd be helpful for me to know, will you tell me?

Praising her mother for all the work she was undertaking, Christabel pleaded, 'She does meet opposition & indifference so splendidly. If you shd be seeing her & shd have any suggestion of advice to offer it will be a great help.'[94] This very frank exchange of views between Christabel and Elizabeth Robins, both celebrities in their day, did not spell the end of their friendship during these suffrage years, although it inevitably became less close. And even though Elizabeth had resigned from the WSPU's Central Committee, she remained a supporter of the women's cause, occasionally sending copy to *The Suffragette*.

The debate over the long-awaited women's suffrage amendment to the Manhood Suffrage Bill had still not taken place, and so the WSPU in London now began to focus upon attracting recruits for the deputation of working women, to be held in the New Year. Working women, many of them from the working classes, had joined the WSPU in large numbers and had taken part in deputations to parliament before; indeed, some of their number, such as Annie Kenney and Flora Drummond, held key positions in the WSPU and were close to Christabel. The improvement of the working woman's daily lot, a theme already emphasised by Christabel, was now given greater prominence by others within the WSPU's inner circle. '[E]nemies of votes for women are saying that the Suffrage movement is a movement of rich women', protested Flora Drummond,

> and that the women workers are taking no real part in it. I, for one, as a working woman, have made up my mind to prove that this is not true, and I am asking other working women to join with me in one great stand for their political rights.

She went on to speak of the broader reform aims of the WSPU that Christabel and her mother had already articulated – the ending of sweating for women workers, the halting of the White Slave Traffic and the stopping of the 'outrages' committed on little girls, a growing evil which 'working-class mothers are determined to stamp out'.[95]

In the Christmas edition of *The Suffragette* Christabel threw her support behind Flora, reinforcing the attractiveness of the WSPU as an inclusive organisation that welcomed women of all classes. 'There is no other woman's society which so entirely disregards class distinction as does the W.S.P.U., nor in which working women, by virtue of their human capacities, hold positions of so much responsibility and authority.' But whereas the working man had become a figure of great importance in the political world, 'voteless working women' had not, even though they were 'more qualified for political leadership than are many of the male Labour leaders of the present day'.[96]

Undoubtedly Flora Drummond and Annie Kenney felt boosted by such sentiments – unlike many socialist men, including Annie's brother, Rowland, a journalist and first editor of the *Daily Herald*. Rowland claimed that the militant suffrage movement was in ruins since it had lost touch with working women and focused on recruiting middle- and upper-class women who could swell the WSPU's funds. The working woman now in the WSPU was 'arrayed in her new silk gown, her speeches fashioned for effective attack on the emotion of sentimental people who had money to spare'. Annie was a typical example, having become 'a splendid marketable commodity', exploited for propaganda purposes.[97]

On 2 December, at a meeting at the London Opera House in honour of George Lansbury, Emmeline Pankhurst, Flora Drummond and Annie Kenney all upheld the new militant policy of attacking pillar boxes. Indeed, Emmeline Pankhurst warned that other forms of militancy would arise 'as necessity develops . . . the woman's civil war is going on and what fresh developments are to come depends upon those who can give us the vote and won't'. Annie, after reading a rallying message from Christabel, received that very morning, added her own. 'Let us go on with the damage, let us go on making public life unbearable . . . our own conscience is telling us we are doing the right thing in the movement.'[98] With such arguments, the inner circle of the WSPU placed responsibility for attacks upon property not upon the militants themselves but upon the all-male Liberal Government that refused women their democratic rights.

Be that as it may, plain-clothes policemen were at this and subsequent WSPU meetings held in public, taking note of all that was said and monitoring those they considered dangerous subversives, especially the fiery and charismatic Emmeline Pankhurst. Henry Nevinson had been present at the Opera House meeting and, despite his admiration for Christabel, noted that faith in Mrs Pankhurst was 'much shaken'. He had heard yet more gossip about the split with the Lawrences who, apparently, at the Boulogne meeting had 'objected' to Christabel's interference with the way Evelyn Sharp edited *Votes for Women*. Making no mention whatsoever of his secret love affair with Evelyn, the handsome womaniser concluded, 'All through, the P.s come out badly – very.'[99]

If such gossip about the 'Peths' and 'Panks' reached Christabel's ears, she was not perturbed by it but by the constant rumours about splits in the Government over the women suffrage issue and, in particular, that Asquith would resign if the women suffrage amendments to the Manhood Suffrage Bill were carried. Since Asquith said nothing to contradict the rumours, Christabel believed it was merely a tactic to force pro-suffrage MPs, including Lloyd George, Chancellor of the Exchequer and Sir Edward Grey, Secretary of State for Foreign Affairs, to choose between their suffrage pledges and the breaking up of the Government. Once again, party loyalty would be put before the women's cause.[100]

Believing that the women's suffrage amendments had little chance of being carried, Christabel again sought the help of Elizabeth Robins who had recently sent an article for *The Suffragette*. On 11 December, Christabel warned Elizabeth not to trust pro-suffrage ministers in the Liberal Government, especially Sir Edward Grey. '[S]uffrage ministers will not resign if W.S. is not carried!' The following day, having read Elizabeth's article, Christabel composed a long letter, offering constructive comments on the essay, as well as lots of praise. Ever ready to defend the work of the WSPU, she asserted:

> The effect we have had on the flame we have lit in women who don't know anything about votes or politics & don't realise that there is any link between us & them is one of the things I am proudest of.

Continuing in a self-reflective vein, Christabel commented, 'I never felt more mistress of myself – more unstrained, more "all there" – more full of grit & vim & everything else of the kind than I do now feel & have felt for months.'[101]

Christabel had already informed Elizabeth that she had completed arrangements to improve the management of *The Suffragette* by bringing in Rachel Barrett, a graduate and former science teacher. 'We have not of course the galaxy of editorial talent that some papers have, but we shall hold our own', she mused. Concern for the well-being of the previous subeditor, the well-meaning but hardpressed Geraldine Lennox, led Christabel to advise her to 'take a good rest at Christmas. Talk the matter over with Miss Kenney and Miss Barrett and see what can be arranged'.[102] Geraldine Lennox was not the only WSPU worker to whom Christabel offered support at this time. In mid-December, the mother of Mary Phillips died. Although Mrs Phillips, a paid-up Union member, had been in failing health for some weeks, she had refused to send for her daughter because she believed her work was more important. On 16 December, Christabel penned a warm letter of sympathy to the bereaved Mary:

> This is just to send you my love and to tell you how grieved I am to hear of your great loss . . . Death is always so hard that one never knows quite how to find words of consolation, but it is not the worst thing because it is not the end of the love that was between you and your dear mother and the memory of that is with you for the rest of your life.[103]

The ink had barely dried from Christabel's pen when Asquith announced that the Manhood Suffrage Bill would have its second reading after Christmas. Millicent Fawcett swung the weight of the NUWSS behind the proposed women's suffrage amendments to the long-hovering bill and put strong pressure on the WSPU to suspend all militant action. Christabel and Emmeline Pankhurst refused to comply. 'Those who persist in saying that Mr Asquith is a "man of honour" are mistaken', thundered Christabel. 'Suffragists who continue to pursue a peaceable and trustful policy are simply playing into the hands of the enemy.'[104]

The approach of the festive season brought Christabel some relaxation. On Christmas Day she dined at the Restaurant Mollard with thirteen other WSPU members – Jessie Murray Clark, Elizabeth Murray, Edith Stuart, Phyllis Keller, Jennie King, Elizabeth Edmonds, Alice Morgan Wright, Lilia Wittler, Hilda and Irene Dallas, Blanche Edwards, Gwendolyn Hensley and Dorothy Habgood. After lunch, an impromptu entertainment took place. Phyllis, a student of dance, displayed some of her skills, Jessie gave recitations to music, while Jennie and Gwendolyn sung some songs. Then all joined in the singing of 'The March of the Women'. Most of those who were with Christabel this Christmas Day had travelled from Britain especially to spend time with her, while others, such as Phyllis Keller, lived in the French capital, as did Alice Morgan Wright, an American sculptor who had cast a head of Emmeline Pankhurst.[105]

Notes

1 Raeburn, Militant suffragettes, p. 171; A. Raeburn, The suffragette view (Newton Abbott, David and Charles, 1976), p. 54.
2 Raeburn, The suffragette view, p. 54.
3 FPL, Fate, p. 98.
4 EPL, My part, p. 278; FPL, Fate, pp. 98–9.
5 VfW, 2 August 1912, pp. 712–13.
6 Standard, 22 October 1912.
7 ESP, TSM, p. 396.
8 For an opposing position to my claim see Bearman, An examination of suffragette violence, pp. 379–80, who supports Sylvia Pankhurst's views in The suffragette movement.
9 VfW, 26 July and 30 August 1912, pp. 697 and 772, respectively.
10 CP, Unshackled, p. 222.
11 VfW, 27 September 1912, p. 832.
12 Coleman, Adela, p. 50.
13 CP to M. Tuke, n.d., Henry Harben Papers, BL Add 58226 (hereafter, Harben Papers).
14 Kenney, Memories, pp. 299–30.
15 Interview with Jessie Kenney, 31 July 1964, DMC.
16 EP to Miss Robins, n.d. [August 1912], Robins Papers, HRHRC.
17 EP to Alice Morgan Wright, 9 September 1912, SSC.
18 Kenney, Memories, pp. 185–6.
19 VfW, 13 September 1912, pp. 793, 797.
20 VfW, 20 September 1912, pp. 810–13.
21 How I escaped arrest, Miss C. Pankhurst's dramatic story, Daily Chronicle, 13 September 1912.

22 *VfW*, 20 September 1912, p. 811.
23 J. Kenney, Notes on Ethel Smyth, Mrs Pankhurst and Christabel, Kenney Papers, KP/5; interview with Jessie Kenney, 2 July 1965, DMC.
24 Kenney, *Memories*, p. 192.
25 EP to Mrs Lawrence, 8 September 1912, draft letter, Craigie Collection.
26 ESP, *TSM*, p. 412.
27 EPL to Mrs Pankhurst, 22 September 1912, copy, P-L Papers.
28 Interview with Jessie Kenney, 2 July 1965, DMC.
29 EPL, *My part*, p. 280.
30 EPL, *My part*, p. 281.
31 CP, *Unshackled*, p. 227; *Pall Mall Gazette*, 8 October 1912.
32 FPL, *Fate*, p. 99.
33 EPL, *My part*, p. 281.
34 Entry for 23 December 1913, Nevinson Diaries.
35 EPL, *My part*, 281; FPL, *Fate*, p. 100.
36 Memo, n.d., signed by C. Pankhurst, E. Pankhurst, F. W. Pethick-Lawrence and E. Pethick-Lawrence, written in Fred Pethick-Lawrence's hand, Craigie Collection.
37 EPL, *My part*, p. 285; FPL, *Fate*, p. 100.
38 Interview with Jessie Kenney, 31 July 1964, DMC.
39 Interview with Jessie Kenney, 31 July 1964, DMC.
40 John, *Elizabeth Robins*, pp. 169–70.
41 ESP, *TSM*, p. 412; ESP, *Emmeline Pankhurst*, p. 114.
42 CP, *Unshackled*, p. 226 notes briefly that the break with the Lawrences was 'a cause of deep regret to all concerned'.
43 CP to Miss Robins, 5 December 1912, Robins Papers, HRHRC.
44 CP to My dear P [Harriet Kerr], n.d. [April 1913], TNA, DPP 1/19, Exhibit 33.
45 Miscellaneous notes, Christabel, KP5, Kenney Papers.
46 CP to Miss Lennox, n.d., Rex v. Kerr & Others File, Schlesinger Library, Radcliffe College, Massachusetts, USA (hereafter Rex v. Kerr).
47 Form letter from EP to Dear Friend, 16 October 1912, SFC.
48 Entry for 25 November 1912, Nevinson Diaries.
49 *The Suffragette* (hereafter TS) and VFW, 18 October 1912, pp. 6 and 34, respectively.
50 TS, 18 October 1912, p. 1.
51 TS, 18 October 1912, p. 6.
52 TS, 18 October 1912, p. 7.
53 TS, 25 October 1912. p. 17.
54 TS, 25 October 1912, pp. 17–18.
55 *VfW*, 25 October 1912, p. 58.
56 *Punch*, 30 October 1912.
57 FPL, *Fate*, p. 101.
58 Crawford, *The women's suffrage movement*, p. 698.
59 *Daily Herald* and *Standard*, 18 October 1912.
60 Kenney, *Memories*, pp. 193–4; ESP, *TSM*, p. 413.
61 Entry for 28 January 1913, Nevinson Diaries; *Daily Herald*, 23 October 1912; interview with Jessie Kenny, 24 March 1964, DMC.
62 John, *Elizabeth Robins*, pp. 170–1; A. J. R. ed, *The suffrage annual and women's who's who* (London, Stanley Paul, 1913), p. 216.
63 ESP, *TSM*, p. 414.
64 Kenney, *Memories*, p. 195.
65 CP to Miss Lennox, 30 November 1912, Rex v. Kerr.
66 CP to Miss Lennox, 3 November 1912 and two letters on the 8th, Rex v. Kerr.
67 *Times*, 6 November 1912.

68 *VfW*, 8 November 1912, p. 85.
69 *VfW*, 25 October 1912, p. 59.
70 CP, Clear case of sex prejudice, *Daily Herald*, 28 October 1912.
71 G. Lansbury, *My life* (London, Constable and Co., 1928), p. 121; Shepherd, *George Lansbury*, p. 115. Lansbury's son-in-law, Raymond Postgate, in *The life of George Lansbury* (London, Longmans, 1951), p. 127, suggests that it was Christabel and Emmeline Pankhurst who 'persuaded' Lansbury to resign his seat. Pugh, *The Pankhursts*, pp. 254–5 suggests that the Pankhursts 'took advantage of Lansbury's good nature by encouraging him to maintain his criticism of his own party leadership'. Such suggestions are not supported in Lansbury's own autobiography.
72 CP to Miss Phillips, 17 November 1912, Mary Phillips Papers.
73 CP to Miss Phillips, 19 November 1912, Mary Phillips Papers.
74 Purvis, *Emmeline Pankhurst*, pp. 204–5.
75 ESP, TSM, pp, 424–5.
76 ESP, TSM, p. 419.
77 CP to Mr Lansbury, 24 November 1912, Lansbury Papers.
78 *Times*, 29, 30 November and 2 December 1912.
79 CP, Burnt letters, TS, 6 December 1912, p. 114.
80 See ESP, TSM, p. 244.
81 See S. Jeffreys, *The spinster and her enemies: feminism and sexuality 1880–1930* (London, Pandora Press, 1985); M. Jackson, *The 'real' facts of life: feminism and the politics of sexuality c1850–1940* (London, Taylor & Francis, 1994); L. Bland, *Banishing the beast: English feminism and sexual morality 1885–1914* (Harmondsworth, Penguin, 1995).
82 TS, 13 December 1912, p. 125.
83 TS, 29 November 1912, p. 94.
84 CP, The lesson of the election, TS, 29 November 1912, p. 98.
85 CP to Mr Lansbury, 8 December 1912, Lansbury Papers.
86 Shepherd, *George Lansbury*, pp. 129–35.
87 ESP, TSM, p. 427; TS, 29 November 1912, p. 94.
88 Entry for 23 November 1912, Nevinson Diaries.
89 Quoted in John, *Elizabeth Robins*, p. 170.
90 CP to Miss Robins, 18 November 1912, Robins Papers, HRHRC.
91 Elizabeth Robins to CP, 23 November 1912 (copy), Robins Papers, HRHRC.
92 CP to Miss Robins, 28 November 1912, Robins Papers, HRHRC.
93 CP to Miss Robins, 2 December 1912, Robins Papers, HRHRC.
94 CP to Miss Robins, 5 December 1912, Robins Papers, HRHRC.
95 TS, 29 November 1912, p. 95; reprinted in *Clarion*, 13 December 1912.
96 CP, Why the Union is strong, TS, 27 December 1912, p. 160.
97 R. Kenney, Women's suffrage: the militant movement in ruins, *English Review*, December 1912, pp. 100–3.
98 TNA, HO 45/10695/231366/2, Metropolitan Police Criminal Investigation Dept, notes on WSPU meeting 3 December 1912.
99 Entries for 2 and 8 December 1912, Nevinson Diaries.
100 CP, *Unshackled*, p. 232.
101 CP to Miss Robins, 11 and 12 December 1912, Robins Papers, HRHRC.
102 CP to Miss Robins, 9 December 1912, Robins Papers, HRHRC; CP to Miss Lennox, 3 December 1912, Rex v. Kerr.
103 CP to Miss Phillips, 16 December 1912, Mary Phillips Papers.
104 TS, 20 December 1912, p. 142, and CP, Ministerial manoeuvres, ibid., p. 146.
105 TS, 20 December 1912, p. 179; Raeburn, *Militant suffragettes*, p. 195; Purvis, *Emmeline Pankhurst*, p. 165.

15

THE ARSON CAMPAIGN
AND MORAL CRUSADE
January 1913–end of September 1913

As planned, Emmeline Pankhurst spent the first week of the New Year of 1913 with Christabel, in Paris. Although both Christabel and her mother believed that the women suffrage amendments to the Manhood Suffrage Bill were foredoomed, they decided to suspend all militant action until the amendments had been debated since, as Emmeline explained, it might give the Liberal Government 'an excuse to put the blame on our shoulders'.[1] While in Paris, Emmeline also discussed with Christabel the 'problem' of Adela, whose agricultural course at Studley was due to finish in March. Sometime earlier Adela had informed her mother of her plan to apply for teaching posts abroad, especially in Australia. 'C & I have considered them & we incline to think that it is best to let her have her own way in the matter', Emmeline informed Helen Archdale on 11 January. 'After all she is old enough & the experience may do her good whether she succeeds or fails. It may help her to stand alone.'[2] Emmeline was keen for Helen and Adela to come to Paris, to discuss everything, and for Helen to arrive sometime before Adela so that matters could be talked over privately. As Emmeline had to return to England, it was left to Christabel to finalise the arrangements.

Shortly after Emmeline had left, Christabel had another visitor, Grace Roe. At Christmas, Christabel had urged the hard-working Grace to take a rest in Switzerland, which she did, travelling there with her father. On her return route, Grace visited Christabel and readily agreed to the suggestion that she should be an understudy for Annie Kenney. Christabel had hoped that Jessie Kenney, who had proved indispensable during autumn 1912, would come to live with her in Paris, as her secretary. But Jessie had developed a threatening lung condition and went to Switzerland to recuperate, returning to Christabel intermittently throughout 1913, as her health improved. Known as 'Constance Burrows' in Paris and as 'Mary Fordyce' in Scotland, where she later supervised the printing of *The Suffragette*, Jessie acted as a courier, going to London and back by a roundabout route.[3] When Jessie was away, other women helped Christabel or sometimes she managed on her own, as seems to have been the case this January when she kept in touch with suffragettes in England by telephone and mail. 'You will remember won't you to arrange for <u>3</u> press tickets for the Deputation [of working women]', wrote an anxious Christabel to Rachel Barrett, recently put in charge of

The Suffragette. 'I can't remember whether we got that down in the last set of notes.'[4] Rachel too now became a frequent visitor to Paris, recollecting that when she spoke to Christabel on the telephone she often heard a click as Scotland Yard listened to their conversations.

Apart from such 'official' business, Christabel also tried to keep up her flow of personal letters to relatives worried about an imprisoned suffragette or to the released prisoners themselves. The crippled May Billinghurst, who propelled herself around in an invalid chair, had been sentenced on 9 January to eight months' imprisonment for attacking a letter-box. Immediately she went on hunger strike and was forcibly fed. The following day, the horrified Christabel wrote to May's mother, 'You must be feeling keenly anxious about her . . . The sentence is so monstrous.' Fortunately, May was released one week later, about the same time as Kitty Marion who had also been forcibly fed during a one-month sentence for setting off a fire alarm. 'Your courage is wonderful and we are full of pride in you', wrote Christabel to Kitty.[5] Then there were congratulations to be sent to Elizabeth Robins, whose novel, *Where are you going to . . .?* had just been published, as well as matters relating to Adela to be organised.[6] 'You shall come here first if you will', Christabel suggested to Helen Archdale:

> The shipping people are putting a double berthed cabin at Adela's exclusive disposal so she ought to be very comfortable. Dr. Hamilton has sent what shd prove a very useful testimonial and tells of a proposed horticultural college in N.[ew] S.[South] Wales which may provide an opening.[7]

Yet, despite the importance of such family matters, Christabel's main focus was always upon winning the vote and mobilising the suffragettes when, as she accurately predicted, the women's suffrage amendments failed to become law.

No hope was drawn from the deputation of working women, led by Flora Drummond and Annie Kenney on 23 January to two Cabinet Ministers, Lloyd George and Sir Edward Grey, their replies being considered 'shifty and vague'.[8] Nonetheless, Christabel was full of praise for the way in which Annie had spoken to the two men, telling Elizabeth Robins, on holiday in Florida, that Annie just 'develops & develops and yet remains the same which is so satisfactory. The stodgy Labour MPs for whose benefit the non militants have raised such sums of money are not fit to black her boots'.[9]

On 23 January, the Speaker of the House of Commons ruled that the women's suffrage amendments to the Manhood Suffrage Bill were out of order since they would so change the nature of the bill that a new measure would need to be introduced. Four days later, Asquith announced that he regretted that the Government would withdraw the bill this session, although facilities would be offered for a private member's bill in the next. Lloyd George conveyed this news to Flora Drummond and Annie Kenney who promptly travelled to France to discuss the offer with Christabel. Believing that the Government had deliberately wrecked the bill to prevent women's suffrage becoming law, Christabel's reply was that 'anything short of a Govt. Bill' should be declined, a view with which her mother and even C. P. Scott agreed.[10]

In advance of the Manhood Suffrage Bill debate, Christabel had left Paris for Calais. 'I am staying here [at the Hotel Terminus] so as to be even more accessible than usual during the crisis', she wrote on 25 January to Elizabeth Robins. 'Mother is here for a short visit.' The Government 'have dished us', Christabel concluded, something they appear to have had 'up their sleeve for some time'.[11] Although Asquith denied any complicity with the Speaker, the WSPU challenged that view, pointing out that 'Mr. Asquith, Mr. Lloyd George, and the rest, are not ignorant of parliamentary procedure . . . they are scoundrels'.[12] Emmeline Pankhurst at various large, enthusiastic meetings denounced the 'trickery' of the Liberal Government and announced that it was 'guerilla [sic] warfare that we declare'.[13] On the evening of 28 January, suffragettes resumed window smashing in London's West End, while two days later a new form of militancy was devised in the Birmingham district when 'Votes for Women' was cut in large letters into the turf and acid poured onto the ground, destroying the grass.[14] When Emmeline met Henry Nevinson, who pleaded for restraint, she told him it was 'impossible for Christabel to return: she had the finest political insight, & the time for great speeches was gone'.[15]

Christabel, in *The Suffragette*, reinforced the call for direct action. The 'torpedoing' of the women's suffrage amendments clearly proved that 'militancy is for women both a political weapon and a means of vindicating their spiritual freedom . . . Fortified by disappointment and inspired by betrayal, the militant women shout their songs of triumph in the face of the enemy'. Nor was she impressed with the Labour Party which stood:

> at the parting of the ways. If they ignore the women's appeal and continue to support the Government, they will meet political ruin. If, on the other hand, they decide to fight the Government in the interests of women, they will find salvation.[16]

The following week, on 7 February, *The Suffragette* put on its front page a cartoon of a fawning Keir Hardie, a fat cigar in his mouth, arm-in-arm with the Prime Minister. Inside the covers, praise was given to the 'guerilla [sic] warfare . . . now in full swing' – which included not only window smashing and damage to letter-boxes and golf greens but also the breaking, in the Tower of London, of the glass case containing the Crown Jewels.[17]

The attack on Keir Hardie angered Sylvia, who had just visited Christabel in Paris. However, Christabel was unrepentant. 'Sylvia has been here . . . & . . . has had some rest from her fight with the Government. Miss Kenney is with me at this moment', she wrote blithely on 9 February to Mrs Belmont, a wealthy American WSPU supporter. 'I have been long on the point of writing to you', she continued, 'but Mother has been here & every available minute I have spent talking to her & going out with her.' Comparing the fight for women's suffrage in the United States with that in Britain, Christabel asserted that the British politicians 'are the worst in the world . . . In America they have their faults but our highest politicians surpass all others in treachery & cruelty'.[18] As the scale and variety of militancy spread, Emmeline Pankhurst during a speech that February admitted that she was 'the head and front' of those who offended the public by destroying orchid houses at Kew Gardens, breaking windows, cutting telegraph wires and damaging golf greens. A plain-clothes detective was at the meeting taking full notes. The Government were biding their time, waiting for the occasion when she would give them cause to arrest her. On 19 February, the day after suffragettes had wrecked with a bomb Lloyd George's empty and partly completed fourteen-roomed house in Walton Heath, Surrey, Emmeline said at a WSPU meeting at Cardiff, 'I accept responsibility . . . I have advised, I have incited, I have conspired.'[19]

The following day, Lilian Lenton and Olive Wharry were arrested on suspicion of setting fire to the refreshment pavilion at Kew Gardens which was burnt to the ground. Emmeline expected to be arrested at any moment, and that came shortly after two o'clock in the afternoon of 24 February. In the police court she refused to give an undertaking not to take part in further agitation, and so the magistrate would not grant bail. Sent to Holloway to await a trial, Emmeline went on hunger strike and, after twenty-four hours, agreed to accept the bail conditions when the Government promised to move her case to the Central Criminal Court at the Old Bailey where it would be heard in the April assizes. Much to Christabel's relief, her mother was released on 27 February.[20]

On the front page of that week's *The Suffragette*, underneath the title 'WHAT MEN DID TO GET THE VOTE', was a picture of the burning of Nottingham Castle during successful male agitation for an extension of the franchise in 1831. In an unsigned statement beneath the etching, Christabel defended the WSPU arson campaign:

> After nearly fifty years of peaceful appeal, after seven years of mild and merely symbolic militancy, women have taken to real violence in order to win the vote. The obstinacy and the treachery of the politicians have convinced women that the Government will never give them the vote except as a means of escape from an intolerable situation . . . the militant acts committed by women in the past few days . . . are trifling when compared to the militancy of men . . . In Bristol [in 1831] they burnt the Mansion House, the Custom House, the Bishop's Palace, the Excise Office, three prisons, and much private property. In many revolutions for political freedom life itself has been destroyed. The Government may indeed be thankful for the moderation shown by women.[21]

Although Christabel defended the arson campaign, she was insistent that all those who fired empty buildings should not endanger human life and regularly asked for reassurances from London headquarters that this was the case. When the *Daily Mail* claimed that suffragettes had caused an explosion at Devonport that hurt a boy, she wrote immediately to the editor, enclosing a copy of a telegram from Harriet Kerr denying it was the work of the WSPU.[22] Nor would Christabel let the constitutional work of the WSPU slip away. She wrote to Flora Drummond proposing a series of public meetings in Hyde Park. At the first, held on Sunday, 1 March, Flora was bombarded with turf and drowned out by rowdies in the crowd.[23]

Meanwhile, Emmeline Pankhurst had travelled to Paris to discuss with her eldest daughter what future direction the WSPU should take if she should be sent to prison after her forthcoming trial. The two decided that militancy had to continue and that Emmeline should make any prison sentence as short as possible, by going on hunger strike. Above all, Emmeline was insistent that even if she was committed to prison, Christabel must remain in Paris to direct the movement. Christabel agreed. 'Mother is in the best fighting spirit that I have <u>ever</u> seen her in & that is saying something', she informed Elizabeth Robins whose recent letter mother and daughter had read together.[24] Christabel and Emmeline also discussed the crucial role of *The Suffragette* for keeping the rank-and-file in touch with the leadership, suggesting various improvements in content and layout. 'Will you see Mrs Pankhurst on her return abt the paper', wrote Christabel in early March to Agnes Lake, the business manager of *The Suffragette*. 'She has ideas on the subject I gather.' Christabel was worried that copy for the paper was going to the printer too late so that it appeared after their main rival, *Votes for Women*, edited by the Lawrences. Just a few days earlier, she had told Agnes that the circulation of the paper had to be increased and enquired, 'Are we getting our posters well shown by newsagents & at tube & other railway bookstalls?'[25]

The worry about the effectiveness of *The Suffragette* at this time was soon tempered by a more personal, family matter. Sylvia, the little sister Christabel had looked after when a child, was being forcibly fed in Holloway. Despite their ideological differences in adulthood, Christabel made sure that extensive coverage about her sister's plight was given in *The Suffragette*.[26] After the failure of the working women's deputation, the WSPU had closed its offices in the East End of London but Sylvia had continued to live there, forming with a few friends a radical, militant organisation allied to the WSPU, the East London Federation of the Suffragettes. A community organisation with close ties to the labour movement, the East London Federation was not solely concerned with votes for women. Nor was it a single-sex organisation, since it also admitted men. Nonetheless, Sylvia hoped the organisation, of which she was Honorary Secretary, would bring in more working-class supporters to the women's movement. She was aided in this task by Zelie Emerson as Honorary Organiser and the wealthy Norah Smyth, niece of Ethel, as Financial Secretary.[27] On 17 February, Sylvia had led an East London demonstration in support of votes for women and broken the windows of an undertaker's shop, and it was for this offence that she was now serving two months' imprisonment in Holloway.

Released on medical grounds, on Good Friday, 21 March, she had served just five weeks of her sentence. In addition to the hunger strike, she had added the protests of thirst and sleep strikes.[28]

The plight of the hunger-striking suffragettes weighed heavily on Christabel's shoulders, especially the case of Lilian Lenton who had been hastily released from prison on 23 February, seriously ill with pleurisy caused by fluid from the nasal tube having entered her lung when being forcibly fed. Henry Harben, a lawyer, Fabian, member of the Men's Political Union and WSPU supporter, advised Christabel that it would be difficult to prove 'carelessness' on the part of the doctor, a view with which she reluctantly agreed. 'Thank you for the trouble you have taken in this matter', she replied on 11 March. 'It will be a great pleasure to see Mrs Harben and yourself when you are here in May.'[29] However, the tone of the front page of *The Suffragette*, published three days later, was less mild:

> For the sake of Justice the militant women have surrendered all thought of self, and that is why the material force of the law fails to subdue them. The law may imprison, may torture, may kill, but it cannot make women afraid, and it cannot make them surrender.[30]

Such comments that stressed women's spiritual strength over men's physical force were particularly apposite. The Liberal Government, determined to stop suffragettes flouting the law, had quickly drawn up legislation that would give the Home Secretary, Reginald McKenna, the power to release into the community, on a temporary licence, prisoners in a poor state of health so that they could recover sufficiently to be re-arrested, if their sentence had not been completed. Under the present law, once the Government had been compelled, because of illness, to release a forcibly fed suffragette, she could not be recaptured unless she again broke the law.

It is highly probable that the Liberal Government's drafting of this new legislation was one of the topics of Christabel's weekly address to the Paris branch of the WSPU at this time, the new branch having been formed in February with the American Alice Morgan Wright as its secretary.[31] As Easter approached, Christabel heard that the chaplain in Holloway was denying Anglican militants the sacrament, unless they admitted the error of their ways. She sent a deputation to the Bishop of London, and shortly afterwards the bar was lifted.[32] On Good Friday, 21 March, she called on the example of Jesus Christ to reinforce her message that prophets were stoned during their lifetime. What would the 'Master' say, she commented, of 'certain public men, who profess to be Christians, calling out for more and yet more punishment for the militant women'. The reply would be, 'Woe unto you Scribes and Pharisees, hypocrites . . . Ye blind guides, which strain at a gnat and swallow a camel!' The suffragettes were engaged in 'wars of liberation, holy wars' which gave them 'a clean conscience and a perfect spiritual freedom'.[33]

As a hasty second reading of the Prisoners' (Temporary Discharge for Ill-Health) Bill approached, soon to be known as the 'Cat and Mouse Act',

Christabel thundered that the Government were acting not because they were compassionate towards women but because they were afraid of being responsible for a prisoner's death. However, the forcibly fed suffragette would triumph since she brought about:

> a rending of prison walls . . . a miracle effected by faith and spiritual power. The attainment of votes for women by such means will teach the world a lesson that is much needed . . . that [the] spirit is stronger than matter, the soul greater than the body . . . that, in fighting against evil, the few are stronger than the many, women stronger than men, and one stronger than all. It will establish for ever the truth that it is not brute force that rules the world.[34]

Such considerations carried no weight with Judge Lush who presided in early April over Emmeline Pankhurst's delayed trial. Although the jury found Emmeline guilty, with a strong recommendation to mercy, she was sentenced to three years' penal servitude.[35] That evening, 3 April, Annie Kenney announced at a WSPU meeting that militancy would be 'more furious than before . . . until our leader is let out' and urged all those who sympathised with militancy to join the Union and 'do one deed within the next 48 hours'. She also informed her audience, 'I was in Paris at Easter, spending a few days with the refugee, and discussing the various phases of work with regard to our movement.'[36] The following day, a fresh wave of secret militancy broke out; empty country houses and railway carriages were set on fire, a bomb exploded at the railway station at the Surrey village of Oxted and the glass of famous paintings was smashed.[37] On 8 April Annie too was arrested but released on £200 bail, paid by Henry Harben, after she agreed temporarily to cease her involvement in the militant campaign.[38]

Christabel greeted the arrests of her mother and Annie as calmly as she could, and set about implementing the plan that had been agreed. Grace Roe was asked to come to Boulogne, in preparation for the time when she would take over Annie's work as Chief Organiser in England. Harriet Kerr, the WSPU's office manager, was invited to travel with her.[39] However, it was not only effective organisation that the WSPU needed in a time of crisis but also financial support. 'I write to ask you to . . . give the very biggest subscription that you can afford at the Albert Hall next Thursday', Christabel pleaded with Myra Sadd Brown on 5 April. 'Mother is very anxious for political reasons that the collection shall be a record one and she has asked me to look after it.'[40] Similar letters were sent to other well-off WSPU members, including Janie Allan, daughter of a shipping magnate, Lady Cook and Mrs Douglas Hamilton. Christabel's persistence but especially her mother's hunger strike, carried on for nine terrible days when Emmeline subsisted on water alone, brought positive results. At the Albert Hall meeting on 10 April, a sum of £15,000, far in excess of all previous records, was raised.[41] The Home Secretary was determined to be tough with these troublesome women whose meetings in Hyde Park, Wimbledon Common and other open spaces were causing grave disorder. On 15 April, the Commissioner of Police of the Metropolis of London sent a letter to WSPU headquarters saying that meetings in public open spaces in the Metropolitan area would no longer be permitted. Nor was that all. The management of the Albert Hall refused to let it to the Union for any further events.[42]

Christabel was deeply concerned about her mother, released on 12 April to Catherine Pine's nursing home, at 9 Pembridge Gardens. But she also knew of her mother's remarkable powers of recuperation, her determination and unconquerable spirit. 'Glad to hear news that all goes well at 9 P. Gdens', the relieved daughter wrote to Harriet Kerr. 'She is a great picker up and besides we will just take things as they come – running no risks of course.'[43] Her mother was not the only person close to Christabel causing anxiety. The frail Mabel Tuke had returned from her trip to South Africa and was keen to take up again her role as Honorary Secretary. But 'Pansy' was still not in good health and Christabel wanted to make sure she did not overwork. She wrote to Harriet Kerr, asking her to arrange for her dear friend to come to Paris where, among other things, she could be briefed on the changing situation.[44]

Pansy met up with Christabel who had a steady stream of visitors that April, including Flora Drummond, Betty Archdale, Jessie Kenney and, unexpectedly, Beatrice Sanders, the financial secretary of the Union. Beatrice complained about the difficulties under which she was operating at Lincoln's Inn House; her department was squeezed into too small a space in a partitioned room and the importance of their work was not recognised by Harriet Kerr, the office manager. Christabel listened patiently and once Beatrice had left for England, tried tactfully to ease the tensions by writing to Harriet about various changes that might free up more space. 'What do you think of an idea that came into my head of serving teas in each office i.e. letting girls on each floor take trays to their respective floor?' she wrote apprehensively. 'It is just my suggestion.' Treading carefully, she praised Beatrice's personal qualities:

> One thing about Mrs S. [Sanders] is that she is quite open and shows her work to you and not behind your back . . . She is a good sort and does her job thoroughly well . . . Have a motherly forgiveness of all their failings won't you even Mrs S.[45]

It is highly probable that Christabel made a clandestine trip to London to sort out the matter.[46]

Amid all these comings and goings and attempts to sort out disagreements at WSPU headquarters, the good news arrived that Adela had passed her gardening diploma. Although she had then tried, unsuccessfully, to find a research post, she had been offered the position of head gardener at Road Manor near Bath, the home of Mrs Batten Pooll, a WSPU supporter. 'I am very very grateful to you for all your kindness about Adela', Christabel was soon writing to Betty Archdale.[47]

On 30 April, a severe but not unexpected blow was struck when the police raided the London WSPU headquarters and arrested Harriet Kerr, Flora Drummond, Beatrice Sanders, Rachel Barrett, Geraldine Lennox and Agnes Lake. The story was widely reported in the press, some newspapers printing photographs of the women on the front pages.[48] Also raided that morning was the flat that Annie and Jessie Kenney shared, at 19 Mecklenburgh Square, as well as Victoria House Press which was printing *The Suffragette* for the first time, the former printer having lost his nerve. When Annie returned to England the following day, after a visit to Christabel, she too was arrested. Further detentions included those of Sidney Drew, the manager of the Victoria House Press, as well as Edwy Clayton, a chemist who was helping the WSPU to make bombs.[49] All were charged with conspiring to damage property.

On the morning of the raid at WSPU headquarters, the young Esther Knowles, one of the office staff, slipped out unseen and travelling far afield, for fear of being followed, rang up Christabel in Paris, giving her the names of those arrested. Grace Roe, who was feeling ill, was in headquarters too that morning and amid the chaos, Marjorie, one of the typists, whispered to her that she had Christabel's article hidden in her blouse, ready for *The Suffragette* which was due to appear in a couple of days. As soon as the opportunity arose, Grace left the building through a back door, withdrew £500 out of her own bank account and set about allocating various necessary tasks. The Information Department, under Cicely Hale's guidance, produced copy for the next issue while two other suffragettes found a new printer. After Grace had dictated a letter to be sent to all organisers and secretaries, telling them that they should carry on as usual, she hurried to Hertha Ayrton's house, where the ill Emmeline Pankhurst was now recuperating. Grace told the frail Emmeline that the paper had gone to press. Since it was important to get news to Christabel, it was decided that Barbara Ayrton, Hertha's daughter, should travel to France that afternoon. Grace followed in the evening, disguised as the wife of Arthur Marshall, the WSPU's solicitor, who accompanied her to Victoria. After a two-hour conversation with Christabel in Paris, Grace decided that it was safer in the future not to correspond directly with Christabel but to use Phyl Keller's Paris address. *The Suffragette* appeared as scheduled on 2 May 1913, with a blank front page bearing the headline in large type, 'RAIDED!!'[50]

Once back in her London flat, Grace felt insecure. Her fears were well founded since her abode was raided one day, shortly after she had left. Meanwhile, Mildred Mansell had travelled to Paris to discuss the situation with Christabel and was given instructions to find Grace a safe haven, which she did, in an old house in Earls Court. 'By this time an underground set-up was being formed', recollected Grace Roe, 'messengers travelling by circuitous routes went between Christabel and myself taking letters and important news.' The Earls Court flat became the heart of the WSPU in London, Lincoln's Inn House being merely:

a wonderful front . . . Mrs. Mansel, as cousin of the Liberal Chief Whip, was virtually immune from arrest and she was now a constant visitor . . . She . . . was the vital link between the commander in exile and the chief organiser in London.[51]

This network of women loyal to Christabel was critical for the successful organisation of the WSPU and for Christabel's leadership at a distance. And Christabel, for her part, was loyal to her supporters, especially at this time of crisis. Thus politely but decisively she delayed meeting the wealthy Mrs Belmont until 9 May, knowing that priority must be given to those arrested at Lincoln's Inn and to the continued efficient running of the WSPU.[52] 'I was so pleased to get your cheery letter', Christabel then wrote encouragingly to Agnes Lake, now on bail. 'You are all so brave and I can't tell you how proud I am of you.'[53] The raids had produced some substantial evidence, but did not crush the movement, even though many of its key personnel had been arrested. Christabel, referred to in the British press as 'the brains of the movement', knew in particular that The Suffragette had to be kept in circulation since it was the most important way of keeping in touch with the rank-and-file.[54] And she was determined to do this.

For someone who, by her own admission, had a personal preference 'always for bed in the morning and work later', Christabel kept irregular hours.[55] 'She would wake up in the middle of the night . . . and suddenly think of a good idea for the leading article', recollected Phyllis Keller. 'She usually didn't have a proper piece of paper but she might have some letters or something like that and she would slit up the envelope and she would write on them.' The articles were all written in pencil, in her difficult-to-read handwriting. 'Untidy wasn't the word for it.' On one occasion, Christabel herself had difficulty deciphering her own writing. On another, Pansy offered to do the typing. 'But she wasn't as proficient as I was', remembered Phyllis:

> She was awfully bad at it . . . and Christabel came in and I said, 'Mrs. Tuke is re-writing your articles for you, Christabel.' She was furious . . . I found them afterwards all scrapped and Christabel just sent her originals in.[56]

Back in England, hunger-striking suffragettes continued to be forcibly fed. Yet MPs seemed unmoved by their plight since on 6 May a private member's bill to enfranchise women of twenty-five years and upwards, who were householders or wives of householders, was defeated by forty-seven votes on its second reading in the Commons. Later that day the arson campaign took a different turn as empty churches, such as St Catherine's, Hatcham, South London, were destroyed by fire.[57] The public condemnation of such militant acts, expressed in all major newspapers, was further fuelled by fears about a bomb in St Paul's Cathedral. Some WSPU members, such as Mary Blathwayt, resigned their membership in protest yet continued to attend union meetings.[58]

Christabel took the news of such resignations in her stride since she was adamant that if militancy had been right for voteless men in the past, then it was a necessity for voteless women in the present. Every suffragette activity, she argued, had been met with violence from the Government, even when women were engaging in peaceful, unarmed protest, as on Black Friday. And now, under the Cat and Mouse Act, forcible feeding – another form of violence which was 'universally recognized as torture' – was being used. 'When people condemn violent methods they ought to remember that the Government are greater sinners than the Suffragettes where violence is concerned.'[59] One suffragette whom the authorities never dared forcibly feed was her fifty-five-year-old mother who was re-arrested on 26 May as she tried to leave for a WSPU meeting. Back in Holloway, Emmeline Pankhurst immediately went on hunger strike and was released four days later, on a seven-day licence.[60] Despite the havoc that repeated hunger strikes caused to her body, she continued to use the Cat and Mouse Act in this way, serving just six weeks of her three-year sentence.

That May of 1913 the arson campaign escalated, causing a considerable amount of damage to property.[61] Yet, at the same time, a fund-raising 'peaceful' event was being organised, a Suffragette Summer Festival with stalls selling toys, books, millinery, antiques, sweets, flowers and summer frocks, to be held at the Empire Rooms, Kensington, from 3–13 June. From the outset, Christabel had been very supportive of the idea, giving helpful advice.[62] On the opening day, Emily Wilding Davison went to the fair with her close friend Mary Leigh. A risk-taker, Emily was fatally injured the following day, 4 June, when she ran onto the race course at the Derby as she tried to grab the reins of the King's horse. Her death four days later stunned and saddened Christabel and the WSPU membership generally.[63] An entire issue of *The Suffragette*, edged in black, was full of praise for the martyr for the women's cause. 'So greatly did she care for freedom that she died for it', wrote Christabel. 'So dearly did she love women that she offered her life as their ransom.'[64] Grace Roe was asked to organise a great procession, which she did in secret. The funeral procession, in which five thousand women marched, was the last and most moving of all the suffragette demonstrations and widely reported in the press. Vast and largely silent crowds lined the streets.[65]

The trial of Annie and her fellow conspirators at the Old Bailey had opened on 9 June and continued after the weekend of the funeral. Christabel had told Annie that it was necessary for her to defend herself. 'I knew what her idea was', recollected Annie:

I had to insist on practically all political articles in the paper [*The Suffragette*] being read, to convert the jury, to cross-examine on those points only which would give a hit at the Government . . . to make myself a nuisance.[66]

While waiting to hear the verdict, Christabel replied on 15 June to another of the conspirators, Agnes Lake, expressing the hope that she would be acquitted

325

and could come and see her soon. Although advising that those left behind in the various WSPU departments should cope as best they could, when their comrades were arrested, Christabel gave short shrift to the suggestion that she should take on responsibility for more mundane matters. 'It is impossible for me to look after the tea selling, cigarette selling side of the Woman's Press', she protested, 'and therefore I want that all to be closed down till the autumn when we can consider the position anew.'[67]

On 17 June all the conspirators were found guilty and Judge Phillimore imposed heavy sentences to be served in the Third Division – twenty-one months for Edwy Clayton, eighteen for Annie Kenney, fifteen for Beatrice Sanders, twelve for Harriet Kerr, nine for Rachel Barrett and six each for Agnes Lake and Geraldine Lennox.[68] The women were hurriedly sent to separate jails. All went on hunger strike and within ten days were released in a severely emaciated condition. After recuperating at 'Mouse Castle', the home of Mrs Brackenbury at 2 Campden Hill Square, some were re-arrested and released again, under the Cat and Mouse Act. 'Congratulations on having won your release so soon', penned a thankful Christabel to Agnes on 24 June. 'It will be a joy to all of us when the time is at an end.'[69]

In *The Suffragette* Christabel condemned the Government's policy in the strongest terms possible:

> Hardly has one victim of the Government's cowardly injustice and obstinacy been laid in the grave when other women are, because of that same obstinacy, brought face to face with death . . . In Mr. Justice Phillimore the Government have found a willing ally . . . This vindictive old man . . . has the astounding impudence to take the name of God upon his lips . . . What are we to think of the sanity of an Englishman who declares . . . that rebellion is 'treason to the Almighty'? We commend to him another saying that is written across the heavens: 'Rebellion to tyrants is obedience to God' . . . They nailed Christ to the Cross, they burnt Joan of Arc, they are bent now upon killing Suffragist prisoners by inches.[70]

Although the women conspirators had been released, their close working relationship with Christabel was now at an end. Harriet Kerr, whose companion was ill with phlebitis, felt obliged to give the authorities an undertaking that she would refrain from further militancy – and left her post as office manager. Geraldine Lennox and Rachel Barrett were forced underground, as was Beatrice Sanders. Agnes Lake's health broke down. As new women came forward to replace these key workers and others who were arrested, the group who deputised for Christabel continually changed.[71]

As the WSPU became increasingly an underground movement, the organisational crisis necessitated that Christabel temporarily leave Paris and stay on the northern French coast to make communication between herself and

London easier. Mrs Belmont offered the use of her luxurious home, Les Abeilles, at Deauville near Le Havre. Christabel hoped that Jessie Kenney, who had been staying with Helen Archdale in Switzerland, was sufficiently recovered to act as her secretary. 'I have wanted to know your address for some time so that I might write and thank you for your kindness to Jessie', wrote the grateful Christabel to Helen in mid-June:

> I shd like her to come to me at the end of this month if she is at all fit for
> it & I am writing to her to say so . . . The work will not be laborious for
> Jessie & it may do her good even.

But that was not Christabel's only concern. As always, she was racked with worry about the effect of repeated imprisonments on her mother. 'Mother <u>took no luggage</u> with her to Holloway so that as you will see she did not intend to stay long!' she commented to Helen. 'I hope this will be the end of their cat & mouse tactics as regards her.'[72]

But it was not so. Emmeline Pankhurst continued to suffer repeated imprisonments, a situation that her daughter Sylvia believed was a result of Christabel's strategy. But Emmeline was not a pawn in Christabel's hand but an active participant in their joint decision-making. Emmeline's increasingly dominant and visible role in the suffragette movement in England made her, not the absent Christabel, the increasingly powerful figure. At the heart of the women's struggle with the British Government, it was Emmeline Pankhurst who became *the* epitome of female militancy, struggling for justice for her sex. And by focusing attention on herself, Emmeline was also protecting Christabel, her cherished daughter, the apple of her eye. She wanted the situation no other way.[73]

While Christabel was at Deauville, Jessie Kenney duly arrived to temporarily help out. One of her first tasks was to write out, at Christabel's dictation, a letter to Mary Phillips telling the experienced organiser, now working in Plymouth, that she was dismissed from her post. For some time Mary had been experiencing difficulties in working up enthusiasm for the WSPU in her district and had recently written to Lincoln's Inn pointing this out. A copy of the letter had been forwarded to Christabel. 'Under the circumstances I do not think that we are justified in having an official Organiser', Christabel brutally informed Mary:

> If local people will provide neither money nor work it is impossible for
> Headquarters to supply them with an Organiser. We have been feeling
> this for a long time and have come to the conclusion that it would not
> be right to let matters drift any longer.

Mary was given four weeks' salary in lieu of notice, a breathing space that gave her the opportunity to look for a new occupation if she so wished.[74]

Mary Phillips found it hard to accept her dismissal and wrote to a friend saying she had lost her post because her district was not considered 'worth working'.

When Christabel received a copy of this letter she immediately dealt firmly with the situation, saying bluntly what she had refrained from saying previously:

> I want to say that if we had thought you wd have made a success of another district we shd have asked you to take one. I did not wish to hurt you needlessly by saying what always has been felt at headquarters that you are not effective as a district organiser.[75]

That Christabel, as Chief Organiser of the WSPU, treated one of her long-serving organisers in this way says much about the strain under which she was living – and about her character. Even though she had previously sent Mary Phillips letters of praise and affection, she could be intolerant of WSPU employees who were not working effectively. And living in France, away from the hubbub of suffragette activity, she sometimes felt insecure in her leadership and suspicious of those who, like Mary, had left-wing or 'extreme Left' sympathies, as Mary later described it, and did not fully embrace the new militant tactics. Mary had been unhappy about the expulsion of Mrs Lawrence from the WSPU and, above all else, was becoming increasingly friendly with Sylvia Pankhurst whose East London Federation she joined immediately after her dismissal, working under the name of 'Mary Patterson'.[76] Christabel was worried that her socialist sister was becoming too powerful and too prominent since, like their mother, she was in and out of prison under the Cat and Mouse Act, organising public protests and writing to the press to publicise her plight.[77] Christabel knew only too well that Sylvia, who disagreed with the secret arson campaign that was still raging, wanted to ally the WSPU to the Labour movement. Such an alliance had to be prevented at all costs. The threat that Christabel felt to her authority was not helped by the fact that well-known male socialists, such as Henry Harben and G. R. S. Taylor, a regular contributor to the *Daily Herald* and the *Clarion*, kept trying to persuade her to change her mind on this issue.

Taylor visited Christabel to state his case. '[H]e even tried to make out that many of our members were in favour of such an alliance', wrote Jessie Kenney as she took notes of the conversation:

> When C. P. asked for names, he mentioned only those of two members who have left the Union . . . He did bring in the General's name [Flora Drummond], and would have been prepared to say more if C. P. had not broken in on the conversation then.

Jessie was even more alarmed when later, in a private conversation with Taylor, as they were both travelling to Le Havre, he confided that he thought that Christabel was 'out of touch' with the socialist movement, had an inflexible style of leadership and had generally failed to understand that 'it was not the Parnell Policy that had got Home Rule, but . . . the Redmond Policy [cooperation with a friendly political party]'.[78] Fearing that Taylor and his friends would attack the

WSPU leadership when it suited them, Jessie immediately informed Christabel about what had been said. It was decided to send copies of Jessie's notes to Annie Kenney in London so that she could enlist the support of Agnes and Henry Harben. However, Henry Harben sided with Taylor.

On 7 August 1913, writing to Harben from Deauville, Christabel gave a clear exposition of her views:

> Between the W.S.P.U. and the Daily Herald League or Movement there can be no connection. Ours is a Woman's Movement and the Herald League is primarily a Man's Movement . . . The great need of this time is for women to learn to stand and to act alone . . . women are working out their own salvation . . . the Herald League tends to be a Class Movement. Ours is not a class movement at all. We take in everybody – the highest and the lowest, the richest and the poorest. The bond is womanhood . . . men must paddle their canoe, and we must paddle ours.[79]

Christabel's refusal to form an alliance between the WSPU and the labour movement would eventually lead to a break with her socialist sisters Sylvia and Adela, early in 1914. But that was still to come. Meanwhile, Sylvia sought some respite from her Cat and Mouse existence by escaping to Finland, with Norah Smyth, in August 1913. She would return to England two months later.[80] The unhappy Adela, on the other hand, without telling her mother, had given up her gardening job at Road Manor. She had not told her family how hard and exhausting her job had been, although she did tell the suffragette Maud Joachim who promptly informed Sylvia. Sylvia then related the tale to her mother. 'Sylvia was as hot against me as all the rest', recollected Adela bitterly some twenty years later; 'she repeated the offending words to mother in order to make her angry with me.'[81] Thus in summer 1913 Adela found herself in a mountain village in Switzerland, acting as a governess to the Archdale children, Alec and Betty. 'It is good news that Adela writes so cheerfully', wrote Christabel to Helen Archdale, hoping that at long last her youngest sister might be settled. 'It is a load off one's mind.'[82]

Christabel was joined at Deauville that August by her mother and Annie. Emmeline had been gaunt and haggard when she first arrived, having endured four hunger strikes since April, but by mid-August had regained some of her strength. The three women were sitting in the casino gardens at the fashionable watering place of Trouville, planning the autumn campaign, when journalists spotted them. Celebrity icons of the early twentieth century, they were described by a Daily Sketch reporter as 'perhaps the most-talked-of women in the wide world . . . the trio that defied a Cabinet and made a Government look foolish'. Emmeline Pankhurst wore a black dress, trimmed with a large, white lace collar, but the 'charming' Christabel had 'quite a French look about her in her pink frock with a dainty hat to match a pretty red jacket . . . Miss Kenny [sic] looked very girlish and cool, and all three appeared to be in perfect physical health'. No one would have suspected, as they chatted in the sunlight, 'that these three fragile women were a trio of conspirators who have spiked the guns of the English law and made a mockery of the most powerful Administration of modern times'. Persistent journalists, trying to interview the three women, pursued them as they strolled along the sea front and visited a gambling saloon. Emmeline was intrigued by a game of 'petits chevaux', and wanted to know what the little horses were for, and how the money was staked. Christabel 'smilingly initiated her mother into the mysteries of the game' although none of the three ventured to make a bet, nor would they divulge details of the next stage of their campaign. In reply to questioning from a reporter with the *New York Herald*, Emmeline denied stories that suffragettes were poisoning dogs and suggested that the bomb found in St Paul's Cathedral had probably been placed there by the police.[83]

The next stage of the campaign, initiated by Christabel, was to bring much more centrally into WSPU policy a moral crusade that highlighted the degrading effects of prostitution, venereal disease and white slave trafficking for women and society generally, a situation that was a direct consequence of men's failure to live up to the moral standards of women.[84] In emphasising the double sexual standard, Christabel was restating a key concern of the women's movement from the 1880s onwards, especially in regard to the work of Josephine Butler, and making it integral to suffragette demands.[85] The time was particularly ripe for an analysis of the ways in which men's sexual behaviour was an intrinsic aspect of women's subordination. Christabel was becoming increasingly concerned about how the White Slavery Act of 1912, passed to target traffickers in women and children, was being used almost exclusively to punish rather than protect prostituted women. Further, venereal diseases were considered such a serious problem that a Royal Commission had recently been established on the subject. A notorious court case, that summer of 1913, only added further fuel to her fire.

On 10 July 1913, a brothel keeper named Queenie Gerald pleaded guilty to the charge of having unlawfully, under the White Slave Traffic Act, exercised control over the movement of three young women in such a manner as to aid and abet them in prostitution. Although the case had received little publicity, there was a widespread belief that Queenie Gerald, sentenced to just three months' imprisonment, was merely a figurehead and that behind her were prominent men involved in sadistic practices. Christabel was determined to expose the facts and the *Daily Sketch* soon took up the cause, claiming:

> Letters have been found, signed by men of high position, revealing an organisation for procuring young girls and little children. The evidence was not produced in the case because the men concerned were person of importance. The law of libel makes it impossible to give names, but the 'Daily Sketch' knows the names.[86]

On 14 July, at a speech at the London Pavilion, Emmeline Pankhurst maintained that the police had raided Lincoln's Inn because they wanted to seize articles 'exposing the wrong doing of the Government'. Referring to the Piccadilly Flat case, as it became known, she pointed out that Queenie Gerald had received a light sentence to protect her clientele. '[T]he people who are most against us in the House of Commons are the men who want things hushed up.'[87] With fury, Christabel elaborated in more detail her own analysis of the situation.

'In the Piccadilly Flat Case, with its foul revelations and its still fouler conceal-ments, is summed up the whole case against Votes for Women', she wrote angrily in *The Suffragette* on 25 July. The anti-suffragist theory of life and of the position of women led straight to such a hideous state, of which this case was merely an illustration. Anti-suffragists, who 'see in woman, sex and nothing more', divide them into two categories, 'wives' and 'prostitutes'. Wives were expected to give birth to legitimate children and yet were not recognised by the law as independ-ent 'persons' or as 'legal parents' of their own children. Prostitutes, who soon became diseased, were used for the physical satisfaction of men whose sex instinct was considered innate, something that could not be controlled. For the rest of womankind, the anti-suffragist held a 'peculiar fear and horror', describing them as 'superfluous women' for whom he saw no use at all. The male patrons of the Piccadilly Flat, Christabel blasted:

> after their share in degrading young girls, after wading through physical and moral filth, went home, and doubtless forbade any 'meddling with the Suffrage question' . . . Heaven help and pity the wife of such a man! She is put in danger of acquiring loathsome disease and the marriage into which she entered in love and trust is desecrated.

The conniving of these male patrons with other men to keep the truth hidden, she asserted, had been a great revelation to women. 'Everybody knows that important men were supporting the Piccadilly flat. A great many people know *who these men are*.' Why were women kept out of the court when this case was being investi-gated? Why were no male clients punished? Why was Queenie Gerald put in the Second Division and Annie Kenney and other suffragettes placed in the Third? Why was she given a mere three months' prison sentence and Mrs Pankhurst three years? Christabel entreated 'all women who want to see humanity no longer degraded by impure thought and physical disease' to come into 'the ranks of the Women's Social and Political Union, and help to win the Vote!'[88]

Christabel's clear message that sexual exploitation and abuse took place not only through prostitution, but also through marriage where the double stand-ards of husbands caused the spread of venereal disease to unsuspecting wives, was expanded in a series of eight articles that ran in *The Suffragette* over summer 1913. Towards the end of the year, the articles were collected together, and woven into a book titled *The great scourge and how to end it*.[89]

In the first of the articles, which appeared on 1 August, Christabel rejected the idea that men were biologically incapable of controlling their sexual appetite, making it inevitable that women were sexually exploited. Men, like women, were rational creatures who could exercise control over their own sexuality:

One is forced to the conclusion, if one accepts men's account of themselves, that women's nature is something very much cleaner, stronger,
and higher than the human nature of men. But Suffragists . . . hope that
this is not really true . . . they believe that a man can live as pure and
moral a life as a woman can.

The woman's ideal, Christabel continued, was 'to keep herself untouched until
she finds her real mate. Let that be the man's ideal, too!'[90] However, that ideal
time had not yet arrived and so further scathing attacks on the man-made cultural constructions of masculinity and femininity continued to stream forth.

'The cause of sexual disease is the subjection of women', Christabel announced
boldly, one week later. The relations between man and woman were those of:

an owner and his property – of a master and his slave – not the relation
of two equals. From that evil has sprung another. The man is not satisfied
to be in relation with only one slave; he must be in relation with many.

This sexual promiscuity had given rise to the 'canker of venereal disease' for
which the only cure was the enfranchisement of women 'which is to say the recognition of the freedom and human equality of women'. Women's enfranchisement
would bring about a transformation in gender roles in Edwardian society since
women would hate 'the very thought of selling themselves into slavery' while
men would be taught that 'women are their human equals'.[91]

Christabel went further, presenting a case that enraged many men at the time
and also 'advanced' women using birth control to enjoy sexual freedom. What
every normal woman believes, she asserted, was that 'Sexual intercourse where
there exists no bond of love and spiritual sympathy is beneath human dignity.'
Until men accept such views on the sex question, until they lived as 'cleanly as
normal women do, the race will be poisoned, as it is to-day, by foul disease'.[92]
Feminists, she warned, would 'fight to the very death' against the re-establishment
of state regulation of vice whereby suspected prostitutes were segregated, controlled and medically examined. Such state regulation would not cure venereal
diseases, nor would advances in medical science. 'The real cure of the great
plague is a two-fold one – Votes for Women, which will give to women more self-
reliance and a stronger economic position, and chastity for men.'[93]

Christabel had read widely on the subject of venereal diseases, consulting
the writings of various medical researchers and doctors, largely American, as
well as British Government reports. From these sources, which she quoted, she
concluded that before the age of thirty, '75 to 80 per cent of men contract gonorrhoea' and possibly 'as many as 20 per cent' syphilis.[94] Such sexual diseases
increased the likelihood of various illnesses developing. Syphilis was a powerful
predisposing cause for tuberculosis and cancer, while gonorrhoea played a big
part in causing not only blindness in offspring but also sterility, miscarriage and
puerperal fever in women.[95]

332

Without hesitation, she challenged those critics who suggested that the reason for sexual vice was because men could not afford to marry until late in life: married as well as unmarried men visited prostitutes. Offering a hard-hitting feminist analysis, she attributed the problem of 'the great evil', as she termed it, to the power of men who, in their own interests, kept women on low wages so that they 'more readily become victims of vice'. Nor did she have any words of comfort for those who believed that a socialist society would eradicate the problem:

> [A] man-made Socialism is not less dangerous to women than man-made Capitalism. So long as men have the monopoly of political power, it will be impossible to restrain their impulse to keep women in economic dependence and so sexually subservient.

Men had to become chaste if prostitution was to be eliminated, and live up to the same moral standard as 'virtuous women' who had come to the conclusion 'that men are not worthy to associate with them who are not of clean mind and of clean life'.[96]

The necessity for a change in men's lifestyle was expanded upon in more detail in an article published in early September. Citing the evidence of a number of medical researchers, Christabel squashed the excuse that chastity for men was dangerous to their health and that immorality was necessary to preserve it. She quoted the words of W. J. Jacobson, Surgeon at Guy's Hospital, London, and James Foster Scott, MD, a late obstetrician to Columbia Hospital for Women in Washington, who argued that 'normal men' could find an innocent means of relief for their semen through involuntary emissions during sleep, a perfectly natural function. 'Chastity for men is not only morally imperative', Christabel insisted, 'but is also physiologically imperative.'[97]

The obvious conclusion to the arguments that Christabel was advancing soon became clear: women should avoid marriage. This was the message in two further articles, published that September:

> Let every woman not yet married remember that the vast majority of men contract sexual disease in one of its forms before they are married. Let every woman learn that to cure a man of such disease is long and difficult and strictly speaking impossible . . . Never again must young women enter into marriage blindfold . . . they must be warned that marriage is intensely dangerous, until such time as men's moral standards are completely changed and they become as chaste and clean-living as women.[98]

Christabel's analysis of the 'great scourge' was strongly supported by her mother who had often spoken of the wrongs of women. Speaking with great passion at the International Medical Congress held in London that summer, Emmeline Pankhurst argued against those who said that prostitution was inevitable:

> If it is true – and I do not believe it for one moment – that men have less power of self-control than women have . . . then I say as a woman, representing thousands of women all over the world – men must find some way of supplying the needs of their sex which does not involve the degradation of ours.[99]

Thus Christabel's cry of 'Votes for women, and chastity for men' was now put forward as a double-edged reason for militancy, a way to ensure justice for women and protect the nation from the forces of vice.

The moral crusade that Christabel had initiated signalled very clearly that the WSPU's campaign was not just about granting female enfranchisement but the much broader aim of abolishing the sexual and economic exploitation of women. Such an agenda appealed strongly to some clergy and social workers, whose work often brought them into contact with girls who had been sexually abused or young women drawn into prostitution.[100] But the moral crusade was even more attractive to those suffragettes, increasingly drawn – as militant deeds became more physically arduous – from the ranks of the young and single. Suffragettes whose fragile bodies had been abused by forcible feeding through the orders of an all-male Liberal Government welcomed Christabel's message, as did many other women angry at the torture inflicted on their comrades and the subordinate status of women generally.

However, a number of feminist commentators in 1913 did not see things this way. The left-wing, heterosexual Rebecca West, who moved in suffrage and socialist circles, was appalled. Miss Pankhurst's remarks on venereal disease 'are utterly valueless and are likely to discredit the Cause in which we believe', she wrote vehemently. The sweeping condemnation of men was particularly regretted. 'Dear lady, behind whom I have been proud to walk in Suffrage processions . . . have you no pity for the immoral men?' The fallen man was as much a victim of social conditions as the fallen woman but the 'scolding attitude of Miss Pankhurst' would only encourage men who had VD to keep it a secret, rather than encourage them to seek medical treatment. Deploring Christabel's 'old-fashioned' puritanism, Rebecca West mused, 'The strange uses to which we put our new-found liberty! There was a long and desperate struggle before it became possible for women to write candidly on subjects such as these.'[101]

Dora Marsden was even more critical. 'Ye Gods and little fishes!' she proclaimed. 'It becomes increasingly difficult to realise that Christabel Pankhurst is a comparatively young woman' since she stood for her ideas in that 'hard, dried-in fashion which ordinarily is found . . . only with extreme old age.'[102] There was more danger to health, Dora asserted, 'from the misery of renunciation and the dull heats of virginity than from the ills of syphilis and gonorrhoea'. Summing up acidly, she noted that if 'Miss Pankhurst desires in the interests of a fad successfully to exploit human boredom and the ravages of dirt she will require to call in the aid of a more subtle intelligence than she appears to possess'.[103]

But Christabel was no fool. In a reply to her critics, she pointed out that her views were not 'puritanical' since what may be described as 'puritanism is not a woman's ideal . . . [but] of men's invention'. Yet again she pointed out that, 'Standards of morality made by men only, do wrong to women and cannot be accepted by women.'[104] What her critics failed to understand was that, for Christabel, militancy was about the dignity of women, about rejecting the male authority to which they were supposed to submit, about women reclaiming their bodies for themselves and demanding their own sexual autonomy. And ever the strategist, she had deliberately linked votes for women with chastity for men as a way to unite and motivate her followers to engage in a sex war against their main enemy, men, in the same way that her earlier friends on the left had excited class hatred 'as a spur to revolutionary violence'.[105] And it worked. The moral crusade did not tame militancy but gave it a fresh impetus. Haystacks and empty buildings continued to be set on fire, telephone wires cut and letter-boxes attacked. Imprisoned suffragettes continued to hunger strike and were forcibly fed. The circulation of *The Suffragette*, which had been merely 10,000 copies a week in January 1913, soared to nearly 30,000. *The great scourge* sold well, receiving positive reviews well into early 1914.[106]

Unsurprisingly, Sylvia in *The suffragette movement* was damning about the moral crusade, despite Christabel's claim that it was the young daughters of the working classes who would benefit from her proposals since such girls did not have, 'owing to the circumstances of their parents, the protection which is accorded to the daughters of the more prosperous classes'.[107] For Sylvia, Christabel's emphasis upon gender rather than class divisions merely preached a 'sex war' that 'did not offend the sensitive class consciousness of those frail hothouse blooms, the Conservative supporters of Women's Suffrage, whom the W.S.P.U. was eager to encourage'. And ignoring the fact that their mother supported Christabel in the social purity campaign, Sylvia claims incorrectly that the strategy came not 'from the speeches of Mrs. Pankhurst, who never lost her gift of sympathy with her audiences, but from the columns of the *Suffragette*'.[108]

Most male historians, too, writing within a masculinist framework, have made disparaging remarks about the WSPU's moral crusade.[109] Although Christabel has been criticised, rightly, for the inaccurate claim that three quarters of men were suffering from venereal disease, few mention that her statistics were culled from the leading medical authorities of her day or engage with the intellectual arguments she was raising. It is mainly radical feminist and lesbian historians who have offered a more convincing analysis of Christabel's feminist thinking and leadership. Thus they argue that the concern with the double standard of morality, prostitution, the sexual objectification and abuse of women – plus the emphasis upon bodily purity for women – meant a rejection of the male authority to which women were supposed to submit, a withdrawal from heterosexuality and the opening up of the lifestyle of spinster. In challenging the dominant, man-made ideology about women's traditional role as wife and mother in Edwardian society, Christabel was seeking a radical transformation of women's place in society, a place that she determined for herself.[110]

Christabel's concern with morality during 1913 was undoubtedly linked to her increasing interest in Christianity, an interest that had deepened during her time in Paris when she began to study the Bible closely.[111] Certainly from late 1912, her articles are sprinkled with biblical quotes, and often her language is Christian in tone. The suffragettes, in their fight against injustice and immorality, were enduring suffering and vilification similar to Christ himself. Their war was a holy war that would morally uplift the nation. Thus male clergy who did not support the suffragette cause or speak out against forcible feeding were accused of not interpreting accurately the scriptures. In a well-known essay published on 8 August and titled 'The appeal to God', Christabel accused the Church of England in particular of degrading itself by becoming a 'hanger-on and lackey of the Government'. It was failing the nation in a time of great crisis since although its seed was 'the blood of martyrs', no pity was shown for the 'martyrs of the present day'.[112]

Five days earlier, during the litany at St Paul's Cathedral, suffragettes had introduced a new form of protest when they had prayed aloud for the life of Emmeline Pankhurst. Although the clergy were not amused, from now on such protests were frequently held not only in places of worship but also in restaurants and theatres. 'In praying that the life of Emmeline Pankhurst, Annie Kenney, and others . . . shall be spared, women have been true to the spirit and example of Christ', Christabel announced. 'Knowing that, they are lifted above all human criticism.' Christ was the Saviour of women as well as of men:

> He never hardened His heart against women and His trust in them was never betrayed as men betrayed it . . . Worldly justice is not yet given to women, but Divine justice is theirs, and if the recognised ministers of religion will not ask it for them, then women will ask it for themselves.[113]

Christabel's words were not entirely ignored by the clergy, especially after the Government recommenced forcible feeding in early October. A sizeable proportion of their number came on her side some two months later when over six hundred and fifty Anglican clergy protested against this particular form of torture.[114]

Notes

1 TNA, HO 45/10695/231366/10, copy of Metropolitan Police account of a WSPU meeting Pavilion Theatre, 13 January 1913.
2 EP to Mrs Archdale, 11 January 1913, Craigie Collection.
3 Crawford, *The women's suffrage movement*, p. 320; interview with Jessie Kenney, 24 March 1964, DMC.
4 CP to Miss Barrett [n.d.], Manchester Public City Libraries Archives.
5 CP to Mrs Billinghurst, 10 January 1913, TWL; CP to Miss Marion, 19 January 1913, SFC.

6 CP to Miss Robins, 15 January 1913, Robins Papers, Fales Library.

7 CP to Mrs Archdale, 31 January 1913, Craigie Collection.

8 TS, 31 January 1913, p. 230.

9 CP to Miss Robins, 25 January 1913, Robins Papers, HRHRC.

10 *Daily News*, 27 January 1913; *Daily Mirror*, 28 January 1913; *TS*, 31 January 1913, p. 240; Wilson, ed, *The political diaries of C.P. Scott*, p. 67, extract from 3 February 1913.

11 CP to Miss Robins, 25 January 1913, Robins Papers, HRHRC.

12 TS, 31 January 1913, p. 230.

13 TS, 31 January 1913, p. 240.

14 *Daily Graphic*, 29 January 1913; *Times*, 1 February 1913.

15 Entry for 31 January 1913, Nevinson Diaries.

16 CP, Inspired by betrayal, TS, 31 January 1913, p. 238.

17 TS, 7 February 1913, pp. 253 and 260.

18 CP to Mrs Belmont, 9 February 1913, National Woman's Party Papers, Group II 1913–74, Library of Congress, Washington.

19 TNA, PRO, HO45/10695/231366/23, copy of Metropolitan Police account of WSPU meeting, London Pavilion, 10 February 1913; HO45/10695/231366/27, transcript by Edward James of WSPU meeting, Cory Hall, Cardiff, 19 February 1913.

20 Purvis, *Emmeline Pankhurst*, pp. 210–11.

21 TS, 28 February 1913, p. 301.

22 CP to Editor of *Daily Mail*, 3 March 1913, Suffrage Papers, Linton Park Plc.

23 CP to Dear General, n.d., Rex v. Kerr, Exhibit 40; TS, 7 March 1913, p. 327.

24 CP to Miss Robins, 7 March 1913, Robins Papers, HRHRC.

25 CP to Miss Lake, 7 and 4 March 1913, Agnes Lake Papers, Girton College Archives, Cambridge.

26 See TS, 21 and 28 March 1913, pp. 364 and 378, respectively.

27 Winslow, *Sylvia Pankhurst*, p. 41.

28 ESP, TSM, pp. 441–50.

29 Mr Harben to CP, 27 February 1913; CP to Mr Harben, 11 March 1913, Harben Papers.

30 TS, 14 March 1913, p. 341.

31 TS 21 February and 21 March 1913, pp. 288 and 371, respectively. On 25 March, she spoke at the house of Dr Ruggles at 3 Avenue Ingres.

32 Richardson, *Laugh a defiance*, p. 85.

33 CP, Stoning the prophets, TS, 21 March 1913, p. 366.

34 CP, The martyr spirit, TS, 28 March 1913, p. 384.

35 *Times, Daily Mirror*, 4 April 1913.

36 TNA, HO45/10695/231366/45, A. Kenney speech at Essex Hall, 3 April 1913.

37 *Times* and *Standard*, 5 April 1913.

38 *Times*, 9 April 1913.

39 CP to My dear P, 9 April 1913, Rex v. Kerr, Exhibit 33.

40 CP to Mrs Sadd Brown, 5 April 1913, TWL.

41 TS, 18 April 1913, p. 448.

42 E. R. Henry, Commission of Police of the Metropolis, 15 April 1913, reprinted in TS, 18 April 1913, p. 455; Rosen, *Rise up women!*, p. 193.

43 CP to My dear P [Harriet Kerr], 16 April 1913, Rex v. Kerr, Exhibit 33.

44 CP to My dear P [Harriet Kerr], 21 April 1913, Rex v. Kerr, Exhibit 33.

45 Two letters from CP to My dear P [Harriet Kerr], n.d. [27 April 1913?], Rex v. Kerr, Exhibit 33.

46 CP to Patricia [Miss Kerr], n.d., 'I am leaving here to-morrow morning at 10.18 a.m. via Dieppe-Newhaven. I expect I shall walk in between 9 and 10 p.m.', copy of letter found on Miss Kerr after her arrest on 30 April 1913, Rex v. Kerr, Exhibit 33.

47 CP to Mrs Archdale, 10 May 1913, Craigie Collection.

48 See *Daily Mirror* and *Daily Sketch*, 1 May 1911.
49 *Times*, 3 May 1913.
50 Quoted in Raeburn, *Militant suffragettes*, pp. 193–5; Cicely B. Hale, *A good long time* (Regency Press, London, 1973), pp. 52–4.
51 Quoted in Raeburn, *Militant suffragettes*, p. 198.
52 CP to Mrs Belmont, 3, 4, 6 May 1913, National Woman's Party Papers, Group II 1913–74.
53 CP to Miss Lake, n.d., Lake Papers.
54 *Daily Sketch*, 3 May 1913.
55 CP to My dear P, 9 April 1913, Exhibit 33, Rex v. Kerr & Others File.
56 Antonia Raeburn interview with Phyllis Keller, c.1964, tape lent to author.
57 *Daily Telegraph*, *Daily Mirror* and *Times*, 7 May 1913.
58 Dobbie, *A nest of suffragettes*, p. 56; J. Hannam, 'Suffragettes are splendid for any work': the Blathwayt diaries as a source for women's suffrage, in C. Eustance, J. Ryand and L. Ugolini, eds, *A suffrage reader: charting new directions in British suffrage history* (London, Leicester University Press, 2000), p. 63.
59 CP, Serious violence, *TS*, 16 May 1913, p. 515.
60 *Daily Sketch*, 27 May 1913; *Standard*, 31 May 1913.
61 Harrison, The act of militancy, pp. 26–7 estimates that during 1913 the suffragettes caused £250,000 worth of damage, and another £250,000 worth in the first seven months of 1914. Bearman, An examination of suffragette violence, p. 369 estimates the total cost to the British economy to be between £1 and £2 million.
62 See CP to My dear P [Harriet Kerr], 19 and 21 April 1913, and one n.d., Rex v. Kerr, Exhibit 33.
63 Morley with Stanley, *Emily Wilding Davison*, pp. 163–6. J. Purvis, Remembering Emily Wilding Davison (1872–1913), *Women's History Review*, 22, 3, pp. 353–62 suggests that it is unlikely that Emily deliberately committed suicide since she was a deeply religious woman and would know that, if she did, she could not be buried in consecrated ground.
64 CP, Emily Wilding Davison, *TS*, 13 June 1913, p. 576.
65 *Sunday Times*, 15 June 1913, *Daily Telegraph*, *Times*, *Daily Herald* and *Daily Sketch*, 16 June 1913.
66 Kenney, *Memories*, p. 227.
67 CP to Miss Lake, 15 June 1913, Lake Papers.
68 *TS*, 20 June 1913, pp. 600–1.
69 CP to Miss Lake, 24 June 1913, Lake Papers.
70 CP, Facing death, *TS*, 20 June 1913, p. 596.
71 Cowman, *Women of the right spirit*, p. 167.
72 CP to Mrs Archdale, 16 June 1913, Craigie Collection.
73 ESP, *TSM*, p. 215; Purvis, *Emmeline Pankhurst*, p. 224.
74 CP to Miss Phillips, 9 July 1913, Mary Phillips Papers.
75 CP to Miss Phillips, 1 August 1913, Mary Phillips Papers.
76 Crawford, *The women's suffrage movement*, p. 546; ESP, *TSM*, pp. 523 and 525.
77 See *TS*, 11 July 1913, p. 655.
78 Enclosure attached to letter from Annie Kenney to Mrs Harben, 4 August 1913, Harben Papers.
79 CP to Mr Harben, 7 August 1913, Harben Papers.
80 Crawford, *The women's suffrage movement*, p. 523.
81 APW, My mother, pp. 40–1.
82 CP to Mrs Archdale, 16 June 1913, Craigie Collection.
83 *Daily Sketch* and *New York Herald*, 22 August 1913.
84 See J. Purvis, Fighting the double moral standard in Edwardian Britain: suffragette militancy, sexuality and the nation in the writings of the early twentieth-century British

feminist Christabel Pankhurst, in F. de Haan *et al.*, *Women's activism: global perspectives from the 1890s to the present* (London and New York, Routledge, 2013), pp. 121–35.

85 See Jackson, *The 'real' facts of life*; Bland, *Banishing the beast*; and J. Jordan, *Josephine Butler* (London, John Murray, 2001). H. Martindale, *Under the surface* (Brighton, Southern Publishing Company, 1908), was the first feminist tract devoted solely to venereal diseases; it was argued that only when women had the parliamentary vote would they earn enough to rid the world of prostitution.

86 *TS*, 25 July 1913, p. 691.

87 *TS*, 18 July 1913, p. 677.

88 CP, The truth about the Piccadilly Flat, *TS*, 25 July 1913, p. 693.

89 CP, *The great scourge and how to end it* (London, E. Pankhurst, 1913).

90 CP, The end of a conspiracy, *TS*, 1 August 1913, p. 717.

91 CP, A woman's question, *TS*, 8 August 1913, p. 737.

92 CP, How to cure the great pestilence, *TS*, 16 August 1913, p. 759.

93 CP, How to cure the great pestilence, *TS*, 15 August 1913, p. 759.

94 CP, Plain facts about a great evil, and The dangers of marriage I, *TS*, 29 August and 12 September 1913, pp. 797 and 829, respectively.

95 CP, The dangers of marriage II, *TS*, 19 September 1913, p. 845.

96 CP, Plain facts about a great evil, *TS*, 29 August 1913, p. 797.

97 CP, Chastity and the health of men, *TS*, 5 September 1913, p. 813.

98 CP, The dangers of marriage, I, *TS*, 12 September 1913, p. 829.

99 *TS*, 29 August 1913, p. 796.

100 ESP, TSM, p. 523. For supportive clergy see *TS*, 19 September and 3 October 1913, pp. 851 and 882, respectively.

101 *Clarion*, 26 September 1913.

102 *New Freewoman*, 15 September 1913, p. 124.

103 *Egoist*, 2 February 1914, pp. 45–6.

104 CP, Attacks answered, *TS*, 3 October 1913, p. 883.

105 Marcus, Introduction, p. 14.

106 Mitchell, *Queen Christabel*, p. 229.

107 CP, Attacks answered, *TS*, 3 October 1913, p. 883.

108 ESP, TSM, pp. 522–3.

109 Mitchell, *Queen Christabel*, pp. 224–30 presents Christabel as pathologically deranged; Rosen, *Rise up women!*, pp. 203–13 suggests that the rank-and-file did not question her idiosyncratic views because they were increasingly drawn from a pool of single women, worried about their socially and economically precarious role in society; Pugh, *The Pankhursts*, p. 273 notes 'Sexual scandal offered a welcome variation from the usual diet of suffragist articles and anti-Labour tirades, and could not easily be ignored by the press. *The Great Scourge* therefore offered a way of stamping her authority on a movement in which she was beginning to become marginalized.'

110 See, for example, Kent, *Sex and suffrage*, p. 7; Sarah, Christabel Pankhurst, pp. 256–84; Jackson, *The 'real' facts of life*, pp. 46–9; L. Martz, An AIDS-era reassessment of Christabel Pankhurst's The Great Scourge and How to End It in *The suffragette and women's history*, Special Issue of *Women's History Review*, ed J. Purvis, 14, 3–4, 2005, pp. 435–46; Purvis, Fighting the double moral standard, pp. 121–35.

111 Interview with Jessie Kenney, 24 March 1964, DMC.

112 CP, The appeal to God, *TS*, 8 August 1913, p. 740.

113 CP, The appeal to God, *TS*, 8 August 1913, p. 740; Metcalfe, *Woman's effort*, p. 301.

114 *TS*, 12 December 1913, p. 194. Leaflet, Against Forcible Feeding. Great Demonstration of the Anglican Clergy. Queen's Hall, December 5th, 1913 (London, National Political League).

16

TROUBLESOME SISTERS

Ousting of Sylvia and a fresh start for Adela:
October 1913–end of August 1914

By early October 1913, Christabel had moved from 9 Rue Roy and was living in a small, dim apartment at 11 Avenue de la Grande Armée. It was from the latter address that she wrote a long letter to Alva Belmont, now back in New York, thanking her for the help and encouragement she had given while *The great scourge* was being written. Two thousand copies of the book, with the American price on them, would be on the steamer conveying her mother to the USA for another paid lecture tour. Christabel also gave details about the domestic arrangements at the new address, as well as news about people Alva knew:

> Mother . . . and I have quite settled down here and the furnishing and arranging of the apartment are all but complete. We have found a domestic treasure who cooks admirably & is in every way to our liking. Miss Burrows [Jessie Kenney] is staying in Paris for the present. She is looking quite well again and I hope the sickness she had in Brittany will not recur. Mrs. Tuke is back in London.[1]

On Saturday, 11 October, Christabel waved goodbye to her mother as she sailed from France to New York on *La Provence*. Accompanying Emmeline on the voyage was Rheta Childe Dorr, a journalist, who had spent the last week in Paris persuading Mrs Pankhurst to write her life story, a commission she had been given by the editor of the American journal *Good Housekeeping*. Emmeline had finally agreed to the idea when Rheta offered to take on most of the drudgery, including writing at her dictation and putting the whole manuscript together. However, when the two women arrived in New York, Emmeline was not allowed to land but was detained at Ellis Island as an 'undesirable alien', guilty of 'moral turpitude'.[2] The roar of indignation from suffragists and the general public alike led President Wilson to overturn the ruling, much to Christabel's delight.[3] But other worries soon engulfed her.

On 19 October, the American Ellen N. La Motte, a WSPU supporter and former Superintendent of the Tuberculosis Division of the Health Department of Baltimore, now living in Paris, wrote to Christabel stating that she feared that Mary Richardson, being forcibly fed in Holloway, had TB. Christabel immediately sent copies of the correspondence to Grace Roe who contacted Henry Harben. Mary Richardson was released on 25 October after consultants called in by the Holloway medical officer confirmed she was ill, not with TB but with symptoms of appendicitis.[4] Fearful that another suffragette might die, Christabel sent a message to Lincoln's Inn House saying that 'no mice' should be present at the next big WSPU meeting, scheduled for 7 December.[5] Yet, as pressing as the plight of forcibly fed hunger strikers was, Christabel was soon plunged yet again into the thick of WSPU organisational problems, this time in regard to one particular branch in London.

Tensions had erupted during summer 1913 in the WSPU Kensington Branch which for some time had been working closely with Sylvia's East London Federation. In July, its secretary, Miss Postlethwaite, had resigned as well as long-established committee members Dr Louisa Garrett Anderson and Barbara Wylie. For a brief period, Sylvia had been the secretary before handing over to Elsa Dalglish. Initially, it was difficult for Christabel, residing in Paris, to know exactly what the problems were and she was reliant on key informants, especially Marion Wallace-Dunlop who kept in close contact. Apparently the Lawrences were actively encouraging disaffected Kensington members to join their rival organisation, the Votes for Women Fellowship, established after their expulsion from the WSPU in 1912. Their views held particular sway with Miss Postlethwaite and her associates. The left-leaning Evelyn Sharp, a key member of the Kensington branch, fiercely loyal to the Lawrences and assistant editor to their *Votes for Women*, was also disenchanted. And there were other complicating factors in Evelyn's case. Unknown to the vast majority of the WSPU membership, she was having an affair with the married, debonair Henry Nevinson, also a subscriber to the Fellowship. Although Evelyn and Henry tried to keep their romance secret, a few eyebrows had been raised in July when, armed with red roses and Muscat, Henry had greeted Evelyn on her release from prison.[6] A few close friends, especially the Lawrences and Hertha Ayrton's daughter Barbara, now married to Gerald Gould, had come to 'appreciate' the situation. All three couples were very critical of WSPU tactics, including Christabel's supposedly 'anti-male' stance, and were looking for an alternative suffrage organisation that would include both men and women.[7]

Christabel, kept well informed of the Kensington situation, decided to exclude Evelyn Sharp from public speaking for the WSPU. An angry Barbara Ayrton Gould visited her in Paris and a 'furious quarrel' took place during which Christabel was accused of acting out of 'jealousy & distrust' because Evelyn was politically able.[8] Unsurprisingly, Henry Nevinson too believed that Christabel was envious of Evelyn's talents and worried about maintaining her power. 'The whole thing is a kind of spy mania, a terror and blindness', he noted in his diary. 'She has actually thought we were plotting to extradite her! It is the nearest thing to insanity I've known in the movement.'[9] But Christabel saw the matter differently.

As the key strategist of the WSPU, Christabel believed she had to deal decisively with the 'disruption and disloyalty' at the Kensington branch.[10] There was a divergence between the policies outlined in *The Suffragette* and in *Votes for Women*, Christabel informed Marion Wallace-Dunlop on 7 November, and it was 'absolutely unthinkable' that the *Votes for Women* faction in Kensington should be in the same organisation and occupy the same shop as those who were selling *The Suffragette* and working for the WSPU. *Votes for Women* had recently praised the Bishop of Kensington for his lecture to the Fellowship in which he condemned the WSPU's policy of destroying property.[11] Christabel was full of praise for Elsa Dalglish, the new secretary of the Kensington branch, for her 'strong and firm stand' in stopping the sale of *Votes for Women* in the WSPU shop and hoped that all those who had no confidence in her leadership would leave the WSPU instantly. 'If the Fellowship is going to draw away all disloyal people and all destructive and uncharitable criticism, it will have served one good purpose at least.' Christabel also told Marion that Dr Louisa Garrett Anderson had made a visit to Paris to ask her to return to England, a view also upheld by Emmeline Pethick-Lawrence. 'I thought this request showed a lack of judgement and if not that, then something even more serious', Christabel opined, fearful of plots to get her back to London and certain arrest. '[T]he Fellowship and those responsible for it are seeking to injure the Union. The talk about my going back is indicative of hostility to the Union and . . . hostility to me.'[12] A few days later, Christabel confided to Marion that WSPU member Barbara Wylie would soon be visiting her. 'I shall be extremely glad to see her of course and to hear what she has to say and talk things over with her.'[13]

Towards the end of October, when Wallace-Dunlop had first begun writing to Christabel, she reported that 'one lady' had said that the problem at the Kensington branch was Sylvia and her East London Federation. Christabel had replied immediately, telling Marion how difficult it was to comment until she knew all the facts. Until then, she made it clear that she was intolerant of any criticism of Sylvia and stoutly defended her sister's work:

> Sylvia, with the whole-hearted and enthusiastic approval of mother, myself and headquarters, is conducting a Campaign in the East End. She arranges the whole thing entirely in her own way. We do not interfere in the least, feeling that she has a special understanding of how the whole thing should be done.[14]

But events moved quickly, and such sisterly loyalty was soon shattered.

On 1 November, Sylvia spoke at a large socialist and trade union rally in the Albert Hall, organised by the *Daily Herald* to protest against a mass lock-out of workers in Dublin and to demand the release of Jim Larkin, one of the key leaders. She stood on a platform with Lansbury, James Connolly, the Irish socialist and a leader of the Irish Transport and General Workers' Union (ITGWU), Delia Larkin, sister of the imprisoned Jim Larkin and organiser of the women's section of the ITGWU, Dora Montefiore, Charlotte Despard and Fred Pethick-Lawrence. Shortly afterwards, the *Daily Herald* reported that Sylvia's East London

Federation, which was supported by WSPU funds, was to form a People's Army of women and men to protect its members from police assault. It also noted that 'every day the industrial rebel and the suffrage rebels march nearer together'.[15]

Christabel was furious. Sylvia had betrayed the trust that she and their mother had placed in her. On 7 November she wrote to her sister saying that she would reply publicly to the statement, repudiating 'any connection between the Herald League & the W.S.P.U. and in this & every possible way shall make it clear that we are absolutely independent of this as of all men's parties & movements'.[16] That Sylvia had been speaking on a socialist platform with Fred Pethick-Lawrence, actively involved in promoting the Votes for Women Fellowship, was troublesome. Christabel saw this as a move to weaken her leadership of the WSPU, deliberately timed to occur while her mother was out of the country. Undoubtedly she was strengthened in her view by a letter received from Henry Harben, who had also spoken briefly at the Albert Hall meeting, in which he noted that most of the speakers 'were obviously giving the women lip-service and dragging them in as an afterthought. There was no real feeling on the woman question. The ovation to Sylvia was to the rebel and not to the woman'.[17]

Christabel acted quickly. On 14 November *The Suffragette* carried a statement saying that 'Miss Sylvia Pankhurst', whose campaign in the East End of London was run on 'independent lines', was present at the Albert Hall meeting 'in her personal capacity and not for the purpose of officially representing the W.S.P.U.'.[18] In the same issue, in her regular column, Christabel outlined again clearly the WSPU's independence policy, so there could be no doubt about future action:

> Independence of all men's parties is the basis of the Women's Social and Political Union ... the 'Daily Herald' League ... is ... a men's organisation, and so long as men are voters and women are voteless it is dangerous to women to co-operate with men. We have seen how other such Leagues have started by holding out the hand of friendship to women. Yet when women have given their money and their service, these leagues have thrown over the women's cause. This is precisely what happened in the I.L.P. which now forms part of the larger Labour Party ... the I.L.P. representatives in the House of Commons are in alliance with a Government that defrauds women of the vote and tortures those who fight for it ... A further reason why the W.S.P.U. stands clear and independent of the 'Daily Herald' League is that League is or tends to be a class organisation, while the W.S.P.U is not. The W.S.P.U. includes in its ranks ... women of all classes, rich women, poor women, women of moderate means, striving together in unity.[19]

Sylvia, for her part, decided that she could no longer keep silent, as in the past, about her differences of view with her sister. It was an opportune time to force the issue. Membership of the WSPU was falling, there was a lot of criticism of Christabel's leadership, as well as her residence in France, and disaffected suffragettes, especially in the Kensington branch, were talking about forming a mixed-sex, non-party organisation that would focus solely on votes for women. Sylvia reasoned that if she could oust Christabel from the leadership now, while their mother was in the USA, she might be able to persuade their mother to toe her line. After all, although Emmeline was extremely critical of the ILP and Labour Party, she had never repudiated socialism.

Sylvia tried to rally support among the suffragettes by sending out a circular to all WSPU branches, claiming that her East London Federation was not forming an alliance with the *Daily Herald* League; she also drew attention to a 'Suffrage School' it was organising with the Kensington branch. Pointing out that she went to the Albert Hall meeting to put the question of Votes for Women before an audience of 10,000 people, she continued:

> There was a time when the W.S.P.U. held far more meetings than any other society. This is not the case today . . . we must surely recognise the fact that the holding of public meetings is an important part of our work, if only for the making of new militants.

The *Herald* League, as well as the ILP, would shortly be holding meetings at which, she believed, 'Miss Annie Kenney, Miss Richardson and others, will, I am sure, be glad to help so far as they can in speaking . . . just as I am ready to do whenever possible.'[20] Sylvia also wrote a letter for publication in *The Suffragette*, defending her position and making it quite clear that she and her Federation were independent of any policy her sister determined in Paris.[21]

This was Sylvia's first public criticism of the WSPU leadership. Gasps of horror came from some Union members and sympathisers alike who feared another split, especially when Annie Kenney entered the fray. On 25 November Annie, not fully recovered from her prison ordeal, sent a letter to all WSPU branches, condemning Sylvia's recent circular, including the fact that she had made use of her name, without her knowledge:

> It is to Mrs. Pankhurst and Christabel Pankhurst that we look for guidance in the constructive and political work of the W.S.P.U. We all know from what source all the political wisdom and marvellous insight which inspires our Union, comes.[22]

Nevinson, at a Men's Political Union meeting where the formation of the new mixed-sex suffrage society (soon to be called the United Suffragists) was being discussed, found that his colleagues argued that the trouble was 'Christabel's suspicion & hatred of all men. I . . . offered to see Mrs. Pankhurst but Harben said I was too deeply suspected, apparently as a friend of the Lawrences'.[23]

Theodora Bonwick, a member of the Hornsey WSPU, wrote privately to Sylvia saying she was 'very cut up about it all'. She cautioned that 'far too much fuss has been made over a small matter', and explained that she had also written to 'Miss Christabel . . . for I cannot bear to think of any further division in our ranks, of what our enemies would think & our members feel'. She begged Sylvia not to take any action until Mrs Pankhurst had returned from the USA but to 'lie low a little while so that the public may not be able to make anything of what must surely be but a passing trifle'.[24] But the matter was not a passing trifle; it involved fundamental differences between the two sisters in regard to feminist activism and to tactics for winning votes for women, fuelled by their sisterly rivalry. On 27 November 1913, Christabel, the elder sister and Chief Organiser of the WSPU, reasserted her authority by writing privately to Sylvia, condemning 'very strongly' her recent circular:

> In a recent letter to me you referred to the fact that we do not ask you to speak at meetings. The reason for this is that it is essential for the public to understand that you are working independently of us.

She continued, 'As you have a complete confidence in your own policy & way of doing things, this should suit you perfectly! There is room for everybody in the world, but conflicting counsels inside the WSPU there cannot be.'[25]

Christabel kept in close touch with her mother on these matters, waiting to discuss them further when she arrived back in Britain. Meanwhile she was also actively promoting the cause of militancy to a wider audience, arguing the case clearly in the *New Statesman*. 'Militancy is . . . the flowering of the woman's movement for equality', the result of women's 'long-existing, hidden discontent with their condition of inferiority' and the unsuccessful law-abiding women's suffrage campaign of the last century.[26] The emphasis upon militancy as a way to cast aside the servility of women to men was emphasised time and time again as Christabel attempted to unite her followers in a show of gender solidarity. Such considerations were especially important now that Sylvia was stepping out of line, emphasising the class rather than gender struggle. However, it soon became apparent that Sylvia was not the only family 'problem'.

Adela had not settled in well as a governess to the Archdale children and had announced that she wanted to move to Canada. Emmeline was displeased with this change of heart and, standing firm, had told her youngest daughter that she must stick to her job – and Adela had agreed to do so.[27] Christabel's prediction that Adela would soon change her mind now came to fruition. With winter approaching, Helen Archdale, the children and Adela moved that autumn into a flat in Milan where a journalist mistook Adela for *the* 'Miss Pankhurst', the strategist of the WSPU who lived in Paris – and asked her to address a meeting. Adela, who, like Sylvia, refused to cut her links with the Labour Party, spoke to the reporter, expressing her socialist bias. The bungled incident attracted press coverage, much to Christabel's irritation.[28] Ethel Smyth, visiting Christabel in Paris en route to Egypt, was told about the 'problem' sisters and once she had reached her destination, communicated this news to Emmeline in early December:

> I think C's one preoccupation – only ½ a one! – was lest Sylvia should get round your maternal heart re their differences of opinion!! While I was in Paris the D.M. [*Daily Mail*] was announcing Adela's Milan affair as having happened to C!! & poor C was passionately wishing her sisters would change their names!![29]

Before her mother's return to England, Christabel was busy drumming up support for a 'Great Collection' which would help the WSPU fight against the Government and be presented to Emmeline when she set foot on British soil. 'Will you in addition to giving yourself, do your very best to collect from others!' she pleaded with, among others, Miss Birnstingl.[30] However, Emmeline Pankhurst was arrested as soon as she arrived back home on 4 December, and then released under the Cat and Mouse Act three days later, a few hours after the welcome meeting planned for her had been held in London. At that meeting, Flora Drummond read out, to great applause, a stirring message from Christabel. 'The arrest of my mother, the danger – the Government's attempt to break our Movement by torturing and killing her – will stir the audience even more than the words she would have spoken from the platform had she been free.'[31] Jewels in large quantities and money were offered that night so that, together with the £4,500 that Emmeline had raised on her American tour, the 'Great Collection' totalled £15,000, a substantial sum that indicates that the WSPU still had a lot of support and was not so unpopular as some historians have assumed.[32] Christabel set about preparing a rousing Christmas message for her supporters, a message with a powerful Christian theme:

> Only those who are taking part in the chief crusade of their day and generation can fully understand the meaning of the life and death of Christ. The women militant are informed by the Christ spirit . . . the Christian doctrine of the sanctity of the body as the temple of the spirit.[33]

As soon as was possible, Emmeline travelled to Paris to confer with her eldest daughter about Sylvia and Adela, but was rearrested on her return, and then released on a licence until 23 December. She had no intention of returning to Holloway just two days before Christmas and gave the police the slip so that she, her brother Herbert and Nurse Pine could spend Christmas in France with Christabel. Mabel Tuke, Annie and Jessie Kenney came for the festive season too, as did Phyllis Keller to whom Christabel gave a book on dancing, saying, 'I thought you would like a Christmas present on something that we were both interested in.'[34] Although Christabel, when on her own, had sometimes practised dancing around the table in the sitting room, there was no space or time for that now with so many visitors present, as well as a Pomeranian dog, a present from her mother who thought the tiny dog would be company for her eldest daughter. The very small dining room, separated from the sitting room by glass doors, was crowded that Christmas Day. Emmeline Pankhurst felt content. 'This is more like home to me than anything I have known for years', she wrote to Ethel Smyth on 26 December, and continued:

> C. has gone out with Mrs. Tuke shopping, and the little dog Fay and I are trying to amuse one another with a paper ball . . . C. is devoted to her and has her to sleep on her bed every night. This morning I looked in at her, fast asleep with the window wide open, the snow almost coming into the room and little Fay curled up almost in her neck, a pretty sight. I am glad she has her. It keeps one human to have the care of a little helpless creature.[35]

Christabel and Emmeline had many conversations about Adela and Sylvia. Some family friends, on their way to Europe, had offered to take Adela with them to Chicago where she might seek a job in agriculture or education. But that was not until the spring and the unsettled Adela had abandoned that plan and now decided she wanted to be a writer, a career move her mother did not favour, fearing that she would be unable to earn her living.[36] Christabel, for her part, was still annoyed with her unsettled, impulsive younger sister, partly because of the damaging stories Adela had told the press in Milan. 'I was anything but pleased [to] read in the English newspapers that I had been trying to speak in French & failing in the attempt', wrote the over-sensitive Christabel to Helen Archdale:

> I don't believe in doing what I know cannot be a success. It seems to be irresponsible & not at all dignified . . . Mother & I ought <u>not</u> to be put in a false position by the action of any related to us.[37]

Christabel and Emmeline agreed that Adela should be given a fresh start in life overseas, while Sylvia and her Federation should be expelled from the WSPU.

Early in the New Year of 1914, Sylvia received many requests to come to Paris. Having recently endured her fifth arrest and release, she was still feeling ill but eventually agreed to go. Travelling in disguise, with Norah Smyth as her companion, she reached her destination without being arrested. There is only one detailed account of the meeting with Christabel and their mother, that written by Sylvia herself in *The suffragette movement*, published nearly twenty years later. Yes, despite the passing of time, it is clear that Sylvia still felt bitter about the event. According to Sylvia, as soon as she arrived at the Paris flat, the business was opened with Christabel taking charge of proceedings while their mother, looking ill, stood aside. Sylvia experienced the humiliation of being told by her elder sister, who was 'nursing a tiny Pomeranian dog', that her East London Federation must become a separate organisation, outside the WSPU. Christabel enumerated her complaints. Sylvia had spoken at the large socialist meeting to celebrate Larkin's release, which was contrary to WSPU policy; her Federation had a democratic constitution, which the WSPU did not agree with; her wish to organise a working women's movement was of 'no value' to the

WSPU who wanted 'picked women, the very strongest and most intelligent!' Adding further insult, Christabel was reported to have told her sister, 'You have your own ideas. We do not want that; we want all our women to take their instructions and walk in step like an army!' The bruised Sylva felt 'grieved' by Christabel's 'ruthlessness . . . I thought of many others who had been thrust aside for some minor difference'.[38]

The discussion stopped temporarily when the sisters and their mother went for a drive in the Bois, 'Christabel with the small dog on her arm, I struggling against headache and weakness', claimed Sylvia, 'Mrs. Pankhurst blanched and emaciated'. The discussion resumed once they were back in the flat. Christabel now turned to the issue of finance, saying that Sylvia's appeals for funds for her own organisation meant that donations intended for the WSPU never reached Lincoln's Inn. At this point, Emmeline became distressed by the discussion and said to Sylvia, 'Suppose I were to say we would allow you something . . . Would you ——?' Christabel cut short the offer of a compromise. 'Oh, no; we can't have that! . . . It must be a clean cut!' The weary Sylvia replied, 'As you will then.' Shortly afterwards, when Christabel suggested to Sylvia that they should meet sometimes, 'not as Suffragettes, but as sisters', the gesture was greeted with disdain. 'To me the words seemed meaningless; we had no life apart from the movement.'[39]

Thus Sylvia represented herself as being expelled from the WSPU against her wishes, the decision forced upon her by her elder sister, the betrayer of socialist feminism, the autocratic, inflexible leader of what she saw as a narrow form of feminism which marginalised social class. But the ousting of Sylvia and her East London Federation from the WSPU merely confirmed what had been reality for some time, namely that the Federation was operating independently of any national campaign. Now that its separate and distinctive status was formalised, Sylvia could go her own way. Soon her East London Federation had its own weekly newspaper, *The Woman's Dreadnought*, and later when it became the Workers' Suffrage Organisation, *The Woman's Dreadnought* became *The Workers' Dreadnought*. But before that could happen, there was considerable tension between Sylvia and Christabel because Sylvia would not leave the WSPU quietly.

Sylvia proposed that her separate organisation should be called 'The East End Federation of the Suffragettes'. This was not acceptable to her relatives. She refused to comply with their wishes, despite her mother's pleading that the title was confusing to the public since the terms 'The Suffragettes' and 'the WSPU' had become interchangeable. Nor would Sylvia compromise on the wording of the draft announcement she had drawn up for publication about the split.[40] The angry Emmeline scolded her stubborn daughter for being 'unreasonable', and sent her a copy of the statement about the separation jointly drafted by herself and Christabel.[41] Undeterred and determined to remain within the WSPU, the defiant Sylvia applied to join the Kensington branch but was refused admittance.[42] Ethel Smyth, commiserating with the worried Emmeline, suggested that Sylvia's refusal to comply might be due to family dynamics – 'when it is a question of obeying one's sister as sole arbiter (for she knows you would do what C. wants & probably doesn't understand it is because your own judgement would go with C's) I suppose its harder'.[43]

News of the split soon reached the national and international press, some of the newspapers reporting erroneously that Sylvia had been expelled from the WSPU because she refused to accept its abandonment of militancy, a change in direction that Christabel wanted so that she could end her exile, return to London and take control of the Union.[44] The annoyed Christabel set the record straight by making a formal announcement in *The Suffragette* and writing a letter to the press stating that the WSPU was 'a fighting organisation' where the:

> policy . . . and the word of command is given by Mrs. Pankhurst and myself . . . those who wish to give an independent lead or to carry out either a programme or policy which differ from those laid down by the W.S.P.U. must necessarily have an independent organisation of their own.[45]

Christabel was determined to keep socialist politics out of the WSPU – and to unite her following. But it was not easy. Sylvia's East London Federation, which attracted only a small membership, was not the only suffrage society now allied to the Labour movement. The NUWSS had an electoral pact with the Labour Party while the new suffrage organisation, the United Suffragists, formed on 6 February 1914, was another attempt to link the women's suffrage cause to 'rebel' socialist politics.[46] Although the United Suffragists, open to men and women, militant and non-militant, claimed to be 'non-party', Christabel was not convinced. It was no surprise that its membership included the Lawrences, Henry Nevinson, Evelyn Sharp and Henry and Agnes Harben – as well as others who had been large contributors to WSPU funds – such as Hertha Ayrton and Dr Louisa Garrett Anderson. Nor was it unexpected that some other well-known social-ists, active in the *Daily Herald* League, held key posts in the new society. Gerald Gould and John Scurr, the dockers' leader, were members of the Committee of the United Suffragists while George Lansbury was one of its Vice Presidents.[47] When Sylvia sent a circular letter to WSPU members, inviting them to join her and the United Suffragists in a Votes for Women procession, the link between the United Suffragists and socialism seemed clear.[48]

There were now over fifty suffrage societies competing for membership and Christabel had to act decisively. Rallying her supporters to remain loyal to the WSPU, she claimed that all Union members were 'determined not to have their energies and their subscriptions divided and sub-divided among a multitude of organisations, and thus frittered away'.[49] Resolute in her belief that the women-only WSPU was the most politically effective of all the suffrage groupings, she attacked as worthless the professed support for women's suffrage from social-ists, especially those in the Labour Party. At a recent Labour Party Conference held in Glasgow, no mention had even been made of votes for women, or of the Government's use of torture for the purpose of coercing women. 'The militant women represent the future, and their policy is one of complete independence of the Labour and Socialist parties no less than of the other men's parties', Christabel insisted. Militant suffragists 'have not only learned to condemn and despise the unfaithfulness of the Labour Party to the cause of women – and above all the working women – but they have also acquired a supreme contempt for their political intelligence and capacity'. Labour MPs, who were supporting the Government's Plural Voting Bill, a measure which dealt with men's franchise without removing the political disability of women, were 'the laughing stock of British politics', spending their time 'fetching and carrying for the Liberal Government'.[50] For the uncompromising Christabel, no exceptions could be made for friends, former colleagues or even sisters who wanted to ally the WSPU to socialist politics. Sylvia had been expelled from the WSPU over this issue. Now the socialist Adela had to be dealt with.

Shortly after she had been ousted from the WSPU, Sylvia wrote to Adela, asking her sister to work with her in the East London Federation. 'I refused at once', recollected Adela, 'seeing that the E.L.F. was in opposition to mother and Christabel.'[51] But Christabel did not know this and suspected that the unpredictable, independent-minded Adela, a compelling speaker, might join forces with Sylvia and form an alternative faction to the WSPU. After the embarrassing incident in Milan, when Adela had expressed her socialist bias to a reporter who assumed she was Christabel, Christabel and Emmeline had sent her a reprimand. Annie Kenney brought the message personally to Adela, who by then had moved to Locarno in Switzerland. Annie had already written to Adela, asking her to promise not to speak on a WSPU platform in England again, and repeated the request. The angry and indignant youngest Pankhurst daughter refused to comply.[52]

Christabel and Emmeline decided that the volatile, twenty-eight-year-old Adela should have a fresh start in life, not in Canada but Australia where Adela had once expressed a desire to live. The majority of Australian female citizens now had the vote, including the much-admired Vida Goldstein, the first woman candidate in the British Empire to stand for election to parliament. Christabel and Emmeline were in contact with the tall, elegant Vida, President of the Women's Political Association of Victoria, who had represented her country in the 1911 Coronation Procession and written several articles and letters in support of the WSPU.[53] Emmeline wrote to Vida, asking her to meet and look after her daughter, a request that was gladly accepted.[54] On 26 January, Adela was asked to come to Paris to talk things over, not knowing that provisional arrangements had been made for the future. At that meeting, she felt that her mother was against her:

> Mother seemed to think I had not tried to get work and wanted to come into the Movement as Christabel's rival. I did not tell her about Sylvia's offer nor my refusal. Had I done so, she and Christabel would probably have thought better about me.[55]

Shattered by the news that her mother, to whom she was devoted, considered her a failure, Adela did not argue against the plan to send her overseas. As a deeply committed socialist, for whom the class struggle towards socialism was her main interest, she felt it was best for all concerned that she made herself independent of the WSPU, in another country. 'Before I could do anything in the Labour Movement', she recollected, 'it was necessary for me to leave England, unless I wished to enter into open warfare with my mother.'[56]

On 2 February, Adela set sail on the *Geelong* with just £20 in her pocket, all the money that her mother could spare after spending £27 on the fare. She was supposed to disembark at Melbourne but impatient with the liner as it made a leisurely pace around the Australian coast, the excited Adela came ashore at Adelaide instead. Travelling by train to bustling Melbourne, she was greeted by Vida Goldstein who offered her work that suited her experience – as an organiser for the Women's Political Association – a post she accepted with her mother's blessing and 'many loving words'.[57] Adela also joined the Victorian Socialist Party. Her expulsion from the WSPU revealed that, yet again, Christabel and Emmeline had exercised iron discipline in regard to a member of their family. The task of imposing unity among WSPU members, who came from differing backgrounds and with differing life experiences, was not easy and it was particularly critical to make no exception for relatives. The independence of the WSPU from all men's parties, including the Labour Party, was above family loyalty and must be preserved. From now on, Christabel never saw Adela again and had very little contact with Sylvia.

Christabel's conviction that her strategy for the WSPU was the right one, coupled with an autocratic style of leadership, attracted an increasing amount of criticism from some WSPU members and supporters alike during these early months of 1914. 'Christabel is too too dictating so I shall have to slip out of that show', wrote Lilian Hicks to a friend.[58] One worker at the Union's headquarters who agreed with this assessment was Katharine Douglas Smith who had recently been dismissed from her post. She complained to Constance Lytton about her treatment, and Constance immediately took the issue up with Christabel. Christabel thought that 'a mountain is being made out of a molehill' since although Katharine had spent some hours in the editorial office, it was not 'by any direct or definite arrangement', her help having been sought by the head of a department. 'It is so much easier to give everybody their own way & one wd probably be more liked', Christabel lamented.[59]

Beatrice Harraden, the well-known writer and committee member of the WSPU Hampstead branch, was another disillusioned suffragette who wrote to Christabel that January of 1914, complaining about the dire state of the Union, as she saw it. She particularly remonstrated with Christabel for allowing Mrs Pankhurst to continue with her hunger strikes, a sacrifice to which she could see no end except her death. And there was more. Beatrice accused Christabel of 'turning away deliberately or else alienating so many of our old and faithful comrades', of shutting the door 'in the faces of all the finest, ablest, and most devoted women' who had helped to make the WSPU the 'very first company of modern women in the world'. She drew a bleak picture of petty infighting and disorganisation. 'Never a week passes but that some one has been slighted, rebuffed, or dismissed.' Nor, she learnt with sorrow, was any 'proper care and forethought . . . being given to the "mice"'.[60]

Christabel, by now hardened to criticisms of her policy, welcomed Beatrice's frankness, and sent an equally frank reply, defending current WSPU policy:

> Everything that the Union does is done with a view to serving the cause . . . I am more in touch . . . than I ever was in the past, because I have time and energy to devote to essentials which was impossible for me to have in the old days when there were so many and often conflicting claims upon me.

Regarding her mother, Christabel pointed out that there were three possible alternative courses of action Mrs Pankhurst could follow – serve her three years' penal servitude, declare that she would no longer be militant or incite others to militancy, or remain in Paris and do the organisational work for the Union while she herself returned to England. Her mother, Christabel insisted, rejected these alternatives. 'I have shown this letter to my mother who is here just now and it meets with her entire approval', she insisted. 'On certain points she would have expressed herself even more strongly especially on the idea of her staying abroad.' Reassuring Beatrice that there was 'no real reason' why she should be 'pained or troubled', she asked her to 'give chapter and verse' about neglect of the 'mice'.[61]

Beatrice duly cited the dismissal of Agnes Lake and the cases of Olive Beamish, Lilian Lenton and her companion, 'sent to some place to await money and instructions which never came; and, on their return to headquarters, sent to Paddington Station and arrested there'. Regretting the loss of those 'old experienced friends and comrades . . . no longer on your list of helpers', she pointedly included among the sixteen names 'Sylvia, Evelyn Sharp . . . Mrs. Ayrton Gould, Mrs Ayrton, Dr. Louie Garrett Anderson, Mr. Nevinson, the Daily Herald'. Beatrice ended her letter by calling on Christabel to 'recall' these friends of the Union 'and restore . . . the old spirit . . . still devoted, though distressed'.[62]

Christabel refused to budge. 'The old spirit of the Union needs no restoration', she replied. 'It is with us stronger and brighter and clearer than ever . . . Elements of weakness have been eliminated. Destructive critics and pessimists have now ceased from troubling except from the outside.' And she repudiated 'with the greatest indignation' the 'false charge' that certain 'mice' had not received proper care.[63] Christabel did not mention Sylvia and like-minded colleagues, some of whom had gathered around the Lawrences and joined the United Suffragists – as Beatrice Harraden herself now did, becoming one of its many vice presidents.[64] Her main aim was to keep the WSPU independent of alliance to any men's political parties, particularly the Labour Party, and to forge unity among the suffragettes so that the WSPU would retain its own distinctive identity among the large number of suffrage organisations. But the fall-out from Sylvia's expulsion from the WSPU continued to plague Christabel that January, as she wrestled to retain control of the Union and to enforce discipline, from a distance. The next critic to voice her opinion was Mary Leigh.

Mary Leigh, who had joined Sylvia's East London Federation, crossed the Channel with two like-minded suffragettes. In no uncertain terms, she told Christabel about the desperate plight of some of her comrades, 'young women on the run with no money, no food, no shelter. I saw two crouching in public phone booths'. Mary recollected that Christabel 'seemed annoyed by our intrusion. She was almost flippant. We were wasting her time'. The no-nonsense Mary replied that the militants were loyal but sick of taking orders from young office girls while the leaders were in prison and Christabel in Paris. 'Had she nothing to say, no message to give? No she had not.' When Mary risked a second visit to Paris, this time alone and in disguise as a widow in heavy mourning, Jessie Kenney was in the flat with Christabel. They did not recognise their visitor and got a terrific shock when she threw back her veil. Yet again, Mary was given short shrift, feeling as though she was treated as 'a crazy intruder'.[65]

Despite such criticisms, Christabel's leadership was not seriously threatened during these early months of 1914. She and her mother were supported by a network of organisers who, while recognising that their employers could be autocratic, believed that the campaign was going in the right direction. Those who resigned from the WSPU left behind loyal workers who regarded militancy, as Christabel did, as the only way to rid women of the indignity and shame of their inequality. One such activist was Kitty Marion who later paid tribute to the way Christabel Pankhurst, with her 'brilliant legal mind', marshalled her 'faithful forces of the W.S.P.U.' through the stormy period of the campaign, from March 1912 to the outbreak of the First World War.[66] Another was Lilian Lenton who recollected that the strong irritation she felt about the disadvantages that girls and women experienced in comparison with boys and men was the main motivation for her continued militancy. She had joined the WSPU after hearing one of its speakers say women were classified alongside lunatics and paupers as not fit to vote.[67] Such feelings about the indignity of women's unequal position ran high among the loyal militants in 1914, and kept Christabel buoyant. 'The Suffragettes have compelled the Liberal Government to feel and look ridiculous', she opined. 'They have made the Government despised and hated by every lover of freedom.' The suffragette refusal to compromise and to defy the law had forced the Government 'to admit that their rule over women rests not upon the consent of women but upon the torture of women'.[68]

That Henry Harben, a former political admirer and now a member of the United Suffragists who gave financial support to *both* the WSPU and Sylvia's East London Federation, should suddenly send Christabel a caustic letter was not unexpected.[69] 'One by one every approach towards you has been cut off . . . and your chief officials at Lincoln's Inn House have been going round the Branches turning people out neck and crop.' With venom, he then added:

People are now saying that from the leader of a great movement you are developing into the ringleader of a little rebel Rump . . . that the quality of your following is not what it was either in ability, originality, spontaneity, human sympathy or any of those characteristics which have been so striking a feature of your Movement until quite recently.[70]

Replying on 15 February, Christabel's tone was polite; after all, Harben had not said he would no longer help the WSPU. 'We who are responsible for the campaign must decide who is most fitted for each particular piece of work', she wrote impatiently. 'Also if we are not satisfied that the person occupying a given position is suitable to <u>retain</u> it, she cannot retain it.'[71]

As the forcible feeding of suffragettes continued and a number of doctors were raising concerns about the barbaric practice, the militants organised deputations to high-ranking Church of England clergy, including the Archbishop of Canterbury, to ask for help in stopping a practice that was contrary to the spirit of Christianity.[72] But the Bishops, who were represented in the House of Lords and could have protested against forcible feeding, refused to do so. 'At present, the Church is in league with the State for the purpose of repressing women', thundered Christabel. 'The State disfranchises women; the Church condones it. The State tortures women; the Church connives at it. An unholy alliance indeed!'[73] *The Suffragette* soon published on its front page a graphic cartoon depicting the Bishop of London with his hand around the neck of a terrified suffragette prisoner, a whitewash brush in his hand. The Bishop, in response to a WSPU deputation, had visited Rachel Peace, Kitty Marion and Phyllis Brady in Holloway but would not intervene on their behalf. The correspondence between him and a worried Marion Wallace-Dunlop, who had consulted with Christabel about the content of the WSPU's response, was published in *The Suffragette*.[74]

Yet, despite horrendous stories about the suffering inflicted by forcible feeding, including the drugging of prisoners with bromide to make them more docile, the practice continued in English prisons and was also adopted in Scotland. The case of Ethel Moorhead, fed in Calton Gaol, Edinburgh, attracted particular attention since she was so ill, after food had been accidentally poured into her lungs, that the prison officials sent for a priest to administer the sacraments. She was released suffering from double pneumonia.[75] Forcibly fed suffragettes laid bare the sexual divisions in Edwardian society, exposing a deep flaw in an all-male Liberal Government that claimed to be 'democratically' elected, yet tortured those women who challenged its legitimacy. Their experiences spurred many of their comrades to continue their arson campaign, as well as attacks on golf courses and pillar boxes, and the setting off of false fire alarms. During late February and early March, Whitekirk Parish Church, East Lothian, and Redlynch, a Georgian mansion near Wincanton, Somerset, were both destroyed while serious damage was done to the Church of St John the Evangelist, Westminster.[76] For Rebecca West, as for many of the public, destruction of empty beautiful buildings was a pointless act of vandalism. But for suffragette Ethel Smyth, 'the time for destroying works of art has come'.[77]

'The Union has passed through difficult seas during the past two years and more and more difficult will our course become', Christabel warned Constance Lytton whose autobiography *Prisons and prisoners* had just been published and would be sold in WSPU shops. 'The people who have guided it must guide it to the end using their best & therefore free judgement . . . Concentration is the watchword for us!'[78] Indeed, 'concentration' was the title for a key article published in early March, in which Christabel rallied the suffragettes to work just for the WSPU, rather than spread their energies too thinly between a competing range of interests:

> [W]omen have been carefully trained by the dominant sex to be 'all abroad' – Jill of all trades and mistress of none . . . This bad old lesson of 'Don't concentrate' women are steadily unlearning . . . by preaching and setting the example of concentration, the W.S.P.U. has amply justified its existence as an emancipator of women.[79]

Although Christabel was preoccupied with the task of leading the WSPU, more personal matters could intrude. 'It is hardly credible that Adela's voyage is nearly at an end', she confessed to Helen Archdale on 4 March:

> It seems yesterday only that she was here . . . Very grateful do I feel to you for your help in the difficult matter of arranging for Adela's future doings. You have been ever since we have known you so very good & very kind about her.

'We are fighting very hard against forcible feeding', Christabel continued, 'I never felt so assured & so hopeful.'[80] However, such optimism was now tempered by the growing crisis over the Irish situation.

The Irish question had become increasingly tense over the last few months. Sir Edward Carson and his followers in the Ulster Unionist Party had declared that if Home Rule were granted to Ireland, with a parliament in Dublin, they would establish a rival, independent Government in Ulster. Arms and ammunition had already been shipped to Ulster, men were being drilled and it seemed as if civil war would break out. The WSPU had approached Carson, asking if his proposed rebel Government would give equal voting rights to women. He declared this would be so. However, Asquith, concerned about the potential scale of Ulster militancy and the setting up of an alternative Government, sought a peaceful solution to the crisis rather than to arrest and imprison the ringleaders. Now in early March, Carson suddenly announced that he could not commit the Unionists to women suffrage since his colleagues were not united upon the matter and he did not wish to cause dissent by introducing the issue.[81]

The way in which the Liberal Government caved into pressure from Ulster Unionists was not lost on Christabel, or the blatant message that militant women were treated differently from militant men. Boldly she announced in *The Suffragette*:

> Sir Edward Carson has declared war upon women, and women in their turn declare war upon him . . . While the Government were finally framing their peace-offering to Ulster, they were giving orders for . . . the arrest of Mrs. Pankhurst. The very fact is an advertisement of the glaring inequality of women's position in the State. This meting-out of concession to men and coercion to women will stir to active indignation all those women who are not spiritually maimed by past subjection.[82]

Soon afterwards, the WSPU mounted an arson campaign in Northern Ireland.

One of the many suffragettes determined to show their displeasure at the double standards the Government adopted, particularly in regard to the treatment of Emmeline Pankhurst, was Mary Richardson. On 9 March, at St Andrew's Hall, Glasgow, the pale Emmeline, whose hair had turned silvery white since her various imprisonments, had just explained that her text for the evening was 'Equal justice for men and women, equal political justice, equal legal justice, equal industrial justice, and equal social justice' when the police burst into the building. During the fierce fighting that broke out, she was hit over the head by a big constable, knocked to the floor and arrested.[83] Before the Glasgow event, Mary Richardson had written to Christabel, outlining what she intended to do. When Christabel's reply – 'Carry out your plan' – arrived on 10 March, Mary did just that. She went to the National Gallery and with a meat chopper she slashed the famous 'Robeky Venus' painting by Velasquez.

Although the press expressed outrage at the act, the *Daily Telegraph* even claiming that it was 'probably the most wicked act of vandalism ever committed in this or any country', Christabel praised the notorious suffragette:

> Humbug and hypocrisy it is indeed to whine at an attack upon the picture of a beautiful woman, while beautiful womanhood is being defaced and defiled by the economic horror of sweating and by that other horror of prostitution. Let the men whose crocodile tears have dewed the editorial columns of the daily press consider . . . the devastation their sex have wrought by the political disenfranchisement, the industrial robbery and the sex exploitation of women.[84]

Christabel's statement held no sway. Mary Richardson was sentenced to six months' imprisonment, and went on hunger strike. As she was suffering from appendicitis, the struggling and violence entailed by forcible feeding was regarded as especially dangerous. Grace Roe sought the help of Henry Harben, hoping he could put pressure on the Home Secretary to release her. Mary was released in early April, about one week before Kitty Marion who had been forcibly fed 232 times.[85]

The brutal treatment by an all-male Liberal Government of Emmeline Pankhurst and other suffragettes campaigning for their democratic rights only increased the determination of many militants to continue following Christabel's advice. The week following the vicious Glasgow attack, an unprecedented amount of militancy took place as suffragettes interrupted church services, made speeches in theatres and restaurants and attacked property. By the end of March, the damage was estimated to be between £25,900 and £27,000.[86] In mid-March, Christabel wrote to Janie Allan, the WSPU organiser in Glasgow, rejoicing in the news that 'so many new members' had joined the Union as a consequence of the Glasgow attack. 'I expect you will be having a talk with mother. You must have been as glad as we were to hear that she was free again.'[87] But Ethel Smyth was far from impressed with the way Emmeline Pankhurst was always in the front line of protest, and complained to Christabel about it. The offended Emmeline sent Ethel a scolding letter, defending her daughter. 'Darling I'm so sorry you should be so put out about my writing to C.', replied the contrite Ethel to Emmeline. 'Now I will ease your mind by promising not to remonstrate to C. again . . . But . . . I don't in the least regret doing it -!' If Christabel did not have any concern, Ethel dared suggest, that her mother's life might be in danger, 'so much the worse for her knowledge of personality (which I have never thought, by the by, up to the level of the rest of her equipment. She thinks too well & too badly of people)'.[88]

Some weeks earlier, Christabel had dealt decisively with a curious incidence which still remains shrouded in mystery. On 8 April 1914, a letter signed 'St John Rowlandson' from 39 St James's Place, S.W. London, had been sent to Henry Harben explaining that the writer was interested in women's suffrage and had, for nearly two years:

> been engaged in marshalling forces with the object of making the objec-
> tive a matter not of supplication, but actually a sine qua non to the
> existence of any Government. My arrangements were completed some
> three days ago and I should very much like to meet you.

Presumably the two men met since the next day St John Rowlandson wrote to Christabel, saying he had enjoyed a conversation with Mr Harben and was anx-ious to meet her, with as little delay as possible.[89]

Christabel was suspicious. Neither she nor Harben knew anything about this man apart from his claim that he worked for the Foreign Office. On 12 April she replied to St John Rowlandson:

> I regret it is quite impossible for me to arrange the interview which
> you suggest. So far as we are concerned there is nothing more to be
> said concerning the Suffrage situation and the steps to be taken for the
> achievement of our object.

To Harben, Christabel explained that she would want to know more about the man before meeting him:

> In my private and personal capacity I should always decline to have any-thing whatsoever to do with shady or dubious characters and I am firmly convinced that what is a valid rule for an individual woman is a sound rule for women acting collectively as a Union.[90]

The curious Harben hired private detectives to find out more about St John Rowlandson, but little came to light. It was reported that he was well liked and respected by the various West End clubs to which he belonged, paid his bills promptly, travelled abroad a lot and was engaged in numerous business enter-prises. But what exactly this business activity involved, no one found out. There was no record of a St John Rowlandson at the foreign office, but only of a Mr Rowlandson who was the Advisor to the ex-Sultan of Zanzibar.[91]

Harben was helpful, yet again, when Christabel asked him if he could find an alternative venue for the holding of the WSPU's large Monday afternoon gatherings. He recommended the Queen's Theatre in Shaftesbury Avenue and Christabel agreed to pay £1,250 for hiring the building weekly throughout the year. 'We shall certainly use the place only for Constitutional meetings', she reas-sured her correspondent:

> A very large number of such meetings were held at the London Pavilion in the past and we never had any disturbances, save on a few occasions, and these disturbances were, as you say in your letter, caused entirely by the police.[92]

Large WSPU meetings were particularly important for raising women's con-sciousness about the necessity of militancy for winning their enfranchisement. 'We want, when the vote comes, to be able to say that we got it ourselves – not that men gave it to us', Christabel emphasised to Constance Lytton. Confident that their cause would triumph, Christabel predicted prophetically that 'women's enfranchisement is inevitable. The utmost the anti-Suffragists can do is to delay it; prevent it they cannot'.[93]

The ill Constance was unable to participate in any further WSPU activ-ity, including the planned deputation to the King, scheduled to take place on 21 May. But Mabel Tuke, whose constitution was never strong, was intend-ing to take part. 'Darling Pansy', Christabel wrote affectionately to Mabel in early May,

> I fear even I harbour a remaining weakness – which is a shrinking from old Pansy going to prison & all that sort of thing. Will you like a dear & darling talk it over with mother & see what she thinks . . . Darling old Pansy flower, if you go I hope you will come & see me first.[94]

Emmeline Pankhurst, due to lead the deputation on 21 May, was still ill that early May of 1914. A fugitive on the run, she sought shelter wherever it was safe, this time in a remote country house. Ethel Smyth, worried that her dear friend was doing irreparable damage to her health, wrote to Emmeline in early May, blaming Christabel for the deplorable state of affairs:

> [O]ften I say to people what I most passionately admire in C. is her quietly accepting that you have to bear the brunt of the fight – & thinking out how best to use you. I often have said she goes one better than God who sacrificed his son – a young person !![95]

Ethel, soon to leave Egypt for Vienna, failed to understand the relationship between Christabel and Emmeline, and the perfect accord between them. Daughter and mother had decided jointly what their respective roles should be in the WSPU, and both accepted Emmeline's willingness to be ruthless with her own body. Nor was Christabel as heartless about her mother's plight as Ethel feared. Jessie Kenney remembered the terrible strain under which Christabel lived, 'not knowing whether her mother, my sister Annie', as well as other hunger-striking suffragettes, might 'die in prison'.[96]

'Alarming rumours about Mother reached me', wrote the worried Christabel to Janie Allan when her mother was arrested on 21 May after leading about one hundred of her followers to Buckingham Palace, to try to present a petition to the King. Although the women had bravely advanced, they were no match for the 2,000-strong foot and mounted police who had orders to turn them back.[97] The frail Emmeline had nearly reached the gates of the palace when the burly Inspector Rolfe lifted her off the ground in his arms, crushing her ribs. The photograph of her, clasped around the waist, her small feet off the ground, her head thrown back and her face grimacing in pain, was widely published in the press. Back in Holloway, Emmeline went on her eighth hunger strike since she was sentenced to three years' penal servitude in April last year. The anxious Christabel explained to Janie Allan that she had telephoned the Governor of Holloway, asking for news:

> His reply was that she was as well as could be expected under the circumstances. As a Cat-and-Mouse prisoner, she was snatched away without our having the opportunity that a police court trial gives, of hearing how she was, and whether or not she was hurt.[98]

Christabel pondered on the failure of this deputation to the King who, she believed, was surrounded by people who gave false impressions of the suffragettes. Could other ways be found to end the suffering of her mother and the militants and bring justice to their cause? 'An idea has just occurred to me', she wrote to the well-connected Victor Duval of the Men's Political Union, two days after her mother's release on 27 May, due to return to prison on 3 June:

The Prince of Wales is at Oxford, and, I should say, rather more accessible than under ordinary conditions. I wonder if you could try to see him, and explain to him the whole militant situation? . . . If the Prince of Wales could be talked to, and made to understand the whole thing, he might do some good with his parents.[99]

But such a suggestion came to nothing, and the double standard the Government used when dealing with her mother and the leaders of the Ulster Unionist Party who were arming with machine guns, drilling and mobilising their followers, was only too obvious.

An appeal to the monarch by militant Irishmen, together with a call to arms, had resulted in the King convening a conference on the Irish question, but no such concession was granted to the suffragettes. Nor did the Government censure Bonar Law, the leader of the Conservatives, who supported the Ulster leaders in their fierce opposition to Home Rule. 'Why is Mrs Pankhurst sent to prison, while Mr Bonar Law is left at liberty?' Christabel asked in a leading article. 'Why is the W.S.P.U. attacked, its offices raided, its paper assailed; while the militant Ulster organisation and its leaders are unmolested, its headquarters not raided, and the Unionist press, constantly inciting to militancy, not attacked?'[100]

The plight of her mother was not Christabel's only worry. Many of those recently arrested were novices, militant for the first time. 'I don't know how much longer we could have stood the strain of using other people's lives', recollected Jessie Kenney.[101] The strain increased when, in an attempt to crush the printing and sale of *The Suffragette*, the police again raided WSPU offices at Lincoln's Inn. Grace Roe was arrested on the charge of conspiracy. Among information seized was a list of subscribers to the Union's funds. On 8 June, temporary offices at 17 Tothill Street, Westminster were raided by police who took possession of the building. Four days later, the police raided the new headquarters at 2 Campden Hill Square. Olive Bartels succeeded Grace Roe as the chief organiser but the police did not know this since she did not appear in the WSPU offices but lived a secluded life in a Bloomsbury hotel, disguised as a recently bereaved young widow, 'Margaret Cunningham'. Dressed in deep mourning, she never went outside without wearing a widow's bonnet and clothes with a thick crepe veil over her face, as was the custom of the time. She had no direct communication with the WSPU but kept in touch by what she termed a 'secret service' that warned her if the police were hot on her tracks.[102] In view of the fluidity of the situation, Christabel never again left her flat in Paris but remained indoors continuously, until the outbreak of war in August.[103] She hired a pianola so that she could play it now and again, for a little recreation.

As the forcible feeding of militants continued, news came through in early June that some of the women, including Rachel Peace, Gertrude Ansell, Grace Roe and Nellie Hall, were being drugged by the prison authorities to lower their resistance against the process. Christabel's attack on the authorities was fierce:

The Government do not . . . stop at kicking women in the open street. They drug them, and they torture them behind the locked doors of prison cells . . . The most revolting aspect of the Liberal Government's unnatural persecution of women is that it is to a large extent a war of old men upon young women.[104]

Christabel's condemnation of forcible feeding had been receiving support from growing numbers of the clergy and medical profession for some time, many arguing that it was being used not to save life but as a form of punishment. In December 1913 the Association of Registered Medical Women had passed a resolution condemning compulsory feeding as a contravention of the rules of medical practice. In 1914, under the leadership of Sir Victor Horsley, a senior member of the British Medical Association, a petition with seventy-one signatures was sent to the Home Secretary.[105] But despite these protests, the Government refused to yield and forcible feeding continued.

After the raid on Lincoln's Inn that May of 1914, *The Suffragette* was printed in Scotland. Jessie Kenney (as 'Mary Fordyce') travelled each week from Paris to Glasgow to see the paper through the press, in the cellar where it was printed. For security, she posted copy for the paper late at night, in a post box near the Gare du Nord. She recollected that she and Christabel 'lived like nuns', thinking of nothing else but the cause:

> C never saw anyone not connected with the job in hand, or who could not in some way help it . . . The tension was terrific. C felt it terribly, though she never showed it much . . . For make no mistake, she kept the Movement together by sheer willpower.

Since Christabel now never left the flat, Jessie was the person who ventured outside, as necessary, sometimes to return and find her in a panic:

> It was one night when I was taking the stuff to the post that I was overcome by the sheer claustrophobia of the life we were leading. I felt I must have a break, some fresh air. So I sat in a little cafe and watched people walking past . . . It must have been about 2 a.m. when I got back to the little flat. For the first time I saw Christabel in a state. Where had I been? Didn't I realise that if I got caught and spirited away by Government agents (for we did not discount this possibility) she would be helpless? I must promise never to do it again, never.[106]

The strain under which Christabel was living was evident only to those closest to her, including Jessie's sister Annie, Christabel's dearest friend. At Christabel's request, Annie had gone to see the Archbishop of Canterbury, to appeal for sanctuary until the vote was won. The Archbishop's response was to call in Scotland Yard. After a six-day hunger strike in prison, Annie was released but then returned to Lambeth Palace in an ambulance van she had ordered. The police once again arrested her and since Annie refused to give an address, took her to the workhouse infirmary from where she eventually made her way back to 'Mouse Castle'. This was Annie's last arrest. From late May 1914 until the outbreak of war in August, she used a variety of disguises to evade the police, speaking at WSPU meetings, raising money for the cause – and visiting Christabel in Paris.[107]

On one such occasion in May, Christabel had a serious talk with her. Afraid that Annie might devote too much energy to the Theosophical Movement, which she had joined in July 1912, Christabel asked her not to align herself with any other cause until the vote was won. The loyal Annie had no difficulty in agreeing to the request and the two parted, on the best of terms. She stood in the street to wave goodbye to Christabel who waved back, from the small balcony of her flat. Jessie recollected that Christabel then suddenly rushed inside, her face 'bathed in tears', something Jessie had never witnessed before.[108] Such displays of emotion were possible only for the most trusted of friends. When Kathleen Kennedy and another suffragette from Southampton visited, Kathleen spoke of how ill Mrs Pankhurst was looking. 'Don't you feel very worried about her?' she asked. The inscrutable Christabel replied, 'A general can have no feelings', a reply that was undoubtedly repeated to her critics in England.[109]

Jessie was firmly of the view that Christabel was not uncaring and that her leadership at a distance was the critical lynchpin of the suffragette movement:

> I often think that it was the saving of the Movement that C did come to Paris. Awful as the tension was, she did have a chance to think and read and get things into some sort of perspective. This she did, and it is unfair to describe her as inhuman because this was her role – as so many people do, comparing her with Mrs. P[ankhurst] . . . I have known Mrs P, who was essentially . . . an evangelist, weakened as she was by . . . illness, break down completely and sob on my shoulder: 'If only I knew what Christabel would do now.' That's what everyone in Britain was waiting to hear, and it was a terrible responsibility for her.[110]

Ethel Smyth observed that after the deputation to the King, a virulent attack was directed against Christabel, 'engineered by the Government, and fed, I fear, by certain disgruntled suffragists who resented Christabel's dictatorship'.[111] On 11 June Reginald McKenna, the Home Secretary, in a long speech suggested four alternatives for dealing with the militant women ('hysterical fanatics') – allowing them to die in prison, deportation, commitment to a lunatic asylum or granting them the franchise. The last alternative he refused to discuss, and dismissed the others as offering no solution to the problem. McKenna defended the Cat and Mouse Act as adequate to deal with the situation and proposed to proceed against WSPU subscribers by criminal and civil actions to make them personally responsible for damage done, so that insurance companies would seek to recover their losses.[112] Christabel responded with a typically robust rebuttal, arguing that the Government's use of forcible feeding was like 'the Inquisitors in the old time', torturing over and over again women who were fighting for justice. 'Hysterical fanaticism – their words do not sting, for so have been called all the saints and martyrs.'[113] She passed no comments on the remarks of Conservative Sir Robert Cecil during the Commons debate, who asked whether it was possible to induce the French Government 'to take proceedings against one of the chief organisers of the W.S.P.U. who lived in Paris'.[114]

Certainly the disgruntled Emmeline Pethick-Lawrence was one suffragist who believed that Christabel should come back to London, criticisms that she too now began to air publicly. On 7 July, at a large public meeting organised by the United Suffragists in Kingsway Hall, to the surprise of many of her friends, Mrs Lawrence recalled her dismissal from the WSPU. She spoke of how all discussion had been 'swept away by the ultimatum of Mrs. Pankhurst' and how the finances and control of the WSPU had been 'placed in the hands of one sole leader in Paris'. Shouts of 'liar' and hisses echoed around the room as indignant supporters of Christabel and Emmeline Pankhurst made their presence felt at regular intervals.[115] Such public denunciations put even more pressure on Christabel who had also to face, yet again, more problems with that 'troublesome' sister, Sylvia.

Sylvia, like her mother, a Cat-and-Mouse prisoner, decided she would attempt to force Asquith to grant votes for women by adopting different tactics to those advocated by Christabel. Released from prison on 18 June, in a severely weakened state, she insisted on being taken to the House of Commons where she was carried from her car within a few yards of St Stephen's Hall, threatening to starve herself to death unless Asquith received a deputation of working women from her East London Federation. Sylvia did not have to wait long on the stone steps where she lay; the besieged Asquith did not want a martyr on his hands, especially with a general election looming the following year. Keir Hardie passed on the message that Asquith would receive a deputation in two days' time, a decision greeted with cheers by all around her, including Henry Nevinson.

On 20 June, the deputation of working women, accompanied by two well-known socialists, John Scurr and George Lansbury, arrived at the Commons. But Lansbury failed to find a single Labour MP who would have anything to do with them and fell back on Sir William Byles, the Liberal MP, who escorted the party into the House.[116] At the meeting with Asquith, the deputation asked for the unconditional release of Sylvia and for a Government measure granting suffrage to all women over the age of twenty-one, not the more limited enfranchisement that the WSPU supported. In his written reply, Asquith emphasised that 'if a change in the franchise had to come, then women should be given the vote on the same terms as men, that it must be a democratic and not a restricted measure.[117] It is clear that at the time the leader of the East London deputation, Julia Scurr, regarded their mission as a failure, as did Sylvia. 'The Prime Minister's letter is a cruel answer to the women workers', Sylvia wrote in the Woman's Dreadnought.

'He pretends to sympathise with these women but he puts them off without saying anything.'[118] Yet, in *The suffragette movement* written many years later, Sylvia claims that Asquith's reply revealed 'an unmistakable softening in his long hostility' to women's suffrage. She presents herself as the key figure, with her socialist male and female comrades, especially the East End working women, who makes the breakthrough after all the years of agitation for the vote. Many people and the press praised her, she notes, in this great step forward, which may be portrayed as a victory for socialist feminism rather than the separatist divisive policies of Christabel and their mother.[119]

Although Christabel made sure that some coverage was given in *The Suffragette* to Sylvia's protest and the deputation to Asquith, she was angry.[120] Socialist MPs, who had recently supported the third reading of a Plural Voting Bill that did not grant votes to women, were no more to be trusted than the Liberal Prime Minister. In particular, she vented her disdain in a scathing attack on Asquith, arguing that it was not 'if' women were to be given the franchise, but 'when':

> Perhaps it was the poor opinion of working-class intelligence that he had formed as the result of his experience of Mr. J. R. Macdonald and the Labour MPs, that made Mr. Asquith think he could afford to talk to the working women he received . . . Mr. Asquith had of course, his word to say about militancy . . . He spoke of the 'criminal methods which have done so much to impede the progress of the cause.' For him, the Great Impeder, the Arch-Impedient – unless we give that title to the crafty, false friend, the Chancellor of the Exchequer [Lloyd George] – to talk of 'impeding the cause', is a piece of unparalleled and unprecedented effrontery.[121]

Unknown to Christabel, Sylvia had asked Lansbury if he could arrange for her to meet with Lloyd George, which he did, also attending himself. Lloyd George assumed that a general election would intervene before the next session of Parliament and, according to Sylvia in *The suffragette movement*, declared he would 'refuse' to join the new Liberal Cabinet unless a Reform Bill should be introduced 'in which . . . a clause giving votes to women on broad, general lines should be left to a free vote of the House of Commons'. Meanwhile, he would introduce a private member's bill on the same lines to indicate his intentions. He asserted that he would 'stake' his political reputation on the passage of votes for women in the next parliamentary session, 'resign' if defeated, give 'written guarantees' of his intentions – but only if, in the meantime, militancy was suspended.[122] Sylvia either incorrectly recalled the facts or changed them to suit her version of events since Lloyd George, as a cabinet minister, was unable to introduce a private member's bill and so was unlikely to make such an offer.[123] Nonetheless, on 6 July Lloyd George wrote to the Home Secretary asking to discuss 'Sylvia Pankhurst', before any steps were taken to re-arrest her:

She & her friends mean to throw in their lot with the Constitutionalists against the Militants. This would be useful & unless she is guilty of some fresh outbreak – which is extremely improbable – would it not be desirable to leave her alone?[124]

Sylvia had decided to keep these negotiations secret. However, Lansbury, excited about Lloyd George's offer of a women's suffrage measure, communicated the news to Henry Harben who promptly rushed to Paris to tell Christabel. Victor Duval also wrote to Christabel, telling her what had happened. 'I too have heard of the interviews with Lloyd George', replied the exasperated Christabel to Victor on 14 July, 'and I most strongly disapprove of them, as I have taken every opportunity of saying.'[125] As soon as Sylvia knew that her sister had been told everything, she wrote to her saying that she intended to interview other Cabinet Ministers and engage in various negotiations, and that when she had done so, she would travel to Paris to see her. Christabel was furious. 'Tell your friend not to come', was her sharp reply, sent by telegram to Norah Smyth.[126] Christabel had already agreed that a small WSPU deputation could wait on Sir Edward Grey, the Foreign Secretary, for the purpose of demanding, not negotiating, the immediate enfranchisement of women and an end to forcible feeding. And as usual, Grey gave the reply that since the Cabinet was divided on the issue of women's suffrage, he could do nothing.[127]

For Christabel that summer of 1914, there could be no cooperation with socialist men, no begging to the Government on the woman question, 'no compromise', which was the title of her leading article on 17 July. 'Militancy will continue unless and until the Lords carry a Votes for Women Bill and that Bill, receiving the Royal Assent, becomes an Act of Parliament.'[128] As harrowing stories about forcible feeding continued to filter through and further protests were made to the Government about its treatment of suffragette prisoners, Christabel held firm, as did her mother who entered her tenth hunger strike.[129] Emmeline Pankhurst, again a fugitive on the run, had been rearrested on 16 July as she set out, on a stretcher, to attend a WSPU meeting at Holland Park Hall. Anticipating such a move, she had prepared a speech to be read out at the meeting. 'There is talk of negotiation and compromise. No negotiation for us. A Government measure giving equal voting rights to women with men is our demand, and we demand it **Now!**' Christabel, working in unison with her mother, had a similar message read out by Mabel Tuke.[130] In *The Suffragette* she reiterated the message again, calling the Government's call for negotiation 'a piece of clap-trap . . . [like] Joan of Arc . . . [her] spiritual descendants, the Suffragettes will no more be negotiated into surrender or compromise than would she'.[131] The total amount of the 'Protest Fund' raised at a recent Holland Park meeting was £15,350. This sum, together with an income of £36,896 that the WSPU had attracted during the last year, an increase of £8,000 upon the previous year, are firm indicators that the policy that Christabel and Emmeline Pankhurst upheld had not cost the Union all public support.

The Government, for its part, responded to such developments by trying to crush *The Suffragette* once more, arresting its printers and issuing proceedings against all persons involved in its publication or distribution.[132] The situation could not continue, especially in times of national uncertainty when the clouds of the First World War were gathering. The outbreak of war enabled Christabel and the Government to get out of an impossible situation without either side granting concessions to the other.

Notes

1 CP to Mrs Belmont, 3 October 1913, National Woman's Party Papers, Group II, 1913–74.
2 *New York Times*, 19 October 1913.
3 CP, Moral turpitude, TS, 24 October 1913, p. 30.
4 Ellen N. La Motte to CP, 19 October 1913, Grace Roe to Mr Harben, 20 October 1913, Mr Harben to Miss Pankhurst, 31 October 1913, Harben Papers.
5 Marie Roberts, Prisoners' Secretary to Dear Friend, [November 1913], Hugh Franklin – Elsie Duval Papers, TWL.
6 John, *Evelyn Sharp*, p. 71. I have inferred that Henry's gifts on this occasion would have aroused suspicions that their relationship was more than friendship.
7 Information gleaned from CP to Miss Wallace-Dunlop, 3, 7 and 10 November 1913, Wallace-Dunlop Family Archive Private Collection (hereafter WDFA).
8 Entry for 16 October 1913, Nevinson Diaries.
9 Entry for 11 October 1913, Nevinson Diaries.
10 CP to Miss Wallace-Dunlop, 7 November 1913, WDFA.
11 *VfW*, 24 October 1913, p. 40.
12 CP to Miss Wallace-Dunlop, 7 November 1913, WDFA.
13 CP to Miss Wallace-Dunlop, 10 November 1913, WDFA.
14 CP to Miss Wallace-Dunlop, 3 November 1913, WDFA.
15 *Daily Herald*, 3 November 1913.
16 CP to Sylvia, 7 November 1913, ESPA.
17 Quoted in R. Cullen Owens, *Smashing times: a history of the Irish women's suffrage movement 1889–1922* (Dublin: Attic Press, 1984), pp. 87–8. CP to Mr Harben, 7 November 1913, Harben Papers, states, 'I am glad to think that Mrs. Harben and yourself will understand our next step which must & will be to get clear of any appearance of an alliance with the Daily Herald League . . . Our appeal is to women as such & to women of all classes.'
18 TS, 14 November 1913, p. 95.
19 CP, Independence, TS, 14 November 1913, p. 102.
20 ESP to Dear Friend, 18 November 1913, ESPA.
21 TS, 21 November 1913, p. 134.
22 Annie Kenney to Dear Friend, 25 November 1913, ESPA.
23 Entry for 28 November 1913, Nevinson Diaries.
24 Theodora Bonwick, 29 November 1913, ESPA.
25 CP to Dear Sylvia, 27 November 1913, ESPA.
26 CP, Militancy, *New Statesmen: Special Supplement on The Awakening of Women*, ed Mrs Sidney Webb, 1 November 1913, pp. x–xi.
27 EP to Mrs Archdale, 2 September 1913, Craigie Collection.
28 Macpherson, *The Suffragette's Daughter*, pp. 44–5; Coleman, *Adela Pankhurst*, pp. 53–4.
29 Ethel Smyth to My darling Em, 9 December 1913, Ethel Mary Smyth Letters, Walton Clinton Jackson Library, University of North Carolina Library, Green Boro, USA (hereafter Smyth Letters).

30 CP to Miss Birnstingl, 27 November 1913, Craigie Collection; see also CP to Mrs Badley, 17 November 1913, TWL; TS, 7 November 1913, p. 77.

31 VfW, 12 December 1913, p. 202.

32 VfW, 12 December 1913, p. 202; see Fulford, Votes for women, Chapter 32; Pugh, The march of the women, pp. 202–23.

33 CP, Christmas comes again, TS, 26 December 1913, p. 250.

34 Antonia Raeburn interview with Phyllis Keller and Grace Roe, c.1964, Raeburn Collection.

35 EP to Ethel Smyth, 29 December 1913, quoted in Smyth, Female pipings, pp. 219–20.

36 EP to Mrs Archdale, 11 December and 26 December 1913, Craigie Collection.

37 CP to Mrs Archdale, 12 December 1913, Craigie Collection.

38 ESP, TSM, pp. 516–17.

39 ESP, TSM, pp. 517–18.

40 EP to Dearest Sylvia, 29 January 1914, ESPA.

41 EP to Dearest Sylvia, n.d. [1 February 1914?], ESPA.

42 Elsa Dalglish to ESP, 17 February 1914, ESPA.

43 Ethel Smyth to EP, 15 and 16 January, 19 April 1914, Smyth Letters.

44 New York Times, 7 February 1914.

45 TS, 13 February 1914, p. 387.

46 Holton, Feminism and democracy, p. 128.

47 VfW, 7 February 1914, p. 281.

48 ESP, TSM, p. 520; ESP to Dear Friend, 16 February 1914, Helen Watts Papers.

49 TS, 13 February 1914, p. 388.

50 CP, The Liberal-Labour Pharaoh, TS, 20 February 1914, p. 418; see also CP, The Labour Party's betrayal of women, TS, 6 February 1914, p. 565.

51 APW, My mother, APWP, p. 42.

52 APW, My mother, APWP, pp. 41–2.

53 See The Suffragette, 16 January 1914, p. 306.

54 EP to Mrs Archdale, 27 January 1914, Craigie Collection.

55 APW, My mother, APWP, pp. 42–3.

56 APW, The story of my life, APWP.

57 APW, My mother, APWP, p. 44; Coleman, Adela Pankhurst, pp. 59–60.

58 Lilian Hicks to Maude Arncliffe Sennett, 24 January 1914, MASC.

59 CP to Constance Lytton, 14 January 1914, P-L Papers.

60 Copies of correspondence Beatrice Harraden (BH) to CP, 13 January 1914, Allan Papers.

61 CP to BH, 16 January 1914, Allan Papers.

62 BH to CP, [n.d. but 20 January 1914], Allan Papers.

63 CP to BH, 26 January 1914, Allan Papers.

64 VfW, 6 February 1914, p. 281.

65 Interview with Mary Leigh, 21 March 1965, DMC; ESP, TSM, p. 523.

66 Kitty Marion, Autobiography, p. 230, SFC.

67 Suffragettes: the battle for the votes, Presented by Rosalyn Ball, BBC website, 19 March 2009.

68 CP, The inner policy of the WSPU, TS, 30 January 1914, p. 353.

69 Harben offered Sylvia £150 down and the loan of another £150 to be repaid during the next two years for erecting a hall at the proposed headquarters in Bow, ESP to Mr Harben, 24 February 1914, and Harben to Miss Pankhurst, 26 February 1914, ESPA. Henry and Agnes Harben during 1913–14 also gave £50 jointly to the WSPU, and Agnes another £108, Beatrice Sanders to Mr and Mrs Harben, 7 March 1914, Harben Papers.

70 Mr Harben to CP, n.d. typescript draft [c.10 February 1914].

71 CP to Mr Harben, 15 February 1914, Harben Papers.

72 TS, 6 February 1914, pp. 372–3.

73 CP, Church and state in unholy alliance, *TS*, 13 February 1914, p. 389.
74 CP notes of draft of Marion Wallace-Dunlop letter n.d. [February 1914], WDFA; *TS*, 13 March 1914, p. 497.
75 *TS*, 6 March 1914, p. 465.
76 *Daily Chronicle*, 27 February 1914; *TS*, 6 March 1914, p. 468.
77 *Clarion*, 13 December 1913; Ethel Smyth to EP, 28 February 1914, Smyth Letters.
79 CP to Constance Lytton, 2 February 1914, P-L Papers.
79 CP, Concentration, *TS*, 6 March 1914, p. 461.
80 CP to Mrs Archdale, 4 March 1914, Craigie Collection.
81 *TS*, 13 March 1914, p. 486.
82 CP, The moral of the Irish situation, *TS*, 13 March 1914, p. 490.
83 *TS*, 13 March 1914, pp. 492–3.
84 CP, Humbug and hypocrisy, *TS*, 20 March 1914, p. 516; *Daily Telegraph*, 11 March 1914.
85 Grace Roe to Mr Harben 14 March 1914, Harben Papers; *TS*, 24 April 1914, pp. 33 and 44.
86 *TS*, 20 March 1914, pp. 518–23; Rosen, *Rise up women!*, p. 229.
87 CP to Miss Allan, 15 March 1914, Allan Papers.
88 Ethel Smyth to EP, 22 April 1914, Smyth Letters.
89 St John Rowlandson to Henry Harben, 8 April 1914 and to CP, 9 April 1914, Harben Papers.
90 CP to St John Rowlandson and to Mr Harben, 15 April 1914, Harben Papers.
91 Mr Campbell to Mr Harben, 18 April 1914, Harben Papers.
92 CP to Mr Harben, 29 April 1914, Harben Papers.
93 CP to Constance Lytton, 1 May 1914, P-L Papers.
94 CP to Mabel Tuke, 2 May 1914, Harben Papers.
95 Ethel Smyth to EP, 6 May 1914, Smyth Letters.
96 J. Kenney, The flame and the flood, p. 343.
97 *Daily Chronicle, Daily News, Daily Telegraph*, 22 May 1914.
98 CP to Miss Allan, 26 May 1914, Allan Papers.
99 CP to Mr Duval, 29 May 1914, Purvis Collection
100 *TS*, 29 May 1914, p. 120. See also CP, How men fight, *TS*, 19 June 1914, p. 165.
101 Interview with Jessie Kenney, 24 March 1964, DMC.
102 *TS*, 12 June 1914, p. 144; Rosen, *Rise up women!*, p. 234; Olive Bartels, Rough notes, DMC.
103 CP, *Unshackled*, p. 276.
104 *TS*, 'Male creatures!', 5 June 1914, p. 130.
105 Geddes, Culpable complicity, pp. 91–2; *VfW*, 10 July 1914, p. 629.
106 Interview with Jessie Kenney, 24 March 1964, DMC.
107 Kenney, *Memories*, pp. 248–51; Archbishop Davison Papers, Lambeth Palace Library, London, Women's Suffrage Box, Memorandum by J. V. Macmillan, 22 May 1914.
108 Kenney, The flame and the flood, p. 388.
109 Kathleen Kennedy Notes, n.d., SFC, 60/60:15/8.
110 Interview with Jessie Kenney, 24 March 1964, DMC.
111 Smyth, *Female pipings*, p. 232.
112 *Times*, 12 June 1914; *TS*, 19 June 1914, pp. 168–9.
113 CP, The remedy, *TS*, 19 June 1914, p. 162.
114 *TS*, 19 June 1914, p. 168.
115 *VfW*, 10 July 1914, p. 633; *Daily Herald*, 8 July 1913.
116 *Daily Herald*, 20 July 1914.
117 Rosen, *Rise up women!*, p. 236.
118 ESP, What we must do, and Mrs Scurr's letter to the Prime Minister, *Woman's Dreadnought*, 18 July 1914, p. 69.
119 ESP, *TSM*, p. 575–6; Marcus, Introduction, p. 6.

120 TS, 26 June 1914, p. 178.
121 CP, Not if, but when!, TS, 26 June 1914, p. 180.
122 ESP, TSM, p. 582.
123 Romero, *Sylvia Pankhurst*, p. 85.
124 Lloyd George to McKenna, 6 July 1914, LG Papers.
125 CP to Mr Duval, 14 July 1914, Purvis Collection.
126 ESP, TSM, p. 583.
127 TS, 17 July 1914, p. 236.
128 CP, No compromise!, TS, 17 July 1914, p. 240.
129 See TS, 17 and 24 July 1914, pp. 239 and 247, respectively.
130 TS, 24 July 1914, p. 262.
131 CP, Down with negotiation!, TS, 24 July 1914, p. 260.
132 TS, 24 and 31 July 1914, pp. 263 and 282, respectively.

16 Emmeline Pankhurst, Emmeline Pethick-Lawrence, Christabel and Mabel Tuke, suffragette procession, 10 June 1911. Author's collection

17 Christabel in her Paris apartment, 1913. Author's collection

18 Christabel in New York, October 1914. Author's collection

19 Emmeline Pankhurst with the four adopted 'war babies', left to right, Elizabeth Tudor (Betty, later adopted by Christabel), Flora Mary Gordon, Joan Pembridge and Kathleen King, 1916. Author's collection

20 Christabel and Flora Drummond campaigning for the Women's Party, Smethwick,
    December 1918. Author's collection

21 Christabel as Second Adventist writer and preacher, 1920s. Author's collection

22 Funeral of Emmeline Pankhurst, from left to right, Enid Goulden Bach (Emmeline's sister), Sylvia Pankhurst and Christabel, outside St Smith's Church, 14 July 1928. © Mary Evans Library

23 Christabel addressed Los Angeles Breakfast Club, invited by Mrs Cutler B. Whitwell, November 1931. Author's collection

24 Grace Roe in USA, July 1932. Author's collection

25 Aurea (formerly Betty), Christabel's adopted daughter, c.1934. Author's collection

26 Christabel, 18 February 1936, leaving for Buckingham Palace to receive Investiture as Dame Commander of the British Empire. Author's collection

27 Jim Taylor, Annie Kenney-Taylor and their son Warwick, 4 September 1941. Author's collection

28 Aurea's American husband, Charles vanHaelen, with his daughter from his first marriage, Joan Elizabeth, c.1938. Nancy Everett Private Papers

29 Christabel at Santa Monica, California, 1957. Author's collection

17

WAR YEARS ABROAD
October 1914–end of April 1917

As international tensions gathered that late July of 1914, Christabel was in Paris packing her suitcases and collecting her papers together, ready to travel to St Malo where she would meet up with her mother and Ethel Smyth. On 1 August she telephoned Lincoln's Inn to report her departure for Brittany.[1] Jessie Kenney, her secretary, had already left for London with a copy of one of Christabel's key articles. Laying the blame for the international crisis on the misuse of power by men, Christabel argued, 'This great war, whether it comes now, or by some miracle is deferred till later . . . is God's vengeance upon the people who held women in subjection, and by doing that have destroyed the perfect human balance.' That which had made men 'for generations past sacrifice women and the race to their lusts, is now making them fly at each other's throats'. In the coming days, it would be enfranchised women – for women must and would be enfranchised – who would save the race. 'Women of the W.S.P.U., we must protect our Union through everything', Christabel pleaded. 'It has great tasks to perform . . . for the saving of humanity.'[2]

Christabel was with her mother and Ethel Smyth in St Malo on 3 August when Germany declared war against France, the country that had given her shelter for over two years. An ardent Francophile, like her mother, the horror they both felt over Germany's action intensified when, the following day, the small, neutral country of Belgium was invaded. That evening Britain declared war on Germany. During her journey to St Malo, Christabel had long pondered on the best way forward for the militant campaign which, she believed, was close to victory.[3] Now Germany's unprovoked acts of aggression necessitated a re-thinking of militant tactics.

The patriotic Christabel and Emmeline decided to support their own nation in its hour of need and halt the militant campaign, otherwise they and their followers were unlikely ever to be granted the parliamentary vote and could even be accused of treason. However, such a course was difficult to adopt while comrades were still in prison. The French Government had immediately released all political prisoners on the outbreak of war but the British Home Secretary, Reginald McKenna, only offered an amnesty to suffragette prisoners (still not regarded as political offenders) who would undertake not to commit further crimes or outrages. Christabel and Emmeline contacted the well-connected Mrs Mansel, cousin of the Liberal Chief Whip, asking her to seek the help of the Archbishop of Canterbury, as an intermediary. Archbishop Davidson met up with McKenna and assured him that the WSPU leaders genuinely wanted to halt militancy at a time of national crisis, but only when all WSPU prisoners had been released. On 10 August, McKenna reversed his previous decision, announcing that within a few days all suffrage prisoners would be released unconditionally.[4]

The conditions were now right for Christabel and her mother to outline the WSPU's new strategy. On 12 August Emmeline Pankhurst sent a circular letter to WSPU members announcing a temporary suspension of militant activities – and of publication of The Suffragette – until further notice. She did not refute 'the most vigorous militancy' that the WSPU had recently engaged in but saw it as less effective in contrast with the 'infinitely greater violence' of the present war, not merely to property and economic prosperity but to human life. The temporary suspension of the WSPU's militancy would allow not only the saving of 'much energy and a very large sum of money' but would also give an opportunity for 'those individual members who have been in the fighting line to recuperate after the tremendous strain and suffering of the past two years'. It was inevitable that Great Britain took part in the war, 'and with that patriotism which has nerved women to endure torture in prison cells for the national good, we ardently desire that our country shall be victorious'.[5] Thus the war enabled Christabel and Emmeline to steer the WSPU in a different direction, as Christabel recollected:

> As Suffragettes we could not be pacifists at any price . . . We offered our service to the country and called upon all our members to do otherwise. The cause of Votes for Women would be safe, provided our country and its constitution were preserved, for on the restoration of peace we should, if necessary, resume the pre-war campaign. To win votes for women a national victory was needed for, as Mother said, 'What would be the good of a vote without a country to vote in!'[6]

On 3 September, accompanied by her mother, Christabel returned to England on a new mission, to rouse the country to serve the national cause at a time when conscription to the army was voluntary, and few British men were at the frontline. 'I feel that my duty lies in England now', she told the Weekly Despatch, one of the many newspapers keen to interview her:

> The British citizenship for which we Suffragettes have been fighting is now in jeopardy . . . We wish to make the whole people understand the tremendous issues that are at stake and rouse our men to action. We must help to save the country and the Empire in the face of the German menace.

To a reporter from the Star Christabel emphasised that Germany was not a democracy since only German men had the vote. German women 'had less influence than English, French or American women', the attitude towards them summed up in the Kaiser's own words that women should be 'restricted to children, kitchen, and church'. Men and women in England, Christabel implored, should cooperate and work together to fight the German peril. Such a call for a unity of interest between the sexes impressed even the conservative *Daily Telegraph* which claimed that the new direction which the 'cheery and energetic' Christabel Pankhurst was taking would 'have the approval and support of every patriotic Englishman and Englishwoman, whatever their attitude to the Suffragist movement, now in abeyance'.[7]

Just how many suffragettes were impressed with the change in WSPU direction is difficult to ascertain. Elsie Bowerman, an enthusiastic organiser for the WSPU since her graduation in medieval and modern languages at Girton in 1911, and a survivor of the *Titanic*, undoubtedly expressed the views of many when she said that she greeted the declaration of war 'almost with a sense of relief . . . as we knew that our militancy, which had reached an acute stage, could cease and we could devote ourselves entirely to the service of our country'. However, Kitty Marion, a rank-and-file fire-starter, was of the view that there was 'much dissatisfaction and withdrawal from the W.S.P.U. on the part of many members at militancy and suffrage propaganda being suspended in favour of war propaganda'.[8] The war brought into sharp focus questions about the relationship of feminism to nationalism and militarism on the one hand, and to internationalism and pacifism on the other.[9] The pro-war patriotic stand of Christabel and Emmeline Pankhurst would cause splits in the WSPU, just as Millicent Garrett Fawcett's pro-war stance caused tensions and resignations among suffragists in the NUWSS.

Most historians have portrayed Christabel's patriotic support for her country as an abrupt about-turn from her suffragette days.[10] However, Christabel had *not* abandoned women's suffrage but changed the context in which she presented the issue. Both she and her mother now began to skilfully present themselves as patriotic feminists as they wove into their speeches themes about the nation, patriotism, imperialism, democracy, internationalism, men's and women's contribution to the war and, in particular, the part that women's loyal war service could make to women's enfranchisement.[11] As Jacqueline deVries points out, a more nuanced analysis of the Pankhurst position reveals a consistency of thought. Christabel and Emmeline Pankhurst's interpretation of war was still feminist and 'gendered', in that they defined Germany as a 'masculine' nation and Britain and her allies as 'feminine'; ideals of purity, sacrifice and national moral regeneration were still upheld, and a belief in women's unique capacity to achieve these goals.[12]

This was evident on 8 September when Christabel celebrated her return home by addressing a big meeting in the London Opera House, her first speech in Britain for several years. Flags of the Allies decorated the room and a women's band played national airs. Standing alone on the vast stage in a gown of pale green, 'a dainty, smiling, blushing figure' according to the *Daily Mail*, she received tremendous applause from the mainly female audience who sang 'For she's a jolly good fellow' and handed up bouquets of roses and lilies. In the streets outside hundreds struggled for admission.[13] '[W]e suffragettes', Christabel began,

> believe that it is our duty to do all we can to rouse the individual citizen to fight for the freedom and the independence of this country and this Empire . . . as militant women, we may perhaps be able to do something to rouse the spirit of militancy in men.

A victory for Germany, where the position of women was the lowest in Europe, would lead to the extinction of democratic Government, she emphasised:

> Therefore, we women are determined that the British citizenship for which we have fought in the past, for which we are prepared to fight again, for which we are prepared to die as readily as any soldier now fighting on the battlefield . . . shall be preserved from destruction at the hand of Germany.[14]

One of the powerful anti-suffrage arguments against granting votes to women had been that women did not fight for their country in times of war, that they took no part in national defence. Christabel directly challenged that view, arguing that women's support on the home front was vital and would be a way to win their enfranchisement:

> For every one who fights you must have a number of non-combatants to feed him, to clothe him and to prevent the State for which he is fighting from crumbling into ruins . . . It is the women who prevent the collapse of the nation while the men are fighting the enemy.[15]

And in a last prophetic statement, Christabel emphasised that once the war was over and England was victorious, women who had taken a full part in the war effort would insist upon 'being brought into equal partnership as enfranchised citizens of this country'.[16]

In this important speech Christabel was emphasising a key theme that she and her mother reiterated throughout the war – that women's war service was crucial to the war effort and would earn them the right to the parliamentary vote. As Nicoletta Gullace has perceptively observed, Christabel and Emmeline Pankhurst were taking control of the discourse, drama and spectacle of war to serve their own feminist ends and further the campaign for female citizenship. In so doing they demolished the anti-suffrage argument against women being enfranchised, and helped to bring about a cultural shift in the definition of citizenship so that it centred on loyal service, patriotic sentiment and British blood rather than manhood, the age of majority or property.[17]

Grace Roe, who had made the arrangements for the exiled Christabel to return to England, was sitting in the London Opera House that evening of 8 September.

She could still recollect, some fifty years later, how Christabel looked 'most beautiful' in her green dress against the background of a darker-green velvet curtain. In particular, it was Christabel's prescience in advocating national conscription and the introduction of food rationing, both of which were eventually adopted, that impressed Grace. 'It was an amazing talk . . . absolutely amazing . . . if they had done what she said at the meeting we would never have gone through what we did.'[18] Emmeline Pankhurst was also in the audience that evening, glowing with pride as she listened to her eldest daughter. But Sylvia, sitting some distance from her mother, was horrified. As a pacifist socialist she believed that the war had been created by greedy capitalists who would exploit the working classes for their own political ends. After the meeting, she went backstage to the speakers' ante-room. 'Christabel was alone there . . . An impenetrable barrier lay between us. "Is Mother here?" I asked her. She answered laconically that she would be coming soon; and occupied herself over some papers, with unraised eyes.' Then Emmeline entered the room and Sylvia exchanged a brief greeting with her. When Sylvia went outside, a small crowd of East End women began cheering her in opposition to the cries for Christabel and their mother. 'I was irritated beyond measure', recollected the middle Pankhurst daughter, 'and hurried home without waiting for my henchwomen.'[19]

The rift between the elder Pankhursts and Sylvia, now very public, was to deepen over the coming months as Christabel and Emmeline returned to Paris and announced that they would shortly come back to England to partake in rallies for recruiting men into the army. Sylvia wept when she read the news, seeing it as a betrayal of everything for which her father had stood. For nineteen years Emmeline had supported her husband in his life-long advocacy of peace and internationalism. And after his death, she had stood firm, her children by her side, against the Boer War. On impulse, the unhappy Sylvia wrote to her mother. 'I am ashamed to know where you and Adela stand', the angry Emmeline replied.[20] Adela, like Sylvia, an ardent pacifist, was now a leading speaker for the Women's Political Association in Melbourne and delivering anti-war speeches and opposing conscription.[21]

All these family tensions did not throw the strong-minded Christabel off her course. There were more important issues with which to deal, namely giving advice to anxious suffragettes who sought her help – and the necessary task of slimming down the organisational structure of the WSPU. Kitty Marion, German by birth, worried by the Government's call for all Germans to register, asked Christabel whether she should lie about her nationality. Make a 'clean breast' of everything, was the sensible reply, and avoid the temptation to register under a false name.[22] Other suffragettes, such as Gertrude Harding, were surprised that Christabel 'advised everyone to follow their own feelings of duty to the country and act as individuals'. Such a goal, of course, did not require the extensive national organisational structure of the WSPU and so most of the organisers and staff were released from their posts and just a few trusted colleagues retained on the payroll – such as Grace Roe, Olive Bartels, Annie and Jessie Kenney,

Flora Drummond, and Gertrude herself. Lincoln's Inn House was retained, for the time being, but given up the following year.[23]

Gertrude Harding and Isabel Cay were soon in Manchester, organising a meeting at which Christabel would speak. The talk was duly delivered and a few men signed up for war service, a recruiting sergeant being also present.[24] But despite her desire to serve her country, Christabel felt uneasy about settling in Britain, primarily because she still feared arrest since her prison sentence had never been served, only suspended. The Government amnesty applied only to all suffragette prisoners and 'mice' on the run who, if they reported to the authorities, could have a remission of their sentences. Christabel fitted neither category and so was constantly on edge. Consequently she spent a considerable amount of time abroad during the war years, leaving her mother in Britain to spearhead the new WSPU strategy. That seemed a sensible solution to the problem – and a wise division of labour between the two women. Keen to develop an international role, where she could rally support for the Allies from neutral countries such as the United States, Christabel contacted Mrs Belmont, now back home in North America, who was willing to sponsor her trip. 'I did not wish to stay in England with a suspended jail sentence over me', Christabel explained to one reporter when she arrived in New York on 14 October 1914. She had travelled incognito, under the name of Miss Margaret MacDonald, on the Red Star liner *Finland*, accompanied by Olive Bartels who took the name Miss Mabel Barton. Christabel's tour of the United States and Canada lasted nearly six months, until late March 1915.[25]

At the outbreak of the war Annie Kenney, accompanied by suffragette Mary Batten-Pooll, had been sent to America to address various suffrage groups. Annie had just completed a suffrage campaign in North Dakota, Montana and Nevada when the surprise news came that Christabel had landed in New York. 'Christabel in America! What was wrong at home? I must go to New York to see if I was needed', recollected the astonished Annie. 'I feel lonely. I want to go home!' Annie complained to Christabel, after warmly greeting her in New York. It was decided that the homesick Annie would return to Britain and do her part for the war effort by organising a campaign explaining the seriousness of the Balkan situation. Once back in London, the earnest Annie spent ten days researching intensely the history, geography and politics of the question before giving, in Huddersfield, her first speech on the Balkan situation.[26]

Meanwhile, Christabel was busy advertising her first public speech to be given in the United States, at the Carnegie Hall, on 24 October, claiming it would be pro-British. New York suffragists, who could afford to be staunchly pacifist at a time when their neutral country was not at war – although they too became riven when, eighteen months later, their country entered the conflict – did not welcome Christabel's patriotic approach.[27] Mrs Raymond Brown, President of the New York State Woman Suffrage Association, returned the ticket she had been sent. However, Harriot Stanton Blatch, an old friend of the Pankhurst family, remained loyal and expressed her intention of attending.[28] On the afternoon of 24 October, the overflowing audience in the Carnegie Hall greeted the notorious suffragette warmly. '[S]he looked so dainty and appealing', a 'pink cheeked slip of a girl', clad in 'a gown of white satin and pale green chiffon' that she generated much enthusiasm, opined the *New York Times*, although more for her gallant and terse style than for the content of her address.[29] As the last notes of a robust singing by a massed choir of the Battle Hymn of the Republic had died away, Christabel began delivering her address, stressing the strong ties between her host country and Britain. Germany wanted to divide and conquer the Allied Nations, she warned, since the Kaiser believed that 'might is right'. Yet this was a doctrine that both the United States and Britain repudiated. 'I am a militant', she continued:

> That is not to say that I prefer war to peace; but it is to say that when people want to govern me by physical force and not by the moral force of justice, then I am prepared to defy their physical force to the very death.[30]

The Allies were engaged in a just war since they were dragged into the conflict out of principles of duty and honour, not naked aggression, and were fighting for democracy, something that was not perfect in Britain where women were disenfranchised. However, to allow Germany, a 'male nation' in which the counsels of women did not prevail, to spread all over the world would be disastrous for humanity. When the war was over, it would not be easy for the British Government to refuse women their political rights. Suffragettes were fighting not only for themselves and for women's right of citizenship but also for 'future generations, for whose liberty, for whose freedom from the aggression of the invader and the enemy we are responsible'.[31]

Taking a warning tone, Christabel pointed out that it was not safe to assume that America was free from attack. Why should the Kaiser love America any more than Britain? Trying to win over the pacifists in her audience, she entreated them to join Britain in the fight against German aggression by referring to America's own war of independence:

> Was your war against a British Government wrong? . . . when you fought us for the principle of freedom, for the right of self-government, you did right. I am glad you fought us and I am glad you beat us . . .We were as much in the wrong in that war as Germany is in the wrong to-day.[32]

Emphasising that the war of 1914 was a war for peace, Christabel finally appealed to the women who were present to stand in solidarity with their British sisters:

> Women! our responsibilities at this time in the world's history are enormous. When this war is over we, as enfranchised citizens, must hold the nations of the world together in friendship. We must prevent

376

the growth of fresh antagonisms. I believe the American and British women have especially a great part to play. American women! hold hands with us of Britain.[33]

It would appear that few women in the audience warmed to Christabel's call. By a strange coincidence Emmeline Pethick-Lawrence, her one-time close friend, was billed to speak in New York in a week's time. Now a pacifist, it was Mrs Lawrence that the American suffragists wanted to hear. Christabel was not down-hearted by this rebuttal since there were plenty of invitations to speak elsewhere, including one from Alice Paul, former member of the WSPU and now a leader of the militant suffragists in the USA. Writing to Alice on 29 October, Christabel explained that she was unable to give a talk in Washington on 8 November since she was only passing through on that particular day:

So many people write asking me to speak that I put the whole affair into the hands of Pond's Lyceum Bureau. They propose to arrange for me to speak in Washington later on when Congress is sitting . . . It will [be] so very interesting to hear all your news & I look forward to seeing you again after all these years.[34]

It was not until the New Year of 1915 that Christabel spoke in Washington, on 24 January, followed by major addresses in Chicago, Indianapolis and Minneapolis, as well as some Canadian cities.[35] However, before she left New York she spoke again at the Carnegie Hall, on 13 January. This time she was subjected to frequent interruptions but revealed, much to the delight of the audi-ence, that she had lost none of her art of repartee, for which she was well known:

Oh, I like these interruptions. But I tell you, sir, this: if you were a suffragette, you would have been thrown out – (laughter and applause) – and then, after you had been thrown out, I should have said I didn't believe in your violent methods. (Laughter and applause.) But you men are always so much indulged. You are the privileged sex, the sheltered ones. We have not the heart to treat you as cruelly and as roughly as you treat us. (Applause.)[36]

The American militant suffragists were in greater number among the Carnegie Hall audience this time, and warmly appreciative of Christabel's talk, even if they did not agree with all she said. The enthusiastic Eleanor Garrison wrote to her mother:

[T]he air was all electric & at no meeting I ever attended has excitement been so high . . . You never heard so much heckling & hissing (never at Christabel, but at Germans who would talk & were drowned out by the audience) & clapping. The great body of the house was with her all the time . . . there was nothing but admiration for the way in which she handled the situation. Always a good answer for everything . . . She must have talked for over two hours, but I bet no one closed an eye.[37]

However, not all in the audience were so impressed.

In particular, two British women were dismissive of Christabel's speech. Edith Ellis, a writer and wife of the sex psychologist Havelock Ellis, in America to deliver some lectures, had gone to Carnegie Hall, out of curiosity. 'I think it abominable to come to a neutral country and make strife', was her verdict. 'It was all buttering of the Americans and vilifying of the Kaiser.'[38] The suffragette Olive Bartels, accompanying Christabel on her American tour, was aghast. 'I hated it, because I hated her line on the war. I hated the whole thing', she recollected.[39] Olive would soon sever her ties with the WSPU. But others back in Britain saw things differently. The powerful British newspaper proprietor, Lord Northcliffe, owner of the *Times* and the *Daily Mail*, which had consistently opposed votes for women, was becoming increasingly impressed with the press reports about Christabel's support for the Allies and advocacy of women's war work as a way to free up men for the war front. His 'conversion' to the women's cause would soon lead his newspaper to adopt a pro rather than anti-suffrage stance, a viewpoint that other newspapers would soon follow.

In March 1915, Christabel returned from her North American tour to her flat in Paris. She found, as expected, her mother, Annie Kenney and Grace Roe waiting to greet her and was glad to have escaped an air raid the previous night.[40] Emmeline was keen to hear about her daughter's plans, especially her wish to resurrect *The Suffragette*, and conveyed all the news to Nancy Astor, an American married to the British aristocrat, Waldorf Astor. 'We feel that a clear lead is needed for women just now', she informed Nancy:

> Their natural love of peace is causing some suffragists to take action greatly to be deprecated. They are being made use of by very doubtful people without knowing it. This must be counteracted & the 'Suffragette' will be useful for the purpose.[41]

While Emmeline Pankhurst continued to be based in London, campaigning for women's war work and equal pay, Christabel set about re-establishing 'a Paris stronghold' for the WSPU, seeing it as a useful point 'of observation and information' since she and her mother were 'constantly mindful of votes for women and watchful in case the war should end leaving a Suffrage agitation still necessary'.[42]

Christabel now employed as her private secretary suffragette Gertrude Harding who had previously drilled and deployed Emmeline Pankhurst's bodyguard. The two women established a business-like routine, preparing copy for the soon-to-be re-launched *The Suffragette*, as well as dealing with general correspondence. Christabel worked at 'an incredibly fast pace', speaking into her dictaphone letters for Gertrude to type up to politicians, lawyers, businessmen and suffragettes. She also gave Gertrude the task of reading every day the three London newspapers sold in Paris so that she was well informed for their daily meeting to discuss the news, and its importance, although Christabel herself did most of the talking. Gertrude, who worked a ten-hour day, six days a week, was of the view that her employer, who did not smoke and rarely enjoyed a glass of sherry, led 'a Spartan existence'. Nonetheless, there were some lighter moments, as when Christabel made the occasional visit to the theatre or to a soiree with Baroness de Brimont or the Princess de Polignac, and gave Gertrude the afternoon or evening off, telling her to have some fun. Although Gertrude may have occasionally longed for the excitement and outdoor work involved in her last job, she found Christabel a 'warmer' person to work for than Emmeline Pankhurst. Christabel, Gertrude suggested, cared more than her mother about losing former friends and members, because of the change in the WSPU strategy. And Christabel would occasionally ask Gertrude, some nine years her junior, for her advice, something Emmeline had never done. Mrs Pankhurst 'never got beyond the stage of formalities' because she would never 'shed her role as leader of a great political movement'.[43]

Living in France, with the WSPU headquarters in Paris, gave Christabel a particular perspective on the war. Unlike Britain, France was not physically separated by a stretch of water from Germany, but a part of the European continent which bordered on that country; furthermore, some of its territory had been invaded. Living physically 'close to the enemy', so to speak, increased Christabel's admiration for the suffering of the French people – and their wish to be liberated. At the same time, her headquarters in Paris, rather than London, gave her the opportunity to observe at a distance the activities of the British Government – and to voice trenchant criticisms. Although she strongly supported the cause of the Allies, she was soon to direct a barrage of criticisms against Prime Minister Herbert Asquith and what she saw as the stupidity of his war policy. However, for the re-launch of The Suffragette, on 16 April 1915, Christabel threw the WSPU's patriotic support behind the Government's recent call for women to join a Register of Women for War Service, which had attracted so far some 33,000 recruits. Militant women, she argued, would not 'be Prussianised' since they knew too well 'what Prussianism has done to . . . kill the spirit of liberty in the German people!'[44] Many examples were cited of women, some of them WSPU members, helping the war effort by nursing the wounded, cooking for camp hospitals, or taking up a range of jobs previously held by men, such as motor van driver, tram conductor, railway porter or ticket collector.[45]

A challenge to this feminist patriotism now became highly visible as the well-known English pacifist, Emily Hobhouse, and some Dutch suffragists began organising an International Congress of Women, to be held in The Hague from 28 until 30 April, with the aim of negotiating a peace. The issue split the women's movement worldwide. In Britain, both Millicent Garrett

Fawcett and Emmeline Pankhurst condemned the event, as did Christabel in Paris.[46] 'Negotiations while the German armies are trampling on the prone body of Belgium! The very idea is monstrous', she thundered. The call of the Congress to the governments of the belligerent countries to define the terms upon which they were willing to make peace would mean 'no protest against the outrage upon Belgium . . . no message of encouragement and hope to the Serbs [who had been invaded by Austria] . . . nor to the Slav population . . . nor to the Poles'.[47] To bolster her argument, Christabel published in *The Suffragette* statements from French women's organisations expressing their refusal to have dealings with the women's peace conference. The British newspapers were impressed. 'It is not often that we have the pleasure of finding ourselves in complete agreement with Miss Christabel Pankhurst', opined the *Globe*, a view upheld by most of the British press. 'Miss Pankhurst does well in urging all sensible women, all women who know what is at stake, and what ideals are trembling in the balance, to have nothing to do with this ridiculous assembly.'[48] Undoubtedly the press also supported Christabel's condemnation of the Union of Democratic Control, the most important of the anti-war organisations in Britain. Although some of Christabel's foes and friends from her pre-war suffrage days were influential figures in this organisation, including Ramsey MacDonald, Henry Brailsford and Israel Zangwill, it was particularly against MacDonald that Christabel aimed her fire. Such attacks made Evelyn Sharp, Christabel's one-time colleague who became more and more a pacifist as the war progressed, 'very unhappy and indignant'.[49]

The Hague Peace Conference not only caused tensions within the women's movement but also highlighted differences between the Pankhurst women. Much to the embarrassment of Christabel and Emmeline, Sylvia had declared her intention of attending the event while Adela, in faraway Australia, was in sympathy with its aims. The British Government refused Sylvia the passport that would enable her to travel and withheld permission generally from other British women wishing to be delegates. One of the few who escaped the ban was Emmeline Pethick-Lawrence. Returning from her recent American tour, accompanied by her husband, she joined the American delegation. Shortly afterwards, the Lawrences returned to England where Fred took up the post of Treasurer of the Union of Democratic Control.[50]

The ardent Francophile Christabel regularly included in *The Suffragette* not only reports on the success of the WSPU's campaign to encourage women into war work but also accounts by French authors and friends, such as Jean Finot, on the joint mission of the British and French people.[51] On Sunday 16 May, the feast of Joan of Arc, the saintly French warrior and patron of the WSPU, Christabel lay flowers at her statue in the Rue de Rivoli. Together, she and Gertrude had carefully chosen a bouquet of colours to represent the Franco-British alliance and the WSPU's colours – white lilies for France, red roses for Britain, complemented by the green foliage of leaves, the whole all tied with a purple ribbon. On the card attached to the flowers Christabel wrote:

From the Women's Social and Political Union of Great Britain A token of honour and reverence for Joan of Arc, the ideal woman, the perfect patriot, and the heroic militant – and a sign of devotion to the Franco-British Alliance which was foreseen and desired by Joan of Arc and now exists as part of that greater Alliance, upon whose coming triumph in the present war, the freedom of humanity depends.[52]

Christabel's resolve to support the Allies stiffened that May when the committee set up to enquire into the extent of the atrocities committed by the Germans against Belgian citizens published its findings. The Bryce Report, as it became known, concluded that 'horror, lust and pillage' had prevailed over many in Belgium on 'a scale unparalleled in any war between civilised nations during the last three centuries'. *The Suffragette* printed excerpts from the Report, citing the murder, rape and mutilation of women, including the cutting off of their breasts, as well as the bayoneting of babies.[53] With such horrendous information at her fingertips Christabel was adamant that a German invasion of England could bring a similar reign of terror. 'If British women are to win a vote worth keeping, if British men are to keep a vote worth having, Germany must be defeated in this war', she emphasised.[54] She found it particularly galling that German men naturalised in Britain had been granted the vote while British women had been denied it. And she reiterated again a point she had made on more than one occasion, that the Kaiser had passed a law which stipulated that naturalised Germans living in a foreign country did not lose their German nationality, unless a desire was expressed to do so. Thus a naturalised German could 'remain a German subject at heart', while enjoying the privileges of a British citizen, and use this power to bring injury to the 'adopted' country.[55]

Soon *The Suffragette* was endorsing the war views of prominent politicians that the WSPU had once fiercely opposed, such as Lloyd George and Sir Edward Carson; like Christabel and her mother, these two men were critical of Asquith's leadership, especially from May 1915 when he decided to form a coalition Government with the Conservative and Labour parties. Yet Lloyd George, the recently appointed Minister for Munitions, had some transparent failings, notably that he appealed only to men to enrol for service in the munitions factories. The disappointed Christabel voiced her concerns in an article published initially in the *Times* and reprinted in the *Observer* on 27 June:

Mr. Lloyd George said . . . there is nothing in shell-making that a fairly intelligent person cannot learn in a very short time; it is not highly skilled work. Then why should women not learn to do this work of shell-making, leaving men of more training and experience to do other work more difficult?[56]

Such views did not endear Christabel, or her mother, to industrialists and trade unionists who opposed the entry of unskilled women into jobs traditionally held by men. Since women usually earned less than half the wages of men, trade unionists feared that women employees would undermine their own wages which were predicated on the notion of the male breadwinner. However, Christabel's article in the *Observer* caught the attention of King George V who sent a letter to Lloyd George 'wondering whether it would be possible or advisable for you to make use of Mrs. Pankhurst'.[57] Lloyd George sent an emissary to visit Emmeline, asking for her help. The astounded Emmeline hesitated for a moment, thinking of all that had happened before the war, but accepted the invitation. Lloyd George explained the problem – men sacrificed at the war front for want of munitions, women excluded from working in the munitions factories. He asked Emmeline to hold a great procession of women, funded by a Government grant of £3,000, a procession which would express women's willingness to enter munitions factories.[58]

With only a fortnight to plan the procession and deputation, Christabel in *The Suffragette* gave a lot of coverage to the event which was to take place on 17 July, under the able direction of the WSPU's Chief Organiser, Grace Roe, assisted by half a dozen of the old WSPU inner circle who were released from their war-time jobs for the purpose. Christabel, still living in France, proclaimed that the event would be not only a 'new pledge of support to our Allies' but also 'a sign to the enemy that British women are determined to work and strive for the freedom of their country and for the freedom of Europe'.[59] Lord Northcliffe, approached for his support, ran large advertisements and promised, when the issue of women's enfranchisement should come up again, that his newspapers would support the women's cause.[60]

The Women's War Service Procession, headed by Emmeline Pankhurst and Annie Kenney, was a great success and reported enthusiastically in the press.[61] Despite a gusty wind and driving rain, about 40,000 women of all social classes, but primarily the middle classes, marched four abreast in their cloaks and mackintoshes in one hundred and twenty-nine contingents. They carried not umbrellas but pennons or flags in the colours of the Union Jack – red, white and blue. Ninety bands played and a wagon of wild flowers bore the inscription 'We Demand the Right to Serve!' Slogans such as 'Women's Work Will Save Men's Lives', 'To Keep the Kaiser Out Let Us Make Shells' and 'Shells Made By A Wife May Save Her Husband's Life' adorned the banners. At six o'clock in the evening, Emmeline and Annie were among the small group of women who met with Lloyd George in the Ministry of Munitions. The shrewd Emmeline made no mention of the vote. 'We make no bargain for serving our country . . . We love our country and desire to serve her.' She then asked for equal pay for women to prevent women becoming a cheap source of labour. Lloyd George regretted the Government could not offer this, pointing out that since women would be unskilled and untrained for some time, they would not be able to produce as much as men who were experienced employees. However, he did agree with Emmeline's suggestion for a fixed minimum wage for women. When the small group of WSPU women joined Lloyd George outside on an especially built platform in the Ministry's gardens, a roar of cheering went up from the crowd. One woman shouted, 'We want the vote.' An amiable, good-humoured Lloyd George immediately replied, to much laughter, 'Yes, but we want you in the shell factory first.'[62]

Emmeline Pankhurst was now hailed by the press as a patriotic heroine, a woman who put her country first in its hour of need.[63] Lord Northcliffe, in the *Times*, even made a reference to the absent Christabel. 'Miss Christabel Pankhurst . . . delivered in the United States a series of admirable lectures which contributed greatly to counteract pro-German propaganda. The demonstration . . . was conceived in the same spirit.'[64] Although the direct aim of the procession was not votes for women, the notion of 'women's right to serve' was inevitably linked to pre-war suffragette agitation.

Soon Lloyd George was erecting a vast network of new munitions factories which would provide work for women.[65] For Christabel, his action on this point and his readiness to turn to her mother and the WSPU for help in the national emergency convinced her that he was in earnest in the country's cause. 'When he became Prime Minister, we supported him . . . We had confidence in his will to win.'[66] Thus began a strategic alliance between the leaders of the WSPU and their old enemy. However, Lloyd George would not become Prime Minister until December 1916, and in the meantime the hated Herbert Asquith still held that office.

For some time now Gertrude Harding had been thinking about returning to England and did so during that August of 1915. Her departure left Christabel without a secretary and so various suffragettes, including Elsie Bowerman, helped out until a more permanent appointment could be made. Armed with a reference from Emmeline Pankhurst, Gertrude was offered a job in the Intelligence Department of the War Office, headed by the Liberal politician, Lord Haldane.[67] Whether her move to the War Office was deliberately planned is difficult to determine.

Although the WSPU was attracting fewer subscriptions, Christabel and her mother now decided on an additional activity for the organisation, namely to set up a home for illegitimate female children. The problem of 'war babies', born to unmarried women who had been made pregnant by soldiers now at the war front, had been widely discussed in the press during the early months of 1915 and was soon taken up by the two WSPU leaders. Most of these mothers, some of them very young, did not qualify for an army allowance and lived on low wages so that the death rate among their offspring was high. In their feminist desire to help, Christabel and Emmeline proposed to adopt fifty female war babies who, for whatever reason, could not be brought up by their mothers. It would be not only an important service to the state, but also:

> a joy and privilege to ensure that a body of children, in such numbers as it may be possible to deal with, shall be brought up to play a worthy part in life. The W.S.P.U. will seek to make compensation to these children, for every disadvantage due to the circumstances of their birth.[68]

Although Christabel was firmly behind this new project, it was Emmeline in particular who was most enthusiastic about it, calling upon the WSPU membership for financial support. Some members initially made generous donations but most were lukewarm and some antagonistic.[69] Undaunted, the disappointed Emmeline, accompanied by Kitty Marshall, visited a Salvation Army orphanage in the early autumn of 1915 and selected four baby girls who were brought back to her London address, namely Nurse Pine's nursing home. The birth certificates of the babies were destroyed and new names were given – Kathleen King, Flora Mary Gordon, Joan Pembridge and Elizabeth Tudor, whom Christabel would later adopt.[70] A group of suffragettes who titled themselves 'Ex-prisoners and Active Members of the W.S.P.U.', angry about the autocratic way in which Emmeline had acted, printed a leaflet protesting that she was 'neglecting the Cause of Votes for Women in order to take upon herself, in the name of the Union, without consulting its Members, responsibilities which belong to the State'. Voteless women were advised to 'think twice' before contributing to the upkeep of the babies and to 'call upon Mrs. Pankhurst to refound the Women's Social and Political Union on a new and democratic basis'.[71] Neither Christabel nor Emmeline responded to these criticisms, despite their anger and hurt at such a response.

As Emmeline continued to tour Britain making rousing speeches calling for universal and obligatory war service for men and women, Christabel was still busy in Paris, writing copy for *The Suffragette*, highlighting what she believed to be German influence in the British Government, especially in departments of strategic importance, such as the War Office, the Admiralty and the Foreign Office. Lord Haldane, Gertrude Harding's employer, had strongly believed that war with Germany could have been avoided. His affinity with and affection for Germany and German philosophy led to him being regarded with suspicion by Christabel – and the general public. Christabel attacked Haldane for having allowed cotton, which was an indispensable ingredient for making weapons, to be sent from America to Germany rather than intercepting it as contraband. Nor did she view favourably some comments he made in a recent speech when he used the phrase 'The great German nation – in some respects rather like our own people.'[72] The charge of pro-Germanism and German intrigue was not limited to Haldane. Since Sir Eyre Crow, an Assistant Under-Secretary for Foreign Affairs, was married to a German and half German himself, the nephew of Admiral von Holtzendorff, Chief of the German Naval Staff, it was argued that there was no room for him in the Foreign Office. Christabel also made a call for the dismissal of Sir Edward Grey, the Foreign Secretary, who had not sent British troops to help the small Balkan country of Serbia, an ally of Britain which the Austrians were determined to destroy.[73]

On 15 October 1915, *The Suffragette* re-appeared under its new name *Britannia*. Edited by Christabel in Paris, *Britannia* with the slogan 'For King, for Country, For Freedom' became not only more fervently patriotic but more critical of what was perceived as the incompetence of the Asquith-led Government. Christabel pointed out that if Britain was to be saved from a German invasion, Asquith had to bring about closer cooperation between the Allies and improve coordination of their policy, establish a diplomatic centre for the whole alliance, and make sure that announcements by the Allies were made jointly, rather than by Britain alone, of any decisions regarding naval, military and diplomatic policy.[74] Be this as it may, the general tone of *Britannia* and the lack of any reference to votes for women was too much for some of the rank-and-file WSPU dissenters.

On 22 October, Rose Lamartine Yates, active in the Wimbledon WSPU branch, chaired a meeting at Caxton Hall. A resolution was passed protesting against the 'action of the W.S.P.U. officials whereby the Union's name and its platform are no longer used for woman suffrage', and calling for an audited statement of the Union's funds. Signed copies of the resolution were sent to Christabel and Emmeline, by registered post. The press gave extensive coverage to the story, the *Daily News and Leader* even quoting from an unnamed inform- ant that Emmeline Pankhurst, as the Honorary Treasurer of the WSPU, had control of funds which probably amounted to between £15,000 and £20,000. 'Many of Mrs. Pankhurst's former supporters feel . . . that her present power over an organisation which she has not moral, or possibly even legal, right to control . . . should immediately cease.' Neither Christabel nor Emmeline acknowledged receipt of the registered letter that was sent. Nor did they make any comment to the press.[75]

At another meeting of disgruntled WSPU members, held on 25 November and chaired this time by Elinor Penn Gaskell, a manifesto was unanimously approved and adopted protesting about the WSPU's name being used for political purposes outside its remit and asking for information about finances. Again, Emmeline was asked to issue a report on how the funds had been deployed since the outbreak of war while Christabel was given an ultimatum about her prolonged absence:

> Christabel Pankhurst . . . should resign her association with the Union as one its leaders, or else should offer a clear explanation to the members of her continued absence from this country, at a time when the services of all women of capacity and goodwill are so sorely needed here.[76]

The manifesto was published and distributed to the press.

Such a public attack on the leaders of the WSPU was unprecedented. Even during the bitter 1912 split, neither the Lawrences nor their supporters had openly expressed their views or spoken to the press. Christabel and Emmeline were contacted by the *Weekly Dispatch* for their comments on the present tensions. Emmeline initially refused to say anything but Christabel was more forthcoming:

> I cannot take the matter seriously . . . If there is any question of a revolt it can only come from an insignificant handful of malcontents who have never quite liked our support of the war. My mother and I founded the union in 1903, and we have been at the head of it ever since. There can- not be any question of our resigning. That is impossible because of the

manner in which the union is constituted. In order to take responsible decisions you must have responsible leaders. No one need follow us who does not want to, and those who do not are free to do otherwise.[77]

Autocratic and inflexible, convinced that she and her mother were taking the WSPU in the right direction, Christabel thus sharply dismissed these critics. She had no sympathy for a more consensual style of leadership. Nor did Emmeline who, one week later, echoed her daughter's sentiments, telling the *Weekly Despatch* that since the war began the WSPU's work had been diverted into new channels, and the funds contributed for suffrage work had been set aside and not touched for the purposes of the war campaign. All the WSPU accounts were periodically audited by a firm of accountants.[78] These statements did not satisfy some of the dissenters who felt strongly enough to set up a breakaway group called the 'Independent WSPU'. In March 1916, another dissenting group formed another separate organisation, the 'Independent Women's Social and Political Union'. Both the new groups sought to revive suffragette agitation by campaigning for the parliamentary vote for women. However, they soon found that fund-raising for such a cause was an almost impossible task during war time. Christabel and Emmeline, in taking the path they did, had shrewdly judged the situation.

During that autumn of 1915, as *Britannia* continued to attack the Government's war policy, the WSPU issued a circular stating bluntly that 'The Prime Minister and Sir Edward Grey are unfit for the responsible positions they hold.'[79] Some of the press, which had once lauded Emmeline, were now critical of her, saying that if Mrs Pankhurst had spoken these words at the planned WSPU meeting to be held on 18 November at the Albert Hall, 'the Huns would have concluded that we were as good as beaten'.[80] But other newspapers, as well as some important social and political figures, including Lord Northcliffe (who kept in touch with Christabel), were strongly behind the WSPU. In addition, Christabel's call for closer cooperation between the Allies, the dismissal from Government of all employees of German origin and the cancellation of all naturalisation certificates issued to Germans, Austrians, Bulgarians or Turks resonated with the public mood. *Britannia's* patriotic message, which may seem extreme to modern ears, was in tune with much of the nation's media and with public opinion.[81]

Prime Minister Asquith, still precariously in power, knew that he could not imprison the patriotic Mrs Pankhurst, or ask for Christabel's extradition to Britain. Nonetheless, he decided that something had to be done to control these dreadful women who were continuing to hassle him. Government pressure was put on the Council of the Albert Hall to cancel the WSPU's planned meeting on 18 November – which it did. The London Pavilion also told the WSPU that it could no longer hold its regular weekly meetings on its premises. Unable to hire any large halls in Central London, the Union had no choice but to hold smaller gatherings in its new headquarters in the West End, in Great Portland Street, the large Lincoln's Inn House building in Kingsway having been put out to let in September. However, Sunday afternoon large outdoor meetings continued to take place in Hyde Park, near the Reformer's Tree.[82]

Strong rumours were circulating that Christabel and Emmeline were in league with Lloyd George and putting pressure on Asquith to resign so that the Minister of Munitions could take his place and give women the vote. This seems plausible. One plain-clothes detective gathering information for the Metropolitan Police took the rumours seriously enough to report on the WSPU, concluding that although it was impossible to ascertain whether the gossip was true, it was certainly the attitude adopted by the WSPU leaders. 'I gathered the same view from a long conversation I had with Mrs Drummond and I have heard other members say the same thing.'[83]

As Christabel continued with her tirades against the Asquith-led Government, she aligned herself with the opponents of its Western-front strategy, particularly Lloyd George, who argued that Britain should use its military force to assault Austria and Turkey, thus undermining Germany and shortening the war.[84] She believed that the war could be won in the East if the Allies cut short the German advance in the Balkans. However, Asquith and his war ministers – 'misleaders', as she termed them – had not done this, thus giving Germany a free hand to invade Serbia and get the Balkans 'under their control'.[85] On 10 December, *Britannia* branded Sir Edward Grey, the Foreign Secretary, a 'Judas' for his betrayal of Serbia:

> Against treachery, even the Son of God was helpless. Judas at the British Foreign Office is to-day bringing to naught the glorious, the Divinely inspired heroism of Serbia. The cold, premeditated, long-calculated treachery of Sir Edward Grey might, indeed, almost make Judas of old time blush![86]

Five days later, the police seized *Britannia*'s printing press which had been installed in a garage in Kensington. Herbert Samuel, Secretary of State for the Home Department, defended such action as necessary under the Defence of the Realm Act (DORA) since the paper was making allegations which were 'absolutely untrue' and 'calculated to prejudice our relations with our Allies'.[87]

The insistent Christabel was not sidetracked. Calmly and logically she wrote to the influential Tory MP Bonar Law, a pro-women suffrage supporter, explaining her case. '[T]his Government, which has Mr. Asquith and Sir Edward Grey at its head, with Lord Haldane as the power behind, is a Government which not only cannot, but will not, win the war', she penned on 18 December, the message being placed in Bonar Law's hands by a trusted intermediary:

> It is time that we left completely our fool's paradise and faced facts. The Balkans simply must be wrested from the German grip . . . we realise how calamitous is the military mistake into which Sir Edward Grey and our Germanised and pro-Germanised Foreign Office have led us.[88]

Determined to press her point, Christabel also arranged for the libellous 'Judas' article to be sold to the general public as a one-penny fly-leaf. H. G. Wells, whom Christabel had once met and never liked, later referring to him as 'a spiteful little worm', acquired one.[89] Presumably unaware that Government officials were already monitoring the situation, Wells promptly sent the leaflet to the Foreign Office, saying it should be suppressed. The Government, having already decided on such action, seized *Britannia*'s printing press for a second time. Although this again failed to prevent its publication, by 30 December New Scotland Yard was taking a more relaxed view of the situation. Thus one of its key officials noted that steps were being taken to prevent *Britannia*'s distribution through newsagents, which very much restricted its sale, and that information had been received:

> to the effect that the paper is moribund. There has been a quarrel in the central Organisation and Miss Christabel Pankhurst and her mother and one or two of the more violent women stand practically alone. There is very little money . . . Owing to these circumstances I do not recommend any action at present.[90]

But Lloyd George saw things differently. He was in France early in the New Year of 1916 and arranged to meet up with Christabel, an indication of the standing in which she was held. 'Perhaps when we meet you will tell me of ways in which you would like us to help', she wrote to him on 2 January, 'and perhaps, also you will let me tell you of some ideas that have come to me.' The following day, after the two had talked matters over, Christabel penned a note of thanks. 'We are all grateful to you for assuming the burden of office in this crisis . . . We want to help as much as we can & thank goodness the whole nation feels as we do.'[91]

But no amount of confidences shared with Lloyd George could protect *Britannia* from raids by the Government. Suffragettes responsible for its printing and circulation were constantly on the alert. A few months after it was founded, the anxious Grace Roe contacted Gertrude Harding, asking her to come immediately to *Britannia*'s aid and take charge of its printing. Gertrude agreed and, telling a half-truth to her boss, managed to leave the Intelligence Department without serving a month's notice.[92] From now on *Britannia*, which continued to be controlled and edited by Christabel in Paris, had to be printed secretly, appearing in a variety of sizes and types, sometimes just two pages of foolscap produced on a manually operated duplicating machine. Initially, the place of printing was frequently moved until finally a stuffy little cellar was found at Catford, about fifteen miles from London. Gertrude recollected, 'We worked day and night . . . to have the paper ready to go on the news-stands early Thursday morning, and our hideout was never discovered by Scotland Yard, although they tried their best.'[93]

The content and tone of the anti-German articles in *Britannia*, especially the emphasis upon the right of small nations to self-determination, encouraged a number of exiled leaders to visit Christabel in Paris. Her home became a political salon where scraps of insider information provided useful copy for *Britannia* and topics of intrigue for her political correspondence.[94] And when in January 1916, Emmeline Pankhurst began a seven-month lecture tour in America and Canada, to raise money for Serbia as well as for the upkeep of the war babies, more useful political contacts were made. Emmeline was accompanied on her trip by Mr Miyatovich, the former Serbian Secretary of Foreign Affairs, his attaché Mr Petrovitch, and Jean Wickham, her secretary. Jessie Kenney had gone in advance to arrange the tour, and on her return home visited Christabel to give her, in a sealed envelope, a report about the activities of the German secret service which had to be passed to Edvard Benes, a Czech exile living in Paris and one of the leading organisers abroad of an independent Czechoslovakia. The message had been given to Emmeline by a Czech exile living in the USA. Christabel was receiving information too about political intrigue in Greece. '[H]ave you heard of a Greek Deputy who is instrumental in conveying supplies to German Submarines?' she wrote to Sir James Murray, an MP who used to bail out arrested suffragettes. 'A Greek from whom I sometimes get news of these parts tells me it is so, and that great surprise is felt that our Foreign Office does not do something to ensure that cessation of this pro-German activity.'[95] But the Foreign Office and the Asquith-led Government, even if they knew of these various activities, were unimpressed with Miss Pankhurst's constant interference.

In mid-March 1916, the Government again seized *Britannia*'s printing press, an action that was condemned by some in high places. Mr Handel Booth, Liberal MP for Pontefract, Yorkshire, asked the Attorney-General in a House of Commons debate:

> whether he is aware that this organ gives support to the country in the present conflict; and if he will say why the staff are continually persecuted and if the Government attacked the 'Britannia' because of its faithful and devoted pleading of the cause of our Allies the Serbians?[96]

But the Government was resolute that *Britannia* had to be silenced and when this latest raid also failed to do that, it arranged for the post office to intercept copies of the paper in the mail.[97] Nonetheless, *Britannia* continued to be published in secret locations and the formidable Christabel continued her tirades against Asquith, Grey and Haldane, as well as the pacifists. 'Lack of patriotism is a disease like any other . . . that besets the body of a nation', she expounded. 'Only Nationalism and Patriotism can save the world from becoming a huge Germany, ruled by the Kaiser'.[98]

Christabel's patriotic views continued to grate against those held by her two sisters, Adela and Sylvia. Adela had recently published *Put up the sword*, an anti-war, anti-British Empire tract in which she was scornful of accounts of German atrocities, but ready to believe those of the British, and prepared to forgive German soldiers but not those of the Allies for any incidents of killing and rape.[99] Sylvia, whose East London Federation of the Suffragettes had recently been renamed the Workers' Suffrage Federation (WSF), had become fiercer in her class loyalties, and even more opposed to the views of Christabel and their mother.

Sylvia had been deeply upset when, the previous year, Christabel had reprinted on the front page of *The Suffragette* a *Punch* cartoon that portrayed her former lover Keir Hardie, who was opposed to the war, receiving a bag of money from the Kaiser. She immediately wrote to her mother, protesting that Hardie was dying. According to Sylvia, her mother never replied.[100] The incident increased Sylvia's contempt for what she saw as the insensitivity of her domineering sister, and the foolishness of their weak mother. On 8 April 1916, Sylvia was a key figure in a 20,000-strong anti-war demonstration in Trafalgar Square against the Government's introduction of conscription – which Christabel and Emmeline had advocated – the Munitions Act and DORA. When Emmeline on tour in North America heard this news, she instantly cabled Christabel, 'Strongly repudiate and condemn Sylvia's foolish and unpatriotic conduct. Regret I cannot prevent use of name. Make this public.' Christabel, only too glad to distance herself from this embarrassing sister and always in accord with her mother, printed the notice on the back page of *Britannia*. The press also covered the story.[101]

Family differences aside, Christabel had more important issues on her mind that spring and summer of 1916. In February the Germans had begun an offensive against Verdun, in north-eastern France. Although there were heavy casualties on both the French and German side, the Germans held the upper hand well into June (the offensive would not end until December). The worried Christabel discussed these developments with Annie Kenney when she came to Paris in the spring. Was there any way the WSPU could persuade President Theodore Roosevelt of the USA to abandon his country's neutrality and fight alongside the Allies? After all, Roosevelt had recently praised a speech Mrs Pankhurst had given urging men and women to join in the war effort and condemning those British workers who went on strike.[102] On 23 June, Christabel made her eloquent plea to Roosevelt:

> Living here in Paris not many miles from the firing lines, one is conscious of the tragic sacrifice that the French people are making for us all . . . will you not . . . [c]ome here . . . calling upon those Americans who are made of the same stuff to come with you and fight for France? . . . When the American people were hard pressed, there came to their rescue Lafayette [French military officer who fought in the American Civil War]. Now that France is fighting a more deadly foe . . . shall she not have the help of an American Lafayette . . . [103]

The letter was given to a homeward-bound American to place in Roosevelt's hands. Although Christabel knew that such an important person as the President of the United States would not necessarily listen to her, she was of the view that her letter 'cannot do any harm. Sometimes when one asks people a big thing which they feel unable to do, they decide to do some smaller and different thing'.[104]

Roosevelt was not the only world leader that Christabel contacted. As the war progressed and fighting on French soil intensified, especially after 1 July, the first day of the battle of the Somme when fourteen British divisions were massacred by German artillery and machine guns without gaining any foothold in German defences, she felt it necessary to voice her strong support for the beleaguered Billy Hughes, the Welsh-born Prime Minister of Australia. In July the Australian army had made its debut on the Somme, taking back a French town from the Germans. Yet the patriotic Hughes, an outspoken critic of a compromise peace, was in trouble at home. Expelled from the Australian Labour Party for advocating conscription, he was challenging his opponents by holding a referendum on the issue. Among his fiercest critics was Adela Pankhurst whose condemnation of conscription led her mother to cable Hughes, saying that she was ashamed of her daughter and repudiated her. Christabel and Emmeline, championing Hughes' case, argued for him to come back to London – where he had shared in the deliberations of the British Government and given rousing 'Wake Up, England' speeches throughout the country – and take his place on the war council.[105] They wanted Hughes to join the Asquith Government, not to prop it up indefinitely but to bring 'some common sense, foresight, sanity, and determination where those qualities were conspicuously absent'.[106]

The WSPU's 1916 Women's War Procession, held on the beautiful summer day of 22 July and witnessed by many thousands of Londoners, included homage to Hughes. Among the banners with messages such as 'God Save our King and Queen' and 'To Fight until Victory is our Duty to the Heroic Dead' were others saying 'We Want Hughes'.[107] In demanding the return of Hughes, opined the *Globe*, the:

> women were doing no more than giving natural expression to the sentiment which nine-tenths of the country feel . . . Women are proving themselves not only patriotic in their actions, but politically shrewd in their judgement on the conduct of the war.[108]

Not unexpectedly Lloyd George, who reviewed the procession, gave a 'friendly welcome . . . to the Hughes banners', commented Christabel to Sir James Murray. 'It is a remarkable thing that little Wales should have given to the Empire the two strong men of the war.'[109] Building on this wave of popular support, Christabel asked Annie to take a Women's Memorial to Hughes in Australia, begging him to return to England to help the Allied cause. But Hughes was preoccupied with the forthcoming referendum and Annie finally agreed with him that his place at that time was in Australia, not England.[110]

Unable to attend the procession in London yet wanting to give a personal touch to the encouragement of women's war effort, Christabel had arranged for a small group of British women war workers to spend a short time in France in mid-July, primarily to tour the munitions factories. Acting as host, she booked the visitors into a hotel in Senlis, near Paris, and also arranged a few cultural trips, including a visit to the Louvre. 'All the girls were very grateful indeed for your kind consideration and thoughtfulness for their every comfort', wrote Annie Buchan appreciatively.[111] Soon Christabel left Paris, to spend most of August by the sea, at the Villa Angele Marie in Deauville, where her mother joined her on her return from Canada, staying only a brief time before travelling back to London.

The introduction of conscription for single men in January 1916 – and its extension to married men three months later – had raised uncomfortable questions about the voting rights of soldiers and sailors. The stringent electoral residency requirement meant that many men in the British armed forces were disenfranchised while thousands of working-class unmarried soldiers had never qualified at all since they did not yet own or rent their own homes. Further, women's invaluable contribution on the home front, as Christabel and Emmeline intended, also gave them a firm basis for political citizenship. On 14 August, in the Commons, Asquith delivered a confusing, convoluted speech in which he stated that although he had no intention of introducing a reform bill, he had had many representations from those authorised to speak for women which represented a 'reasonable' case for their enfranchisement, after the war, based on their service to the state. Nonetheless, he also warned that 'nothing could be more injurious to the best interests of the country . . . than that the floodgates should be opened on all those vast complicated questions of the franchise . . . at this stage of the War'.[112]

Christabel and Emmeline were furious. Long distrustful of the hated Asquith, they disliked intensely the way he was using the cause of votes for women to disfranchise men fighting for their country. Christabel, in a letter to Renee de Brimont, outlined their thinking:

> Asquith's latest performance is to say that he will not arrange for all the soldiers and sailors to vote at the next election, because that would not be fair unless women were also allowed to vote[,] and at the same time he will not give women the vote, so that we all suffer together. We are protesting against this method of exploiting our cause.

She continued angrily:

> because if we cannot vote ourselves, we at least want the soldiers and sailors to do so. We believe that they deserve the vote and we also think that they will vote to put an end to certain weaknesses and abuses that endanger victory and the proper utilisation of victory.[113]

Asquith's position as Prime Minister was growing more precarious daily, and hoping to delay the issue of franchise reform he asked the Speaker of the Commons, James Lowther, to form an all-party committee that would report on the matter. The Speaker's Conference, as it became known, first met in October 1916 and reported early in the New Year. Both Christabel and Emmeline held aloof from the negotiations that attended the group since, as Christabel explained, they both believed:

> that a certain detachment on our part would give more effect to the potential, post-war militancy . . . We therefore left it to others to discuss such points as the differential age limit for women voters, designed to prevent them from becoming at once an electoral majority.[114]

By autumn 1916, Christabel was living at a different address in Paris, 1 Avenue du Trocadero. After leaving Avenue de la Grande Armée in June she had stayed at 103 Rue al Boétie but never really settled there. 'I gave up the other flat before going to Deauville', she later told a friend,

> & now have taken this one which is much more airy. In the other flat I did not feel very well perhaps because it was rather shut in & rather stuffy in its construction and I am such a 'fresh air fiend' as they say in England.

The new flat belonged to an American woman who had gone home until the end of the war. 'If you are still in Paris won't you come & see me', Christabel pleaded. 'Mother is here until 4 o'clock tomorrow when she returns to London. How nice if you can come while she is here.'[115]

It was from her new address that Christabel continued with her tirades against the Asquith-led Government, condemning its policy towards Greece and claiming that it was giving Germany a free hand in the Balkans. Believing that the main aim of the Foreign Office was a compromise peace, Christabel particularly attacked Grey, the Foreign Secretary, and Sir William Robertson, Chief of the Imperial General Staff, who were accused of being pro-German and hostile to Serbia and Romania. On the evening of the 31 October, two suffragettes were arrested and taken to Canon Row Police Station for breaking windows in Government offices in Whitehall.[116] All this was part of Christabel's strategy, to force the resignation of Asquith and his 'incompetent' Government and to give credence to the threat that the WSPU, once peace had been established, could take up militancy again.

A few days later, *Britannia* was raided again but, nonetheless, it still appeared in print shortly afterwards. The futile attack upon *Britannia* was regarded as a 'high honour', proclaimed the triumphant Christabel, especially when contrasted with 'the immunity and protection accorded by the Government to the pro-German, pro-Compromise Peace publications . . . Britannia's policy is one of perfect loyalty to Britain and her Allies'.[117] That widespread food shortages were now apparent, forcing the Government to talk about introducing food rationing, something the WSPU had advocated in 1914, only increased Christabel's contempt for Asquith and his ministers.[118]

Christabel and Emmeline were not alone in their criticisms of the Asquith Coalition Government. Dissatisfaction was evident among the general population as well as among some leading Government figures, including Lloyd George and Bonar Law. In early December Asquith resigned, and Lloyd George became Prime Minister. Christabel and Emmeline were delighted. Lloyd George, who was not in favour of a compromise peace but keen to press for a victory for the Allies, was their man. On the day that Asquith resigned, Emmeline had hastened to speak to Lord Northcliffe, who claimed that the campaign he had conducted in his right-wing press had brought about the Prime Minister's fall. When Emmeline said that Grey, the Foreign Secretary, was the worst of the ministers and was still in post, Northcliffe leapt to his feet, crying, 'Don't you worry, my dear girl, I'll get 'em all out!'[119] But things did not work out quite to plan. Christabel and Emmeline, much to their consternation, read in the press that two Conservatives they did not trust were to form part of the new administration – Lord Robert Cecil was to be reappointed to the Foreign Office while Arthur Balfour was to replace Grey. The anxious Emmeline immediately wrote a polite letter to Lloyd George, asking to see him before he finalised his Cabinet, saying that the news was 'most disquieting'.[120]

The confidences shared between Christabel, Emmeline and the new Prime Minister did not stop Christabel from continuing to publish in *Britannia* scathing attacks on Britain's foreign policy, when it followed the Asquith line, and nor could Lloyd George shield her newspaper 'from the penalties of its own exuberance'.[121] Angered by what she saw as the folly of the British Higher Military Command, Christabel accused Sir William Robertson, Chief of the Imperial General Staff, of being 'Hindenburg's partner', the 'military accomplice and tool' of the 'traitors' Grey, Asquith and Cecil in that they all wanted a 'Compromise Peace and the downfall of the British Empire'.[122] Since Lloyd George did not agree with Robertson's strategical direction of the war, he probably enjoyed reading these broadsides. On 14 January 1917, the police and military raided the WSPU's private printing press at Catford, its offices in Great Portland Street and the flats occupied by Annie Kenney and Grace Roe.[123]

Christabel was unrepentant. Although the next four issues of *Britannia* were all rolled into just three mismatched pages, they were published. Why was *Britannia* victimised? asked the defiant Christabel, as she accused the authorities of double standards. When the *Times* and the *Daily Mail* had attacked Lord Kitchener, there were no raids on their offices, or on the private residences of their editors and staff, or on the home of the proprietor of these newspapers, Lord Northcliffe.[124] Northcliffe, who had recently visited Christabel in Paris, believed that a sinister 'Unseen Hand' was operating in Lloyd George's Government, a suspicion that both Christabel and Emmeline supported.[125] 'This problem of the two Govts within the Govt. is a most serious one', she confided to Mr Ellis-Griffith, a barrister and Liberal politician who had served under Asquith. The elimination of 'Asquithism' was necessary to prevent injury to the new Government, upon whom victory depended. 'Some of us firmly believe that Mr. Lloyd George's policy was such that if carried out by the ex Govt., it would have saved the Balkans, including the Roumanian situation.'[126] The practical Emmeline, always of one mind with her eldest daughter, wrote to WSPU members, asking for donations to make up the financial loss that the Union faced in its 'Victory Fund', after the recent raid. 'The very fact that "Britannia" has been raided is a further proof of the sinister influence which is endeavouring to counteract every patriotic effort to support and strengthen the new National Government.'[127] At a WSPU meeting held in Trafalgar Square in early February 1917, Emmeline again expressed her faith in the new Premier.[128] Lloyd George did not forget this loyalty on the part of the elder Pankhursts. Nor did Christabel and Emmeline cast aside their faith in him. Lloyd George was *the* man who would bring both victory in war and votes for women.

A test to that loyalty was soon to come in regard to one of the more bizarre incidents of the First World War, one that Christabel feared could bring notoriety to the WSPU at a time when she and her mother were working hard to present it as a patriotic organisation. On 10 March 1917, Emmeline Pankhurst was in the dock at the Old Bailey again, but this time as a witness in the trial of anti-war campaigner Alice Wheeldon and her daughter Hettie, militant socialist feminists and former WSPU members, accused of plotting to assassinate Lloyd George and Arthur Henderson, a Labour member of the Cabinet. The astounded Emmeline, keen to promote the WSPU as a supporter of the new Prime Minister, emphatically denied a statement made by a witness for the prosecution that the WSPU had spent £300 trying to murder Lloyd George by smuggling a chambermaid into his hotel equipped with a nail dipped in poison that was to be driven through the sole of his boot.[129] Christabel, in a letter published in several newspapers in France, emphatically supported her mother's plea: '[O]ur new Prime Minister, has no more loyal supporters than the suffragettes, who regard his life as one of the most precious necessities, not only for Great Britain but also for noble France, which is so dear to us.'[130] Although Alice Wheeldon, but not Hettie, was found guilty and sentenced to ten years' penal servitude, she was later released on Lloyd George's order after serving just nine months, undoubtedly because he knew or discovered that the 'plot' was a set-up by undercover agents.[131] However, this was not revealed to Christabel and Emmeline at the time. Instead Lloyd George, extremely pleased with the public statements of support from the elder Pankhursts, sent a personal note of thanks to Emmeline.[132]

Christabel now knew for certain that if she did return to England, she would be safe and not under threat of arrest. This was particularly pressing since, after the latest raid, *Britannia* was being printed under very difficult conditions. The heaviest burden fell on Grace Roe who had to visit Christabel each week – despite the difficulty of obtaining passports – and retain all the instructions in case of a search. Annie wrote to Christabel, explaining the gravity of the situation. 'My place is in London', Christabel decided before she had finished reading the letter.[133]

Notes

1 CP, *Unshackled*, p. 287.
2 CP, The war, *TS*, 7 August 1914, p. 301.
3 CP, *Unshackled*, pp. 287–8.
4 *Evening News and Evening Mail*, 10 August 1914; Cowman, *Women of the right spirit!*, p. 179.
5 Form letter from EP to Dear Friend, 12 August 1914, Goode Collection.
6 CP, *Unshackled*, p. 288.
7 *Weekly Despatch*, 6 September 1914; *Star* and *Daily Telegraph*, 4 September 1914.
8 Elsie Bowerman statement 11 October 1964, DMC; Kitty Marion, typescript autobiography, SFC.
9 Caine, *English feminism*, p. 133; A. Ronan, The legacy of the suffragettes: women, peace and the vote in Manchester 1914–18, in *Suffragette legacy: how does the history of feminism inspire current thinking in Manchester*, eds C. Mork Rostik and E. L. Sutherland (Newcastle upon Tyne, Cambridge Scholars Press, 2015), pp. 1–15.
10 Rosen, *Rise up women!*; Mitchell, *Queen Christabel*; Pugh, *The march of the women*; J. Vellacott, *Pacifists, patriots and the vote: the erosion of democratic suffragism in Britain during the First World War* (Houndmills, Palgrave Macmillan, 2007).
11 Purvis, *Emmeline Pankhurst*, Chapter 19; A. K. Smith, *Suffrage discourse in Britain during the First World War* (Aldershot, Ashgate, 2005), pp. 31–5. J. Purvis, The Pankhursts and the Great War, in *The women's movement in wartime: international perspectives, 1914–19*, eds A. S. Fell and I. Sharp (Houndmills, Palgrave Macmillan, 2007), pp. 141–57.
12 J. deVries, Gendering patriotism: Emmeline and Christabel Pankhurst and World War One, in *This working-class world: women's lives and culture(s) in Britain 1914–1945*, ed S. Oldfield (London, Taylor and Francis, 1994), p. 77.
13 *Daily Mail*, 9 September 1914.
14 CP, *The war, a speech delivered at the London Opera House, on September 8th, 1914* (London, The Women's Social & Political Union, n.d.), pp. 3 and 6.
15 CP, *The war*, p. 12.
16 CP, *The war*, p. 16.
17 N. F. Gullace, *'The blood of our sons': men, women, and the renegotiation of British citizenship during the Great War* (Houndmills, Palgrave Macmillan, 2002), pp. 118–19.
18 Interview with Grace Roe, c.1964, Raeburn Collection.
19 ESP, *The home front: a mirror to life in England during the World War* (London, Hutchinson, 1932), p. 66.
20 ESP, *The home front*, p. 67.
21 Coleman, *Adela*, p. 63.
22 Kitty Marion, Autobiography, SFC, p. 274.
23 G. Wilson, *With all her might: the life of Gertrude Harding, militant suffragette* (New Brunswick, NJ, Goose Lane Editions, 1996), p. 170.
24 Wilson, *With all her might*, pp. 170–1.
25 *Evening Sun* (New York), 14 October 1914; Pugh, *The Pankhursts*, p. 305.
26 Kenney, *Memories*, pp. 266–70.
27 Dubois, *Harriot Stanton Blatch*, p. 173.
28 *New York Tribune*, 24 October 1914.
29 *New York Tribune*, 25 October 1914.
30 CP, *America and the war, a speech delivered at Carnegie Hall, New York, October 24th, 1914* (London, The WSPU, n.d.), p. 3.
31 CP, *America and the war*, p. 6.
32 CP, *America and the war*, p. 12.
33 CP, *America and the war*, p. 17.

34 CP to Miss Paul, 29 October 1914, National Woman's Party Papers, Group I.
35 See *Speech delivered by Miss Christabel Pankhurst at Washington, USA, January 24th, 1915* (London, WSPU, n.d.); Mitchell, *Queen Christabel*, p. 253.
36 CP, *International militancy: a speech delivered at Carnegie Hall, New York January 13th, 1915* (London, WSPU, n.d.), p. 5.
37 Eleanor Garrison to her mother, 14 January 1915, SSC.
38 Quoted in Mitchell, *Queen Christabel*, pp. 254–5.
39 Brian Harrison interview with Olive Bartels, 27 March 1976, TWL.
40 Interview with Phyllis Keller and Grace Roe, c.1964, Raeburn Collection.
41 EP to Mrs Astor, 26 March 1915, Nancy Astor Collection, University of Reading.
42 CP, *Unshackled*, p. 289.
43 Wilson, *With all her might*, pp. 172–4.
44 CP, We will not be Prussianised, TS, 16 April 1015, p. 6.
45 TS, 16 April 1915, pp. 12–13.
46 Purvis, *Emmeline Pankhurst*, p. 274.
47 CP, Let none be Kaiser's Cat's paws, TS, 23 April 1915, p. 22.
48 *Globe*, 23 April 1915.
49 CP, The Union of Democratic Control, TS, 30 April 1915, p. 38; entry for 3 May 1915, Nevinson Diaries.
50 Purvis, *Emmeline Pankhurst*, p. 274; FPL, *Fate*, p. 113.
51 Jean Finot, The Franco-British people, TS, 14 May 1915, p. 71.
52 Wilson, *With all her might*, p. 174.
53 The Germans in England, what an invasion would mean, TS, 21 May 1915, p. 92; see commentary in S. Kingsley Kent, *Making peace: the reconstruction of gender in interwar Britain* (Princeton, NJ, Princeton University Press, 1993), pp. 25–6.
54 CP, Keep the flag flying, TS, 21 May 1915, p. 86.
55 CP, Universal national service, TS, 28 May 1915, p. 102.
56 CP, Women and war, *Observer*, 27 June 1915.
57 Buckingham Palace to Lloyd George, 28 June 1915, LG Papers.
58 Purvis, *Emmeline Pankhurst*, p. 277.
59 TS, 9 July 1915, pp. 197 and 195.
60 Interview with Grace Roe, 22 September 1965, DMC.
61 *Daily Chronicle, Daily Telegraph* and *Times*, 19 July 1915.
62 *Observer*, 18 July 1915.
63 *Daily Chronicle* and *Daily Telegraph*, 19 July 1915.
64 *Times*, 19 July 1915.
65 See *Daily Sketch*, 6 October 1915, Women's services soon to be used. Mrs. Pankhurst condemns male treachery.
66 CP, *Unshackled*, p. 291.
67 Wilson, *With all her might*, p. 177.
68 TS, 7 May 1915, p. 51.
69 Smyth, *Female pipings*, pp. 237–8.
70 Purvis, *Emmeline Pankhurst*, p. 279.
71 The Women's Social and Political Union leaflet, n.d. [c.1915], photocopy, DMC.
72 TS, 25 June and 16 July 1915, pp. 163 and 214, respectively.
73 CP, No Germanised bureaucracy for us, TS, 6 August 1915, p. 254; CP, The betrayal of Serbia, *Britannia*, 5 November 1915, p. 42.
74 *Britannia*, 15 October 1915, p. 5.
75 *Daily News and Leader*, 18 and 17 November 1915.
76 Mrs. Pankhurst and the W.S.P.U. The Manifesto, MASC, Vol. 26.
77 Christabel Pankhurst replies to the rebels, *Weekly Dispatch*, 28 November 1915.
78 *Weekly Dispatch*, 5 December 1915.

79 ESP, *The home front*, p. 270.
80 *Morning Advertiser*, 17 November 1915.
81 Mitchell, *Queen Christabel*, p. 258; Smith, *Suffrage discourse*, p. 26.
82 ESP, *The home front*, p. 270.
83 PRO, H045/10796/2, 6 December 1915; *Britannia*, 14 April 1915, p. 166.
84 Pugh, *The Pankhursts*, p. 319.
85 *Britannia*, 3 December 1915, p. 85.
86 CP, Judas!, TS, 10 December 1915, p. 102.
87 B. Wasserstein, *Herbert Samuel: a political life* (Oxford, Oxford University Press, 1992), p. 190.
88 CP to Bonar Law, 18 December 1915, Bonar Law Papers.
89 CP to My Dear, 24 February 1917, de Brimont Papers.
90 B. Thomson, New Scotland Yard, to Montgomery, 30 December 1915. Thanks to John Partington for this reference and for the Wells letter which is undated but stamped 21 December 1915, PRO, FO 371/1277 69211.
91 CP to Lloyd George, 2 and 3 January 1916, LG Papers; *Britannia*, 17 November 1916, p. 303.
92 Wilson, *With all her might*, pp. 177–8.
93 Wilson, *With all her might*, p. 179.
94 Mitchell, *Queen Christabel*, p. 259.
95 CP to Sir James Murray, 28 July 1916, LG Papers.
96 PRO HO45/10796/303883/10, Daily debates, 15 March 1916.
97 Minute dated 5 May 1916, PRO HO45/10796/303883/13.
98 Lack of patriotism a disease!, *Britannia*, 14 April 1916, p. 165.
99 A. Pankhurst, *Put up the sword* (Melbourne, Cecilia John, 1917, third edition, first pub. 1915); Coleman, *Adela*, p. 67.
100 TS, 30 July 1915, front page; ESP, *The home front*, pp. 228–9. Hardie died on 26 September 1915.
101 *Britannia*, 28 April 1916, p. 174; Winslow, *Sylvia Pankhurst*, 85.
102 *Britannia*, 26 May 1916, p. 188.
103 CP to Mr Roosevelt, 23 June 1916, de Brimont Papers.
104 CP to Renee de Brimont, 5 July 1916, de Brimont Papers.
105 Purvis, *Emmeline Pankhurst*, p. 287; *Britannia*, 21 July 1916, p. 219.
106 *Britannia*, 25 August 1916, p. 240.
107 *Daily Telegraph*, 24 July 1916.
108 *Globe*, 24 and 25 July 1916.
109 CP to Sir James Murray, 28 July 1916, LG Papers.
110 Kenney, *Memories*, p. 281.
111 Annie Buchan to CP, 23 July 1916, copy, LG Papers.
112 Rosen, *Rise up women!*, pp. 258–9.
113 CP to Renee de Brimont, 16 August 1916, de Brimont Papers.
114 CP, *Unshackled*, p. 293.
115 CP to Baronne Renee de Brimont, 21 September 1916, de Brimont Papers.
116 *Britannia*, 3 November 1916, p. 294.
117 *Britannia*, 24 November 1916, p. 308.
118 Food rationing was not introduced until early 1918.
119 C. St John, *Ethel Smyth: a biography* (London, Longmans, 1959), p. 221.
120 EP to Lloyd George, n.d. [10 December 1916?], LG Papers.
121 Mitchell, *Women on the warpath*, p. 62.
122 *Britannia*, 15 December 1916, pp. 320–1; Mitchell, *Women on the warpath*, p. 62.
123 *Daily Express*, 16 January 1917.
124 *Britannia*, 22 and 29 January, and 5 and 12 February 1917, p. 328.

125 CP to My Dear, 27 February 1917, de Brimont Papers.
126 CP to Mr Ellis-Griffith, 26 February 1917, Ellis-Griffith Papers.
127 EP to Mr Franklin, 23 January 1917, Franklin-Duval Papers, TWL.
128 *Observer*, 18 February 1917.
129 S. Rowbotham, *Friends of Alice Wheeldon* (London, Pluto Press, 1986), p. 52.
130 *Britannia*, 12 and 19 March 1917, p. 345; CP letter, cutting in de Brimont Papers, English translation in Mitchell, *Queen Christabel*, p. 261.
131 MI5 behind suffragette plot to kill PM, *Guardian*, 28 November 1997.
132 Lloyd George to Mrs Pankhurst, n.d. [c.16 March 1917], de Brimont Papers.
133 Kenney, *Memories*, p. 282.

18

CO-LEADER OF THE WOMEN'S PARTY

May 1917–end of October 1918

On returning to England in early May 1917, Christabel initially stayed with her mother at 50 Clarendon Road, Holland Park, London. The fifty-nine-year-old Emmeline Pankhurst had rented and furnished the house the previous summer since it was in a pleasant area and large enough to accommodate the four adopted babies and Catherine Pine, who looked after them. This was the first settled home that Emmeline had known since she left 30 Upper Brook Street in Manchester some ten years earlier and, to her surprise, she was greatly enjoying the experience although worried about her financial situation and increasing age. 'Sometimes I feel appalled at the responsibility I have undertaken in adopting these four young things at my time of life', she confessed to Ethel Smyth, now working at a military hospital in France. 'I'll go on as long as I can, in the faith that help will come when it's needed. The cost of living increases from week to week. How the poor live God only knows.'[1] That her ever-optimistic mother had to live frugally was no surprise to Christabel who had led a Spartan existence herself in Paris. Yet, despite her joy at being reunited with her mother again, Christabel did not find life at Clarendon Road easy. She had lived on her own for five years and was unused to the interruption and noise of small children. But above all else, she chafed under the strict discipline that Catherine Pine imposed on the household – and on her young charges.

Emmeline, accompanied by Jessie Kenney, was shortly to leave for a three-month trip to Russia where the Tsarist regime had been overthrown in the February 1917 revolution. The visit was provoked by the news that the pacifist Ramsay MacDonald, a key Labour figure, had been allowed by the British Government to travel with some like-minded socialists to Russia, one of Britain's allies. Both Christabel and Emmeline feared that MacDonald would try to negotiate a peace on German terms with Alexander Kerensky, the head of the democratically elected but fragile Provisional Government, which would take from the Russian people the freedom for which they had fought in their revolution. Further, a premature peace would weaken the Eastern front, leading to Russia's and Britain's withdrawal from the war and the collapse of the Allied strategy. Emmeline wrote to Lloyd George, asking for passports for herself and Jessie to visit Russia so that they could contact various women's groups and persuade them to keep their menfolk fighting. The request was granted, money for the trip being raised through appeals in *Britannia*.[2]

Christabel was firmly of the view that MacDonald's trip to Russia had been deliberately engineered by the Foreign Office as a way to seek a compromise peace. She believed that her mother and Jessie could challenge such defeatism since they would express 'the view of the patriotic women of England', widely shared by both women and men outside the WSPU.[3] Knowing that Jessie had few suitable clothes for such a trip, Christabel set about helping her. 'Go through my wardrobe and choose what you fancy . . . There are one or two things that are almost new', she said to her trusted friend. A small purse with five pounds in it was also given to Jessie, to keep around her neck, for use in emergencies. '[M]oney talks, even in Revolutions', Christabel warned. 'Should anything happen that may separate you from Mother you will be able to get some kind of help.' Such thoughtfulness and generosity, Jessie remembered, were 'a trait in Christabel's character which endeared her to the hearts of those who worked very closely with her'. Jessie was asked to keep a diary of her trip and, if possible, to fill it in daily, recording her impressions of events and people she met – which she did.[4]

Before her mother and Jessie left for Russia in early June, Christabel had enthusiastically returned to the public platform, addressing an appreciative and crowded WSPU meeting at the Queen's Hall on 22 May. With Emmeline absent from Britain for some three months, Christabel took her place as the WSPU's star attraction, holding At Homes every Tuesday afternoon in the Aeolian Hall, New Bond Street, often with Annie presiding.[5] The women's cause was now in a relatively strong position since most of the population acknowledged that women, through their varied war work in factories, on the land and in public life, were vital to the war effort. Shifts in public opinion and in the press, influenced by suffragist arguments, helped to make the anti-suffrage arguments seem 'increasingly outdated and foolish'.[6] Indeed, the legislative process to bring in franchise reform, including a limited women's suffrage measure based on age and property restrictions, was well advanced. On 19 June 1917, the House of Commons voted overwhelmingly (by three hundred and eighty-seven votes to fifty-seven) in favour of the women's clause in the Representation of the People Bill which would confer the parliamentary vote on certain categories of women aged thirty and over. Since all men aged twenty-one and over were to be granted the vote, younger if they had served in the war, irrespective of their property-owning status, the bill fell short of that full electoral equality with men that the WSPU had demanded before the war. The marginalisation of women's enfranchisement within the overall scheme of suffrage reform was galling to Christabel but, like her mother, she had reluctantly accepted Lloyd George's argument that this bill would be acceptable to the majority of Parliament who regarded an equal franchise as too radical.[7] She knew that the long, hard fight to break the sex discrimination that disqualified women from voting was now over, provided the House of Lords ratified the bill in the New Year.

Younger, fitter and much more vigorous than her absent mother, Christabel enthusiastically delivered patriotic speeches that were well received by the press and general public. Elaborating upon themes already articulated in *Britannia*, she welcomed the new Government under Lloyd George but felt it was not homogeneous enough and, in particular, that it had to get rid of the many Asquith sympathisers with their policy of a compromise peace. For Christabel the old political issues that had once divided the political parties were dead, destroyed by the war. The political conflict was now between the party of compromise peace and the party of victory.[8] And it was the party of victory that would serve women well.

Thus Christabel was contemptuous of those male socialist workers who went on strike over the 'dilution' of skilled labour when women entered the factories. 'We should all like to hear no more of strikes . . . There is too much selfishness even in labour politics.'[9] Although most historians label such sentiments as a move to the right of the political spectrum, it is important to remember that Christabel's feminism was independent of the socialist movement and of Marxist concepts of class and class conflict.[10] Rather than emphasising class, she put women and their needs first, democratic needs which were conflated with the needs of the country. She argued that women were against class war since such a stand could jeopardise, at this critical time, the granting of the parliamentary vote to their sex:

> We women have not been fighting for the vote to have anarchy established when we are on the eve of victory. The talk of settling industrial problems by strikes is nothing more nor less than anarchy . . . Some Pro-Germans have tried very hard to get the women in munition factories to strike, but they will not succeed. The woman civilian has been at least as patriotic as the man . . . you can rank . . . [her] with the British soldier, and point to both as examples of patriotism in the highest sense.[11]

It was foolish, Christabel continued in a prescient statement, to assume that when peacetime came, a 'democratising' Germany would no longer be a threat. The Kaiser could not have held out for so long if he had not been helped by the German bankers, financiers, manufacturers, workmen, socialists and Germans of all classes. The Allies had to ensure that Germany was permanently weakened in regard to manpower, coal and iron, so that arms would not be taken up again. Further, the necessary guarantees against future German war had to include 'the restoration to France of Alsace Lorraine . . . and the break-up of the Hapsburg Empire, which would remove the Slav millions of Austria-Hungary from Austro-German control'.[12]

Christabel's fear of what German victory would mean for British citizens, especially British women, was evident in one particular speech delivered in mid-June. She saw the war with Germany as a conflict between good and evil, and in gendered language reminiscent of her suffrage days, emphasised that women's role was to sacrifice their bodies, if need be, for the greater spiritual contribution to the nation:

402

[T]his war is essentially a spiritual conflict . . . between God and the Devil . . . women's part must be to keep the spiritual side of the conflict foremost. It is women who must see that the last sacrifice of body is made if that is needed that the human spirit may remain free.[13]

By the time this speech was delivered, Christabel was living at a different address. When the down-sized WSPU had moved its offices from Portland Street to much smaller and cheaper premises at William Street, Knightsbridge, she had jumped at the chance to occupy the flat on the top floor – and escape Catherine Pine's strict regime. 'My dear, I have moved into my new home and am delighted with it', she wrote in fluent French to Renee de Brimont on 16 June.[14] This was not the only change in Christabel's life. She had decided to take responsibility for one of the war babies of whom she had become very fond, the red-haired ('Betty') Elizabeth Tudor, named after Queen Elizabeth I. Christabel wished to give Betty, Kathleen, Joan and Mary the best start in life and so favoured raising them, with other children, on the progressive, non-directive Montessori method of education with which Catherine Pine, 'a stern traditionalist', had little sympathy.[15] Brimming with energy, she decided to use the money left in WSPU funds to purchase Tower Cressy, a large house in Aubrey Road, Kensington, for conversion into a day school for children from three to six years of age. The new venture would not only be a service to the public but also provide employment and accommodation for three of the Kenney sisters – Annie, Jessie and the Montessori-trained Jane who was soon brought over from Washington to be the school's Director.[16] Carefully managing the budget, Christabel furnished the premises at a very small cost; material for curtains and covers was bought at the sales and made up, without charge, by volunteers while other furnishings were bought second hand.[17] Soon Annie and Jane moved into Tower Cressy, as did Catherine Pine and her niece who was employed as an assistant to the four babies.

While waiting for her mother and Jessie to return home, Christabel continued her platform speaking, arguing against Home Rule for Ireland on the grounds that an Ireland separate from Britain would be unable to defend itself and would fall victim to Germany. She also travelled to South Wales, pleading for a vigorous prosecution of the war.[18] Sometimes she would relax at weekends by taking Betty to an old cottage she rented called 'High Edser' in Ewhurst in the Surrey countryside. From here the two would visit the nearby Marion Wallace-Dunlop who had also adopted a little girl named Dawn but whose nickname was 'Wings'. A country cottage, Christabel enthused to Marion, was just the place 'for getting ideas for the ensuing week's campaign. O! lovely Surrey! There is nothing like it'.[19] Some recent family news, that the left-wing Adela, in far-away Australia, had married on 30 September a middle-aged widower with three daughters, Tom Walsh, an Irish working-class, ex-Catholic, radical socialist and trade unionist, was undoubtedly discussed with Marion – and especially with the exhausted Emmeline when she finally arrived back home in October. That Adela should choose such an 'unsuitable' husband was no surprise to Christabel.

Christabel accompanied her ailing mother to a breakfast meeting with Lloyd George where Emmeline told the Prime Minister about the desperate situation in Russia, urging him to intervene against the forces of Bolshevism by sending Allied troops to help the Cossacks and other loyal sections regain control.[20] The armed Bolsheviks who would soon overthrow the first, weak attempt at parliamentary Government in Russia were, she believed, German agents. She feared that an unelected, communist dictatorship calling for world revolution would soon be established, as did Christabel. Christabel's criticisms of the tyranny of the emerging communism and socialism generally were relentless. The 'Socialist Internationale', she cried, was 'nothing more or less than a German Sausage Machine . . . British, French, Italians, Russian Socialists who enter that Germanised affair, the Socialist Internationale, are denationalised and demoralised, and simply become fuel to feed the fire of German World-Domination.'[21] Such condemnation of the Bolsheviks, when they came to power in the October revolution, were not isolated statements but part of a worldwide concern as governments and peoples feared that their revolutionary ideas could be exported elsewhere, destabilising the old order.[22] In particular, many feminists who shared such concerns were driven to the right.[23]

For some time Christabel had been thinking that, with the imminent arrival of women's enfranchisement, the WSPU was redundant. Further, with the foundation of rival organisations such as the 'Suffragettes of the WSPU' and the 'Independent WSPU', it was time to think about a change of name. Believing that there was a 'woman's vote' that could be secured in the next general election, a vote that would be based on appeals to gender rather than class or political affiliation, Christabel discussed her ideas with her mother about the need for a new organisation that could be influential in post-war politics. Like the WSPU, the new organisation should not be integrated into any of the main discredited political parties of the day but stand on its own and attract women voters. On 2 November 1917, the WSPU was relaunched as the 'Women's Party'.[24] As Christabel explained in her inaugural speech at the Aeolian Hall:

> We have formed the Women's Party because our opinion has been, and is, that it would not be a good thing for women, the new brooms in politics, to go into those hopelessly dusty old places known as men's political parties. (Applause.) What would our fight for the vote, and our dreams of what it would enable us to do, be worth if we were simply to go into the party political grooves which men have made, and which now the best of them are so anxious to get out of? It is no good to put the new wine of women's votes into the old bottles of party politics, and we are not going to do it. (Applause).[25]

Emmeline elaborated further, noting that women needed a party of their own because 'men had grown so accustomed to managing the world in the past that it had become rather difficult for women in politics to hold their own if they were associated with men'.[26] Thus the Women's Party, which would serve the nation by keeping clear of men's party political machinery, was positioned as the voice of women within British politics, a voice that would bring a new spirit, a new form of democracy, of equality and of morality within the public sphere. Its foundation must be located, however, not only within the local British context but also within the global politics of a world war and the arrival of Bolshevism in Russia.[27] Given Christabel's and Emmeline's scathing criticisms of Bolshevism, it is no surprise that the Women's Party, like the WSPU, conflated the winning of the war with the women's cause. 'Victory, National Security and Progress' was its slogan.

An account of the campaigning platform of the Women's Party was signed by its four key members – Emmeline Pankhurst, the Honorary Treasurer: Christabel, Editor of its official newspaper, *Britannia*: Anne Kenney, the Honorary Secretary, and Flora Drummond, the Chief Organiser, in that order.[28] The campaigning literature and various speeches, which reiterated many of the ideas that Christabel and Emmeline had earlier articulated, set out an ambitious plan not only for victory in war but also for industrial and feminist reforms that would bring progress and security to British society. Thus 'Down with pacifism everywhere' was one of the chief cries of the Women's Party, a demand that would be fortified by the pursuit of more radical war measures, including better coordination of the Allied command, food rationing and the reduction of non-essential industry.[29] Efficient and loyal public service could be guaranteed, it was argued, by ridding all Government departments of officials who had enemy blood or connections or pacifist and pro-German leanings. The Naturalisation Laws should be changed too, to prevent Germans and their allies acquiring British nationality and exploiting it after the war, as they had done in the past. On the Irish question, the Women's Party was strictly Unionist while support was voiced for strengthening the British Empire so that its natural resources and transport system came under British ownership and control. Placing faith in the democratic process rather than the dictatorship of the Bolsheviks, it was argued that since:

> the interest of the community as a whole transcends that of the employer . . . and the employed . . . Parliament as the sole representative of the nation, must have the last word in all questions affecting the relations between Capital and Labour and industrial questions generally.

Further, the authority of Parliament should not be surrendered to any 'so-called League or Council of Nations' in which Germany would be included.[30] 'The Women's Party will use the vote to make Britain strong for defence against the outside foe', editorialised *Britannia*, 'and to strengthen Britain from within by securing more prosperous and more harmonious national development in its education, industrial, political and social aspects.'[31]

Such sentiments echoed those of most Conservatives of the day. But the Women's Party diverged widely from Conservative thinking in regard to the progressive feminist and industrial programmes that it advocated. Thus in regard to

'Special Women's Questions', equal pay for equal work was demanded, as well as equal marriage and divorce laws, equality of parental rights, equal opportunity of employment, and equal rights and responsibilities in regard to the social and political service of the nation. A system of maternity and infant care was called for, with parents making a financial contribution according to their income, as well as a guarantee that all children would receive a state-sponsored system of health care and education that would make them worthy citizens. A cooperative system of housing was also considered necessary in all state housing schemes to lift the burden of the overworked working-class wife and mother – complete with communal kitchens, central heating and hot water supply, communal laundry, medical services and, if desired, a crèche, nursery school, gymnasium and reading-room. Such changes, it was alleged, 'would enable the standard of living of the mass of the people to be enormously raised'.[32]

Importantly, both Christabel and Emmeline believed that all this could be achieved, not through emphasising the class divisions and class hatred so central to Marxism and the emerging communism in Russia, but through class coopera-tion. 'We are opposed to the Class War', cried Christabel to a packed, cheering meeting in the Queen's Hall. 'We are in favour of class harmony, and of outgrow-ing class distinctions.'[33] Class warfare divided rather than united women in the service of the nation. In particular, Christabel articulated that industrial reform should come not from the socialist-inspired notion of worker control of industry – which the Women's Party strongly opposed – but through increasing industrial output, cutting working hours and improving working conditions. The socialist cry of 'Up with the Proletariat and down with the Bourgeoisie!' was nonsense, 'indeed, madness', she asserted.[34] As democrats, the leaders of the Women's Party could not tolerate such a system under which workers would be marked off from their fellow citizens by peculiarities of speech and deportment, by uncouthness, by all the limitations evident in the class system of its day. The solution was to abolish the proletariat, not the bourgeoisie, and this could be done by bringing the comforts, refinements, and luxuries that had hitherto been the monopoly of the few to the masses.

Pre-war trade unions had deliberately restricted production in the wrong belief that it would involve 'over-production' and consequent unemployment. But increased production did not involve this danger if it was accompanied by increased consumption. In this process of moving towards a more equal society, the paid employment of women, 'so greatly dreaded by the fossilised and reaction-ary element among the men trade unionists', was an economic boom.[35] Women workers had a crucial part to play since they not only increased the prosperity of the nation but, through their purchasing power, provided employment for others.[36] Christabel concluded her plan for 'Industrial Salvation', as she termed it, by not-ing that in the happier time towards which the Women's Party was striving, the high standard of living of the upper classes would be 'as natural and as open to all, without distinction of class, as the free air of heaven'.[37] Thus the Women's Party, in its economic plan, emphasised the material benefits of capitalism, consumption and rising living standards rather than the levelling down that would accompany communism and socialism.

The Women's Party, at its launch, received enthusiastic reviews from a right-wing press concerned about the growing influence of the Labour Party and the rise of Bolshevism. 'We realise that patriotism is the inspiration of Mrs. Pankhurst's new organisation', opined the *Daily Express*:

> The Labour Party is already angling for the woman vote, and the Labour Party is still liable to fall under the sway of Mr. Ramsay MacDonald. Mrs. Pankhurst intends to use woman suffrage to save the country from MacDonaldism, and for that reason we wish her God speed.[38]

Not unexpectedly, the Women's Party appealed too to 'well-born' Conservative women, such as Lady Sybil Smith and Mrs Peggy Macmillan, sister-in-law of Harold Macmillan, a future Prime Minister currently serving with the Grenadier Guards.[39] And, more significantly, the anti-Bolshevik campaign attracted Government approval as well as the support of leading industrialists, such as Lord Vincent Caillard, the Financial Director of Vickers, and Lord Leverhulme, the soap manufacturer.[40] On 4 October 1917 an official in the Ministry of Munitions sent a note to William Sunderland, a Lloyd George aide, stating:

> I have been asked by Miss Pankhurst to assist the W.S.P.U. in the Anti-pacifist propaganda by giving letters of introduction to some of the leading men in Liverpool and I have obtained the consent of the Lord Mayor and others to see the ladies . . . They assured me that the Prime Minister supported their efforts and I am glad to know from you that this is the case.[41]

Additionally, the British Commonwealth Union (BCU), a recently formed protectionist organisation that aimed to influence the post-war Conservative Party, courted the Women's Party. Monies were paid to the Pankhursts' new organisation to help fund its campaign against industrial militancy and, on at least one future occasion, the Women's Party in its turn asked for help settling debts that had been incurred. In a preposterous claim, Pugh asserts that this 'new element of corporatism', combined with Christabel's 'well-established belief in the principle of leadership and discipline', suggests that by 1917 she was 'on the high road that leads to fascism'.[42]

But if many on the political right welcomed the Women's Party, for many on the left, such as Sylvia Pankhurst, now a revolutionary socialist who had changed the title of the *Women's Dreadnought* to the *Workers' Dreadnought*, the Women's Party was an object of contempt. Dismissively, she told the delegates at the Women's Civic and Political Responsibilities conference that 'too much importance' should not be attached to the new organisation, which was 'using the name "Women's" in a way which none of us could accept'. Similarly, Labour

Party member Susan Lawrence scornfully noted that 'there was an objection to a Party really political calling itself a non-party organisation'.[43] Such criticisms were not only directed against Christabel and Emmeline, as the co-leaders of the Women's Party, but also at the formidable team of speakers they had gathered around them – Annie Kenney, Flora Drummond, Phyllis Ayrton, Cynthia Maguire, Isabel Green and Elsie Bowerman.

On 10 January 1918 the women's suffrage clause in the Representation of the People Act was passed in the House of Lords by the large majority of one hundred and thirty-four to seventy-one. The Act conferred enfranchisement on women aged thirty and over who were householders, the wives of householders, occupiers of property of £5 or more annual value, or university graduates.[44] A few weeks later, on 6 February, when the Act received the Royal Assent, nearly eight and a half million women were enfranchised, about two thirds of the female adult population aged thirty and over. Christabel chafed at the age and property restrictions placed on women. Too many women would be voting not in their own right but because of their relationship to a man, while about one third of women over thirty were excluded as well as those under the age limit. She was in her small flat that cold winter day when the news of the suffrage victory came through. 'I remember sitting with her there, both huddled in our coats over a tiny fire, when we heard about the Vote', recollected Jennie Kenney. 'It's funny, but it was an anti-climax. We were both so tired with our war work.'[45]

Despite the disappointment, for Christabel the much bigger issue was the war; it was still raging and its outcome uncertain so that the limited suffrage success was subsumed within the crisis of wider global issues. Reflecting on the suffrage victory forty years later, Christabel's comments were subdued:

> We had pictured national rejoicing, a great public celebration of our Votes for Women victory. It had come in time of public mourning and deepening war danger. Our only celebration of women's enfranchisement was a greater devotion to war service in defence of the country in which we now were citizens and in defence of the national and constitutional liberties in which women now had obtained their part.[46]

Despite her tiredness, Christabel continued campaigning vigorously for the Women's Party. She became energised when on the platform. In weekly meetings in London or in speeches made elsewhere in cities such as Liverpool, Manchester, Cardiff or Glasgow, she hit back at the socialists, pounding the message that it was the Women's Party that was *the* party of progress for women, not the Labour Party, a view commonly reiterated by her co-workers.[47] Thus at Nottingham that January, she fiercely denounced Labour's pacifist leaders, particularly Ramsay MacDonald, pointing out that women owed these men no gratitude for their enfranchisement. 'Mr. Ramsay MacDonald led his flock into the same lobby as the Government when it was refusing to give them the vote.'[48] Even now, when women's long fight for the vote had culminated in victory, the Russian communist Leon Trotsky, so 'ardently admired and faithfully followed by the Bolsheviks of Britain', such as MacDonald, had said that 'Universal Suffrage is out of date'.[49]

The revived Christabel was in good form when she spoke alongside her mother, Annie and Flora Drummond at a crowded Women's Party meeting held in the Albert Hall on 16 March to celebrate the suffrage victory. According to Louisa Garrett Anderson, the energetic Christabel looked 'so fresh & vital' as she spoke of how newly enfranchised women must use their power wisely.[50] Warning that the exercise of the suffrage depended upon victory in war, she advised women not to be lured by the false promises of Britain's Bolsheviks but to vote for responsible leaders. 'We have got to show that . . . consideration for the good of the community comes before the good of the individual', she cried, to loud cheers.[51] Christabel then put a resolution that was unanimously passed, calling upon the Government, the captains of industry and patriotic working men to cooperate in retaining women in factories and workshops during and after the war, on the basis of the equal right to work and equal pay for equal work.[52]

Christabel's message of sex equality, patriotism, improvement in women's working conditions and industrial peace rather than strikes and disruption appealed to a wide range of the female population, including middle-class and working-class employees such as schoolteachers and munitions workers. To schoolteachers she stressed that the Women's Party was against the 'excessively large classes' to be found in Britain's state elementary schools which put an undue strain upon both teacher and pupils, robbing working-class children of the chance to develop their potential. The Women's Party, she announced, stood for raising the school leaving age and for equal pay for equal work, a view that was heartedly endorsed by women teacher associations.[53]

The highly paid munitions workers, often noisy and boisterous, were frequently a target of criticism in both the right and left-wing press, chastised for their high wages and frivolous spending habits. But Christabel championed their cause. Under the headline, 'Million Loyal Women Determined to Defy "Bolshies" in Munition Shops', the Empire News commented that the women had 'a strong and far-seeing leader in Miss Christabel Pankhurst, who understands the psychology of her sex, and can diagnose a labour situation more correctly, probably, than any other woman'.[54] Christabel appealed not only to the patriotism of the munitionettes; she inspired them with her rhetoric about sex equality, encouraged a sense of pride in their accomplishments and spoke up forcefully against their dismissal and demobilisation.[55] On more than one occasion, as at Woolwich Arsenal in March 1918 where eight thousand women workers had been dismissed, Christabel received an ovation from the large female audience. Her fighting speech was interrupted with frequent applause as she praised the loyalty of the women and condemned those men who were shirkers, strikers or pacifists:

These miserable creatures threaten to strike. Well, if they do go out, lock the gates on them and never let them back. (Applause). They are holding their country to ransom . . . Keep the women in the factories, and send these 'skilled' workers to the Western front . . . The women can turn out more stuff than these slackers will. (Applause).[56]

Demanding equal pay for equal work, Christabel insisted that demobilised women should be treated the same as demobilised men. Condemning the Amalgamated Society of Engineers for its sexist practices – it would admit any man, even bookmakers and public housekeepers, as members but not women – she emphasised the discriminatory nature of its ruling that the relaxation of trade union rules to admit women to the factories should be discontinued after the war. 'We intend to see that sex distinctions shall be done away with', Christabel asserted. 'There must be no aristocracy of labour; we shall all be working men and women.'[57]

That the trade unions, with their emphasis upon a class war, had the audacity to ask women to join the Labour Party and help send their candidates to Parliament was a theme frequently reiterated by Christabel. '[W]omen owe the vote to no men's political party', she claimed, 'but to their own pre-war agitation (and, above all, militant agitation), crowned by their patriotic policy and national service during the war.'[58] Dismissive of socialists who condemned working women such as the munitionettes who tried to better themselves, Christabel praised such women for their initiative:

The I.L.P. lecturer works himself up into a frenzy in his efforts to incite the working woman to the class war. He tries to rouse her to class jealousy by his denunciation of 'the employer's wife in her silk dress'. But the working woman simply and calmly adheres to her determination, not to prevent the employer's wife from having a silk dress, but to have a silk dress too! . . . The working women who spend their earnings on silk dresses, silk stockings, shapely shoes, fine underwear, fur coats, pretty hats, and all the rest of it, are far better social reformers than all the men's Socialist or Labour organisation rolled into one . . . They are raising their standard of living, and they are doing their best to break down class distinctions, which are so largely a question of dress, speech, and deportment.[59]

The women munitions workers, for their part, were among the most ardent sellers of *Britannia* and frequently contributed significant sums of money to the Women's Party. During early 1918, munitionettes from Coventry and Birmingham subscribed £880 to the latest appeal for funds while workers in Wales and on the Clyde gave £400 and £1,335, respectively. Overall, £8,000 was collected.[60] However, Christabel's popularity with the female munitions workers has rarely been commented on by historians, and certainly not by her sister Sylvia in *The suffragette movement*.[61] Yet her shrewd tactic in emphasising that women's war work would help to bring victory *and* female enfranchisement attracted a number of new influential allies, including right-wing press entrepreneurs and industrialists. As Gullace has persuasively argued, the patriotic Christabel and Emmeline Pankhurst were not so much a feminist anomaly as the feminists 'most in tune' with the cultural climate of wartime Britain. Demolishing the anti-suffrage argument that women were unable to aid the defence of the nation, they had helped to bring about a cultural shift in the definition of citizenship so that it centred on the idea of loyal service, patriotic sentiment and British blood rather than manhood, the age of majority or property qualification.[62]

In September 1918, Christabel travelled to Derby where the Women's Party was holding a special campaign because the Trade Union Congress was being held in that town. She met up with Mr Hughes, the Prime Minister of Australia, and with Havelock Wilson, the patriotic leader of the Seamen's and Firemen's Union. Wives of the members of the latter had already shown their support for the Women's Party by contributing £500 to its funds.[63] 'The Women's Party is the one and only real Trade Union for Women', proudly proclaimed *Britannia*.[64] When Hughes then travelled to Glasgow, Christabel made sure that the Women's Party took part in the enthusiastic reception given to him there – and again, in Manchester, when Lloyd George visited that city in September, over two thousand people waiting in the rain to greet him.[65] 'Mr. Lloyd George among his former enemies, the Suffragettes', ran the caption under one photo in the *Daily Sketch*. 'The Prime Minister and the munitionettes understand each other' ran another caption under a photo showing Lloyd George inspecting a guard of women munitions workers, with Flora Drummond and Cynthia Maguire, the Manchester organiser for the Women's Party, by his side.[66]

Emmeline had been in North America for some months now, having sailed there in late May on a mission to rouse the American public in favour of Japanese intervention in Russia. Russia had withdrawn from the war after peace had been agreed with Germany in March 1918, but at a heavy cost since the western portion of its former Empire came into German hands. The strengthening of German military power led to an Allied offensive on the Western front which Christabel and Emmeline feared would not be successful unless Japan intervened on the Eastern front. Such a move would compel Germany to send reinforcements from the Western to the Eastern front, thus relieving pressure on the Allies and, hopefully, helping the Russian people to bring down their unelected Bolshevik leaders.[67]

However, by the time Emmeline had returned to England in mid-October 1918, the balance of power had shifted to the Allies. 'Is it not wonderful news that the Allies now have it in their power to make a complete & lasting job of the war?' she wrote optimistically to Lady Muriel Paget, who had founded an Anglo-Russian hospital in Petrograd. 'I return to find the Women's Party very vigorous & prosperous & I feel very hopeful that we shall overthrow the demon of Bolshevism.' One week later, Emmeline reiterated her views, informing her correspondent that she was 'certain' that the politically independent Women's Party was:

the way to save Civilisation from Bolshevism & to get real social improvement. I don't know what the future has in store for men & women but I am sure that for the present we must stand alone & show what women can do.

Since Muriel Paget was anxious about which career her eldest daughter might take up, Emmeline suggested tactfully:

When she is next in London would you like her to talk to Christabel? Girls will often unfold to girls and Christabel although much older than your daughter is very young in everything apart from politics & her mission in life.[68]

Whether Christabel met up with Muriel Paget's daughter is not known. However, like her mother, Christabel was greatly relieved to know that the war was drawing to an end although the armistice was not called until 11 November.

Notes

1 EP to Ethel Smyth, 3 May 1917, quoted in Smyth, *Female pipings*, p. 242.
2 J. Kenney, Miscellaneous notes on Russian visit, Introduction, p. 22, KP5, Kenney Papers.
3 *Britannia*, 13 June 1917, p. 10.
4 J. Kenney, Miscellaneous notes on Russian visit, Introduction, pp. 23–4, KP5, Kenney Papers; J. Kenney, Diary of her trip to Russia 1917, Craigie Collection, pp. 13–14.
5 *Britannia*, 6 June 1917, p. 4.
6 Gullace, 'The blood of our sons', p. 187.
7 Woman suffrage a necessary war measure, *Britannia*, 23 April 1917, p. 364.
8 CP, *No peace without victory! The report of a speech delivered in the Queen's Hall on June 23rd, 1917 with some extracts from speeches delivered at a series of Meetings in the Aeolian Hall* (London, WSPU, n.d.), p. 8.
9 CP, *No peace without victory!*, p. 6.
10 See, for example, Pugh, *The Pankhursts*, p. 332.
11 CP, *No peace without victory!*, p. 6.
12 CP, *No peace without victory!*, pp. 17 and 4.
13 *Britannia*, 22 June 1917, p. 24.
14 CP to Renee de Brimont, 16 June 1917, de Brimont Papers; English translation in Mitchell, *Queen Christabel*, p. 262.
15 Mitchell, *Queen Christabel*, p. 263.
16 Purvis, *Emmeline Pankhurst*, p. 300.
17 CP, Typescript, The Projected Memoir of Dame Ethel Smyth, p. 6, DMC.
18 *Britannia*, 17 August 1917, pp. 84 and 86.
19 CP to Marion Wallace-Dunlop, 4 October 1917, WDFA.
20 Purvis, *Emmeline Pankhurst*, p. 301; H. Rappaport, *Caught in the revolution Petrograd 1917* (London, Hutchinson, 2016), pp. 107–206.
21 CP, The 'international' danger, *Britannia*, 12 October 1917, p. 151.
22 See R. Service, *Spies & commissars: Bolshevik Russia and the West* (London, Macmillan, 2011). According to the modern calendar, the Bolsheviks took control in November, not October.

23 E. C. Dubois, Woman suffrage and the left: an international socialist-feminist perspective, in her *Woman suffrage and women's rights* (New York, New York University Press, 1998), pp. 272–3.
24 *Britannia*, 2 November 1917, p. 171.
25 *Britannia*, 30 November 1917, p. 207.
26 *Britannia*, 23 November 1917, p. 196.
27 J. Purvis, The Women's Party of Great Britain (1917–1919): a forgotten episode in British women's political history, *Women's History Review*, 25, 2016, pp. 638–51.
28 *Britannia*, 2 November 1917, pp. 171–2.
29 *Britannia*, 22 March 1918, p. 386.
30 *Britannia*, 2 November 1917, pp. 171–2; *Britannia*, 16 November 1917, p. 189.
31 *Britannia*, 11 January 1918, p. 241.
32 *Britannia*, 2 November 1917, p. 172.
33 *Britannia*, 9 November 1917, p. 190.
34 CP, Industrial salvation, *Britannia*, 30 August 1918, p. 107.
35 CP, Industrial salvation, *Britannia*, 30 August 1918, p. 108.
36 N. F. Gullace, Christabel Pankhurst and the Smethwick election: right-wing feminism, the Great War and the ideology of consumption, *Women's History Review*, 25, 2014, p. 332 makes the over-exaggerated claim that the Women's Party upheld a 'consumer-based feminism'.
37 CP, Industrial salvation, *Britannia*, 30 August 1918, p. 109.
38 Cited in *Britannia*, 15 March 1918, p. 377.
39 Mitchell, *Queen Christabel*, p. 265.
40 See *Report of proceedings at dinner given by Sir Vincent Caillard at Claridge's 29th May, 1918*, which both CP and Annie attended, Leaflet, Kenny Papers, KP/1/4.
41 Burton Chadwick to Mr Sutherland, 4.10.17, LG Papers.
42 Pugh, *The Pankhursts*, p. 342.
43 *Labour Woman*, November 1918, p. 76.
44 Rosen, *Rise up women!*, p. 266.
45 Interview with Jessie Kenney, 24 March 1964, DMC.
46 CP, *Unshackled*, p. 294.
47 See comment by Annie Kenney, *Britannia*, 15 March 1918, p. 372.
48 *Britannia*, 25 January 1918, pp. 269–70.
49 *Britannia*, 1 February 1918, p. 274.
50 Quoted in John, *Evelyn Sharp*, p. 87.
51 CP, Women and the war, *Britannia*, 22 March 1918, pp. 395–8.
52 *Daily Telegraph*, 18 March 1918.
53 *Britannia*, 1 and 15 February 1918, pp. 278 and 308–10, respectively.
54 Reprinted in *Britannia*, 16 August 1918, p. 24.
55 Gullace, 'The blood of our sons', p. 137.
56 *Woolwich Herald*, 8 March 1918, reprinted in *Britannia*, 15 March 1918, p. 1918.
57 *Woolwich Herald*, 8 March 1918, reprinted in *Britannia*, 15 March 1918, p. 1918.
58 Editorial, The plain truth, *Britannia*, 17 May 1918, p. 458.
59 CP, To abolish the proletariat, *Britannia*, 6 September 1918, p. 116, reprinted in CP, *Industrial Salvation* (London, The Women's Party, 1918), pp. 12–13.
60 *Britannia*, 22 March 1918, p. 386.
61 Historians guilty of this omission include G. Braybon, *Women workers in the First World War* (London, Routledge, 1981); A. Woollacott, *On her their lives depend: munitions workers in the Great War* (Berkeley, CA, University of California Press, 1994); D. Thom, *Nice girls and rude girls: women workers in World War I* (London, Tauris, 1998); Vellacott, *Pacifists, patriots and the vote*, pp. 112–16; and A. Hochschild, *To end all wars: how the First World War divided Britain* (London, Macmillan, 2011). For an exception to this general rule see Gullace,

'*The blood of our sons*'. Sylvia, in *The suffragette movement*, pp. 596–609, presents herself as the only member of the Pankhurst family in Britain popular with working women during the First World War and pressing for equal pay and safeguards for their employment, a view that too many historians have followed.

62 Gullace, '*The blood of our sons*', pp. 141 and 118–19.
63 *Britannia*, 6 September 1918, p. 115 and ibid., 22 March 1918, p. 386.
64 *Britannia*, 13 September 1918, p. 123.
65 *Britannia*, 6 September 1918, p. 118.
66 *Daily Sketch*, 13 and 14 September 1918.
67 Purvis, *Emmeline Pankhurst*, p. 309; *Britannia*, 21 June 1918, p. 3.
68 EP to Muriel Paget, 21 and 28 October 1918, Lady Muriel Paget Papers, Special Collections, University of Leeds, Correspondence Box S. Thanks to Eve Colpus for these references.

19

PARLIAMENTARY CANDIDATE
AND SINGLE PARENT

November 1918–end of July 1921

The war had profoundly changed Christabel. When the war was still raging, during Easter 1918, she had been browsing in a bookshop when she came across *The approaching end of age viewed by the light of history, prophecy and science* by Dr Grattan Guinness, a writer of historicist biblical prophecy. The book foretold that Jesus Christ was coming again and that His return would initiate an age of righteousness, peace and happiness that would be the answer to the world's problems. The disillusioned Christabel, searching for an understanding of the upheavals in the shattered international order, continued to read avidly on the subject, a search that became critical as yet more news emerged of the carnage among young men, especially in the trenches. By the time of the Armistice on 11 November, she had become a Second Adventist; that is, a Christian who is expecting the imminent coming of Christ.[1] This was to become her second great campaigning cause – after women's suffrage – but a few years were to elapse before that was so.

Christabel did not speak about her conversion to her friends. 'For a long time . . . mine seemed too fragile a flower of belief to speak of, and expose to the cold wind of other people's possible scepticism.'[2] Nor did she seek out like-minded believers. However, she did tell her mother when she arrived back home that October. Emmeline was not entirely surprised. She herself had gladly gone back to an open expression of her Christian faith, after the influence of her long-dead agnostic husband had waned.[3] Some three years earlier, in the midst of war, Emmeline had attended the Temple Church, London, where she loved the 'beautiful music and the exquisite singing' but felt hurt by the knowledge that the Church of England was male dominated, excluding women from the pulpit.[4] Emmeline kept Christabel's secret while Christabel read keenly on biblical prophecy, deepening her knowledge of the subject. Such a period of private reflection seems to have lasted for three years from around the summer of 1918 to the summer of 1921.[5] In the meantime, life continued along some predictable and less predictable lines.

Christabel was buzzing with some other unexpected news when her mother Emmeline returned home that October: speculation was mounting that women could stand for election to the House of Commons in the forthcoming general election, something that not even she – or any of the pre-war suffragists – had dared to ask for. The Parliament (Qualification of Women) Bill passed into law on 21 November 1918, giving the Women's Party the short space of just over three weeks to field any candidates for polling day on 14 December. Yet despite this drawback, the new Act was far more radical than the 1918 Representation of the People Act in that it allowed women to stand on equal terms with men for a Parliament they could not elect! Although some of Emmeline's friends urged her to stand for election, Emmeline was adamant that the much younger Christabel, her favourite and talented thirty-eight-year-old daughter, should be the candidate even though there were just over three weeks to put everything in motion.

At a Women's Party meeting on 19 November, the proud Emmeline introduced the parliamentary candidate in heartfelt words – and to much cheering. 'The movement which has resulted in the possibility of there being a woman candidate at all was started not by me, as many of you think,' she humbly observed, 'but by my daughter. (Cheers). I am her most ardent disciple.' Christabel was not only the strategist who had taken the question of the citizenship of women 'out of the region of fads into practical politics'; her war record was another proof that she was the woman of the hour. '[H]ad her war policy prevailed in those early years of the war, many thousands of lives would have been saved.' Emmeline continued:

> [P]utting aside my own feeling as her dearest friend and her mother
> ... she is, in my opinion, in this critical hour of our country's fortunes, necessary in the House of Commons and the best representative our party can find.[6]

Christabel, for her part, responded warmly to her mother's praise in a rare public statement that described their working relationship:

> Ladies and Gentlemen, – I do not think that any candidate, and certainly no daughter, could have listened without emotion and without gratitude to the words that have just been addressed to you. I want to say that my feeling has always been that my mother and myself are simply two sides of the one coin. Both of us have worked in so close partnership that we do not really distinguish between each other; we are absolutely one, and always have been, and always shall be, in our fight. (Cheers). It is a great honour to me that she and you should have the confidence in me which you are expressing to-day.[7]

The next speaker was Annie Kenney who appealed urgently for both personal and financial help in running the Women's Party campaign. 'If there could only be a few people like Miss Christabel Pankhurst in Parliament we could redeem this Empire and build it up on the bases that we should all be proud of.'

Flora Drummond too was fulsome in her praise. 'Miss Pankhurst should be in the House of Commons. She has taken her degree in International Law, and during the war has done all she could for the small nations.' Further, Christabel's pamphlet titled *Industrial Salvation* had made a tremendous impression in industrial areas and offered a useful blueprint for success in times of peace.[8]

Initially Christabel was to stand for the Westbury Division of Wiltshire and, as she expected, had the backing of Lloyd George. Both Emmeline and Annie had been to see him, to plead her case. Lloyd George had been in a dilemma about the forthcoming general election: although he led the Coalition Government, many of the Liberal MPs remained loyal to Asquith. He had decided therefore to fight the election in conjunction with the Conservative Party, led by Bonar Law, their preferred candidates being given a 'coupon' or letter of approval which greatly increased the chances of success (the Labour Party had left the Coalition Government before the election and was campaigning on its own). Of the seventeen women standing as parliamentary candidates, Christabel was the only one to receive the coveted coupon.

On 21 November 1918, Lloyd George wrote to Bonar Law, asking him to see Miss Pankhurst. 'I am not sure that we have any women candidates, and I think it is highly desirable that we should', he remarked:

> The Women's Party, of which Miss Pankhurst is the Leader, has been extraordinarily useful, as you know, to the Government . . . They have fought the Bolshevist and Pacifist element with great skill, tenacity and courage, and I know especially in Glasgow and South Wales their intervention produced remarkable results.[9]

On that very same day, Christabel wrote to Lloyd George, telling him that she had changed her mind about Westbury. 'I want to see you about my candidature. Something very much better than Westbury is now available but for one little difficulty which you can clear away for me.' And in a rare expression of implied criticism of her mother, she noted, 'Mother, who is absolutely bent upon my getting elected, was coming herself to see you and is still prepared to come, but we felt you would think it quite enough to see me for a minute or two.'[10]

Christabel now wanted to fight the new working-class constituency of Smethwick, close to Birmingham, an industrial town with massive engineering works, as well as glass factories and large breweries. As Emmeline explained, she and Christabel had gone through the full list of seven hundred seats and decided upon Smethwick since no one political party could lay claim to it, nor was there a sitting member to be ousted.[11] Although the new constituency had been carved out of the old Handsworth division, which used to be Conservative and Unionist, the Trades and Labour Council in the town had gained considerable influence during the past three years and so this seemed a suitable seat to contest with the aim of defeating the Labour candidate, Mr J. E. Davison, an experienced trade union official and national organiser for the Ironfounders' Society.

417

The over 32,000 electors on the register of voters included 14,789 men and 12,736 women, many of the latter being industrial workers who might be interested in the Women's Party. There were also an additional 5,393 absent voters in the armed forces entitled to a postal vote.[12] The 'one little difficulty' that Christabel spoke about was Major S. N. Thompson who the local Conservatives had already chosen as their candidate.

Christabel hoped that Lloyd George could use his influence with Bonar Law to persuade Major Thompson to withdraw in her favour. On 23 November, Bonar Law gave Christabel his guarded approval. 'I have greatly appreciated the way in which you and your friends have sunk all considerations in order to help the Nation in the terrible struggle which has ended so victoriously', he penned politely. 'For that reason I should personally be glad to see you returned to the House, and hope you will be able to find a suitable Constituency.'[13] Northcliffe, the powerful press proprietor, who had already promised Annie he would give special coverage to the constituency that Christabel decided upon, had already intervened in the matter.[14] At the end of October he had written to William Sutherland, one of Lloyd George's aides:

> I wish that you would tell him my respectful opinion that the best possible seat should be got for Miss Pankhurst, who has more brains than the rest of these women put together, and is a lday [lady] into the bargain – and also pleasant to look upon – and will therefore have power over the men in the House.[15]

Under pressure of time to mount the Women's Party election campaign, Christabel tried to sort out the 'one little difficulty'. P. G. Hosgood, a respected and well-known solicitor in Birmingham, was recommended to her as a possible election agent. Together with her mother and Annie, the hopeful Christabel travelled to Birmingham where an intermediary asked Hosgood if he would take on the task. He declined, mainly because he was good friends with Major Thompson, the Conservative candidate. However, he arranged for the three women to meet Thompson, to talk things over. Christabel asked the Major if he would withdraw from the contest but he declined, saying he had been nursing the constituency for some time and therefore thought it more appropriate that she should retire. The determined Christabel would not compromise, explaining that she had the chance of being the first woman to be elected to Parliament. Both the Prime Minister and Bonar Law had stated that she should be found a seat as a Coalition candidate – and hoped she would succeed. Thompson agreed to discuss the matter with his local committee which decided that the final decision should rest with the Prime Minister and the leader of the Conservative Party. Lloyd George and Bonar Law soon settled the disagreement by writing to Major Thompson, explaining that there was a danger of the seat being lost if both he and Miss Pankhurst went to the poll. '[I]f you could see your way to retire you would be doing . . . a real public service, for which we should be grateful.'[16] Thus Thompson stepped down and only Christabel competed against the Labour candidate, Mr J. E. Davison.

The relieved Christabel, at the opening of her election campaign, paid warm tribute to the 'very patriotic action' of Major Thompson.[17] Her headquarters, decked out in the Women's Party colours of red, white and blue, was a rented room at 112 the High Street, Smethwick. An official photo of Christabel in her academic gown and cap, described as 'Patriotic Candidate and Supporter of the Prime Minister and the Coalition', adorned the walls.[18] A constant stream of women volunteers from all parts of the country, including Phyllis Ayrton, Cynthia McGuire, the crippled May Billinghurst, Joan Dugdale and Barbara Wylie, came to canvass enthusiastically alongside stalwarts such as Flora Drummond and Emmeline Pankhurst herself. 'You can be the first to return a woman to Parliament', Barbara Wylie entreated the voters. Miss Pankhurst is 'a woman with a brain as good as any man's – and better than any man's whom I know', cried out Phyllis Ayrton.[19] Elsie Bowerman, a former WSPU organiser, was Christabel's agent while Joan Dugdale, a former suffragette, was drafted in as her deputy.[20] Jessie Kenney, who by now was listed as the Honorary Parliamentary Secretary of the Women's Party, could not travel to campaign in Smethwick since her health was still poor. So she stayed in London, as did her sister Annie who had the task of raising the necessary election expenses, including donations from many sympathetic women as well as £1,100 given by the British Commonwealth Union.[21]

Christabel pledged, if elected to Parliament, to work for two main objectives: first, to secure a lasting peace based on material guarantees against future German aggression and second, to improve the social conditions of the working classes through a levelling up of society, by social reform, industrial salvation and wealth production. In an attempt to woo the electors, she spelled out clearly her ideas:

We must in future have not only Britain for the British, but a Britain worthy of the British. The Abolition of Poverty is an ideal which can and must be realised by means of increased Wealth Production, so that there may be enough to go round and provide the comforts and refinements of life for all . . . Indeed, my determination to work for the Abolition of Poverty, by increasing Wealth Production, and Democratising Prosperity, is one of my main reasons for seeking election to Parliament . . . As a Woman Member of Parliament, I shall, if elected, give special attention to the Housing Question, because, as every woman knows, a good home is the foundation of all well being. It is necessary that all New Housing Schemes shall help the woman in the home and relieve her burden of drudgery, by introducing bathrooms, and various labour-saving arrangements, and also co-operation in the form of central hot water supply, central kitchens and laundries where these are desired . . . The welfare of children is a foremost consideration with me . . . A Good Education is the birthright of every child, and I shall do my utmost to give equal education opportunities to all, and to improve the system of Education.[22]

Christabel also supported the provision in public houses of music and refreshments, as a way to make them 'fit places' that women would want to enter.[23]

Press reports reveal that such views were received favourably by women in the audiences, especially when Christabel, as in her suffrage days, put down male hecklers. 'Have you yourself ever worked in a factory?' asked one such nuisance at one of the Women's Party's packed evenings. 'No, I have not', was Christabel's pert reply, as accompanied by cheering she added, 'neither have your friends, Ramsay MacDonald or Philip Snowden.' When the heckler then commented, 'Two blacks don't make a white', she retorted, 'I am glad to hear that you think Mr. MacDonald and his friends are black.'[24] Local schoolchildren too, out of lessons since schools were closed because of an outbreak of influenza, added to the election excitement by singing to a marching song a ditty they had been taught. 'Vote, vote, vote for Christabel/ Christie's sure to win the day/ When the soldiers come with a double-barrelled gun/ They'll blow old Davison away.'[25] Christabel herself caught the 'flu that was killing many but fortunately survived, although it left her with the unwanted complication of depression and tiredness. Nonetheless, she did her best to keep on campaigning, and to rally her supporters.

Dressed in 'lovely Liberty velvets – suits & frocks – greens browns and deep heliotrope', Christabel with her 'red gold hair' cut a handsome figure.[26] Dubbed by the press as 'The Portia of the Suffragists and their most brilliant orator', she addressed about sixty indoor and outdoor meetings in the short time to polling day.[27] She has a 'good array of clever speakers', it was noted, 'Mrs. Pankhurst being regarded as her greatest asset on the platform.'[28] The proud and determined Emmeline worked feverishly to assist her favourite daughter's passage to Parliament, even on one occasion climbing in the rain upon a table in front of a beerless public house to deliver her impassioned speech.[29] She often emphasised that Christabel was not only the best candidate to represent the women and men voters but also the person whose international status would make Smethwick known to the whole of the British Empire and the whole of the world.[30] That Sylvia was now a Communist repudiating the whole election process and the very notion of parliamentary government had deeply upset Emmeline – and Christabel. Sylvia was disgusted by what she saw as the 'unrevolutionary timidity' of the Labour Party, and had refused an invitation to stand as its candidate for the Hallam division of Sheffield, a view not apparently shared by Emmeline Pethick-Lawrence who was contesting, as a Labour candidate, the Rusholme division of Manchester.[31]

In the midst of the election hubbub at Smethwick, Jessie Kenney wrote to Christabel in late November saying that she had developed a problem with her lungs and was still not fit enough to help out. Writing on notepaper from the

Midland Hotel, Birmingham, where she was staying, Christabel replied immediately, comforting her friend as well as giving news about the election campaign:

My darling old Jessie

I am so very sorry about the news your letter brings, but I hope you are better by now. The weather here is damp & horrid – only one gleam of sun . . . has visited us so far. But the Smethwick people's friendliness seems to make up for it. You can imagine what work it has been to set the organisation side going. 5000 absent voters to circularise, committee rooms hard to get through the political views of their landlords etc etc But all is smoothing out & in the next two weeks we shall reap the fruits of all this constructive work . . . My first meeting was last night & was most encouraging . . . I have written to Dr. Strode asking if it is really impossible to get the stuff Mother had when she is in [the] U.S.A. If he arranges anything I will let you know so that you may share the benefit. What you need is . . . dry weather, for dampness is the worst thing for your troubles.[32]

Reflecting many years later on this letter, as she re-read it, Jessie commented, 'Those who think that Christabel was as "hard as nails" are generally those who know the least about her. Her affections were strong and deep.'[33]

As the Women's Party campaign gathered speed, Christabel reached out to a wide spectrum of the electorate including the absent voters in the armed forces to whom she sent a special address.[34] Her photograph frequently appeared in the press with groups of mothers and children, members of the general public or sailor and soldier supporters.[35] A photograph of May Billinghurst in her invalid tricycle talking to Christabel even appeared on the front page of the *Daily Sketch*.[36] Joan Dugdale was enthusiastic. She had been out and about a great deal and talked to many people, she told her sister Una, and:

most of them are amazed & thrilled with C.P. She has spoken marvel-lously – a revelation even to me, & her answers to the heckling . . . have been inspired. She looks bursting with health, perfectly turned out & abt. 20 years of age.[37]

The gallant Major Thompson added his weight to the campaign, chairing a large Women's Party meeting in the Theatre Royal.[38]

At a crowded meeting at the Empire Picture house, over which Emmeline presided, Christabel dealt satisfactorily with questions asked by the local peo-ple, including representatives of tenants' and allotments' associations. When another member of her audience queried whether she would promote legislation for requiring railway offices to be kept up to the standard of modern requirements, in the interests of public health, she tactfully agreed. To much laughter, she wit-tily added that even if the ventilation of the House of Parliament itself wanted immediate improvement she would see whether it could not be done. 'I want free air letting into the place in every sense of the word – physical, mental, moral, and spiritual.'[39] However, it was mainly on the inadequacies of the Labour Party that Christabel directed her attack.

'The Women's Party is the true Labour Party', she reiterated on a number of occasions. 'We aim at the abolition of poverty by the increased production of wealth so that there may be enough wealth for all.'[40] When she denounced the Labour Party as a party corrupted by Bolshevists and led by Bolsheviks and told the voters that the choice was between the Red Flag or the Union Jack, charges that were commonly made by Conservative candidates during the 1918 election, the exchange of views became particularly fiery.[41] Davison angrily retorted that the Labour Party stood for social reform on constitutional lines, 'without breaking a single window, firing a single pillar-box, or burning down a single church'. Christabel and her women supporters were smeared contemptuously as 'Christabelligerents' who were famous for 'all things by turn and nothing long'. Great play was made of the fact that it was from a 'haven of safety in Paris' that Miss Pankhurst had incited her followers to violence.[42]

On the eve of the general election, the *Times* was of the view that such charges against the Women's Party's candidate had fallen flat. 'Miss Pankhurst is a fighter . . . [who] has made steady progress . . . It is believed her majority will be large.'[43] Joan Dugdale was of the same view. 'The Lab. People said we had 300 workers in fr. outside & are getting v. furious because C.P. has turned 100s of Labour voters with her speeches . . . I believe she will get in.'[44] But Christabel was not optimistic. She felt it was 'a completely foregone conclusion' that she would not be elected, and that it would take some time 'before a woman did'.[45] Although the general election took place on 14 December, the results were not declared until two weeks later. Christabel lost by just nine hundred and fifteen votes. A recount was demanded and she had to concede defeat to Davison by a majority of seven hundred and seventy-five.[46]

'It was a dreadful blow', recollected Jessie Kenney. 'Annie and I weren't able to be with her. She said later that she thought she would have won if we had been. There was something almost telepathic in our closeness.'[47] Although the deflated, tired Christabel was upset by her defeat, she took the news much better than her mother; for Emmeline it was the bitterest disappointment of her life.[48] Elsie Bowerman believed that Christabel had lost the election because she was 'rather aloof and perhaps had not the gift of establishing the homely human contacts which win votes'. Local connections with the constituency were lacking too, thus making her task that much harder. There was also, Elsie insisted, 'prejudice against a woman candidate'.[49] Voter turnout was low too, since less than 55% of the electorate voted. And, of course, many men may have felt unable to support a political party with such a gendered name. Whatever the reasons for her failure, Christabel took comfort in the fact that, despite the short time allotted to her campaign, she had polled more votes than any of the other fifteen women candidates apart from Countess Markievicz who had been returned for a

Dublin constituency but, as a member of Sinn Fein, had pledged not to take her seat at Westminster.

A few days after the general election results were known, Christabel spoke to the press. 'This election has not provided a fair test of the will of the electors with respect to women in Parliament', she pointed out:

> The patriotic women candidates had not a proper chance of success compared with the men candidates because they only became eligible practically at the last moment . . . In my own case I had only three weeks in which to get the organisation going.

Christabel made it clear she still had political ambitions. 'I intend to become a candidate again at the first available by-election. My opponent's majority was so small that I consider it justifies my again seeking election at the earliest possible moment.'[50]

Despite such high hopes, the exhausted Christabel's immediate concern was to take time out to rest – and look after little Betty. She had been campaigning tirelessly now for nearly fourteen years. While Emmeline travelled with Catherine Pine to Paris, primarily to keep an eye on the Peace Conference whose negotiations with thirty-seven nations would spread over six months, Christabel retreated to High Edser at Ewhurst where Mrs Crowe helped with the care of Betty. '[O]f course it is certain that she will become a member of Parliament', the optimistic Annie claimed.[51] However, to make this happen, the Women's Party had to stay in the news and, since it was in debt, find ways to increase its income.

Widespread industrial strikes in Britain at this time gave resolve and purpose to Christabel's mission, especially as the crisis deepened.[52] She advertised in the *Times* for a private secretary and chauffeuse and appointed Muriel Cook, who had been an ambulance driver in France during the war. Muriel found her employer and Mrs Pankhurst, who was among the many visitors to the 'nice, neat house' at Ewhurst, 'perfectly charming' but did not know exactly what Christabel did in London when she went to the Women's Party headquarters:

> She was a very vague naïve sort of person, especially as regards money & if anyone came to do the smallest repair job . . . or deliver a note even, she always said to me give him a shilling or two dear, for himself.

Christabel had a mania for sleeping out at night, to enjoy the fresh country air, and tried to persuade her secretary to do the same. Muriel refused, recollecting how once or twice, when three or four of them slept outside, 'it poured with rain in the night & they disturbed the rest of the household, dragging their bedraggled selves & bedding indoors & then out again if it stopped raining. Quite mad, I thought'.[53]

Christabel enjoyed these weekends at High Edser, when she often had friends to stay or visited friends herself, including Marion Wallace-Dunlop. 'Betty &

I will arrive chez vous on Friday afternoon', she wrote to Marion from William Street on 7 February 1919. 'It will be delightful to present each other's treasure for inspection & admiration & have a good "motherly" talk.' Once back home, Christabel got caught up for a couple of weeks in the whirl of Women's Party business so that she apologised profusely to Marion for not thanking her earlier for her warm hospitality. 'I have been here & there . . . & every day about to write to you to tell you how very much Betty and I enjoyed our stay with you.'[54] Such close female friendships that had helped to sustain and nourish Christabel during the suffrage campaign continued to be important to her, especially now that she and Marion shared alike the experience of being a single parent. But, as always, political work could impinge on such pleasures.

Thus during that early February, Christabel was busy writing two high-profile articles soon published in the *Daily Sketch*. The first was titled, '"If A Woman Were Premier!" Famous Suffragist Leader Shows How She Would Solve The Strike Crisis In Britain. Fewer Hours: Increased Output'. Christabel sent a copy to Bonar Law, assuring him of the 'readiness of the Women's Party' to help the Government and the country during this time of industrial difficulty.[55] A second article, 'Bolshevism's Menace To Women. Will Labour Leaders Repudiate Infamous Russian Doctrines – Blunders in Industrial Policy', appeared on 14 February.

Within a few weeks, Christabel had decided that the time was right to make an announcement: she would contest the Westminster Abbey constituency at the next general election, despite the fact that the present incumbent, William Burdett Coutts, a Conservative, had not stepped down but only stated that he was considering retiring, given his poor state of health. However, a new election campaign required more resources, and putting the Women's Party finances on a more stable footing proved problematic. Flora Drummond applied to the British Commonwealth Union for £3,130 to pay outstanding debts to the printers while Annie Kenny warned one of its key members, Sir Vincent Caillard, that the costs of the Women's Party (including the retention of its headquarters in London and £100 for salaries) were such that they would have to restrict their industrial campaign until they had Christabel's effective voice in Parliament.[56]

Patrick Hannon, the General Secretary of the British Commonwealth Union, was irritated by Flora Drummond's request. 'Our relations with the Women's Party here have been unsatisfactory beyond words', he complained in late March. 'We were rushed at a critical moment in the industrial situation some months ago into giving very substantial assistance, and that substantial assistance has been continued week by week up to the present.'[57] The British Commonwealth Union had tried, unsuccessfully, to impose certain conditions on the Women's Party in return for financial support, including the submission of statements of income, expenditure and policy for perusal, as well as receipt of proofs of each forthcoming issue of *Britannia* which had to be seen at least two days before publication, for its veto.[58] Much to Hannon's annoyance, Christabel had ignored the requests. 'We have been totally unable to get any information of any sort or kind from these women', he commented, 'and I have had to tell them this morning that unless Mrs. Drummond sees me to-day I shall be obliged, acting with the authority of my Committee, to stop supplies.' Hannon was enraged that Christabel and her supporters would not dance to his tune. '[T]he pretensions of Miss Pankhurst and her worshippers who surround her are becoming almost unbearable', he wrote angrily:

> I don't believe for one moment that Miss Pankhurst stands the ghost of a chance of being adopted as the official Unionist candidate for the Abbey Division, and whatever may be the future of women MPs I most earnestly hope for the sake of the peace and quiet of those who are now in the House that Miss Pankhurst will not be returned.[59]

Emmeline returned home from Paris that March of 1919, very excited about her daughter's prospects. 'We look upon Westminster as an ideal constituency for us to contest', she stated in a circular letter to supporters, as she pleaded for donations and workers. 'When John Stuart Mill introduced the question of Women's Suffrage in the House of Commons he was its Member; it is, therefore, historically fit that woman should represent this constituency now that the Cause he championed is won.'[60] But Emmeline, like Christabel, was fearful about the peace proceedings currently being conducted in Paris. Although peace had returned to the Western fronts, fighting was still being waged elsewhere, particularly in Russia where there was a civil war. Neither the old Russia nor the new Soviet Union had sent delegates to the talks over which the threat of a 'Bolshevik tide' hovered.[61] Further, it appeared that too much was being given away to the defeated enemy at the cost of weakening the alliance between Britain and France.

Christabel was determined to make her voice heard. 'Are We Forsaking France? Why Britain Must Be Loyal To Her Ally In Demanding Frontiers Essential To A World Peace' was the title of her article in the *Daily Sketch* on 4 April, the very day she travelled to Paris, accompanied by Flora Drummond, to seek to influence the peace proceedings. The following day, while staying at the Hotel Westend in the Champs Elysees, she wrote to Lloyd George saying she had come to the French capital specifically to see him:

> about the Peace discussions and public feeling at home. I hope that you can arrange to spare time <u>today</u> for a good long talk. I can tell you what is the point of view of those people who gave their loyalty and active support to you in your management of the War.[62]

It is doubtful whether the hard-pressed Lloyd George did meet up with Christabel but she did confer with some of the important delegates, including the Prime Minister of Australia, Billy Hughes, who wanted Germany to repay the estimated £364 million that the war had cost his country.

425

By 10 April Christabel was back in England, ready to give the first of a series of six talks as the prospective candidate for the Abbey Division of Westminster. The small Women's Party headquarters at William Street buzzed with activity so that it took over Christabel's top-floor flat, forcing her to find alternative temporary accommodation at a rented house nearby, at 6 South Street, where she stayed for just two months. 'There is no room for me at 4 William Street because of our ever-expanding political campaign', Christabel explained excitedly to Renee de Brimont. 'It makes life a bit too hectic to be always under the same roof as our office!'[63] Life was more leisurely during weekends spent at High Edser with Betty, socialising and tending to the vegetable plot. But now another blow fell.

Annie Kenney, Christabel's closest friend and a key fundraiser, was too tired to continue with Women's Party work. 'I was exhausted to death', recollected Annie. 'I had been on the social pilgrimage for fourteen years . . . For the first time in my life I yearned for death. I felt no bodily life would give me the rest I needed.'[64] Annie and her sister Jessie, still unable to help because of ill health, had never really settled in Tower Cressy and missed the comforts of their home in Mecklenburgh Square. '[W]e had nothing we could call our own', remembered Jessie, 'no flat, not many clothes and no money.' The two sisters decided they had to live their lives on their own terms, break temporarily with the Women's Party, and take a three-month trip abroad, to recuperate. 'Annie asked me to go down [to High Edser] and see Christabel to break the news, she simply could not do it', wrote Jessie many years later.[65] Christabel was deeply upset, but understood the reasons. Annie met up with her, for a long talk. They would always be the dearest of friends, even if they were no longer working together. 'My heart ached for Christabel as I was leaving her in the midst of a difficult situation', recorded the sad Annie, 'and yet had I stayed I could not have helped.'[66] By mid-May, Annie and Jessie were in touch with Frances Stevenson, Lloyd George's secretary and secret mistress, seeking testimonials that would ease their journeying to and around Europe. Frances, an 'ardent suffragist' who had attended WSPU meetings, commented that Miss Annie Kenney 'is well known to me'.[67]

That two of her oldest and closest friends were no longer by her side made Christabel feel very vulnerable. Jessie believed that without the old inner circle of the WSPU and then the Women's Party around her, Christabel was 'lost, and in some way, stifled by [her] mother's possessiveness'.[68] Certainly Emmeline was keener than the Women's Party candidate herself that she should be elected to Parliament. Christabel was taking a more realistic view of the situation and enjoying particularly the time spent in her own home, at Ewhurst. 'Mother will be here for Whitsuntide', she cheerfully informed Marion Wallace-Dunlop on 2 June, 'so if you could bring Wings over one day while she is with me it would be very nice.' Occasionally one or more of the three small children that Emmeline had adopted came to stay, to benefit from the healthy country air. 'Joan [Pembridge] has rejoined her two "sisters" [Kathleen King and Mary Gordon] in London & tomorrow they all go with Miss Pine to stay in Kent', Christabel continued, giving Marion all the latest family news. 'Joan grew tall & got much stronger during her stay here. Betty is growing & flourishing. Tomorrow is her fourth birthday.'[69]

On 16 June, Christabel was back in London again, speaking at the Caxton Hall. Shortly afterwards arrangements were made for the Women's Party to participate in a Women's Procession and Demonstration to be held in Trafalgar Square on Saturday, 28 June, as part of the Victory Loan Campaign.[70] But all the efforts of the Women's Party came to nothing. No by-election was called in the Westminster Abbey Division and worse, there was no money to support any future parliamentary candidature for Christabel. The British Commonwealth Union had stopped all financial contributions while donations from other supporters dried up. And it was only too apparent that Lloyd George, who had fallen out with Lord Northcliffe, was making no effort to 'push' Christabel into a political career.[71] The Women's Party faded away.

Christabel was shaken by the whole experience. She had spent all her adult years in the women's movement and been one of its key players. Now it all seemed to be crashing around her. Writing over twenty years later to Esther Greg, a former member of the Women's Party who had become a close friend, she reflected how she knew she had come 'to the end of my political days', something she might not have discovered but 'for the jolt I received at that time'. Elaborating further, Christabel reminisced how after the First World War she and her mother had been shunned by many for their patriotic stand so that the loyalty of old comrades became 'a very costly . . . & a risky thing' for those living in a world 'that wanted none of the two virtually exiled leaders & thus did not want any of their followers who were "too loyal" '.[72] The women's movement that had once focused on the struggle for the vote was now allying itself to a number of differing causes with which Christabel had little or no sympathy, including pleasurable sex within marriage, birth control, free love, socialism and pacifism.

In March 1918, Dr Marie Stopes, one-time member of the WSPU, had published *Married love*, a book that legitimised female sexual pleasure and gave ignorant husbands instructions how to bring it about. A sensational success, the book had reached its seventh edition by summer 1919.[73] The link between the suffragists of the NUWSS (now called the National Union of Societies for Equal Citizenship) and the Labour Party had been long standing while the Women's Freedom League had strong socialist leanings too. A pull towards socialism, communism and pacifism was evident among a number of other feminists, including Christabel's own sisters, Sylvia and Adela. Indeed, some of these women were scorning the 'spinsterly ideals' of the older generation of feminists.[74] Christabel and her mother with their attacks on socialism and Bolshevism, and their silence on the issue of birth control, were out of tune with the times. The *Daily News* had noted late in 1918 that 'the Pankhurst coterie has for some time been a spent force in Feminist circles', and it would appear to be so.[75]

With the collapse of the Women's Party, both Christabel and Emmeline lost their small salaries as its co-leaders and key speakers. To this unwelcome situation was added the financial burden of Tower Cressy. It was decided to present the latter to the National Children Adoption Association of which Princess Alice was a patron. Christabel long contemplated her own future. She knew she could write and that there was a demand, in some of the press, for what she had to say and so hoped to support herself and little Betty, at least for a short time, by such means. The sixty-year-old Emmeline, on the other hand, knowing that at her age she would not find employment in Britain, planned for that autumn another lucrative lecture tour of North America – and other economies. She gave up her London home and brought Kathleen, Joan and Mary to live, temporarily, at High Edser. During the summer, Ethel Smyth came to visit the family and, having been a tomboy in her childhood, was horrified to see the Pankhurst children at tea time dancing in an affected manner. They 'flitted about like fairies, offered you scones with a curtsey, and kissed their hands to you when they left the room'. Ethel had assumed that Christabel had taught the children these airs and graces but, after conversing with Emmeline, suspected that she was the culprit.[76]

That August of 1919, to help ease the congestion at High Edser, Christabel took her small daughter on a seaside holiday, to Looe in Cornwall. Initially Christabel and Betty lodged for two weeks at 'Halycon', with a Mrs Brown. 'At this present moment I am by the sea – to celebrate, if you will, this great <u>Peace</u> which I hope will prove to be worthy of its name', she wrote apprehensively to Renee de Brimont on 6 August 1919. Christabel feared, unlike the statesmen of their respective countries, that a 'Russo-German peril' was bound to emerge in the future. 'Our Prime Minister knows very well what Mother & I & the rest of us think on the subject.' Nonetheless, comfort could be found 'in the belief that Dieu est avec nous [God is with us] . . . Certainly if we had to trust <u>only</u> in the wisdom of our rulers we might feel rather pessimistic'. Thanking Renee de Brimont for writing to her on 14 July, the anniversary of the fall of the Bastille, Christabel closed her letter with warm expressions of their friendship. 'And how are you my dear friend whom I think of always with so much affection. Are you ever coming to see us?'[77]

That very same day, Christabel penned another letter, this time focusing on domestic rather than international issues, to another female friend whom she persistently addressed as 'Miss Wallace-Dunlop'. 'Our lodging looks on to the river & mill pond & wooded slopes & we get lovely reflections in the evening', she wrote contentedly from Looe:

> There is good safe bathing & there are delightful excursions to be made by river, sea & land. We find ourselves in the ideal, old fashioned seaside place – with no 'attractions' except the right ones. You can imagine how Betty blooms in these conditions. There is nothing like the sea once a year.

However, the high price of food in Cornwall was a cause for concern. 'Vegetables being scarce here & very dear, we get them sent by parcel post from High Edser but this supply is scanty & we are having, and were having before we left, very disappointing results.'[78] For the third week of their stay, the holidaymakers moved to another address 'Glenrise', on West Looe Hill, where they lodged with a Mrs Smith. 'We are still at Looe but at a different address as we got the other place for a fortnight only', Christabel explained. Sympathising with Marion's difficulties in finding good domestic help, she advised her to peruse the pages of The Lady – and gratefully accepted the offer of some fresh honey. 'I . . . will let you know on our return when we shd like to go over & fetch it in Betty's "Pram". Hope you will have luck in your search for a domestic angel.'[79]

By the time Christabel had returned to High Edser, Emmeline was busy preparing for her voyage. Knowing that they would soon be oceans apart, Christabel and Emmeline had already taken the precautionary measure of each making their wills which stated that, subject to the payment of funeral expenses and debts, the estate of each was bequeathed to the other who was also appointed the executrix.[80] Kathleen, Joan and Mary were taken back to Tower Cressy, to be looked after there until Emmeline returned to England with enough money to support them and herself. In September, accompanied by Catherine Pine, the sixty-one-year-old Emmeline sailed for the USA and Canada, not envisaging that she would be obliged to remain continuously at work for some six years. Christabel put her own financial affairs in order. Since she could no longer afford the rent of High Edser, she had to give up the cottage. For the next ten months she led a nomadic life as she too struggled to make ends meet, staying in the homes of various friends and relatives, eking out an existence for herself and Betty.

By early December 1919, Christabel was staying in Chipping Ongar, Essex. 'Betty is with me & flourishes exceedingly', she told 'Miss' Wallace-Dunlop. 'How is Wings?'[81] A number of old suffrage friends, including Sybil Rhondda, Kitty Marshall, Elsie Bowerman, Lady Constance Lytton, Ada Wright, Barbara Wylie and May Billinghurst, knowing of the financial plight of Christabel and her mother, set about, in confidence, to raise a testimonial fund in recognition of their service to the women's cause and to the nation:

> It is to the policy which they initiated, and to the inspiration of their leadership that we owe the ultimate granting of votes to women, and it is felt that not only members of the W.S.P.U. but many others will be glad to have an opportunity of showing their grateful appreciation of this fact.[82]

The situation was all the more poignant since, on 28 November, Viscountess Nancy Astor had been elected by a huge majority as the Coalition MP for the Sutton constituency of Plymouth. A woman who had never been active in the women's suffrage campaign or known for her feminist activities, Nancy Astor was an outsider, an American, who had been elected on the strength of her husband's achievement when, on the death of his father, he had been elevated to the House of Lords. Nancy herself seemed to acknowledge the injustice of the situation since she said that the first woman to take her seat in the Commons should have been Millicent Fawcett or Christabel herself.[83]

The testimonial fund raised just £3,000 rather than the hoped-for £10,000. More than half of this was spent on buying and furnishing a country house in Westwood Ho!, a seaside village near Bideford, Devon, where Christabel and Betty were living by the summer of 1920. The rest of the fund was sent to Emmeline in North America. Some of Christabel's supporters were of the view that she would come 'to the front again' and 'get into Parliament'.[84] But it was not to be. Nor did Christabel stay long at Westward Ho! which neither she nor her mother could afford to maintain. It was soon let and then sold. On Christmas Day 1920 Christabel was staying at Graffham, West Sussex, in a cottage lent to her by a Mrs Peters. 'I quite understand & valued your kindness about wanting me to be with you', she wrote pensively to Marion Wallace-Dunlop. 'But it really is best in the circumstances to have one's own quiet Christmas . . . I could not have added much to the gaiety of matrons I fear.'[85] When Marion questioned why the general public seemed so ignorant about the part the WSPU had played in winning the vote, Christabel replied:

> From my personal point of view I don't mind, but for the sake of wom-en's moral backbones if nothing else, the truth ought to be known and admitted, & ought to go down in prosperity who will certainly think the emancipation of British women . . . a fact of greater importance than most of the other facts of history.[86]

Throughout her lifetime, Christabel never wavered in her view that it was the suffragettes of the WSPU who had won the vote and that it was herself and her mother who had led them to victory.

Now forty years old and untrained for any profession, despite her First Class Honours degree in law, the worried Christabel had to find employment. She was too old – and not rich enough – to take up a legal career and other openings were few and far between, despite the passing of the 1919 Sex Disqualification Removal Act. On 19 January 1921 the following advertisement was found in the personal column of the *Times* – 'Miss Christabel Pankhurst (owing to the victorious ter-mination of her leadership in the Cause of Women's Political Enfranchisement) seeks remunerative non-political work.'

That very day Christabel wrote to Marion Wallace-Dunlop from a differ-ent address, 122 Ashley Gardens, Westminster. 'I am staying in Sybil Lady Rhondda's flat which she has lent me while I am looking out for the "job" I am so widely advised to "get" & I have advertised for this job', she wrote sarcastically. Despondent about the lack of a private income which would allow her to take up a political career, she commented, 'The next "Christabel" who comes along will really have to build up her own personal position <u>before</u> she takes to politics & gives her <u>later</u> years to a cause.' The main comfort seemed to be her little daughter. 'Betty is quite well, happy & comfortable here.'[87] Unfortunately, the advertisement brought in nothing suitable or permanent. Christabel turned down several offers from film companies as well as a more bizarre one, from a music hall artiste who offered her the grand sum of £20 a week or £5 a performance if she would become the 'victim' in his sawing-through-a woman act.[88]

Christabel was still in close touch with Lord Northcliffe and now, with Grace Roe by her side, he came to the rescue, offering her a second series of articles, this time in the *Weekly Dispatch*. 'I have undertaken some writing which means that I must first go quietly away & surround myself with papers & absorb myself in my task for some months', she wrote apologetically to Marion on 22 January 1921. 'So there it is and we shan't be meeting for a bit.'[89] But life did not continue without a few interruptions. On 4 February Annie Kenney, who had married Jim Taylor on 24 April the previous year, safely gave birth by caesarean section to a son, Warwick Kenney Taylor. The anxious Christabel, staying at the Abinger Hatch Hotel, Abinger, near Dorking, Surrey, was overjoyed when she heard the news since Annie's health was not robust. She wrote back immediately, with warm congratulations:

My dearest Annie

I am very happy to have your news & to know that your son and you are both well. He will be a great joy to you now & always and you have much to give him – not only the gifts you have unconsciously handed on to him but also the training that your past experience has fitted you to give him . . . Take care of yourself & your health so that you can be more to him . . .

With my best love
C. P.[90]

Christabel visited Annie and Warwick as soon as possible, in between focusing on her articles which were mainly about the suffragette movement and would appear weekly, from 3 April, and number eight in all.[91] On 1 March 1921, now staying at 2 The Esplanade, Seaford, East Sussex, she wrote another affectionate letter to Annie, asking for her comments on the draft of an essay she had written about her flight to Paris in 1912:

If you find that any facts or reflections come spontaneously to your mind, they will be very welcome but I don't want you to force yourself in any way . . . I hope your precious son is going forward as well as ever you could hope & that you are gaining strength too.[92]

It is the first article that Christabel wrote for the *Weekly Dispatch*, titled 'Why I never married', that is the most reflective and revealing of the series. One of the 'surplus' women who survived after the slaughter of men in the trenches in the First World War, the forty-year-old Christabel explained that she had not married because the women's movement had demanded her absolute concentration and her followers would have felt deserted if she had taken a husband. Further, if she had married, the Government 'would have persuaded themselves that a husband's influence would in the end prevail and weaken my militant purpose'. A husband too would have felt neglected 'as mine would have been', and been exposed to retaliation in respect of his wife's militancy. The birth of any children from such a union would have made suffrage work difficult. Besides, the community of women in the WSPU were her family:

> [I]n a sense the women were my children. Children indeed they seemed to me who was born a pioneer, in advance of the time . . . I always felt so motherly towards them and took a mother's pride in seeing them develop and gain confidence through working in our wonderful movement.[93]

Although the work of the suffragettes had increased the happiness of many marriages, because it had awakened in women and in men a new and greater respect for women, 'we unmarried women have also our importance', insisted Christabel, as she offered a robust defence of the celibate single life. Challenging the common assumption that spinsters were unhappy creatures because they lacked a husband and children, she claimed instead that unmarried women had the most time and perhaps the most heart to give to the care of the sick, the friendless and social reform generally. The unselfish work of Florence Nightingale and Edith Cavell were but two examples. Nuns who made vows of celibacy and devoted themselves to a secluded religious life were honoured just as those:

> of us who, without making formal vows of celibacy, live up to the same ideals and, because it has not been our destiny to marry and found a family, live singly in dignified happiness and usefulness, content if we can leave the world even a little better than we found it.[94]

Christabel dismissed as 'ridiculous' the question she had sometimes been asked: whether she was a man-hater. Displaying her radical feminist credentials, she pointed out that in *The great scourge* she had merely advocated that the cure for VD and prostitution was a pure and equal moral standard for both men and women. Reflecting on her past life, she continued:

> Looking back I consider it has been worth while to sacrifice other interests and joys – romance included – to public duty! . . . I could have done no other, the whole force of my nature having urged me to that course I took. One can but fulfil one's destiny, and that I have done. Done it with joy too. For I have always declared and believed myself to be the luckiest person in the world and the happiest.[95]

She had seen women develop powers they hardly knew and had achieved what she set out to do: win the parliamentary vote for her sex. Nor did she subscribe to the commonly held view that spinsters were emotionally unfilled. 'I have known passion, that strengthens one for endurance, makes the heart swell, shakes on with its mighty force, makes humans god-like, fills them with creative fire. The passion of my life has been for the freeing of women.' This was not just for political and economic reasons. 'I always knew that such a fight as ours had its highest significance elsewhere – was simply the dim reflection of a far struggle on some celestial battlefield where greater hosts than ours clashed in the eternal struggle for Right.'[96] Ethel Smyth had always believed that in Christabel she saw 'a born bachelor'.[97] 'Why I never married' is certainly a celebration of the celibate single life.

Christabel ended her article on 'Why I never married' by noting that having lived a life of 'inspiration' meant to wake every morning, 'thanking God for the new day and for the work to be done in it'.[98] That was an acknowledgement, highly visible in the press, that she had become a Christian, a change in her life that only her mother and now a few close friends knew about. With the proceeds from her articles in the *Weekly Dispatch* and a share of the monies from the sale of the house at Westward Ho!, Christabel decided to visit her mother in Canada, where Emmeline had settled, and also to spend some time in California, a place she had always wanted to visit. Grace Roe, who did not agree with Christabel's conversion to Second Adventism but nonetheless greatly admired all Christabel had done for women, agreed to accompany her.[99]

During late July 1921, just before she was packing for her trip to North America, Christabel saw an advertisement for the monthly meeting of the Advent Testimony Movement, a conservative evangelical organisation that proclaimed the imminent return of Christ. She decided to make contact with like-minded people. 'I went to the Kingsway Hall, and got in just in time to hear Dr. Meyer.'[100] Dr Meyer, a Baptist, chair of the Advent Testimony Movement, a director of the evangelical newspaper the *Christian*, and the most prominent conservative evangelical in England, also had wide contacts in North America, including influence with the evangelical publishing house Morgan and Scott with whom Christabel was later to publish. As Larsen observes, he was an 'ideal person' to serve as Christabel's 'sponsor'.[101]

Notes

1 T. Larsen, *Christabel Pankhurst: fundamentalism and feminism in coalition* (Woodbridge, Boydell Press, 2002), pp. 36–7; D. Todman, *The Great War: myth and memory* (London, Hambledon, 2005), p. 44 notes that overall, ten million people had died, one tenth of whom were the war dead for Britain and her Empire.
2 CP, '*The Lord Cometh': the world crisis explained* (London, Morgan & Scott, 1923), p. 13.
3 APW, The philosophy of the suffragette movement, p. 12.
4 EP to M. A. R. Tuker, 11 March 1915, TWL. Thanks to Jacqueline deVries for this reference.

433

5 Larsen, *Christabel*, p. 24.
6 EP, To win the peace, *Britannia*, 22 November 1918, p. 203.
7 CP, The candidate's speech, *Britannia*, 22 November 1918, p. 205.
8 *Britannia*, 22 November 1918, pp. 206–7.
9 Lloyd George to Bonar Law, 21 November 1918, LG Papers.
10 CP to Lloyd George, 21 November 1916, LG Papers.
11 *Britannia*, 6 December 1918, p. 219.
12 *Times*, 28 November 1918.
13 Bonar Law to Miss Pankhurst, 23 November 1918, LG Papers.
14 Kenney, *Memories*, pp. 286–7.
15 Northcliffe to Mr Sutherland, 31 October 1918, LG Papers.
16 Notes from the unpublished memories of the late P. G. Hosgood taken by David Mitchell, July 1975, DMC; quote from *Britannia*, 6 December 1918, p. 218.
17 *Britannia*, 6 December 1918, p. 218.
18 Covers of *Britannia*, 22 and 29 November 1918.
19 *Britannia*, 6 December 1918, p. 219; *Smethwick Telephone*, 7 December 1918, p. 3.
20 Joan Dugdale to Una Duval, 14 December [1918], Purvis Collection.
21 Kenney, *Memories*, p. 287; P. J. Hannon, General Secretary of the BCU to Miss Jessie Kenney, 29 November 1918, Patrick Hannon Papers, HLRO.
22 Miss Pankhurst's Election Address, General Election December 14th, 1918, leaflet published by E. E. Bowerman, Smethwick, n.d., Kenney Papers.
23 *Smethwick Telephone*, 7 December 1918.
24 *Weekly Dispatch*, quoted in *Britannia*, 6 December 1918, p. 222.
25 *Daily Mail*, 6 December 1918.
26 Mary Kenney [niece of Annie and Jessie], to Miss Raeburn, 21 June 1965, Raeburn Collection.
27 *Smethwick Telephone*, 7 December 1918.
28 *Smethwick Telephone*, 30 November 1918.
29 *Britannia*, 29 November 1918, p. 212.
30 *Smethwick Telephone*, 14 December and 30 November 1918.
31 Mitchell, *Women on the warpath*, pp. 369–70; Purvis, *Emmeline Pankhurst*, p. 313.
32 CP to Jessie Kenney, 29 November 1918, Kenney Papers.
33 Jessie Kenney Notes, n.d., Miscellaneous papers, Kenney Papers, Box KP5.
34 Miss Christabel Pankhurst's Election Address to the Absent Voters of Smethwick, *Britannia*, 20 November 1918, p. 211.
35 See *Daily Mirror*, 9 and 12 December 1918; *Daily Sketch*, 9 December 1918.
36 *Daily Sketch*, 7 December 1918.
37 Joan Dugdale to Una Duval, 14 December 1918, Purvis Collection.
38 *Britannia*, 13 December 1918.
39 *Smethwick Telephone*, 14 December 1918.
40 *Daily Mail*, cited in *Britannia*, 6 December 1918, p. 222.
41 Mary Hilson, Women voters and the rhetoric of patriotism in the British general election of 1918, *Women's History Review*, 10, 2001, p. 334.
42 *Times* and *Smethwick Telephone*, 14 December 1918.
43 *Times*, 14 December 1918.
44 Joan Dugdale to Una Duval, 14 December 1918, Purvis Collection.
45 Mary Kenney to Miss Raeburn, 21 June 1965, Raeburn Collection.
46 Dennis Barker, Pankhurst at the polls, *Guardian*, 30 September 1964.
47 Interview with Jessie Kenney, 24 March 1964, DMC.
48 Smyth, *Female pipings*, p. 246.
49 Statement by E. E. Bowerman, 11 October 1964, DMC.
50 *Daily Sketch*, 30 December 1918.
51 Annie Kenney to Sir Vincent Caillard, 27 January 1919, Hannon Papers.

52 Pugh, *The Pankhursts*, p. 351 notes that during 1919 thirty-five million working days were lost compared with five and a half million in 1918.
53 Muriel Wortham (nee Cook) to David Mitchell, 11 August and 16 October 1975, DMC.
54 CP to Miss Wallace-Dunlop, 7 and 25 February 1919, WDFA.
55 *Daily Sketch*, 7 February 1919; CP to Bonar Law, 7 February 1919, Bonar Law Papers.
56 Women's Party, Memo for General Purposes Committee, n.d. and Annie Kenney to Sir Vincent, 27 January 1919, Hannon Papers.
57 Patrick Hannon to Manville, 21 March 1919, Hannon Papers.
58 Memorandum, Relations with Women's Party, 23 January 1919, Hannon Papers.
59 Patrick Hannon to Manville, 21 March 1919, Hannon Papers.
60 Form letter from EP to Dear Friend, The Women's Party headed notepaper, n.d., Purvis Collection.
61 Zara Stenier, The peace settlement, in *The Oxford illustrated history of the First World War*, ed H. Strachan, p. 291.
62 CP to Lloyd George, 5 April 1919, LG Papers.
63 CP to Renee de Brimont, n.d., de Brimont Papers; Mitchell, *Queen Christabel*, p. 278.
64 Kenney, *Memories*, p. 288.
65 Jessie Kenney notes, The three phases of the pioneer, Kenney Papers, KP5.
66 Kenney, *Memories*, p. 288.
67 Ffion Hague, *The pain and the privilege: the women in Lloyd George's life* (London, Harper, 2008), p. 164; F. L. Stevenson to Private Secretary Sir Rennell Rodd, British Embassy, Rome, 16 May 1919, Kenney Papers.
68 Interview with Jessie Kenney, 2 July 1965, DMC.
69 CP to Marion Wallace-Dunlop, 2 June 1919, WDFA.
70 C. Wilbraham Ford, 12 June 1919 and 24 June 1919, to Dear Madam and Dear Friend, respectively, Hugh Franklin-Elsie Duval Papers, TWL.
71 Interview with Grace Roe, 22 September 1965, DMC.
72 CP to Esther Greg, Easter Day 1938 and 12 March 1928, Purvis Collection.
73 M. Carmichael Stopes, *Married love: a new contribution to the solution of sexual difficulties* (London, Putnam's Sons, 1918).
74 Mitchell, *Queen Christabel*, pp. 278–9.
75 *Daily News*, 9 December 1918.
76 Smyth, *Female pipings*, pp. 248–9.
77 CP to Renee de Brimont, 6 August 1919, de Brimont Papers.
78 CP to Miss Wallace-Dunlop, 6 August 1919, WDFA.
79 CP to Miss Wallace-Dunlop, 13 August [1919], WDFA.
80 Wills of Emmeline and Christabel Pankhurst, 23 July 1919, former in Principal Probate Registry, London, copy of latter in Purvis Collection.
81 CP to Miss Wallace-Dunlop, 5 December 1919, WDFA.
82 Sybil Rhondda *et al.*, Testimonial letter, n.d. [December 1919?], DMC; see A.V. John, *Turning the tide: the life of Lady Rhondda* (Cardigan, Parthian, 2013), p. 381.
83 C. Sykes, *Nancy: the life of Lady Astor* (London, Collins, 1972), pp. 190–1.
84 Mrs Cameron Swan quoted in Vida Goldstein to Adela Pankhurst, 7 July 1902, APWP.
85 CP to Miss Wallace-Dunlop [Christmas 1920?], WDFA.
86 CP to Miss Wallace-Dunlop, 8 January 1921, WDFA.
87 CP to Miss Wallace-Dunlop, 19 January 1921, WDFA.
88 Mitchell, *Queen Christabel*, p. 283.
89 CP to Miss Wallace-Dunlop, 22 January 1921, WDFA.
90 CP to Annie Kenney, 4 February 1921, Kenney Papers.
91 CP, Why I never married, *Weekly Dispatch*, 3 April 1921, and subsequently mainly weekly, My war chest: how we gathered and spent £100,000, 10 April; Politicians I have met: tussles and flattery, 17 April; 'Cat and Mouse' days: our friendly war with the police: the men we liked: their raids and ours, 1 May; My escape to Paris: a night in hiding, 8 May; Young

jurywoman and unsavoury cases, 15 May; Turning the vote to good account, 22 May; How I held audiences, 29 May.

92 CP to Annie Kenney, 1 March 1921, Kenney Papers.
93 CP, Why I never married, p. 7. This article was written many years before marriage between same-sex couples became legal in the UK.
94 CP, Why I never married, p. 7.
95 CP, Why I never married, p. 7.
96 CP, Why I never married, p. 7.
97 Smyth, *Female pipings*, p. 253.
98 CP, Why I never married, p. 7.
99 Grace Roe interview, 22 September 1965, DMC.
100 *Christian*, 16 September 1926, p. 5.
101 Larsen, *Christabel*, p. 24.

20

SECOND ADVENTIST MINISTRY
August 1921–end of June 1928

On 7 August 1921, Christabel, Betty and Grace arrived on the steamer *Magantic* in Montreal, Canada en route to Victoria, on Vancouver Island, where Emmeline was now living in a rented one-storey house, 1428 Beach Drive, Oak Bay. Christabel explained to the eager press that she had come to Canada only for a holiday and had no plans to address meetings, although she hoped to gather information about the possibilities for British women in Canada. One reporter, knowing of Christabel's worldwide reputation as an 'intrepid and fearless leader who drove the ingenuity of Scotland Year to the utmost', was surprised by her feminine, youthful appearance – 'graceful girlish figure, merry blue eyes . . . a musical well-modulated voice, and curly brown hair'.[1] Although Christabel said that the question which now most interested her was the abolition of poverty, the conversation inevitably turned to women's suffrage.

None of the wild fears that anti-suffragists had raised when women got the vote had come about, Christabel insisted, and in Quebec, where women still did not have the provincial vote, the situation would right itself in time. The methods of the militant suffragettes in England were a 'disagreeable necessity' because England, before the war, was such an 'intensely conservative' country. Men and women now had votes and what they had to do was 'to forget old grievances and work together in a spirit of co-operation for the new future that lies in front of them'.[2] From now till the summer of 1940, Christabel led a nomadic life before finally settling in the USA.

There was great excitement when Christabel, Grace and Betty finally arrived at 1428 Beach Drive. Victoria, a small city of about 38,000 inhabitants, with its English-looking homes set close to the sea, complete with tennis courts and neatly tended gardens, was considered the most British of all the Canadian cities. About one year earlier, Emmeline had finally saved enough money to bring Kathleen, Joan and Mary out to Canada and so the children were particularly delighted to meet up again with their 'sister', the six-year-old, auburn-haired Betty. At a time when North America was at the height of a 'Red Scare', the popular Emmeline had been earning a living lecturing on a range of topics, particularly Anti-Bolshevism, sometimes addressing crowds of 70,000. In April 1921 she had taken a new post as a lecturer on social hygiene for the Canadian

National Council for Combating Venereal Diseases and by mid-October was to be lecturing in Toronto.[3] Christabel, Grace and Betty stayed in Victoria for just over two months before all three travelled to California. As devoted as she was to her mother, Christabel did not want to join her in her 'social purity' campaigning but to forge her own independent path, talking, writing and evangelising about her religious faith. Like Grace Roe, Emmeline was not particularly enthusiastic about this new direction in Christabel's life but she loved her daughter enough to understand.

Once in California, Christabel, Grace and Betty stayed first in Santa Barbara and then rented a cottage called 'The Little Mission', in the Hollywood Hills. Alma Whitaker, a leading reporter for the *Los Angeles Times*, interviewed Christabel here in late November and was surprised to find that the former militant suffragette who had once shaken the British establishment was now 'sweetly passive, gently neutral'. The once stormy petrel had 'metamorphosed into almost a Jane Austen heroine . . . I expect to see her taking to tatting and fine embroidery. I feel sure she darns Crystal's [Betty's] stockings and sews her buttons on'. When Christabel, dressed in flowered georgette with a pink sash, was pressed about solutions to the world problems, she emphasised the importance of 'understanding and co-operation' for which 'religion is so necessary'.[4]

Rallying wonderfully in the warm Californian sunshine, the renowned British suffragette was courted not only by the press. Christabel turned down offers to play herself in a film, and 'was absolutely against it', much to Grace's regret.[5] The expanding Hollywood movie business held no appeal for her. Constantly invited out to speak, especially to the wealthy women's clubs, Grace arranged the engagements, introducing the celebrity to her admiring audiences. Although Christabel might talk about feminism and past suffrage battles, as she did at the influential Friday Morning Club in Los Angeles, she wanted to move on, carve out a new life, say something about her conversion to Second Adventism.[6] 'She always brought in her Second Coming message', recollected Grace, 'perhaps right at the end after a survey of world affairs, and it did not always go down well . . . I could hardly bear to listen to her, it was so awful for me. But I didn't see why if Christabel wanted to do it, she shouldn't do it'.[7] Keen to make contact with like-minded Christians, Christabel was soon writing to Dr Meyer, asking for his help. This was not an unusual request given that religious fundamentalism was flourishing in the USA, particularly in Los Angeles.[8]

In January 1922, Emmeline moved to Toronto at the request of the Canadian National Council for Combating Venereal Diseases, which had its headquarters there. Initially she rented a house in St George Street and then moved to 78 Charles Street West.[9] Cherishing the idea that Christabel would live with her again, she wrote to her eldest daughter, asking her to join the family. Christabel was happy to accept, although she pointed out that, first of all, she had to honour various speaking engagements. In April and May Christabel was back in Victoria, giving talks at Canadian Women's Clubs on topics such as the rights of women and the suffragette movement, and Christianity and the social order.[10]

Since she never earned much from the collections taken at such events, Grace and other supporters always made sure she was never out of pocket. Yet, despite being in Canada, Christabel never forgot her old friends in England, such as Annie Kenney and Rangeley Stride, and still kept in touch with them. Perhaps such continuity helped her to cope with her rootlessness. Thus in April she replied to the questioning Annie, reassuring her that since they had both accomplished what they set out to do, 'to move on', in a different direction, was the right path:

> To have had a great interest and inspiration was a happiness that lasted many years. It would not have lasted for ever, and mercifully our task was fulfilled and we were set free. You, my true friend and helper of past years, I send my thanks and love.[11]

Vancouver was the next place that Christabel visited. And while staying here she had a tremendous surprise: she had not heard from Emmeline Pethick-Lawrence since she and her husband had been ousted from the WSPU in 1912 and now, out-of-the-blue, a letter appeared from this once close friend. Emmeline Pethick-Lawrence, a Christian who had always emphasised that the fight for the vote involved women's spiritual as well as political enfranchisement, was keen to make contact with the 'reborn' Christabel. Christabel was overjoyed to hear from her. Her reply, dated 4 May 1922, is couched in warm and loving words:

> Dearest,
>
> Your letter filled me with joy. In an instant ten years were gone and they have never been. Our love united us all the time and only the surface of it was moved . . . It was like your generous heart to write. I am so glad you did. All that morning we (Grace Roe and I) had been joggling along in motor stages and interurban trains through a lovely bit of Washington State and the thought of you and Godfather and our wonderful years of work together came to me so strongly and remained with me and for a long time I talked to Grace of it . . . Then we arrived at Bellingham and when I entered the hotel a letter was put into my hand. I knew the writing at once! I can only say again with what joy I read it . . . The envelope was so frayed and covered with hotel redirection . . . it might so easily have been lost . . . All the more must I let you know by telegram safely and at once that I had the dear letter & that my heart met yours in all you said.

Christabel went on to explain how she had had great experiences, inward rather than outward, and been unhappy. But that was all past. She was thankful that she had learnt many lessons and now had 'a real freedom of spirit' that she never knew before. 'I depended too much upon humanity – upon myself and other people. One has to find the bed-rock. And these turning points in one's life always &

only come after a time of inward stress. Rebirth is painful.' Now she was absorbed in 'viewing the great world situation' and was convinced 'that Jesus Christ will come again and that soon . . . Dear Godfather, give him a big message from me. With all my love – your same Christabel'.[12]

Christabel probably told her mother that she had heard from Mrs Lawrence when, in early summer 1922, she, Grace and Betty finally arrived at Charles Street West. Like her sisters, Betty was taught to memorise her new address, something in which the girls were always instructed, in case they got lost. Emmeline was released from lecturing for the National Council during the summer so that she could speak on social hygiene in the smaller, Western Canadian settlements on the Chautauqua circuit and, to her great delight, Christabel agreed to accompany her. It was like old times for daughter and mother to be together, sharing stories about the past. Travelling by car, Emmeline and Christabel began their tour at the small community at Admiral, Saskatchewan, and completed it at The Pas, Manitoba, where the railway ended and many Indians and prospectors gathered to take the river road to the wilderness.[13] Although the trip was pleasant, it was good to be back home again, away from all the bustle, in Charles Street West. '[W]e had a quiet home and were happy in Toronto, city of churches, trees, and kind hearts', Christabel reflected.[14] There was plenty to interest her, including making new friends and keeping in touch with old ones. 'I still have a letter to write to you, & meant it to be a longer, fuller one than this, replying to what you said about "base materialism", but opportunity for that seems lacking at this moment', she penned Marion Wallace-Dunlop on 25 October. Enclosing details about the Advent Preparation Movement which held monthly meetings at the Kingsway Hall, London, Christabel pointed out that its adherents believed that the present age would end and that Jesus Christ would return.[15] Involvement in Second Adventism was increasingly taking up her time.

News had spread among North American conservative evangelicals that Christabel Pankhurst, the famous suffragette, had converted to their cause – and was a remarkable speaker. The Rev. J. G. Inkster, the minister of the evangelical, large and powerful Knox Presbyterian Church in Toronto, asked her if she would give a sermon. Initially Christabel refused, feeling she needed more time for communing with the Lord before taking up 'public service again'.[16] But Inkster prevailed, and Christabel eventually consented. Her first sermon, preached on 12 November 1922, drew such great crowds that the doors were closed long before the service began. Discussing the text 'Without Me ye can do nothing', Christabel told how these words had changed her life. In pre-war days she believed that the emancipation of women would settle the world's difficulties, and that man-made laws were at fault rather than human nature. But early in 1918, when the Allies were in despair, she had a vision of the reality behind the Great War, that the lust, greed, hatred and bitterness produced by it would continue until nations were at peace with God and with each other. In simple words of 'passionate eloquence', noted the local press, Miss Pankhurst told of her study of the Bible, of her finding Christ as her Saviour, of her unquestioning faith in the absolute accuracy of the Scriptures, of her vision of the world as it was in God's sight, and of her certain conviction of the coming again of Christ as the hope and solution to the world's problems.[17]

Such a message may have been particularly welcomed by many residents in Toronto as Christmas drew near, a time when the Pankhurst household itself received some more earthly news. Early that December, the balance from the sale of the house at Westward Ho! in Devon was finally sent to Emmeline. Such welcome news enabled a move to a larger rented house at 76 St Mary Street, in time for Christmas. That Christmas of 1922, as usual, a big Christmas tree was bought for the children who were very excited since it was only at Christmas and birthdays they received presents. 'At Christmas, Christabel was, of course, very religious', remembered Kathleen, the eldest of Emmeline's adopted daughters. 'When I said I had read most of the Bible . . . she was so delighted.' The eight-year-old Kathleen used to borrow Aunty Kate's Bible 'which had a lot of notes at the bottom of the page and lovely maps. That is what made me read the Bible, because I had the maps and I could follow the trips where these people went'.[18] Neither Christabel nor Emmeline, however, attempted to influence the children's religious views, although Aunty Kate did teach them their prayers. Bible stories that were learnt by heart were taught as history, rather than as religion.[19]

Christabel and Betty, or Elizabeth as the girls always called her, went with Emmeline, Kathleen, Mary and Joan to the theatre that winter, to see the famous Russian ballerina Anna Pavlova, and to the pantomime where, between the acts, two clowns played games with an umbrella and sausages. The family, who always sat in a box at the theatre, also went to the circus where the children were thrilled to be given gas-filled balloons. On another occasion, when the children were at home, they came across an old photograph album with Emmeline and Christabel in prison clothing. Aunty Kate hastily took the album from them, explaining nothing about the suffragette past about which the girls knew nothing. Catherine Pine's care for the children was now complemented by the services of a daily Scottish governess, Mrs Jean Cookson. 'We were told we must be very good to her because she only had one arm', recollected Kathleen. 'She lost her left arm in a skating accident. Of course we tried, but it did not last long.'[20]

Such happy family times refreshed Christabel who was delighted, after her successful debut at Knox Presbyterian Church, to be asked to deliver more Sunday evening addresses, seven in all. The freshness and earnestness of her testimony was admired by many. Several visiting ministers, among them two theological professors, expressed their admiration for 'the gifts of the speaker and her unique method of presenting truth, but wondered chiefly at the speaker's wonderful knowledge of the Scriptures'.[21]

Christabel was now beginning her second career, as a Second Adventist minister. Over the next thirty years or so, until her death in 1958, she became an enormously popular preacher, writer and evangelist in both North America and Britain. She wrote six popular books (which ran into reprints) on biblical

441

prophecy – 'The Lord cometh': the world crisis explained, first published in 1923, Pressing problems of the closing age in 1924 (with some minor changes this book was published for the American market under the title Some modern problems in the light of Bible prophecy), The world's unrest: visions of the dawn, first published in 1926, Seeing the future in 1929, and The uncurtained future in 1940.[22] Additionally, Christabel published innumerable articles in the evangelical press and, from 25 November 1926 to 12 May 1927, wrote a weekly column for the Christian news-paper, twenty-five articles in total under the general heading of 'On the Watch Tower. Signs of the Lord's Return'. From 1925 to 1941 she was a regular con-tributor to the Sunday School Times, the articles she penned being advertised in advance with a special deal for new subscribers. In 1934, she edited and wrote the articles for her own free journal, Present & Future, not as a commercial enter-prise but as a means to make her voice heard in public debate. As Larsen notes, Christabel Pankhurst, who repeatedly preached from the pulpits of some of the most important churches in major cities in North America and Britain, was num-bered among the elite on the fundamentalist platforms as well as the great annual Bible conferences that brought thousands of the faithful together. Her ministry was held in high regard by an 'impressive array of the most well-respected leaders of fundamentalism at that time, as well as by innumerable rank-and-file support-ers of the movement'.[23]

While Christabel was beginning her career as a minister, her sisters were going in differing directions. By early 1923 Adela had had her third child, a second daughter, and had rejected communism, Marxism and the Soviet Union, although she remained committed to socialism and unionism.[24] Sylvia too had left the Communist Party, having been forced to do so in September 1921.[25] For Sylvia, a lifelong atheist, Christabel's embrace of religion was incompre-hensible, merely a search for a 'solution of this world's problems by cataclysmic supernatural means'.[26] In her influential The suffragette movement, she notes that their father would often say to his children, 'If you ever go back into religion you will not have been worth the upbringing', a comment that at least implies that Christabel's Second Adventist career was a waste of time and certainly incompatible with feminist activism.[27] Sylvia's condemnation of her sister's religious faith has become the standard reading of events, endlessly recycled by historians who continue this secularist bias in their analyses of the suffragette movement. Thus Mitchell, who sneeringly asserts that Christabel 'groped her way to a new Cause', portrays her ministry as a rejection of her feminist suf-frage days. Barbara Castle claims that Christabel's religious writings show 'the complete reversal of her views on the women's struggle', while Rita Pankhurst asserts that by 1921, three years after women in Britain had obtained a limited franchise, Christabel 'had turned away from feminism'. Similarly, Pugh con-demns Christabel's religious life as a product of 'the shallowness of Pankhurst politics and their ceaseless search for self-promotion', confidently observ-ing that Christabel 'went so far as to repudiate the whole suffrage cause after 1920'.[28] Joyce Marlow aptly sums up this secular viewpoint when she notes that

442

the socialist Sylvia Pankhurst is 'the most popular Pankhurst' for present-day feminists, Christabel's post-war activities being a 'difficult' subject.[29] Such views in regard to Christabel's religious faith must be challenged.

Even in the nineteenth century, close links existed between religion and feminist activism, a link that was also present in the suffragette movement.[30] In particular, for Christabel Pankhurst the campaign for the vote was never just about political reform but also about moral and religious change. As we have seen in an earlier chapter, in *The great scourge* she argued that votes for women and chastity for men were the means not only to a more just society but also a purer, more godly nation which upheld the Christian ideal of sexual purity before marriage. Indeed, at the height of the suffrage struggle, Christianity became an important element in Christabel's feminism. In 1914, when imprisoned suffragettes were being forcibly fed in prison, she wrote passionately of the 'militant women crusaders' in whom 'the spirit of Christ is living today'. Like the early Christian martyrs, the militants were re-enacting Christ's crucifixion, their spirit triumphing over physical torture.[31] As Joy Dixon has emphasised, historians need to re-think the assumptions about distinctions between the secular and the sacred in women's politics in the Edwardian era. For Christabel Pankhurst, as for a significant minority of the women, feminism was a 'kind of theology as much as a political ideology'.[32] Now, in 1923, as Christabel embarked on her religious career, she was not repudiating her feminism but merely extending it in a different direction, 'transforming the pulpit', as one author terms it.[33]

When asked by the *Toronto Daily Star* if she believed that women should take their place in the pulpit, Christabel unhesitatingly replied, 'It has always been open to women to do this. In the early church women played a great and honoured part. This is what I shall do. I shall testify to my experience.'[34] Thus rather than seeing Christabel's religious career as the negation of her suffrage feminism, one may interpret it as an extension of her feminist politics, a continuation of the struggle for women's equality but in a different context, that of church organisation. By carving a career for herself as a preacher and religious writer, she was helping to lead the way in opening up Christianity to women's spiritual leadership.

Although Christabel regarded herself as an Anglican, a member of the Church of England, she had to pursue her ministry in another denomination since the Church of England was vehemently opposed to women preachers.[35] The openness, at this particular point in time, of the conservative Protestant evangelical movement to women who were called to minister was something she embraced – despite the absence of gender equality within its structures. In great demand on both sides of the Atlantic, as a speaker in churches probably mainly in Baptist or Reformed contexts, she combined her prophetic message about the Second Coming of Christ with the theme that laws and suffrage alone could not solve the world's problems.[36] A single woman with no formal theological training but a First Class Honours Degree in Law, an 'outsider' whose Britishness and crisp English accent set her apart, a well-known 'militant' feminist who was clever with words, the talented Christabel entered the male-dominated profession of Christian ministry and carved out for herself a place 'not just as a participant, but as a star'.[37]

In July 1923, Christabel published her first and most successful book on religion, 'The Lord cometh'. With a foreword by the well-known Rev. F. M. Meyer, the print run reached some 21,000 copies within a year: a seventh edition was issued in 1928 and a 'popular' edition in 1934.[38] In this book Christabel proclaimed that biblical prophecy was simply future history:

> It is awe-inspiring to watch current history fitting into the very mould of prophecy. Once you have the clue to the meaning of the existing world crisis you marvel that everybody else does not also see how prophecy is fulfilling itself in the world-events of the passing days.[39]

Jesus' birth at Bethlehem had been foretold through the Prophet Micah just as Christ himself told of His own death and resurrection. Christabel noted how she watched current events and interpreted some of them as 'Signs of the Times' that Christ and other biblical characters had predicted would mean the end of human history and the establishment of Christ's kingdom on earth, a Millennial Age marked by 'righteous peace and happiness'.[40] Since it had been predicted that at the end times, Jerusalem would return to Jewish control once again, she suggested that the recent ejection of the Turks from Palestine and 'the Zionist plan, already in active operation, for the return of the Jews to the Promised Land' was a sign that Christ's return was imminent.[41] Similarly, '[w]ars and the existence of wars', which had been foretold by Christ to be incident to the 'closing years of this Age', and the rise of an anti-Christ (although she did not use that particular word in 'The Lord cometh' but spoke of an earthly dictator who would exalt himself above all that is called God), were taken as signs of the Second Coming.[42] In particular, prophecy indicated that the Roman Empire of old would revive itself and have at its head:

> a leader, president, emperor, call him what you will . . . the 'Man of Sin', who, for a brief space of time, shall wield that predominant world-power that has ever been the goal of super-ambitious men. Several prophecies in the Bible concur in witness to the rise, and to the short but drastic and evil rule, of this personage.[43]

Although Christabel, like many Second Adventists of her day, was careful not to give specific dates for when Christ would return, she nonetheless claimed that the time was 'very near', a view that she modified over time; if the end was not imminent, then this meant that the world was destined to exist through even more intense periods of wars, earthquakes and other major disasters.[44]

Rather than spending the second half of her life turning away from feminism, Christabel's feminism is particularly evident in 'The Lord cometh' in the emphasis upon equality for women, although it is a discussion that is embedded in a much wider articulation of her religious views. In the very first chapter of this book she notes that women's political enfranchisement was a necessary measure of justice. However, she now believed that political equality between the sexes was not enough on its own to solve the world's problems, that women had become increasingly aware of this and that there was now a great reliance upon God.[45] Women's entry into national politics did not bring the moral uplifting of societies that she had hoped for. Christabel's feminism in 'The Lord cometh' is also evident in the importance she places on women in Christian ministry. It was women who first saw the resurrected Christ after His crucifixion and it was to these women that Jesus first spoke, asking them to spread the good news.[46] In so doing, Christabel directly challenged sex discrimination in the priesthood, a bastion of male privilege, especially in the Church of England, and opted for the greater openness in the conservative evangelical Protestant wing. Christabel was wise enough to fulfil her call to Christian ministry where she was welcomed.

Not unexpectedly, the evangelical Protestant press lauded 'The Lord cometh', calling it a 'very remarkable book' that 'thousands will read . . . with profound thanksgiving to God'. It is a 'wonderful work in many ways', commented another reviewer; 'it comes from the pen of an accomplished woman, and is characterized by vision and force in a remarkable degree'. The 'name and reputation of the writer' will assuredly attract the interest of those who might not read about Christ's Second Coming 'if in a book written by a theologian', pronounced the Sunday School Times.[47] But a number of the women's journals, especially in Britain, were sceptical. The Woman's Leader, for example, which had emerged from the NUWSS's the Common Cause, was deeply critical. '[W]e find ourselves on the verge of wondering whether the author is really serious or, less cynical suspicion, whether this conversion to a new gospel is indicative of a lamentable mental unbalance', wrote the caustic reviewer.[48] This reaction was not uncommon among many former suffragists and suffragettes in Britain who did not want to know anything about Christabel in 'her changed attitude'.[49] Even theologically liberal Christians did not proclaim that certain 'Signs of the Times' heralded the Second Coming of Jesus Christ. Nonetheless, the carnage of the First World War and the upheaval created by the Russian Revolution were seen as 'doomsday' moments by a large number of women who required divine solutions to earthly problems.[50]

Even if negative criticism about the new cause in her life did reach Christabel, she was too busy to worry about it – and too embedded within the evangelical community to be concerned. That summer of 1923 she was one of the key speakers at some revivalist gatherings in New York. 'It was a quiet, slender little figure in gray that preached the sermon last night which held the rapt attention of a large audience', opined the New York Times of her first address at the popular Old Tent Evangelical. Similar praise was lavished on her addresses at the conference organised at Stony Brook, New York, by A. A. Gaebelein, one of the leading speakers on biblical prophecy who had met Christabel earlier in California.[51]

SECOND ADVENTIST MINISTRY

But if Christabel's message of the Second Coming was appreciated by her audiences in New York, the doughty Catherine Pine was not impressed.

Catherine Pine, with her impish sense of humour, was apt to joke privately to Emmeline that if Christabel's gloomy prediction about the Second Coming of Christ was so imminent, it was hardly worthwhile cooking the dinner.[52] But more troublesome than such comments were the differing approaches that Christabel and Miss Pine adopted when upbringing children. Catherine Pine was an old-fashioned disciplinarian, with sanctions such as no jam or reading of a favourite book or other treats for a week if Kathleen, Mary or Joan were naughty. Christabel, who usually took the much-loved Betty with her wherever she went, was much more lax with her adopted daughter, an approach that created tensions within the household when she was at home. 'Elizabeth [Betty] wasn't punished at all', remembered Mary:

> Auntie Christabel would say to her 'Why did you do it, darling?' and we were furious in our little baby minds. We used to stand on the sidelines all bereft of whatever treat it was, and there was Elizabeth eating her strawberries and cream.[53]

Matters came to a head during the late summer of 1923. Catherine Pine decided to leave and sail back home to England.

Christabel continued with her Second Adventist preaching and was invited herself, by Mr Jensen, to return to England so that she could preach her religious message at Newton Solney, South Derbyshire. 'The difficulty is that I can fix no date for my return to England yet', she replied on 13 November:

> At present I am busy in Canada – at the end of this month I go to Chicago & district to speak at the Moody Church [the most important of all the many fundamentalist Bible institutes in North America which trained Christian workers] & elsewhere. In the early year I am likely, though I am not yet irrevocably committed, to undertake a good deal of speaking in the United States.[54]

That Christabel was invited to address the students at the Moody Institute in Chicago says much about the esteem in which she was held.[55] After Chicago, she then travelled that early New Year of 1924 to Springfield, Massachusetts, on the east coast of America, where she met up with an old suffrage friend from England, Rangeley Stride. The two women, who used to correspond almost weekly, had much to talk about. When they parted, Christabel gave Rangeley a Bible, inscribed with a personal message.[56]

Christabel's next port of call was New York where she was invited to speak at another popular venue, the Calvary Baptist Church at which the well-known Dr John Roach Straton, one of the most important leaders of American fundamentalism, was the minister. 'I am still a politician', she said on this occasion, 'but I have given up earthly politics for the higher politics. I am working for God.'[57] Straton, a firm supporter of Christabel's ministry, frequently relinquished the pulpit so that his large congregation could listen to her.[58] Helen Fraser, a former WSPU organiser who had resigned in 1908 and joined the NUWSS, was sitting in the audience on one such occasion. Christabel 'looked very little older than when I last saw her', wrote the astonished Helen, 'beautifully gowned and wearing a big becoming softly-feathered hat with the same tilt of her head, the same upward fling of long eloquent hands – unbelievably the same, incredibly different, she enunciated her new faith'.[59] By April Christabel had returned to Los Angeles where she gave a series of free evening lectures at the Bible Institute. On 4 May, at the invitation of the Reverend J. A. Hubbard, she preached two sermons at the Church of the Open Door, an interdenominational evangelical church, the afternoon address being based on the text 'This Same Jesus Shall Come', while the topic for the evening was the familiar 'Some Signs of the Times'.[60]

When Christabel returned to Toronto after such travels, she was often courted by the local press. In an interview for the *Toronto Star Weekly* in March 1924, which also featured a photograph of the four little girls in the Pankhurst household, she spoke enthusiastically about adopting fatherless children:

> I feel that there are a great many unmarried women who have inherited or developed an income of their own, and a great many well-to-do married women without children who could bring a great deal of joy into their lives by adopting a family of children. It is both a privilege and a duty.[61]

But despite this expression of commitment, all was not running smoothly in the household.

After Catherine Pine's departure, a series of nurses and governesses were employed to look after the children, including Mrs Jean Cookson. But more worrying was Emmeline's failing health. After four and a half years of arduous work, she was looking 'very tired and worn', recollected Christabel, and not relishing the idea of more meetings travelling in Canada in far from warm weather. 'I feared one of the chills which, so rare with her, seemed, when they came, to affect her the more. Complete rest, change, warmth, were what she needed.'[62] The Canadian government granted Emmeline six months' leave of absence. At Toronto's famous annual exhibition, she had noticed the Bermuda stall and fallen in love with this British colony with a warm, balmy climate. It seemed the ideal place to rest and regain her health. By May 1924, Christabel, Emmeline and the children, together with Mrs Cookson, had moved there.[63]

Initially the family stayed at Glencoe, a guesthouse in Paget, Salt Kettle. Christabel was now the main breadwinner and so it was important that she continued with her writing. It was at Glencoe, on 18 August 1924, that she signed the contract with Fleming H. Revell Company of New York and Chicago for *Some modern problems in the light of Bible prophecy*, a book aimed at the American market and, apart from some minor changes, largely the same as *Pressing problems of the closing age*, for which a contract was signed on 27 September.[64] Upon publication of *Pressing problems* Christabel would receive the grand sum of £25 and royalties of 15% on each volume sold after the first one thousand had been bought.

In both books, published later that year, we find discussion of the decline of democracy in the world and the rise of dictatorships in countries such as Russia, Italy and Spain. Since, as Christabel noted, the prophet Daniel had predicted that the Roman Empire would be in existence at the end of this Age, she gave some coverage to the fascist Mussolini's attempt to resurrect that Empire, not unusual for an Adventist of her time.[65] The Adventist movement generally was very interested in the rise of Mussolini since biblical prophecy had predicted that a newly revived Roman Empire, under the anti-Christ, would play a central role in the end times. Thus Christabel's interest in explaining the qualities and arguments that Mussolini might use to aid his success, an interest based in theological 'exuberance', was not seen as a 'solution' to the world's problems but a 'counterfeit and ultimately doomed one'.[66] For Pugh to claim, therefore, that Christabel 'expressed great admiration for Mussolini and his efforts to resurrect the Roman Empire' is to misinterpret the situation.[67]

The decay of democracy, Christabel pointed out, accounted for the debasement of the women's franchise. In a chapter titled 'The Votes of Women' in *Pressing problems* she outlined how in the pre-war days, it was never doubted that 'constitutional democracy would be adhered to in the letter and in the spirit . . . we believed the vote would give to women a power, a practical influence upon events and conditions'.[68] But that had not happened. 'The rifle of a black-shirted Fascist, the industrial weapon of the striker, these are more potent in national affairs than the vote of a woman, and the balance is turning more against the vote as the days pass.' Some hoped for more from woman suffrage 'than is ever going to be accomplished', Christabel lamented. 'My own large anticipations were based partly upon ignorance . . . of the magnitude of the task which we women reformers so confidently wished to undertake when the vote should be ours.'[69] Such statements reveal that Christabel had not turned away from feminism; she was merely pointing out that women's entry into national politics had not solved society's problems. That she spoke about the women's suffrage campaign reveals that it was still a subject close to her heart. Nor was her suffrage past denied by her fellow Adventists, but welcomed.

On numerous occasions, generous language was used to describe Christabel. 'Those who have heard this brave, heroic woman do not doubt the sincerity of her purpose and aim', enthused the *Moody Bible Institute Monthly*. 'As a politician and militant suffragette she showed her willingness to endure scoffs, jeers, imprisonment and suffering of every kind. Now the Man of Galilee has so gripped her heart that she sees as a student of the Word.'[70] The positive appraisal given to Christabel's preaching and writings was partly because the suffrage cause was seen as a just cause, a cause that had been won sooner in the USA than in Britain. After all, some women had been voting in American federal elections as early as 1869 and in California since 1911.[71] Those Americans who read that autumn of 1924 Annie Kenney's newly published memoirs would find their praise for Christabel vindicated. 'Without her there would have been no real Women's Movement', opined Annie. 'Christabel Pankhurst has done more than any other woman to make British women not only think, but act . . . She united thousands upon thousands of women in a bond of fellowship' to demand their democratic rights.[72]

Shortly after publication of *Pressing problems* Christabel wrote to Lloyd George, thanking him for his kind message about her book and asking if he had read it. '[Y]ou have a knowledge of the Bible dating from your boyhood and that is a wonderful equipment for the higher Statesmanship – for the heralding of the Kings of Kings', she flattered him as she tried to enlist his support for the imminence of the Second Coming:

> [Y]ou are capable, as no other public man of your standing is, of receiving and acting under inspiration. You were raised up to bring us through the war to victory. I feel that God has an even bigger thing for you to do.[73]

With the healthy proceeds from the sale of Christabel's books and Emmeline's remaining savings, the household was able, in early 1925, to leave the guesthouse and move to a rented house called Roche Terre on a slight hill overlooking the Sound near Buena Vista. 'We had about 96 steps to get up to it', recollected Kathleen. 'And on the 84th, or something like that, there was a seat . . . It took a long way to go down to the beach, which we did nearly every day.'[74] The house had two floors. Christabel and Emmeline lived on the second floor where the doors of the lounge could be pulled back, making a large open space that opened into the dining room and library. The children stayed in the bottom floor with Mrs Cookson. Christabel was still often away from home, preaching on the mainland, her activities reported frequently by the English press. Miss Christabel Pankhurst was in a 'mournful mood', noted the *Daily Herald*, when early in 1925 she spoke at the Ascension Memorial Episcopal Church, New York, predicting that the day of judgement was close at home and forecasting that a large federation of nations would soon come into being, under a dictator who would be the anti-Christ.[75] In May Christabel was in New York again, at the Church of the Stranger, speaking under the auspices of the National Bible Institute on 'What the Bible Means to Me Today'. 'When I was fourteen years old I suddenly realized that I knew nothing of philosophy', she reminisced. 'I immediately started to study it. But I found like many an older and wiser student that the question "What is Truth?" remained unanswered. The Bible answers that question.'[76]

Christabel rarely took Betty with her now when she preached on the mainland since she was acutely aware that her daughter needed a regular education. One day, when Christabel was away, Emmeline decided that it was time the children had swimming lessons. She gladly accepted the offer of an elderly Bermudan to undertake the task. The man put the children in a small boat, rowed out a short distance from the shore and then, to her horror, threw them into deep water, one by one, telling them to swim after him as he rowed away. The children survived the ordeal and were soon thriving in the more conventional lessons offered by Mrs Cookson. 'She taught us swimming', recollected Kathleen. 'In four days we were all swimming.' Now confident in the water, the girls would sometimes take themselves out in a rowing boat, attached to a long rope, and glide to the yachts moored nearby. At other times they would go fishing with home-made fishing rods made out of a hairpin and a piece of string. However, the arrival of Mrs Cookson's husband from Alaska, to join the household, brought about an unwelcome change. 'We could not forget him', remembered Kathleen, because she, Mary, Joan and Betty 'woke at five o'clock in the morning full of spirits, and woke them up.' After listening to Mr Cookson's complaints, Emmeline punished each girl by spanking her with a slipper. Soon the disgruntled Mr and Mrs Cookson left, and then another governess was employed.[77]

When she was home at Roche Terre Christabel often withdrew from family life to write, even leaving the table suddenly during the middle of a meal, something the children were forbidden to do. Mary thought she was eccentric, 'not the same as other people', using 'very dramatic speech' and wearing 'flowing garments' with her hair in the same style as in her suffragette days. But neither Christabel's or Emmeline's suffragette past was even spoken about to the children, although they were encouraged to think for themselves, to stand up for their convictions and never to be talked down. When the girls chanced one day on a photograph album with Emmeline and Christabel in prison clothing, Aunty Kate had hastily taken the album from them, explaining nothing. That was not the only secret. Shortly after this incident, Betty and Kathleen accidentally locked themselves in a cupboard. Betty had previously, on a number of occasions, taken the door handle off and it had not been screwed on again securely. So when they entered the cupboard and the door was banged shut, the handle on the outside fell off. It took the two frightened girls a long time to free themselves. They both felt so ashamed that they said nothing about their ordeal.[78]

Christabel was delighted that these months resting in Bermuda had restored her mother's health but concerned that financial matters had become pressing again. The sixty-six-year-old Emmeline could not face the prospect of returning to her lecturing job in Canada, travelling on draughty trains in the cold Canadian winter, despite her dwindling savings. Since Christabel found that her own earnings were insufficient to support their large household, she tried her hand at popular journalism again, writing various articles for the British press. The very fabric of civilisation was being challenged, she noted, in an article on 'The sexless life' for the *Daily Express*. There was talk, she observed, of a 'new morality for women' but the best morality was Christian morality, the morality taught by Christ. 'At the marriage feast at Cana of Galilee, Jesus was there and . . . honoured the union of man and woman, safe-guarded by marriage.' Nevertheless, Christ also showed that 'the destiny of some individuals is a life without sex activity. He blessed this life by living it Himself'. Although the world was a hard place, especially for young people of the day who faced many difficulties, problems and temptations would not be solved by throwing over Christian morality.[79] Such views suggest strongly that Christabel was almost certainly not a sexually active lesbian, even if her main friendships were with women. But the emphasis upon traditional Christian morality undoubtedly did not find favour with many feminists in Britain, particularly those on the Left who favoured 'free unions' and 'free love'. Christabel Pankhurst was considered out of touch with progressive, feminist thinking. She was no longer making the news.

Emmeline came up with an idea to solve all their financial problems. She and Christabel could open a family business, with perhaps a close woman friend, somewhere on the warm, Mediterranean coast. Christabel could continue with her writing while she and the friend ran the business. That way they could earn enough to support themselves and also have a home. Christabel was not keen on the idea. Nonetheless, Emmeline persevered with the plan and wrote to their old friend Mabel Tuke, one-time Honorary Secretary of the WSPU. Mabel, who had a steady income from her husband's military pension, was enthusiastic about the scheme and suggested that they open a tea-shop on the French Riviera where tourists and British expatriates would be plentiful. Her enthusiasm, plus the offer to put up the capital to fund the venture, won over Christabel. But before the three women could embark on this new challenge, Emmeline had to make some hard decisions. Reluctantly she decided she could no longer afford to support all three of her adopted children, and so arranged for Kathleen and Joan to be sent back to England where they would be adopted by better-off people who could give them the chances in life she could not. She did not part with the fiery, red-headed Mary who was not only her favourite child but had also been left a small legacy, in trust, by Mary Dickson Home.[80]

In pursuit of their new venture, Christabel, Emmeline, Mary and Betty arrived in Avonmouth, near Bristol, on the S S Changuinola on 14 June 1925, en route for France. Then they all travelled to Paris, to stay in Christabel's flat at 27 Avenue Victor Hugo. 'I hope that you are having a delightful holiday and I look forward to seeing you again when you return to Paris, when we can talk to our hearts' content', Christabel wrote to Renee de Brimont from her Parisian address in early August. 'I rejoice that we are not "lost" to one another any longer!'[81] While in Paris, Christabel continued with her writing commitments, penning a series of articles for the Sunday School Times, a task that kept her absorbed.[82] Betty and Mary, dressed in big floppy hats, pretty Kate Greenaway dresses and kid boots with small buttons, were greatly admired by the Parisians. Emmeline bought them each a pair of roller skates, and since she and Christabel were frequently out, the two ten-year-olds had a lot of freedom. On one occasion, 'We skated all round the boulevards alone for hours and hours, nearly all day', remembered

Mary, 'Christabel and Mother did not know where we were.' Christabel and Emmeline would have been extremely worried if they had known, so the girls were careful when they returned home not to speak of what they had been doing, but to behave like 'little angels'.[83] However, it was not all play for Betty and Mary. They had always been encouraged from an early age to read avidly and were soon enrolled in the local libraries where they found the English classics. On one occasion, the quiet pursuit of reading at home was interrupted when a fight broke out between them, some furniture even being broken. Mary recollected how Christabel, with her Montessori approach, stopped the rumpus, more out of sorrow than anger, an approach of which she was envious. Christabel's question to Elizabeth, 'Now why did you do that darling?' contrasted sharply with the stern sanctions imposed by Emmeline.[84]

On 25 August, Christabel was writing again to Renee de Brimont, this time from the Hotel Pavillon Rivoli, Nice:

> You will see that we have moved again. Mother decided to come to this coast for the winter and wanted to be sure of getting a suitable dwelling before everybody else arrives . . . So we sublet the apartment, finding a tenant who wanted it no later than last Thursday and came away in quite a rush.

Christabel was sitting on the beach as she wrote, delighted to be by the sea in which Betty and Mary were 'swimming like fish . . . (At this moment a very wet small girl has sat down beside me & splashed the paper which I hope will be excused)'. Christabel regretted leaving Paris without seeing Renee but hoped they could keep in touch by letter writing:

> It is too bad not to see you face to face but, as I reflected while driving to the Gare de Lyon, we are united by so real an affection and so deep an understanding that we cannot be 'lost' or separated by kilometres . . . do you not think that a visit to the Cote d'Azur would do you good?

Another letter penned to the Baronne on 8 September contained a lot more discussion about the Second Coming of Christ, in which her friend was interested. It was immensely fascinating to watch public events, Christabel suggested, as she commented on the state of world affairs. The world was moving towards a 'confederacy of nations' that would be predominant during the last years of this Age.[85]

Juan-les-Pins was finally chosen for the business venture, the English Tea-Shop of Good Hope which looked very elegant with its tangerine-clothed tables, big window-seat and window box filled with bright flowers. Mabel Tuke cooked the cakes and scones while Christabel continued with her writing, working on the manuscript of *The world's unrest: visions of the dawn*, sections of which were published in the *Sunday School Times*. But few customers called. Emmeline now had little money left and hearing of her plight, Lady Rhondda, back in England, guaranteed her an income of £400 per annum for three years, if she returned home and worked with the Six Point Group, a feminist pressure organisation that campaigned for equality for women, including an equal franchise. The proud Emmeline, disdaining anything that smacked of 'charity', politely refused. She also felt it was unpatriotic to re-open the franchise question at a time of world crisis when women already had 'enough voting power . . . to secure the various ends to which the vote is a means'.[86] When her mother developed bronchial symptoms induced by the bleak French winter, Christabel suggested they should all return to England. Christabel and Betty arrived early in the New Year of 1926, via a stop in Paris. They went to live with Christabel's Aunt Ada Goulden Bach at 2 Elsham Road, Kensington. Emmeline and Mary, who had arrived a few weeks earlier, were already living at the same address.

Christabel and Emmeline had returned to an England in which industrial disputes were endemic, a situation of which they were both critical. Yet although Christabel was in touch with old friends, such as Flora Drummond, Elsie Bowerman and the wealthy Esther Greg, she was not drawn into the work of the Women's Guild of Empire, founded by Flora and Elsie in 1920 with financial backing from Esther.[87] Nor did Christabel get drawn closely into her mother's political work. Impressed with the way that the Conservative Prime Minister, Stanley Baldwin, had handled the General Strike declared on 1 May, in which some 2,500,000 workers were eventually involved, Emmeline had decided to re-enter politics and stand as a Conservative parliamentary candidate, a decision that set the newspapers buzzing.[88] Christabel did not take much interest either in suffrage reunions or accompany her mother in the women's franchise demonstration, held on 3 July to demand votes for women on the same terms as men. To Elsie Bowerman, she seemed 'very far away'.[89] What was occupying Christabel was her new cause of Second Adventism, as well as the necessity of earning a living to support herself and Betty.

The world's unrest, published in July 1926, was very well received within the Adventist community. One commentator asserted that rather than being a 'divisive controversialist', Christabel was an 'effective popularizer', circumnavigating the issues that divided Adventists and offering her own take on many issues, particularly modernity.[90] Whereas the majority of fundamentalists saw modernity as the work of the devil, she embraced scientific innovation and technological change, weaving it into her analysis.[91] 'The account of Creation in Genesis has been a stumbling-block to Science, but it claims reconsideration in the light of the latest thought', she boldly claimed. The doctrine of relativity might do something to illumine for the scientist the time references in Genesis:

> The constitution of matter, as now understood, was a sealed book to those who initiated the 'scientific' objections to biblical statement. It is not so much the Bible, but the whole body of the sciences, and geology and biology in particular, that need review in the light of modern scientific doctrine as to the constitution of matter.[92]

453

The influential Rev. F. B. Meyer, one of the leading voices in the Adventist world, was so impressed with *The world's unrest* and with Christabel generally that he asked her to be the key guest speaker in the British autumn campaign of the Advent Testimony and Preparation Movement, held from September 1926 to February 1927.

In this capacity, Christabel, the only female voice among a group of male clergy, addressed audiences in many towns and cities in England – Bristol, Ipswich, Liverpool, Manchester and London – as well as Cardiff and Porth in Wales, Edinburgh in Scotland and Dublin in Ireland.[93] She always drew large crowds, as at Bristol where over two thousand people gathered to hear her. Although her evangelistic speeches focused on the 'signs of the times' that foretold the Coming of Christ, other themes were present too, including the denouncing of anti-Semitism. 'The Jew is being made the scapegoat of the world', she told one audience, a theme to which she frequently returned.[94] Indeed, her status as a friend to the Jewish community was such that she was invited on a number of future occasions to speak to Jewish groups, including the twelve sections of the Women's League for Palestine at the Temple Emanu-El in New York.[95]

Undoubtedly the meetings she attended at the Free Trade Hall in Manchester in mid-October 1926 brought back memories for Christabel of past suffrage campaigning. 'One seems to have been cradled in the Free Trade hall – a home of noble aspirations and great ideals', she announced poignantly, after remarking that it was good to be home again. 'But how to realize them – that is the great problem. I think I have now found the way, through the One who alone can give effect to all the striving and endeavours of mankind.' Going on to speak of the ruined hopes of political idealists, such as herself in former days, she described the world in 1926 as being in a more dangerous state than in August 1914. The true task for preachers was not to take a more prominent part in public and political life but to warn the heedless that Christ is coming, and that only He could cleanse and regenerate.[96]

Meetings in the afternoon and evening of 2 November 1926 at the Queen's Hall, London, another suffrage haunt, were similarly packed to overflowing. When Christabel, sitting on the platform with a score of clergymen, stood up to speak in the afternoon gathering, the audience 'rose to her greet her', noted the *Manchester Guardian*, 'an indication that it included great numbers of the suffrage women, who perform this simple rite when they wish to show special honour to a leader'. The reporter noted that Christabel, her face hidden by a wide hat:

> looked smaller and slighter than one had remembered, and less self-possessed. But when she got up to speak one recognised in her the same Christabel, as convinced as ever that she knew the truth. She had the old mannerisms . . . Most of the time she leant forward, running her hands along the rail before her, but she had the free, dramatic gestures of arms flung out or raised in emphasis. Hers is a wonderful voice, carrying every word to the back of the hall, a little shrill sometimes, but

with a trick of almost singing at times, yet a voice without sympathy or poetry . . . She read glorious prophetic passages of scripture as if she were quoting from a catalogue.[97]

Emmeline, who was in the audience on both occasions, glowed with a mother's pride when she recounted the story to Esther Greg. Christabel 'was wonderful at both meetings . . . hundreds were turned away'. There was to be an Albert Hall meeting in January, and already applications were 'pouring in'.[98]

The Royal Albert Hall, with its ten-thousand capacity, had been another important meeting place in Christabel's suffragette past. Yet again, she filled to overflowing the two meetings held here, so that it become the apogee of her present tour in England.[99] Christabel had proved to herself and to fellow Adventists that she was a popular, engaging speaker. Indeed, the *Sunday Chronicle* considered her important enough to be included among the four 'distinguished people' of differing views who were asked to give their opinion about the suggestion that Christ was soon to reappear on this earth.[100] And as Christabel spread her Christian message of hope she embraced new forms of communication, such as radio, speaking on the BBC in Cardiff and, on another occasion, predicting a bright future for the invention of television. 'Radio-vision . . . soon will enable spectators all round the globe to watch . . . lawn tennis at Wimbledon.'[101]

Yet historians ignore such positive assessments of Christabel, preferring to engage in negative criticism. Thus David Mitchell, her biographer, claims that his subject attacked the 'new' sexual and moral climate in England, despite the fact that there is little evidence of this in her speeches or writings. For example, in none of the popular twenty-six columns 'On The Watchtower' that she wrote for the *Christian* during 1926–7 did she once highlight the problem of public mores.[102] Christabel had very little to say publicly about immorality, which is surprising given that it was regarded as one of the biblical signs of the times.[103] The assertion too of biographer Martin Pugh, that Christabel was a 'prophet of doom', must be questioned.[104] Christabel herself tried to answer this charge in her lifetime, pointing out that proclaimers of the Second Coming were prophets of salvation and sunshine. 'The real pessimists are not we', she claimed, 'but they who cannot believe this Gospel of the kingdom. We are the true optimists, because we believe in the best – and our optimism has a sure, because a divine, foundation.'[105] Indeed, one theological scholar suggests that Christabel's religious views may be described as 'extraordinarily upbeat'.[106]

By early December 1926 Emmeline Pankhurst heard that she could expect to be formally adopted, in the New Year, as the Conservative candidate for the East End constituency of Whitechapel and St George's in the 1929 general election. Although it was a poor, socialist constituency that she had little chance of winning, Emmeline was keen to contest such a seat since she believed that it was the working classes, especially the women, who were most exploited by communism.[107] When Sylvia heard the news of her mother's plans, she wept. She was now advocating the communism which her mother and Christabel so detested.

With typical aplomb, Sylvia wrote to the socialist journal *Forward* denouncing her mother for deserting 'the old cause of progress'.[108] The press took up the story, giving wider coverage to what was already a public family feud. A few months earlier, even the North American newspapers had discussed the divergent ideological paths of the Pankhurst women. 'Trio of Pankhursts Far Apart In Ideals', ran the *Toronto Daily Star*. 'Mrs. Pankhurst Against Communism, Sylvia Teaches It. Christabel Very Religious.'[109] Christabel, for her part, always protective of her mother, saw Sylvia's action as yet another indication of how intolerant and vindictive this sister could be.

Now leading her own independent life, Christabel was supportive but not drawn into her mother's political work. Her main base was not London, where Emmeline lived, but Upwood, 10 Florence Road, Boscombe, Bournemouth, a boarding house run by a kindly but elderly Adventist couple who looked after the eleven-year-old Betty while she was away, as well as some aged blind persons. Sometimes too Rangeley Stride, to whose daughter Christabel was godmother, helped out with Betty who was remembered at this time as being 'very quiet, no trouble, always reading'.[110] That Christmas of 1926 Christabel spent with Betty in Bournemouth rather than with her mother and Esther Greg in London.[111]

Throughout 1927 and well into 1928, Christabel continued with her ministry, travelling up and down Britain, spreading her Second Adventist message. Her speech to the annual conference of the International Christian Police Association in London, on 29 April 1927, revealed that she was at ease with her militant past, still a feminist, and had lost none of her power to captivate an audience. 'When I was asked to speak at these Christian Police Association gatherings, I said I would come, because it *is* a Police Association', she began jokingly. 'You see, there was a time when we – well, when we worked together!'[112] In one section of her speech, where Christabel pleaded that 'we must feel proud of being women', she elaborated upon the limitations of what politicians of any political hue could achieve, even if in the future Britain had a government of all women:

> And whether it be a Lloyd-George or a Macdonald, a government violently Red or ultra-conservative or moderate or liberal, or a government of women – and you know we may some time have a government of women even – any British government in these days will have a burden upon its shoulder which can only be borne by the Son of God of whom it is said by the prophet that when He comes the government shall be upon His shoulder.[113]

In early December 1927, some secret family news was conveyed to Christabel's Aunt Ada who had moved to 35 Gloucester Road, a location that was much more convenient for the frequent journeys of the sixty-nine-year-old Emmeline to her constituency. Ada was told that on 3 December her unmarried niece Sylvia Pankhurst, who was cohabiting in Woodford, Essex with the Italian socialist and anarchist, Silvio Erasmus Corio, had given birth to a son in a Hampstead nursing home. The stunned Ada contacted Christabel who was deeply shocked by the revelation. Christabel upheld the Christian notion of chastity before marriage and had never been in favour of 'free love' unions. At a time when unmarried mothers were stigmatised as sexually promiscuous, she feared in particular that such news would break the heart of her ageing mother. Christabel and Ada, fiercely protective of the ailing Emmeline, decided it was best to keep the family secret private for as long as they could. Each morning, the cautious Ada would vet any post that came for her sister. When a letter arrived addressed in Sylvia's hand she hastily secreted it away to the bafflement of Emmeline's secretary, former suffragette Nellie Hall-Humpherson.[114] Despite the best intentions of Christabel and Ada, such a family secret could not be kept forever and would soon erupt in a most cruel way.

In early April 1928, when Emmeline was addressing a constituency meeting, she was interrupted by a working-class woman who asked about one of her daughters who had had a baby out of wedlock. The devastated Emmeline, having been warned just minutes beforehand that such a question would be raised, composed herself sufficiently to reply that she was not in the habit of discussing private matters in public – and continued with her speech. But the news had a devastating effect on her and it would be the last time she ever spoke in public. On Easter Sunday, the News of the World, not considered a respectable newspaper even in that day, carried an article on its front page titled '"Eugenic" Baby Sensation. Sylvia Pankhurst's Amazing Confession.' The forty-five-year-old Sylvia advocated 'marriage' without a legal bond, explaining that her 'husband', whom she refused to name, was an old and dear friend, a foreigner, fifty-three years old. Described as 'one of the leaders of the suffragette movement', Sylvia considered her son a 'eugenic' baby since both his parents were intelligent and healthy people. The baby was called Richard Keir Pethick Pankhurst, the first name after the child's grandfather, Keir after the Labour leader Keir Hardie and Pethick after Emmeline Pethick-Lawrence, the wife of Fred Pethick-Lawrence, now an MP. Sylvia had given the baby her own surname, not that of the father, and professed that she could not understand why her family in Britain had broken ties with her. She had written 'to her mother about the birth of the child, but there was no reply'.[115] The sensational story was spread around the world, especially in the tabloid press. The following week Sylvia published an article titled 'My Baby – and Why' in the Sunday Chronicle, giving a further robust defence of her actions.[116]

Christabel was outraged by the sheer vulgarity of it all – and particularly the effect on their ill mother who, overcome with distress at the shame to the Pankhurst name, had sunk into a deep depression, her political career cruelly ended. The fear that Sylvia's actions would have fatal consequences for Emmeline Pankhurst was a view shared by many former suffragettes, including Elsa Gye. 'It was wicked to advertise his birth as she did', Elsa complained to Adela, 'glaring posters everywhere & coarse jokes in the music halls. Your Mother never got over it.'[117] Christabel herself also felt tainted by the whole tawdry business since many people thought she, a Second Adventist minister, was the 'Miss Pankhurst'

457

named in the newspaper, the unmarried daughter who had given birth to a son out of wedlock. '[F]riends in and out of the Suffragette ranks were quick and emphatic to tell me, the world in general thought the whole story related to <u>me</u>', she told Grace Roe twenty-three years after the event, still vividly remembering the pain and embarrassment of it all, 'and the repercussions have not really ceased.' Christabel firmly believed that the publicity Sylvia had deliberately sought was 'skilfully engineered to harm me'.[118] One year before her death, in 1958, she was still haunted by the story. 'It was difficult to say anything that would mean attacking my sister. I had to be silent', she told another friend:

> At the time the news broke, I was speaking in Churches a great deal. Those religious people were put into a difficulty naturally . . . and many of their people shared the idea <u>that I was the one</u>. It was the biggest blow of my career.[119]

As Christabel grappled with this setback to her ministry and tried to reassure people that she was not *the* 'Miss Pankhurst' mentioned in the tabloid press, the health of the increasingly hard-up Emmeline declined rapidly. Emmeline decided that she could not look after the twelve-year-old Mary, the adopted daughter she loved, and so Christabel arranged for Mary to stay with Marion Wallace-Dunlop for a short time, before she went to Wallington, Surrey, to the Coleridge Taylors who had adopted Kathleen. Christabel continued with her preaching as best she could but hid away, whenever possible, showing her face only to those she knew well. When she was unable to visit her mother, she wrote her long, weekly letters which the loyal Nellie read out to the ailing Emmeline. Adela wrote to her sick mother too, saying that she now shared her opposition to the class struggle. Overjoyed to hear from her youngest daughter, Emmeline replied 'full of regret for the long rift' between them.[120] However, Sylvia's requests to visit her mother were firmly refused. Neither Emmeline nor Christabel would forgive Sylvia for the disgrace she had brought on the Pankhurst name, or for the vindictive way in which she had implicated Christabel in shameful publicity.[121] Emmeline would never see the grandchild whose first name was that of her husband.

In late May, the anxious Christabel and Ada transferred Emmeline, who had had a relapse, to a nursing home in Hampstead. '[I]t is hoped she will show a definite improvement tomorrow & if not further advice will have to be taken', wrote the worried Christabel to Esther Greg. 'I gave her messages from you.'[122] By 1 June Christabel's tone to Esther was more fretful:

> After a very anxious week I have put Mother under the treatment of the Doctor [Chetham Strode] who 14 years ago, after 13 hunger strikes, restored her to health & enabled her to do fourteen year strenuous service in the war & after . . . He . . . understands as no one else can, her constitution. She so greatly wished to have him, that I must have

458

put the case in his hands even had my own judgment not also dictated that course . . . She is very seriously ill of course and has suffered & lost strength. It is too soon to know how things will turn.[123]

Soon Emmeline was moved to another nursing home, at 43 Wimpole Street, to be closer to Dr Chetham Strode's abode. On 5 June Christabel conveyed to Esther more hopeful news. '[S]he shows this morning an improvement – in her sensations at any rate & this is a great relief after nearly 14 days continuous nausea & misery . . . It will be a stiff climb up to health at the best.'[124] Emmeline spoke often to Christabel now about Richard and Harry, her 'greatest griefs', and said that she had never recovered from their deaths. She expressed no bitterness about the suffrage struggles of the past but merely said, 'After all, I have had a wonderful life.'[125] It was a comfort to know that an Equal Franchise Bill, which lowered the voting age for women to twenty-one, on the same residence terms as men, had now passed both Houses of Parliament and was awaiting royal assent.

But strength was ebbing from Emmeline's body. On 13 June, after thanking Esther for the sweet peas she had sent her mother, Christabel noted, 'She can just show her pleasure, but she is very, very weak & in a very critical condition.' The devoted daughter sat reading to her mother a letter from Mrs Baldwin, thanking Emmeline for all she had done for women, saying that she was needed to guide them in the future, words that 'pleased' greatly the gravely ill patient.[126] But no amount of comfort and medical help could save the broken spirit of Emmeline Pankhurst. On Thursday morning, 14 June 1928, she died. 'My greatest comfort is the look of joy on her face that I saw when I went back into the room where we had watched beside her to the end', a sorrowful Christabel informed Esther. 'It seemed to fade afterwards & just peace & contentment & beauty were left – as I have never seen them on any other. But that first look of great joy I shall always have before me.'[127] Although septicaemia due to influenza was listed as the cause of death, Ethel Smyth was firmly of the view that it was 'that obscene little monster of a Sylvia who killed her'.[128]

The British and international press reported extensively on Emmeline Pankhurst's death, praising her courage and vision. Former suffragettes from far and wide wrote letters of condolence to Christabel, including Ethel Froud and Jessie Kenney who was working far away from home as a steward on cruise liners.[129] 'Your dear Mother was a very wonderful personality, for she combined courage[,] dignity and charm to the highest degree', sympathised Emmeline Pethick-Lawrence. 'I regret the break that came in our comradeship.'[130] The sorrowful Christabel wrote for the British press her own warm tribute to her mother:

The greatest sacrifice she made for women was that she was willing to be falsely reckoned an eccentric, a virago. To make votes for women a question of practical politics and to break into the closed circle of citizenship she was willing to *seem* to be the thing that she *was not*. She disliked eccentricity; she was reserved, sensitive – above all she had a wonderful, innate dignity. But she sacrificed all that and faced mockery and hostility, because she sincerely believed it necessary to win the vote for women . . . she had on the eve of the war created such a situation and made the women's vote so urgent a political question that a Cabinet Minister, once an anti-Suffragist, pleaded with the House of Lords to pass the Woman Suffrage Measure of 1918 . . . The vote was granted, and so the suffrage truce that mother had declared when war broke out became a lasting peace . . . In the very year that sees her work for women crowned, she has passed from the scene of her victory.[131]

On Sunday, 17 June, Emmeline's body lay in state on a purple catafalque so that people could pay homage. Christabel returned several times, unable to believe that the devoted mother who had always been there was no longer by her side. Later that day the coffin was conveyed to St John's Church, Smith Square, close to the Houses of Parliament, where a vigil was kept that night.[132] The following day, Christabel, Aunt Ada and Sylvia, who defiantly brought her baby son, were among the key mourners. Adela, in faraway Australia, could not afford the fare to England. More than one thousand women dressed in WSPU colours followed the funeral cortege to Brompton Cemetery. At the graveside, the tearful Christabel was supported by a friend and carefully avoided contact with Sylvia.[133] When Christabel went through her mother's papers at Aunt Ada's, she found the loving courtship letters her father had written to her mother so many years ago.[134] Emmeline had little else to leave, her estate of just £86. 5s. 6d. being granted to Christabel. After spending a much-needed stay with Annie, Christabel took Betty to a cottage in Sussex from where she wrote to her dear friend. '[M]any thoughts of old times.'[135]

Notes

1 *Montreal Star*, 8 August 1921.
2 *Montreal Star*, 8 August 1921.
3 Purvis, *Emmeline Pankhurst*, pp. 321, 327 and 331.
4 A. Whitaker, Christabel in placid role, *Los Angeles Times*, 28 November 1921.
5 Interview with Phyllis Keller and Grace Roe, c.1964, Raeburn Collection.
6 *Friday Morning Club Bulletin*, No. 6, Los Angeles, California, 22 March 1922. I am grateful to Cathy Cherbosque, the Curator, and Lenora Shull, Curatorial Assistant at The Huntington in 1995, for bringing this to my attention.
7 Interview with Grace Roe, 22 September 1965, DMC; interview with Phil Keller and Grace Roe, Raeburn Collection.
8 S. Bruce, *Fundamentalism* (Cambridge, Polity, 2000), p. 67 notes that the religious fundamentalist movement in the USA at this time was marked by a number of beliefs, particularly the proposition that the Bible was the inerrant word of God and that anything that challenged biblical teaching, such as Darwin's theory of evolution, was not just wrong but sinful. Another belief was 'premillennialism', the idea that the world would get worse before the Day of Judgement, which was imminent. Such views held important implications for political action. If life was due to become less pleasant until the righteous were

lifted out of the world at what was called 'the rapture', there was little point in engaging constructively with the world: better to remain 'pure and clean' by remaining aloof. Thus the operating principle for the fundamentalist movement was separatism, an idea that was embodied in the creation of alternative institutions – not only sects and congregations, but also schools, colleges, publishing houses and radio stations.

9 Purvis, *Emmeline Pankhurst*, pp. 330–1.
10 *Victoria Times*, 12 April and 10 May 1922.
11 CP to Annie Kenney, 10 April 1922, quoted in Kenney, *Memories*, pp. 289–90.
12 CP to EPL, 4 May 1922, P-L Papers.
13 *Victoria Daily Times*, 31 August 1922.
14 CP, *Unshackled*, p. 296.
15 CP to Miss Wallace-Dunlop, 25 October 1922, WDFA.
16 Quoted in Larsen, *Christabel*, p. 26.
17 *Globe, Toronto* and *Mail and Empire, Toronto*, 13 and 14 November 1922, respectively.
18 Telephone conversations with Kathleen King and especially interviews with her on 30 May 1992 and 1 July 2000 (hereafter referred to as Kathleen King interviews) at the author's home in Portsmouth. Kathleen, who died in 2011, believed that her birth name may have been Eveline Bennett but was never sure of this.
19 Brian Harrison interview with Mary Hodgson (Gordon) at her home 60 Glenholt Road, Crownhill, Plymouth, 2 July 1976, copy in DMC.
20 Kathleen King interviews, Purvis Collection.
21 *Christian*, 29 March 1923, p. 20.
22 CP, *'The Lord cometh': the world crisis explained* (London, Morgan and Scott, 1923), *Pressing problems of the closing age* (London, Morgan and Scott, 1924), *Some modern problems in the light of Bible prophecy* (New York, Fleming H. Revell, 1924), *The world's unrest: visions of the dawn* (Philadelphia, PA, Sunday School Times Company, 1926), *Seeing the future* (New York, Harper and Brothers, 1929) and *The uncurtained future* (London, Hodder and Stoughton, 1940).
23 Larsen, *Christabel*, p. viii.
24 Coleman, *Adela Pankhurst*, pp. 92–3.
25 Romero, *Sylvia Pankhurst*, pp. 154–5.
26 ESP, *Emmeline Pankhurst*, p. 171.
27 ESP, TSM, p. 16. Larsen, *Christabel*, pp. 17–19 suggests that Richard Pankhurst may have been committed to organised Christianity for most of his adult life, first as a Baptist and then as a Congregationalist.
28 Mitchell, *Queen Christabel*, p. 285; Castle, *Sylvia and Christabel Pankhurst* p. 158; R. Pankhurst, Introduction to reprint of C. Pankhurst, *Unshackled* (London, Cresset Library), p. 7; Pugh, *Women and the women's movement*, p. 47; Pugh, *The Pankhursts*, p. xv.
29 Marlow ed, *Votes for women* (London, Virago, 2000), p. 293.
30 J. Dixon, *Divine feminine: theosophy and feminism in England* (Baltimore, MD and London, Johns Hopkins University Press, 2001); A. Summers, *Christian and Jewish women in Britain, 1880–1940: living with difference* (Houndmills, Palgrave, 2016).
31 CP, 'Thou That Killest the Prophets', TS, 10 April 1914, p. 590.
32 Dixon, *Divine feminine*, p. 205.
33 J. R. deVries, Transforming the pulpit: preaching and prophecy in the British women's suffrage movement, in *Women preachers and prophets through two millennia of Christianity*, eds B. Mayne Kienzle and P. J. Walker (Berkeley, CA, University of California Press, 1998), pp. 318–33.
34 *Toronto Daily Star*, 18 November 1922.
35 *Present and Future*, May 1934, p. 2 she states she was 'simply a member of the Church of England'.

36 Janette Hassy, *No time for silence: evangelical women in public ministry around the turn of the century* (Grand Rapids, MI, Zondervan Publishing House, 1986), p. 136.
37 Larsen, *Christabel*, p. 138.
38 Larsen, *Christabel*, p. 27.
39 CP, 'The Lord cometh', p. vii.
40 CP, 'The Lord cometh', p. 5.
41 CP, 'The Lord cometh', p. 98.
42 CP, 'The Lord cometh', pp. 99 and 102. In *The world's unrest*, Christabel devotes a whole chapter to 'Christ and Antichrist'.
43 CP, 'The Lord cometh', p. 75.
44 CP, 'The Lord cometh', p. 97; Larsen, *Christabel*, pp. 50–68.
45 CP, 'The Lord cometh', pp. 6–7.
46 CP, 'The Lord cometh', pp. 116 and ix.
47 *Christian*, 12 and 19 July 1923, pp. 2 and 26, respectively; *Sunday School Times*, 23 February 1924, p. 134.
48 M. D. S., Christabel Pankhurst, *Woman's Leader*, 17 August 1923, p. 229.
49 Moyes, *A woman in a man's world*, p. 35.
50 See J. Shaw, *Octavia: daughter of God* (London, Jonathan Cape, 2011).
51 *New York Times*, 16 and 19 August 1923.
52 Smyth, *Female pipings*, p. 257.
53 B. Harrison interview with Mrs Mary Hodgson, 2 July 1976, DMC.
54 CP to Mr Jensen, 13 November 1923, Purvis Collection.
55 *Christian*, 13 March 1924, p. 5.
56 Interview with Mrs Stride, 25 August 1975, DMC. She states that she destroyed all CP's letters since they were mostly on Second Adventism and she did not think anyone would be interested in them.
57 *New York Times*, 10 March 1924.
58 Larsen, *Christabel*, pp. 100–1.
59 H. Fraser, A new Christabel Pankhurst, *Glasgow Bulletin*, 29 April 1924.
60 *Los Angeles Times*, 26 April and 3 May 1924.
61 *Toronto Star Weekly*, 8 March 1924.
62 CP, *Unshackled*, p. 296.
63 Purvis, *Emmeline Pankhurst*, p. 335.
64 Book contracts in Craigie Collection.
65 CP, *Pressing problems*, p. 91.
66 Larsen, *Christabel*, p. 58.
67 Pugh, *The Pankhursts*, p. 342.
68 CP, *Pressing problems*, p. 39.
69 CP, *Pressing problems*, pp. 38–9.
70 Quoted in Larsen, *Christabel*, p. 115.
71 L. Martz, Moved to minister: Christabel Pankhurst and Aimee Semple McPherson in Los Angeles, in *Women on the move: refugees, migration and exile*, eds F. Reid and K. Holden (Newcastle upon Tyne, Cambridge Scholars Publishing, 2010), p. 87.
72 Kenney, *Memories*, pp. 300–2.
73 CP to Lloyd George, 8 December 1924, LG Papers.
74 Kathleen King interviews.
75 *Daily Herald*, 6 January 1925.
76 *New York Times*, 4 May 1925.
77 Kathleen King interviews; Harrison interview with Mary Hodgson.
78 Harrison interview with Mary Hodgson; Kathleen King interviews.
79 CP, The sexless life, *Daily Express*, 20 July 1925.

80 Adoption was lax until 1926, when it became legal. Kathleen was eventually adopted by John Coleridge Taylor, an *Evening Standard* journalist, and Joan by a wealthy couple in Scotland; Purvis, *Emmeline Pankhurst*, p. 337.
81 CP to Renee de Brimont, 4 August 1925, de Brimont Papers.
82 See *Sunday School Times*, 31 October 1925, p. 684.
83 Harrison interview with Mary Hodgson.
84 Interview with Mary Hodgson, 19 April 1975, DMC.
85 CP to Baronne Renee de Brimont, 26 August and 8 September 1925, de Brimont Papers.
86 Smyth, *Female pipings* (1934, revised second edition), p. 259.
87 The Guild, which aimed to promote cooperation between employers and workers, and to campaign against communism and trade union tyranny, had grown to more than thirty branches by 1926 with a membership of about 40,000 women, mainly wives of working men – Mitchell, *The fighting Pankhursts*, pp. 163–5.
88 Purvis, *Emmeline Pankhurst*, pp. 341–2.
89 Elsie Bowerman to Grace Roe, 3 April 1966, Craigie Collection.
90 Larsen, *Christabel*, p. 41.
91 Martz, Moved to minister, p. 88.
92 CP, *The world's unrest*, p. 191.
93 *Christian*, 23 September 1926, p. 6.
94 *Christian*, 23 September 1926, p. 5.
95 Larsen, *Christabel*, p. 64.
96 *Christian*, 21 October 1926, p. 23.
97 Miss Pankhurst as Missioner, *Manchester Guardian*, 3 November 1926.
98 EP to Esther Greg, 4 November 1926, Purvis Collection.
99 Larsen, *Christabel*, p. 94. Unfortunately, the sound system was faulty so that few of the audience could hear clearly the words of any of the speakers.
100 Is Christ coming?, *Sunday Chronicle*, 26 December 1926.
101 *Christian*, 4 November 1926, p. 12; *Sunday School Times*, 11 December 1926, p. 755.
102 Mitchell, *Queen Christabel*, p. 301. The first of these appeared in the *Christian*, 25 November 1926, p. 6.
103 Larsen, *Christabel*, p. 113.
104 Pugh, *The Pankhursts*, p. 382.
105 *Sunday School Times*, 21 December 1929, p. 739.
106 Larsen, *Christabel*, p. 71.
107 Purvis, *Emmeline Pankhurst*, p. 344.
108 Mitchell, *The fighting Pankhursts*, p. 177.
109 *Toronto Daily Star*, 2 October 1926.
110 Interview with Mrs Stride, 25 August 1975, DMC; Mitchell, *Queen Christabel*, p. 309.
111 Purvis, *Emmeline Pankhurst*, p. 345.
112 *Christian*, 5 May 1927, p. 22.
113 *Moody Bible Institute Monthly*, September 1927, pp. 10–14, quoted in Larsen, *Christabel*, p. 118.
114 Statement by Nellie Hall-Humpherson, DMC, 73.83/36 (c).
115 *News of the World*, 8 April 1928; the story was also reported in the *Sunday Chronicle* and other tabloid newspapers.
116 *Sunday Chronicle*, 15 April 1928.
117 Elsa Gye to Adela Pankhurst, 10 November 1934, APWP.
118 CP to Grace Roe, 2 April 1950, Craigie Collection.
119 CP to Christopher St John, 21 December 1957, Craigie Collection. I have corrected CP's typing errors.
120 Purvis, *Emmeline Pankhurst*, p. 351; Coleman, *Adela Pankhurst*, p. 108.

121 Norah Walshe to David Mitchell, 2 November 1964, DMC; Purvis, *Emmeline Pankhurst*, p. 351.
122 CP to Esther Greg, 29 May 1928, Purvis Collection.
123 CP to Esther Greg, 1 June 1928, Purvis Collection.
124 CP to Esther Greg, 5 June 1928, Purvis Collection.
125 CP, *Unshackled*, p. 298.
126 CP to Esther Greg, 13 June 1928, Purvis Collection.
127 CP to Esther Greg, 20 June 1928, Purvis Collection.
128 Ethel Smyth to Lady Astor, 6 July 1928, Nancy Astor Papers, University of Reading.
129 CP to Miss Froud, Records of the National Union of Women's Teachers, University of London, Institute of Education; CP to Jessie Kenney, 7 September 1928, Kenney Papers.
130 EPL to CP, 17 June 1928, Craigie Collection.
131 CP, Mother, *Daily Mail*, 15 June 1928.
132 *Daily News*, 18 June 1928.
133 *Daily Telegraph* and *Daily Express*, 19 June 1928; *The Vote*, 22 June 1928.
134 As noted earlier, it seems these letters are lost, although they are referred to in CP, *Unshackled*, pp. 21–2.
135 CP to Annie Kenney, 27 June 1928, Kenney Papers.

21

ELIZABETH/BETTY/AUREA
July 1928–end of June 1940

The death of her mother was a formative moment in Christabel's life. Although she still had Betty to love and care for, Christabel wanted to honour the woman she had been close to all her life, her companion and friend as well as her mother. On 22 June 1928 she had placed an advertisement in the *Times*, stating she had arranged to write a 'memoir' of her mother and would be grateful to receive any useful material that people might want to send her. She also wrote to individual former suffragettes, such as Una Duval, asking for 'any letters of Mother's that you have kept & also your recollections of work with her'.[1] Undoubtedly Christabel spoke to more former WSPU members when she attended a suffragette reunion that December of 1928. 'We have been able to help Christabel in the book she is writing on your Mother's life', a member of the Suffragette Club (formed in 1926 and later called the Suffragette Fellowship) later informed Adela. 'She found references that otherwise she would never have been able to obtain without tremendous difficulty.'[2] However, Sylvia was also busy writing a history of the suffrage struggle which would be published in 1931, whereas Christabel's memoir would be printed posthumously in 1959, one year after her death.

As the New Year of 1929 dawned, Christabel sent affectionate greetings to Esther Greg, glad that her friend was taking part in the Memorial Fund, set up by Kitty Marshall, Rosamund Massy and Lady Rhondda, to commemorate her mother. The plan was to raise £2,500 which would pay for a headstone for Emmeline's grave in Brompton Cemetery, the purchase of a portrait that had been painted by Georgina Brackenbury for presentation to the National Portrait Gallery, and a statue to be erected in Victoria Tower Gardens, close to Parliament. Esther had said that she might leave London and spend a few days in the Norfolk countryside, a suggestion that triggered in Christabel fond memories of her time in rural Surrey. She told Esther how she wished she could find rooms there 'in some oak beamed cottage in a high & dry spot. To miss the birds as the spring comes on & all the sprouting green things is a cruel deprivation'. But such a plan would have to wait until April when 'my adopted has her Easter holiday'.[3] Christabel wanted the best in life for the bright thirteen-year-old Betty and so had decided it was time for her adopted daughter to attend Headington Girls' School, Oxford, an independent school founded by a group of evangelical Christians in

1915. Headington Girls' School, with its nineteen acres of farmland, claimed to offer a sound academic, Christian education in spacious surroundings. Betty was a boarder here, at Napier House, from 1929 to 1932.

Christabel now had an additional reason to keep working hard, namely that she had to earn enough to pay Betty's not inconsiderable school fees. Although she received some income from her writings, any money derived from preaching was unpredictable since it was in the form of an honorarium, usually given without mentioning an amount, let alone agreeing to one.[4] As she continued with her Adventist ministry Christabel also kept in touch with Kitty Marshall about the proposed statue of her mother, for which Mr Walker – who had forged a statue of Florence Nightingale – was commissioned. 'The last time I saw Christabel', noted Mabel Tuke, 'she told me how greatly she liked the work . . . & is jealous that all the power & dignity & true womanliness of Mrs Pankhurst's character should be worthily perpetuated.'[5] Indeed, her mother was often on Christabel's mind, even when spreading her Adventist message. 'I had such a wonderful Mother myself I wish she could have come among you', she told one group of poor women in the East End of London that she spoke to that January of 1929:

> [T]his country now needs the very hand of God to lift us out of our difficulties . . . the biggest thing we shall ever do as women is to pray that Christ will keep his promise and return to this earth . . . His coming . . . is not a long way off.[6]

The other nine addresses that Christabel gave at the Aeolian Hall, Bond Street, London, on 'World problems: and the outlook from a woman voter's point of view', were so well attended that a further series was arranged for the summer. By this time the Revd. F. B. Meyer, whose friendship and support she greatly valued, had died. During his final days, Meyer had read and endorsed Christabel's latest book *Seeing the future* in which she makes statements about women's enfranchisement that echo those in earlier writings. 'Emphatically, we are not disappointed in votes for women', she asserted, 'but government, in this modern world especially, is a more than superhuman task: it is truly a task beyond all save God in person.'[7] Emphasising the limitations of all human beings, whether male or female, Christabel suggested that women entering the doors of Government office now opening to them would not be 'one bit worse' than their male counterparts.[8]

With the gossip still ringing about the unmarried Sylvia's illegitimate baby, Christabel decided it was time to confront her sister. Even Betty, with the surname Pankhurst, was being asked questions by curious fellow pupils, something that worried Christabel who was about to set in motion the process for legally adopting the girl. Christabel visited Sylvia, now living in Woodford, urging her to give baby Richard his father's surname, not that of Pankhurst. A furious row broke out between the sisters, with Sylvia insisting it was none of Christabel's business.[9]

The upset Christabel discussed the situation with Betty who was beginning to enquire about her own birth parents. Perhaps Christabel told her that her birth mother, Edith Bathe, a servant, had been deserted by her lover, Louis Lurashi, and that at birth she had been named Dorothea Joan Bathe. Or, given the mores of the time, perhaps Christabel said nothing about the matter. However, over the following months Betty asked if she could have a new Christian name. Christabel, ever indulgent of the fourteen-year-old she loved dearly, agreed. In early 1930, Betty was legally registered as 'Aurea Elizabeth Pankhurst' and Christabel listed as her adopter.[10] Shortly after this, Christabel also agreed that Aurea could even change her surname to 'Clifford', the name by which Aurea became known at her school. 'Clifford' was chosen because the red-haired Aurea considered it a 'sort of Tudor name'.[11] All four adopted girls had been promised the surname 'Pankhurst' and it is ironic that the one girl who legally was given that name rejected it.

Christabel had earlier agreed to undertake a six-month lecturing tour in Canada and the United States, during autumn 1929 and spring 1930, on the topic of prophecy and the Second Coming of Christ. Such a long-distance venture was possible since Rangeley Stride, a close friend, had promised she would visit Betty regularly at Headington Girls' School. Before she left for North America, Christabel wrote for the *Sunday School Times* the first of several articles on 'Current World Events Which Are Heralding Our Lord's Promised Return', the essays appearing in print during the time she was away.[12]

On 27 September 1929, Christabel sailed from Liverpool on the *Duchess of Bedford*, bound for Montreal. Her headquarters during her tour was listed as being in this Canadian city, at the home of a friend, Mrs T. C. Thomson, Chateau Apartments, Sherbrooke Street. Churches, Bible schools and other organisations keen to ask Christabel to address audiences were asked to contact her as early as possible at this address.[13] 'Politics Boring to Miss C. Pankhurst' ran the headline in the *Montreal Star*, as Christabel explained to a disappointed reporter that she did not want to talk about women's suffrage but the Second Coming of Christ.[14] By early December Christabel was in Baltimore in the USA, from where she wrote to Renee de Brimont:

> I have been travelling almost constantly. Last week I was in Washington. The National Woman's Party founded by American women who were in sympathy with our movement of pre war days was holding its Convention . . . & on Sunday afternoon in the Capitol they held a memorial service for Mother. This was a wonderful occasion & a very moving ceremony. Mother was greatly loved in America & everywhere I go people tell me that they heard her speak & remember her. Even a coloured train attendant in charge of the Pullman car said to me one day: 'I remember Mrs Pankhurst: she travelled in my car. She was a mighty sweet lady.'

Christabel also commented on world affairs to Renee, such as the terrible storms in England, earthquakes and the stock market crash in the USA which 'led to the ruin of many with the suicide of several people'. She also gave news about her 'precious adopted . . . at boarding school in Oxford' whom she hoped to meet up with in Paris, after leaving North America at the end of March. Rangeley Stride was taking her own daughter and Betty to Switzerland and, en route, would bring them both to Paris for a few days. Christabel expected Miss Pepper to join them, and hoped Renee would too.[15]

Unfortunately, Christabel was still in North America on Thursday, 6 March 1930, the date that had been arranged for the unveiling of her mother's statue in Victoria Gardens, London. She sent a golden wreath and a telegram, which was read out by Flora Drummond who presided over proceedings.[16] The day before, Christabel was in Chicago from where she sent to Grace Roe, now in San Francisco, a telegram outlining her thoughts:

> Loving Thoughts With You Dear Grace Thursday Remembering As Always Your Courage Firmness Loyalty I Know How You Are Rejoicing In Justice Done And Honour Paid to Mother In London You And I There In Spirit Ever In Faithfulness To The Past & Hope For Future.[17]

Christabel was not the only absent daughter on this important day. Adela in far-away Australia was unable to attend too. She could not afford the fare. Of Christabel's two sisters, it was only Sylvia who was present, with baby Richard in her arms, despite the fact that she had been shunned by those organising the memorial proceedings.

After returning to England on 1 April 1930, Christabel had gladly accepted the invitation of Edith How Martyn of the Suffragette Fellowship to make a pres-entation to Kitty Marshall of a replica of the statue of her mother. But finding a convenient time for the event was problematic. Christabel had been invited to the USA again and, ever restless, greatly enjoyed such visits – and the income she earned. A recent small legacy from the estate of Gladys Emily Sophy Compton Shedden was very welcome but, combined with the earnings from writing and preaching, it was not enough to keep herself and Aurea, who had expressed a wish to study for a degree at Oxford.[18] 'I will postpone my sailing for a week & can give you October 1st', Christabel finally suggested, in desperation, to Edith How Martyn. 'This really is the very latest day & I hope all interested can be present including Mrs Marshall herself.'[19] The criticism that was frequently being voiced in Britain about her conversion to Second Adventism was hurtful to Christabel. 'Miss Pankhurst started off impressively', wrote St John Ervine in *Time and Tide* of one of Christabel's addresses, but 'steadily declined in authority until at the end she became wearisome, for she did not know when to stop and she repeated herself. It was the sermon of a disillusioned and disappointed woman.'[20]

Once back in the USA again, Christabel was soon mixing with like-minded people on the Second Adventist circuit and corresponding with old acquaintances, including Harriot Stanton Blatch.[21] She initially went to California where, on 18 January 1931, she was billed to speak at the Calvary Church, Placentia, Los Angeles, with a broadcast over KGER Radio.[22] This willingness to embrace new forms of communication in an effort to bring more people to the Christian faith served Christabel well. With her distinctive English accent, clear enunciation and crisp sentences, attractive to many American listeners, she became a popular religious speaker on the air. In an interview for the *Los Angeles Times* she made it clear that she did not recant her past suffrage work but now believed that more than feminist activism was necessary when trying to solve the problems of the world:

> The suffrage work is over and there is no longer any need to promote it. I believe that after a certain amount of political and governmental service, there is a higher work to be done and, right now, I am sure the world needs prophets more than politicians. The world needs ideals and hope rather than reform and that is what I have chosen for my work – to try to bring vision to the world, to turn people back to the Bible and faith in the coming of a kingdom of God on earth.[23]

As her tour continued, Christabel continued to speak out against the rise of anti-Semitism, a worrying feature of the world political situation, especially in Germany. She was also an invited main speaker at the annual conference of the World's Christian Fundamentals Association which met in Philadelphia that May of 1931.[24] In contrast to St John Ervine in Britain, one of the Los Angeles-based journalists would come to describe Christabel's sermons as 'lucid, gently reasonable and obviously spoken in abiding faith'. Her understanding of all Christian faiths, Alma Whitaker claimed, made her popular across a broad Christian spectrum, 'Baptist, Presbyterian and Methodist audiences or any others who accept the Bible teaching'.[25]

When Christabel was back in Britain again, by the end of May 1931, relatives and friends pleaded with her to start writing her account of the suffragette campaign. While she had been away, Sylvia had published her book *The suffragette movement* in which she stingingly attacked Christabel and their mother, portraying her sister as the evil genius of the movement who had led Emmeline and the WSPU away from socialism. Christabel was upset by the content of Sylvia's book but decided, generously, that she would not disagree with her sister in public. What purpose would be served by yet another family feud? Many former suffragettes were critical of Sylvia's book too. 'It is extraordinary how her jealousy of Christabel comes out', wrote Elsa Gye. 'The book has created rather a bad feeling & most of us were terribly disappointed . . . Sylvia . . . is still the same intolerant person.' Geraldine Lennox, once a subeditor of *The Suffragette*, was outraged. 'It is a pity that Sylvia has not emulated her elder sister's loyalty and greatheartedness and kept a fine book free from a personal bitterness that had nothing to do with the Movement', she wrote angrily in a letter published in the press.[26]

Christabel welcomed such loyalty as she picked up again the threads of her life in England. She renewed her acquaintance with Lloyd George when they both spoke at the same service at a Welsh Baptist chapel in London in summer 1931. And from September, she also met up several times with Winston Churchill.[27] Both Christabel and Churchill, who had rejoined the Conservatives after spending some twenty years on the Liberal benches, were stern critics of Bolshevism. However, Christabel knew she could not earn enough in England to support Aurea and herself, and so soon she was back in North America again, saving as much as she could. She did not feel able to return until early January 1934.[28]

Tired after her strenuous but necessary tour, Christabel found herself immediately embroiled in another conflict situation. Late in 1933 Ethel Smyth had published a memoir titled *Female pipings in Eden* in which she quoted freely from letters sent to her by Emmeline Pankhurst who had asked, without success, for their return. Foolishly, Ethel had not asked Christabel, Emmeline's literary executrix, for permission to quote. But, more importantly, Christabel objected strongly to what she saw as libellous and false statements about herself. She met up with Ethel in the offices of the publisher, Peter Davies. Weary and exhausted, she was no match for the aggressive Ethel who threatened to strike her with her umbrella – forcing the publisher to intervene. The outcome was that the first edition of the book was withdrawn from circulation and agreement was reached for a revised, second edition. 'Unwilling . . . that the letters should not be lost to the world', wrote the reluctant Ethel in the preface to the second edition, 'Miss Pankhurst, while not, of course, committed to all I have written in this monograph, has most generously made me a gift of the copyright in these particular letters, and now permits their publication.'[29] Ethel made no mention of the passages she edited out or of the many re-written sentences. Surprisingly, Sylvia had supported Christabel in her protest. Although both sisters may have been jealous about the close relationship Ethel had enjoyed with their mother, it is also highly probable that they were deeply concerned what the public might make of such revelations, given that Ethel was now known as a 'lesbian'.[30] Ever since late 1928, when Radclyffe Hall's lesbian novel *The well of loneliness* had been condemned as obscene and banned, there had been much greater awareness about the possibility of physical love between women. Whatever the reason for Christabel's objections to the first edition of Ethel's book, she was never happy with the revised version, an issue that would haunt her in later life. Nonetheless, from now until mid-1940 Christabel spent most of her time in England, apart from a few occasional visits to North America.

If Aurea was to fulfil her dream of becoming a student at Oxford University that autumn of 1934, then she needed some tuition to prepare her for the entrance exams. Christabel engaged a private tutor for that very purpose. St Hugh's College was chosen as the ideal place since it was a women's college with which the WSPU had unofficial links. The suffragette Emily Wilding Davison had briefly been a student there, in its early days, while another former WSPU member, the wealthy Clara Mordan, was its first major patron and a member of

470

the College Council. However, Aurea's tutor found his eighteen-year-old pupil very naïve and innocent and suggested that she spend a year abroad, gaining some experience of life before entering college.[31] But Aurea did not want this delay; nor could Christabel afford it.

While Aurea was being coached, Christabel published a prophecy journal, *Present and Future*, the first issue of which appeared in May 1934. The new journal was free, intended for non-believers – although voluntary contributions towards its cost were welcome. Yet wherever Christabel travelled in Britain she was inevitably asked about her bewildering turn from politics to prophecy. She preached prophecy, she wrote, because 'the hope it gives endures and brightens, while other hopes fade into darkness'.[32] As she elaborated further to her congregation at Union Chapel, West Gorton, Manchester on 13 May, 'her work in the women's suffrage movement had taught her how much could be done by human agency and how much could not'. Everywhere she looked today she saw evidence of noble endeavour and self-sacrifice but also of the 'adverse side' of human nature. Every form of political and economic experiment was being tried, 'except one – theocracy. It was true we needed leadership, but it was the leadership of Christ. His form of government would mean the end of unemployment, of war, of cruelty, of injustice to women, and wickedness towards children'.[33] While staying in Manchester, at the Midland Hotel, Christabel sent to Churchill a copy of her new journal, enclosing also a letter that argued along similar lines to her sermon.[34]

Despite her new mission in life, suffrage comrades were not forgotten. 'I was very happy to be among the old friends, to have that opportunity of expressing my love for them', she wrote to Edith How Martyn after a gathering of the Suffragette Fellowship at her mother's statue on 14 July 1934. 'It meant much work for you & the other officers of the Suffragette Fellowship, including Miss Gye who so recently had that operation! We all appreciate it!'[35] And Christabel sent affectionate thanks to Edith when, on behalf of the Fellowship, she was sent a birthday telegram.[36] But with other people who did not appreciate her suffrage work, Christabel could be short-tempered. The young Margaret Grant, recently appointed acting editor of the *Life of Faith*, met Christabel in the office of her publisher, Marshall, Morgan and Scott, and remembered her as 'a rather dowdy middle-aged woman with a dominant personality, restless and frustrated because her work was done, the results had not been what she expected, and she herself had been forgotten'. She offered Christabel a chair, which was refused while Margaret remained seated. Pacing up and down the room, Christabel said impatiently, 'Young woman, do you realise that you would not be sitting in that chair if it had not been for me and my friends?' When Margaret tried to reply that she was not unaware of the suffrage struggle since her mother had been a suffrage sympathiser, Christabel turned abruptly, enquired if she used her vote, and when the reply was in the affirmative, asked, 'Do you vote for the most good-looking candidate? Most women seem to.' The overwhelmed Margaret said nothing.[37]

Much to Christabel's delight, in October 1934 Aurea passed her 'Modern Greats' entrance exam for St Hugh's and then began studying for a degree in Philosophy, Politics and Economics. Still hurt by the content of Sylvia's *The suffragette movement*, Christabel now tried to settle to work on her own manuscript. Having led an active nomadic life for a number of years, she confessed to a friend that she found it hard sitting down, just writing. She was particularly anxious about whether what she wrote would only generate more unwelcome controversy. 'It must be all right to <u>set down the facts at least</u>', the frustrated Christabel believed.[38] One 'fact' that Jessie Kenney did not want Christabel to endlessly repeat was that her sister, Annie, should be described as an Oldham 'cotton operative', a phrase that Sylvia had used:

> Now Christabel, you know Sylvia – and I know Sylvia. I know as you know her consuming jealousy of you and of other Suffragettes, especially Annie . . . I am writing to you about Annie and to say that I do trust you will give Annie a rest, and her family too, from this cotton operative and mill-girl business.[39]

Christabel replied immediately, reassuring Jessie that she would do all in her power to meet her wishes:

> My strong opinion is that all those who strove for the vote . . . should stand together loyally . . . None more than Annie deserve this loyalty and I would not for the world have a word said or published that could wound her or be of the slightest disadvantage to anyone related to her. The old friends have ever the same place in my heart and in my words that they had in the old days.

Christabel was shocked to hear from Jessie that two years ago Annie had been gravely ill with a brain fever. 'I did not know', she confessed, 'I was in America and Canada and my stay lasted 2 and half years during which I had little or no news from this side of the world.'[40]

By the time this exchange of letters took place, Aurea had completed a year at St Hugh's. But Christabel made no mention of her to Jessie. Her relationship with Aurea, who was not doing well academically, was beginning to show signs of strain. Christabel's frequent absences and lack of a settled home life in England had not helped matters. A single parent, Christabel had coped better with Aurea when she was a young child who could be taken with her on her travels. Perhaps, too, the relationship between Christabel and Aurea had become less close because the young woman was developing her own resilient personality and becoming less malleable as she grew older.

When Aurea first entered St Hugh's she was still very much 'like a schoolgirl in her thinking', even wearing her auburn hair in 'a kind of pigtail', remembered one of her contemporaries.[41] At a meeting of first-year women students, called by the authorities to discuss what sports might be taken up, Aurea caused laughter when she naïvely suggested 'gym classes', something more appropriate for school than university. More astonishment erupted when she confessed that she had never been to the cinema since her 'Auntie' [Christabel] did not approve of it. Eager to have some freedom and appear 'grown up', Aurea wanted to know how to meet men.[42] Soon she had her long hair cut and waved in a short style.

The freckle-faced Aurea, with her slim figure, thick auburn hair, brown eyes, enchanting smile and creamy skin, was considered an attractive young woman, despite her stubby hands and thick ankles. She always looked 'very elegant', remembered another of her contemporaries, had a 'natural grace, spoke and acted in an "upper class" manner'. Her 'devil-may-care' attitude and Micawberish attitude to life, that something would always turn up, led many of her fellow students to excuse her hedonism and unreliability. Despite the fact that the lively, friendly Aurea was considered 'wild', there was a vulnerability about her that inspired sympathy and a desire to protect her. Molly Gaminara, the wealthiest student at St Hugh's and Aurea's closest friend, was her 'motherer'.[43] But Aurea's tutors were not impressed. During her first year at Oxford, her English Political History tutor complained that her essays were 'badly arranged and sometimes almost incoherent', a criticism that was frequently aired over the next two years.[44] The situation was not helped by the fact that during Hilary Term 1935 Aurea had to take time out because of contact with mumps.

Aurea, the university student, became caught up in the social world of adult living. Extravagant with money, her allowance from Christabel was never enough to cover her expenses, as fellow students remembered. Wenda Reynolds recollected how Aurea was 'always putting down the deposit on clothes and not going back for them', frequently in debt and borrowing money. Beryl Davies recalled how she lent Aurea 7/6 d. during the last week of term, insisting that she must have the money back as soon as possible. Aurea sold her bike for the paltry sum of 10/- to repay the debt.[45] Rather than studying, Aurea enjoyed partying and, at a time when contraception was not freely available to women, became pregnant. She pleaded with her doctor to arrange an abortion. The German baron who got her pregnant drove her up to London for the necessary operation. On the way back, the next day, he said to her, 'Don't you know I would have married you?' Aurea burst into tears. Her women friends at St Hugh's rallied around to support the vulnerable young woman. 'Christabel would kill me if she knew', she told them.[46]

Aurea's friends had covered for her during her night's absence. Miss Gwyer, the Principal of St Hugh's, was in the habit of knocking on Aurea's bedroom door every night, peeping into the bedroom and asking 'Are you alright?' This was something that she never did with the other women students. On the night in question, it was arranged that a red-headed substitute would sleep in Aurea's bed. When Miss Gwyer, as expected, peeped into Aurea's room, calling out, 'Good night, Miss Clifford', the substitute, with most of her head apart from her hair under the bedclothes, murmured a reply.[47]

While this distressing incident was hidden from Christabel, Aurea's poor academic record at St Hugh's could not be. But Christabel, ever indulgent of the young woman she loved dearly, hoped things would improve. She did not want to be too judgemental, but modern in her approach. The excitable, exuberant Aurea, recollected one of her fellow students, became 'a very different person' when Christabel visited, 'very demure' with 'Yes, Auntie' and 'No, Auntie'. Keen to create a good impression, Aurea became terrified when, on one occasion, she lost a ten-shilling note that Christabel – whom she saw as a 'meal-ticket' – had given her, afraid she would be asked about it. Although Christabel, whom Aurea described as her 'Guardian', gave her adopted daughter an adequate allowance, the amount could vary, depending on how much money she could afford. If the cheque was just for £5, Aurea would say 'she might as well not have bothered to send it'.[48]

As the relationship between Christabel and Aurea became increasingly uneasy, some unexpected news arrived – Christabel was made a Dame Commander of the Order of the British Empire in the 1936 New Year's honours list. 'I do think this is the happiest of New Years for me', she told a reporter:

I have always been proud of the part I played in helping to secure enfranchisement for women, and I feel that this honour is shared by all those who struggled with my mother and the rest of us through most difficult times . . . mother would have been so pleased.[49]

The conversation was constantly interrupted by telephone calls from jubilant supporters as well as telegrams, including one from the Suffragette Fellowship. Letters of congratulations arrived in profusion. 'The King, in this his Jubilee year, has set the seal of approval on your wonderful leadership', wrote sisters Hannah and Caroline Townsend, former members of the WSPU and Women's Party. 'Would that women had followed the lead you then gave them!'[50] 'There will be in the future no need to be continually explaining which Miss Pankhurst was the leader of the suffragettes', voiced an emotional Annie, who expressed a 'profound thankfulness that I met you and that you chose me as a worker and a companion for so many years.'[51] Although Christabel thanked all the letter writers, it was particularly to the former members of the inner WSPU circle, especially Annie, that she sent her warmest replies. 'Your congratulations have a particular meaning to me no other congratulations could have', she replied in a fourteen-page letter to 'Dearest Annie'. Annie, Christabel noted, had never failed her in the hour of need. 'I trusted you, with the implicit, perfect unquestioning trust that I give to the rising of the sun tomorrow. My memory of our work together is unshadowed.'[52] Unexpectedly, a congratulatory letter also arrived from Emmeline Pethick-Lawrence whom Christabel thanked for her 'generous and loving message . . . I feel & know, like you, that there is no inward change in the love which has once united us in the service of the same ideal, the same cause'. The honour bestowed upon her, Christabel insisted, 'was our Honour, shared by all who, with

474

mother & me, had a part in the great movement for whose victory we may be so thankful to God'. She ended her letter with 'loving thanks' to Emmeline and Fred for the 'power & inspiration' that they had given to the movement.[53]

Christabel had been staying at 50 Pembridge Villas, Ada Wright's flat, when she wrote all these letters. Never once had she made reference to Aurea, even to Annie. In the early summer of 1936, Annie (who now lived in Letchworth) invited Christabel to Warwick's speech day at Stratton Park School, Bricken-donbury, Hertfordshire, a private preparatory school for about fifty boys. Annie was not happy with the school's academic standards and wished to discuss the situation with Christabel. Perhaps Christabel told Annie then about the 'troublesome' Aurea. But there is notably no mention of Aurea in a letter she wrote shortly after the visit but of Annie's son:

> Your boy is the greatest success – a gentleman in every sense of the word. You may well be proud & happy in regard to him. You have brought him up very wisely . . . God bless him! He will always be your joy & give you increasing happiness & pride, I know.[54]

By autumn 1936, when Christabel was writing on notepaper headed 'From Dame Christabel Pankhurst, 5 Vincent Square, Westminster S.W.1.', the new address of her Aunt Ada, there was still no mention of Aurea in letters to former suffragettes. Christabel was speaking on biblical prophecy in relation to wars and rumours of wars in the current world crisis and informed former suffragette Ada Flatman that she had recently visited Stoke-on-Trent and would soon be in Jersey. 'I am glad that you wrote as you did to the BBC', she commented, adding:

> It is well for all concerned to know that those who took part in the WSPU campaign are vigilant. You will be glad to know that the General is in touch with those responsible for the broadcast & is going to take part in it so we shall be well represented.[55]

Well into the New Year of 1937, when Christabel was still travelling and still writing to Ada 'I am almost as busy just now as in WSPU Days!', there was still no mention of Aurea. Christabel was not speaking about her adopted daughter to her old suffragette friends because the twenty-one-year-old university student was causing great embarrassment. 'Miss Clifford is unbelievably lazy & a most trying pupil', wrote one tutor. 'She is sufficiently intelligent & could do quite well, but she hardly even begins to make the necessary effort.'[56] In addition, Aurea had appeared in court, summoned for dangerously catching a lift by standing with a foot on each of two bicycles being ridden down the road by two young men. The incident was reported in the press.[57]

Aurea was now in the third year of her university studies but, inevitably, failed to be awarded a degree in summer 1937. Anxious about Aurea's future, Christabel contacted friends in the USA to see if they could help. On 5 August 1937, Aurea boarded the SS *Champlain* at Southampton, bound for New York. She was listed as a 'student' and her English address was given as 5 Vincent Square, London, the home of Christabel's Aunt Ada Goulden Bach. From September 1937 to January 1938, the young woman was enrolled as a non-matriculated student at Colombia University where she took classes in Economics and Public Law. Living locally at 500 Riverside Drive, her non-school mailing address was c/o Mrs Hyde, Hydewood Hall, Plainfield, New Jersey. Although Aurea was not awarded a degree at Columbia University, the courses studied helped her obtain an au pair/teaching post with the family of the British naval attaché in Washington.[58] However, the posting was not a success and on 7 June 1938 Aurea arrived back in England to stay at 44 Harlech Road, Old Southgate, London, the address of Mrs Kate Pepper, a former private secretary to Christabel.

While Aurea was in the USA, Christabel had continued writing her manuscript on the suffragette movement as well as engaging in her Second Adventist work. During late 1937 and early 1938 she was booked as one of the main speakers of the Bible Testimony Fellowship's national campaign. But the rise of fascism in Spain plus the growing international crisis posed by Nazi Germany worried her, even though she believed that the triumph of General Franco could be prophetically interpreted as the arrival of the 'Anti-Christ' who would precede the Second Coming of Jesus.[59] A few days before Christmas 1937 Christabel wrote to Winston Churchill, reminiscing about the First World War and the current political situation:

> Unhappily, Christmas 1914 was followed by nearly four years of bitter fighting, the use of poison gas & other breaches of the laws of warfare. This was bad enough, but worse still, nearly quarter of a century later, the world, as you truly say is arming on a scale never before imagined & forging itself weapons more ever deadly to be used not only against armies, but whole populations.[60]

The only answer to such threatened destruction was the return of Christ, with His kingdom of peace and justice.

A letter from Esther Greg, received early in 1938, revived nostalgia about the suffragette past. Esther spoke of how she no longer trusted one of Christabel's former close suffrage friends (probably Flora Drummond). Christabel, although distressed by this news, was not too judgemental, suggesting that such behaviour might be explained in terms of the hardship and stresses of both the suffrage years and post-war life:

> After all the years of battling with Asquith followed by the war & then being obliged to face life anew – I wonder we were not each one a nervous wreck . . . So perhaps nerve strain may have accounted for something. I don't <u>know</u>. I only <u>feel</u> unhappy that any of our true and trusted ones of the suffrage years shd be <u>anything</u> else . . . In the

movement I came to look at people as gold bearing ore – & had to get out the <u>gold</u> & leave the <u>dross</u>. Perhaps we extracted so much gold from them all that the vein was drilled out in that part of them . . . Some of them were not what are counted <u>big</u> people but they did big things in the days of need & thus we conquered. They went through hard things & risked & suffered . . . Some of them are rank Pacifists now & advocating things mother & I disapproved & making it almost a principle not to follow us in our ideas of what is good for the country . . . But we never forgot what they were & did at the time.[61]

Deeply appreciative of how Esther had always supported her and her mother, trying to persuade them to stay in England after the war and then, when they lived in the USA and Canada, begging them to return home, Christabel thanked Esther for her 'love & loyal true friendship'. Feeling keenly the loss of many former suffrage friends, Christabel pleaded, 'Esther, dearest, your love means much to me, so never be angry with me, will you . . . do forgive <u>me</u> for anything you have suffered from anyone of our followers.'[62]

Occasionally, when she had the time, Christabel met up with Esther or even accompanied her to a classical concert. But even though they both had London addresses, the two women appear to have kept in touch mainly through letter writing. Writing on Easter Day 1938 to thank Esther for an enjoyable evening the night before, Christabel again thought about the past, recalling how grateful she was for the 'jolt' that ended her political career in the Women's Party and for Esther's support at that time in her life. She claimed:

I am doing what makes me far happier than I shd have been doing politics & being in Parliament – and is, I believe, more <u>really</u> useful to others than my political activities would have been. To you Esther, true & very dear friend, I am . . . grateful for having made the <u>jolt not too severe</u>![63]

After the First World War, Christabel had warned that Germany would rise again. Such fears were uppermost in her mind when, on 11 March 1938, German troops entered Austria and encountered popular support. Under the Versailles Treaty, union of the two countries had been forbidden as well as restraints upon military armaments. 'My thoughts are much with our Prime Minister at this most difficult time', Christabel wrote anxiously to Esther. 'He is faced by a harvest not of his own sowing. God help him & us!'[64] The British Prime Minister, Neville Chamberlain, hoping to avoid war, was adopting a policy of appeasement in regard to Nazi Germany and the aggressive expansionist plans of its dictator, Adolf Hitler. But the incorporation into Germany in early September of the German-speaking Sudeten areas of Czechoslovakia, comprising 3 million people, could leave no doubt as to Hitler's intentions. Chamberlain paid three visits to Hitler that September, as the world braced itself for another war. There was widespread relief when, at the end of the month, agreement was reached between the Germans, Italians, British and French over the geographical extent and timetable for the Sudetenland's absorption into Nazi Germany. The Munich agreement between Hitler and the Four Powers brought hope that war had been averted – and widespread praise in Britain for Chamberlain, including praise from Christabel.

Christabel began a brief correspondence, not with Chamberlain but with his wife, Anne, hoping that she would convey her thoughts to her busy spouse:

> May I tell you how grateful I am to the Prime Minister for this effort to preserve world peace. Though I have long ceased to take any part in politics, I am moved by the clamour of his misguided critics to send, through you, this assurance of loyalty & thanks.

Believing she spoke for the voiceless, Christabel noted, 'The vast, silent majority of the people are certainly of the same way of thinking.' Her hope for a 'complete & lasting peace', she continued, 'is based on the promised return of the divine Prince of Peace, as the ultimate if not imminent remedy for war'.[65]

With the Munich agreement very much on her mind, Christabel was determined to attend the important Congress of the Church of England held that autumn in Bristol and have her say. Since the Anglican Church had closed its doors to women preachers, she took advantage of the invitation open to any member of the Congress to speak to the limit of five minutes on any relevant topic. The dissent that had been expressed at the Congress on the Munich policy for preventing war, she stated, illustrated the great danger the Church faced in becoming divided against herself on social and international policy. The Church could not bring in the millennium but it could pray that until the millennium came 'God would inspire King and Government and Parliament. The recent crisis had shown us a little about prayer. The nation must keep on praying'.[66] That a woman spoke in this hallowed patriarchal setting astounded a number of the delegates, including the reporter for the Anglican *Church Times*.[67] The point underlined something Christabel knew only too well – despite the fact she considered herself an Anglican, she could not pursue her ministry within an Anglican context where sex discrimination was rife.

After Aurea's arrival back in Britain in June, Christabel had discussed with her various employment options and was now paying for her to attend a secretarial college. But the course was not completed. Aurea found it difficult – and had other priorities. Seeking independence and a whirl of social activity, she was soon sharing a flat in Gloucester Road with Wenda Reynolds. Aurea cooked the evening meal, Wenda the breakfast. Aurea's interest in partying and having a good time continued, sometimes landing her in trouble. She returned home one night with a black eye. At a party, she had made a pass at the host, a married man whose wife was also there. A male friend of the couple hit Aurea, and made her apologise for her behaviour. 'She then crept back to our flat at dawn. She was a bit silly like that. If she made a set at someone she would be quite open about it when it was not wise to be so.'[68] Such reckless behaviour continued to strain the relationship between Aurea and Christabel who visited occasionally. To Wenda Reynolds, Christabel appeared 'very dogmatic', the kind of person who would not tolerate discussion. 'She seemed like an old lady to me . . . elderly rather plump woman. I can remember seeing her sitting on a sofa wearing a broad brimmed hat, wearing very homely clothes, not very elegant at all.'[69] But Christabel, who could not afford to spend a lot on clothes anyway, had more weighty matters on her mind.

The New Year of 1939 brought her some unexpected news – she had been left a legacy of £1,000.[70] 'Yes it was a great surprise', Christabel informed Annie shortly after she had returned from South Wales, '& as is apt to happen it comes at a needed moment. Thank you for writing about it in such a loving way.' Although her first book 'The Lord cometh' had sold well, Christabel was not well off and Aurea had not found a steady job. Annie had asked Christabel if she had read Mrs Lawrence's autobiography, published the previous year, in which she had spoken about the ousting of herself and her husband from the WSPU in October 1912. Christabel replied that she had not read the book. 'It is not always a happy thing to read of these great past days – one's memories are often the most satisfying. By this I do not mean your book', she hastily added, 'which stands out as a worthy contribution. But since mother went & we entered upon the present troubled period . . . [I] feel more sensitive about any written revivals of the past.'[71] The hurt tone in which Christabel wrote to Annie indicates, perhaps, that even if she had not read My part in a changing world, published in 1938, she had been told about its content. Christabel knew that, after the 1912 split, she was not 'a complete stranger' to Emmeline Pethick-Lawrence as she had claimed.[72] Mrs Lawrence had written to her in 1922 and in 1928, on the death of her mother, and sporadically since then, most recently on the occasion of the award of her DBE in 1936. On each occasion, Christabel had sent warmly worded replies. But Mrs Lawrence was now close not to Christabel but the hard-up Sylvia Pankhurst to whom she regularly sent money.[73] And still smarting from the pain of the 1912 split, she preferred her own version of events, undoubtedly supported by Sylvia.

There was some small comfort for Christabel in the various suffragette celebrations taking place that year: it was her name and especially that of her mother which were given prominence, not Sylvia's. 'Days when, led by Christabel Pankhurst, they fought for votes for women, were recalled last night in Manchester by 40 old members of suffragette organisations, who celebrated the twenty-first anniversary of women's enfranchisement', ran the Daily Dispatch on 10 May 1939. 'I was Christabel Pankhurst's first associate, and she always christened me "No 1"', proclaimed Mary Helen Harker, one of the socialist women present at the founding of the WSPU in 1903.[74] 'Mrs. Pankhurst's "Veterans" Celebrate Tonight', ran a headline in the Evening News on 14 July, as it told how ex-suffragettes were united with other women's societies in keeping green the memory of the woman 'America called the Gentle Amazon' whose birthday was that very day. The article was illustrated with photographs of Emmeline and Christabel in prison dress and Emmeline being arrested outside Buckingham Palace in May 1914.[75]

As welcome as such stories were to Christabel, she had decided that her future lay in the USA rather than Britain. Only in a country far away that welcomed her could she escape the shadow of Sylvia's narrative of the suffragette movement and suspicion that 'she' was the 'Miss Pankhurst' who had had an illegitimate child in 1927. Christabel discussed her plans with Aurea who was thrilled at the prospect of living abroad. A move to the USA, of course, could not take place until Christabel had completed her commission to write another religious book to be titled *The uncurtained future*. But before all this happened the fragile world peace was shattered.

Nazi Germany, since 1933, had been following a domestic policy of 'strengthening' and 'purifying' the German race by marginalising and persecuting German Jews. On 9 November 1938, a dramatic shift occurred in that policy when state-sponsored violence against Jewish individuals and their property became widespread. Synagogues and businesses were attacked or burnt, nearly one hundred people killed and a further 30,000 arrested and sent to concentration camps. Hundreds of thousands of Jews fled into exile. Over the coming months, Hitler advanced his expansionist programme in Eastern Europe. Again the anxious Christabel wrote to Anne Chamberlain, expressing her 'confidence' in her husband's efforts to find a peaceful solution to the tensions.[76] But the crisis in Europe deepened over the summer of 1939. On 31 August, Christabel was attending a British Association conference at Roosie Priory, near the village of Inchture, Perthshire, when she felt compelled to express once again her thoughts to Anne Chamberlain. 'I still hope that the Prime Minister's great-hearted & wise endeavour for peace will have the crown of success. God grant it!'[77] It was not to be. On 3 September 1939, two days after Hitler had invaded Poland, Britain and France declared war on Germany in support of their ally.

Aurea, who had not settled to any work, decided to join the Women's Auxiliary Air Force (WAAF). Although she had difficulty in passing the necessary medical, because of bronchial asthma induced by her heavy smoking, she was accepted. One of her former friends at St Hugh's remembered meeting her, dressed in a WAAF uniform, in a restaurant near Holborn. The proud Aurea – in a 'typical touch' – pulled out her knitting from a gas-mask container.[78] Christabel, on the other hand, who had now completed her manuscript on the suffragette movement, continued as best she could with her religious writing and preaching, travelling around when appropriate to earn enough to keep herself and her adopted daughter. In March 1940 she visited Truro, Cornwall, staying with Ida Copeland, a former Unionist MP for Stoke-on-Trent, a Commissioner for the Girl Guides and wife of the Director of Copeland China Works. But soon Christabel was back to her new London address, 7 Collingham Road, and catching up with old suffrage friends including Elizabeth Robins whose memoirs of her life before the suffragette campaign had just been published. 'I shall enjoy entering the time of which you have just written – before world wars and gigantic contests for power and before this great upheaval of nations and civilizations and challenges to Christianity', Christabel wrote to Elizabeth on Good Friday 1940. Reflecting on the past, the fifty-nine-year-old Christabel pondered:

> Life is a pilgrimage – and a voyage of discovery . . . Trials, and disappointments one finds by the way – but they are salutary one must believe . . . If human hopes fail – that leaves one reliant on God as otherwise one would not be.[79]

On the last day of May 1940, staying at a house in Bickley, Kent, a house that belonged to St Hugh's, Christabel put the final touches to *The uncurtained future* which appeared later that year and would be her last book.

Although Pugh claims *The uncurtained future* is 'a rather stale volume', largely a '*rechauffe*' of Christabel's earlier works, he fails to observe that it is the only book published during her life that contains substantial reflections about her past life.[80] Having now completed her manuscript on the suffragette struggle, some of this material was uppermost in her mind. In *The uncurtained future* she devotes one chapter each to her father and mother, describing with great affection her happy childhood and her parents' all too brief marriage during which they were trying to make the world a better place. She speaks too of her part in the suffrage agitation, downplaying her own contribution as her mother's 'right hand' and writing fondly of her mother and the countless women involved:

> Human agency I . . . saw at its best during our Suffragette campaign, in the unselfish devotion of numberless women, many of unknown or today forgotten name[s], to a movement which, to them personally, brought only sacrifice and loss . . . Mother . . . put her health and her life in the balance, that the women of future generations might be free.[81]

The winning of the vote was not the WSPU's only accomplishment. With the outbreak of war, the WSPU's leaders declared a truce to suffrage agitation and 'claimed and gained a wider sphere for women's war-work, advocated conscription of man-power, food rationing, unity of command . . . individual Suffragettes were active in many fields'.[82] There can be no doubt that Christabel Pankhurst, although now a Second Adventist, was still a feminist.

Some of Christabel's thoughts about the Second Coming of Christ had developed over the passing years, with differing interpretations being given to prophecies about the doom of the end times. Whereas in her first book, '*The Lord cometh*', she had asserted that the prophecies of the end times could not be avoided, seventeen years later, in *The uncurtained future*, she emphasises that such a state of affairs was not inevitable. 'The prophets bring, above all, good tidings . . . [they] say nothing of unconditional and inevitable judgement and doom. Their message forewarns: it does not foredoom.'[83] Nor did looking forward to the Second Coming mean that one should abandon all reform work or be inactive in the face of social and international wrongs. 'The classical disproof of this is Lord Shaftesbury, who, deeply interested in the Second Advent doctrine, was also the pioneer of social reform. Without a vision the people perish, and there is no human need so great as the need of faith in the essential justice of things . . .'[84] Christabel would soon preach such messages of Christian hope in the United States. On 28 June 1940, Christabel and Aurea – en route to the USA – sailed to Montreal on the *Duchess of Richmond*, with Christabel being listed as a 'Housewife' and Aurea as a 'Secretary'. Both gave 5 Vincent Square as their English address.[85] Neither was ever to return to Britain again.

Notes

1 CP to Una Duval, 29 June 1928, Purvis Collection.
2 Elsa Gye to Adela Pankhurst, 10 November 1934, APWP. The club had been formed in 1926 to perpetuate the memory of the pioneers for women's emancipation, especially the militant suffragettes.
3 CP to Esther Greg, 5 January and 2 March 1929, Purvis Collection.
4 Thanks to Timothy Larsen for this information.
5 Mabel Tuke to Miss Robins, 28 January 1929, Robins Papers, Fales Library.
6 Miss Pankhurst, East End Meeting for Poor Mothers, 21 January 1919, Craigie Collection.
7 CP, *Seeing the future*, p. 116.
8 CP, *Seeing the future*, p. 208.
9 Interview with Charlotte Drake, 2 September 1965, DMC.
10 Entry in the Adopted Children Register, 18 January 1930, General Register Office.
11 Interview with Wanda Reynolds at her home in Wantage, Oxon, 12 March 1999, Purvis Collection.
12 See, for example, CP, 'Who can speak to the nations?' and 'The wailing wall that circles the globe', *Sunday School Times*, 26 and 30 November 1919, pp. 591 and 689, respectively.
13 *Sunday School Times*, 7 September 1929, p. 485.
14 *Montreal Star*, 7 October 1929.
15 CP to Renee de Brimont, 9 December 1929, de Brimont Papers.
16 *Evening Standard*, 6 March 1930.
17 Telegram from CP to Grace Roe, 5 March 1930, Craigie Collection.
18 For details of the beneficiary see *Daily Express*, 12 October 1929. This was to be one of a few small bequests left to Christabel.
19 CP to Edith How Martyn, 25 July 1930, SFC.
20 St John Irvine, Notes of the way, *Time and Tide*, 13 September 1930, pp. 1140–2.
21 Dubois, *Harriot Stanton Blatch*, p. 261.
22 Advertisement in *Los Angeles Times*, 17 January 1931, p. A8.
23 Miss Pankhurst Here, *Los Angeles Times*, 1 January 1931, p. 10.
24 Larsen, *Christabel*, pp. 63 and 101.
25 A. W., Sugar and spice, *Los Angeles Times*, 8 August 1943, p. D8.
26 Elsa Gye to Adela Pankhurst, 10 November 1934, APWP; G. Lennox letter to the editor, *Everyman*, 5 March 1931.
27 Mitchell, *Christabel*, pp. 299–30; Larsen, *Christabel*, p. 60.
28 *Daily Telegraph*, 11 January 1934.
29 Smyth, *Female pipings* (1934 second edition), p. vi; interview with Van Thal, March 1965, DMC.

30 In Purvis, *Emmeline Pankhurst*, p. 160 it is claimed that it was 'unlikely' that Emmeline Pankhurst and Ethel Smyth were lovers in any physical sense. See Rachel Lumsden, 'The music between us': Ethel Smyth, Emmeline Pankhurst, and 'Possession', *Feminist Studies*, 41, 2, 2015, pp. 335–70 for a nuanced reading of how Ethel 'wrote' her relationship with Emmeline by drawing on the generic opportunities that music offered.
31 Interview with Wenda Reynolds, 20 November 1975, DMC.
32 *Present and Future*, June 1934, p. 6.
33 *Manchester Guardian*, 14 May 1934.
34 CP to Winston Churchill, 14 May 1934, Churchill Archives Centre, Churchill College, Cambridge.
35 CP to Mrs How Martyn, 16 July 1934, SFC.
36 CP to Mrs How Martyn, 28 September 1934, SFC.
37 Margaret Grant, A meeting with Miss Pankhurst, n.d. [1934], DMC.
38 CP to unknown recipient [Grace Roe?], Christmas 1934, Craigie Collection.
39 Jessie Kenney to CP, 12 October 1935, Kenney Papers.
40 CP to Jessie Kenney, 15 October 1935, Kenney Papers.
41 Interview with Wenda Reynolds, Purvis Collection.
42 Mitchell, *Queen Christabel*, p. 310. Mitchell does not name his informant but it was probably Wenda Reynolds whom he interviewed on 20 November 1975. I subsequently also interviewed Wenda who told me differing stories to those Mitchell recorded, as did Eric Midgley in correspondence with me, 26 February 1992, Purvis Collection.
43 Interview with Mrs Beryl Davies, 13 September 1975, DMC.
44 Report for Hilary Term 1935. Thanks to Amanda Ingram, Archivist, St Hugh's, Oxford, for this information and to the Principal and Fellows for permission to quote.
45 Interview with Reynolds, Purvis Collection; interview with Mrs Beryl Davies, 13 September 1975, DMC.
46 Interview with Reynolds, Purvis Collection; Mitchell, *Queen Christabel*, p. 310. In Mitchell's 1975 interview with Reynolds she says that it was David Huxley, Christ Church College, who drove Aurea up to London and who told her afterwards that he would have married her.
47 Interview with Reynolds, Purvis Collection.
48 Interview with Beryl Davies, DMC.
49 *Evening News*, 1 January 1936.
50 Hannah and Caroline Townsend to CP, 1 January 1936, SFC.
51 Copy of letter from Annie Kenney to CP, n.d., Kenney Papers.
52 CP to Annie Kenney, 14 January 1936, Kenney Papers.
53 CP to EPL, 5 January 1936, P-L Papers. Christabel wrote a separate letter to Fred, 9 January 1936, thanking him for his congratulations but as the letter is in the Craigie Collection it may not have been sent or may be a copy.
54 CP to Annie Kenney Taylor, 2 June 1936, Kenney Papers.
55 CP to Miss Flatman, 7 October 1936, SFC.
56 CP to Miss Flatman, 22 February 1937, SFC; Report by Miss Bickley, St Hugh's, Hilary Term 1936.
57 Interview with Beryl Davies, DMC.
58 Thanks to Elizabeth Crawford and Elizabeth Hodgson, daughter of Flora Mary Gordon, for this information.
59 J. Gottlieb, *'Guilty women': foreign policy, and appeasement in inter-war Britain* (Houndmills, Palgrave Macmillan, 2015), p. 176 quotes from the diary of a Miss Rose Dartle who noted that her friend Miss Elizabeth Prig had heard Christabel Pankhurst address a crowded meeting in which she announced 'she had always foreseen General Franco's triumph and that this event would shortly be followed by Our Lord's Second Coming'.
60 CP to Winston Churchill, 23 December 1937, Churchill Archive, Churchill College.

61 CP to Esther Greg, 12 March 1938, Purvis Collection.
62 CP to Esther Greg, 12 March 1938, Purvis Collection.
63 CP to Esther Greg, Easter Day 1938, Purvis Collection.
64 CP to Esther Greg, 12 March 1938, Purvis Collection.
65 CP to Mrs Chamberlain, 23 September 1938, Neville Chamberlain Papers, University of Birmingham. Thanks to Julie Gottlieb for bringing these letters to my attention.
66 *Times*, 7 October 1938.
67 *Church Times*, A woman speaks, 7 October 1938.
68 Interview with Reynolds, DMC; interview with Reynolds, Purvis Collection.
69 Interview with Reynolds, Purvis Collection.
70 *Daily Telegraph*, 9 March 1939. The legacy was from the will of Miss Elizabeth Mary Strelley Yates.
71 CP to Annie Kenney Taylor, 19 March 1939, Kenney Papers.
72 EPL, *My part*, p. 285.
73 See, for example, EPL to ESP, 14 October 1939, ESPA.
74 Suffragettes fight their battles again, *Daily Dispatch*, 10 May 1939.
75 *Evening News*, 14 July 1939.
76 CP to Mrs Chamberlain, 12 April 1939 and 1 May 1939, Chamberlain Papers.
77 CP to Mrs Chamberlain, 31 August 1939, Chamberlain Papers.
78 Interview with Wenda Reynolds, DMC.
79 CP to Miss Robins, Good Friday 1940, Robins Papers, Fales Collection.
80 Pugh, *The Pankhursts*, p. 454.
81 CP, *The uncurtained future* (London, Hodder and Stoughton, 1940), pp. 44–5. Mitchell in *Queen Christabel* makes no reference to this volume, even in the listing in the bibliography of Christabel's books.
82 CP, *The uncurtained future*, p. 24.
83 CP, *The uncurtained future*, p. 120.
84 CP, *The uncurtained future*, pp. 142–3.
85 Thanks to Elizabeth Hodgson for this information.

22

LIVING IN THE UNITED STATES
July 1940–December 1956

Christabel spent the last eighteen years of her life in the United States, mainly in the vicinity of Los Angeles on the sunny East Coast. When she first arrived in 1940 it was announced that she was:

> open for speaking engagements before churches and other organizations, and . . . may be addressed in care of Fleming H. Revell Company, 158 Fifth Avenue, New York City. She makes no fixed charge for such services, but gladly leaves that to be cared for by the free will offerings of the Lord's people.[1]

Within a year of her arrival, Christabel was preaching regularly on the Second Adventist circuit and writing a series of articles for the *Sunday School Times*.[2]

In summer 1941, Christabel was one of twenty-three main speakers at the forty-seventh annual summer Winona Lake Bible Conference, and by the winter of that year was a house guest at the palatial home of Mrs Francis de Lacy Hyde, in Plainfield, New Jersey, where Aurea had initially stayed after leaving Oxford.[3] Many years later, the writer Marjorie Greenbie, a fellow guest, remembered the sixty-one-year-old Christabel as a 'rather gentle little lady, slender, with reddish . . . hair'. Christabel never spoke of her suffrage activities but expounded at length about the Second Coming of Christ, arguing that the 'the world could not be saved except by the return of Christ and things were reaching the point of final destruction'. Another thing that struck Marjorie was that Christabel, who had certainly thought the British Government less than perfect in the days when suffrage was refused to women:

> now seemed to think it perfect in relation to India . . . she was convinced that Great Britain was destined to carry the white man's burden for all colored races, and was almost childishly amazed that 'all lesser breeds without the law' were not immediately grateful to them for it.

However, despite such imperialist attitudes, Marjorie Greenbie also noted that Christabel was:

never shrill or difficult in argument, always gentle and courteous but utterly impervious. Apart from what seemed [to] us her fixations, she was shrewd and apt in her comments. I remember one of her remarks about the American standard of living. 'The Americans', she said, 'are wealthy because they have discovered the secret of insatiable desire.'[4]

Over the next couple of years, Christabel continued with her preaching and travelling, also engaging in outreach pastoral work with young soldiers. After the Japanese attack on Pearl Harbour in December 1941, America had been drawn into the war and churches of many denominations became involved in caring for combatants, wounded or otherwise. In July 1943 she returned to the Los Angeles area when she was one of eleven high-profile speakers at the Christian Fellowship Bible Conference. 'British Suffrage Leader Here for Religion Talks' ran the headline in the local press. 'Victory will be won by the Allied nations and material prosperity shall increase but if sin remains in human hearts the return of strife and poverty is inevitable', declared Christabel. Even if international wars were abolished, 'permanent peace will not come until Christ returns to build His kingdom on earth'.[5] By September, Christabel had her own half-hour weekly show on Radio KMTR where she spoke about present-day events, analysing them as harbingers of the better world that was promised.[6] Alma Whitaker, a local reporter, was impressed. 'Women owe a great debt to Christabel', she asserted. 'The least we can do is to further her crusade against the devil to the extent of our ability.'[7]

One woman who felt she did not owe a great debt to Christabel was Aurea. Although both enjoyed living in the United States, the tensions between them had not been resolved. Aurea, who had taken American citizenship and was living in New York, had difficulty keeping a job. When the twenty-seven-year-old met American Charles vanHaelen, a personnel director, thirteen years her senior, and married him in Boston on 7 April 1943, Christabel hoped her adopted daughter would become more settled. After all Charles, who lived at 44 Pickney Street, Boston, had graduated from the Sheffield Scientific School at Yale University in the 1920s. It is doubtful if Christabel attended the wedding since the marriage certificate yields some fictitious information, at least on Aurea's side. Aurea's father was listed as 'John Clifford' while the maiden name of her mother was given as 'Elizabeth Pankhurst'.[8] Nonetheless, Christabel was happy for her adopted daughter and conveyed the welcome news of the marriage to friends in England, including Olive Duran-Deacon. 'I hope she is fortunate & will be very happy & that he meets with your approval', replied the cheery Olive. 'How nice for you that Aurea & her husband are motoring your way', Olive commented one year later. 'I am so much interested in hearing about her.'[9] But it would soon appear that Christabel did not want to say too much about Aurea. Charles, who had a daughter, Joan Elizabeth, with his first wife, Jeanne Stevens, had difficulty finding permanent employment and was often on short-term government contract work, for the navy. In between contracts, he had to travel around, taking whatever job he was offered, even hotel work.[10] It seems that Aurea did not cope well with her husband's frequent absences and their financial insecurity. She began to drink heavily – and to pester Christabel for money. In one such meeting, when Christabel refused the request, Aurea physically assaulted her, breaking her wrist. The shaken Christabel decided to terminate all contact with her adopted daughter who had become a 'great embarrassment'.[11]

The welcome that Christabel had received in Los Angeles convinced her that this was a place where she could settle, a place where no one knew about Aurea. Her celebrity status – both as a well-known suffragette and as a gifted preacher – meant that many people, especially those among the British community, warmly accepted her. In 1945 she became a paying guest at 2172 Vista Del Mar Avenue, a fine two-storey, mock-Tudor house with an old-fashioned garden and a caretaker's cottage, the home of an English friend, Shirley Carson Jenney. Mrs Jenney, whose mother had worked for the WSPU, had written some fifty novelettes before her marriage to an American; she now enjoyed fame as a psychic who claimed to be in touch with the poet Percy Bysshe Shelley whose communications she wrote down and published in book form, including communications about Christ.[12] Christabel would live happily with the much older Jenneys for five years, enjoying their cheery hospitality. She had the fireplace bedroom on the second floor, above the living room, from where she had a rustic view of the tree-studded canyon nearby. The Jenneys often held teas for their many visitors, and friends of Christabel remembered how the former suffragette was always ready to debate almost any topic, 'from soup to nuts, from politics to book reviews, and from earthquakes to the idiosyncrasies of the English colony in California!'[13] Since Christabel never learnt to drive – nor did Mrs Jenney – she mostly walked everywhere, taking the bus or being given a lift for longer distances across the sprawling metropolis. Determined to put the painful incidence with Aurea behind her, and enjoy the social life that had been denied her during young womanhood, she immersed herself in the local cultural life.

Christabel read widely, developed a reputation as a current affairs commentator and appeared regularly on television, either being interviewed or on discussion programmes. Other pastimes included opera and classical music concerts in the famed Hollywood Bowl, conserving the environment and supporting young writers and artistes. Above all, Christabel's main interest centred on the activities of the Writers' Round Table, whose quarters were in Hollywood, and to which Shirley Jenney also belonged. Here she met such well-known British authors as James Hilton and Richard Llewellyn, both novelists, and Alfred Noyes, the poet. Jaime Palmer, the president of the Hollywood writers' group at that time, recollected how occasionally Christabel 'acted as hostess for me, pouring tea, and was most gracious in that capacity'. A slender, graceful figure, Christabel always dressed unostentatiously although for evening events she wore 'lacey black with modest décolleté, and favoured long skirts'. The word 'lovely', it was suggested, particularly summed up the former suffragette:

She had a flower-like quality, with clear white skin, and a soft Madonna face. She was kind but her eyes had an aloofness, as though finding it necessary to guard against a constant invasion to her privacy. She always maintained this reserve, not inviting intimacy.[14]

For most Americans this reserve was considered a natural British characteristic that did not detract in any way from Christabel's charms. 'Every time I heard Christabel speak', noted another friend, 'her English was flawless and her delivery melodic to the ears, while her logic, her analysis from experience and literature along with her biblical allegories were superb.'[15] Loving the vibrancy of American society, and the warmth and openness of its people, Christabel rarely, if ever, offered any criticism. 'I am not a citizen but a guest of this great country', she would say.[16]

Meanwhile, back in England Jill Craigie was interested in making a film about the suffragette movement and had met a number of former WSPU members, including Lilian Lenton, Helen Archdale and Emmeline Pethick-Lawrence. But the old tensions between Christabel and Sylvia soon began to make their mark as those who were loyal to each particular sister took sides. 'I should have told you something which I quite forgot at the moment and that is that Christabel may make difficulties', Emmeline Pethick-Lawrence warned Jill. The Christabel question should be 'be settled at once', she advised, to avoid disappointment.[17]

Jill Craigie heeded the advice and wrote a carefully worded letter to Christabel:

> I am anxious that the film should be historically accurate and this would naturally mean re-enacting some of the great scenes in which you played the leading role. It is also necessary that your mother should be included. I trust you will have no objection to this. I have a very great admiration for your past achievements . . . Perhaps you could kindly cable me your reply.[18]

Christabel replied by telegram. 'PLEASE CONFER COMMITTEE REPRE-SENTING ME CONCERNING PRESENTATIONS MOTHER AND MOVEMENT' [sic].' The committee should comprise Olive Durand-Deacon, Ada Goulden-Bach, Annie Kenney Taylor, Flora Drummond, Mabel Tuke and Kitty Marshall.[19] However, Annie, who was to represent Christabel's side of the story, kept putting off Jill's pleas for a meeting. Neither she nor Christabel wanted a film made about the suffragette movement during wartime. As Christabel explained:

> Those who revive the unfortunate history of how the former Liberal Government, with the assent of the Labour and Conservative leaders treated the women and their cause, are taking a grave responsibil-ity . . . Such a film will do no good to anyone . . . I do not want it and I know that Mother would not have wanted it . . . Some members of the

Government who resisted us so unjustly are still living and politically active . . . foremost among these being Winston Churchill [who had succeeded Chamberlain as Prime Minister in May 1940].[20]

Sylvia Pankhurst was not happy about the proposed film either. She complained that she had not seen an outline of the proposal and insisted that she should make 'certain stipulations in the interest of the movement and the part in it of myself and family.'[21] When Helen Archdale, who had been close to Christabel and Emmeline Pankhurst, accepted Jill's invitation to become her official and paid advisor, the situation became yet more complicated. Sylvia, fearful of the direction in which things were moving, demanded that she be given that role:

> I do not think a film about the Suffragette Movement can possibly be a success without one who took an active part in the Movement having a considerable share in the production . . . As I have written the history of the Movement it was of course quite natural that I should present the Movement also in another medium.[22]

Sylvia, like Christabel, was also unsure as to whether a suffragette film should be made during wartime but for differing reasons to her sister: she thought the sufferings of the suffragettes would be 'dwarfed' by the present conflict. She also claimed that she herself had intended to make such a film, and that it was only the Ethiopian war that had prevented her from doing so. Emmeline Pethick-Lawrence waded further into the debate by strongly supporting Sylvia and criticising Annie Kenney, telling Jill that, in her opinion, Annie had 'nothing much to give' since she was merely 'a register of Christabel's mind & will'.[23] Unable to reconcile the Christabel and Sylvia contingents, Jill Craigie eventually abandoned the project.

Annie Kenney, who regularly wrote to Christabel, told her the news. Unsure whether Christabel had completed her manuscript on the suffragette movement, she pleaded with her to do so, and to publish her book:

> Is Sylvia's book of your family and early life to be the only family book to which film writers, historians, etc., have to go for the history of your family and the history of the work that absolutely changed the position of women?

Christabel must put her book in the public domain:

> I feel in every fibre of my being that this is what your Mother would have wished . . . Oh, Christabel, when we pass the border it is the records that we have left behind that will mar or help in the task that others will have to perform.[24]

But Christabel would not change her mind. She had had a contract for her book and even placed the manuscript in the publisher's hand, but then decided not to publish it. To do so while the darks clouds just before the advent of the Second World War were gathering would be irresponsible and embarrassing; her manuscript would be bad propaganda for Britain, since it exposed the disgraceful way a Liberal Government, which once included Winston Churchill, the present Prime Minister, had treated women fighting for a just cause.[25]

Christabel continued keeping in touch with friends and relatives in England, including her Aunt Ada Goulden-Bach who would regularly send her snippets about what Adela and Sylvia were doing. In March 1942, the now right-wing Adela had been arrested and interned for her pro-Japanese talk while the left-wing Sylvia, no longer a communist, had taken up the cause of Ethiopia. Although the British had supposedly liberated Ethiopia in 1941, after it had been invaded by Mussolini's fascist troops, it still kept the country under foreign occupation, a situation against which Sylvia protested. 'I hear nothing of A. [Adela]', Aunt Ada informed Christabel in November 1944. 'Whether she is now free I do not know. I fear she is the scapegoat for her husband's sayings & doings, tho A. herself has a chatty tongue . . . I heard the son is greatly annoyed & left home.' Aunt Ada, who still blamed Sylvia for hastening the death of her sister, Emmeline Pankhurst, had little news either about this other Pankhurst daughter:

> S. I never see though 'The Times' announced she has had an invitation to Addiss Abbaba [sic] & she has gone. She certainly deserves this for she's steadily supported them in bad & good times. All my good wishes to her but no desire for paths to cross.[26]

Amidst all this news, Christabel had another letter from England informing her that Tower Cressy, the adoption home that she had given to Princess Alice, had been completely destroyed by a flying bomb. 'I regret the demolished Tower & and the view it gave of London & the country beyond & sometimes even the sea', she replied nostalgically to a Mrs Bullivant, 'but after the war, another building can arise, designed especially for its own beautiful purpose.' Since Christabel still legally owned the site, she now generously gave it to the three trustees.[27]

The end of the war against Germany in Europe, on 8 May 1945, was a great relief, although the idea of a 'Victory Parade' in London, Olive Durand-Deacon informed Christabel, seemed absurd given that people had none of the 'fruits of victory' and few of the bare necessities of life.[28] For some time, Christabel had supported the right of the Jewish people to their own independent state and this seemed more imperative now as the horrors of the Holocaust, in which over 6 million Jews had been exterminated by Hitler's Nazi regime, became known. America, however, was still at war and victory over Japan would not come until 2 September. Meanwhile, Christabel continued with her philanthropic work with wounded or traumatised American soldiers. 'We often think of your kindness to this family and your great desire to help my brother', wrote one grateful man.

490

Norton, his thirty-seven-year-old brother, had had the DTs badly and died on 31 May. 'I wish I could see you and talk with you . . . If you ever come to Rochester we want you to stay with us.'[29]

Such philanthropic work attracted little attention from the press and brought no financial income to the not well-off Christabel. Yet she preferred to be useful in this way and shunned the chance to earn a high income, even when the opportunity arose. As she explained to Annie, 'I have been approached over here with the idea of making a film and financial advantage was suggested, but I would not agree to the idea.' News was given to Annie too about Grace Roe who was still living in the United States, and had not yet returned to England:

> Grace is in these parts but not so near that I see her often. She is just the same Grace. I suppose we all who worked so closely together shall always feel that we remain the same – inwardly the same certainly, & even outwardly not too much changed.

And knowing that Annie's health was not robust, especially during a time of post-war food shortages, the concerned Christabel advised her to take a vitamin supplement, as she did:

> I fear things are not too easy over there [England] . . . Did I write to you about Supavite SUPAVITE. It is a preparation of vitamins & minerals sold in England . . . It is the best way to supplement a slender diet. I use the same sort of thing here because, tho' food is abundant it is quite high in price & because I don't like to be bothered with marketing & cooking.[30]

Living in Los Angeles, after the war with Japan had ended, had its compensations. Christabel continued to be well liked – and her celebrity suffrage past was not forgotten. In February 1948 she was invited to give a talk at the Los Angeles Public Library in commemoration of the birthday of the influential American suffragist Susan B. Anthony whom she had met in Manchester, in 1904. The organiser of the event found Christabel 'most charming and so unassuming'.[31] And at a world affairs group too that met monthly in the late 1940s, Christabel was one of three hostesses who were very popular. She often spoke about her earlier political life – although rarely its militant aspects – and characteristically, in her closing remarks, returned to the theme of the return of Christ.[32] There was greater tolerance in the United States than in England for Christabel's religious views, something of which she was only too acutely aware. 'I know that you & many others do not agree with me in expecting the second coming', Christabel wrote to Annie, back in England. 'Well time will show as I used to say when people told me that our methods would lose the vote for women, & not win it.'[33]

Christabel's religious faith stood her in good stead when early in 1948 she was involved in a serious car accident as she was being driven by a female friend to

Ojai, a small town north west of Los Angeles. The friend was killed but the badly injured Christabel survived, despite a broken hip and leg, plus multiple fractures. Now sixty-seven years old, the upset Christabel bore the sadness in a stoic manner. 'You know, I am the one who should have died. I am not afraid of death, I believe in Heaven. But she *was* afraid', she told one friend.[34] '[T]hank God you are spared', penned the eighty-year-old Esther Greg back in England, on hearing the news. 'I have been long in writing to give you my sympathy.'[35] As Christabel recovered from her injuries, her many friends helping as best they could, news arrived that another acquaintance had died, Dame May Whitty, the well-known English actress who had lived in California for a number of years.

'I have just returned from hearing those beautiful words from the Bible which so illumine death', Christabel wrote to Dame May's daughter, Margaret, after attending the funeral:

> I shall miss your beloved mother – though I did not see her nearly as often as I should have liked – because I feared to trespass on her time and strength but I cherish the memory of the times I spent with her – & with your father.

Christabel, who had known Dame May when she was active in the Actresses Franchise League, reminisced about the past:

> You and I have been extraordinarily blessed in our parents, father & mother both, have we not! . . . I am so happy to think that she was with my own mother in that campaign [for women's enfranchisement] and that they both lived to see its triumph . . . I sympathise with you in such a present loss – even though I believe that the best is yet to be & that these sorrows & partings are but for a little while & the world's ills are destined to have a glorious happy end.[36]

Yet, despite her faith in a better life after death, Christabel was facing a particular problem in her earthly existence: her income was meagre. For some time she had been embroiled in an extended correspondence with the respective authorities in the United States and England about the continuing deduction, in England, of income tax from her annuity with the Prudential Company. The issue had eventually been settled in her favour when she was informed that she was entitled to recover in full income tax deducted from instalments paid since April 1945.[37] Christabel had to be careful with her spending. American friends, though not told directly of her financial situation, nonetheless deduced that the reserved former suffragette was not well off. '[W]e were unhappy that such a dear person might have financial worries', recollected one couple:

> Her dress was not quite in style, and often when we invited her for tea she came in a long flowing dress and large picture hat with a rose on it. She look[ed] as though she had come from the early 1900 years![38]

Friends in England may have pondered too about Christabel's financial situation, but dare not mention it. Many of these friends belonged to the Suffragette Fellowship whose newsletter *Calling all Women* Aunt Ada regularly sent to Christabel, often reminding her niece when a message to former suffrage comrades was due. 'A Happy New Year to friends everywhere', wrote Christabel for the 1949 issue of this publication, 'and greetings to all enfranchised women. May God give them wisdom in the use of that precious possession, the Vote.'[39] The greeting had barely been published when news arrived that Flora Drummond had passed away. It was a great shock. 'Grace and I feel that this is the first break in the circle of you and me and the General and Grace herself, upon whom a good deal depended in the good days of the WSPU', Christabel wrote sorrowfully to Annie:

> Shall I ever forget that the General was the first to greet me when I came out of Holloway . . . I am so glad that she had so much happiness in the later years with the husband who was so sadly killed in the war . . . A chapter has closed for us.[40]

Christabel also told Annie that she had received yet another letter from someone who wanted to write a combined life of her mother and a history of the WSPU. As before, she discouraged such a project, although it prompted her to send for her own manuscript which she had left in the safe keeping of Aunt Ada, in London. Yet, despite continued appeals from her aunt to publish the manuscript – 'It can do no harm and <u>may do good</u>' – Christabel would not do so.[41]

Olive Durand-Deacon, a rich widow, wrote regularly to Christabel but suddenly the letters stopped. Then the horrendous news arrived – Olive had been murdered by John George Haigh, a serial killer who came to be known as the 'Acid Bath Murderer'. After Haigh killed his victims, he dissolved the bodies in a bath of concentrated sulphuric acid and then forged the necessary papers so that he could claim any possessions and large sums of money. A charmer, Haigh lived at Onslow Court Hotel in South Kensington, as did Olive. On 18 February 1949, he had invited her to visit his business in Sussex. It was here that he shot her in the back of the head and, after removing her jewellery and an expensive black Persian lamb coat, placed her body in a tank of sulphuric acid. He confessed all when he was arrested some ten days later.

Christabel wept when she heard the story and prayed for Olive's soul. The horrified Aunt Ada sent relevant newspaper cuttings and speculated about the grisly murder. 'Please God that Haigh may have done it without her being aware of it.' After thanking Christabel for advice about the rheumatism she had in her hands, Aunt Ada closed with more news about Adela. 'Heard that Adela was not too well placed & complains bitterly that she had no chances in youth!!!! Adela has more words than sense or reason.'[42] But such snippets of family news were, for some weeks, always interspersed with the haunting topic of Olive's murder. 'That man H. didn't get her money only what was in bag & sale of her jewellery.'[43]

Christabel thought of the many times she and Olive had expressed the wish to meet up again. Perhaps she even re-read an earlier letter from her now dead friend – 'I sometimes wish I had gone to America with you. Your idea of my coming out after the war & touring with you & then flying back together sounds very thrilling!'[44] But it was impossible now, in this earthly life.

The annuity of £300 that Olive Durand-Deacon left Christabel in her will was useful, especially since there were legal bills to be paid regarding the accident at Ojai over a year ago; the defendant in the court case had still not paid the damages that had been awarded.[45] The sad circumstances surrounding Olive's death and the gloomy worldwide political situation appeared to deepen Christabel's religious beliefs. 'My own belief in the personal and powerful return of the Lord Jesus Christ is unshaken and in fact daily confirmed', she confessed to Annie in December 1949, 'the fact that we have the atomic bomb and one world crisis after another and the Red Terror behind the Iron Curtain and the spread of it now to China.' Reflecting on the past, which she often did now in her correspondence, Christabel continued:

> Jessie did well to recall what we did in the first world war and after to try to win the war and resettle the world in peace at home and abroad. I wonder how much was understood by our own women at that time and women in general of what we did in the realm of international affairs . . . and whether they knew that we helped to shorten the war and so spare lives . . . [if only] the politicians [had] listened to us in the matter of keeping the victorious Allies permanently united (instead of being torn apart by that futile League of Nations . . .) and kept always at least one gun stronger than Germany so that it would have been plain that another war would mean her defeat more quickly . . . It is tragic to look back on that . . . especially in this present cold war, as they call it, with Russia. Russia would never have achieved the menacing position and power that she now has, if we had averted the Second World War.[46]

The times that Christabel and Annie had shared together, especially their 'militant' activity at the Free Trade Hall on 13 October 1905 when they had interrupted a Liberal Party political meeting, been arrested and chosen prison rather than pay a fine, were now frequently mentioned in Christabel's correspondence. 'On Oct 13', she wrote to Annie in her Christmas greetings for 1950, 'I suddenly remembered that it was the anniversary of you and my great day when we struck the fetters from the women of the world.' Perhaps thoughts of Aurea were in Christabel's mind when she mused, 'I like to think of your peaceful happy home life . . . Warwick . . . is his mother's own boy . . . his father must be very proud of him.'[47]

Back in England, interest continued to grow in the history of the militant women's suffrage movement in the Edwardian era. On 13 March 1951, BBC radio broadcast a play written by Jill Craigie titled *The women's rebellion: a dramatized impression of the suffragette movement.* Apart from the narration, the entire dialogue was taken from historical accounts and testimonies that had been gathered during the 1940s. The play was sympathetic to the views of Christabel and her mother, emphasising that the Labour movement was insufficiently attuned to the injustices that women experienced. Sylvia had a very minor role in the drama and was, unsurprisingly, very critical, as were Annie and Jessie Kenney, although for differing reasons.[48]

Although a number of former suffragettes praised the play, for Jessie the portrayal of Annie as a Northern mill-girl was 'a caricature . . . vulgarised . . . a belittling' of her important leadership role in the WSPU.[49] Christabel tried to console the hurt Annie who agreed with her sister. 'As for anything . . . unfavourable to you and false to the truth about you, I too know what that sort of thing means.' She went on to remind Annie she herself had been hit hard when her unmarried sister, Sylvia, gave birth to a son in December 1927 and, sensationally, told the press her story in a blaze of publicity, the general public thinking she was the 'Pankhurst' involved.[50] The pain and shame of that incident still haunted Christabel, as she made abundantly clear to Grace Roe:

> I sympathise with Annie if she feels that she was mis-represented. Unfavourable publicity is painful . . . [t]he one who has had the worst and most painful personal publicity is myself . . . at the time of the S. affair . . . when the whole country was placarded with Sunday newspaper posters. 'Miss Pankhurst's Confession' . . . and as friends in and out of the Suffragette ranks were quick and emphatic to tell me, the world in general thought the whole story related to me. That was the biggest blow I ever received and the repercussions have not really ceased. The whole publicity was skilfully engineered to harm me.[51]

But life had to continue, despite the pain and embarrassment.

In addition to her usual round of religious and social activity, Christabel now began to meet regularly and correspond with Elsie Hill who had been active in the American National Women's Party. She suggested to Elsie:

> Every work and plan of humankind . . . whether it be Catholicism, Protestantism, Democracy, Internationalism, or any other, always has been, and is now and always will be marred by the human nature which invents and operates all the various systems, religious, economic, political, social.

'There is much in the current world news to suggest that Armageddon, literal and historical and not merely symbolical, is approaching', she warned characteristically.[52] Although such predictions were common to Second Adventists, Grace Roe always insisted that Christabel attended a wide range of churches and was not narrow in her focus:

She had all sorts of friends around her . . . [and] would go with one friend to . . . the Roman Catholic Church, and with another . . . to the High Episcopal [Church of England], and with somebody else . . . to the Fundamentalist . . . she seemed to be very universal.[53]

For over a year, Christabel had been living at a different address, Apartment 300, on the third floor at 2020 North Beachwood Drive, Los Angeles. Since she had been very happy living with Mr and Mrs Jenney at 2172 Vista del Mar Avenue, the move was probably prompted by the need to find cheaper accommodation. However, some structural damage occurred at the new apartment when a leak also affected the floors of the living quarters below, and so by July 1951 Christabel was obliged to move temporarily to 1734 North Ogden Drive, while repairs were carried out.[54] It was from this address that she informed Elsie Hill that she had been caring for a blind woman of a friend, Ivy de Verley, a portrait painter, a task she found very demanding:

How thankful we may be for our eyes – our ability to <u>see</u>. That lesson I have learnt – or learnt anew, for already I have left my eyes by will to whomsoever they may help to see, when I need them no longer![55]

Christabel's contact with Elsie Hill soon led to a particular invitation – would she become an 'Honorary Chairman' of the National Woman's Party? The request was endorsed by none other than the American Alice Paul, once a WSPU member, who explained the situation to Christabel:

We are trying to form a small Round Table of women, from all countries, who are outstanding in their service and devotion to the woman's cause. We all feel . . . that you belong, more than almost any other living woman, on such a list. Without you we can never have the kind of group that we are seeking to create. It would be a great joy to me personally to be associated with you again. All that I have tried to do, all my life, for the freedom of women, has been due in large measure to your inspiration and leadership, and to that of your Mother and Mrs. Lawrence. I began under your guidance and should like to feel myself always one of your followers. I enclose the text of a new article – Article 60 – on Equality for Women that has been added recently to the draft Covenant on Human Rights, by the Human Rights Commission. Our next big task is to make certain that political and civil equality are also in the Covenant.[56]

Unfortunately, Christabel did not receive the letter, which was sent to her old address. She was still chasing it, some nine months later.[57]

For some months Christabel had been distracted, grieving over some devastating news: in early 1952 Aurea had died from alcoholism.[58] After her marriage to the gregarious Charles had collapsed, Aurea had taken to drink. Deeply upset, Christabel pondered long on happier times. What had gone wrong with the little child she had dearly loved, the little girl who, with her adopted sister Mary, could recite verses from the Bible? What had caused Aurea to turn to alcohol? The sad Christabel hid the cause of Aurea's death from even close friends such as Annie, Rangeley Stride being one of the few to know the truth. 'I was grieved for Christabel when I heard of the death of her darling', Annie commiserated with Grace Roe, 'but she is in a safe place and free from this unsettled world.'[59]

Shirley Carson Jenney, whose husband had died in 1948 when Christabel was still living with her, was seriously ill herself some four years later, with incurable cancer. The compassionate Christabel had returned to 2172 Vista del Mar Avenue, by May 1952, to help care for this friend who died later that year. 'I'm not sure what we should have done without your help in those many trying circumstances which were yours, rather than ours', wrote the grateful son Dr Ross Jenney, from Madrid. Since Christabel stayed on to look after the house, Dr Jenney proposed that she lived there rent free, until he returned in late February 1953. 'Bless your heart for your kindness', he wrote appreciatively.[60] 'My love for your father & mother has made me only too glad to do anything I could', Christabel replied. 'I will look after things here until your return . . . & will try to find a tenant for the house . . . the loss of your so loving mother . . . is my loss too of a true and beloved friend.'[61]

Once everything was sorted out at Vista del Mar Avenue, Christabel then stayed for a short time with a Mr Bernard Hambledon, a composer, and his wife.[62] After the Hambledons left for England, Christabel decided it was time to fulfil a wish she had had for some time, to live by the sea. So she moved a few miles away to a rented seafront apartment at 1317 Ocean Avenue, Santa Monica, which Grace Roe, who now lived at Ventura further along the coast, helped her find. Since Christabel had little spare money and few possessions, Grace furnished the flat and sent her gardener to tidy the lawn.[63] It was to be in Ocean Avenue that the nomadic Christabel was to live for the last four years of her life, although not all the time at number 1317. By 1955 she had moved to flat 943 in Ocean Avenue, in a lovely house with fine views of the Pacific Ocean.

Some three years earlier, Aunt Ada Goulden-Bach had passed away so that Christabel's contact with her mother's side of the family now seems to have been continued mainly through correspondence with her cousin Lorna Goulden-Bach, the eldest of Aunt Ada's three daughters and living in England. In April 1953, Lorna told Christabel all about the preparations for the Coronation of Queen Elizabeth II and the high cost of the seats lining the route along The Mall and Oxford Street. Some family news was also conveyed. 'Sylvia . . . has been very ill – heart . . . I believe she is better now but thought I had better warn you. She is very friendly with the P-Ls [Pethick-Lawrences] still.'[64]

The news of Sylvia's heart attack shocked the seventy-two-year-old Christabel into action. Ever since April 1928, when so many people thought that it was she, the Second Adventist preacher, who was the 'Miss Pankhurst' who had given birth to an illegitimate child, Christabel had been tormented. But what was the point now of holding onto all that pain? Sylvia was just two years younger and both of them might not have much longer to live. Christabel was determined to put this particular demon to rest. She found out Sylvia's address in Woodford Green, Essex, England, and on 5 May 1953 wrote her bed-ridden sister an affectionate letter:

> Sylvia dear,
>
> This is your birthday and I am writing to wish you, with my love, many happy returns of the day. I hear that you are not as well as usual and I hope that you are improving and feeling stronger in this spring and your birthday month. Your mind often goes back, I know, as mine does, to those good years of our childhood, when we still had Father & Mother & the home they made for us ... We had wonderful parents for whom we can be always thankful ... Your son must be a great joy & comfort to you & I am sure that there is a beautiful bond between you & him ... The years are passing by & what strange ... unexpected events & conditions they have brought & are bringing to the world. I view the things that are happening all over the globe with concern, but with strong, with invincible hope in the final triumph of goodness & justice & of glory surpassing all human dreams.
>
> God's in His heaven: all must & will be right with the world.
> Again my birthday love
>
> > Your sister
> > Christabel[65]

Sylvia replied almost immediately and Christabel's second letter to her, just under three weeks later, asks if she still has papers relating to their father's family tree. Thanking Sylvia for the photo of her son, Richard, which had arrived recently, she concludes, 'Again, I am so sorry to hear of your illness and hope it is passing from you ... I am well & feeling much as I always did ... Affectionately, your sister, Christabel.'[66] Thus began a correspondence in old age between these once warring sisters, a correspondence that continued intermittently until late summer 1957, some six months before Christabel's death.[67]

In the midst of this unexpected joy at 'finding' her sister Sylvia again, Christabel received yet more sad news. On 9 July 1953 Annie died peacefully in hospital at 11.25 a.m., her husband Jim (James), her son Warwick and her sister Jessie at her bedside. She had been ill for some time with diabetes, telling few people of her condition. 'DEEP SYMPATHY LOVING MEMORIES. WRITING' said Christabel's telegram to Annie's husband.[68] The letters of condolence said more about how Christabel felt. 'My true & deep sympathy goes out to you & to your father', she wrote to Warwick:

> Yes, I know that your mother had a complete belief in life beyond this world & I am happy to know that you share it & that you can turn to Him who is the Resurrection & the Life for comfort in the inescapable pain of losing the presence of the wonderful wife, mother & friend who has gone ahead of us.

But, Christabel added, Annie was much more than all this, in particular, 'a pioneer & a liberator of women'. Christabel recalled that day in autumn 1905 when she and Annie went to a Liberal Party meeting at the Free Trade Hall, determined to get an answer to their question about votes for women:

> Then followed all the years that led on to victory in which your mother did more than will ever perhaps be known to win justice for women . . . You have an inheritance of which you can be most highly proud & I know that Annie's record & example will be an inspiration to you through your whole life.[69]

After Annie had been cremated and her ashes scattered on the Lancashire moors, Jessie sent to Christabel a sprig of moor heather. 'I have put [it] in a little transparent bag', penned an emotional Christabel, touched by this precious reminder of her dear friend. Trying to support Jessie, Christabel continued:

> Jessie dear, now that you (& the rest of her family) have completed all that remains to be done for Annie in this world, you will feel the loneliness & reaction that comes after the first period of a bereavement is over – but you are just as brave & strong now as you always were.[70]

And more than this, as Christabel continued over the coming years to comfort Jessie about the death of 'our beloved Annie', as she called her life-long friend, she reminded her about the Christian promise of the greater life to come. '[T]he best is yet to be & we can see above the present & beyond it, by our faith in God's glorious tomorrow.'[71] This devout Christian faith in an afterlife was to sustain Christabel over the coming months as yet more friends and loved ones passed away.

As expected, Christabel wrote a short piece for the Suffragette Fellowship's newsletter, mourning the loss of Annie and other suffrage workers.[72] Sometimes nostalgic for her homeland, she usually listened to the Queen's Christmas Day message, broadcast on American radio, as she did this December of 1953. Since the Queen was travelling around the world, Christabel felt obliged to write an appreciative note to Queen Elizabeth, the Queen Mother:

> May I express . . . the happiness I felt at hearing the Royal Christmas broadcast, which for us British and for foreigners too, has become a precious part of the world-wide Christmas celebration. I thought that our Queen made beautifully clear her sense of being Queen of the Commonwealth . . . and of every land and people composing it.[73]

For Christabel, her identity as a 'British' citizen, an outsider in North America, was important to her and a very positive asset that American friends welcomed.

In the spring of the New Year of 1954 Emmeline Pethick-Lawrence, another former suffrage friend living in Britain, died. 'I cabled Lord Pethick-Lawrence a message of sympathy & of appreciation of what they both did for votes for women', Christabel informed Sylvia, adding cheerfully, 'I gather that your <u>health</u> is <u>better</u> now & am very glad.'[74] Christabel also wrote an appreciation of Emmeline's life for *Equal Rights*, a feminist journal, an action which brought Fred Pethick-Lawrence much pleasure.[75] Sylvia confided to her sister that she and Mrs Lawrence had successfully petitioned the publisher G. Bell and Sons about a libel in the first edition of Ray Strachey's book *'The cause': a short history of the women's movement*, published in 1928. Strachey, a member of the NUWSS and a friend of Millicent Garrett Fawcett, had claimed that no full financial accounts had been kept by the WSPU; the publisher had agreed to insert two new pages into every copy of the book, correcting the text, although this did not always happen.[76]

Sylvia's initiative in correcting untruths about the much-maligned WSPU strengthened the bond between the two once warring sisters. Yet, even so, Christabel cautioned her sister about going to the press about the Strachey book. '[I]t would be a <u>mistake</u> (<u>however fair & just</u>) to have statements in the <u>daily newspapers</u>, because it would be rubbing in her unwarrantable statement & calling attention to something that the general public <u>have never noticed</u>.' Christabel concluded:

> The great outstanding fact is that the women's cause was brought to life & brought to victory (& not by the Stracheys), & all who subscribed to the WSPU <u>got their money's worth</u> & those responsible for the direction of the WSPU <u>made nothing out of it for themselves</u> & no one has suggested that they <u>did</u>.[77]

Sylvia, an agnostic, had nothing to say to Christabel about the successful visit to Britain that year of 1954 of the North American evangelist Billy Graham, but Ida Copeland, a fellow Christian, did. In his various crusades around the world, Graham asked his audience to accept Christ as their personal saviour and Ida had gone to one such event, attended by some 11,000 people.[78] But even Billy Graham's success could not tempt Christabel to visit her homeland, or the Advent Testimony and Prophetic Movement. When the latter asked her, in early 1955, to come and speak for them, she politely declined.[79] Now seventy-four years old, Christabel did not want to make the necessary long journey, or engage in the strenuous tours that would be necessary when other, younger, able people could easily undertake such a task.

Christabel had barely turned down the Advent Testimony's request when news of a different kind arrived from her homeland – the Minister of Works had announced that plans that autumn for the reconstruction of Victoria Tower Gardens would necessitate the re-siting of her mother's statue from its central position to a comparatively remote one, near the children's sandpit. Deeply upset at what she interpreted as a slight to her mother, Christabel expressed her strong disapproval, as did the Suffragette Fellowship and other supporters, including Sylvia who sent press clippings about the protest to her sister in Santa Monica.[80] The Suffragette Fellowship, which for many years had been organising the lying of a wreath at Emmeline Pankhurst's statue on the anniversary of her 'birthday', swung into action. It made sure that, when the statue was moved, it was placed in an even more prominent place, close to the entrance to the House of Lords.

The new siting of the statue greatly pleased both Christabel and Sylvia, yet another issue that united the sisters. Yet none of the Pankhurst daughters attended the small rededication ceremony held on the rainy Saturday, 14 July 1956. The previous month, the seventy-four-year-old Sylvia and her son had moved to Ethiopia where Richard was to teach at the University College of Addis Ababa. Both Christabel in the USA and Adela in Australia were no longer accepting invitations for long-distance travel. Instead Grace Roe flew from the USA to read out a message from Christabel which spoke of how the ceremony would revive vivid memories of all the women – and men – who had fought for the emancipation of women. As the small group of former suffragettes stood in silence on 14 July, above them was a rain-drenched flag of the WSPU, the one that Emily Wilding Davison had carried that fatal day when she ran onto the Derby race course in 1913.[81]

'July 14th is over and I think Enid [Goulden-Bach] & Charlie Marsh who really have carried the brunt of <u>everything</u> are to be highly congratulated', Grace informed Christabel after the event:

> The statue is on the exact spot the Burghers of Calais were on [this statue had been moved to another site] & is surrounded by a beautiful flower bed. The inscription is on a marble stone at the base . . . It can be seen well from the Road & there is a continuous flow of visitors.

The tactful Grace also told Christabel how she thought it best to expand upon the message she had been given to read out, to keep happy the friends and relatives of dead former suffragettes who were present. Thus she added the names of Annie Kenney, Emmeline Pethick-Lawrence and 'The General', among others. 'Jim [Kenney Taylor] thanked you with tears in his eyes for remembering A.K. and not only was your message received with much applause but as I stepped back many in the audience said "Thank you".'[82] After the ceremony, the small group went to Caxton Hall where messages were read out from a number of people including Fred Pethick-Lawrence, Lady Churchill and Mabel Tuke. Fred was now a Labour member of the House of Lords and a contented Christabel wrote to him. 'Dear Lord Pethick-Lawrence', she penned, addressing him by his title and thanking him for the part he had played in the upper chamber of Parliament in winning the new and better position for her mother's statue. Although the soon-to-be eighty-year-old Fred replied, he did not suggest that Christabel abandon the formality of addressing him as 'Lord'.[83]

This renewal of contacts with past suffrage friends and relatives brought additional joy to the ageing Christabel's life, perhaps most of all when Mabel Tuke suddenly made contact. Mabel, living in South Africa, had not been in touch for many years. However, when in late 1953 she had acquired Christabel's address, she had written to the former organiser of the WSPU – and been anxiously awaiting a reply. 'I feel tired darling S.A.L. [Christabel's pseudonym when she escaped to Paris in 1912] so excuse brevity, but I'm anxious to be in touch with you again', she penned apprehensively on New Year's Day 1954. 'Ever with dearest love . . . Your own Pansy'.[84] Soon the two old friends were corresponding regularly, Mabel expressing her affection openly, despite the distance of the years. 'No one could possibly take or even share your place with me, either in want or mind', she confessed some eighteen months later,

> & I seem to face a fresh gush of life pulsing through me whenever I see the envelope addressed by you . . . Even if we shared religious convictions [Mabel was a Roman Catholic] I doubt whether we could be nearer each other than we are . . . if only we could meet![85]

But the two dear friends were never to meet up again. Nor did Christabel, who had now added drawing and painting to her leisure interests, correspond often enough for the emotional, lonely Mabel. 'Do write me dearest Christabel', she pleaded:

> it seems long since I had the welcome sight of your handwriting. There is only one Christabel, bless her now & ever & always & she remains & always must remain, the bright particular star in our women's firmament of those great days.[86]

Pondering on past times, Mabel wistfully noted, 'I can see you in my mind's eye as I write in that lovely apple green silk dress chosen by Sybil Smith . . . you looked such a treat on the . . . platform.'[87]

But no such compliments were forthcoming from Teresa Billington-Greig who was not only collecting information to write the obituaries of still living suffrage leaders but also, as she informed Christabel in autumn 1956, intending to give lectures on 'The Pankhurst Family'. Knowing of the past problems Teresa had caused in the WSPU, Christabel panicked. 'I do not consider suggested theme advisable', she hastily cabled back. 'Please keep lecture title and topic of the movement itself.' In a long letter Christabel explained that she had made this request so as to avoid any suggestion that the suffragette movement was a 'family party'. From the early days of the campaign, 'this was the allegation of critics and opponents. Furthermore . . . politically, the Pankhurst family has never existed', she insisted:

> Each person of that name has always been an independent person . . . there actually have been, at times, emphatic differences of opinion & divergences of action on important public issues . . . The army of women who sought the vote was the only 'family' involved in the movement.[88]

The prickly Teresa was not impressed, accusing Christabel of being unrealistic:

> Your main objection seems to be that considering the five of you together in one speech, book or article, would mean the presentation of a sort of undifferentiated octopus of feminist militancy. But surely that is what has happened already, so that the name carries to the common mind just that sort of picture.[89]

Teresa ended her caustic letter by asking Christabel, yet again, to send to her the facts about her post-suffrage career. Christabel did not oblige. The old tensions between the two women flared up again as Christabel commented sarcastically:

> I should have thought a woman of your brains, Teresa, and of your presumably forward-looking eye, would, in this crisis of human destiny, have been immersed in the consideration of the serious national and international situation . . . Why not address women on that great theme?[90]

Notes

1 *Sunday School Times*, 14 December 1940, p. 1025.
2 See *Sunday School Times*, 10, 17, 24 and 31 May, and 7 June 1941.
3 Larsen, *Christabel*, p. 99.
4 Marjorie Greenbie to David Mitchell, 19 March 1965, DMC.
5 British Suffrage Leader Here for Religion Talks, *Los Angeles Times*, 9 July 1943.
6 Martz, Moved to minister, p. 84. The radio show ended in March 1944.
7 Alma Whitaker, Pankhurst Tradition Whets Christabel's Steel for Satan, *Los Angeles Times*, 13 July 1943.
8 Grateful thanks to Elizabeth Crawford for locating Aurea's marriage certificate. And thanks to Nancy Everett for further information about Charles, her grandfather, and copies of some of his surviving letters to Jeanne O. Stevens, his first wife and her grandmother, and to Joan Elizabeth, their daughter, her mother. Charles was born on 6 May 1902. His father, a diamond cutter from Antwerp, Belgium, was a naturalised American. His mother, Jennie Estella Greene, was born in New York c.1879. Charles died on 4 September 1998.

9 Olive Duran-Deacon to CP, 23 April 1944 and 17 March [1945], Craigie Collection.

10 In December 1949, Charles was in Miami seeking work; from July to October 1950 he was staying at the Gordon Hotel in Washington and by August 1950 was in New York where he was listed as a 'Technical Writer'. There is just one reference to Aurea in the extant letters he wrote. While in Miami, writing to his first wife Jeanne on 31 December 1949, he states, 'I am very anxious to hear how you made out with Aurea and the apartment. I feel like a heel for running out and leaving it all to you but I guess there really was little that I could do', Nancy Everett Private Papers.

11 Interview with Rangeley Stride, 25 August 1975, DMC.

12 Douglas Field to David Mitchell, 6 October 1964, DMC; *The Fortune of Eternity* by Percy Bysshe Shelley, *Transmitted wholly through clairaudient dictation* by Shirley Carson Jenney (New York, William-Frederick Press, 1945), p. 117. 'I who am the poet Shelley transmit now to my clairaudient some pages of Christ-Script intended for the Earth-World.'

13 Douglas Field to David Mitchell, 6 October 1964, DMC.

14 Jaime Palmer to David Mitchell, 8 July 1965, DMC.

15 Jay Trevor Weiss to David Mitchell, early June 1965, DMC.

16 Douglas Field to David Mitchell, 6 October 1965, DMC.

17 EPL to Jill Craigie, 7 June 1944, Craigie Collection.

18 Jill Craigie to CP, copy, 9 June 1944, Craigie Collection.

19 CP to Jill Craigie, 2 July 1944, Craigie Collection.

20 CP to Annie Kenney Taylor, 19 November 1946, Kenney Papers.

21 ESP to Jill Craigie, 12 July 1944, Craigie Collection.

22 ESP to Jill Craigie, 14 September 1944, Craigie Collection.

23 EPL to Jill Craigie, 23 September 1944, Craigie Collection.

24 Annie Kenney Taylor to CP, c.1944, DMC.

25 CP to Annie Kenney Taylor, 25 January 1949, Kenney Papers.

26 Ada Goulden-Bach to CP [November 1944], Craigie Collection. Adela had been released in late 1942, with restrictions placed on her activities.

27 Copy of letter from CP to Mrs Bullivant, 9 January 1945 and telegram from CP to HRH Princess Alice, c.March 1945, both Craigie Collection.

28 Olive Durand-Deacon to CP, 17 March 1945, Craigie Collection.

29 Douglas Buell to Christabel Pankhurst, 15 June 1945, Craigie Collection.

30 CP to Annie Kenney Taylor, 19 November 1946, Kenney Papers.

31 Una Winter, Director of the Susan B. Anthony Memorial Library Committee of California, to Mrs Jackman, 20 February 1948, DMC; *Los Angeles Times*, 8 February 1948.

32 Jay Trevor Weiss to David Mitchell, June 1965, DMC.

33 CP to Annie Kenney Taylor, 15 April 1947, Kenney Papers.

34 Doris Szekely to David Mitchell, 5 October 1964, DMC.

35 Esther Greg to CP, 17 February 1948, Craigie Collection.

36 CP to Margaret Webster, 2 June 1948, TWL.

37 Principal of Westminster Bank, Income Tax Department, London, 25 May 1948, to CP, Craigie Collection. The issue revolved around whether Christabel was considered resident in the UK or the USA.

38 Rudolf and Doris Szekely to David Mitchell, 21 October 1964, DMC.

39 *Calling All Women*, February 1949, p. 2.

40 CP to Annie Kenney Taylor, 25 January 1949, Kenney Papers. Flora Drummond died on 17 January 1949.

41 Ada Goulden-Bach to CP, 27 January 1949, Craigie Collection.

42 Ada Goulden-Bach to CP, 28 March 1949, Craigie Collection.

43 Ada Goulden-Bach to CP, 4 April 1949, Craigie Collection.

44 Olive Durand-Deacon to CP, 22 April 1944, Craigie Collection.

45 Manager of Westminster Bank, 12 December 1950 to CP, Craigie Collection; copy of letter from CP to Mr Moser, her lawyer, 17 June 1949, Craigie Collection.
46 CP to Annie Kenney Taylor, 11 December 1949, Kenney Papers.
47 CP to Annie Kenney Taylor, 9 December 1950, Kenney Papers.
48 Rollyson, *To be a woman: the life of Jill Craigie* (London, Aurum Press, 2005), pp. 126–9; ESP to Mr Mansfield, 15 March 1951, Purvis Collection.
49 Jessie Kenney to Charlie Marsh, 2[2] March 1951, Kenney Papers; Ada Flatman to Jill Craigie, 15 April 1951; Lilian Buckley [nee Dove-Willcox] to Jill Craigie, 16 March 1951, noted that Annie's voice had very little Yorkshire or Lancashire accent in it, both in Craigie Collection. On 14 July 1951 a play titled 'The Suffragette', written and produced by Norman Swallow, was shown on British TV. It explored the women's movement through the eyes of a rank-and-file suffragette.
50 CP to Annie Kenney Taylor, 17 April 1951, Kenney Papers.
51 CP to Grace Roe, 2 April 1950, Craigie Collection.
52 CP to Elsie Hill, 11 May 1951, National Woman's Party Papers, Group II.
53 Interview with Grace Roe, c.1964, Raeburn Collection.
54 Mrs Darer, owner of Beachwood Manor, to CP, 29 June 1951, Craigie Collection.
55 CP to Elsie Hill, 14 July 1951, National Woman's Party Papers, Group II.
56 Alice Paul to CP, 31 August 1951, National Woman's Party Papers, Group II.
57 CP to Elsie Hill, 5 May 1952, National Woman's Party Papers, Group II.
58 Interview with Rangeley Stride, 25 August 1975, DMC.
59 Annie Kenney Taylor to Grace Roe, 22 January 1952, Kenney Papers.
60 Dr E. Ross Jenney to CP, 30 December 1952, Craigie Papers.
61 CP to Ross Jenney, 14 January 1953, Craigie Papers.
62 Pugh, *The Pankhursts*, p. 473.
63 Grace Roe to unknown person, n.d. [1958], Craigie Collection; Grace Roe interview with Brian Harrison, 4 October 1974, TWL.
64 Lorna Goulden-Bach to CP, 25 April 1953, Craigie Collection.
65 CP to ESP, 5 May 1953, Richard Pankhurst Private Collection.
66 CP to ESP, 25 May 1953, Richard Pankhurst Private Collection.
67 See R. Pankhurst, Suffragette sisters in old age: unpublished correspondence between Christabel and Sylvia Pankhurst, 1953–57, *Women's History Review*, 10, 3, 2001, pp. 483–537.
68 Telegram dated 13 July 1953, Kenney Papers.
69 CP to Warwick Kenney Taylor, 20 July 1953, Kenney Papers.
70 CP to Jessie Kenney, 2 October 1953, Kenney Papers.
71 CP to Jessie Kenney, 9 April 1954, Kenney Papers.
72 *Calling All Women*, February 1954, p. 2.
73 CP to Dear Madam, 19 January 1954, Royal Archives, Clarence House, London, SW1A 1BA; Jean Rankin, Lady-in-Waiting, Sandringham, Norfolk, England, to CP, 29 January 1954, Craigie Collection
74 CP to ESP, 22 April 1954, Richard Pankhurst Private Collection. EPL died on 11 March 1954.
75 FPL to Grace Roe, 7 December 1954, Craigie Collection.
76 The Virago 1974 reprint of Strachey's '*The cause*' nonetheless used the original version, thus repeating the libel.
77 CP to ESP, 1 June 1954, Richard Pankhurst Private Collection.
78 Ida Copeland to CP, 24 April 1954, Craigie Collection.
79 Copy of letter from CP to Mr Buckhurst Pinch, 19 March 1955, Craigie Collection.
80 CP to ESP, 13 August 1955, Richard Pankhurst Private Collection.
81 *Times*, 14 July 1956.
82 Grace Roe to CP, 15 July 1956, Craigie Collection.

83 CP to Lord Pethick-Lawrence, 15 December 1955 and FPL to CP, Christmas Eve 1955, Craigie Collection.
84 Mabel Tuke to CP, 1 January 1954, Craigie Collection.
85 Mabel Tuke to CP, 8 July 1955, Craigie Collection.
86 Mabel Tuke to CP, 11 December 1956, Craigie Collection.
87 Mabel Tuke, 20 September 1956, Craigie Collection.
88 CP to Teresa Billington-Greig, 4 October 1956, TWL.
89 Teresa Billington-Greig to CP, 26 October 1956, TWL.
90 CP to Teresa Billington-Greig, 13 November 1956, TWL.

23

FINAL YEARS
1957–8

That Christmas of 1956, Christabel wrote a festive greeting to Jessie Kenney and Fred Pethick-Lawrence, reflecting not only on past times but also the present-day tyranny of the communist Soviet Union which, since the end of the Second World War, had occupied Eastern Europe. The uprising in Hungary that autumn of 1956 against Soviet-imposed policies had been brutally crushed, as had protests earlier in the year in Poland. Christabel and her mother had always detested communism and now their warnings, sneered at by many on the left, were coming to fruition. Christabel wrote movingly to Fred:

> When I read of the gallant & incredibly heroic fight for freedom by the women of <u>Hungary</u>, I like to think that they have in mind the record of the British Suffragettes – though the Suffragettes had not the same dangers to face & the same terrible price to pay . . . The men & women of Hungary teach us that in their heart[s] the love of liberty lives in greatest strength [,] & self sacrifice for country and humanity burns as brightly as they ever did.

Sensitive about the representation of her mother and family, as well as to the oppressive nature of communism, Christabel also asked Fred if he had read the section on Emmeline Pankhurst in the *Encyclopaedia Britannica* which omitted some important things, including mention of her mother's statue in Victoria Tower Gardens, but dragged in 'Sylvia's <u>communism</u> etc'. Defensive of her sister, Christabel commented, 'Sylvia does not, I suppose, call herself a communist now.'[1]

In Christabel's Christmas letter to Jessie, there was no mention of such family embarrassment, merely a reference to the Second Coming of Christ as the only way to make wars cease on earth and to put an end to the 'cruel tyranny' suffered by the Hungarians, Poles '& millions of other human beings'. However, feminist considerations were not entirely absent from the analysis:

> If we all had our time to live over again & the vote were already ours as it should have been a hundred years before we set out to win it, our

507

task would be to get some women in Parliament & some women in the Cabinet . . . That would have meant a less warlike world in the whole 20th century.[2]

Christabel's life now entered a slower pace. Friends would drive her to the market to buy fresh food, to the library to borrow another book, to her bank in Los Angeles or to visit Grace Roe in Ventura – although more often Grace came to visit Christabel. Although Christabel still socialised in the British ex-patriot community, letter writing to friends, near and far, was still an important part of her daily existence as she exchanged news about people known in common and causes dear to her heart. 'Nothing from Enid & Sybil [Goulden Bach, Christabel's cousins] for a long time', she informed Grace in late January 1957. 'Sybil is on her own very much, I think . . . since Lorna died.' Lamenting the early death of this cousin, Christabel commented, 'What a beautiful character Lorna was – strong, selfless & wise – she had a quite definite sense of humour too.'[3] To Fred Pethick-Lawrence, grateful thanks was expressed for supporting the women's cause when the Lords debated the admission of women to its chamber.[4]

However, like the rest of the former WSPU members, Christabel was greatly surprised when she heard that the eighty-five-year-old Fred had decided to re-marry, the bride-to-be none other than former suffragette Helen Craggs, at one time her brother Harry's sweetheart. Helen, a widow since 1936, had emigrated to the USA and then Canada after the Second World War, her two children now both married and living in California. 'Helen and I were so pleased to get your cordial telegram', the happy Fred wrote to Christabel after the wedding on 14 February 1957. 'Apart from a sea of press cameras we had a very quiet wedding in the Caxton Hall, and went to Worthing, where Helen has relations, for a week-end honeymoon.' They were now back at 11 Old Square, Lincoln's Inn, where they hoped to live until the sixty-two steps up to their flat proved too difficult to climb.[5] 'I am so glad to have your letter so expressive of hope and happiness in the new chapter of your life', replied a chirpy Christabel. 'Long may you both be equal to the sixty-two steps.'[6]

But Christabel was far from happy about another issue that took up the bulk of her letter to Fred. A book on the British votes for women campaign, written by a man whose name she did not know, had been published in England. 'What does he know about our policy, our motives and even our doings?' she queried. Anxious that the book might contain inaccurate statements and misunderstandings about the WSPU, Christabel asked Fred:

Do you think that it is generally understood by those who look back on the activities of the W.S.P.U. that the basis of our policy . . . and its truly original character . . . was that for the first time in the history of the women's movement we held the Government responsible for giving or withholding the enfranchisement of women[?]

For two generations, the constitutional suffragists had neglected to place responsibility upon the Government and the leaders of the political party in power; never did they develop a policy of 'opposing' a Government which refused to give women the vote or adopt the WSPU's 'anti-Government policy'.[7] But it was not just the publication of a book about the British women's suffrage campaign that made Christabel anxious.

The BBC had contacted her, saying they were making a TV programme about the suffragette movement and would send over a crew to Santa Monica to interview her. Doubtful whether such a project would accurately capture the past, Christabel declined the offer. 'I have been given "instructions" about how to frame and what to put into my discourse, which do not fit in with my own ideas of what it will be helpful and needful to say', she lamented to Fred.[8] Reflecting upon the matter over the next couple of days, she elaborated further, noting that one reason she did not wish to participate was that the 'two beloved Emmelines, Annie Kenney, the General, are no longer here to stand with me in that programme'. But, above all else, Christabel emphasized that if ever she were to address the British public again, she would wish to do so on the 'present national and world condition and the prospects for the future. I know that you and dear Helen will understand, and sympathise and approve my decision'.[9]

However, Helen Pethick-Lawrence did not agree with Christabel on this point and sent her a telegram, outlining her views. 'It saddens me to disappoint you and other friends over there', the chastened Christabel replied:

> If the B.B.C. promoters of the television programme greatly want me on it, they have at their disposal the gramophone record I made directly on leaving prison after the trial in which I had Lloyd George and Herbert Gladstone in the witness box . . . that recorded speech will represent me quite well.

Additionally, photographs such as the one 'of me speaking in Trafalgar Square and standing on the plinth of London Nelson's statue' could be shown on the screen.[10] When Helen remonstrated further, Christabel pointed out:

> I cannot compromise regarding what is truth and justice where Mother and indeed all of us who were with her, are concerned. My position in the matter as her Prime Minister, shall I call myself, she being the Queen of the WSPU, is a special one and imposes a special responsibility upon me. The resistance of the BBC to my perfectly reasonable and historically sound request that the programme end with the Statue [of Emmeline Pankhurst] is beyond respectable justification or explanation . . . What they will say in the script is another and somewhat doubtful point . . . I have asked to see the script and have met refusal there also.[11]

509

Deeply upset about the way she was being treated by the BBC, Christabel asked Grace Roe to send the corporation a telegram on her behalf stating that she would only take part if the complete commentator's script was sent to her, she spoke the final words and a picture of her mother's statue closed the programme.[12] After some delay, the BBC reluctantly agreed. The seventy-six-year-old Christabel was now keen to air her views on TV since, at long last, she knew the name of the male author who had published a book on the British women's suffrage campaign. It was Roger Fulford. In England, on 8 April 1957, the *Evening Standard* had published the first of a series of extracts from his book titled *Votes for women* which had won their £5,000 Book Prize. Copies of the extracts, as well as a copy of the book, had been sent to her. Widely reviewed in the British press, one commentator noted that Fulford had a 'slight distaste for the Pankhursts . . . with a special emphasis of admiration on Mr. Pethick-Lawrence'.[13] Fulford was a member of the Liberal Party and had stood unsuccessfully for election to Parliament.

The BBC half-hour programme was duly transmitted on 14 May 1957. 'We were all delighted to see you and hear your voice again when we were rehearsing', wrote an elated Jessie. 'You looked very charming and we saw little touches with the movement of the head of our beloved Christabel, once more.' Jessie lamented how the contribution of most of the former suffragettes, including herself and Charlotte Marsh, had to be cut down to make space for the views of Lady Violet Bonham Carter, daughter of the arch-opponent of the WSPU, Herbert Asquith. 'I have never heard in the whole of <u>our</u> history such a vindictive diatribe against us, for the way in which <u>we</u> treated <u>her</u> father.'[14]

Jessie also gave Christabel some other interesting news – it was Stella Newsome of the Women's Freedom League and now Honorary Secretary of the Suffragette Fellowship who had been in touch with Fulford, given him the address of another League member, Teresa Billington-Greig, and recommended he read Sylvia's books on the suffragette movement. There had been a three-hour 'bust-up' at the last Fellowship meeting about such biased sources, but Stella refused to resign. 'You remember in one of your speeches in the height of our Movement saying that the Liberal Party would go in the wilderness for many years for the way they had treated the Suffragette Movement', Jessie observed. 'This is what has happened. Fulford cannot get into Parliament as a Liberal . . . So of course Fulford's book is a white washing of the Liberal Party under Asquith.'[15] Although such background information helped Christabel to understand why Fulford took the line he did, it did not lessen her anger. She was so agitated by his book that Grace Roe feared she would have a stroke. Fortunately, this did not happen. Instead, Christabel wrote to friends in England, such as Jessie Kenney and especially the Pethick-Lawrences, listing her criticisms of *Votes for women*, hoping they would complain to the publisher.

'As for the author of <u>that book</u>', the indignant Christabel told Jessie, 'he [is] just a <u>party political Liberal</u> – 3 times a Liberal candidate – who knows what the WSPU did to the last Liberal Govt – last in two senses of the word.'[16] 'Not one member of the W.S.P.U., including myself, was consulted by this author', she complained to Fred to whom she detailed all her criticisms. In particular, Christabel was 'utterly shocked . . . by the tone and content' of the chapter about her parents; even their marriage, when her mother wore not the expected white bridal gown but a brown velvet dress, was subject to the author's 'rudeness' since he ignored the fact that, since her father's parent had died recently, a white gown was considered inappropriate. Just as appalling were the numerous errors in Fulford's account of the WSPU. Sylvia was not in the inner circle of management of the WSPU while the references to her mother and herself were 'quite scandalous'. The split of 1907, when Fulford claimed that Emmeline Pankhurst autocratically took control of the WSPU and Mrs Despard, Mrs Billington-Greig and Mrs How Martyn left to form the Women's Freedom League, was inaccurate. 'I recall that it was our Hon. Treasurer in the WSPU [Fred's first wife, Emmeline] who advised and indeed insisted as the condition of her remaining Treasurer . . . that mother took the action she did', she reminded Fred. Angry and pained, Christabel continued, 'The author's whitewashing of that Liberal Government's denial of votes for women, the tricks with which they avoided keeping their deceptive pledges, the coercion they directed against the women militants, make this anything but a valid book of history.'[17]

However, there was one particular paragraph in Fulford's book that wounded Christabel more than any other and about which she wrote to Helen, rather than Fred. It referred to the time in March 1912 after she had fled to France and the police ransacked the office at Clement's Inn and searched her flat. 'As sometimes happens on these occasions', Fulford commented, 'the police contrived to give an extra twist to public prejudice by letting it be known that they had found a bookshelf in the flat "with a rather mixed selection of works, many of them French".'[18] 'Very much do I resent the insinuation . . . accusing me of a taste for dirty books', the distressed Christabel, a devout Second Adventist, confided to Helen. 'I have never in my whole life had any collection of books or any single book of an unclean, immoral nature. I have only one mind and aim to keep it clean.' Christabel explained that the flat she occupied at that time was sub-let to her by a suffragette, Jessie Stephenson, 'and she was not the woman to acquire books of the kind Fulford reports, falsely, were in the flat. Had there been any such books there, I should have had them removed.' Deeply upset, Christabel asked Helen to speak about it to Fred who was a defendant at the 1912 trial, so that he could confirm or deny Fulford's statement. 'Hoping for an early reply', Christabel ended her letter, 'as this matter touches me painfully.'[19]

Helen replied that Fred could not remember any statement about obscene books and politely pointed out that neither she nor Fred interpreted Fulford's words as she did. Fulford, Helen suggested, 'just wants to belittle the Pankhursts! I fancy the majority of readers will miss the implication – & it surely wd be unwise to give the matter any publicity in the press'. Helen continued:

511

I understand that you have objections to publish your own book, you are probably right – you usually are!! – but certainly it would be a consolation to your old followers if we know that [at] least you had appointed a literary executor who will eventually publish it. After all, the real assessment is for future historians and one does hope there will be an authoritative record which may be consulted. Who else can give it but yourself?[20]

Christabel gave the matter some thought and decided that the best way to counteract any influence of Fulford's insulting and inaccurate book was to republish her mother's autobiography, My own story, collated from articles that had originally appeared in a Hearst Newspaper publication. Written before the partial enfranchisement of women in 1914, Christabel proposed to Hearst Newspapers that the book should be reprinted, with a supplementary chapter possibly written by herself.[21] But although the project was discussed with Grace Roe and Mabel Tuke – who were asked to contribute to an additional preface – the updated reprint did not come to fruition.

Christabel was not the only Pankhurst daughter deeply upset by Fulford's Votes for women. Sylvia too, in Ethiopia, read the book with seething indignation, especially since Fulford claimed to have 'unashamedly drawn' on her books, especially The suffragette movement.[22] 'I am horrified by the book and by the manner in which he expresses "a deep sense of obligation" to me while distorting everything I have written', she wrote angrily to Christabel. Like Christabel, Sylvia was deeply wounded by the denigration of their father and the inaccuracies about the WSPU. Nonetheless, she expected Christabel, her elder sister rather than herself, to shoulder the burden in dealing with the matter. 'I consider it is your duty to act.' And untruthfully, she then claimed, 'I have done my best to defend the W.S.P.U. on other occasions which means defending Mother and you.' Sylvia continued:

It is your turn to come forward in the interests of historic truth even apart from your personal reputation. While I am handicapped here I will still do anything which occurs to me. I have written Lord Pethick Lawrence my opinion that it ought not to pass unchallenged.[23]

Old grievances on Sylvia's part were now aired again as she recollected that when Annie Kenney came to rouse London women in 1906, all the WSPU women were frequent visitors to her two rented rooms in Park Walk. 'They monopolised my workroom . . . That was why I had to leave the place and I resigned from the Hon. Secretaryship at the same time.' Commiserating with Christabel that Teresa Billington-Greig was not a suitable person to write an obituary of either of them, Sylvia ended her letter with some personal news, namely that her son Richard was getting married to a Romanian woman with an Oxford MA:

He asks me to send you his love: he is family conscious. Having been an only child he likes the idea of having relations and was amused by Zuleika Dobson [the heroine of the 1911 book of this name, modelled on Christabel and written by the British author and caricaturist Max Beerbohm] and is interested in the lady concerned. He is a Professor and is considered a great man by the students. I suppose you know Richard's father is dead.[24]

Christabel, in her reply, said nothing to her sister about the hostile portrayal of herself and their mother in Sylvia's influential *The suffragette movement*. It appears that since making contact with Sylvia, after so many years of estrangement, Christabel had now let bygones be bygones. 'I wonder whether Sylvia, if she were writing now, would have provided RF [Roger Fulford] with so much ammunition' as she had earlier done, Christabel confided to Jessie. 'I fancy that she would not . . . however the harm is done though he had no right to pick up and use everything hostile that he could.'[25] The ageing Christabel, who had looked after Sylvia when they were children, assumed the older sister caring role again; she was not going to let any differences of view between them split asunder their newly rediscovered family ties and their shared loyalty to their beloved parents.

'First of all I must send my congratulations to Richard upon his approaching marriage and my love to both of them', Christabel began affectionately in her long reply to Sylvia. 'During the first world war, I became and have remained deeply interested & sympathetic with Romania and all that group of nations. How interesting that your new daughter is an Oxford M.A.' Striking a conciliatory note in 'big sister' style, Christabel responded sympathetically to Sylvia's complaint about the invasion of her rented rooms at Park Walk, so many years ago:

I sometimes regret that I went on with my work for the LL.B. degree and did not go straight to London . . . that would have spared you a good deal in the way of the invasion of your abode, and other difficulties. It was a hard case for you. I knew nothing about it at the time . . . I do not know how long it went on . . . surely not after the funds began to come in . . . after Mrs. Lawrence became the treasurer.[26]

Despite such shared concerns, the bulk of Christabel's letter focused on her utter distaste for the Fulford book. Christabel reiterated to Sylvia many of the points she had already made to Fred and Helen Pethick-Lawrence. 'The book is anti-W.S.P.U. and anti-Pankhurst . . . and I may say anti-me.' Like Sylvia, Christabel resented Fulford's claim that the WSPU had divided the Pankhurst family:

The Pethick-Lawrences begged Mother to resign her appointment [Registrar of Births and Deaths] her earned income in order to be free to concentrate on the movement & they guaranteed her an income – which . . . did not replace her govt. salary and pension. What did I get – 3 little pounds a week. Heavens! I earned them!

Christabel similarly attacked Fulford's assertion that she and her mother had a partiality for Conservative drawing rooms.[27] She argued instead:

> It is well known that mother and I were no respectors of persons . . . Countesses and charwomen, mill girls and millionaires were all one to me . . . But what I did notice was that Cabinet Ministers and M.Ps were more impressed by protests from women from the West End than by protests in the East End and that was especially true of Labour M.P.s and next to them Liberals.

Nor did Christabel agree with Fulford's claim that when the WSPU's constitution was annulled and the annual conference abandoned, in 1907, it became a dictatorship.[28] She believed that Fulford wrote as he did because of the 'jealous spite' of Teresa Billington-Greig who had spoken to him about the split, putting the side of the breakaway faction that became the Women's Freedom League. Christabel informed Sylvia that she had written a very long detailed commentary on the book and sent it to Fred Pethick-Lawrence, hoping he would show it to Fulford's publisher, Faber and Faber. Despite her concerns, Christabel concluded her letter on an optimistic note:

> All over the world votes for women and the Pankhurst names are identified and I do not think the Fulford's book will change that . . . Mother's statue is my great consolation. It will stand when Fulford's pages have long crumbled.[29]

Christabel's long, discursive letter to Sylvia only temporarily lessened her anxieties about the way in which suffragette history was being written. Pondering on the past, she considered she had not said enough to her sister about how male MPs in the Edwardian era, including those in the Labour Party, had failed to support the women's cause and so penned another letter a few days later. Asquith could not have remained in office, Christabel insisted, without the support of the Labour Party. '[W]here votes for women was concerned we owe <u>nothing</u> to any of the men's parties, but all to our own efforts – which is a good thing, after all!!' Perhaps reflecting that Sylvia, a deeply committed socialist, might be offended by her forthright condemnation of Labour, Christabel added, '[W]hatever any of us has done politically has been done out of a sense of principle & duty.'[30]

Sylvia, also mellowed by old age, soon replied in conciliatory tone:

> [W]e all have our failings and lack the gift to see ourselves as others see us . . . I have tried in my life to follow and to learn what I imbibed from Father and not to desert the cause to which he dedicated his life and energy – Human welfare and progress . . . I was probably mistaken in giving up my art.

In regard to Fulford's book, Sylvia expressed exasperation that the author had not been asked, when the book was first published, to expunge the offending pages. It was too late now to do much other than write complaining letters to the publisher. 'I passed your message to my children: Rita seemed pleased', Sylvia ended her letter. 'They will get married on September 17 this year, in just a few weeks.' Although signing off in a business-like way – 'As ever Sylvia P.', rather than 'Affectionately', a word both Sylvia and Christabel had previously used in this recent correspondence – the two sisters were at ease with each other.[31] Neither discussed with the other the causes of the rift that had earlier divided them.

It would appear that Christabel made no attempt to make contact with her youngest sister Adela, in Australia, although there were people with whom she still corresponded that autumn of 1957 who had known Adela, including Mabel Tuke, Charlie Marsh, Jessie Kenney and Rangeley Stride. Mabel Tuke, recovering in St Joseph's hospital in Port Elizabeth, South Africa, gladly accepted Christabel's decision not to proceed with a re-printing of an updated version of her mother's autobiography. Although Mabel, as asked, had duly written a few sentences for the additional preface, she did not feel up to the task. The admiring Mabel reminisced:

> Everyone of us who knew & loved Mrs. Pankhurst & you, my darling Christabel, know the feelings which surge within us as we turn over our memories of the years when we fought together for a most just & righteous cause . . . The personal, (Christabel & Pansy) part of your dear letter, filled my heart to overflowing, but dearest C, you never really thought I had changed from what I was in those days, except physically? . . . In becoming a Catholic, that did not carry me further away, but brought you nearer in a certain sense, i.e. in prayer and thanksgiving for your wonderful leadership & the amazing un-selfish character of it . . . What an amazing & destined pair you were![32]

Rangeley Stride, who had been so helpful in looking after the young Aurea, was less emotionally expressive in her letters to Christabel but nonetheless greatly valued their long friendship. 'Bless you, my precious changeless friend for all you have meant to me all these years.' Since Christabel was urgently seeking an extra copy of one of her own publications, Rangeley was only too happy to search for the book in England and send it to Santa Monica when found. Both women, with increasing age, were now experiencing in common various pains in their shoulders, neck and back and were visiting chiropractors, although Rangeley considered the service Christabel was receiving far superior to her own.[33] Meanwhile, other more mundane activities intruded into Christabel's life, including the breaking down of her TV set. An American friend, Mrs Limberg, brought the repaired item to Christabel's apartment that autumn of 1957 and then drove both of them, in her new Thunderbird car, to a 91st birthday party.[34]

Such happy moments were soon punctuated with yet more worrying news about the writing of suffragette history. Late that October of 1957 Christabel heard that a Mr Herbert van Thal was writing a biography of Ethel Smyth who had died in 1944. Fearful that the author would draw upon Ethel's distorted references to herself and her mother in *Female pipings*, especially in its first edition, the anxious Christabel wrote to Ethel's publisher, hoping they could locate the author. 'None of my Mother's letters do I wish to have re-published. I regret that I ever agreed to the publication of any of them.' Hoping that van Thal was a 'sympathetic and well-bred man' who would wish to avoid including 'anything wounding' to her mother's family, friends and followers in the suffragette movement, Christabel wanted the biography to focus on Ethel's musical life and to exclude any reference to Emmeline Pankhurst.[35] Fortunately, Peter Davies, the publisher, found the address of van Thal and Christabel was soon writing a polite letter to him, setting out her concerns as well as enclosing a detailed account of her objections to Ethel's book.[36] Van Thal gave way. 'I am so glad to have your friendly & very understanding letter', replied Christabel. 'It has greatly relieved my mind.' However, the news that former suffragette Christabel Marshall, now called 'Christopher St John', was writing a biography about Ethel was less welcome. 'By this mail I am writing to her explaining my point of view.'[37]

The necessary letter was duly written and sent to Charlie Marsh, back in England, asking her to forward it to Christopher St John. The latter's reply did not satisfy the anguished and increasingly dogmatic Christabel. In particular, Christabel did not want repeated from Ethel Smyth's book the 'false libel' that it was herself and not Sylvia who had given birth to an illegitimate child in December 1927. 'It was the biggest blow of my career . . . No one knew better than she did that it was not I, but my sister. This was <u>no mistake</u> on Ethel Smyth's part.' Based upon this libel, the review in the *Times* had remarked, Christabel recalled, that it was 'strange and sad' that the daughter who had been the closest partner to Emmeline Pankhurst in the campaign for the vote 'should have broken her heart by her act'. Perhaps, Christabel reflected sadly, she should have sued the *Times*, Ethel Smyth and her publisher, but 'that would have meant involving my sister and I could not do it'. Nor did Christabel want Christopher St John to repeat from *Female pipings* any of the remarks her mother was alleged to have made about various personalities. 'These were all what the lawyers would call privileged communications and must of course not be published without my consent as Mother's legal representative.' Deeply pained by the thought that the contents of *Female pipings* might be publicly aired again, Christabel pleaded with her correspondent:

> [I]f this Memoir comes out it will cloud my remaining years . . . My friend, let me live the rest of my days in peace regarding what is past . . . the revival of past dissension . . . and the possible exploitation of the history of our campaign by the enemies of our country and of freedom everywhere in the world would torment me for the rest of my life . . . without doing the least good to the cause of women.[38]

Christopher St John was very upset by such requests:

> It is of course out of the question for me as an honest biographer to com-
> ply with your request that neither your name nor your mother's should
> be mentioned in my book. Forgive me for saying that you have no right
> to make it.

Assuring Christabel that there was nothing that could possibly be construed as
'derogatory' to herself or her mother in her manuscript, she explained that it had
already been sent to the publisher and that her literary adviser would correct any
references he might think indiscreet or give offence. 'My affectionate and admiring remembrances of you have not been affected by your attacks on Ethel Smyth.
Some of them seem to me justified, others not.'[39]

Christopher St John was not the only person offended by Christabel's demands.
Charlie Marsh was furious. 'I have always had the greatest admiration & love for
CP', she confided to Grace Roe:

> but really this business has shaken me as to her judgment [underlined
> twice] . . . Knowing Christopher [who was in her eighties] I can tell you
> that she is most loyal to the Pankhursts as leaders & is proud to have
> been in the W.S.P.U. . . . I am really most annoyed that CP should lec-
> ture a woman of her stature as though she was a schoolgirl.

Could they not encourage Christabel to put her energies into writing her own
account of the suffragette movement, Charlie queried:

> Enid [Goulden Bach] says the book is written & that the family sent it
> on to C.P. & it needs revising & bringing more up to date. C.P. owes this
> to her family & to her comrades, I feel, as I think you agree.[40]

That Christmas of 1957, the last that Christabel would be alive, passed
much the same as usual. But although she appeared outwardly calm and serene,
Christabel was still in turmoil about the way suffragette history was being written and how she and her mother were being represented. Keen to counter the
unstoppable tide of criticism, she had written to Charlie Marsh asking her to
send a picture of her mother's statue in its new position since she wanted to give
copies of it, at Christmas, to friends in the USA. But the only picture Charlie
had was being used as a frontispiece for the next issue of *Calling All Women*, the
newsletter of the Suffragette Fellowship, and might not be returned in time.[41]
The necessary photograph did eventually arrive, belatedly, and copies sent to
Christabel's friends who wanted to know details about the statue and the sculptor himself. Since Christabel could not remember clearly all the information she
sought Grace's help.[42]

The New Year of 1958 brought the additional hassle of a bus strike in Santa Monica. On 15 January Christabel explained to Grace the inconvenience this caused her and, yet again, asked for her help:

> This bus strike is keeping me tied to Santa Monica as there are no buses and no Santa Monica person having a car ever wants to drive to Los Angeles . . . So I cannot get to my bank to cash a check. I have cashed a few small ones with the Papins [next door neighbours], but I do not want to overdo that . . . That account is too small to be divided between the Los Angeles and Santa Monica branches, and anyhow I do not particularly want to advertise my affairs in Santa Monica . . . So I am wondering whether you will very kindly send me three five dollar bills in exchange for the enclosed returned cheque [sic] in separate letters, one after another if you think that safer.
>   There is such a fuss about identification at the Post Office where money orders are concerned unless one has a driver's licence.[43]

Undoubtedly Grace helped as best she could.

Rain storms that January prevented Christabel being driven by a friend to Ventura to see Grace. But there were some compensations. 'Who should come to my door two days ago but Lady (Helen) Pethick Lawrence driven here from Reseda [in Los Angeles] by a pretty American daughter-in Law, Mrs. Alec McCombie', the excited Christabel wrote to Grace on 24 January. 'They stayed about an hour & a bit more . . . She will be here again next year, if not before, as this is her pre-marriage arrangement with Lord P-L.'[44] As the bad weather continued into early February, another planned trip to see Grace had to be cancelled again. 'I am sorry', wrote the apologetic Christabel to her life-long friend, 'but it is a pleasure postponed until an assuredly lovely sunshiny day.'[45] It was Christabel's last letter to Grace.

Unexpectedly, aged seventy-seven years old, she died late in the evening of 12 February 1958 from a heart attack (coronary sclerosis), although the death certificate listed the following day as the date of death. Grace was informed immediately and travelled to Santa Monica to arrange the funeral and sort out Christabel's effects. It was from here that she sent telegrams and letters to relatives and friends. Grace informed Enid Goulden Bach:

> Her passing was just as she would have most wished – no illness – no thought that she was going – she was watching T.V. and sewing and the doctor, I gather, stated it must have been around 11pm Wed Feb 12 Pacific Time, that she stopped breathing.

During that Wednesday evening Christabel had had a cheerful telephone conversation with the Papins. Although her lungs had been giving her some trouble during the last few months – she had been bothered with phlegm and would sometimes get pain when she coughed – 'she was always active & about – & had visits with friends'. At about ten o'clock on the following day, the Papins noticed that Christabel had not taken her paper in and so knocked on her door, as they always did. When they had no reply, they broke in and found Christabel dead, sitting in a chair. 'I have not Sylvia's or Adela's address, so, dear Enid, please cable both of them if you have not already done so', Grace pleaded.[46]

Notes

1 CP to FPL, 15 December 1956, P-L Papers.
2 CP to Jessie Kenney, 15 December 1956, Kenney Papers.
3 CP to Grace Roe, 29 January 1957, Craigie Collection.
4 CP to FPL, 24 January 1957, P-L Papers.
5 FPL to CP, 26 February 1957, Craigie Collection.
6 CP to FPL, 10 March 1957, P-L Papers.
7 CP to FPL, 10 March 1957, P-L Papers.
8 CP to FPL, 4 April 1957, P-L Papers.
9 CP to FPL, 6 April 1957, P-L Papers. Christabel had also written to Charlie Marsh, airing her grievances about the programme – see extract from this letter, dated 4 April 1957, 'Proposed TV- BBC Suffrage programme', P-L Papers.
10 CP to Helen PL, 17 April 1957, P-L Papers.
11 CP to Helen PL, 19 April 1957, P-L Papers.
12 Quoted in CP to Helen PL, 22 April 1957, P-L Papers.
13 Margaret Lane, Women on the march, *Daily Telegraph*, 12 April 1957.
14 Jessie Kenney to CP, 17 April 1957, Craigie Collection. The title of the programme was 'First Hand (no. 4) – The Suffragettes'.
15 Jessie Kenney to CP, 17 April 1957, Craigie Collection.
16 CP to Jessie Kenney, 16 May 1957, Kenney Papers. Fulford had stood unsuccessfully as a Liberal parliamentary candidate for the Woodbridge division of Suffolk in 1929, the Holderness division of Yorkshire in 1945 and Rochdale in Lancashire in 1950.
17 CP to Lord Pethick-Lawrence, 25 May 1957, P-L Papers.
18 R. Fulford, *Votes for women* (London, Faber and Faber, 1957), p. 251.
19 CP to Helen PL, 15 June 1957, Craigie Collection.
20 Helen PL to CP, 4 July 1957, Craigie Collection.
21 Undated letter from CP to Head of Hearst Newspapers, only page 2 extant, Craigie Collection.
22 Fulford, *Votes for women*, p. 15.
23 ESP to CP 10 July 1957, Craigie Collection.
24 ESP to CP, 10 July 1957, Craigie Collection.
25 CP to Jessie Kenney, 25 May 1957, Kenney Papers.
26 CP to ESP, 3 August 1957, Richard Pankhurst Private Collection.
27 Fulford, *Votes for women*, p. 274, 'Mrs. Pankhurst's and Christabel's partiality for Conservative drawing-rooms, may have deflected the Union from its original loyalty to the Labour movement, and no doubt helped to widen the breach with the Lawrences, who were Labour party sympathizers from the earliest days.'
28 Fulford, *Votes for women*, pp. 165–7.
29 CP to ESP, 3 August 1957, Richard Pankhurst Private Collection. CP to Jessie Kenney, 25 May 1957, Kenney Papers, notes that Fred P-L had spoken to Fulford who was willing to make some changes. Christabel's detailed commentary of Fulford's book is not extant in the P-L Papers.
30 CP to ESP, incomplete and undated letter [August 1957?], Richard Pankhurst Private Collection.

31 ESP to CP, n.d. [August 1957?], Richard Pankhurst Private Collection.
32 Mabel Tuke to CP, n.d. [4 September 1957?], Craigie Collection.
33 Rangeley Stride to CP, 12 September 1957, Craigie Collection.
34 CP to Grace Roe, 6 October 1957, Craigie Collection.
35 CP to Dear Sir, 1 November 1957, DMC.
36 CP to van Thal, 5 November 1957 and CP 'The Projected Memoir of Dame Ethel Smyth', DMC.
37 CP to van Thal, 14 November 1957, DMC.
38 CP to Christopher St John, 21 December 1957, Craigie Collection.
39 Christopher St John to CP, 7 January 1958, Craigie Collection.
40 Charlie Marsh to Grace Roe, 7 January 1958, Craigie Collection.
41 CP to Grace Roe, 4 December 1957, Craigie Collection.
42 CP to Grace Roe, 3 February 1958, Craigie Collection.
43 CP to Grace Roe, 15 January 1958, Craigie Collection.
44 CP to Grace Roe, 24 January 1958, Craigie Collection.
45 CP to Grace Roe, 3 February 1958, Craigie Collection. The visit had been planned for the following day.
46 Grace Roe to Enid Goulden Bach, 14 February 1958, Craigie Collection.

24

LEGACY

The news of Christabel's death was greeted with much sorrow by her friends in America, many of whom wrote to Grace Roe. '[T]he valiant lady, has certainly left her footprints not only in "the sands of time", but in the hearts of her many friends who loved & appreciated her true goodness', commented Ivy de Verley, a portrait painter.[1] But it was the letters sent to Grace from former suffragettes who had been close to Christabel in her suffrage days that were particularly poignant. 'I've just this minute heard on the radio this terribly sad news that our darling Christabel has gone', wrote Kathleen Pepper. 'I feel so shocked & stunned that I can't write any more now . . . Mrs. Stride [Rangeley] & I . . . feel – as you will be – heartbroken – I just cannot realize it.'[2] For Rangeley, who was sixteen years old when she first met Christabel, had helped to look after Betty/Aurea as a young girl and been close to Christabel all her life, her deceased close friend was 'as perfect as any human being could be . . . She always asked us to destroy her letters, so I did, but nothing can ever destroy the memories'. Shattered by the dreadful news, Rangeley confided to Grace, 'No words can describe her as we knew her. I truly believe that you & I loved her more than anyone else has ever done.'[3]

For former suffragette Charlie Marsh the news of Christabel's death was a particular shock, since she had recently received a letter from her. In touch with many of the former WSPU members, Charlie remembered past times. 'Una Duval rang me up this am & we were both much upset – I saw Dorothea Rock & Zoe Procter (aged 90) also & later Decima Moore.'[4] Cecily Hale similarly reflected on the 'grand old days. Christabel so young, & so brilliant . . . one can't realize that she was growing old'.[5] The grieving Mabel Tuke was devastated:

> I feel struck suddenly to the ground . . . it never ever remotely occurred to my mind that she would pass from the dreadful mess which is being made of the world today, before I did . . . oh dear dear Grace what a blow to all who loved her for her splendid fearless qualities & were full of admiration for her clear sighted statesmanlike attitude to all questions of world politics . . . I haven't shed a tear – tears & Christabel don't match somehow; but the heartache is woeful . . . God rest her most precious soul.[6]

Adela in Australia and Sylvia in Ethiopia made no public statement about their sister's death but undoubtedly were upset by the news. 'Poor Christabel "blotted her copy book" by turning to religion', the insightful Adela had written sympathetically to another former suffragette some weeks earlier.[7] For Sylvia, Christabel's death brought back not only memories of the early days of the WSPU but 'of our childhood together, when we did everything together and went everywhere together', she told Fred Pethick-Lawrence. The advances women had made in the twentieth century would not have happened but for the great struggle 'in which Christabel took a leading part . . . which had wide publicity throughout the world', Sylvia emphasised generously to Pearl Murcheson. 'I much regret to learn that she was alone with no friend present when the end came – one can never know what that meant to her', Sylvia wrote sadly to the parents of her daughter-in-law. She also recollected that Christabel had adopted a little girl during the First World War, but that girl had grown up and died soon after her marriage, a long time ago. 'My sister never mentioned the girl in later years but she had been very fond of her when she was a little child.'[8]

None of the newspaper obituaries mentioned Aurea either. The British press mainly focused on Christabel's suffrage days. The *Times* described her as 'the driving force' behind the militant section of the women's suffrage movement, 'and possibly its most brilliant orator'. Her power sprang from:

> a magnetic personality. A most attractive young woman with fresh colouring, delicate features, and a mass of soft brown hair, a graceful figure on the platform, she spoke with a warmth, a passion, and a highly effective *raillerie*, which few who were prepared to give her a hearing could resist.

Although the crowds did not always spare her, the most familiar cry they uttered was 'We want Chris'. Courageous and resourceful, 'she was a force to be reckoned with'. A brief reference was also made to the time when Christabel, as a member of the Women's Party, stood for election to Parliament as well as to her crusade for Second Adventism in her later life. A shorter notice by the *Daily Telegraph* told a similar story.[9]

The obituaries in the American press were more effusive, highlighting Christabel's contribution to the women's cause but also giving more attention to her evangelical and humanitarian work. 'Dame Pankhurst probably did more than any other one individual to make woman suffrage come true in Britain in 1918', ran the *New York Times*. After converting to Second Adventism, she came to the USA where she 'lectured widely at Bible conferences . . . [and] made many speeches favoring improved British-American relations'.[10] An active member of the Episcopal Church, Dame Christabel Pankhurst was a 'militant campaigner for Christ and women's suffrage', claimed the *Santa Monica Outlook*. Those who knew Dame Christabel in later life as 'a sweet and gentle woman', asserted Wingate White, found it hard to believe that she had ever been 'such an

LEGACY

iron-souled character' in the suffragette movement.[11] 'A noble crusader has gone home', wrote Mrs Kent Allen for the *Los Angeles Times*:

> Dame Christabel was a great humanitarian. Among her many kind deeds, there is one outstanding in my memory: when she nursed a blind woman night and day for months with dedicated devotion until Dame Christabel herself became ill from exhaustion but would not leave the blind woman until someone capable could take over.[12]

Grace set about arranging the funeral for 17 February, contacting Christabel's cousin Enid Goulden Bach about the wishes of the family who wisely left all decisions to her. 'I have ordered sprays in "the colours" but each one different for you, Enid & Sybil, Charlie Marsh & Pansy', Grace informed Jessie.[13] Christabel had left no instructions regarding her burial but Grace managed to secure a plot in Woodlawn Cemetery, Santa Monica, overlooking the Pacific Ocean, a spot that Christabel had visited and liked. For some years, Christabel had been attending the small St Augustine By-the-Sea Episcopal Church and so its rector, the Revd. Clifford E. Barry Nobes, was asked to officiate. Grace Roe and Grace Harris, an American friend, had been appointed executrixes of Christabel's will, made in 1951 and written in her own hand, with Ethel Jenny and Irene C. Buell, both of Vista Del Mar Avenue, Hollywood, being the witnesses. Christabel had no property to leave, and the small annuity on which she had lived for several years ceased at her death. But she did have papers and manuscripts she wanted preserved and so the executrixes, who were the beneficiaries, were requested to deal with literary copyrights and any unpublished manuscripts. 'I leave my eyes to the Eye Bank', Christabel had stipulated, 'so that having served me perfectly during my whole lifetime, they may serve to restore sight to others.'[14]

Among the seventy-five or so personal friends present at the funeral was the British Consul who had given permission for the coffin to be draped in the British flag, as Grace had requested. Flowers were received from many countries, including a laurel wreath of white gardenias, white gladiolas, lilies of the valley and purple ribbon from the Suffragette Fellowship and friends in London. Although Rangeley Stride, on receiving a copy of the funeral service, was upset to learn that it had ended not with a funeral march but a secular song, 'The Rose Still Grows', most of those present were impressed.[15] '[Y]ou did a fine piece of work and everything seemed to work so smoothly', Edna Dunrobin complimented Grace. Edna and Marion Brink, a worshipper at St Augustine, fondly recounted some memories about Christabel, even remembering how she had make a big fuss of a 'cute' baby who once lived nearby, buying him on one occasion a rubber fish.[16]

Relatives and former suffrage friends in England were soon arranging a memorial service to be held at St Martin-in-the-Fields, London, on 14 March at 12.30 p.m. A congregation of about five hundred people turned up on the day, including many elderly white-haired former suffragettes wearing their hunger-striking medals, as well as Marion Reeves, Vice Chair of the Suffragette Fellowship and President of the Women's Freedom League. A number of women MPs attended too, including Eirene White, Lena Jeger and Joyce Butler.[17] Grace Roe, Sylvia and Adela were unable to attend. The Reverend Austen Williams officiated, Adeline Bourne, a former member of the Actresses Franchise League, read the lesson and the hymns 'The Lord's my Shepherd', 'He who would valiant be' and 'Now thank we all our God' were sung. In his eulogy from the pulpit, Fred Pethick-Lawrence praised Christabel's 'great life work' in bringing about the enfranchisement of women. 'There are few people of whom it can be said that they changed the course of human history and that they changed it for the better.'[18] In the afternoon, after the service had ended, Woman's Hour, a popular BBC radio programme, included a talk by Una Duval about Christabel. 'She only had 5 minutes on air', Kathleen Pepper informed Grace, 'but gave such a true & sincere & spontaneous & loving appreciation of our darling Christabel that it made me weep.'[19]

Helen Pethick-Lawrence was keen that a permanent memorial to Christabel should be established and set up a Memorial Fund Committee with herself as the Treasurer, Nancy Astor as Patron, Vera Laughton Mathews as Chair, and Enid Goulden Bach as Secretary; Grace Roe, Charlie Marsh and Dame Sybil Thorndike, the actress, were among the other ten members. The aim was to raise £1,500 to have Christabel's name added to the statue of her mother in Victoria Tower Gardens, adjacent to the House of Lords. The proposal, approved by the Ministry of Works, was for the addition of a semi-circular low wall which would terminate in two piers showing on one a bronze relief of Christabel and, on the other, a replica of the WSPU's prison brooch. 'The design appears to be particularly appropriate', it was argued, 'for in as much as Christabel and her mother jointly led the militant campaign so should they be remembered together by future generations.'[20]

Helen worked tirelessly to raise the necessary monies for the memorial, despite problems with her back. On 6 July 1959, a week before the unveiling, she and Fred held a party in their flat in Lincoln's Inn. Grace Roe travelled from the USA to join the commemorations. Grace had unearthed from a London shop a recording of Christabel speaking in 1908 after she had left prison, defending militant methods. Now thirty years after that event all the party guests listened to the voice of the Chief Organiser of the WSPU saying:

> Men got the vote not by persuading, but by alarming the legislators. Similar measures must be adopted by women. The militant methods of women today are clearly thought out and vigorously pursued. We have waited too long for political justice; we refuse to wait any longer.[21]

On Monday, 13 July 1959 the Lord Chancellor, Lord Kilmuir, unveiled the memorial, about eighty former suffragettes being present, many wearing their prison brooches and prison medals on ribbons of purple, white and green. Mary Leigh held high a WSPU flag that had cheered on the Pankhursts and their supporters so many years ago. In her opening address, Dame Vera Laughton

Mathews, who had taken over as subeditor of *The Suffragette* in 1913 when the staff of the newspaper had been imprisoned for conspiracy, noted that, 'Fifty years ago the name of Pankhurst was on everybody's lips . . . if Mrs. Pankhurst was the heart and inspiration of the Movement, Christabel was the political genius.' Lord Kilmuir spoke of Christabel as a 'truly dynamic and remarkable personality' who, with her mother, inspired their followers to a 'passionate and profound feeling that it was an injustice and an insult to women that they could not have a part in choosing the representatives of the country in Parliament'.[22]

This was not the last event the Christabel Pankhurst Memorial Committee Fund organised. On 19 May 1960, a plaque to Christabel and Annie was unveiled in the Free Trade Hall, Manchester, to commemorate the first militant protest that had been held there in 1905.[23] Later that year, on 10 October, Dame Sybil Thorndike unveiled a tablet at Clement's Inn, the former WSPU headquarters.[24] And then, in spring 1962, a small bronze statuette of Christabel, fashioned by Sir Charles Wheeler, was exhibited at the Royal Academy.[25]

Meanwhile, three years earlier, in 1959, Christabel's book on the suffragette movement had been published. When cleaning up Christabel's flat shortly after her death and going through her papers, Grace had found no trace of the manuscript, although she did find several letters referring to it. Suspecting that the document might be elsewhere, she visited Edna Dunrobin who some time earlier had rescued boxes that had once belonged to Christabel when she had lived with Shirley Carson Jenney. The now very dilapidated, torn boxes were found in Edna's cellar. Grace piled them into her car to take home. On arriving in Ventura she seized one of the boxes and quite at random found inside the missing manuscript.[26] Overjoyed at her find, Grace decided to bring the precious manuscript to England, hoping that Fred Pethick-Lawrence would see it through to publication. The hesitant Fred, soon assured of the high quality of the material and recalling the 'warm esteem' in which he held the author, agreed to do so. Except for a new subdivision of chapters, the omission of a few repetitive paragraphs and a short postscript, the manuscript was published as Christabel had written it.[27] Since it had no title, Fred supplied one: *Unshackled: the story of how we won the vote*. He also chose as the frontispiece a photograph of Christabel in a straw hat with flowers that he had bought her. The book was published in June 1959, a few weeks before the unveiling of the memorial.

As noted in the Introduction, *Unshackled*, written in a matter-of-fact style, was no literary match for the socialist-feminist Sylvia's *The suffragette movement*.[28] Although Sylvia had only played a minor role in the suffragette campaign, in *The suffragette movement* she had exaggerated her own importance, presenting herself as the 'heroine' of the campaign, the Pankhurst daughter who, with her East London women, won votes for women. Furthermore, Christabel and their mother are portrayed in a negative, hostile manner, as discussed throughout this book. As Craigie has noted, Sylvia was not above 'feathering her nest in posterity by filching her mother's and elder's sister plumage'.[29] However, in *Unshackled* Christabel presents her mother and herself in a positive light, as *the* leaders of the

WSPU who worked in unison for the good of the women's cause and not for self-aggrandisement. In particular, Christabel understates her own importance and emphasises the valiant role of her mother.[30]

Unlike *The suffragette movement*, no mention is made in *Unshackled* of the East London Federation of the Suffragettes and the break with Sylvia and Adela in 1914.[31] It offered a narrative about a political campaign and did not deal with the minor diversions of family tensions, so evident in Sylvia's account. When Adela read *Unshackled*, she found it 'well written, accurate as far as it goes & very fair to all concerned'. But she was annoyed that she had not been consulted about its publication. 'As long as Sylvia & I are alive, it is wrong for us to be ignored by those who deal with the Suffragette Movement.'[32] Sylvia had been sent a copy of the book by Fred Pethick-Lawrence. 'I am neither surprised nor distressed at not receiving much mention', she observed. 'It could not be otherwise as Christabel did not like the East End campaign.' Sylvia also pointed out some errors that would need to be corrected if the book went into a second edition.[33]

Although Fred himself had nothing but praise for *Unshackled*, commenting especially on its 'remorseless objectivity', reviewers were unimpressed.[34] Since Christabel's attitude was 'my mother, right or wrong', opined the *Times*, not too much faith should be placed 'in her historical judgment or accuracy . . . [in] this lively but tendentious book'. Felicia Lamb in the *Daily Telegraph* condemned the book's 'one-sidedness' and asserted that the short-sighted Christabel and her comrades never foresaw that the suffragettes would become 'one of the comic sideshows of history, like some of the Puritan sects'. The socialist Margaret Cole, in the *Listener*, thought *Unshackled* revealed 'a delight in the generalship of guerrilla warfare and a contempt of the methods of democracy'.[35]

Such comments were not unexpected. By 1959, when *Unshackled* was published, Sylvia's *The suffragette movement* had become the standard reading of the WSPU and of Pankhurst family life. *Unshackled*, with its emphasis upon sisterhood and marginalisation of class, appeared in a climate when such views were not welcomed in historical circles. The development of women's history in Britain, from the late 1960s, did little to challenge this situation since it was primarily socialist-feminist historians who set the parameters and who praised Sylvia's book – which highlighted the conflicts between the WSPU and the Labour and socialist movements, and between middle-class and working-class suffragettes. Sylvia, who stressed not the unity but the tensions among the militants, between those like herself who abhorred physical violence and those who advocated attacks upon property, between those who wanted a women's movement allied to socialism and those who did not, became a heroine of a left-leaning women's history. Christabel, on the other hand, was seen as right wing, as her sister had portrayed her. And since feminism was seen (and still is) as owned by those on the left, she became a 'problematic figure' in the history of British feminism.[36] Committed to a cause rather than party politics, Christabel was despised by the left, disliked by the Conservatives and hated by the Liberals. There was no political party to claim her as a 'heroine'.

The problem was particularly compounded by David Mitchell's hostile biography, *Queen Christabel*, which appeared in 1977. Two years earlier Mitchell had published a letter in the press asking for the loan of letters and documents that might be helpful for the book he intended to write. A reply soon followed from Enid Goulden Bach, stating that Christabel's family, Grace Roe, her executor, and the Trustees of the Suffragette Fellowship 'wish to dissociate themselves from his request . . . This book will be written without the approval of those who knew and worked with her'.[37] Thus began a feud that became increasingly bitter over the time that Mitchell was writing the biography. In particular, Grace Roe told Mitchell, in no uncertain terms, that she objected to the mistakes and fiction about his subject in his previous publications. '[A]s Christabel Pankhurst's executor', she insisted, 'I do have some obligation in seeing, so far as it lies within my power, that an author does not misrepresent all she stood for.' Informing Mitchell that she had made arrangements with her lawyer and executors to take action on any breach of copyright, the ninety-year-old firmly asserted, 'It would be an abrogation of my responsibility if I continued to co-operate with one whom I think unfitted to write on the subject.'[38]

The refusal of the Goulden Bachs, Grace Roe and some of the other suffragettes to cooperate with Mitchell undoubtedly helped to shape his already jaundiced masculinist view of the Chief Organiser of the WSPU. Mitchell particularly disliked Christabel's radical feminism, as did the liberal feminist Ray Strachey before him, and the socialist-feminist Sylvia Pankhurst. Thus from the 1930s, the dominant representations of Christabel Pankhurst have been persistently negative, a negativity that this biography has questioned.

It was the intelligent, energetic and charming Christabel Pankhurst who revitalised the women's suffrage campaign, transforming it from a pressure group formed in the 1860s, before her birth, into a vibrant political movement. Acutely aware of the discrimination that women experienced in Edwardian society – and of the long feminist struggle for the parliamentary vote – she was not prepared any longer to tolerate another generation of women wasting their lives begging for a democratic measure that was justly theirs. The subordinate and inferior position of women, she argued, was due to the power of men, including socialist men who could be as unjust to women as men of other political persuasions. Men would never give up that power voluntarily, unless forced to do so. Such a message roused thousands of women from a variety of backgrounds to demand their citizenship rights in a mass movement that has been unparalleled in British history.

Together with her widowed mother Emmeline, Christabel was a charismatic and fearless leader of the single-sex WSPU, its key strategist. Realising that peaceful campaigning was bringing no results, she had the political insight to decide on a new militant strategy of confrontational and assertive tactics that would force the Liberal Government of the day to take notice. The duty of women as voteless citizens was to resist such tyrannous governments which denied them their democratic rights, a principle that was at the heart of her notion of militancy. Militancy meant rebellion against submission, the casting aside of what she called the 'slave spirit'. This emphasis upon the 'dignity of womanhood' was a form of consciousness raising about the wrongs that vote-less women shared in common, irrespective of their class or income, a means whereby women could develop their own backbone. Militancy changed women's perceptions of themselves and people's perception of the vote. It pushed the issue of women's enfranchisement into the mainstream political agenda so that it became a foremost political question of the day.

A brilliant and captivating orator, Christabel roused and persuaded women from all social classes and all ages to join the women-only WSPU. She had a 'keen and rapier-like gift of repartee', recollected Clara Codd. 'No heckler stood any chance with her. She could turn the tables on him, sometimes to such an extent that I have seen men literally foaming at the mouth with impotent rage.'[39] Even when the WSPU's 'unladylike' tactics made it unpopular, Christabel's influence over a crowd was still 'almost irresistible', remembered Henry Nevinson: 'her youthful elegance, her rapid wit and vehement repartees played more than music's charm upon the savage breast'.[40]

As an intransigent Liberal Government refused to yield on the women's question, the form and nature of militancy changed, especially from March 1912 when, fearing arrest, Christabel fled to France and directed the WSPU from her temporary home in Paris. Although the WSPU still engaged in constitutional tactics, it increasingly adopted illegal, violent forms of protest, including damage to public and private property – although never to human life. Christabel became a controversial figure. But the aims of the WSPU had never been just the granting of the parliamentary vote to women but a radical transformation of society, and these wider issues now became increasingly important. The destruction of mail in letter-boxes, she asserted, had as its object the abolition of the sexual and economic exploitation of little girls and women. Such reasoning, as well as her articles on venereal disease, alarmed her critics, who accused her of rousing a sex war. But Christabel was unrepentant. Men in the past had not been given the vote by asking nicely; it was only by using such militant methods that the WSPU would win.

When the First World War broke out, Christabel supported the war effort, arguing that women's war work would help to bring them their political citizenship. Her patriotic support for the war and fervent criticisms of Bolshevism and the emerging communism have made her unpopular with many feminists who associate feminism with peace movements and with the left. But feminism and patriotism are not mutually exclusive categories. Nor, as noted earlier, is feminism 'owned' by the left. The feminist movement has always been more complex than this, and has had many differing ideological strands. For Christabel, who wanted to unite women in an independent women's movement, the cause had to be above party politics. Her condemnation of Bolshevism and communism proved not to be misplaced. Bolshevism, which had set out to emancipate working people throughout the world, became, especially in Stalinist Russia, one of the most oppressive tyrannies of the twentieth century.

Many historians have blamed suffragette vandalism for the failure of women to be granted the parliamentary vote before 1918.[41] But, as David Morgan has argued, Prime Minister Herbert Asquith had no intention of including women's suffrage in a franchise bill and if the question had come to a vote, Conservatives, Liberal dissidents and the Irish would have killed it for reasons other than the behaviour of the militants. Similarly, both Harold Laski and Fred Pethick-Lawrence claim that militancy was necessary for winning the vote. Constance Rover notes, 'While one would like to say that law and order should always be maintained, it is almost impossible to find a legal means of protest, open to those outside the constitution, which is effective.' Without subscribing to the doctrine that 'the end justifies the means', she continues, 'it is possible to hold the opinion that the end was a worthy one and that as suffragette methods stopped short of endangering human life, they were justifiable'.[42]

It is often said, in an attempt to deny greatness to Christabel Pankhurst and her mother, that women won partial enfranchisement in 1918 not because of militant tactics but because of their 'good behaviour' during the First World War when they encouraged women to be patriotic and engage in war work. But as John Grigg has pointed out, that is only half of the truth. '[T]he all-male political establishment remembered the harassment inflicted by the suffragettes before the war and had no wish to return to it afterwards.'[43] Moreover, it is often forgotten that Christabel and her mother, during the war years, did not abandon votes for women but interwove into their speeches themes about patriotism, democracy, men's and women's contribution to the war effort – and women's enfranchisement. This change of strategy helped to bring about a cultural change in the understanding of suffrage.

Although the driving force of Christabel's life was to win women's suffrage, she did have a life after 1918. However, her conversion to Second Adventism and later successful career as a fundamentalist preacher and writer have added to the negative assessments about her. Pugh disparagingly condemns this phase of her life as the product of 'the shallowness' of her politics, while Helen Rappaport sums up the uncomprehending attitude of many feminists when she notes that Christabel's life as 'a born-again Christian' was a 'dramatic U-turn for a woman who was, during the period 1903–1914, one of the most radical voices in British feminism'.[44] But religious belief and feminist subjectivity have been strongly linked in the past, just as they were in Christabel's rhetoric during the 'moral crusade' against the double sexual standard. Rather than seeing her post-suffrage career as a repudiation of her radical feminist past, we should see it as an extension of her feminism. Recognising that winning female enfranchisement would not necessarily bring about equality for women and the moral uplifting of society, she felt called to a new field of influence where she could exercise spiritual leadership and extend the public sphere. Christabel Pankhurst became one of the most significant female Anglican preachers during the first half of the twentieth century.

Six years after Christabel's death, Jessie Kenney, her one-time former suffrage colleague and a close friend, was asked to sum up Emmeline and Christabel Pankhurst in one word. 'For Mrs Pankhurst, this is easy. I say "Dignity". It's not so easy for Christabel. She had dignity, but there was something more. She embodied an idea.'[45] That idea, that found its fullest expression in the suffragette movement, was that women should no longer be subservient to men but be confident, assertive, autonomous beings in their own right who could choose, if they so wished, the fulfilled single life, a lifestyle that was an alternative to the expected heterosexual destination of wifehood and motherhood.

Christabel Pankhurst's important contribution to the history of feminism must be acknowledged. In advocating a separatist feminism and in articulating the difficulties of fitting feminism 'into' any of the male-dominated political parties of the day, she was one of the key feminist thinkers of the twentieth century. Her emphasis upon the sisterhood of women, trenchant critique of male power and insistence that socialism could be just as injurious to women as capitalism may have been out of tune with feminism in Britain in the 1920s and 1930s, but was echoed strongly in the women's liberation movement in Western Europe in the 1970s. Her ideas shook up Edwardian society, challenging perceptions about what women should and could do. Arguably, she did more than any other woman of her generation to change society's attitudes towards her sex and women's perceptions of themselves. Her place in the narrative about the making of a modern, democratic Britain is assured.

Notes

1 Ivy de Verley to Grace Roe, 10 March 1958, Craigie Collection.
2 Kathleen Pepper to Grace Roe, 14 February 1958, Craigie Collection.
3 Rangeley Stride to Grace Roe, 24 February and 16 March 1958, Craigie Collection.
4 Charlie Marsh to Grace Roe, 14 February 1958, Craigie Collection.
5 Cecily Hale to Grace Roe, 18 February 1958, Craigie Collection.
6 Mabel Tuke to Grace Roe, 14 February 1958, Craigie Collection.
7 APW to Helen Fraser, 3 January 1959, Helen (Moyes) Fraser Papers, Museum of London.
8 ESP to FPL [late February 1958?], P-L Papers; ESP to Miss Murcheson [14 February 1958?], Purvis Collection; ESP to Mr and Mrs Eldon, 21 February 1958, Richard Pankhurst Private Collection.
9 Dme. Christabel Pankhurst Votes for Women and Dame C. Pankhurst Suffragette and Evangelist, *Times* and *Daily Telegraph*, 15 February 1958, respectively.
10 *New York Times*, 15 February 1958.
11 Dame Pankhurst, Noted Suffrage Leader Dies, *Santa Monica Outlook*, 14 February 1958; Wingate White, The Pankhurst era, *Los Angeles Times*, 19 February 1958.
12 *Santa Monica Outlook*, 14 February 1958; In Memoriam, Mrs Kent Allen, *Los Angeles Times*, 27 February 1958.
13 Grace Roe to Jessie Kenney, 15 February 1958, Craigie Collection. 'The colours', of course, refer to the white, purple and green of the WSPU.

14 Thanks to Elizabeth Crawford for informing me that a copy of the will was listed for sale for £125 in the early 1980s by a now extinct bookseller. We have been unable to trace who bought it. Six copies of the will had been made and distributed, and Jill Craigie told me the Goulden Bach family had sold one copy.

15 Rangeley Stride to David Mitchell, 13 September 1975, Purvis Collection.

16 Edna Dunrobin, 23 February 1958, Craigie Collection.

17 Memorial Service Dame Christabel Pankhurst, *Times* 15 March 1958; Cicely Hale to Grace Roe, 16 March 1958, Craigie Collection. Former suffragettes who attended include Jane Brailsford, Lilian Dove-Willcox, Una Duval, Cecily Hale, Jessie Kenney, Mary Leigh, Lilian Lenton, Charlie Marsh, Mary Phillips and Kathleen Pepper.

18 Address by Lord Pethick-Lawrence at the Memorial Service for Dame Christabel Pankhurst DBE at St Martin-in-the-Fields, March 14th 1958, Craigie Collection.

19 Kathleen Pepper to Grace Roe, 22 March 1958, Craigie Collection. Kathleen had been one of Christabel's former private secretaries. Cecily Hale to Grace Roe, 16 March 1958, Craigie Collection notes: 'I nearly wept when, after the service, the March of the Women was played on the organ as we filed out, to meet and greet old friends . . . a wonderful occasion.'

20 Letter published in *Times* and *Los Angeles Times*, 22 October and 9 November 1958, respectively, signed by Helen P-L, Nancy Astor, Thelma Cazalet-Keir, Rose Heilbron, Vera Laughton Mathews, A. Lousie McIlroy, Mary Stocks and Sybil Thorndike.

21 A voice from the past, *Manchester Guardian*, 6 July 1969.

22 Speech by Dame Vera Laughton Mathews, DBE, at the Unveiling of the Christabel Pankhurst Memorial on 13 July 1959 and Summary of a Speech by the Lord Chancellor Lord Kilmuir before Unveiling the Dame Christabel Pankhurst Memorial in Victoria Power Gardens on Monday, 13 July 1959, Craigie Collection.

23 The twenty-three who attended included many of the dwindling band of former suffragettes as well as supporters and sympathisers – including Mary Leigh, Charlie Marsh, Dorothy Bowker, Teresa Billington-Greig, Enid and Sybil Bach, Lilian Dove Wilcox, Lilian Lenton, Una Dugdale, Fred Pethick-Lawrence and Jim Taylor, husband of Annie Kenney. The words of the plaque are 'At an election meeting in the Free Trade Hall on 13th October, 1905, Christabel Pankhurst, of this city, and Annie Kenney of Saddleworth, asked whether the incoming Liberal Government would give votes for women. Thrown out without an answer, they continued their protest outside; were arrested and imprisoned in Strangeways Gaol. Thus was born the suffragette campaign which was crowned with victory in 1918.'

24 *Times*, 11 October 1960.

25 *Calling All Women*, February 1963. The Christabel Pankhurst Memorial Fund was wound up in 1964 with a balance of £71.16s. 5d.

26 Grace Roe to Fred P-L, 23 October 1958, Craigie Collection. Grace explained that after Shirley's death her house was rented out to 'rather undesirable people, with all C's papers in it. Many, I fear, were scattered'. This may explain the absence of the letters that Christabel's father wrote to her mother, when he was courting her, from which Christabel quotes in her manuscript.

27 FPL, Preface, p. 13 of CP, *Unshackled*.

28 See J. Purvis and M. Wright, Writing suffragette history: the contending autobiographical narratives of the Pankhursts, *Women's History Review*, 14, 3 and 4, 2005, pp. 405–33.

29 Jill Craigie, Additional Notes, Mrs Pankhurst's Bad Press, unpublished manuscript, n.d., Craigie Collection.

30 CP, *Unshackled*, p. 239.

31 CP, *Unshackled*, p. 69.

32 APW to Helen Fraser Moyes, 22 January 1960, TWL.

33 ESP to FPL, n.d. [early 1959, documents 79, 78 (1), 83 and 85], P-L Papers.

34 FPL, Preface, p. 12 of CP, *Unshackled*.

35 *Times*, 18 June 1959; *Daily Telegraph*, 15 June 1959; *Listener*, 16 July 1959.
36 Helen Rappaport, *Encyclopedia of women social reformers Vol 2* (Santa Barbara, CA, ABC-Clio, 2001), p. 509.
37 Letters from David Mitchell and Enid Goulden Bach to the editor, *Daily Telegraph*, 21 and 30 July 1975, respectively.
38 G. Roe to D. Mitchell, 19 September 1975, DMC.
39 Clara Codd, *So rich a life* (Pretoria, Institute for Theosophical Publicity, 1951), p. 45.
40 Nevinson, *More changes, more chances*, p. 312.
41 See Harrison, *Separate spheres*, p. 147; Pugh, *The march of the women*; Adams, *Women and the vote*.
42 David Morgan, *Suffragists and Liberals: the politics of woman suffrage in Britain* (Oxford, Blackwell, 1975), p. 160; H. Laski, *The militant temper in politics*, typescript of a lecture given on 18 November 1932 to the Suffragette Fellowship, SFC; FPL to Professor G. M. Trevelyan, 3 October 1949, reprinted in V. Brittain, *Pethick-Lawrence: a portrait* (London, Allen & Unwin, 1963), pp. 215–18; C. Rover, *Women's suffrage and party politics in Britain 1866–1914* (London, Routledge, 1967), p. 99.
43 J. Grigg, *Lloyd George: from peace to war 1912–1916* (London, Harper Collins, 1997, first pub. 1985), p. 294.
44 Pugh, *Women and the women's movement*, p. 382; Rappaport, *Encyclopedia of Women Social Reformers*, p. 509.
45 J. Kenney interview, 24 March 1964, DMC.

SELECT BIBLIOGRAPHY

Collections of papers

Janie Allan Papers, National Library of Scotland
Nancy Astor Collection, University of Reading
Jennie Baines Papers, Fryer Library, University of Queensland
A. J. Balfour Papers, British Library
Baronne Renee de Brimont Papers, Bibliotheque Marguerite Duran, Paris
Neville Chamberlain Papers, University of Birmingham
Winston S. Churchill Papers, Churchill College, Cambridge
Selina Jane Cooper Papers, Lancashire Record Office
Jill Craigie Collection, The Women's Library at the London School of Economics
Archbishop Davison Papers, Lambeth Palace Library, London
Wallace-Dunlop Family Archive, Private Collection, London
Elibank Papers, National Library of Scotland, Edinburgh
Ellis Jones Ellis-Griffith Papers, National Library of Wales
Elizabeth Wolstenholme Elmy Papers, British Library
Franchise League Minute Book, Special Collections, Northwestern University Library, Illinois
Hugh Franklin/Elsie Duval Papers, The Women's Library at the London School of Economics
Alfred George Gardiner, 1865–1946, Journalist, Editor of *Daily News* 1902–19, British Library
    of Political and Economic Science, London School of Economics and Political Science
Mary Gawthorpe Papers, Tamiment Library, New York University
Lloyd George Papers, House of Lords Record Office
Viscount Gladstone Papers, British Library
Bruce Glasier Diaries, Sydney Jones Library, University of Liverpool
Philip and Myrna Goode, Private Collection
Henry Harben Papers, British Library
Patrick Hannon Papers, House of Lords Record Office
John Johnson Collection, Women's Suffrage, Bodleian Library, Oxford
Jessie and Annie Kenney Papers, Archive Collections, University of East Anglia
Knebworth House Archives
Agnes Lake Papers, Girton College Archives, Cambridge
George Lansbury Papers, British Library of Political and Economic Science, London School of
    Economics
Bonar Law Papers, House of Lords Record Office
Linton Park Plc., Suffrage Papers
Constance Lytton Papers, Knebworth House Archives
Manchester Guardian Archive, John Ryland University Library, University of Manchester
Manchester Public City Libraries Archives, Suffrage and other relevant Papers

Manchester High School for Girls Archives
Harriet McIlquham Papers, British Library
Dora Marsden Papers, Princeton University
David Mitchell Collection, Museum of London
Hannah Mitchell Papers, Manchester Public City Libraries Archives
National American Woman Suffrage Association Papers, Library of Congress, Washington, DC
The National Archives, Various Documents
National Woman's Party Papers, Group II 1913–74, Library of Congress, Washington DC
Evelyn Sharp Nevinson Papers, Bodleian Library, Oxford
Henry Woodd Nevinson Diaries, Bodleian Library, Oxford
Lady Muriel Paget Papers, Special Collections, University of Leeds
Richard Pankhurst Private Collection
Pethick-Lawrence Papers, Trinity College, University of Cambridge
Caroline Phillips Papers, Watt Collection, Aberdeen Art Gallery and Museum
Mary Phillips Papers, Linton Park plc., Linton, Maidstone
June Purvis Private Suffrage Collection
Antonia Raeburn Private Suffrage Collection
Eleanor Rathbone Papers, Sydney Jones Library, University of Liverpool
Rex v. Kerr & Others File, Schlesinger Library, Radcliffe College, Massachusetts
Elizabeth Robins Papers, Harry Ransom Humanities Research Center, University of Texas
    at Austin
Elizabeth Robins Papers, Fales Library at the Elmer Holmes Bobst Library, New York University
Royal Archives, Clarence House, London
John Rylands Library, University of Manchester, Suffrage Papers
C. P. Scott Papers, *Manchester Guardian* Archive, John Rylands University Library, University
    of Manchester
Maud Arncliffe Sennett Collection, British Library
G. B. Shaw Papers, British Library
Sophia Smith Collection, Northampton, Massachusetts
Ethel Smyth Letters, Walter Clinton Jackson Library, University of Northern California
    Library, Green Boro, North Carolina
Suffragette Fellowship Collection, Museum of London
Adela Pankhurst Walsh Papers, National Library of Australia, Canberra
Helen Watts Papers, photocopies, Nottinghamshire County Record Office, Nottingham
Women's Social and Political Union, various booklets, leaflets etc., The Women's Library at
    the London School of Economics
Women's Suffrage Collection, including Autograph Letter Collection, The Women's Library at
    the London School of Economics

Journals and newspapers consulted

Calling All Women
Christian
Christian Commonwealth
Clarion
Daily Graphic
Daily Herald
Daily Mail
Daily Mirror
Daily News
Daily News and Leader
Daily Telegraph

East Kent Times
Evening News and Evening Mail
Evening Standard and St. James's Gazette
Evening Sun (New York)
Fort Wayne Journal Gazette
Friday Morning Club Bulletin
Globe (UK)
Globe Toronto
Illustrated London News
Labour Leader
Labour Record and Review

Liverpool Courier
Los Angeles Times
Mail and Empire Toronto
Manchester City News
Manchester Evening News
Manchester Guardian
Montreal Star
Morning Advertiser
Morning Leader
Nation
Newcastle Daily Chronicle
New Freewoman
New York Times
New York Tribune
Observer

Pall Mall Gazette
Review of Reviews
Salford Reporter
Smethwick Telephone
Standard
Star
Sunday School Times
Sunday Times
The Suffragette
Times
Toronto Daily Star
Tribune
Victoria Times
Votes for Women
Woolwich Pioneer

Books and articles

(Place of publication is London unless otherwise stated)

Adams, J., *Women and the vote: a world history* (Oxford, Oxford University Press, 2014).
A. J. R. ed., *The suffrage annual and women's who's who* (Stanley Paul, 1913).
Anand, A., *Sophia, princess, suffragette, revolutionary* (Bloomsbury, 2015).
Atkinson, D., *Rise up women! The remarkable lives of the suffragettes* (Bloomsbury, 2018).
Balfour, Lady F., *Ne obliviscaris dinna forget, Vol. 2* (Hodder and Stoughton, 1930).
Balfour, F. ed., *Letters of Constance Lytton* (William Heinemann, 1925).
Banks, O., *The biographical dictionary of British feminists, Vol. 1 (1800–1930)* (Brighton, Harvester Press, 1985).
Bartley, P., *Votes for women 1860–1928* (Hodder and Stoughton, 1998).
Bartley, P., *Emmeline Pankhurst* (Routledge, 2002).
Bearman, C. J., An examination of suffragette violence, *English Historical Review*, CXX No. 486, 2005.
Beerholm, M., Miss Christabel Pankhurst, *Saturday Review*, 24 October 1908.
Benn, C., *Keir Hardie* (Hutchinson, 1992).
Bennett, J., 'Lesbian-like' and the social history of lesbianisms, *Journal of the History of Sexuality*, 9, 2000.
Billington-Greig, T., *The militant suffrage movement: emancipation in a hurry* (Frank Palmer, 1911).
Bland, L., *Banishing the beast: English feminism and sexuality morality 1885–1914* (Harmondsworth, Penguin, 1995).
Bosch, M. and Kloosterman, A. eds, *Politics and friendship, letters from the International Woman Suffrage Alliance 1902–1942* (Colombia, OH, Ohio State University, 1990).
Bostridge, M., The Conservative suffragette, *Times Literary Supplement*, 16 August 2002.
Braybon, G., *Women workers in the First World War* (Routledge, 1989, first pub. Croom Helm, 1981).
Bruce, S., *Fundamentalism* (Cambridge, Polity, 2000).
Bullock, I. and Pankhurst, R. eds, *Sylvia Pankhurst: from artist to anti-fascist* (Houndmills, Macmillan, 1992).
Burton, A., *Burdens of history: British feminists, Indian women and imperial culture, 1865–1915* (Chapel Hill, NC, University of North Carolina Press, 1994).
Bush, J., *Women against the vote: female anti-suffragism in Britain* (Oxford, Oxford University Press, 2007).

Caine, B., Vida Goldstein and the English militant campaign, *Women's History Review*, 2, 3, 1993.

Caine, B., Feminist biography and feminist history, *Women's History Review*, 3, 2, 1994.

Caine, B., *English feminism 1780–1980* (Oxford, Oxford University Press, 1997).

Castle, B., *Sylvia and Christabel Pankhurst* (Harmondsworth, Penguin, 1987).

Cockin, K., *Edith Craig (1869–1947): dramatic lives* (Cassell, 1998).

Cockin, K., *Edith Craig and the theatres of art* (Bloomsbury, 2017).

Codd, C., *So rich a life* (Pretoria, Institute for Theosophical Publicity, 1951).

Coleman, V., *Adela Pankhurst: the wayward suffragette 1885–1961* (Melbourne, Melbourne University Press, 1996).

Connelly, K., *Sylvia Pankhurst: suffragette, socialist and scourge of empire* (Pluto Press, 2013).

Copelman, D., *London's women teachers: gender, class and feminism 1870–1930* (Routledge, 1996).

Cossart, M. de, *The food of love: Princess Edmond de Polignac (1865–1943) and her salon* (Hamish Hamilton, 1978).

Cousins, J. H. and Cousins, M. E., *We two together* (Madras, Ganesh, 1950).

Cowman, K., What was suffragette militancy? An exploration of the British example, in *Suffrage, gender and citizenship*, eds I. Sulkunen, S-L. Nevala-Nurmi and P. Markkola (Newcastle upon Tyne, Cambridge Scholars Publishing, 2009).

Cowman, K., *Women of the right spirit: paid organisers of the Women's Social and Political Union (WSPU) 1904–18* (Manchester, Manchester University Press, 2007).

Cowman, K., 'Incipient Toryism'? The Women's Social and Political Union and the Independent Labour Party, 1903–14, *History Workshop Journal*, 53, 2002.

Craigie, J., Sylvia, the revolutionary who ended in a feudal palace, *Times*, 1 May 1982.

Crawford, E., *The women's suffrage movement: a reference guide 1866–1928* (UCL Press, 2000).

Dangerfield, G., *The strange death of Liberal England* (MacGibbon and Kee, 1966, first pub. 1935).

Davis, M., *Sylvia Pankhurst: a life in radical politics* (Pluto Press, 1999).

Delap, L., *The feminist avant-garde: transatlantic encounters of the early twentieth century* (Cambridge, Cambridge University Press, 2007).

deVries, J., Gendering patriotism: Emmeline and Christabel Pankhurst and World War One, in *This working-day world: women's lives and culture(s) in Britain 1914–1945*, ed. S. Oldfield (Taylor and Francis, 1994).

deVries, J., Transforming the pulpit: preaching and prophecy in the British women's suffrage movement, in *Women preachers and prophets through two millennia of Christianity*, eds B. Mayne Kienzle and P. J. Walker (Berkeley and Los Angeles, CA, University of California Press, 1998).

deVries, J., Sounds taken for wonders: revivalism and religious hybridity in the British women's suffrage movement, in *Material religion in modern Britain*, eds T. Willem Jones and L. Matthews-Jones (New York, Palgrave Macmillan, 2015).

DiCenzo, M., Militant distribution: *Vote for Women* and the public sphere, *Media History*, 6, 2, 2000.

Digby, A., Victorian values and women in public and private life, in *Victorian values*, ed. T. Smout (Oxford, Oxford University Press, 1992).

Dixon, J., *Divine feminism: theosophy and feminism in England* (Baltimore, MD, Johns Hopkins University Press, 2001).

Dobbie, B. M. Willmott, *A nest of suffragettes in Somerset* (Batheastern, The Batheastern Society, 1979).

Dodd, K., Cultural politics and women's historical writing: the case of Ray Strachey's 'The cause', *Women's Studies International Forum Special Issue: British Feminist Histories*, ed. L. Stanley, 13, 1/2, 1990.

Dodd, K., Introduction: the politics of form in Sylvia Pankhurst's writing, in her edited *A Sylvia Pankhurst reader* (Manchester, Manchester University Press, 1993).

Dubois, E. C., *Harriot Stanton Blatch and the winning of woman suffrage* (New Haven, CT, Yale University Press, 1997).

Dyhouse, C., *Feminism and the family in England 1880–1939* (Oxford, Oxford University Press, 1989).

Eustance, C., Meanings of militancy: the ideas and practice of political resistance in the Women's Freedom League, 1907–14, in *The women's suffrage movement: new feminist perspectives*, eds M. Joannou and J. Purvis (Manchester, Manchester University Press, 1998).

Fletcher, I. C., 'A star chamber of the twentieth century': suffragettes, Liberals, and the 1908 'Rush the Commons' case, *Journal of British Studies*, 35, 1996.

Fletcher, I. C., Mayhall, L. E. Nym and Levine, P. eds, *Women's suffrage in the British Empire: citizenship, nation and race* (Routledge, 2000).

Francis, H., 'Dare to be free!': the Women's Freedom League and its legacy, in *Votes for women*, eds J. Purvis and S. Stanley Holton (Routledge, 2000).

Fulford, R., *Votes for women: the story of a struggle* (Faber and Faber, 1957).

Garner, L., *Stepping stones to women's liberty: feminist ideas in the women's suffrage movement 1900–1918* (Heinemann, 1984).

Gawthorpe, M., *Uphill to Holloway* (Penobscot, ME, Traversity Press, 1962).

Geddes, J., Culpable complicity: the medical profession and the forcible feeding of suffragettes, 1909–1914, *Women's History Review*, 17, 1, 2008.

Gleadle, K., *British women in the nineteenth century* (Houndmills, Palgrave, 2001).

Gottlieb, J., *'Guilty women': foreign policy, and appeasement in inter-war Britain* (Houndmills, Palgrave Macmillan, 2015).

Griffith, E., *In her own right: the life of Elizabeth Cady Stanton* (Oxford, Oxford University Press, 1984).

Grigg, J., *Lloyd George: from peace to war 1912–1916* (Harper Collins, 1997, first pub. 1985).

Gullace, N., *'The blood of our sons': men, women and the renegotiation of British citizenship during the Great War* (Houndmills, Palgrave Macmillan, 2002).

Hague, F., *The pain and the privilege: the women in Lloyd George's life* (Harper, 2008).

Hale, C. B., *A good long time* (Regency Press, 1973).

Hall, L., *Sex, gender and social change in Britain since 1880* (Houndmills, Macmillan, 2000).

Hannam, J., *Isabella Ford* (Oxford, Oxford University Press, 1989).

Hannam, J., Women and the ILP, 1890–1914, in *The centennial history of the Independent Labour Party*, eds D. James, T. Jowitt and K. Laybourn (Halifax, Ryburn, 1992).

Hannam, J., 'Suffragettes are splendid for any work': the Blathwayt diaries as a source for suffrage history, in *A suffrage reader: charting directions in British suffrage history*, eds C. Eustance, J. Ryan and L. Ugolini (Leicester, Leicester University Press, 2000).

Hannam, J. and Hunt, K., *Socialist women Britain, 1880s to 1920s* (Routledge, 2002).

Hannam, J., Auchterlonie, M. and Holden, K. eds, *International encyclopedia of women's suffrage* (Santa Barbara, CA, ABC-CLIO, 2000).

Hardie, K., *The citizenship of women: a plea for women's suffrage* (ILP, 1905).

Hardie, K., Women and politics, in *The case for women's suffrage*, ed. B. Villers (T. Fisher Unwin, 1907).

Harrison, B., The act of militancy: violence and the suffragettes, 1904–1914, in his *Peaceable kingdom: stability and change in modern Britain* (Oxford, Oxford University Press, 1982).

Harrison, B., *Prudent revolutionaries: portraits of British feminist between the wars* (Oxford, Oxford University Press, 1987).

Harrison. S., *Sylvia Pankhurst: a crusading life 1882–1960* (Aurum Press, 2003).

Hatton, B., A chat with Christabel Pankhurst, LL.B., *Sunday Times*, 8 March 1908.

Hilson, M., Women voters and the rhetoric of patriotism in the British general election of 1918, *Women's History Review*, 10, 2, 2001.

Hochschild, A., *To end all wars: how the First World War divided Britain* (Macmillan, 2011).

Holledge, J., *Innocent flowers: women in the Edwardian theatre* (Virago, 1981).

Holton, S. Stanley, *Feminism and democracy: women's suffrage and reform politics in Britain 1900–1914* (Cambridge, Cambridge University Press, 1986).

Holton, S. Stanley, *Suffrage days: stories from the women's suffrage movement* (Routledge, 1996).

Holton, S. Stanley, Now you see it, now you don't: the Women's Franchise League and its place in contending narratives of the women's suffrage movement, in *The women's suffrage movement: new feminist perspectives*, eds M. Joannou and J. Purvis (Manchester, Manchester University Press, 1998).

Holton, S. Stanley, Manliness and militancy: the political protest of male suffragists and the gendering of the 'suffragette' identity, in *The men's share? Masculinities, male support and women's suffrage in Britain, 1890–1920*, eds A. V. John and C. Eustance (Routledge, 1997).

Holton, S. Stanley, Challenging masculinism: personal history and microhistory in feminist studies of the women's suffrage movement, *Women's History Review*, 20, 5, 2011.

Howlett, C. J., Writing on the body? Representation and resistance in British suffragette accounts of forcible feeding, *Genders*, 23, 1996.

Hunt, K., Why Manchester? Why the Pankhursts? Why 1903? Reflections on the centenary of the Women's Social and Political Union, *Manchester Region History Review*, xvii, 2004.

Jackson, M., *The 'real' facts of life: feminism and the politics of sexuality c.1850–1940* (Taylor & Francis, 1994).

Jacob, N., *Me: a chronicle about other people* (Hutchinson, 1932).

Jeffreys, S., *The spinster and her enemies: feminism and sexuality 1880–1930* (Pandora Press, 1985).

Jenkins, L., *Lady Constance Lytton: aristocrat, suffragette, martyr* (Biteback, 2015).

Joannou, M. and Purvis, J. eds, *The women's suffrage movement: new feminist perspectives* (Manchester, Manchester University Press, 1998).

John, A. V., *Elizabeth Robins: staging a life 1862–1952* (Routledge, 1995).

John, A. V., *Evelyn Sharp: rebel woman, 1869–1955* (Manchester, Manchester University Press, 2009).

John, A. V., *Turning the tide: the life of Lady Rhondda* (Cardigan, Parthian, 2013).

Jorgensen-Earp, C. R., *'The transfiguring sword': the just war of the Women's Social and Political Union* (Tuscaloosa, AL, University of Alabama Press, 1997).

Jorgensen-Earp, C. R., *Speeches and trials of the militant suffragettes: the Women's Social and Political Union, 1902–1918* (Cranbury, NJ, Associated University Presses, 1999).

Kahn, S., *Music's modern muse: a life of Winnaretta Singer, Princess de Polignac* (Woodbridge, Boydell and Brewer, 2003).

Kean, H., *Deeds not words: the lives of suffragette teachers* (Pluto Press, 1990).

Kenney, A., *Memories of a militant* (Edward Arnold, 1924).

Kenney, R., Women's suffrage: the militant movement in ruins, *English Review*, December 1912.

Kent, S. Kingsley, *Sex and suffrage in Britain, 1860–1914* (Princeton, NJ, Princeton University Press, 1987).

Kent, S. Kingsley, *Making peace: the reconstruction of gender in interwar Britain* (Princeton, NJ, Princeton University Press, 1993).

Knowles, E., Born under a lucky star, *Calling All Women*, 1975.

Lansbury, G., *My life* (Constable, 1928).

Larsen, T., *Christabel Pankhurst: fundamentalism and feminism in coalition* (Woodbridge, Boydell Press, 2002).

Lawrence, J., Contesting the male polity: the suffragettes and the politics of disruption in Edwardian Britain, in *Women, privilege and power: British politics, 1859 to the present*, ed. A. Vickery (Stanford, CA, Stanford University Press, 2001).

Leneman, L., *A guid cause: the women's suffrage movement in Scotland* (Aberdeen, Aberdeen University Press, 1991).

Lewenhak, S., *Women and trade unions: an outline history of women in the British trade union movement* (Ernest Benn, 1977).

Lewis, G., *Eva Gore Booth and Esther Roper: a biography* (Pandora Press, 1988).

Liddington, J., *Rebel girls: their fight for the vote* (Virago, 2006).

Liddington, J., *Vanishing for the vote: suffrage, citizenship and the battle for the census* (Manchester, Manchester University Press, 2014).

Liddington, J. and Norris, J., *One hand tied behind us: the rise of the women's suffrage movement* (Virago, 1978).

Lumsden, R., 'The music between us': Ethel Smyth, Emmeline Pankhurst, and 'Possession', *Feminist Studies*, 41, 2, 2015.

Lytton, C. and Warton, J., *Prisons and prisoners: some personal experiences* (London, Heinemann, 1914).

Macpherson, D., *The suffragette's daughter: Betty Archdale, her life of feminism, cricket, war and education* (Dural Delivery Centre, NSW, Australia, Rosenberg Publishing, 2002).

Maguire, G. E., *Conservative women: a history of women and the Conservative Party, 1874–1997* (Houndmills, Macmillan, 1998).

Marcus, J., Introduction: re-reading the Pankhursts and women's suffrage, in her edited *Suffrage and the Pankhursts* (Routledge, 1987).

Markino, Y., *My idealised John Bullesses* (Constable, 1912).

Marlow, J., ed., *Votes for women* (Virago, 2000).

Martindale, H., *Under the surface* (Brighton, Southern Publishing Company, 1908).

Martz, L., An AIDS-era assessment of Christabel Pankhurst's *The great scourge and how to end it* in *The suffragette and women's history*, Special Issue Women's History Review, ed. J. Purvis, 14, 3 and 4, 2005.

Martz, L., Moved to minister: Christabel Pankhurst and Aimee Semple McPherson in Los Angeles, in *Women on the move: refugees, migration and exile*, eds F. Reid and K. Holden (Newcastle upon Tyne, Cambridge Scholars Publishing, 2010).

Mayhall, L. E. Nym, Defining militancy: radical protest, the constitutional idiom, and women's suffrage in Britain, 1908–1909, *Journal of British Studies*, 39, 1994.

Mayhall, L. E. Nym, *The militant suffrage movement: citizenship and resistance in Britain, 1860–1930* (Oxford, Oxford University Press, 2003).

McPhee, C. and Fitzgerald, A., eds, *The non-violent militant: selected writings of Teresa Billington-Greig* (Routledge, 1987).

Mercer, J., Making the news: *Votes for Women* and the mainstream press, *Media History*, 10, 3, 2004.

Metcalfe, A. E., *Woman's effort: a chronicle of British women's fifty years' of struggle for citizenship (1865–1914)* (Oxford, Blackwell, 1917).

Mitchell, D., *Women on the warpath: the story of the women of the First World War* (Jonathan Cape, 1966).

Mitchell, D., *Queen Christabel: a biography of Christabel Pankhurst* (MacDonald and Jane's, 1977).

Mitchell, G., ed., *The hard way up: the autobiography of Hannah Mitchell, suffragette and rebel* (Faber and Faber, 1968).

Montefiore, D., *From a Victorian to a modern* (E. Archer, 1927).

Morgan, D., *Suffragists and Liberals: the politics of woman suffrage in Britain* (Oxford, Blackwell, 1975).

Morgan, K., *Keir Hardie: radical and socialist* (Weidenfeld and Nicholson, 1975).

Morgan, S., Theorising feminist history: a thirty-year retrospective, *Women's History Review*, 18, 3, 2009.

Morley, A. with Stanley, L., *The life and death of Emily Wilding Davison* (The Women's Press, 1988).

Moyes, H., *A woman in a man's world* (Sydney, Alpha Books, 1971).

Mukherjee, S., *Indian Suffragettes: female identities and transnational networks* (Oxford, Oxford University Press, 2018).

Murphy, C., *The women's suffrage movement and Irish society in the early twentieth century* (Hemel Hempstead, Harvester Wheatsheaf, 1989).

Neville, D., *To make their mark: the women's suffrage movement in the North East of England 1900–1914* (Newcastle upon Tyne, Centre for Northern Studies, University of Northumbria, 1997).

Nevinson, H. W., *More changes more chances* (Nisbet, 1925).

Nevinson, H. W., *Fire of life* (James Nisbet in association with V. Gollancz, 1935).

Oram, A., *Feminist teachers and feminist politics 1900–39* (Manchester, Manchester University Press, 1996).

Owens, R. Cullen, *Smashing times: a history of the Irish women's suffrage movement 1889–1922* (Dublin, Attic Press, 1984).

Pankhurst, A., *Put up the sword* (Melbourne, Cecilia John, 1917, third edition, first pub. 1915).

Pankhurst, C., The story of women's franchise, *Labour Record*, May 1906.

Pankhurst, C., *Why we protest at Cabinet Ministers' meetings* (pamphlet, NWSPU, 1907).

Pankhurst, C., The truth about adult suffrage, *Labour Record*, February 1907.

Pankhurst, C., The adventures of a suffragette: VI. In prison for the vote, *Penny Magazine*, 445, XXV, 1907.

Pankhurst, C., The legal disabilities of women, in *The case for women's suffrage*, ed. B. Villiers (T. Fisher Unwin, 1907).

Pankhurst, C., The movement week by week, *Women's Franchise*, 27 June 1907.

Pankhurst, C., Women's votes: the history of a crusade, *Vanity Fair*, 18 March 1908.

Pankhurst, C., What we women want, *Daily Mail*, 13 June 1908.

Pankhurst, C., Women's fight for the vote, *Weekly Dispatch*, 26 July, 2 August, 9 August and 16 August 1908.

Pankhurst, C., *The militant methods of the N.W.S.P.U., being the verbatim report of a speech by Christabel Pankhurst, at the St. James's Hall, on October 15th, 1908* (Woman's Press, 1908).

Pankhurst, C., *Broken windows* (WSPU, 1912).

Pankhurst, C., Militancy, in *New Statesman: special supplement on the awakening of women*, ed. Mrs Sidney Webb, 1 November 1913.

Pankhurst, C., *The great scourge and how to end it* (Lincoln's Inn, E. Pankhurst, 1913).

Pankhurst, C., *America and the war: a speech delivered at Carnegie Hall, New York, October 24th, 1914* (Kingsway, the Women's Social and Political Union, 1914).

Pankhurst, C., *The war, a speech delivered at the London Opera House, on September 8th, 1914* (The Women's Social and Political Union, 1914).

Pankhurst, C., *Speech delivered by Miss Christabel Pankhurst at Washington, USA, January 24th, 1915* (WSPU, 1915).

Pankhurst, C., *International militancy: a speech delivered at Carnegie Hall, New York January 13th, 1915* (WSPU, 1915).

Pankhurst, C., *No peace without victory! The Report of a speech delivered in the Queen's Hall on June 23rd, 1917 with some extracts from speeches delivered at a series of Meetings in the Aeolian Hall* (WSPU, 1917).

Pankhurst, C., *Industrial salvation* (The Women's Party, 1918).

Pankhurst, C., Why I never married, *Weekly Dispatch*, 3 April 1921.

Pankhurst, C., My war chest: how we gathered and spent £100,000, *Weekly Dispatch*, 10 April 1921.

Pankhurst, C., Politicians I have met: tussles and flattery, *Weekly Dispatch*, 17 April 1921.

Pankhurst, C., 'Cat and Mouse' days: our friendly war with the police: the men we liked: their raids and ours, *Weekly Dispatch*, 1 May 1921.

Pankhurst, C., My escape to Paris: a night in hiding, *Weekly Dispatch*, 8 May 1921.

Pankhurst, C., Young jurywoman and unsavoury cases, *Weekly Dispatch*, 15 May 1921.

Pankhurst, C., Turning the vote to good account, *Weekly Dispatch*, 22 May 1921.

Pankhurst, C., How I held audiences, *Weekly Dispatch*, 29 May 1921.

Pankhurst, C., *'The Lord Cometh': the world crisis explained* (Morgan and Scott, 1923).

Pankhurst, C., *Pressing problems of the closing age* (Morgan and Scott, 1924).

Pankhurst, C., *Some modern problems in the light of Biblical prophecy* (New York, Fleming H. Revell, 1924).

Pankhurst, C., *The world's unrest: visions of the dawn* (Philadelphia, PA, Sunday School Times Company, 1926).

Pankhurst, C., *Seeing the future* (New York, Harper, 1929).

Pankhurst, C., *The uncurtained future* (Hodder and Stoughton, 1940).

Pankhurst, C., *Unshackled: the story of how we won the vote* (Hutchinson, 1959).

Pankhurst, E., *My own story* (Eveleigh Nash, 1914).

Pankhurst, E. Sylvia, *The suffragette: the history of the women's militant suffrage movement 1905–1910* (New York, Sturgis and Walton Co., 1911).

Pankhurst, E. Sylvia, *The suffragette movement: an intimate account of persons and ideals* (Longmans, 1931).

Pankhurst, E. Sylvia, *The home front: a mirror to life in England during the world war* (Hutchinson, 1932).

Pankhurst, E. Sylvia, Those elfin days, in *Little innocents: childhood reminiscences* (Cobden-Sanderson, 1932).

Pankhurst, E. Sylvia., *The life of Emmeline Pankhurst: the suffragette struggle for women's citizenship* (T. Werner Laurie, 1935).

Pankhurst, E. Sylvia, Sylvia Pankhurst, in *Myself when young*, ed. Countess of Oxford and Asquith (Frederick Muller, 1938).

Pankhurst, R. Marsden, The right of women to vote under the Reform Act, 1867, *Fortnightly Review*, September 1868.

Pankhurst, R., *Sylvia Pankhurst: artist and crusader, an intimate portrait* (Paddington Press, 1979).

Pankhurst, R., Suffragette sisters in old age: unpublished correspondence between Christabel and Sylvia Pankhurst, 1953–57, *Women's History Review*, 10, 3, 2001.

Paxton, N., *Stage rights! The Actresses' Franchise League, activism and politics 1908–1958* (Manchester, Manchester University Press, 2018).

Pedersen, S., *The Scottish suffragettes and the press* (Palgrave Press, 2017).

Pethick-Lawrence, E., *My part in a changing world* (Victor Gollancz, 1938).

F. W. P. L. (Fred Pethick-Lawrence), Character sketch: Miss Kenney, *Labour Record and Review*, April 1906.

Pethick, F., *Fate has been kind* (Hutchinson, 1943).

Porter, B., *The origins of the vigilant state: the London Metropolitan Police Special Branch before the First World War* (Weidenfeld and Nicholson, 1987).

Postgate, R., *The life of George Lansbury* (Longmans, 1951).

Pugh, M., *Women's suffrage in Britain 1867–1928* (Historical Association, 1980).

Pugh, M., *Women and the women's movement* (Houndmills, Macmillan, 1992).

Pugh, M., *The march of the women: a revisionist analysis of the campaign for women's suffrage 1866–1914* (Oxford, Oxford University Press, 2000).

Pugh, M., *The Pankhursts* (Penguin, 2001).

Purvis, J., Prison experiences of the suffragettes in Edwardian Britain, *Women's History Review*, 4, 1, 1995.

Purvis, J., A 'pair of infernal of . . . infernal queens'? A reassessment of the dominant representations of Emmeline and Christabel Pankhurst, First Wave feminists in Edwardian Britain, *Women's History Review*, 5, 2, 1996.

Purvis, J., Christabel Pankhurst and the Women's Social and Political Union, in *The women's suffrage movement: new feminist perspectives*, eds M. Joannou and J. Purvis (Manchester, Manchester University Press, 1998).

Purvis, J., *Emmeline Pankhurst: a biography* (Routledge, 2002).

Purvis, J., The Pankhursts and the Great War, in *The women's movement in wartime: international perspectives, 1914–19*, eds A. S. Fell and I. Sharp (Houndmills, Palgrave Macmillan, 2007).

Purvis, J., Christabel Pankhurst and the struggle for suffrage reform in Edwardian Britain, in *Suffrage, gender and citizenship*, eds I. Sulkunen, S-L. Nevala-Nurmi and P. Markkola (Newcastle upon Tyne, Cambridge Scholars Publishing, 2009).

Purvis, J., The power of the hunger strike, *BBC History Magazine*, June 2009.

Purvis, J., Emmeline Pankhurst (1858–1928), suffragette leader and single parent in Edwardian Britain, in *Lone Mothers: Special Issue Women's History Review*, eds T. Evans and P. Thane, 20, 1, 2011.

Purvis, J., Fighting the double moral standard in Edwardian Britain: suffragette militancy, sexuality and the nation in the writings of the early twentieth-century British feminist Christabel Pankhurst, in *Women's activism: global perspectives from the 1890s to the present*, eds F. de Haan, M. Allen, J. Purvis and K. Daskalova (Routledge, 2013).

Purvis, J., Gendering the historiography of the suffragette movement in Edwardian Britain: some reflections, *Women's History Review*, 22, 4, 2013.

Purvis, J., The march of the women: a BBC drama from 1974 highlights the tensions in writing feminist history, *History Today*, November 2014.

Purvis, J., Christabel Pankhurst – a Conservative suffragette? In *Women, gender and the Conservative Party, 1880s to the present*, eds C. Berthezene and J. Gottlieb (Manchester, Manchester University Press, 2017).

Purvis, J. and Holton, S. Stanley eds, *Votes for women* (Routledge, 2000).

Pye, D., *Fellowship is life: the National Clarion Cycling Club 1895–1995* (Bolton, Clarion Publishing, 1996 reprint, first pub. 1995).

Raeburn, A., *The militant suffragettes* (Michael Joseph, 1973).

Raeburn, A., *The suffragette view* (Newton Abbot, David & Charles, 1976).

Rappaport, H., *Encyclopedia of women social reformers, Vol. 2* (Santa Barbara, CA, ABC-CLIO, 2001).

Rappaport, H., *Caught in the revolution Petrograd 1917* (Hutchinson, 2016).

Rendall, J., Citizenship, culture and civilisation: the languages of British suffragists, 1866–1874, in *Suffrage and beyond*, eds C. Daley and M. Nolan (Auckland, Auckland University Press, 1994).

Richardson, M., *Laugh a defiance* (Weidenfeld and Nicolson, 1953).

Rollyson, C., *To be a woman: the life of Jill Craigie* (Aurum Press, 2005).

Romero, P. W., *E. Sylvia Pankhurst: portrait of a radical* (New Haven, CT, Yale University Press, 1986).

Ronan, A., The legacy of the suffragettes: women, peace and the vote in Manchester 1914–18, in *Suffragette legacy: how does the history of feminism inspire current thinking in Manchester*, eds C. Mork Rostik and E. L. Sutherland (Newcastle upon Tyne, Cambridge Scholars Press, 2015).

Rosen, A., *Rise up women! The militant campaign of the Women's Social and Political Union 1903–1914* (Routledge, 1974).

Rowbothan, S., *Friends of Alice Wheeldon* (Pluto Press, 1986).

Rowland, P., *Lloyd George* (Barrie and Jenkins, 1975).

Rubinstein, D., *A different world for women: the life of Millicent Garrett Fawcett* (Hemel Hempstead, Harvester Wheatsheaf, 1991).

Rupp, J., *Worlds of women: the making of an international women's movement* (Princeton, NJ, Princeton University Press, 1997).

Sarah, E., Christabel Pankhurst: reclaiming her power, in *Feminist theorists: three centuries of women's intellectual traditions*, ed. D. Spender (The Women's Press, 1983).

Sen, S., *Memoir of an octogenarian* (Simla Anjali, 1971).

Service, R., *Spies and commissars: Bolshevik Russia and the West* (Macmillan, 2011).

Sharp, E., *Hertha Ayrton 1854–1923: a memoir* (Edward Arnold, 1926).

Sharp, E., Emmeline Pankhurst and militant suffrage, *Nineteenth Century*, April 1930.

Sharp, E., *Unfinished adventure: selected reminiscences from an Englishwoman's life* (John Lane, Bodley Head, 1933).

Shaw, J., *Octavia: daughter of God* (Jonathan Cape, 2011).

Shepherd, J., *George Lansbury: the heart of old Labour* (Oxford, Oxford University Press, 2002).

Smith, A., *Suffrage discourse in Britain during the First World War* (Aldershot, Ashgate, 2005).

Smyth, E., *Female pipings in Eden* (Edinburgh, Peter Davies, 1933).

Smyth, E., *Female pipings in Eden* (revised sec. ed., Edinburgh, Peter Davies, 1934).

Snowden, Viscount P., *An autobiography, Vol. 1* (Ivor Nicholson, 1934).

Spender, D., *Women of ideas and what men have done to them: from Aphra Behn to Adrienne Rich* (Routledge, 1992).

Stanley, L., *The auto/biographical I: the theory and practice of feminist auto/biography* (Manchester, Manchester University Press, 1992).

Stanley, L., Romantic friendship? Some issues in researching lesbian history and biography, *Women's History Review*, 1, 2, 1992.

Steiner, Z., The peace settlement, in *The Oxford illustrated history of the First World War*, ed. H. Strachan (Oxford, Oxford University Press, 1998).

St John, C., *Ethel Smyth: a biography* (Longmans, Green & Co., 1959).

Stocks, M., *Fifty years in every street: the story of the Manchester University Settlement* (Manchester, Manchester University Press, 1945).

Stopes, M. Carmichael, *Married love: a new contribution to the solution of sexual difficulties* (Putnam's, 1918).

Stott, M., The missing years, *Guardian*, 6 October 1977.

Strachey, R. *'The cause': a short history of the women's movement in Great Britain* (Bell & Sons, Ltd., 1928, reprinted by Virago 1978).

Summers, A., *Christian and Jewish women in Britain, 1880–1940: living with difference* (Houndmills, Palgrave, 2017).

Swanwick, H., *I have been young* (Victor Gollancz, 1935).

Taylor, A., *Annie Besant: a biography* (Oxford, Oxford University Press, 1992).

Taylor, R., *In letters of gold: the story of Sylvia Pankhurst and the East London Federation of the Suffragettes in Bow* (Stepney Books, 1993).

Thom, D., *Nice girls and rude girls: women workers in World War I* (Tauris, 1998).

Thompson, L., *Robert Blatchford: portrait of an Englishman* (William Clowes and Sons, 1951).

Thorpe, V. and Marsh, A., Diary reveals lesbian love trysts of suffragette leaders, *Observer*, 11 June 2000.

Tickner, L., *The spectacle of women: imagery of the suffrage campaign 1907–14* (Chatto & Windus, 1987).

Tiernan, S., *Eva Gore Booth: an image of such politics* (Manchester, Manchester University Press, 2012).

Todman, D., *The Great War: myth and memory* (Hambledon, 2005).

Toye, R., *Lloyd George and Churchill: rivals for greatness* (Houndmills, Macmillan, 2007).

Tusan, M. E., *Women making news: gender and journalism in modern Britain* (Urbana and Chicago, IL, University of Illinois Press, 2005).

T. W. G., In bohemia, citizen Pankhurst, *Manchester City News*, 12 April 1913.

Vellacott, J., *Pacifists, patriots and the vote: the erosion of democratic suffragism in Britain during the First World War* (Houndmills, Palgrave Macmillan, 2007).

Vicinus, M., *Independent women: work and community for single women 1850–1920* (Virago, 1985).

Vicinus, M., Fin-de-siecle theatrics: male impersonation and lesbian desires, in *Borderlines: genders and identities in war and peace 1870–1930*, ed. B. Melman (Routledge, 1998).

Villiers, B., ed., *The case for women's suffrage* (T. Fisher Unwin, 1907).

Ward, G. Whiteley, Women of the hour, 1, Miss Christabel Pankhurst, *Throne and Country*, 18 April 1908.

Wasserstein, B., *Herbert Samuel: a political life* (Oxford, Oxford University Press, 1992).

West, R., Mrs. Pankhurst, in *The post Victorians*, with an Introduction by the Very Rev. W. R. Inge (Ivor Nicholson, 1933).

Wilson, G., *With all her might: the life of Gertrude Harding militant suffragette* (New Brunswick, NJ, Goose Lane Editions, 1996).

Wilson, T. ed., *The political diaries of C. P. Scott 1911–1928* (Collins, 1970).

Winslow, B., *Sylvia Pankhurst: sexual politics and political activism* (UCL Press, 1996).

Wollacott, A., *On her their lives depend: munitions workers in the Great War* (Berkeley and Los Angeles, CA, University of California Press, 1994).

Wright, M., *Elizabeth Wolstenholme Elmy and the Victorian feminist movement: the biography of an insurgent woman* (Manchester, Manchester University Press, 2011).

Unpublished typescripts

Kenney, J., The flame and the flood, Kenney Papers, University of East Anglia

Marion, K., Autobiography, Suffragette Fellowship Collection, Museum of London

INDEX

Note: References in *italics* are to plate numbers; those in roman are to page numbers. CP and EP refer to Christabel and Emmeline Pankhurst respectively.